**PERFORMANCE**
**Maximum speed:** 106.6 mph
(172 kph)
**Acceleration 0-60 mph:** 13.5
seconds
**Fuel consumption:** 25.7 mpg

**BELOW** The layout of the last of the 356s, the 356C, still owed an obvious debt to the VW Beetle on which the original 356 was based. The 356 maintained the VW's torsion bar suspension front and rear along with a rear-mounted flat four engine

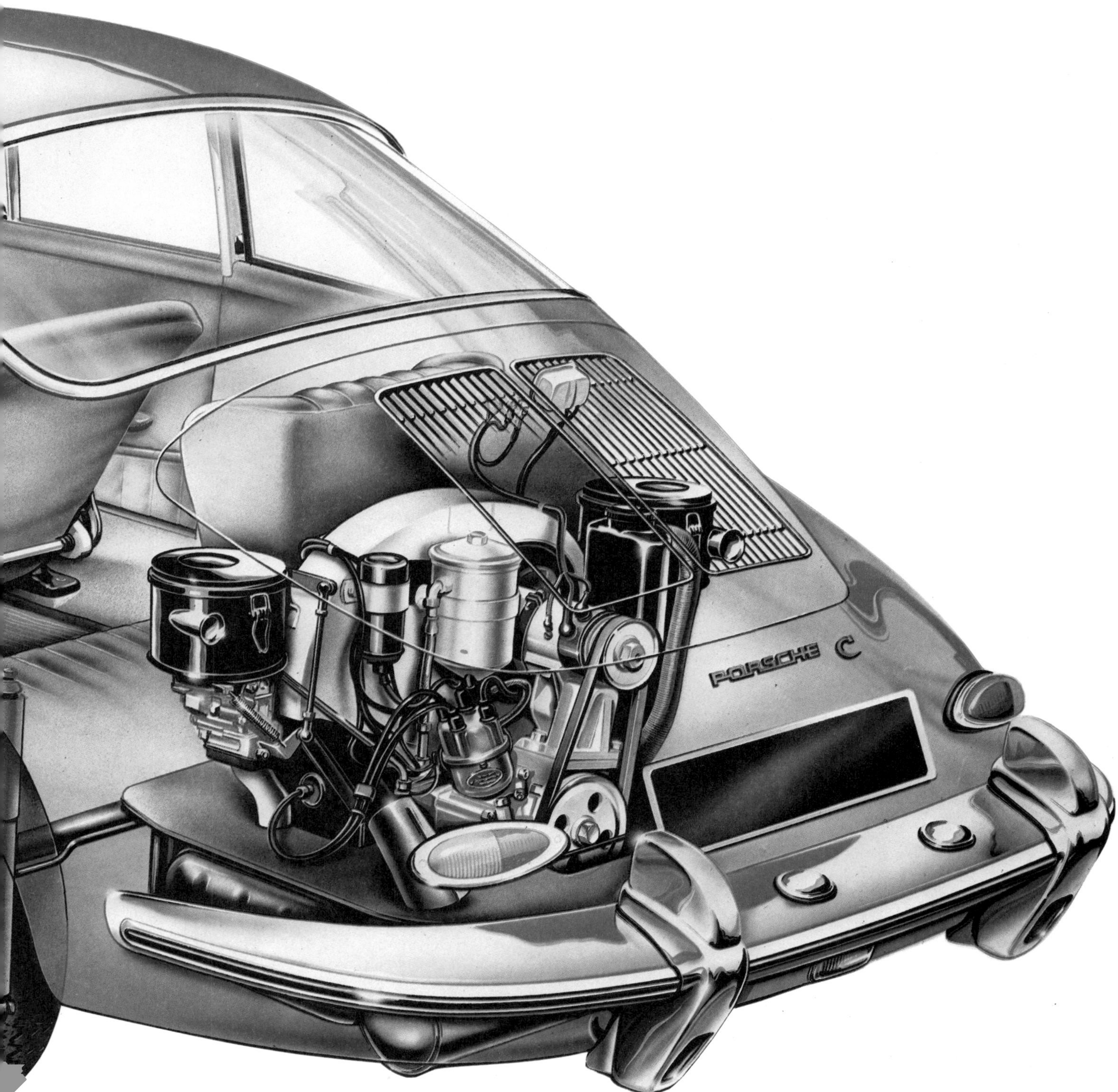

# ENCYCLOPEDIA OF
## —— THE ——
# CAR

© 1993 Orbis Publishing Ltd

Published by Grange Books
An Imprint of Grange Books PLC
The Grange
Grange Yard
London
SE1 3AG

Published 1993

ISBN 1 85627 342 3

Printed in Hungary

# ENCYCLOPEDIA OF
## — THE —
# CAR

Grange
BOOKS

# A-Z
# A-Z OF THE CAR

## ABADAL
**Barcelona, Spain**
**1913–1930**

Don Francisco Serramalera y Abadal (known as Paco Abadal) was a racing driver as well as Barcelona concessionaire for Hispano-Suiza (he is said to have introduced the famous Spanish marque to King Alfonso XIII). In 1912 Abadal decided to found his own marque, but oddly enough his first cars were built in Belgium by Imperia.

Two models of Abadal were offered, the 18-24 hp four and the 45 hp six, cars in the same sporting idiom as the Hispano, with elegant vee radiators. A very elegant Labourdette-bodied 'skiff torpedo' in riveted wood – complete with boat fenders – caused a minor sensation at the 1913 Paris Salon and a second Abadal on show boasted a doorless 'boat' body by Alin & Liautard, which featured a polished brass bonnet.

The 45 hp six was so well built that one completed a 20,000 km observed trial in Spain without any of its components needing replacement. With the outbreak of war in 1914, Belgian production understandably ceased, and Abadal built two light cars, a 12 hp and a 15 hp, in Spain until, in 1916, he took on the agency for Buick, subsequently building sporting variants under the name Abadal-Buick.

Imperia resumed production of Abadals at their Nessonvaux factory after the war, building an estimated 170 cars between 1919 and 1922, including one

prototype 5.6-litre overhead-cam straight-eight in chassis form only.

During the 1920s Paco Abadal concentrated more on his General Motors dealership, while Abadal cars were built in Belgium, Imperia finally dropping the name in 1923. The last Abadal however, appeared in 1930, in Barcelona, but the prototype, a 3.5-litre Continental-engined and rather American looking saloon never went into production.

### 1912 ABADAL

**Engine:** in-line four cylinder
**Bore × stroke:** 80 mm × 180 mm
**Capacity:** 3619 cc
**Maximum power:** 18–24 hp (rated)
**Transmission:** four-speed manual
**Chassis:** pressed steel
**Suspension:** non-independent, semi-elliptic leaf springs all round
**Brakes:** rear only
**Bodywork:** to order
**Maximum speed (approx):** 70 mph (112 kph)

## ABARTH
**Turin, Italy**
**1950–**

Carlo Abarth was born in Yugoslavia of Italian parents and grew up in Austria before moving at the end of World War II to Italy, where he worked as an engineering consultant, met Ferry Porsche and became Porsche's

**Abadal 18/24hp**

Italian representative. When Porsche assisted in producing the Cisitalia racing cars with Piero Dusio, Abarth became involved as well. Cisitalia soon went under, due to financial problems, and Abarth took over the racing side of the company, forming his own company in 1949. After a spell racing Cisitalias Abarth began building his own racers with tubular backbone chassis. He also produced a successful range of tuning equipment (first silencers, then valves and manifolds).

Abarth's first car, the 204 Berlinetta, appeared at the 1950 Turin Show with a four-cylinder 1100 cc Fiat engine (with an Abarth manifold) and Porsche-type torsion bar suspension. It was a taste of things to come, being capable of 114 mph (183 kph) and it provided the legendary Nuvolari with his last win (in a 204 Spyder in 1950). In 1952 came the Vignale-bodied 205 and the aerodynamic Scaglione-bodied 1500 two

seater. Abarth started his collaboration with Fiat in 1956 and from then on most of his cars were Fiat based. First came the little Fiat 600 saloon which Abarth turned into a high-performance 750. Further development turned it into the 850TC and 1000TC and finally to out and out Group 2 competition saloons. During the '50s Abarth's silencer business boomed providing him with a sound financial base and Abarth indulged himself in producing cars like the tiny Zagato coupés which enjoyed a very successful racing career. With their twin-cam engines and two-seat Zagato bodies the coupés were a world away from their Fiat origins.

In 1960 Abarth introduced the 2000, based on the enlarged Fiat engine of the time and the resulting Bialbero (twin-cam) GT became virtually unbeatable in Europe. Although Abarth began to move more and more towards producing his own engines (the

**Abarth Bialbero**

1

four-valve-per-cylinder 2-litre of the late '60s was perhaps the best) the company still modified Fiats, producing a 137 mph (220 kph) 1.6-litre derivative of the Fiat 850 in 1964. In 1966 Abarth branched out and built the Abarth-Simca 2000, a 200 bhp, 168 mph (270 kph) two-seater coupé.

By 1971, however, Abarth's enthusiasm for complicated racing cars saw the company in financial trouble and Fiat stepped in and took over the tuning section of the company, retaining Carlo Abarth's services as technical consultant. The Abarth name lived on in much the same way as did Gordini's at Renault, as a label on high-performance and rally cars.

**AC Ace**

## 1966 ABARTH BIALBERO

**Engine:** in-line four cylinder, double overhead cam
**Bore × stroke:** 65 mm × 74 mm
**Capacity:** 932 cc
**Maximum power:** 97 bhp
**Transmission:** four-speed manual
**Chassis:** integral
**Suspension:** independent with double wishbones and transverse leaf spring front and trailing arms rear with coil springs
**Brakes:** discs all round
**Bodywork:** Zagato coupé
**Maximum speed (approx):** 130 mph (208 kph)

## ABC
### Hersham, England 1920-1929

The first ABC appeared in 1920 and its main feature was its air-cooled flat-twin engine designed by that erratic genius Granville Bradshaw. Consequently it combined pleasure and pain in virtually equal proportions, the long, fragile, exposed pushrods being particularly problematical.

When the car was running, its performance was lively and handling good. Racing versions appeared in the 200 Miles Race at Brooklands in 1921, 1922 and

1923, but their engines were just too large for the 1100 cc category and consequently the ABCs had to run against 1500 cc cars and were consequently outclassed.

The valve gear was strengthened after 1925 and the lubrication improved, but by then the car had been overtaken by its rival marques, and was lagging behind market trends – right to the end of production in 1929, four-wheel brakes and electric starting were still extra cost options.

## 1920 ABC

**Engine:** flat twin, overhead valve
**Bore × stroke:** 96 mm × 91.5 mm
**Capacity:** 1203 cc
**Maximum power:** 40 bhp
**Transmission:** four-speed manual
**Chassis:** pressed steel
**Suspension:** non-independent with quarter elliptic leaf springs all round
**Brakes:** rear drums only
**Bodywork:** two-seater convertible
**Maximum speed (approx):** 65 mph (105 kph)

**ABC**

## AC
### Thames Ditton, England 1908–

The origins of AC go back to 1903 and the unlikely partnership between engineer John Weller and pork butcher John Portwine. The company took its name from the little 'Auto-Carrier' delivery tricycles built between 1905-14 (a passenger version was announced for 1908); conventional cars first appeared in 1913. The overhead-cam six-cylinder engine announced in 1919 was a classic power unit, surviving in AC cars until 1963.

Following an enforced seven-year sabbatical after his parting with Napier, super-salesman S. F. Edge became chairman and managing director in 1921, a move followed by active AC participation in long-distance record-breaking. Commercial success wasn't as easily achieved as endurance records, however, and between 1929 and 1931, AC was in liquidation and no cars were built.

Acquisition of AC by the Hurlock brothers in 1930 resulted in revival of the trusty six in an intelligently updated chassis. The post-war AC had eye-catching styling combined with archaic

leaf-spring front suspension and it wasn't until the appearance of the 1953 Ace – and its descendant the Cobra – that the AC name became a household word. The 1967 428 was a Cobra derivative clothed elegantly by Frua, replaced for 1974 by the mid-engined ME3000.

By the early 1980s, AC had virtually ceased to build cars, but in 1984 came news that the marque would be constructed in Scotland.

Although it was announced that production of the ME3000 would continue, there was a strong rumour that the exciting AC-Ghia, an aerodynamic sports car commissioned as a design study by Ford, would actually enter production.

## AC ACE

In 1953, the old AC six, now developing over twice as much power as when it had been introduced 34 years earlier, was fitted in the new Tojeiro-designed Ace, whose elegant two-seater body had overtones of the Ferrari 166 Barchetta.

## 1953 AC ACE

**Engine:** in-line six cylinder, overhead valve
**Bore × stroke:** 65 mm × 100 mm
**Capacity:** 1991 cc
**Maximum power:** 105 bhp
**Transmission:** four-speed manual
**Chassis:** tubular ladder frame
**Suspension:** independent all round with wishbones and transverse leaf springs
**Brakes:** drums all round
**Bodywork:** two-seater sports
**Maximum speed (approx):** 100 mph (161 kph)

Its 'ladder' chassis marked a definite break with tradition, for it was made up from welded 3 in (76 mm) steel tube with independent suspension all round. Its clean lines contributed to a top speed in excess of 100 mph (161 kph).

Joined a year later by the handsome Aceca coupé, the Ace marked the first step away from the old six-cylinder model when the 125 bhp Bristol 2-litre six was offered as an option. The AC-Bristol enjoyed racing success in Britain and the United States, winning the Autosport Championship outright in 1957 and taking its class at Le Mans. From 1961 the Ruddspeed-converted 2.6-litre Ford Zephyr six was also available, in five stages of tune but the Ace was about to turn into the much fiercer Cobra.

Ditton, Surrey, factory and shipped to the Shelby plant in Los Angeles for installation of the engines and finishing. Their leaf-sprung chassis was built around two parallel 3 in (76 mm) tubes, with structural stiffness added by welded-on cross-members, suspension mounts and body framing. Before long, the 289 cu in (4735 cc) Ford V8 had been standardised, and eventually 427 cu in (6996 cc) engines were fitted; road-going versions had cast-iron cylinder heads, competition versions aluminium. Coil spring suspension was specified on racing Cobras built from February 1965, and on normal production cars from 1966.

Shelby's ambition in building the Cobra was to build a sports car that would outperform the Chevy Corvette and Ferrari, and production levels were initially targeted

declared in 1964. Shelby Cobras dominated SCCA Class A racing from the time they won their first race in 1963 until 1969. The racing programme benefited the road cars by revealing shortcomings in the chassis and suspension: corrective actions such as the replacement of the imprecise worm-and-sector steering by rack-and-pinion were rapidly incorporated on the production line.

The performance and endurance available from the Cobra were amply demonstrated in the model's first assault on the Le Mans 24-hour race in 1963, when a Cobra entered by AC Cars finished seventh (behind six Ferraris) and established a new record in the over-3-litre GT class. Then in 1965, Cobras won America's first-ever (and only) World Manufactur-

plete cars, equipped with high performance 289 cu in engines: 27 AC289s were built between mid-1966 to early 1969, mostly in right-hand-drive form. Even after production had ended, the Cobra mystique continued unabated – one British enthusiast has developed what he claims to be the ultimate road car round a 1968 Cobra 427, equipped with twin Garrett turbochargers, which boost its power output to over 700 bhp – and replicas of varying quality have been built by kit car companies.

The ultimate accolade was given to this 20-year-old design when AutoKraft of Brooklands began manufacture of the Mark IV in the early 1980s, using the original AC body jigs and the rights to put the AC badge on 'Cobra-shaped cars' for 25 years.

AC Cobra 427

## AC Cobra

As early as 1957, the American racing driver Carroll Shelby had attempted to interest General Motors in the production of a lightweight sports car combining a European chassis with a small-block American V8 power unit, but without success. Then, when he learned that Bristol had ceased production of their 2-litre engine, Shelby decided to realise that ambition and unleash the latent performance capability of the AC Ace. He had two 221 cu in (3621 cc) Ford V8 engines shipped to AC in England and the first Cobra prototypes were built in February 1962.

Ford approval meant that a production version with the 260 cu in (4260 cc) engine went into production the following June. The cars were built in AC's Thames

### 1966 AC COBRA 427

**Engine:** V8, overhead valve
**Bore × stroke:** 108 mm × 96 mm
**Capacity:** 7010 cc
**Maximum power:** 390 bhp
**Transmission:** four-speed manual
**Chassis:** tubular ladder frame
**Suspension:** independent all round with wishbones and coil springs
**Brakes:** discs all round
**Bodywork:** two-seater sports
**Maximum speed (approx):** 162 mph (261 kph)

tion levels were initially targeted only at the 100-car minimum necessary for homologation. Making money was not Shelby's prime motive: 'I build the Cobra with my heart rather than for a profit,' he

ers' Championship for Grand Touring Cars. Thereafter, the team Cobras were withdrawn from FIA competition as Shelby became increasingly involved with the Ford GT project.

A total of 1011 Cobras was built between 1962-67, a third of them equipped with the 427 cu in engine (or the less-powerful, cheaper 428 cu in Special Police Interceptor unit normally specified for road cars). The ultimate road-going Cobra was the 427 S/C, with 162 mph (261 kph) performance in standard trim. Two special Cobras were built, one for Shelby, one for comedian Bill Cosby, with dual Paxton superchargers and automatic transmission. Top speed was 'over 182 mph' (293 kph); 0-60 mph took just 3.8 seconds.

Near the end of production, AC Cars assembled the remaining chassis and body parts into com-

## AC 428

The success of the various Cobras with their huge American V8s led AC to carry on the theme, in gentler vein, with the 427 (427 standing for 427 cu in, the displacement of the engine used). Italian coachbuilders Frua were commissioned to design and build a body on what was basically one of the coil-sprung Cobra chassis lengthened 4 inches in the wheelbase. Stretching merely involved lengthening the two main 3-inch tubes in the ladder chassis.

The car appeared as an elegantly purposeful 2+2 convertible or fastback coupé. It was only the switch to the slightly larger 428 cu in (7016 cc) V8 from the American Ford Galaxie which led to the model change to 428. That high-compression (10.5:1) engine produced an enormous amount of

power, with 345 bhp available at 4400 rpm, and even more torque (462 lb ft at just 2800 rpm). Consequently, although the 428 was not designed as an out and out sports car like the Cobra it was still capable of reaching nearly 140 mph (225 kph), taking just 5.9 seconds to achieve 60 mph (96 kph) and 14.5 seconds to reach 100 mph (161 kph), even with the optional automatic transmission.

It was a big heavy car, but despite that huge iron V8 it actually had a rearward weight bias, helping to avoid the understeer usually associated with large front engines. In fact the 428's handling was considered to be quite neutral and predictable and the double-wishbone suspension all round and the Dunlop SP tyres coped well with the power once the right damper settings were finalised. The 428 had a lot in its favour – even the fuel consumption was not too horrendous for the time and size of engine, at around 17 mpg. Unfortunately only 80 cars were built, basically to order, between 1967 and 1974. AC found it difficult to maintain a good supply of bodies from Frua and the quality of Italian steel was then too poor for AC's standards on a car significantly more expensive than the contemporary Aston Martin DB6. That combined with the oil crises of the '70s which put paid to 7-litre American V8s in Europe, led AC to end production in 1974 in favour of the smaller 3000ME.

AC 3000 ME

## AC3000ME

After a troubled gestation period the 3000ME finally appeared in actual production in 1979, powered by a 138 bhp Ford 3-litre V6 with chain drive to the five-speed gearbox. It was notable for its mid-engined layout and the particularly solid perimeter box chassis under its glassfibre skin. The Peter Bohanna design originally appeared as a Unipower prototype in 1969, first with a Triumph Stag V8 and then an Austin Maxi 1.7-litre four.

AC spent many years in its development before starting production, so long that press and public alike began to lose faith. Consequently demand for the car was light after so many false starts but the 3000ME gradually overcame its early teething troubles and by the early 1980s it was becoming accepted as a worthy contender in the mid-range sports coupé market where it competed on price with versions of the Porsche 924 and BMW five series cars.

Its performance never quite matched the car's striking looks, however, and the maximum speed around 115 mph (185 kph) with a 0-60 mph time of just under 9 seconds was a little disappointing. The mid-engine layout and double-wishbone suspension all round also promised a lot without really delivering and the 3000ME was never one of the world's great

---

### 1967 AC 428

**Engine:** V8, overhead valve
**Bore × stroke:** 105 mm × 101 mm
**Capacity:** 7017 cc
**Maximum power:** 345 bhp
**Transmission:** three-speed automatic or four-speed manual
**Chassis:** tubular ladder frame
**Suspension:** independent all round with unequal length wishbones, coil springs and telescopic dampers
**Brakes:** discs all round
**Bodywork:** Frua two-seater convertible or coupé
**Maximum speed (approx):** 140 mph (225 kph)

---

### 1979 AC 3000ME

**Engine:** V6, overhead valve, mid mounted
**Bore × stroke:** 93.6 mm × 72.4 mm
**Capacity:** 2994 cc
**Maximum power:** 138 bhp
**Transmission:** five-speed manual
**Chassis:** perimeter box type frame
**Suspension:** independent with double wishbones and coil springs front and rear
**Brakes:** discs all round
**Bodywork:** two-seater glassfibre coupe
**Maximum speed (approx):** 114 mph (183 kph)

---

mid-engine cars. It demonstrated typical characteristics for the type, with nimble and neutral handling before increasing understeer turned into rather sudden oversteer at the limit.

Given AC's limited capacity, production was never high, but at its peak it was probably no more than two per week and by mid 1984 that had slowed to nearer one a month although the new factory in Scotland continued to take orders.

## ADLER
**Frankfurt, Germany**
**1900-1939**

The fortunes of Adler of Frankfurt were founded on bicycles and typewriters long before the age of motoring. The firm's first move into the automotive sphere taking the form of a contract to supply wire wheels for the Benz Velo of the 1890s. The firm then contracted

to build De Dion tricycles under licence to be sold by Cudell of Aachen, but when its proprietor, Heinrich Kleyer, saw the new Renault voiturette in Paris in 1899, he decided to go into car manufacture on his own account.

Up to 1903, there was nothing remarkable about Adler cars, but in that year a Bohemian engineer, Edmund Rumpler, joined the firm, and new engines, like a 12 hp twin and 24 hp four appeared (though his bolder innovations, like the swing axle suspension he patented in 1903, were unappreciated by the Adler management).

Engines built in unit with the gearbox and roller tappets were two Rumpler innovations that *were* adopted, and the reliability of the cars proven by a third placing in the 1908 Prince Henry Trials, behind works Mercedes and Benz cars. Adlers, especially the smaller models, enjoyed much export success, particularly in Britain, where coachbuilders Morgan of Leighton Buzzard held the agency.

Recovery was slow after World War I and it was not until 1925 that the company's first six-cylinder cars appeared, in both 2.6 and 4.7-litre form to be followed by the 1.9-litre Favorit in 1929. The Favorit was a four-cylinder machine with hydraulic braking and it was followed by the first eight, the Standard 8 with a side-valve 3.9-litre engine. Its resemblance to the contemporary Chrysler was ironic because during the Depression when Germany's economic situation was quite desperate Chrysler saw their chance to buy into the European market. Unfortunately General Motors had the same idea at the same time and acquired Opel whereupon the Deutsche Bank vetoed Chrysler/Adler negotiations.

The succession of dull, American-inspired cars was

AC 428

**Adler Trumpf**

brilliantly followed by the advanced front-wheel-drive Trumpfs of the 1930s and, with excellent *autobahn* performance achieved by the use of aerodynamic bodywork, Adler soon had a name for advanced technology. Unfortunately the Adler factory in Frankfurt was destroyed during the war, and although it was planned to revive the Trumpf range no more cars were built, the company concentrating on typewriters, becoming part of the Grundig group.

## Adler Trumpf

Hans-Gustav Rohr, one of Germany's most advanced automotive engineers, joined Adler in 1930, fresh from the failure of his own company. His clean-sheet-of-paper approach produced a front-wheel-drive 1.5-litre car with all-round independent suspension, aptly called 'Trumpf' (trump). It was in full production by 1933,

### 1933 ADLER TRUMPF

**Engine:** in-line four cylinder, side valve
**Bore × stroke:** 71 mm × 95 mm
**Capacity:** 1505 cc
**Maximum power:** 30 bhp
**Transmission:** four-speed
**Chassis:** pressed steel punt
**Suspension:** independent all round with transverse leaf springs front and swinging arms and torsion bars rear
**Brakes:** drums all round, mechanically operated
**Bodywork:** two-seater sports
**Maximum speed (approx):** 62 mph (99 kph)

## Aerodynamic Trumpf

The opening of Germany's *autobahn* network in the 1930s gave the nation's motorists unparalleled

**Adler Aerodynamic Trumpf**

comfortably ahead of Citroën's *traction avant*. Its relatively small side-valve engine was not particularly powerful, but the Trumpf made up for that with its incredibly agile handling and cornering.

A 1.7-litre derivative appeared in 1934, in which year the range was further widened by the announcement of the Trumpf Junior, with a 996 cc four-cylinder engine. A sports version was available in 1936-38, with a lowered chassis and an alloy cylinder head boosting power output to 28 bhp. Two other sports versions were built, but all were underpowered although well balanced.

opportunities for high-speed cruising; and Adler were among the leading exponents of achieving high speed through scientific design. 'It is now possible,' wrote a visitor to the Adler stand at the 1938 Berlin Motor Show, 'to have a three-seater car with ample luggage accommodation that will travel at 90 mph (145 kph) with an engine developing only 80 bhp. This is a reduction of 33 per cent as compared with normal practice.'

The benefits of wind-tunnel-developed streamlining were demonstrated during 1935-36, when Adler streamliners established no fewer than 22 international re-

cords. The 1936 Autobahn was a production derivative of the record-breakers, with a four-seat body panelled in aluminium over a thin-wall steel tubular framework welded to the chassis; plexiglass curved side windows helped cut 550 lb (250 kg) off the all-up weight compared with a conventional 2500 lb (1134 kg) saloon. Top speed was 80 mph (129 kph) – almost 20 mph (32 kph) faster than the standard model – with a high-geared sports coupé capable of 93 mph (150 kph).

The ultimate Adler was the 2.5-litre six designed by Rohr's successor, the Austrian Jentschke, which replaced the 1.7-litre Trumpf and the 3-litre Diplomat in 1937. This new rear-wheel-drive streamliner was both fast – 95 mph (153 kph) could be achieved by the triple-carburettor Sport version – and endowed with good roadholding, aided by independent suspension all round with swing axles.

### 1937 AERODYNAMIC TRUMPF

**Engine:** in-line six cylinder, side valve
**Bore × stroke:** 71 mm × 105 mm
**Capacity:** 2494 cc
**Maximum power:** 80 bhp
**Transmission:** four-speed
**Chassis:** platform frame
**Suspension:** independent all round with swinging half axles
**Brakes:** drums all round
**Bodywork:** four-seater coupé
**Maximum speed (approx):** 95 mph (153 kph)

## AERO
**Prague, Czechoslovakia**
**1929–1939**

Bretislav Novotny was a Czech engineer who entered car production with the friction-drive two-stroke DISK after World War I; he retained both features on the little single-cylinder 499 cc ENKA,

launched in 1928 and taken over the following year by the Aero aircraft works in Prague. The original Aero was said to have been Czechoslovakia's smallest car and its specification was as basic as the car was tiny. Electric starting was an extra on this little car, the standard method being a rope starter like that of a marine outboard engine, mounted beside the driver's seat.

The elektron rear axle was devoid of a differential, suspension was quarter-elliptic all round, and there were no front wheel brakes. But the Aero was durable, and in a stunt timed to coincide with the opening of the 1929 Prague Show, Bohumil Turek covered the 3050 miles (4900 km) from Prague–Brest–Prague–Hamburg–Prague in 184 hours 35 minutes, an average of 16.5 mph (26.6 kph).

A 660cc vertical twin was the next Aero model, followed by another twin, this time of 998cc, developed in 1934 into a front-wheel-drive four-seater. Aero's last model was a 1997 cc four-cylinder, front-wheel-drive model, the Type 50. Even in 2-litre form it was still only a two stroke.

While the early Aeros had been stark and basic the later models grew to be quite handsome beasts, particularly the convertibles. The Aero came to an end in 1939 with the outbreak of World War II.

### 1929 AERO

**Engine:** single cylinder, two stroke
**Bore × stroke:** 85 mm × 88 mm
**Capacity:** 499 cc
**Maximum power:** 10 bhp
**Transmission:** friction drive
**Chassis:** integral punt
**Suspension:** non-independent by quarter elliptic leaf springs all round
**Brakes:** rear drums only
**Bodywork:** two-seater coupé
**Maximum speed (approx):** 50 mph (80 kph)

**Aero**

# A-Z
## A-Z OF THE CAR

## ALDA
**Courbevoie, France**
**1912–1922**

Probably the only marque ever to be named by the readers of a daily newspaper, the Alda took its name from the initials of the phrase *Ah – La Delicieuse Automobile*, chosen by the readers of *L'Auto*. it was produced in the old ENV factory at Courbevoie on the Seine by Fernand Charron after Charron had left the CGV company. The strange name was adopted to avoid a clash with CGV who were also known as Charron.

Just like the cars Charron built for CGV the Alda had the rather odd feature of a dashboard radiator and a 3187cc four-cylinder engine capable, it was claimed of '6 to 47 mph in top gear'. Both open and closed bodies of great luxury were available, and the Alda sold for £395 in chassis form in England.

Despite its sponsor's distinguished racing career, the Alda had a mediocre competition record, achieving sixth place in the 1913 Coupe de l'Auto and retiring in the 1914 Grand Prix. An unusual technical feature of the touring Aldas was the employment of either normal poppet valves or Henriod rotary valves; Charron having acquired rights to the Henriod valve along with the ENV factory in 1912.

A six-cylinder version was listed before World War I, but subsequently only the four, bored-out to 3563cc, was available. In 1920 Alda was absorbed by the Farman luxury-car company, also based in Billancourt (Seine) but production only continued for another two years before the marque expired.

### 1913 ALDA

**Engine:** in-line four cylinder, side or rotary valve
**Bore × stroke:** 85 mm × 140 mm
**Capacity:** 3187 cc
**Maximum power:** 15 hp
**Transmission:** four-speed
**Chassis:** pressed steel
**Suspension:** non-independent with semi-elliptic leaf springs
**Brakes:** rear drums only
**Bodywork:** to order
**Maximum speed (approx):** 47 mph (76 kph)

## ALBA
**Trieste, Austria**
**1906–1908**

Before World War I the free state of Trieste was an enclave of the Austro-Hungarian Empire and in the autumn of 1906, a group of wealthy automobile enthusiasts decided to found a car manufacturing company to take advantage of its considerable financial attractions, quickly building a 215,300 sq ft (20,000 sq m) factory. Alba's chief engineer was S. Bauer, who proposed the construction of two chassis types, an 18/24 hp and a 35/40 hp but only the larger model reached production. At the 1907 Paris Salon, the 35/40 hp was praised for its perfect finish, but orders were not forthcoming, and production ceased in 1908 after only nine chassis had been assembled. Liquidation was long and painful and it was not until 1911, three years later, that the company was finally wound up.

### 1908 ALBA

**Engine:** in-line four cylinder
**Bore × stroke:** 125 mm × 140 mm
**Capacity:** 6868 cc
**Maximum power:** 35/40 hp
**Transmission:** four-speed
**Chassis:** pressed steel
**Suspension:** non-independent with semi-elliptic leaf springs
**Brakes:** rear only
**Bodywork:** to order
**Maximum speed (approx):** 60 mph (97 kph)

**Alba**

## ALFA ROMEO
**Milan, Italy**
**1910–**

In 1906 a branch factory of the French Darracq company was incorporated in Naples, moving before the year was out to a large new plant in Milan. The 8-10 hp twin-cylinder cars it built were of poor quality, and the venture was wound up in 1909, the works being acquired by the Anonima Lombarda Fabbrica Automobili, a consortium led by Ugo Stella.

Chassis of 2.4 and 4.1-litres, both side-valve fours designed by the company's newly appointed designer, Giuseppe Merosi, were produced, while an overhead valve 6.1-litre model was made in limited numbers. Next the company was acquired in 1915 by the wealthy industrialist Nicola Romeo, who reformed the company in 1918, its products now bearing the name Alfa Romeo. Merosi was retained and designed the post-war 20/30 hp of 4.2 litres, and its sporting derivative the 20/30ES. A 3-litre model, the RL, appeared in 1921, and won the 1923 Targa Florio.

Merosi was a designer of somewhat patchy capability, and his 1923 P1 Grand Prix car – which took the life of works driver Ugo Sivocci in practice at Monza – was too slow and never even started a race. So it was somewhat of a coup when Enzo Ferrari (then an Alfa team driver) persuaded Vittorio Jano to leave Fiat and join Alfa, where his first design was the sensationally successful P2 GP car.

The lessons that Jano learned on the track were translated into an outstanding series of sports cars which started with the 6C 1500, and progressed through the twin-cam 2.3 supercharged straight-eights of the 1930s; these outstanding cars were built, ironically, when the company was in the financial difficulties that resulted in its becoming Government-controlled.

As a result, Alfa Romeo's racing cars represented Italy in international motor racing during the 1930s with outstanding success – until, that is, the Nazi-backed teams of Mercedes and Auto-Union really got going.

Though the Alfa factory was three-quarters destroyed in World War II, the company was quickly back in production, a six-cylinder

**Alda**

2.5 litre called the Freccia d'Oro and derived from the pre-war 6C 2300 appearing in 1947. It was joined in 1950 by the all-new 1900, designed by Alessio, which was Alfa's first four-cylinder model since the mid-1920s; Super and Sprint derivatives soon appeared, plus the exciting Disco Volante, built as a publicity exercise in limited numbers.

In 1954 came the first of the Giuliettas, a handsome 1300cc twin-cam four, followed in 1962 by the slightly larger Giulia. The following year construction work began on a vast new factory at Arese, outside Milan, to replace the old Portello works, followed in 1968 by the development of a plant near Naples in an ultimately disappointing attempt to extend car manufacture to the impoverished south of Italy. The Naples plant built a new, cheaper car line known as the Alfasud, a front-wheel-drive 1186cc overhead-cam flat four designed by Rudolf Hruska, one-time collaborator with Porsche. The Alfasud was an inspired creation but plagued by poor quality control and a truly frightening tendency to rust in short order.

The cars built in the north at Alfa's main factory were not immune either, which was a shame as the Alfetta range had many desirable qualities. These new models were originally all twin-cam fours, with the de Dion rear suspension and transaxle, and then in 1981 came the GTV 6, with the alloy 2.5-litre V6 first used in the Alfa Six saloon.

This 160 bhp, fuel-injected unit gave a top speed of 129 mph (208 kph). In the late 1980s, the sleek Pininfarina-styled 164 saloon range was launched, with alloy 2-litre four-cylinder and 3-litre V6 engines. The 146 bhp, 1955 cc 164 Twin Spark had twin sparking plugs and variable valve timing, and was capable of 130 mph (209 kph), yet had fuel consumption of

**Alfa Romeo 8C 2300**

28-48 mpg.

The 155 range was similarly styled but smaller, with 1.8 and 2-litre Twin Spark engines, a 2.5-litre V6 and the Integrale-based Cloverleaf 4, with dramatic acceleration up to 139 mph (224 kph).

Following Fiat's take-over of Alfa Romeo in the late 1980s, the marque's sporting heritage was re-emphasised with the bizarre-looking 152 mph (245 kph) SZ.

## 6C 1750

The 6C 1750 was a direct descendant of Vittorio Jano's first touring car design for Alfa after leaving Fiat, the 6C 1500. That was announced in 1925 and appeared two years later in 1927 with (as the 6C suggests) a six cylinder, single-overhead-cam, fixed-block engine which produced 44 bhp. It was noteworthy for introducing Alfa's distinctive tappet adjustment by collars threaded on the valve stems. A twin-cam Gran Turismo version appeared in 1928 and was known as the Super Sport, one of which won the Mille Miglia in 1928.

In 1929 both the bore and stroke of the 1500 engine were increased to give a displacement of 1752 cc but a power increase of just 2 bhp! In typically confusing Alfa style the 1750 appeared in various guises as

both a single-overhead-cam and double-overhead-cam machine, normally aspirated and super-charged. The unsupercharged twin cam was known as the Sport until 1930 when the name was changed to Gran Turismo. At the same time the supercharged Super Sport became the Gran Sport. All the Gran Sports and all except the first fifty Super Sports were fitted with a large direct-drive blower rather than the smaller geared-up example of the 1500. The net result was a power output of 85 bhp.

For 1933, the 6C 1750 SS was fitted with a synchromesh gearbox

---

**1929 6C 1750 SS**

**Engine:** in-line six cylinder, twin cam
**Bore × stroke:** 65 mm × 88 mm
**Capacity:** 1752 cc
**Maximum power:** 85 bhp
**Transmission:** four-speed
**Chassis:** pressed steel, five cross-members
**Suspension:** non-independent with semi-elliptic leaf springs all round
**Brakes:** rod-operated drums
**Bodywork:** to choice (normally sports roadster)
**Maximum speed (approx):** 95 mph (152 kph)

---

and freewheel, features also found on the ultimate development of the original 1500 line, the rare 6C 1900 Gran Turismo, which appeared in 1932, with the engine bored out to give a capacity of 1918cc, and an aluminium cylinder head. The effect of these modifications was to boost power output to 68 bhp, against the 55 bhp of the standard 1750 GT.

Not only did the 1750 look the part it was a very effective competition car and the 95 mph (163 kph) Super Sport took the Mille Miglia in 1929 and the Spa 24 hour race the same year. Alfas went one better in 1929 winning the Mille Miglia, the Tourist Trophy and the Spa 24 Hours.

Although Alfa were at pains to make the road and race cars look as similar as possible, race car performance was not really available for the road. Nevertheless a typical Zagato-bodied two seater sports would be able to reach 60 mph (96 kph) in under 14 seconds with a top speed of over 90 mph (145 kph). The cars were light and responsive to drive with high geared steering (with only 1¾ turns lock to lock) which needed a delicate touch to drive the car straight. The centrally mounted gear lever needed the same precise touch and the engine's pick-up was dramatic when the throttle was depressed. Luckily the 1750 would stop as well as it went as the rod-operated drum brakes were smooth and powerful with lots of feel.

The line came to an end in 1934, not because the cars were obsolete but because Alfa Romeo changed their policy, drawing in its horns during the Depression.

## 8C 2300

Produced alongside the 1750 six between 1931 and 1934, the 8C 2300 series was unquestionably Jano's masterpiece, though it was also a hopelessly uneconomic car to produce during the Depression. It had a straight-eight engine with the cylinders cast in two blocks of four; the train of gears which drove the twin overhead camshafts was mounted between them. Apart

**Alfa Romeo 6C 1750 Zagato**

### 1931 8C 2300

**Engine:** in-line eight cylinder, twin cam
**Bore × stroke:** 65 mm × 88 mm
**Capacity:** 2336 cc
**Maximum power:** 130 bhp
**Transmission:** four-speed
**Chassis:** pressed steel
**Suspension:** non-independent, semi-elliptic springs all round
**Brakes:** 16 in light-alloy drums
**Bodywork:** to choice
**Maximum speed (approx):** 110 mph (176 kph)

from the very first cars, which had cast-iron blocks, alloy blocks with dry liners were used, and the one-piece alloy heads incorporated hemispherical combustion chambers in typical Alfa fashion.

The crankshaft was made in two halves, with twin helical gears separating them; one gear drove the camshafts, the other the Roots-type supercharger, and both the water and oil pumps (dry sump lubrication was standard).

In standard form, this power unit developed 130 bhp, though the racing Monza version could achieve 178 bhp. Some engines, particularly when used for competition work, were bored out to 2.6 litres, though a 2.6-litre version was never catalogued.

There were two road-going versions, the long-wheelbase Le Mans (8C 2300 Alfas won the Le Mans 24-hour race in 1931-2-3-4) and the short-wheelbase Mille Miglia (the model won the 1000-mile classic in 1932-3-4). In all, a total of 188 8C 2300 Alfas was built between 1931 and 1934, and to drive one of the surviving cars is to experience a rare combination of vehicle dynamics. The roadholding and performance are still outstanding, even after over half a century.

## 6C 2300

After the years of extravagance, the introduction of the Jano-designed 6C 2300 in 1934 showed that the reality of the harsh economic conditions had at last reached Alfa Romeo. The new models were

well enough designed, but lacked that artistry and inspiration that had characterised Jano's earlier Alfas: indeed in its later forms its cheap pressed steel bodywork and banal instrumentation attracted much criticism.

It retained the twin cams of its predecessor, but the supercharger was a thing of the wasteful past. The engine was available in two stages of tune, the less powerful (68 bhp) normally being fitted in the long wheelbase chassis, which generally carried five-seat saloon coachwork, while the more powerful (76 bhp) appeared in the short-wheelbase chassis, which, as a rule, had four-seat coupé coachwork.

In 1935, these six-cylinder models were replaced by the 6C 2300B, with all-round independent suspension, and available in three forms: Lungo (70 bhp, 128 in/325 cm wheelbase), Corto (76 bhp, 118 in/300 cm wheelbase) and Pescara (95 bhp, 118 in/300 cm wheelbase). When the Second Series 6C 2300B appeared in 1937, a lightweight 'Mille Miglia' model was added to the range.

In 1939, the 6C 2500 made its debut, in Sport and Super Sport forms; it went back into production after the war and survived until 1953.

## 8C 2900

If the 2.3-litre Alfas seemed prosaic in comparison with what had gone before, the 2.9-litre series introduced in 1936 elevated the company's stock considerably. The original model, Tipo 8C 2900A, was derived from the Tipo B Grand Prix car, one of which had won the 1935 Mille Miglia fitted with road equipment. Though a catalogue model, probably less than a dozen Tipo 8C 2900A cars were built, using a 170 bhp engine in a 108 in (274 cm) wheelbase chassis with all-round independent suspension.

Actively campaigned during 1936 by Alfa's racing team, Scuderia Ferrari, the 8C 2900A took the first three places in the Mille Miglia and won the 24 Hours of Spa. The 8C 2900B appeared late in 1937: its 2.9-litre supercharged engines were reputed to be the surplus factory stock of Tipo B GP

**Alfa Romeo 8C 2900**

### 1936 8C 2900

**Engine:** in-line eight cylinder
**Bore × stroke:** 68 mm × 100 mm
**Capacity:** 2905 cc
**Maximum power:** 180 bhp
**Transmission:** four-speed
**Chassis:** box section
**Suspension:** twin trailing arms and coil springs front with swing axles and transverse leaf spring rear
**Brakes:** drums all round, hydraulically operated
**Bodywork:** two-seater sports
**Maximum speed (approx):** 140 mph (225 kph)

power units, which limited the production run to 30 cars. The chassis was a much stiffer version of the 6C 2300B, with trailing link front suspension and rear swing axles controlled by a transverse leaf spring. The transmission was in unit with the final drive, and two chassis lengths were available.

In 1938 the 8C 2900 took the first three places in the Mille Miglia and won the Spa 24 Hours. An aerodynamic coupé was entered for the Le Mans 24 Hours and proved to be the fastest car running, lapping at over 96 mph (155 kph). It was leading by 115 miles (185 km) after 18 hours, when a tyre burst on the Mulsanne straight, damaging the bodywork.

Probably the fastest production sports car of the 1930s, the 2.9 Alfa

### 1935 6C 2300 PESCARA

**Engine:** in-line six cylinder
**Bore × stroke:** 70 mm × 100 mm
**Capacity:** 2309 cc
**Maximum power:** 95 bhp
**Transmission:** four-speed
**Chassis:** twin box section
**Suspension:** independent all round by trailing links and coil springs at the front and swing axles and torsion bars at the rear
**Brakes:** steel drums all round
**Bodywork:** lightweight saloon
**Maximum speed (approx):** 98 mph (156 kph)

was superseded in 1939 by the 4.5-litre Tipo 412, with a V12 power unit. This promising model was never fully developed due to the war and post-war conditions dictated a return to the likes of the 6C 2300.

## Giulietta

Announced late in 1954, the Giulietta was a 1300cc saloon designed on similar lines to the larger 1900 introduced for the 1950 season. That bald statement should not hide the fact that the Giulietta was an inspired creation, a car that was exactly right from the word go.

It had a five-bearing four-cylinder engine with two chain-driven overhead camshafts. The standard four-door Berlina, with factory bodywork, developed only 60 bhp, but alongside it was offered a Bertone-bodied two-door coupé, the Sprint, with a 91 bhp engine. The first Giuliettas suffered from transmission trouble, but this fault was rectified by the introduction of a new gearbox with Porsche-type baulk-ring synchromesh on all gears.

Two Farina-bodied open two-seaters, the Spyder and Spyder Veloce, appeared in 1957, as did the four-door TI (Turismo Internationale). In 1959 came a 114 bhp Sprint Speciale, bodied by Bertone, but the ultimate Giulietta was the 1960 SZ, a lightweight Zagato-bodied two-door fixed-head coupé. In July 1962 all models except the TI gained an enlarged, 1570 cc, power unit as well as a five-speed gearbox with overdrive fifth: in this form the car was renamed Giulia. Most notable of the new Giulias was the TZ (Tubolare Zagato) with multi-tube space frame, all round independent suspension and disc brakes.

The basic design and layout of the Giulietta was so good that in essence it lived on well into the '70s as the basis for Alfa's coupés and saloons. In saloon form it was damned by one of the ugliest bodies ever foisted on an Alfa but the Bertone-bodied coupé was one of his best designs.

In typical Alfa Romeo fashion there was a plethora of names for very similar cars, Giulia Sprint, Giulia Sprint Veloce, GTV, GTA (with lightweight bodywork like

**Alfa Romeo 6C 2300 Pescara**

**Alfa Romeo Giulietta Sprint**

**Alfa Romeo Disco Volante**

## 1954 GIULIETTA SPRINT

**Engine:** in-line four cylinder, twin cam
**Bore × stroke:** 74 mm × 75 mm
**Capacity:** 1290 cc
**Maximum power:** 103 bhp
**Transmission:** four-speed manual
**Chassis:** integral
**Suspension:** independent front with wishbones coil springs and telescopic dampers, rear live axle
**Brakes:** drums all round hydraulically operated
**Bodywork:** two seater–sports
**Maximum speed (approx):** 112 mph (183 kph)

the TZ before it and more power) and GT Junior. All shared the same well located live axle, the five-speed transmission, superb disc brakes all round and that alloy twin-cam four in 1290 cc, 1570 cc, 1779 cc, and 1962 cc form in the last of the line, the GTV 2000. The classic of the line was probably the GTV 1750 as the twin cam lost some of its free-revving sparkle when it was bored out to two litres to give over 120 bhp. Carburation was usually twin Webers or Dellortos but US models used the sometimes troublesome Alfa mechanical fuel injection.

Running parallel with Bertone's coupés were his rival Pininfarina's equally attractive spyders using the same running gear and engine sizes. In fact that range has outlived the coupés with the 2-litre spyders still on sale in 1984.

## Disco Volante

The Disco Volante has generated far more interest and attention that its production run (if one could call it that) warrants and that shows just how successful it was in its own way.

It was primarily a show car, a car to get Alfa noticed and talked about, but secondly it was built as a test-bed for a new 3-litre six-cylinder power unit. It was also meant to earn its keep in sports car racing, where it was intended that

the model would gain even more useful publicity for Alfa. It took its name (which translates as 'flying saucer') from its voluptuous two-seat coachwork, built by Touring in association with Alfa engineers Colombo and Satta.

Six were built and tested during 1952, two of them short-wheelbase models with the 1900 four-cylinder engine. As a result of this development programme, the car was extensively modified for 1953, when a team of four coupés was entered in the Mille Miglia, one a 2-litre four, the others powered by 3.6-litre six-cylinder engines. The 2 litre retired early in the race, but the other three cars all held the lead at some time during the event. However, engine failure eliminated one car, a transmission oil leak another, while the third car, driven by Fangio, suffered a partial steering failure, only the right-hand wheel responding. As a result, the car could only be driven slowly round bends, was overtaken by a Ferrari and finished second.

At Le Mans that year, all three Disco Volante coupés retired with mechanical problems. The sole entry in the Spa 24 Hours spun off while lying third and retired, and the model's only racing victory was in the Supercortemaggiore Grand Prix at Mercano, where a 3-litre Disco Volante with more conventional bodywork, driven by Fangio, won when the Lancias retired.

One of the 1953 works cars was then sold to Jo Bonnier and fitted with an open two-seater Zagato

body, in which form it was raced during 1955. It should be remembered that the competition models did not have the same rather outrageous bodywork of Touring's original, the car that everyone thinks of as *the* Disco Volante.

## 1953 DISCO VOLANTE

**Engine:** in-line six cylinder, twin cam
**Bore × stroke:** 88 mm × 98 mm
**Capacity:** 3576 cc
**Maximum power:** 260 bhp
**Transmission:** five-speed
**Chassis:** tubular space frame
**Suspension:** independent with double wishbones and coil springs front and de Dion axle and coil springs rear
**Brakes:** drums all round,
**Bodywork:** aerodynamic open or coupé two seater

## Alfa Romeo SZ

The SZ was the brainchild of Fiat chairman Vittorio Ghidella, and revived the marque's tradition of building low-volume models with existing mechanical components. Design work on what Alfa Romeo called their `alternative supercar' began in 1987 and resulted in one of the most remarkable-looking road cars ever made. The SZ body, which was styled in-house and then refined by Zagato, was of ICI Modar composite glassfibre panels over a

steel monocoque.

Despite the bluff front end and high slab sides, the car had a very low drag coefficient (Cd) of 0.30.

Underneath, power was from Alfa's 3-litre 60-degree V6, with tuning changes to the timing and fuel injection to raise power to 210 bhp, with 181 lb ft of torque at 4500 rpm. This was longitudinally mounted, with drive to the rear wheels through a five-speed transaxle. Handling was superb, thanks to suspension designed with help from Alfa's racing engineers and aided in part by special Pirelli asymmetrically treaded P Zero tyres. Performance, in a car weighing 2778 lb (1260 kg) was excellent, with 0-60 possible in 6.9 seconds.

## 1990 ALFA ROMEO SZ

**Engine:** V6 single overhead cam per bank of cylinders
**Bore × stroke:** 93 mm x 72.6 mm
**Capacity:** 2959 cc
**Maximum power:** 210 bhp
**Transmission:** five-speed transaxle
**Chassis:** Alfa 75 floorpan
**Suspension:** independent front with struts, transverse links, anti-roll bar, rear de Dion axle, watt parallel links, anti-roll bar, rear de Dion axle and Watt parallel links
**Brakes:** ventilated discs
**Bodywork:** composite 2 + 2
**Maximum speed:** 152 mph (245 kph)

**Alfa Romeo SZ**

# A-Z
## OF THE CAR

**Allard J2**

## ALLARD

**London, England**
**1937–1957**

'Sydney Allard didn't have much of a sense of humour,' said racing commentator James Tilling recently. 'well, you wouldn't, living in Clapham and building a car like that . . . .' But actually the Allard, despite its somewhat agricultural styling, was a most effective motorcar, with quite surprising reserves of performance.

Sydney Allard was born in 1910, son of a well-to-do builder but instead of following his father into the family business, he decided to make the motor industry his career and eventually acquired a garage in Putney. His spare time activity was motor sport, first with a Morgan three wheeler, then with a Model A Ford, but it was the acquisition of a Ford V8 that had competed (unsuccessfully) in the 1934 Tourist Trophy which led him to build a trials special powered by a Ford V8 engine. This was so successful, despite a start-to-finish construction time of only three weeks, that friends asked him to make replicas for them.

Allard and a friend, Ken Hutchinson, whose replica had a Lincoln Zephyr V12 engine, formed a highly-successful trials team known as the Tail-Waggers; out of 75 events entered in three years, Allard won awards in 71 . . . The first production Allards – in reality, highly-modified Ford V8 chassis fitted with two-seat bodies – appeared in 1937, but production was hardly under way before war broke out in 1939 and car manufacture was shelved 'for the duration'.

After the hostilities, Allard shifted his company to Clapham High Street and began production of a new range of Allards in 1946. All Ford-powered, there were three models available – J1, K1 and L – with Ballamy divided-axle independent front suspension and a box-section chassis. Gearing for road work was kept low to aid

acceleration at the cost of top speed, and the aluminium bodywork was invariably designed by 'Gop' Imhof.

J1 was a sports two-seater, with the option of a 3.9-litre Mercury V8 engine, K1 was a two-seat roadster and L was a four-seat tourer. In 1949 the J2 appeared, and quickly gained a reputation in competition; with a 4.4-litre Mercury V8 as standard, the J2 could also be had with a Mercury power unit converted by Zora Arkus-Duntov. Its overhead valve Ardun cylinder heads helped boost power output to over 140 bhp.

The prestige being quickly earned by Allard was enhanced by the P-Type coupé of 1949: in 1952 one of these cars won a difficult Monte Carlo Rally. Penalised by misguided 'luxury taxes' which hit all cars costing over £1000, Allard attempted to widen the appeal of his marque with a new model, the Palm Beach, powered by four- or six-cylinder Ford power units, but by 1957 Allard production had ceased, though there were ventures into sub-economy three-wheelers and, at the other extreme, dragsters.

After the death of Sydney Allard in 1966, the company continued its involvement in 'alternative motoring' with the sale and supply of racing and rally tuning equipment.

## Allard J2

Unmistakeably a sports car, the J2 Allard was advertised as 'the Sportsman's Choice'. Its two-seat body was streamlined in the manner of the day, and cycle wings were standard. Its de Dion rear end layout was inspired by a special hill-climb car that Sydney Allard had built using an air-cooled Steyr-Puch V8. These cars were exported engineless to America, where enthusiasts could implant power units of their choice, the 5.4-litre Cadillac V8 being an especial favourite. In 1950 there were victories for these Yankee Allards at Bridgehampton, Santa Ana and Watkins Glen, and one of the most successful American Allard drivers, Tom Cole, partnered Sydney Allard at Le Mans, where a creditable third place was secured at an average of 87.75 mph (141.2 kph). Because of the sterling crisis, Allard couldn't sell the Cadillac-engined cars in Britain; nevertheless, the works raced them to good effect, setting a new record at the Brighton Speed Trials in 1950. The following year, Sydney and his wife achieved the remarkable 'his and her' double of firsts in the sports car class and in the ladies class with Cadillac-Allards. Moreover, Sydney's time was not only a new sports-car record, it was within a second of the time set by the AJB racing car.

The J2 was very much a car of

the 'point-and-squirt' breed, and by the end of 1952 more sophisticated sports cars, such as the Jaguar XK120, had pushed it from pre-eminence, even in America, where it had achieved its most notable victories. Though the model ceased production in the 1950s, the 1980s saw a revived Allard company, now based in Canada, offering J2 replicas.

## Palm Beach

In 1952 with the intention of reaching a wider clientele, Allard announced a lower-priced model, the Palm Beach, which cost under £1200 compared with the £2000-plus of the contemporary Allard P2 Monte Carlo. Power was again by Ford, but this time the in-line Consul Four and Zephyr Six power

### 1950 ALLARD J2
**Engine:** Cadillac V8 overhead valve
**Capacity:** 5420 cc
**Maximum power:** 160 bhp
**Transmission:** three-speed manual
**Chassis:** tubular ladder frame
**Suspension:** independent front with divided axle and coil springs, rear de Dion axle
**Brakes:** drums all round
**Bodywork:** two-seater sports
**Maximum speed (approx):** 110 mph (176 kph)

**Allard Palm Beach**

units of 1508cc and 2622cc respectively were utilised. However, the expected demand failed to materialise, and a more up-to-date example, the Palm Beach Mk II, was brought out in 1956. Though a choice of the newly-introduced Zephyr II six-cylinder power unit or the 3.4-litre Jaguar XK six was given, and the split-axle front suspension was replaced by proper torsion-bar independent front suspension, demand was minimal.

A performance derivative, the J2R, had a 270 bhp Cadillac V8 of 5.4-litres as export customers could still fit their own choice of power unit. In 1956 the company announced that its cars would henceforth only be built against individual orders; these, it seems, were not forthcoming, and the company turned to its other activities from 1957 on.

### 1952 Allard Palm Beach
**Engine:** Ford in-line four cylinder overhead valve (in-line six optional)
**Bore x stroke:** 79.37 mm x 76.2 mm
**Capacity:** 1508 cc
**Maximum power:** 47 bhp
**Transmission:** three-speed manual
**Chassis:** tubular ladder frame
**Suspension:** independent front with Bellamy divided front axle with coil springs
**Brakes:** drums all round
**Bodywork:** two or three-seater open sports
**Maximum speed (approx):** 80 mph (128 kph)

# ALMA
**Paris, France**
**1926–1929**

Etablissements Alma was a short-lived company based at Courbevoie (Seine) near the Alda plant. It was only in business for four years between 1926 and 1929 and was known chiefly for the Alma Six. That was powered by a small six-cylinder engine developed by an aircraft engineer

### 1926 ALMA 6
**Engine:** in-line six cylinder, overhead valve
**Bore × stroke:** 66 mm × 80 mm
**Capacity:** 1642 cc
**Maximum power:** not known
**Transmission:** two-speed
**Chassis:** pressed steel
**Suspension:** non-independent with semi-elliptic leaf springs
**Brakes:** drums all round
**Bodywork:** two-seater coupé
**Maximum speed (approx):** not known

Alma 6

named Vaslin.

Beautifully made, this 1.6-litre pushrod overhead valve power unit had a seven-bearing crankshaft and each cylinder possessed one exhaust valve and two inlet valves serving entirely separate induction systems, each with its own porting and carburettor. At low speeds, only one inlet system per cylinder came into operation, while at high speeds both systems were used. The engine was so flexible that only a two-speed transmission was deemed necessary by the confident manufacturers.

based on the 4CV, starting work in 1954: his first car, the A106 Mille Miles, used 4CV running gear housed in a glass fibre 2+2 coupé body. The name 'Alpine' was chosen simply because Rédélé enjoyed driving on the winding roads of the Alps.

An improved version of the A106 with the newly announced 850cc Dauphine engine (soon increased to 904cc) appeared in 1956, winning its class in the 1956 Mille Miglia. A cabriolet derivative, A108, appeared in 1957; two years later, Rédélé introduced a Sport version of the

Alpine A110

# ALPINE
**Dieppe, France**
**1955–**

Jean Rédélé, son of a Dieppe garage proprietor, began competition motoring after World War II with highly modified Renault 4CVs, even competing in long-distance events like the Coupe des Alpes and the Mille Miglia, winning the 750cc class in the latter event in three consecutive years, 1952-53-54. He decided to build a sports car

A108 with a new tubular steel chassis.

It was in 1961, however, that he launched the archetypal Alpine chassis with a central backbone carrying a steel subframe for the rear-mounted engine and suspension; it was first used on the 2+2 A108 Berlinette Tour de France which, despite its swing-axle rear suspension and tail-heavy weight distribution, was a consistent class-winner in competition. New versions of 998cc and 1108cc, still with modified Renault engines, appeared in 1963 in response to

the competition offered by the new Bonnet cars. It was eventually available with the double-overhead-cam conversion designed by Amédée Gordini.

While Alpine had many successes in rallies and road racing, particularly at Le Mans, the company's attempts to build Formula 2 and 3 racing cars were not quite so successful, and that side of Alpine's activities was discontinued in 1969. A rally development of the A110 road car, the Berlinette 1600S, used the Renault 16 engine and had 130mph-plus (209kph) performance. In 1969, Alpine

### 1963 ALPINE A110 BERLINETTE TOUR DE FRANCE
**Engine:** in-line four cylinder, twin cam
**Capacity:** 1108 cc
**Maximum power:** 100 bhp
**Transmission:** four or five-speed manual
**Chassis:** tubular steel backbone
**Suspension:** independent with double wishbones, coil springs front and swinging axles rear
**Brakes:** discs all round
**Bodywork:** glassfibre coupé
**Maximum speed (approx):** 135 mph (217 kph)

A110 cars took the first three places in the Coupe des Alpes. Other sporting successes led to an announcement by Renault that Alpine were to be responsible for all the Regie's competition programme.

At the 1971 Geneva Show, Alpine unveiled a new luxury road car, the A310, with a rear-mounted Renault 16TS engine and a 130mph (209kph) top speed: a 2.7-litre V6 power unit was later introduced. In 1976, Alpine and Renault jointly launched the Renault 5 Alpine (sold as the Gordini in the United Kingdom).

# Alpine A110

Alpine and the A110 are synonymous. The distinctive and elegant glassfibre coupé bodywork was designed by Marcel Hubert and clothed a bewildering range of engines, from the humble 956cc unit right up to the powerful 1796cc four, with 1100, 1150, 1300, 1470 and 1600cc versions in between. The key to the car was its sturdy tubular steel backbone chassis. This gave it the strength for its innumerable rally victories which included a famous 1-2-3 in the Monte Carlo in 1970. Originally hung on to that chassis was the prosaic running gear from the boxy Renault R8 saloon. That determined the car's layout with its rear mounted engine and swinging semi-axle rear suspension. The A110's pronounced negative rear-wheel camber was there to overcome the limitations of that rather basic suspension design, which it did successfully.

Although renowned as a rally car, the 110 was a desirable road car too, most popular in its 1300cc

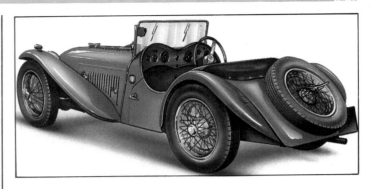

form. Then it could be ordered with twin Weber 40DCOE carburettors, 90 bhp and the potential for 128 mph (206 kph). It had drawbacks of course, a lack of headroom and too much mechanical and road noise among them. The gear linkage was not one of the 110's strong points either although the car's handling and roadholding more than made up for details like that. Despite its rear-engine layout the 110 displayed none of the vices associated with rear engine cars; the very firm suspension and negative camber saw to that.

Production peaked in 1970 when 1000 A110s were built and the ultimate 110 was the 1796cc rally version with 170 bhp on tap which brought Alpine Renault the World Rally Championship in 1973.

# Alpine A310

The A310 arrived with a whimper rather than a bang and lacked the rally heritage of the famous A110. That, plus the fact that it was never exported to Britain, makes it a rather unknown quantity in the UK. It was introduced in 1971 with a 1.6-litre four closely based on the Renault 16 TX engine. That powerplant had done a fine job in the lighter A110, but the 310 was somewhat bulkier and, rather more to the point, aimed considerably further upmarket where a four-cylinder engine was not really appreciated.

The switch to the Douvrin 'co-op' 2.6-litre, overhead-cam V6 transformed the car. Its 150 bhp at 6000 rpm (allied to 151 lb ft of torque at a convenient 3500 rpm) gave the 310 the ability to reach 137 mph (220 kph) and sprint to 60 mph (96 kph) in 6.4 seconds.

Although it was rather different

### Alta

in character from the 110, it shared the same rear engine layout, with a five-speed manual transmission and independent wishbone suspension all round with anti-roll bars front and rear. That V6 may have been of all light-alloy construction, but it was still mounted *behind* the rear axle line and Alpine's engineers found it advisable to fit larger (205/70) Michelins at the rear to counter the terminal oversteer which was a definite feature of the car. Like the Porsche 911, however, the Alpine only misbehaved in extremis or through mistreatment when a driver lifted off in mid corner.

Normally its road behaviour was exemplary and its neutral handling characteristics permitted high cornering speeds without fuss. Its stylish glassfibre body was finished to a very high standard indeed, but the 310 was certainly not a soul-less car and had more than enough idiosyncracies to make it interesting. Hard braking made it feel unstable and broken or bumpy surfaces did not help its composure, while the attractive shape was too easily affected by side winds. Although it was never produced in large numbers it was desirable enough to stay in production for 13 years.

---

**1973 ALPINE A310**
**Engine:** V6 overhead cam
**Bore × stroke:** 88 mm × 73 mm
**Capacity:** 2664 cc
**Maximum power:** 150 bhp
**Transmission:** five-speed
**Chassis:** steel backbone
**Suspension:** independent by wishbones and coil springs all round with anti-roll bars front and rear
**Brakes:** discs all round
**Bodywork:** 2+2 glassfibre coupé
**Maximum speed (approx):** 137 mph (220 kph)

---

**1935 ALTA**
**Engine:** in-line four cylinder
**Bore × stroke:** 68.75 mm × 100 mm
**Capacity:** 1485 cc
**Maximum power:** 65 bhp
**Transmission:** four-speed Wilson pre-selector
**Chassis:** pressed steel
**Suspension:** non-independent with quarter elliptic leaf springs
**Brakes:** drums all round
**Bodywork:** two or four-seater sports
**Maximum speed (approx):** 100 mph (160 kph)

---

# ALTA
**Kingston-upon-Thames**
**1931–1954**

'Combining brawn and brain to a remarkable degree' as he put it, Geoffrey Taylor built his prototype Alta in the stables of his father's house at Surbiton, Surrey, in 1928, fitting an engine of his own design into an old ABC frame. The design was developed for production, which started in 1931, using Taylor's double-overhead-cam alloy-block 1074cc engine in chassis supplied by Rubery Owen. The open two-seater Alta had a sharply raked radiator and was an uncompromising sports car in which comfort was definitely subservient to performance. In 1935, 1.5-litre and 2-litre power units were offered, while in 1937 a 1.5-litre 'special supercharged racing model' was listed; it cost £1250 against £500 for the standard 1.5-litre. Altas were renowned for their acceleration – under factory test the 1.5-litre had to accelerate from 3000-4500 rpm in top (58-95 mph/93-153 kph) in 7 seconds, the 2-litre in 4.8 seconds. A 3-litre V8 (Taylor's ideal sports car) was under construction in 1938, but apparently was never finished. After the war Alta built a 1.5 litre Grand Prix car, but development was slow, and Taylor subsequently just supplied Alta engines for Connaught and HWM.

**Alpine A310**

# ALVIS
Coventry, England
1920-1967

The name 'Alvis' was coined by Geoffrey de Freville, former manager of the London agency for the French DFP car, which was fitted with aluminium pistons (then the latest in automotive technology), the potential of which was realised by the marque's importer, W.O. Bentley, who tuned and raced DFPs with some success. When war broke out in 1914, de Freville set up his own company to make aluminium pistons; he called these pistons 'Alvis', a meaningless word coined because it sounded good in any language. Towards the end of hostilities, de Freville drew up designs for a light car, which he sold, along with the rights to the Alvis name, to a Welsh marine engineer named T.G. John, whose previous experience of the motor industry was limited to the manufacture of the 1919 Mobile Pup motor scooter.

The de Freville design was developed at John's Coventry factory as the Alvis 10/30, and made its debut at the 1920 Scottish Motor Show that March. Regarded as a sporting light car, it was fitted in two-seat form with the ingenious Morgan Zephyr coachwork, in which aluminium panels were fastened to a light, wire-braced tubular metal framework. Its performance – top speed was around 60 mph (97 kph) – was sufficiently above average for the car to be described by one owner as 'extremely hot'; production was soon running at two cars a week.

When the post-war boom ran out of impetus, Alvis supplemented its normal production by building 1096cc vee-twin cyclecars for J.F. Buckingham, inventor of the tracer bullet used with such devastating effect against marauding Zeppelins during the Great War. Inevitably, when Buckingham offered a coupé version, it was known as the Palace . . . .

In 1922, Captain T.G. Smith-Clarke joined Alvis from Daimler as chief engineer: two weeks later he was joined by W.M. Dunn, who became chief designer.

By that time, production was approaching 20 cars per week, and the first sporting models fitted with what became known as duck's back bodywork in polished aluminium appeared. The first

**Alvis 12/50**

production models (10/30 and 11/40, later reclassified as 12/40) had side-valve engines, but in 1923 Smith-Clarke and Dunn collaborated to produce the overhead-valve 12/50, which achieved immediate fame when a racing version won the Junior Car Club's 200 Mile Race at Brooklands.

Nevertheless, Alvis ran into financial troubles in 1924, and for several months, the company was in receivership, with nearly £200,000 owed to its suppliers. The high esteem in which Alvis was already held carried the company through, and once deliveries of the 12/50 attained a steady rhythm, the firm was viable enough to be reconstructed early in 1925. At one stage, the company was operating on such narrow margins that John would ring the company's London Agents, Henlys, on a Thursday morning to ascertain whether they had sold enough cars – seven in one week was the magic figure – to enable him to pay the wages bill . . . .

The return from the abyss seemed to inspire Alvis; in 1925 they built their first front-wheel-drive car, using a 12/50 power unit turned back-to-front, followed the next year by a 1.5-litre straight-eight Grand Prix car, with twin overhead camshafts and a supercharger. It never ran in a Grand Prix, but showed great potential – sufficient for a production four-cylinder Alvis front-wheel-drive car to be catalogued from 1928.

The same year saw the introduction of a six-cylinder model, with a swept volume of 1870cc; the following year the capacity was increased to 2148cc and the model was named the Silver Eagle.

That was the start of a

distinguished line of Alvis sixes like the Speed 20 and 25, 4.3-litre, Crested Eagle and Silver Crest. The 4.3-litre was one of the very few British cars of the 1930s capable of over 100 mph (161 kph) in saloon form.

That distinguished designer George Lanchester was largely responsible for the 1938 12/70 four-cylinder model, which was the basis of the post-war TA14, replaced in 1950 by the 3-litre, six-cylinder TA21 which was developed into the high-speed TA21/100.

This formed the basis for the last Alvis car line, fitted with stylish coachwork designed by Graber of Switzerland. In 1965 Alvis was acquired by Rover and private car production ceased two years later in favour of the more profitable manufacture of specialised military vehicles, a field in which Alvis are still famous.

## Alvis 12/50

The first overhead-valve Alvis engine was announced in June 1923 and fitted in the 10/30 sports chassis, which carried duck's back aluminium bodywork; the prototype went straight out and lapped Brooklands at 86 mph (138 kph), no mean feat for a 1460 cc car of the period. Later that year, a 1496 cc development of the 10/30 appeared, designated the 12/50 and available in two chassis, the SA (108.5 in/275.6 cm) and the SB (112.5 in/285.7 cm). A larger engine of 1598 cc was offered in the same choice of chassis in 1924-25, and designated type SC. For 1926, the design of the 12/50 was modified, and two types were available, the TE touring chassis of 1645 cc and the TF sports chassis of 1496 cc.

**1923 ALVIS 12/50**
**Engine:** in-line four cylinder, overhead valve
**Bore × stroke:** 68 mm × 103 mm
**Capacity:** 1496cc
**Maximum power:** 50 bhp
**Transmission:** four-speed manual
**Chassis:** pressed steel channel section
**Suspension:** non-independent with semi-elliptic leaf springs all round
**Brakes:** drums all round
**Bodywork:** choice of eight body styles
**Maximum speed (approx):** 70 mph (112 kph)

Their power units were of identical design but the greater capacity of the touring model was obtained by increasing the crankshaft throw. These new models also had a re-designed, stronger chassis, with improved steering (lignum vitae joints were a primitive form of lubrication-free bearing) and the cone clutch gave way to a single-plate design. The two-engine policy continued until 1929, when the 12/50 was briefly dropped, then revived in updated form; from 1930 to 1932, only the larger engine was available, and the model was designated the TJ 12/50 in single-carburettor form, or 12/60 with twin carburettors. In terms of performance and durability, the 12/50 was one of the great vintage sports cars.

## Alvis 12/50 fwd

In 1923, the Alvis company achieved perhaps its biggest sporting victory by winning the Junior Car Club's 200-Mile Race at Brooklands with a 16-valve racer derived from the 12/50. The competition soon became keener, however and during 1924 the Alvis was outclassed by lighter, more powerful rivals like Joyce's 16-valve AC. So Smith-Clarke and Dunn began experimenting with supercharging to gain more power, then decided that they could reduce weight and improve stability by the pioneering use of front-wheel drive, hitherto only used on racing cars by the eccentric Walter Christie in America in the first decade of the century. The front-wheel-drive Alvis racer was unveiled in the spring of 1925, with such advanced features as a chassis frame entirely made of duralumin, and powered by a modified 12/50 engine turned back-to-front to drive the front wheels. The front axle consisted of two tubes linked by four vertical supports, and carried on two quarter-elliptic springs; standing a mere 3 feet (0.9 m) high, the car weighed 9.5 cwt (983 kg). The first front-wheel-drive Alvis cars showed sufficient potential – one of them lapped Brooklands at 104.4 mph (265 kph) – to warrant the development of a team of two straight-eight cars to meet the 1 5-litre Grand Prix formula extant in 1926, but the cars were dogged by ill-luck, and consequently were extensively redesigned for 1927. Although they were very fast – said to be capable of 120 mph (305 kph) – the 1927 GP cars were plagued by piston trouble. Before this could be cured, the 1.5-litre GP formula was wound up: so Alvis turned to the production of a super-sports front-wheel-drive car intended for experienced drivers who wanted to compete in sports car races. The first production front-wheel-drive Alvis appeared in 1928, powered by

**Alvis front-wheel-drive racer**

### 1928 ALVIS FWD
**Engine:** in-line four cylinder, overhead cam
**Bore × stroke:** 68 mm × 102 mm
**Capacity:** 1482cc
**Maximum power:** 50 bhp
**Transmission:** four-speed
**Chassis:** pressed steel
**Suspension:** independent with eight-leaf transverse quarter elliptic leaf springs (two pairs per side) at the front with torque arms and reversed quarter-elliptic leaf springs
**Brakes:** drums all round (inboard at front)
**Maximum speed (approx):** 85 mph (137 kph)

a 1482 cc overhead-cam engine and costing £597 unsupercharged or £625 supercharged. Two of these unsupercharged cars competed at Le Mans in 1928, and won the 1.5-litre class – finishing sixth and ninth overall – while five 'blown' front-wheel-drive Alvis competed in the Ulster Tourist Trophy the following August, Leon Cushman desperately trying to wrest the lead from Kaye Don's Lea-Francis and only missing victory by 13 seconds after making up 7 minutes and 27 seconds in the last ten laps. A long-chassis version of the front-wheel-drive Alvis followed, available with saloon or tourer coach work: originally intended for limited sales to a specialist market, the front-wheel-

### 1937 ALVIS SPEED 25
**Engine:** in-line six cylinder, overhead valve
**Bore × stroke:** 83 mm × 100 mm
**Capacity:** 3571 cc
**Maximum power:** 110 bhp
**Transmission:** four-speed manual
**Chassis:** pressed steel with cruciform crossmember
**Suspension:** independent front with live axle rear and semi-elliptic leaf springs
**Brakes:** drums all round, mechanical with vacuum servo
**Bodywork:** to order
**Maximum speed (approx):** 95 mph (153 kph)

**Alvis Speed Twenty-five**

drive Alvis was now in demand by the general public thanks to its attractive appearance and highly-acclaimed technical specification. One clergyman even purchased a supercharged front-wheel-drive saloon to visit his parishioners, though what they thought of his noisy progress is not recorded. Since many of those who were buying front-wheel-drive Alvis lacked the experience necessary to drive them safely, production was curtailed after less than 150 had been built. However, ten straight-eight sports cars were built in 1929-30, and raced by the works as well as being used for the investigation of independent suspension and the handling problems associated with front-wheel-drive.

## Speed Twenty
## Speed Twenty-five
## 4.3 Litre

Late in 1932 Alvis unveiled a high-performance 2.5-litre six derived from the Silver Eagle, and known as the Speed Twenty; it broke new ground for the marque in having the gearbox in unit with the engine. In its price class (a chassis alone was £600 and a sports tourer £695), the Speed Twenty offered unrivalled performance and handling; it was, however, a sign of the times that most of its purchasers ordered roomy closed bodies. For 1934, the Speed Twenty was considerably modified, with a massive cruciform cross-brace incorporated in the chassis, which now featured

independent front suspension, Andre Telecontrol dampers at the rear and the first all-synchromesh gearbox fitted to any British car. Despite all these improvements, chassis price was unchanged, and the price of complete cars was actually reduced. For 1935, the power output was raised by increasing engine capacity to 2762cc, and the Speed Twenty was discontinued during 1936. From 1935, a big-bore 3.5-litre derivative had been sold alongside the Speed Twenty: it had a longer wheelbase in order to accommodate more luxurious bodywork. It was a clear improvement on the Speed Twenty, and was developed into the Speed Twenty-five for 1937. Costing the same in chassis form as the car it supplanted, the Speed Twenty-five was regarded as the finest pre-war Alvis, capable of over 95 mph (153 kph) with saloon bodywork. For 1938, a boxed and stiffened

### 1962 ALVIS TD21
**Engine:** in-line six cylinder
**Bore × stroke:** 84 mm × 90 mm
**Capacity:** 2993cc
**Maximum power:** 120 bhp
**Transmission:** ZF five-speed or
**Chassis:** steel box members
**Suspension:** independent front with double wishbones and coil springs, live rear axle with semi-elliptic leaf springs
**Brakes:** discs front and drums rear
**Bodywork:** Graber four-seater
**Maximum speed (approx):** 106 mph (170 kph)

chassis was specified, along with a dual exhaust system for improved exhaust extraction coupled with greater silence and each tailpipe was fitted with three silencers! Built alongside the Speed Twenty-five was the 4.3-litre (its capacity was actually 4.4-litres), which sacrificed some of the refinement of the smaller car on the alter of high performance, and in those terms the 4.3-litre was unmatched in its price class, offering speeds only otherwise attainable by the Lagonda V12 and 4.25-litre Bentley, both of which cost half as much again as the Alvis. Servo-assisted brakes were fitted from the start, a feature incorporated in the Speed Twenty-five from late 1937. The 4.3-litre could attain a genuine 100 mph (161 kph) in saloon form; on test by monocled journalist Tommy Wisdom a stripped and tuned 4.3-litre tourer lapped Brooklands at over 115 mph (185 kph) and reached a top speed of 119 mph (192 kph).

## Graber TD 21

In 1950 the TA14 was replaced with the all-new TA21 six-cylinder, a refined 3-litre luxury car. Some TB21 roadsters, similar to the TB14, but with the Alvis radiator, were built in 1952, and around 25 Healey cars were fitted with the 3-litre engine. At the 1953 London Show, a performance version of the 3-litre, the TC21/100 'Grey Lady', made its debut but the 3-litre itself ceased production in 1954 when its body makers, Mulliners of Birmingham, were absorbed by the Standard Motor Company. For a while, the

future of Alvis car production hung in the balance; then, at the end of 1955, the 'Gran Turismo Alvis' was unveiled, with bodywork designed by the Swiss coachbuilder Herman Graber of Berne, who had built a number of special 3-litres for Continental customers. 'Owing to the lower frontal area and greater structural stiffness of this body, both the performance and handling characteristics of the car have been considerably improved,' commented *The Motor*. In fact, after the model's Paris Show debut, the Graber coachwork was built in Britain under licence by Willowbrook of Loughborough, better known as makers of motor coach bodies. At £3500, the Gran Turismo understandably had only limited appeal, and orders amounted to just 16 cars. Alvis subsequently bought Graber's jigs and drawings, and a modified version of the Graber body was built by Park Ward on a strengthened chassis known as the TD21, the first production car to be equipped with Lockheed disc front brakes. A choice of Austin Healey manual or Borg-Warner automatic transmissions was available. In March 1959 the car was offered with an improved cylinder head for better breathing, and the Series II TD21 appeared in August 1962, featuring Dunlop disc brakes all round and modified coachwork with all-aluminium doors and resin-bonded laminate (instead of wood) door pillars. An overdrive ZF five-speed gearbox was standardised, with the Borg-Warner automatic as an option. The 21 went out of production in 1967.

**Alvis TD21**

# A-Z OF THE CAR

## AMERICAN BANTAM
### Butler, USA
### 1930-1941

If ever there was a lost cause, it was the American Austin, launched in 1930 in the forlorn hope of creating a large market of small-car enthusiasts in the United States. It was a forlorn hope even during the Depression; beneath its natty styling, which resembled a miniature Chevrolet with horizontal bonnet louvres like the contemporary Stutz or Marmon, the American Austin was pure Austin Seven, with all that that entailed. The company, based in Butler, Pennsylvania, was headed by the youthful Roy S. Evans, aged 21, who attempted to market the little car using hard-sell techniques that can have left him little margin for profit, especially considering the basic price of $435. Any purchaser living in the area of Butler and Pittsburgh was offered free motoring – all maintenance, fuel and oil paid by American Austin – for the first year (or 7500 miles/ 12,000 km). As Americans could

buy used 'full-size' cars for less than that the car was regarded as a joke – and featured as such in a Laurel and Hardy film. Only 8000 buyers came forward during the American Austin's first year on the market, and that was the peak. From then on, sales tailed off to the point that the company went into receivership in 1934. It was revived in 1937 as the American Bantam Car Company, and the car was given a pretentious restyling by Count Alexis de Sakhnoffsky, better

### 1930 American Bantam
**Engine:** in-line four cylinder, side valve
**Bore x stroke:** 56mm x 76.2mm
**Capacity:** 747.5cc
**Maximum power:** 10.5bhp
**Transmission:** three-speed manual
**Chassis:** pressed steel
**Suspension:** non-independent with transverse semi-elliptic sping front and quarter elliptic leaf springs rear
**Brakes:** drums all round
**Bodywork:** two-door sedan
**Maximum speed (approx):** 50mph (80kph)

known for his work with luxury car makers such as Peerless. A full range of body styles was offered, including light trucks and a station wagon. Annual production capability was a never-to-be-realised 44,000 vehicles a year, and the Bantam remained nothing more than an oddball curiosity. In 1940, Bantam designed the original Jeep for the US Army, but was incapable of producing it in the required volumes, so the orders went to their rivals Willys and Ford instead. In 1956, long after production had ceased, the American Bantam plant was purchased by Armco Steel.

## AMILCAR
### St. Denis, France
### Boulogne-sur-Seine, France
### 1921-1939

Regarded in its native France as the poor man's Bugatti, the Amilcar began life in 1921 as just an average cyclecar designed by

Edmond Moyet and Andre Morel, proteges of the famous Jules Salomon, formerly of Le Zebre and designer of the immortal 5CV Citroën. The Amilcar venture was backed by two shareholders in the Le Zebre company named Lamy and Akar, who chose the name Amilcar as a near conjunction of their two surnames. The Amilcar power unit was closely modelled

### 1926 AMILCAR CGSS
**Engine:** in-line four cylinder, side valve
**Bore × stroke:** 57 mm × 95 mm
**Capacity:** 985 cc
**Maximum power:** 23 bhp
**Transmission:** three-speed manual
**Chassis:** pressed steel
**Suspension:** non-independent with semi-elliptic leaf springs front and quarter elliptic leaf springs rear
**Brakes:** drums all round
**Bodywork:** two-seater sports
**Maximum speed (approx):** 72 mph (115 kph)

**Amilcar CGSS**

on the Zebre and Citroën engines, having the same bore, the same sidevalve and splash-lubricated two-bearing crank configuration, and the chassis design was a neat exercise in weight-saving. A differential-less back axle permitted the footbrake and handbrake to occupy only one drum each, yet at the same time act on both rear wheels, while the chassis was carried on quarter-elliptic leaf springs all round. Early models even had a wooden front axle, though that was soon supplanted by metal.

Amilcar's first model was the 903 cc Type CC, followed by the more sporting 985 cc CS and the more commodious 1004 cc C4, which had a rudimentary dickey seat in its tail.

The potential of this somewhat basic little machine was shown in 1922 when joint designer Morel won the first Bol d'Or endurance race in the Foret de St Germain,

**American Bantam**

followed by third and fourth placings in the Voiturette Grand Prix at Le Mans, behind two double-overhead-cam Salmsons – the marque that was to become Amilcar's greatest rival.

Most famous of the Amilcars was the CGS Grand Sport with four-wheel brakes and a 1074 cc side-valve engine which later grew into the lower, more sporty CGSS Grand Sport Surbaisse. Real motor racing came in 1926 with the six-cylinder Amilcar, with a supercharged double-overhead-cam 1100 cc engine and it was capable of a true 125 mph (200 kph). Well known Amilcar driver De Gavardie used the twin cam to take a 24 hour record at an average speed of 84 mph (135 kph). In 1933 50 C6 racers were built for Le Mans homologation with slightly 'softer' specification for road use.

After more than 15,000 side-valve Amilcars had been built, the company ventured an overhead-cam 2-litre straight-eight in 1929 which was a total disaster. Amilcar tried again the late 1930s with the 14CV Pegase, whose four-cylinder engine was supplied by Delahaye, but it could not halt the company's slide into disaster. Hotchkiss acquired the remnants and brought out an advanced 1185 cc light car with a monocoque Alpax light alloy frame and front-wheel drive. Unfortunately for the revival of Amilcar, World War II intervened before this bold project got off the ground.

# ANSALDO
**Turin, Italy**
**1920-1931**

At the end of the World War I Italy's leading metalworking company was Ansaldo of Genoa: its factories employed 80,000 people; it produced cannon, aero engines, armaments and railway engines. It made its own iron and armour-plating and even had shipyards at Sestri Ponente and Voltri.

Peace obviously left Ansaldo at somewhat of a loose end, with a sudden cessation in demand for many of its more profitable products. So the director of its aero-engine division suggested to the company's president that some of the idle plant capacity could be utilised to manufacture cars.

The suggestion was immediately accepted, with one condition: the prototype had to be ready within a year . . . .

In fact, the deadline was comfortably met, for the prototype Ansaldo car was ready in August 1919. An utterly conventional four-seat tourer, the only surprise about the Ansaldo Model 4A was that it was powered by an overhead-

**Ansaldo 4C**

camshaft engine rather than the side-valve unit its prosaic appearance suggested it possessed. The 1.8-litre four-cylinder engine gave – for the day – a good power-weight ratio (the engine developed 35 bhp in a chassis weighing 1428 lb/647 kg). Production began in 1920, based in a former Ansaldo aero-engine factory in Turin. The cars – particularly the sporting 4CS version – quickly gained a reputation for their lively performance. 'The engine sounds as quiet at sixty miles an hour as at twenty,' claimed a contemporary motoring correspondent.

However, in 1922 the Ansaldo group suffered a shattering blow when its principal shareholder, the Banca Italiana di Sconto, collapsed: for a while the future of the automobile division seemed in doubt, but in 1923 it was reformed as a separate company in a rescue bid by a syndicate from Varese.

In 1924, a 2-litre six was added to the range, the model remaining in production until 1928. An economy four – the 1.5-litre Tipo 10 – next appeared, with a single transverse front spring *a la* Model T Ford, then, in 1928, came the Tipo 22 – a de luxe 3.5-litre straight-eight conceived in the forlorn hope of gaining a substantial foothold in the European luxury car market –

---

**1922 Ansaldo 4CS**
**Engine:** in-line four cylinder, overhead cam
**Bore × stroke:** 72.5 mm × 120 mm
**Capacity:** 1980 cc
**Maximum power:** 48 bhp
**Transmission:** three-speed manual
**Chassis:** pressed steel
**Suspension:** non-independent with semi-elliptic leaf springs all round
**Brakes:** drums all round, mechanically operated
**Bodywork:** four-seater torpedo
**Maximum speed (approx):** 68 mph (110 kph)

---

and then finally the Tipo 18, a 2.7-litre six.

But by now Ansaldo was in deep financial trouble; it was reformed and recapitalised a couple of times, then in 1931 the Ansaldo name was absorbed by OM. Two years later, OM itself was taken over by Fiat. When Ansaldo production ceased in 1932, there were some 400 chassis in the course of construction: a company called CEVA (Ansaldo construction and sales) was set up in the vain hope of selling those cars.

## Ansaldo 4CS

Built from 1922 to 1926, the 4CS was the sporting derivative of the original Tipo 4A. Swept volume increased to 2 litres and tuning boosted power output by some 25 per cent. Priced at 26,000 lire in chassis form, the Ansaldo was a relatively economical way to go motor racing, and Tazio Nuvolari gained a number of his early successes at the wheel of an Ansaldo. 'There is,' wrote *The Autocar* in 1923, 'a certain clean look about the engine, a nice manner of disposing of auxiliaries so that they are not at first apparent to the eye, though they are accessible for adjustment. The engine, in fact, looks the sort one would take pleasure in keeping clean at all times, while its overhead valves and overhead camshaft spell efficiency.'

# APOLLO
**Apolda, Germany**
**1910-1926**

From 1904 to 1912, the German firm of Ruppe & Son of Apolda (Thuringia) produced the air-cooled Piccolo voiturette, then in 1910 launched a new marque, the Apollo. The company's first

---

**1911 Apollo Type B**
**Engine:** in-line four cylinder, overhead valve
**Bore × stroke:** 60 mm × 92 mm
**Capacity:** 1040 cc
**Maximum power:** 12 bhp
**Transmission:** Three-speed manual
**Chassis:** pressed steel
**Suspension:** non-independent with semi-elliptic leaf springs all round
**Brakes:** drums on rear wheels and transmission
**Bodywork:** to order
**Maximum speed (approx):** 47 mph (75 kph)

---

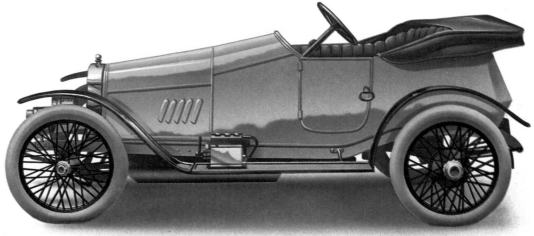
**Apollo**

product, the air-cooled Mobbel, was a 624 cc single-cylinder model of little interest; then the engineer/ racing driver Karl Slevogt, formerly with Cudell, Laurin & Klement and Puch, designed a neat sporting light car, the Type B, with an overhead-valve engine, originally of 996 cc, enlarged in 1911 to just over a litre. The model was, apart from the Bugatti Type 13, the only high-performance small car built in Germany before World War I and, starting with the 1910 Ostend Week (when Slevogt won the 20 km race and the 1.6-litre class of the Circuit d'Ostend), enjoyed many successes in international competition. Apart from Slevogt, the most successful Apollo driver was the Baron de Viscaya (an odd thing, because his father's bank were Bugatti's financiers and his brother was a notable Bugattiste). De Viscaya won the 1913 San Sebastian meeting with a 2-litre Apollo Rekord, a larger version of the Type B. An improved version of the Type B, the 4/20PS, was Apollo's mainstay after World War I. It had split-axle independent front suspension with a transverse leaf spring acting against air springs in front, with quarter-elliptics at the rear, and was available in two wheelbase lengths. Like the French Salmson, the post-war Apollo had only four 'push-and-pull' rods, so that the same rocker operated both inlet and exhaust valves for its cylinder. A streamlined 4/20, driven by Slevogt, averaged 73 mph (117 kph) in a 1924 race on the Berlin AVUS track. From 1924, Jaray streamlined coachwork was available on Apollos — but at a price! Slevogt moved to Selve in 1924, but not before he had built a prototype 12/50 V8 with four-wheel brakes. Apollo lasted only a couple of years after his departure.

## APPERSON
Kokomo, USA
1902-1926

In 1898 the brothers Edgar and Elmer Apperson, of Kokomo, Indiana, joined forces with Elwood Haynes (who claimed to have built America's first car) and manufactured the Haynes-Apperson car. In 1902 the partnership was dissolved, and the brothers began making Apperson cars, which at first had a flat-twin engine like the Haynes-Apperson, then progressed to a horizontal four, and finally, in 1904, to vertical power units of considerable size — 24 and 40 hp models were listed in 1904. A 95 hp four costing $10,500 joined the lineup in 1906, while a year later the first of the famous 'Jack Rabbit' speedsters, a 60 hp four selling at $5000, was catalogued. The entire range was known as Jack Rabbits for some

time: in 1913-14 Jack Rabbits were listed with 5212 cc four-cylinder, and 5971 cc six-cylinder engines. In 1914 a 5502 cc Jack Rabbit V8 appeared, while in 1916 the Roadaplane six- and eight-cylinder Appersons made their debut. That flamboyant stylist Conover T. Silver created the Silver-Apperson sports tourer in 1917; after 1919 this model became known as the Anniversary. By the early 1920s, however, Apperson cars had become as prosaic as the rest of the US industry's offerings, and a proprietory power unit, the 3204 cc Falls six, was fitted from 1923, a Lycoming eight being offered in 1924. The last new Appersons of 1926 were fitted with four-wheel brakes, but this failed to halt the company's slide into oblivion. Apperson raced a good deal early on, albeit unsuccessfully.

### 1913 Apperson Jack Rabbit series XXI

**Engine:** in-line six cylinder
**Bore × stroke:** 92.25 mm × 139.7 mm
**Capacity:** 5971 cc
**Maximum power:** 33.7 hp (rated)
**Transmission:** three-speed manual
**Chassis:** pressed steel and tubular frame
**Suspension:** non-independent with semi-elliptic leaf springs front and three-quarter elliptic rear
**Brakes:** Contracting and expanding band, on rear only
**Bodywork:** four-seater open tourer
**Maximum speed (approx):** 60 mph (97 kph)

**Apperson Jack Rabbit 33.8hp**

## AQUILA ITALIANA
Turin, Italy
1906-1914

In 1906 the Marquis Giulio Pallavicino di Priola and the young engineer Giulio Cesare Cappa transformed the little works they had established in Turin for the repair of motor vehicles and the design of engines into a fully-fledged manufacturing company. They decided to call their products Aquila (eagle) and were compelled by the German Adler company — whose name also meant Eagle — to add the Italiana suffix to avoid there being any confusion between the two marques in international markets. They had built only a few Cappa-designed cars — big fours and sixes with inlet-over-exhaust valve systems — before the Marquis Pallavicino was run down by a railway locomotive on a level crossing. His death provoked an

immediate crisis, and Aquila Italiana went into liquidation in 1908 and production ceased. However, a rescue operation was mounted by the Marsaglia Bank of Turin, and the company was reconstituted in 1909, with Cappa again as chief engineer. The revived Aquilas were

cars of intense technical interest: above all, they were the world's first production vehicles with aluminium pistons. Moreover, their ball-bearing crankshafts and an advanced form of unit construction in which radiator, engine and gearbox were all carried on the 'Baty-carter', a sort of extended aluminium sump casting.

Between 1910 and 1914, Aquila Italiana cars had many competition successes; the works team consisted of Meo Costatini (later *Chef d'Equipe* of Bugatti), Eugenio Beria d'Argentina and Giovanni Marsaglia, son of the banker who controlled the company. Giovanni Marsaglia, who was killed in 1917 test-flying a military aeroplane, came second in the 1913 Targa Florio driving an Aquila, and won his class in the Mont Ventoux and Gaillon hillclimbs and in the Parma-Poggia di Berceto event. A team of three technically-advanced overhead-cam hemi-head sixes was built for the 1914 French Grand Prix, but two of them were forced to return to Turin after seizing their engines while being driven on the roads prior to the race, while the third, driven by Costatini, only lasted ten laps. With the outbreak of war, Aquila Italiana turned to the production of military vehicles, staff cars and aero engines; in 1917 they were taken over by SPA and the marque discontinued.

### 1907 Aquila Italiana H6 35/50

**Engine:** in-line six cylinder, inlet-over-exhaust valve
**Bore × stroke:** 80 mm × 130 mm
**Capacity:** 3921 cc
**Maximum power:** 50 bhp
**Transmission:** four-speed manual
**Chassis:** pressed steel
**Suspension:** non-independent with semi-elliptic leaf springs
**Brakes:** rear drums only
**Bodywork:** to order
**Maximum speed (approx):** 80 mph (130 kph)

**Aquila Italiana**

## 1926 Arab Super Sports

**Engine:** in-line four cylinder, overhead cam
**Bore × stroke:** 70 mm × 127 mm
**Capacity:** 1955 cc
**Maximum power:** not known
**Transmission:** four-speed manual
**Chassis:** pressed steel
**Suspension:** non-independent with semi-elliptic leaf springs
**Brakes:** drums all round
**Bodywork:** two or four-seater sports
**Maximum speed (approx):** 95 mph (153 kph)

**Arab Super Sport**

# ARAB
### Letchworth, England
### 1926-1928

Reid Railton was assistant to Parry Thomas at Leyland Motors at the beginning of the 1920s, when Leyland were building the Thomas-designed Leyland Eight. After that project finished in 1923, Railton realised his ambition to enter production with a quality sports car. His opportunity came when a Leyland project to build high-speed newspaper vans powered by Hooker-Thomas engines was shelved, leaving the company with a batch of fifty cylinder blocks. Railton built up a prototype power unit which was fitted into an Enfield-Allday sports car and entered in various race meetings to establish its potential. In 1926 Railton began production in a factory in Letchworth, Hertfordshire, offering high-chassis two- and four-seaters priced at £525, and a super-sports at £550, 'guaranteed to attain 90 mph'. The overhead cam engine bore the typical Parry Thomas trademark of leaf – rather than coil – valve springs, and, despite the high performance it offered, had only a two-bearing crank. Production was extremely limited – no more than ten or a dozen high-chassis Arabs

were built. Railton lost interest in the project after the death of Parry Thomas in his land speed record car Babs on Pendine Sands in March 1927, and the two low-chassis Super Sports Arabs which survive today were probably built by Thompson & Taylor at Brooklands after the Letchworth factory had been closed down.

# ARIEL
### Birmingham, England
### Coventry, England
### 1898-1925

In their two brief incarnations (1900 to 1915 and 1922 to 1925), Ariel of Birmingham encompassed just about every conceivable type of motor vehicle. They started

production with motor tricycles and quadricycles of the most basic and spidery sort but by 1902 their first car, a 10 hp twin with automatic inlet valves, had appeared. The following year came their first four-cylinder models, of 16 hp and 20 hp, priced at £550 and £1000 respectively. A new crocodile-bonneted 12 hp with mechanical inlet valves appeared in the summer of 1903: 'This car was driven 1300 miles in Ireland during the Irish tour and the stoppages for adjustments of any kind to car only amounted to four minutes, two punctures not counted,' boasted the company, adding proudly, 'This, too, over IRISH ROADS.'

By now the sales agency was in the hands of Harvey Du Cros, Jr, whose father controlled the Dunlop Tyre Company. An odd

design feature of these early Ariels was that the leather cone clutch was separate from the flywheel.

A new 15 hp four appeared at the beginning of 1904, and was promptly driven almost to the summit of Snowdon up the rack railway. Soon after a 30/35 hp six (whose tubular chassis appeared totally inadequate) was launched, and reckoned to be one of the most strikingly-finished exhibits at the Crystal Palace motor show that February. The engine speed was controlled by varying the lift of the inlet valves.

The company changed direction again at the end of 1905, with a completely new range along Mercedes lines called Ariel-Simplex: these were four-cylinder cars of 15 hp and 25/30 hp with a six of 35/50 hp. The 50/60 hp six introduced during 1907 was one of the biggest-engined private cars ever built in Britain, offering 15.9-litres for £950. At the end of 1907, Ariel sold their Bournbrook, Birmingham, factory to British Lorraine-Dietrich. Thereafter, Ariels were assembled in the Coventry Ordnance Works, (who subsequently made one of the first aircraft-carried cannon). An 11.3-litre racing car was built for, but did not compete in, the 1908 Grand Prix. Smaller cars were offered from 1910, including 10 hp twin of just 1630 cc. After World War I, the company concentrated mainly on motorcycles, but an economy flat-twin Nine was offered in 1922, followed by a more refined 1100 cc Ten two years later.

## 1907 Ariel 50/60

**Engine:** in-line six cylinder
**Bore × stroke:** 150 mm × 150 mm
**Capacity:** 15,904 cc
**Maximum power:** 83 bhp
**Transmission:** four-speed manual
**Chassis:** pressed steel
**Suspension:** non-independent with semi-elliptic leaf springs all round
**Brakes:** drums on rear wheels and transmission
**Bodywork:** to order
**Maximum speed (approx):** 70 mph (112 kph)

**Ariel**

# A-Z OF THE CAR

## ARIES

**Courbevoie, France
1903–1938**

When 22-year-old Baron Charles Petiet presented his senior thesis at the Ecole Centrale in Paris in 1901, it was described as 'utopian' because it dealt with the organisation of a car factory. Nevertheless, two years later, after compulsory military service and a few months with Panhard & Levassor, young Petiet did establish an automobile works at Villeneuve-la-Garenne, just to the north-west of Paris.

With a fairly modest capital of half-a-million francs (£20,000), his Ariès company began building two- and four-cylinder cars, manufacturing a batch of 20 chassis at a time. These shaft-drive cars used a curious double rear axle, with engines supplied by Aster, whose factory was just across the

---

### 1925 ARIES 3 LITRE

**Engine:** in-line four cylinder, overhead cam
**Bore × stroke:** 82 mm × 140 mm
**Capacity:** 2957 cc
**Maximum power:** 96 bhp
**Transmission:** four-speed
**Chassis:** pressed steel
**Suspension:** non-independent with semi-elliptic leaf springs all round
**Brakes:** drums all round
**Bodywork:** sports tourer
**Maximum speed (approx):** 100 mph (161 kph)

---

Seine in St Denis.

In 1904 Ariès, by now employing some 95 workers, doubled its original capital to a million francs. In 1907, a compact V4 with desmodromic valves was offered, with a swept volume of 1131 cc, although particular praise was reserved for the 14–18CV Ariès introduced in November 1907: this model did away with the traditional Ariès double axle, using a conventional live axle braced by a stay rod.

Like so many French companies at the time, Ariès established a British company, which was formed at the end of 1907 with a capital of £10,000: its manager, R.Lee Philpot, announced a plan for Ariès chassis to be built in the Wembley factory of Aster Engineering. The company planned to sell fours of 16–20 hp, 30–35 hp and 40–50 hp, plus a 45–55 hp six.

In 1910 Ariès expanded its commercial vehicle activities, mainly supplying the French army: during the war, the works built many military lorries as well as Hispano-Suiza aero engines.

In the 1920s, Ariès offered a wide range, most notably a 7CV overhead-cam 1085 cc four-cylinder and a 15CV 3-litre four offered in two versions: a tourer with a side-valve Aster unit and a sports car with their own overhead-cam engine. It was just such a car that nearly won the Le Mans 24 Hours in 1927... .

During the 1930s Depression, Ariès stopped production of the 1100 cc and 3-litre cars, which had become outdated. They were replaced by inlet-over-exhaust-valve-engined 1.5, 1.8 and 2-litre

models designed by Touté; the six-cylinder 10CV Super of 1934 to 1938 boasted the curious arrangement of a three-speed gearbox augmented by two-speed gears in the back axle to give six forward speeds. Very few were made, and car production was superseded by trucks in 1938. After World War II Ariès briefly made moped engines under the ABG name. Baron Petiet died in 1950.

## Aries 3-litre

The overhead-cam 3-litre Ariès never quite fulfilled its sporting promise; in the 1925 24 Heures du Mans, one Ariès was eliminated by a ruptured head gasket, while the other only managed to finish sixth. Both 3-litre team cars retired in 1926, but in 1927 an Ariès 3-litre almost won at Le Mans; its only opposition was the battered Bentley of Davis/Benjafield, limping round after being extricated in less than pristine condition from the famous multiple pile-up at Maison Blanche. The Ariès was four laps ahead when, after 22 hours 30 minutes, the camshaft drive seized and the car had to retire, but a 3-litre Ariès was second in the Circuit des Routes Pavees three years in succession (1925–6–7), and won the Boillot Cup at Boulogne in 1927. The Ariès was probably more powerful than the Bentley, and the last of the sports racers were so low-built that they were instantly nicknamed 'Punaises' (creeping bugs).

## ARMSTRONG SIDDELEY

**Coventry, England
1919–1960**

In 1919 Siddeley-Deasy of Coventry merged with the car manufacturing division of the massive Armstrong-Whitworth engineering and shipbuilding group to create a new

company known as Armstrong Siddeley.

The first offspring of this union was a massive 5-litre 30 hp, whose six cylinders, somewhat archaically, were cast in two blocks of three. A vee-radiator of architectural proportions was to become the hallmark of Armstrong Siddeley throughout its 41-year lifespan.

A smaller 18 hp six of 2.3 litres appeared in 1922; the 2-litre 14 hp four which came along in 1923 was regarded as a – relatively – cheap line, and hence had merely a flat-fronted radiator.

So clumsy and ungainly were the Armstrong Siddeley cars that it seemed a little incongruous to promote them as 'cars of aircraft quality'; however, the aero-engine division of Armstrong Siddeley provided power units for the front-line fighter biplanes of the RAF, and was one of Britain's largest manufacturers of aero engines.

1928 was a pioneering year for the marque with the Wilson preselector gearbox being offered as an optional extra – it became standard equipment from 1933, and was subsequently supplied to makers of such potent sporting machinery as ERA, HWM and Connaught. That year also saw the introduction of a 15 hp six of only 1.9 litres, joined the following year by an even smaller 12 hp six of just over 1.2 litres.

In 1930 four models – 12, 15, 20 and 30 hp – were marketed and that range of six-cylinder cars with overhead-valve engines upheld Armstrong Siddeley's staid image throughout the 1930s, although a four-cylinder 12 hp was also produced until 1936, and sports coupé versions of this and the 1935 17 hp six were offered.

A reminder of Armstrong Siddeley's aeronautical skills came in 1933 when the 5-litre six-cylinder Siddeley Special was announced, with an aluminium-alloy engine. The model cost £950.

During the week of VE Day, Armstrong Siddeley announced their first post-war models: the Lancaster four-door saloon and the Hurricane drophead coupé, bearing the names of aircraft built by the parent Hawker Siddeley Group during the war, and powered by 2-litre six-cylinder engines (the capacity was increased to 2.3-litres in 1949). Typhoon and Whitley models were subsequently added to the line-up, again named after aircraft.

The company launched the Sapphire in 1953, with a six-cylinder engine of 3435 ccc. In 1956, the range was increased to include the 234 (a 2.3-litre four) and the 236, with the older 2.3-litre six-cylinder engine.

Armstrong Siddeley's ultimate model was the Star Sapphire of 1958; it had a 4-litre engine and automatic transmission. In 1959,

**Aries**

**Armstrong Siddeley Special**

however, Hawker Siddeley merged with Bristol Aero Engines to form Bristol Siddeley; Armstrong Siddeley cars failed to survive this union, and the last one left the Coventry works in 1960.

## Siddeley Special

Launched as a last-minute surprise at the October 1932 London Motor Show, the Siddeley Special made extensive use of the company's experience in aero-engine design. Its 5-litre engine had cylinder block, crankcase, cylinder head, sump, pistons and connecting rods made from Hiduminium alloy, which combined lightness with great strength; hard iron cylinder liners were used as were aero-engine-inspired bronze valve seats. The massive crankshaft ran in seven main bearings. A four-speed self-changing gearbox was standard, and, because of the good power-to-weight ratio, the overall gearing was high; top gear was 3.64:1. The car was low-built – the top face of its double-drop chassis frame was only 17 inches (43 cm) above the road, and there was a centralised lubrication system. Permanently-fitted DWS jacks were an optional extra. Though it was designed for high performance, the Siddeley Special was in no way a compact car. The standard wheelbase was 132 inches (335 cm), with a 144 inch (366 cm) wheelbase available for 'particularly roomy coachwork'. The Siddeley Special was catalogued for four years in which time 140 cars were sold.

---

### 1932 ARMSTRONG SIDDELEY SPECIAL

**Engine:** in-line six cylinder, overhead valve
**Bore × stroke:** 88.9 mm × 133.4 mm
**Capacity:** 4968 cc
**Maximum power:** 29.8 hp (rated)
**Transmission:** four speed pre-selector
**Chassis:** pressed steel
**Suspension:** non-independent with semi-elliptic springs
**Brakes:** drums all round (Bendix)
**Bodywork:** to order
**Maximum speed (approx):** 90 mph (144 kph)

---

## Armstrong Siddeley Sapphire 234

The four-cylinder Sapphire 234 sports saloon launched at the 1955 Motor Show was, in effect, a scaled-down development of the six-cylinder Sapphire 346: it had hemispherical combustion chambers and inclined valves actuated by unequal-length pushrods and tappets from a camshaft mounted high up on the right of the cylinder block. The engine was derived from the power unit of the Sphinx sports-racing car campaigned during 1954 by Tommy Sopwith, son of Sir T.O.M. Sopwith, chairman of the Hawker Siddeley Group, while the stiff X-braced chassis had been de-

veloped on a special test-rig which measured deflection under load.

A lightweight body with Hiduminium 22 panels was developed by High Duty Alloys and Armstrong-Whitworth Aircraft both members of the Hawker Siddeley Group. Flashing indicators were fitted, one of the first installations of a feature that has since become universal. A Laycock de Normanville overdrive was an optional extra as were wire wheels, a rare sight on an Armstrong Siddeley. Both the 234 and its more sedate sister car, the 236, were tested not only on a normal test track but also 'over many hundreds

---

### 1955 ARMSTRONG SIDDELEY SAPHIRE

**Engine:** in-line four cylinder, overhead valve
**Bore × stroke:** 90 mm × 90 mm
**Capacity:** 2290 cc
**Maximum power:** 120 bhp
**Transmission:** four-speed
**Chassis:** X-braced pressed steel
**Suspension:** independent front with coil springs and wishbones. Live rear axle with semi-elliptic leaf springs. Anti-roll bars front and rear
**Brakes:** drums all round, servo assisted
**Bodywork:** Hiduminium alloy saloon
**Maximum speed (approx):** 100 mph (161 kph)

---

of laps of Silverstone where weaknesses were brought to light (and cured) which did not make their appearance when the cars were driven flat out on the high-speed circuit'.

Unfortunately, the appearance of the cars did not live up to the care taken during the development programme, and sales were disappointing; both 2.3-litre Sapphire models were discontinued after a couple of seasons.

## ARNOLT

**Chicago, USA**
**1953–1964**

S.H. 'Wacky' Arnolt of Chicago began car production by fitting Italian steel and aluminium Bertone coachwork to MG chassis to produce stylish four-passenger coupés and convertibles. Before long, however, Wacky Arnolt discovered the British Bristol 404. This potent chassis, equipped with a six-cylinder 130 hp engine, formed the basis of the Arnolt Bristol, with two-seat sporting bodywork again supplied by Bertone; touring and GT coupè coachwork was also offered. Prices started from $6000. Fred Wacker's Arnolt-Bristol tied for the 1954 Sports Car Club of America Class 'E' modified national championship with Boynton's Frazer Nash, while Arnolt-Bristols also won their class at Sebring in 1955–56. There was a repeat performance at Sebring in 1960, when the Arnolt-Bristol of Durbin/Goldman took the up to 2-litre class. Production ended in 1964 after a total of 340 cars had been built.

## ASA

**Milan, Italy**
**1962–1967**

The ASA was one of Ferrari's orphans, a project for a small, high-efficiency dream car, the Ferrarina, powered by an overhead-cam 1032 cc four-cylinder engine; in effect, it was a scaled-down Testa Rossa. Though it was exhibited at the 1961 Turin Show, with coachwork by Bertone, Enzo Ferrari made it quite clear that he had no intention of producing it in his own works. A licence was taken out by the De Nora Electrochemical Group and the car was prepared for production by Bizzarini and built in a small factory at Milan. Racing versions of the 1000GT Coupè had 1092 cc, 95 bhp power units, later developed to produce 105 bhp. Two cars with 1292 cc six-cylinder engines ran at Le Mans in 1966, but without success. Financial troubles hit ASA, and in 1967 a new model,

**Armstrong Siddeley Sapphire**

Arnolt-Bristol

## 1958 ARNOLT-BRISTOL

**Engine:** in-line six cylinder, overhead-valve
**Bore × stroke:** 66 mm × 96 mm
**Capacity:** 1971 cc
**Maximum power:** 105 bhp
**Transmission:** four-speed manual with overdrive
**Chassis:** steel fabricated
**Suspension:** independent front transverse leaf spring and double wishbones, live rear axle with torsion bars
**Brakes:** drums all round
**Bodywork:** sports or coupé
**Maximum speed (approx):** 120 mph (193 kph)

## 1962 ASA

**Engine:** in-line four cylinder, overhead cam
**Bore x stroke:** 69 mm x 69 mm
**Capacity:** 1032 cc
**Maximum power:** 97 bhp
**Transmission:** four-speed manual with overdrive
**Chassis:** tubular space frame
**Suspension:** independent front with double wishbones and coil springs, live rear axle with trailing arms and coil springs
**Brakes:** discs all round
**Bodywork:** GT coupé
**Maximum speed (approx):** 113 mph (181 kph)

the Rollbar GT Spyder, appeared with the 1292 cc six-cylinder engine. Although only a few ASA cars were made – 1964 production amounted to just 52 cars for example – they were successful in Italian sporting events. A few larger four- and six-cylinder cars, mainly prototypes, were also individually built to order, all with glassfibre bodywork.

# ASTON MARTIN

London, England
Newport Pagnell, England
1914–

Lionel Martin and Robert Bamford, garage owners in Henniker Mews, Kensington, built the original Aston Martin in 1914, using a 1.4-litre Coventry-Simplex engine in an Isotta-Fraschini voiturette chassis. The Aston prefix derived from the Aston Clinton hillclimb where Martin had competed successfully with a specially-tuned Singer 10.

The first all-Aston Martin car was completed at the end of 1919; the company moved to Abingdon Road, Kensington, in January 1920 and production started in 1921.

The first cars had side-valve 1.5-litre engines, but more exciting developments came in 1921 when Robb created an overhead-cam racing engine for the Brooklands 200 Miles Race (but it was defeated by the side-valve Aston racer 'Bunny'). The following year, a four-cylinder 16-valve car was designed by Gremillon for Count Lou Zborowski, who financed the company. Unfortunately, it failed to live up to expectations on the race tracks, partly due to engineering shortcomings, but nevertheless became available to private customers the following year.

After Zborowski's death at Monza at the wheel of a Mercedes in 1924, the company struggled on until the 1925 Motor Show, but was wound up a few weeks later.

At the end of 1925, the company was purchased for just £6000 by W.S. Renwick, and production transferred to Feltham, Middlesex, where it remained, through several financial crises and changes of management, until 1957.

Renwick and his partner, A.C. 'Bert' Bertelli, had previously formed an engineering concern which produced just one car, the R & B, with an overhead-cam 1.5-litre four-cylinder engine. Nevertheless, this was the basis for the Bertelli-designed Aston Martins up to 1936.

The new model competed at Brooklands, Le Mans and in the Mille Miglia, establishing a distinguished sporting pedigree. Finance still remained a problem however; after a brief liaison with Frazer Nash in 1931, then with L. Prideaux Brune, the company came under the control of R.G. Sutherland in 1933. A new 2-litre model succeeded the 1.5-litre for 1937; although superficially resembling the smaller car, it lacked its commercial and competition success.

The first post-war Aston Martin had a Claude Hill-designed pushrod 2-litre engine and independent front suspension, but only a few were made before the company was taken over by the David Brown group in 1947. Experiments continued in 1948 and 1949, when a space-frame model of advanced concept was created and dubbed the DB1. David Brown had also acquired Lagonda, and the twin-cam 2.6-litre six-cylinder engine which W.O. Bentley had designed for the post-war Lagonda was fitted in the square-tube space frame, clothed with an aerodynamic body and entered – unsuccessfully – in the 1949 Le Mans. The car achieved production status as the DB2.

The DB3 of 1954 was a sports-racer, actively campaigned by the factory to gain publicity; Eberan von Eberhorst, late of Auto Union, designed the curvaceous DB3S, with ladder chassis and de Dion rear end, which enjoyed a moderately successful sporting career.

Nevertheless, it was the successor to the DB3S, the DBR that gave Aston Martin victory at Le Mans in 1959 along with the Sports Car Constructors' Championship.

However, for the 1960 season Aston Martin produced a completely new car, the DB4, with a Tadek Marek-designed all-aluminium double-overhead-cam 3.7-litre engine in a platform-frame chassis with trailing link and coil rear suspension and handsome Superleggera (lightweight) coachwork in hand-beaten aluminium over a tubular cage.

Announced in 1963, the DB5 had a 4-litre engine from which painstaking development had eliminated many of the troubles that had plagued the earlier DB4s. True four-seater motoring coupled with sensational performance came with the 1966 DB6, while the following year saw the DBS and DBS Vantage, the latter a more expensive and powerful variant that was to remain in production until 1973.

A new 5.4-litre all-aluminium V8 appeared in the DBS V8 of 1970; it was ultimately also used to power the Lagonda model which reached full production in 1978.

David Brown sold out to Company Developments Ltd in 1972, the 'DB' part of the product

ASA

**Aston Martin 11.9 hp**

name being naturally dropped: the company has since had several changes of management yet seems to be coping well with the thorny problem of surviving profitably in the post-energy-crisis world. In 1984 the company was under the control of the American concern Automotive Investments after a three year spell of ownership by Pace Petroleum, and CH Industrials. Pace Petroleum's Victor Gauntlett was retained as Executive Chairman.

The mid-eighties saw Aston Martin offer the 5.3-litre V8 four-seater coupè as the mainstay of production with fast Vantage (good for 170 mph/274 kph) and drophead Volante versions also available. The four-door Lagonda continued to be the company's flagship.

In the early 1980s Aston Martin became involved in endurance racing once more, on a semi-works basis until the 1984 Le Mans race saw both AM Nimrods involved in the same serious crash.

## Aston Martin 11.9 hp

'Bert' Bertelli's 11.9 hp Aston Martin was one of the most highly-regarded British sports cars throughout its production life, from 1926 to 1935. It was, said *The Autocar*, 'One of those cars which make the heart of the enthusiast rejoice, not only because the lines of the little machine suggest the joys of the open road, but because the whole chassis has that indefinable air of breeding which is partly due to careful finish, partly to a design suggesting inevitable durability such as few small cars possess.' The car was exceptionally low-built, thanks to the adoption of worm final drive, and the overhead-cam engine had dry-

### 1926 ASTON MARTIN 11.9 hp

**Engine:** in-line four cylinder, overhead cam
**Bore × stroke:** 69 mm × 99 mm
**Capacity:** 1481 cc
**Maximum power:** 70 bhp
**Transmission:** four-speed
**Chassis:** pressed steel
**Suspension:** non-independent with semi-elliptic leaf springs
**Brakes:** drums all round
**Bodywork:** two-seater sports
**Maximum speed (approx):** 84 mph (134 kph)

sump lubrication as standard from 1930, a testimony to the model's competition breeding. Astons ran in every Le Mans 24 hour race from 1931 to 1964, and Bertelli won the Biennial Cup there in 1932, justifying the production of a range of 'Le Mans' models. Bevel drive and a unit gearbox were introduced at the 1932 Olympia show. Mk IIs were built from 1934 to 1936.

## Aston Martin DB2/3

In 1949, Aston ran an aerodynamic coupé at Le Mans; its 2.6-litre six-cylinder twin cam had been designed for Lagonda (now also part of the David Brown empire) by W.O. Bentley. The model reached production status in 1950 as the DB2, with a choice of power units: 107 bhp, or 123 bhp for the powerful Vantage. In 1950 John Wyer ran a team of three DB2 saloons at Le Mans, finishing fifth (and winning the Index of Performance) and sixth; in 1952, DB2s came first and second in their class in the Mille Miglia, taking 12th and 13th position overall.

That year, too, a new sports-racer designed by Eberan von Eberhorst, the DB3 appeared, and took second, third and fourth places in the Silverstone Production Car Race. The DB2 then won the Nine Hours Race at Goodwood. The sleek DB3S won the Isle of Man Tourist Trophy outright, driven by Reg Parnell, and also took the Daily Express Silverstone race and the Goodwood Nine Hours (for the second time). Privateer Beauman

won the Dutch Sports Car GP at Zandvoort. Driving a DB2/4, Maurice Gatsonides and Marcel Becquart won their class in the Monte Carlo Rally, finishing seventh overall. In 1953, the Aston works team ran in a particularly fetching shade of almond green, with the grilles painted different colours to identify the individual cars. DB3S upholstery was – oddly enough – in tartan.

### 1949 ASTON MARTIN DB2

**Engine:** in-line six cylinder, double overhead cam
**Bore × stroke:** 78 mm × 90 mm
**Capacity:** 2580 cc
**Maximum power:** 125 bhp
**Transmission:** four-speed
**Chassis:** square tubular steel space frame
**Suspension:** independent with wishbones and coil springs front and rear
**Brakes:** drums all round
**Bodywork:** coupè
**Maximum speed (approx):** 110 mph

**Aston Martin DB2**

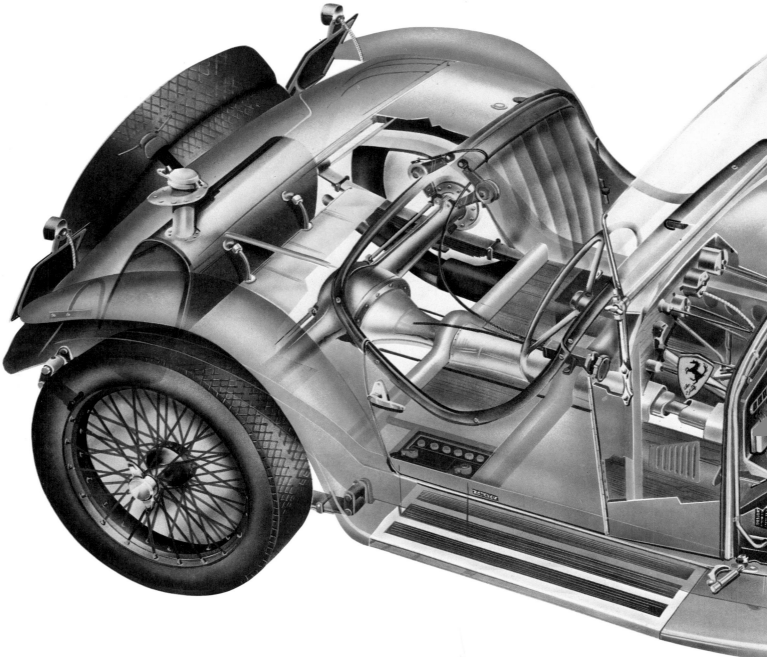

## MODEL
Alfa Romeo 8C 2300 (1932)

**UK price when announced:**
£1700 (chassis only)

### ENGINE
**Location:** Front, longitudinal
**Type:** Water-cooled in-line eight cylinder with two four-cylinder blocks with alloy heads in line.
**Cubic capacity:** 2336 cc
**Bore × stroke:** 65 mm × 88 mm
**Compression ratio:** 5.75 : 1
**Valve gear:** 2 inclined valves per cylinder operated by two gear-driven overhead camshafts.
**Fuel supply:** Single Memini carburettor with single Roots type supercharger
**Ignition:** Mechanical with Bosch coil and distributor
**Maximum power:** 142 bhp at 5200 rpm

### TRANSMISSION
**Layout:** Clutch and gearbox in unit with engine driving rear wheels
**Clutch:** Multiplate, wet
**Gearbox:** Four speed manual without synchromesh
    1st 3.65 : 1    3rd 1.39 : 1
    2nd 2.03 : 1    4th 1.06 : 1
**Final drive:** Spiral bevel
**Ratio:** 4.25 : 1

### SUSPENSION
**Front:** Non independent with semi-elliptic leaf springs and adjustable friction dampers
**Rear:** Live rear axle located by torque tube semi-elliptic leaf springs and adjustable friction dampers

### STEERING
**Type:** Worm and wheel

### BRAKES
**Type:** Finned alloy drums front and rear, rod operated

### WHEELS AND TYRES
**Type:** Wire spoked wheels with 5.50 × 19 in tyres

### BODY/CHASSIS
**Type:** Pressed steel channel separate chassis with two outer longitudinal members and cross members. Two or four-seat open sports bodywork by various coachbuilders.

### DIMENSIONS AND WEIGHT
**Length:** 156 in (3962 mm)
**Width:** 65 in (1651 mm)
**Wheelbase:** 109 in (2768 mm)
**Track – front:** 54 in (1372 mm)
    – rear: 54 in (1372 mm)
**Weight:** 2464 lb (1117 kg)

### PERFORMANCE
**Maximum speed:** 112 mph (180 kph)
**Acceleration 0–60 mph:** 9.4 seconds
**Fuel consumption:** 14 mpg

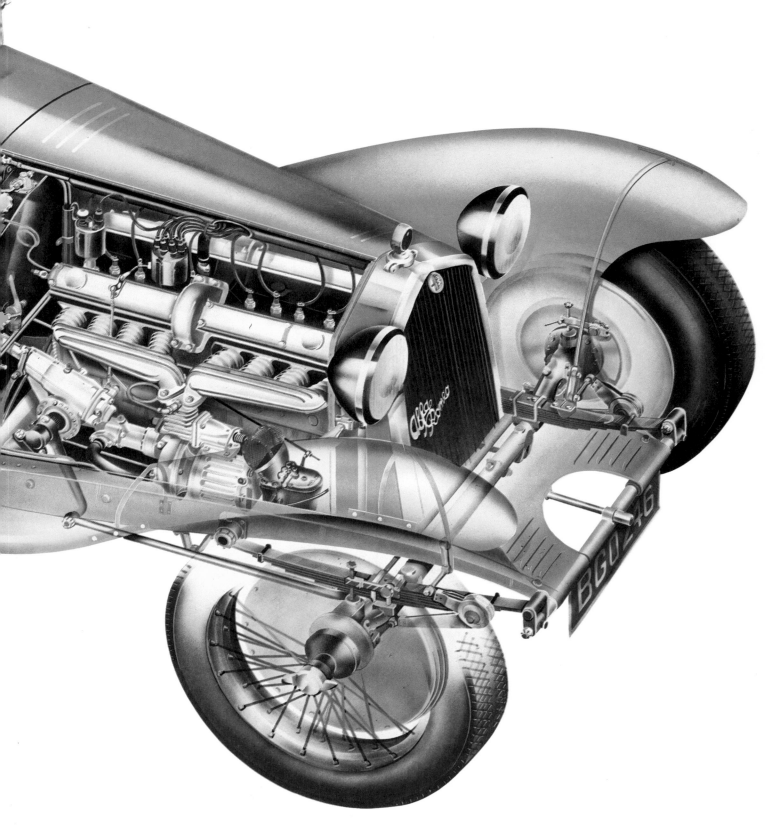

# A-Z OF THE CAR

GT race at Silverstone with a DB4 saloon shortly after the model's introduction. The power unit was Aston's first production engine with a light-alloy block, while the bodywork utilised the Superleggera construction, with hand-beaten aluminium panelling over a tubular steel cage. Later in the year production of the potent DB4GT began and 75 examples in all were built. A 35 gallon fuel tank occupied that part of the luggage boot that wasn't taken up by the spare wheel, and claimed power output was 302 bhp, a figure that put the engine on a par with contemporary Grand Prix units.

Most potent of all the DB4GTs was the Zagato-bodied version, which could cover a standing quarter-mile in less than 15 seconds and achieve a remarkable 0–100–0 mph inside 20 seconds.

## Aston Martin DB4GT

Introduced in 1959, the DB4 had a detuned version of the Tadek Marek-designed double-overhead-cam 3.7 litre-engine from the DBR sports racer: that this still left a potent motorcar was underlined when Stirling Moss won an International

### 1959 ASTON MARTIN DB4GT

**Engine:** in-line six cylinder, double overhead cam
**Bore × stroke:** 92 mm × 92 mm
**Capacity:** 3669 cc
**Maximum power:** 302 bhp
**Transmission:** four-speed
**Chassis:** boxed sheet steel platform
**Suspension:** independent front with double wishbones and coil springs. Live rear axle with coil springs and five links
**Brakes:** discs all round
**Bodywork:** Superleggera coupé
**Maximum speed (approx):** 170 mph (272 kph)

**Aston Martin DB4GT**

## Aston Martin Vantage

The current Aston Martin V8 has been around for many years now and although it can be regarded as an anachronism, years of development have led to a car that can live with its far more modern exotic Italian and German rivals. It can be regarded as the pinnacle of the traditional front-engine, rear-drive sports coupé.

The light-alloy four-cam V8 produces enormous power without the excessive weight penalty of American iron V8s. In fact in its most powerful Vantage form it produces 390bhp and yet the car has a near ideal weight distribution of 51 per cent front and 49 per cent rear. That has a lot to do with making its performance as usable as any modern supercar and its classic suspension system of double wishbones, coil springs and anti-roll bar at the front and de Dion axle, trailing arms and Watts linkage at the rear means that the Vantage handles very predictably while truly massive low profile tyres (275/15 VR 15) hold it securely on the road.

Secure roadholding and excellent handling are obviously necessary with a car that can achieve its maximum speed of 170mph (273kph) without great strain. Despite its light alloy engine and alloy body panels of its Superleggera-type construction, the Aston is still a great deal of car, tipping the scales at 4000lb (1815kg) yet the ventilated discs do as good a job in stopping the car as the superb engine does in making it go.

### 1984 ASTON MARTIN V8 VANTAGE

**Engine:** V8, double overhead cam per bank
**Bore × stroke:** 100 mm × 85 mm
**Capacity:** 5340 cc
**Maximum power:** 390 bhp
**Transmission:** five-speed manual
**Chassis:** steel box-type platform
**Suspension:** independent front with wishbones and coil springs. De Dion rear axle with trailing arms, Watt linkage and coil springs.
**Brakes:** ventilated discs all round
**Bodywork:** alloy two-door 2+2 coupé
**Maximum speed (approx):** 170 mph (273 kph)

**Aston Martin V8 Vantage**

# Aston Martin Lagonda

The Lagonda, Aston Martin's striking flagship, first appeared in 1974 to receive instant bad publicity because of its adventurous use of electronic digital instrumentation. While such systems are commonplace in the mid '80s Aston Martin were breaking new ground in '74 and its unreliabilty and shortcomings were not well received in a car so expensive. With those teething problems fully sorted out the Lagonda took its rightful place as one of the very best of exclusive high-speed four-door saloons. Exclusive it certainly is as the bulk of the limited production goes either to the Middle East or to the USA.

Although it looks wide and flat, almost to excess, it is actually narrower than the V8 it is based on, although naturally it is substantially longer overall and in the wheelbase to allow for proper rear seating. Despite its strikingly different appearance it is basically the same under the skin as the V8 with the same (lengthened) platform chassis and suspension. Its extra length makes it an even more massive 4550lb (2063kg) which gives a top

**Aston Martin Lagonda**

### 1984 ASTON MARTIN LAGONDA

**Engine:** V8, double overhead cam per bank
**Bore × stroke:** 100 mm × 85 mm
**Capacity:** 5340 cc
**Maximum power:** 320 bhp
**Transmission:** three-speed automatic with torque converter
**Chassis:** steel box-type platform
**Suspension:** independent front with wishbones and coil springs. De Dion rear axle with trailing arms, Watt linkage and coil springs
**Brakes:** discs all round, power assisted
**Bodywork:** aluminium alloy four-door saloon
**Maximum speed (approx):** 140 mph (225 kph)

speed of 'only' 140mph (225kph) but with handling and roadholding well up to the task. As one would expect from a car costing the best part of £70,000 such niceties as air conditioning and leather upholstery are standard.

# ATALANTA

### Staines, England
### 1937–1939

Like the Lagonda, the low-slung Atalanta sports car of 1937 to 1939 hailed from Staines; unlike the Lagonda, it had independent suspension all round. The first Atalantas used Albert Gough's temperamental 1.5 and 2-litre overhead-camshaft power units with three valves per cylinder. Gough, director of Atalanta, had

previously designed engines for Frazer Nash. The power output (78 or 98 bhp) of these engines could be augmented by fitting an Arnott supercharger.

More popular than the supercharger, however, was the option of a 4.4-litre V12 Lincoln-Zephyr engine, which gave far greater performance at much the same cost. Indeed, the supercharged 2-litre coupé cost £787, while the V12 coupe was £750 (although the equivalent Lincoln-Zephyr was only £645).

The Atalanta was available with sports two-seater, coupé or saloon coachwork.

The marque gained a number of competition successes, a leading driver being Margaret ('Madge') Wilby, another director of the Atalanta company.

After the war Richard Gaylard Shattock revived the name with the RGS Atalanta, though a different

choice of power units was offered, initially converted Brooke marine engines; subsequently available were Lea-Francis, Ford or Jaguar power units. Shattock offered complete cars or kits of parts, latterly with glassfibre bodywork,

### 1937 ATALANTA

**Engine:** V12, overhead valve
**Bore × stroke:** 70 mm × 95 mm
**Capacity:** 4387 cc
**Maximum power:** 110 bhp
**Transmission:** four-speed manual
**Chassis:** tubular steel
**Suspension:** independent with coil springs front and rear
**Brakes:** drums all round
**Bodywork:** two-seater sports, saloon or coupé
**Maximum speed (approx):** 95 mph (152 kph)

**Atalanta**

until 1958. Though the C-Type Jaguar-engined RGS-Atalanta was a good design customers were not forthcoming, and sales amounted to a dozen or so units, most of them sold as kits.

# ATS

**Bologna, Italy
1962–1964**

The 'Scuderia Serenissima' Formula One racing team was established in Bologna by Count Giovanni Volpi di Misurata and Jaime Ortiz-Patino in February 1962. Unfortunately in December that year Volpi withdrew his backing and the Serenissima organisation was reformed as ATS (Automobili Turismo Sport) to produce racing and sports cars to the design of Carlo Chiti. The Formula One racer was a failure which even drivers of the calibre of Phil Hill and Giancarlo Baghetti could not redeem.

---

### 1963 ATS

**Engine:** V8, double overhead cam
**Bore × stroke:** 76 mm × 68 mm
**Capacity:** 2467 cc
**Maximum power:** 260 bhp
**Transmission:** five-speed manual
**Chassis:** tubular steel space frame
**Suspension:** independent with double wishbones front and rear
**Brakes:** discs all round
**Bodywork:** two-door, two-seater alloy sports coupé
**Maximum speed (approx):** 160 mph (255 kph)

---

**Auburn Cabin Speedster**

Production of the mid-engined 2500GT and 2500GTS began in 1963, but only a handful of these V8 sports coupés with overhead-cam engines up to 245 bhp was built. There was a choice of quadruple Webers or Lucas fuel injection.

Production ran from 1963 to 1964 (when two ATS ran in the Targa Florio without success), and then Count Volpi reappeared on the scene and revived the ATS sports coupé under the name Serenissima, now with two overhead camshafts per bank of cylinders. However, even in this new incarnation, the design was never fully developed. The original ATS company subsequently built prototype racing and GT cars producing as much as 350 bhp fefore finally ceasing car production in 1969.

# AUBURN

**Auburn, USA
1900–1937**

Frank and Morris Eckhart's father founded the Eckhart Carriage Company in Auburn (Indiana) in

1874; the brothers formed the Auburn Automobile Company as an offshoot in 1900 and built a number of 'one-off' cars for local consumption. They went into production with a 'one-lunger' chain-driven two-seater runabout launched at the Chicago Automobile Show in 1903. It was followed in 1905 by a twin-cylinder model; in 1909 Auburn built its first 'real' car, with a 25/30 hp Rutenber four-cylinder engine. In 1911 Auburn absorbed the Zimmermann company, builders of high-wheeler buggies, continuing manufacture of these basic vehicles until 1914.

A handsome 6–50 hp Rutenber-engined six with such

sophistications as electric lighting was added to the Auburn range in 1912, and it was proprietary-engined sixes (with power by Rutenber, Teetor or Continental) that took Auburn through to a change of ownership when a

---

### 1929 AUBURN CABIN SPEEDSTER

**Engine:** in-line eight cylinder, side-valve
**Bore × stroke:** 82.5 mm × 114.3 mm
**Capacity:** 4893 cc
**Maximum power:** 115 bhp
**Transmission:** three-speed manual
**Chassis:** pressed steel, underslung at rear
**Suspension:** non-independent with semi-elliptic leaf springs all round
**Brakes:** drums all round, hydraulic
**Bodywork:** cabin speedster'
**Maximum speed (approx):** 100 mph (161 kph)

---

syndicate of Chicago businessmen took over in 1919; the new proprietors retained Morris Eckhart as President.

The changeover was followed by the launch of the Continental-engined 26 hp Beauty-Six. But the new-look Auburn failed to achieve real sales success, and in 1924 the dynamic Errett Lobban Cord arrived, first as general manager, then as President. A vigorous sales campaign shifted the unsold

**ATS**

Beauty-Sixes while Chief engineer James Crawford prepared a new range.

Early in 1925 came the 4273 cc Eight-in-Line, developed later that year into the 4523 cc 8–88 with a range of striking body styles, mostly built by the Limousine Body Company of Kalamazoo, which was incorporated into Cord's growing empire, along with Duesenberg and Lycoming Motors, in 1926. In 1927, stock car racing was revived in America, and works driver Wade Morton underlined the merits of the 8–88 by covering 1000 miles (1600 km) in less than 16 hours at an average speed of 63.4 mph (102 kph) averaged nearly 90 mph (145 kph) to win a 100-mile race on a board track at Salem, New Hampshire, and came third in the stock car race up the 12-mile (19 km) Pikes Peak hill climb. He exceeded 108 mph (174 kph) over a measured mile on Daytona beach, then put 2033 miles (3273 km) into 24 hours at the Atlantic City track.

In 1928 the first of the boat-tailed Auburn Speedsters appeared, styled by Count Alexis de Sakhnoffsky and capable of over 108 mph (174 kph), thanks to revised inlet manifolding which enabled its Lycoming power unit to develop 115 bhp.

In 1929, over 22,000 Auburns were sold, but the onset of the Great Depression at the end of that year drove the company's sales down to under 14,000 in 1930.

However, 1931 sales were boosted to a record 28,000 by restyled coachwork on the new 8–98 model. The 6407 cc Lycoming-powered V12 of 1932–33 was a near-flop; even Gordon Buehrig's all-time classic supercharged outside-exhaust 851/852 Speedsters of 1935 and 1936 sold at a loss.

## Auburn Cabin Speedster

In 1929 the Auburn company unveiled the remarkable Cabin Speedster, an aerodynamic saloon 'sky-styled' by Wade Morton. It had an underslung chassis and two wicker aircraft seats; further weight reduction was achieved by panelling the body in aluminium. Its streamlining was further enhanced by fitting a full belly-pan to enclose the underside of the chassis. Close-fitting cycle wings rose and fell with the wheels and the spare wheel was housed in the tapered tail. The car stood only 58 inches (147 cm) high, and its top speed was guaranteed to exceed 100 mph (161 kph). Unfortunately, this bold attempt to market 'a racing car with the comfort of a closed car' coincided with the start of the Great Depression, and this remarkable project, catalogued at only $2195, was still-born.

## Auburn 851/852 Speedster

The Speedster versions of the Auburn had become such a hallmark of the range that it came as something of a shock when the 1934 range appeared without a Speedster in it. But the discontinuation was only temporary: in January 1935 a range of bodies was announced on the newly-introduced supercharged 851 chassis (launched in unsupercharged form the previous September); and it included a new Speedster styled by Gordon Buehrig.

Where the old Speedster had been handsomely flamboyant, the new one went truly over the top. It had a deep, sloping radiator, teardrop wings, a tiny two-seat cockpit set back behind a raked windscreen, a tapered tail containing the exiguous luggage compartment (to which there was no external access) and flexible exhaust pipes of drain-like dimensions emerging from the left-hand side of the bonnet. The Schwitzer-Cummins centrifugal supercharger ran at six times crankshaft speed, boosting power output by 30 per cent. A small pointer on the steering column controlled the dual-ratio back axle ('LOW ratio means terrific acceleration and power...HIGH ratio gears you up for speeds up to 100 mph with low revs and consequent lower running costs'). 'Mormon Meteor' Ab Jenkins set several new stock car records with the 851 Speedster in July 1935, covering a standing mile at an average of 69.4 mph (112 kph), a flying mile at 104.17 mph (168 kph) and averaging 102.9 mph (166 kph) for twelve hours, the first American car ever to exceed 100 mph (161 kph) for twelve hours in stock form. And every speedster carried a plaque on the dashboard certifying that Ab Jenkins had driven it at over 100 mph (161 kph) before delivery.

The Model 852, introduced during 1936, was little changed from the 851, and with good reason, for the Cord magic was running out of impetus. Only some 500 Auburns of all types were built during 1936, and the marque finally collapsed in 1936 as Cord's house-of-cards empire crumbled in on itself. Nevertheless the design remained highly regarded, and in recent years several American and Canadian companies have offered replicas of the Auburn Speedster, using modern running gear and glass-fibre bodywork.

### 1935 AUBURN 851/852 SPEEDSTER

**Engine:** V8, side-valve
**Bore × stroke:** 77.8 mm × 120.6 mm
**Capacity:** 4586 cc
**Maximum power:** 150 bhp
**Transmission:** three-speed manual with dual ratio axle
**Chassis:** pressed steel channel
**Suspension:** non-independent with semi-elliptic leaf springs all round
**Brakes:** drums all round, hydraulic
**Bodywork:** speedster
**Maximum speed (approx):** 105 mph (169 kph)

**Auburn Speedster 851**

# A-Z OF THE CAR

## AUDI
Zwickau, Germany
Ingoldstadt, Germany
1910–1935
1965–

After August Horch (creator of Horch cars) quarrelled with his directors over his entering competitions he resigned in 1909 and founded Audi in 1910. Both companies were based at Zwickau in Saxony. Because he now was unable to use his own name on the cars, he adopted the name Audi, because in Latin it meant the same as Horch in German: Hearken.

His first Audi was a 2612 cc four which bore a suspicious resemblance to the last car he had designed for the Horch company; nevertheless, Audi prospered as the fortunes of Horch cars declined.

Other four-cylinder models of 3562 cc, 4680 cc and 5720 cc followed, and proved very successful in major sporting events.

Pre-war models had inlet-over-exhaust-valve engines; a new side-valve 8/28PS four of 2071 cc was designed before the Great War but not introduced until after the Armistice, along with an overhead-valve 3500 cc 50 hp, Model K. This had unit construction incorporating radiator, engine (with a block of silumin alloy), steering box and gearbox; standard equipment included a folding steering wheel.

Type M, the first six-cylinder Audi, appeared in 1924, with a seven-bearing 4655 cc overhead-cam engine, again with silumin block incorporating steel liners. Valves were operated directly by the camshaft without the intervention of rockers. Hydraulic servo-assisted brakes on all four wheels were justified by the 75 mph (120 kph) top speed. The

DKW – bought Audi.

Rasmussen had bought the remains of the American Rickenbacker car works from the receiver and soon began building Rickenbacker eight-cylinder engines in Germany. In 1929 Rickenbacker eights of 4371 cc and 5130 cc were used in the Audi Zwickaus, followed in 1931 by the Dresden 3838 cc six-cylinder and a small four with a 1.1-litre Peugeot engine in a DKW chassis. Most Audis were fitted with luxurious – and heavy – special coachwork.

Audi joined Wanderer, DKW and Horch in the newly formed

## Audi Alpensieger

August Horch's insistence on his cars taking part in competition bore early fruit when he drove a 2.6-litre Type B in the 1911 Alpine Trials and finished without incurring a single penalty point. In 1912 the Type C appeared; its 3.5-litre engine had a *desaxé* crankshaft (to reduce angular loads on the conrods); its inlet-over-exhaust-valve engine had angled exhaust valves to allow a more efficient shape of combustion chamber. The engine drove through a leather cone clutch to a three-point suspended gear-

**Audi Alpensieger**

### 1912 AUDI ALPENSIEGER

**Engine:** in-line four cylinder, inlet over exhaust valve
**Bore × stroke:** 90 mm × 140 mm
**Capacity:** 3562 cc
**Maximum power:** 40 bhp
**Transmission:** four-speed
**Chassis:** pressed steel
**Suspension:** non-independent with semi-elliptic leaf springs all round
**Brakes:** drums, rear only
**Bodywork:** tulip-sided tourer
**Maximum speed (approx):** 60 mph (97 kph)

first straight-eight Audi, the side-valve Type R Imperator of 4872 cc appeared in 1928. It was the last true Audi to be built before Joergen Skafte Rasmussen – the head of

Auto-Union in 1932, and the 1933 1963 cc Audi Front had a 2.3-litre Wanderer six-cylinder overhead-valve engine. It was followed by a 3281 cc car with an overhead-cam Horch six-cylinder engine.

Audi was nationalised in 1945, and became defunct until 1965, when the marque was revived at the 'new' Auto-Union works at Ingoldstadt in Western Germany. Mercedes controlled Audi in the mid-1960s and also designed the first post-war Audi engine, a high-compression 1.7-litre four-cylinder but before the new Audi was on the market, Mercedes had sold Auto-Union to VW. With recent models like the aerodynamic Audi 100 and the four-wheel-driven Quattro, Audi has become one of Germany's leading marques, and is now a profitable partner in the massive VAG Group, the country's biggest company.

box. The normal wheelbase was 120 in (305 cm) but the competition version had a shorter wheelbase and lightweight tulip-sided aluminium coachwork. It became known as the Alpensieger because of its success in the Austrian Alpine Trials, where two cars returned clean sheets in 1912 and the marque won the team prize in 1913 and 1914 (though it had to share the honours with Hansa in the latter year).

## Audi Front
There was a good deal of cross-fertilisation between the component companies of the Auto Union. Wanderer, for example used DKW front-wheel-drive technology on a larger scale – as well as sharing some parts. In this set-up, which to some extent mirrored the organisation of General Motors, Audi was positioned between Wanderer and

**Audi Front**

Horch in terms of prestige. The Audi Front Type 225, introduced in 1934, was powered by a six-cylinder Wanderer engine and was built in the Horch plant, with a unique backbone chassis. The model was in production until 1939, having survived a somewhat inauspicious start in which annoying teething troubles plagued steering, suspension and gear-changing. Front suspension, by two parallel transverse leaf springs, was on similar principles to the front-wheel-drive Alvis. Of the Audi's front-wheel-drive layout, the press commented: 'It undoubtedly gives many advantages, as a large and unobstructed body platform is provided'; and on that large platform, Audi generally provided Teutonically overblown cabriolet or saloon bodies that inhibited any pretensions the car might have had to performance. However, at the 1938 Berlin Show, a wondrously impracticable sporting three-seater with tapered tail and disappearing hood was displayed, in which the third passenger sat sideways in the well behind the front seats. 'By this means,' said an unquestioning journalist, 'good lines can be coupled with a comfortable seat...'.

**Audi Quattro**

## 1934 AUDI FRONT

**Engine:** in-line six cylinder, overhead valve
**Bore × stroke:** 71 mm × 95 mm
**Capacity:** 2257 cc
**Maximum power:** 55 bhp
**Transmission:** four-speed manual
**Chassis:** square-tubular steel backbone
**Suspension:** independent with twin parallel transverse leaf springs front and single transverse leaf spring rear
**Brakes:** drums all round
**Bodywork:** cabriolet or saloon
**Maximum speed (approx):** 70 mph (112 kph)

## Audi Quattro

According to Audi's Ferdinand Piech, the move to permanently engaged four-wheel drive for the road is as inevitable as the transition from rear-wheel to four-wheel braking before World War II. That remains to be seen but Piech's creation, the Audi Quattro, is without doubt one of the modern greats It was mostly a combination of parts already available from other Audis or VWs and yet has a character greater than all its stablemates. The four-wheel drive system was a development of that used on the military Iltis, a VW off-road vehicle. It was naturally robust, and far more simple than most and in its Quattro application it featured a hollow lower transfer shaft through

## 1980 AUDI QUATTRO

**Engine:** in-line five cylinder, overhead cam, turbo
**Bore × stroke:** 79.5 mm × 86.4 mm
**Capacity:** 2144 cc
**Maximum power:** 200 bhp
**Transmission:** five-speed manual with permanent four-wheel drive
**Chassis:** steel, unitary with front subframe
**Suspension:** independent front with MacPherson struts and anti-roll bar and rigid rear axle with trailing links
**Brakes:** discs all round
**Bodywork:** two-door, coupe
**Maximum speed (approx):** 136 mph (219 kph)

which the drive shaft from centre differential to front differential ran.

Power was supplied by the company's five-cylinder in-line engine, turbocharged of course to give the Quattro the performance potential Piech and his colleagues decided was necessary to advertise their idea. The transmission was a five speed manual and both centre and rear differentials could be locked to provide extra performance in loose or slippery conditions.

Despite its very definite front weight bias (the result of using the existing front-wheel drive parts) the Quattro immediately turned into an almost unbeatable rally car. In its first year, 1981, it took Hannu Mikkola to third place in the World Championship for Drivers and the next year Audi became World Rally Champions with Michelle Mouton second in the Drivers' Championship. The success continued the year after as Mikkola took the Drivers' Championship.

As a road car it was almost as great as the rally cars, bringing new standards to high performance motoring. Its enormous capabilities meant that for most drivers it was merely their lack of terminal courage that put a limit on the Quattro's cornering power. It was so sure-footed that it produced a

sense of invincibility in many drivers and the car certainly needed the excellent brakes that were developed for it as drivers realised that there were some corners even the Quattro could not get around.

It was criticised in some quarters for being quite unmanageable at the limit but that was very much the minority view and really the car's only weak point was its interior which lacked the appropriate instrumentation and trim.

## Audi 100 Coupé S

The 100 Coupé S was one of Audi's most attractive designs of the early '70s, having a passing resemblance to the contemporary Aston Martin, although in reality it was merely the fastback version of the Audi 100 saloon. Nevertheless it was a good drivers' car and is now well on the way to becoming a minor classic.

Its 1.9-litre overhead-valve four-cylinder engine showed its Mercedes heritage, particularly in the shape of the combustion chambers, and the 112 bhp (and 118 lb ft of torque) it produced was enough to propel the stylish coupé at up to 115 mph (185 kph) and accelerate it to 60 mph (96 kph) in around 9.5 seconds.

Like the 100 saloon, the coupé was front-wheel drive and the engine was mounted longitudinally ahead of the front wheels which were located by a sophisticated suspension system featuring double

wishbones with relatively short struts operating on the top wishbones. The whole of the front end, in fact, was quite sophisticated with an anti-roll bar, rack and pinion steering and in-board front disc brakes.

Although the 100 Coupé S was a solid well-built machine, Audi did not have the same up-market image it has now. The car was not fully appreciated and commercially it was not a huge success.

## 1974 AUDI 100 COUPE

**Engine:** in-line four cylinder, overhead valve
**Bore × stroke:** 84 mm × 84.4 mm
**Capacity:** 1871 cc
**Maximum power:** 112 bhp
**Transmission:** four-speed manual
**Chassis:** steel, unitary
**Suspension:** independent front with double wishbones, struts, and anti-roll bar. Beam rear axle with trailing arms, torsion bars, Panhard rod and anti-roll bar
**Brakes:** disc front and drums rear mounted inboard at front
**Bodywork:** two-door, four-seat coupe
**Maximum speed (approx):** 115 mph (185 kph)

**Audi 100 Coupé S**

**Austin Seven**

# AUSTIN
**Longbridge, England
1906–**

Wolseley's general manager, Herbert Austin, resigned in 1905 to establish his own company, based in an old printing works at Longbridge, south of Birmingham. Production of conventional but well-made cars with side-valve T-head engines having separately-cast cylinders, began the following year.

The first Austin was a chain-driven 25/30 hp, but within three years the company could offer a range of 15, 18/24 and 40 hp four-cylinder models plus a 60 hp six-cylinder. The latter model was the basis of a racing Austin entered for the 1908 French Grand Prix, in which the marque took 18th and 19th places.

A single-cylinder 1100 cc 7 hp Austin (in effect a re-radiatored Swift) appeared in 1909, precursor of a far more famous 7 hp model. There was also an odd-looking 15 hp cab-over-engine town-carriage chassis used, among others, by Suffragette leader Mrs Pankhurst.

In 1910 a 1.6-litre four-cylinder car, initially for export, was announced, becoming available for home consumption 12 months later.

At the outbreak of war in 1914, Austin was offering three four-cylinder models, the largest a 60 hp of nearly 6 litres swept volume.

After the Great War, Austin's marketing philosophy underwent a pronounced change: he offered just one model, the American-inspired 3.6-litre 20 announced in 1919. Unfortunately, this big car failed to sell in sufficient numbers, and the company was quickly placed under receivership. A new model, the solid and reliable 1.6-litre Twelve – effectively a scaled-down 20 – was rushed into production in 1921.

This admirable car remained in production until 1936; it was enlarged and the swept volume increased to 1861 cc in 1927.

The famous Austin Seven was announced in 1922. When it appeared, the Seven was the smallest British four-cylinder car, with a 696 cc engine; this was soon increased to 747 cc.

A fashionable 3.4-litre six-cylinder 20 went on sale in 1927, the original four-cylinder model remaining in production for another year.

In 1928 the new six was scaled down to produce a 2.3-litre Sixteen, but a less felicitous version was the gutless 12/6 of 1931. A well-received 1125 cc Ten and 1535 cc Light 12/4 were introduced the

following year, and remained in the range until 1947.

The famous Seven was replaced in 1939 by the 900 cc Eight, which was phased out over ten years later in 1947.

Austin's first overhead-valve power unit was fitted in the 1940 12 body and chassis in 1945 to create the 2199 cc Sixteen.

Independent front suspension appeared for the first time on an Austin in 1948, fitted to the Princess and Sheerline and the 1.2-litre A40. The A90 Atlantic was an unsuccessful bid for export dollars with curious 'transatlantic' styling that appealed to few customers.

Old rivalries were slaked in 1952 when Austin and Morris merged to form the British Motor Corporation; that year saw the appearance of Longbridge's first unitary construction car, the A30, with an 803 cc overhead-valve engine.

The curiously styled Metropolitan, another Longbridge bid to break into the American market, and made initially for Nash (later part of American Motors) appeared in 1954. It was powered by a 948 cc A40 engine.

New in 1955 were the Cambridge, with A40 or A50 engines, and the 2.6-litre six-cylinder Westminster.

The 1959 range was styled by Farina, whose Austin Cambridge theme was repeated on badge-engineered versions of the MG,

### 1922 AUSTIN SEVEN

**Engine:** in-line four cylinder, side valve
**Bore × stroke:** 56 mm × 76.2 mm
**Capacity:** 747 cc
**Maximum power:** 10.5 bhp
**Transmission:** three-speed manual
**Chassis:** pressed steel inverted channel
**Suspension:** non-independent with transverse semi-elliptic leaf springs front and live axle with quarter elliptic leaf springs rear
**Brakes:** drums all round
**Bodywork:** two-door tourer or saloon
**Maximum speed (approx):** 40 mph (64 kph)

Morris, Wolseley and Riley. That year, too, the revolutionary Mini appeared, and was initially sold as the Austin Seven. Designed by Alec Issigonis, it featured a transversely-mounted 848 cc A-series power unit with a four-speed gearbox in the sump. Unconventional features of the design were Moulton rubber suspension, 10 inch wheels and a distinctive boxy shape.

The Mini was followed in 1964 by the 1100, with Hydrolastic suspension (also sold as a Morris), with the less successful 1800 following two years later.

BMC was swallowed by

Leyland in 1968 to form British Leyland; the following year the Maxi appeared, with a 1485 cc overhead-cam engine.

Rear-wheel drive was phased out in 1971, when the short-lived 3-litre ceased production.

## Austin Seven

When the one-model policy which followed World War I failed, Sir Herbert Austin first produced the Twelve. Then, working in the billiard room at his home with an 18-year-old draughtsman, Stanley Edge, he designed a tiny car to replace both the motorcycle and sidecar and the minimalist cyclecar. Inspired by the Peugeot Quadrilette, he created a little four-seater with a 696 cc splash-lubricated four-cylinder power unit (the swept volume was soon increased to 747 cc, but the price cut from £225 to £165). A full-size car in miniature, the Austin Seven had four-wheel brakes, transverse suspension at the front and quarter elliptics at the rear. It remained in production until 1939, by which time 290,000 had been made: it was manufactured under licence in France, Germany, Japan and America. BMW and Datsun both had their car production roots in the Seven. The Seven with Swallow sports saloon coachwork led first to SS and then to Jaguar. There were sporting derivatives, too, like the Ulster and the Nippy; the Seven's sporting successes included a third place in the 1929 TT and a win in the 1930 500 Miles Race at Brooklands.

## Austin Atlantic

'Export or die' was the slogan of the late 1940s in Britain: and the Austin A90 was certainly intended for the export market – hence the name Atlantic. Its styling fell unhappily between fashions current in Britain and America, with the net result that it found insufficient buyers in either market. It appeared first in 1948; oddly enough, it was launched as a convertible, with 'the hood operated by hydraulic-electric mechanism at the touch of a switch, a feature which is now demanded in certain overseas markets'. The hardtop Sports Saloon didn't appear until 1949; promoted as 'the alternative A90 styling... has an elegant rigid-built roof with an extra wide rear window and seats five in complete comfort, it had side windows controlled by quick-action levers.' An unkind journalist wondered whether these were intended for passengers affected by the soggy motion of the 'intentionally supple' suspension. A bold sales-promotion scheme in April 1949 saw an Atlantic Convertible taking 63 American Stock Car records by travelling 11,850 miles (19,000 km) in seven days at Indianapolis, averaging over 70 mph (113 kph) de-

spite appalling weather. But even this evidence of the car's stamina failed to attract sufficient customers and the model was quietly dropped. Its power unit, however, later saw more distinguished service in the first Austin Healeys.

### 1948 AUSTIN ATLANTIC

**Engine:** in-line four cylinder, overhead valve
**Bore × stroke:** 87.3 mm × 111.1 mm
**Capacity:** 2660 cc
**Maximum power:** 88 bhp
**Transmission:** four-speed
**Chassis:** steel, integral
**Suspension:** independent front with wishbones and coil springs. Live rear axle with semi-elliptic leaf springs
**Brakes:** drums all round
**Bodywork:** two-door convertible or sports saloon
**Maximum speed (approx):** 84 mph (134 kph)

**Austin Mini**

## Austin Mini

The Mini, or Austin Seven as it was originally known, was a creature born of two fathers, the post-Suez energy crisis and the brilliant designer Alec Issigonis.

BMC chief Sir Leonard Lord instructed Issigonis to build an economy car using any engine as long as it was one produced by BMC. There was little choice but to use the A-series engine from the Morris Minor, cut down to 848 as 948 cc was thought to be too much for the tiny car to handle! The small engine produced just 34 bhp (and 44 lb ft of torque) and that was sufficient to push the compact box along to an eventual 72 mph (116 kph), even if it did take 24 seconds to reach 60.

When it appeared in 1959 the Mini broke new ground, not because it was front-wheel drive – there was nothing remotely new in that – but because it assembled so many unusual features together in such a small package. The gearbox tucked under the engine sharing its sump and the space saving rubber cone suspension helped make the

### 1959 AUSTIN MINI

**Engine:** in-line four cylinder, overhead valve
**Bore × stroke:** 63 mm × 68 mm
**Capacity:** 848 cc
**Maximum power:** 34 bhp
**Transmission:** four-speed
**Chassis:** integral
**Suspension:** independent with wishbones, rubber cone springs and telescopic dampers front with swinging longitudinal trailing arms, rubber cone springs and telescopic dampers rear
**Brakes:** drums all round
**Bodywork:** two-door saloon
**Maximum speed (approx):** 72 mph (116 kph)

Mini the most efficient packaging exercise the industry had seen. The wheel-at-each-corner approach and that rubber suspension helped give the Mini truly incredible handling and roadholding for the times and it was inevitable that it would be

**Austin Atlantic**

taken racing and rallying. Cooper variants, in 997, 998, 1071, and 1275 cc form (in 'S' guise) were much faster than the standard cars with the most powerful Cooper Ss producing 75 bhp and capable of over 100 mph (161 kph) while the rally versions were more potent still with outright wins in the Monte Carlo Rally (in 1964), Austrian Alpine, Acropolis and RAC Rallies.

Over the years the Mini grew up in many ways, although it never lost its original flavour. The sliding windows were eventually replaced by the wind-up variety while, much earlier the original wand-like gearlever was pensioned off to be replaced by a remote change. Evolution brought front disc brakes and the suspension went through the hydrolastic 'wet' phase and back to the dry with rubber.

For all the Mini's appeal it was certainly not without some serious faults and they ranged from being far too expensive to produce in relation to the price that could be asked, to the excessive noise, uncomfortable ride and bus-like driving position. It also had a bodyshell rather too prone to serious rusting. Perhaps the true measure of the Mini is that not only did it spawn a host of imitators and a move to a small car for the masses from numerous other manufacturers but it outlived some of its more modern rivals, such as the Hillman Imp and the original Renault 5, continuing in production during the mid '80s.

# AUSTIN HEALEY
**Longbridge, England**
**1953–1971**

Donald Healey, who originally ran a garage in Perranporth in Cornwall, moved into the mainstream of the motor industry in 1930 when he joined the design team of Invicta, at Cobham in Surrey. When Invicta folded, Healey joined Triumph in Coventry, where he was appointed chief designer, responsible for the Gloria range, as well as for the Alfa Romeo-inspired Dolomite.

After the war, with Triumph swallowed by Standard, Healey established his own company in

## 1952 HEALEY 100

**Engine:** in-line four cylinder, overhead valve
**Bore × stroke:** 87.33 mm × 111.1 mm
**Capacity:** 2660 cc
**Maximum power:** 90 bhp
**Transmission:** three-speed with overdrive
**Chassis:** steel, fabricated
**Suspension:** independent front with wishbones and coil springs. Live rear axle with semi-elliptic leaf springs
**Brakes:** drums all round
**Bodywork:** two-seater sports
**Maximum speed (approx):** 111 mph (179 kph)

Warwick, building cars under his own name. At the London Motor Show in 1952, their graceful, if rather sturdy Healey 100 was the undisputed star: a deal was quickly struck for the car to be produced by Austin as the Austin-Healey 100. Progressively developed, the muscular 'Big Healey' was produced until December 1967 by which time nearly 74,000 cars had been built. The Austin-Healey badge was also seen on the cheeky 'Frog-Eye' Sprites, precisely 48,999 of which were built, as well as on the thousands of Mks II–IV Sprites, which were mechanically identical and bodily similar to the contemporary MG Midgets although the MGs outlived the Sprites.

## Austin Healey 100

When the handsome and competitively priced Healey 100 appeared at the 1952 London Motor Show, it caused an immediate sensation and provoked a rush of orders that the little Healey company was totally unfitted to meet. Sir Leonard Lord of Austin, seeing the crush round the Healey stand, realised the potential of the car (which was powered by the 2.6-litre four-cylinder engine from the Austin A90) and quickly negotiated with Healey for the car to be built by Austin at Longbridge. Within a couple of days, the car on the Motor Show stand bore a new

name – Austin Healey 100. A virtually-standard Austin Healey 100 finished 12th at Le Mans in 1953, while a modified version equipped with disc brakes came third in the 1954 Sebring 12 Hours; in honour of this, a special 100S (S for Sebring) Austin Healey appeared later that year. Its engine was uprated to 132 bhp (from 90) and it had a new remote-change four-speed box (instead of three speeds plus overdrive) and disc brakes, as well as modified bodywork with much aluminium panelling. These cars were built in the Healey works at Warwick, not Longbridge: in November 1954 Donald Healey took a specially-streamlined supercharged 100S to Bonneville, where it attained 192.6 mph (310 kph). The following year, the ordinary Austin Healey 100 also got the four-speed transmission (overdrive was still available); the tuned derivative, the 100M, was principally intended for the American market. In October 1956 the 100 was superseded by the 100/6, equipped with the six-cylinder Austin 2.6-litre engine: longer and heavier, it appealed to a wider public, not least because there was now accommodation for two children (or legless midgets) behind the two bucket seats. A special version of this car, again driven by Donald Healey, topped 200 mph (322 kph) at Bonneville that year. The 100/6 became the 3000 in 1959, as it was now fitted with a 2912 cc engine.

*Austin Healey 100*

**Austin Healey Sprite**

# Austin Healey Sprite Mk I

Late in 1956, Sir Leonard Lord suggested that Healey should develop a new small sports car to fill the gap left by the disappearance of the old Austin Seven Nippy and Ulster – 'a cheap two-seater that a chap could keep in his bike shed'. A two-seater body (inspired by Jaguar's D-type) was designed by Healey's Gerry Coker. He originally planned retractable headlamps to meet American regulations; when this proved impracticable, the characteristic frog-eye lamps were fitted. Mechanically, the Sprite was a child of the BMC parts bin, with A35 engine and front suspension plus Morris Minor steering rack. Chassis were pressed in Wolverhampton, transported to Swindon where the bodies were made and spot-welded into position, then taken to Cowley for painting before arriving at Abingdon for final assembly. Despite this 150 mile trek, the Sprite still cost only £690, about fifty per cent of the price of other specialised sporting cars. The 948 Sprite was not very fast, capable of 83 mph, but that wasn't really the point. Ultra-precise handling made it one of the most enjoyable cheap sports cars ever.

Late in the Mk I's life a highly-modified competition variant appeared, known as the Sebring Sprite, named for the Sprite's various class wins in sports car races at the Sebring circuit. An aluminium hardtop gave the car a purposeful look far removed from the normal frog-eye; the engine was highly tuned, too, bringing the top speed to 100 mph (161 kph). The modifications effectively doubled the price of the Sprite: nevertheless, it was still a remarkably cheap way to go motor racing.

## 1959 AUSTIN HEALEY SPRITE MK I

**Engine:** in-line four cylinder, overhead valve
**Bore × stroke:** 62.9 mm × 76.2 mm
**Capacity:** 948 cc
**Maximum power:** 43 bhp
**Transmission:** four-speed manual
**Chassis:** steel, unitary
**Suspension:** independent front with wishbones and coil springs. Live rear axle with quarter elliptic leaf springs
**Brakes:** drums all round
**Bodywork:** two-seater sports
**Maximum speed (approx):** 81 mph (130 kph)

# AUSTRO-DAIMLER
### Wiener-Neustadt, Austria 1899–1936

Founded in 1899 as a branch of the German Daimler company, the works at Wiener-Neustadt began by building lorries; its first engineering director was Paul Daimler – son of Gottlieb Daimler – who created the 8/9 hp PD model with a twin-cylinder engine of 1411 cc mounted transversely at the front. Young Daimler was succeeded in 1905 by the 30-year-old Ferdinand Porsche – who had already created the petrol–electric Mercedes-Electrique-Mixte (produced from 1902–07), driven by electric motors in the hubs.

Austro-Daimler became financially independent of Cannstatt in 1906, and built some outstanding cars under Porsche's direction. The factory competed in sporting events; success here led to the Prince Henry model of 1911 with an overhead-cam 5715 cc four-cylinder power unit, followed by the similar side-valve 6967 cc 27/60, which developed 60 hp at only 1200 rpm. Both were Porsche designs. The smallest pre-war Austro-Daimler model was a 2212 cc four cylinder.

Porsche was succeeded as chief designer in 1923 by Karl Rabe after a series of policy arguments with the Austro-Daimler board.

The outstanding Austro-Daimler production car of the 1920s was the ADM, created by Porsche and perfected by Rabe, with overhead-cam six-cylinder power units of 2540 cc, 2650 cc and 2994 cc. The last model – ADM111 – developed 110 hp at 4000 rpm and was one of the outstanding cars of its day. The 100 hp ADR was less sporting.

In 1928 Austro-Daimler amalgamated with Puch and in 1930 with Steyr. Porsche, who in 1923 had joined Daimler at Stuttgart, later designed a big car for Steyr, shortly before Steyr merged with Austro-Daimler...

The year 1931 saw the launch of the last great car from Wiener-Neustadt, the six-cylinder Bergmeister with an overhead-cam 3614 cc power unit developing 120 hp at 3600 rpm and a top speed of 90 mph (145 kph). It was followed in 1932 by the short-lived 4624 cc eight-cylinder Austro-Daimler, a superb, and very expensive luxury car. Production of Austro-Daimlers officially ended in 1935, though the odd Bergmeister was still built to bespoke order.

# Austro-Daimler Prince Henry

The works team entered for the 1910 Prinz Heinrich trials represented the true ancestor of the sports car: their power units were derived from those Porsche had designed for the Parsifal airship, with separately-cast steel cylinders and valves inclined at 45 degrees. For the period, they were high-revving, capable of achieving 2300 rpm, and had pressure lubrication and steel pistons for high-speed work. Because the regulations of the event only dictated a minimum width for the bodywork at the top, body designer Neumann-Neander swept the

## 1911 AUSTRO-DAIMLER PRINCE HENRY

**Engine:** in-line four cylinder, overhead cam
**Bore × stroke:** 105 mm × 165 mm
**Capacity:** 5715 cc
**Maximum power:** 95 bhp
**Transmission:** four-speed manual
**Chassis:** pressed steel, channel
**Suspension:** non-independent with semi-elliptic leaf springs all round
**Brakes:** drums, rear only
**Bodywork:** tulip-sided tourer
**Maximum speed (approx):** 90 mph (145 kph)

**Austro-Daimler Prince Henry**

sides in at the bottom to reduce frontal area; a vee-radiator was another concession to aerodynamic efficiency. The cars swept the board, taking the first three places in the trial; fittingly, Porsche drove the winning car. Two more Austro-Daimlers finished in the first ten, and the team took nine of the twelve trophies for which they were eligible. The Prince Henry model was the only German car entered in the trials to go directly into production as a sports model, and some 200 were produced, mostly for export to Britain and the USA. The original cars had chain drive, but shaft drive was used from 1911. A more practical derivative, the 27/60 hp, had a side-valve engine of 6967 cc and carried more comfortable coachwork; top speed was around 60 mph (97 kph)

# Austro-Daimler Sascha

In the early 1920s Porsche created the twin-cam Sascha sports-racing cars. Though this project was opposed by the Austro-Daimler board, Porsche went ahead anyway, financed by Count 'Sascha' Kolowrat, a colourful Bohemian film magnate and industrialist, whose motorsport career included driving the entire 1500 miles (2415 km) of the 1913 Alpine Trial accompanied by a piglet – plus many race and rally victories. In-

**Austro-Daimler ADR**

tended to extract maximum performance out of a minimum engine capacity, the Sascha was perhaps Austria's equivalent of the Bugatti. Built in the Austro-Daimler factory, it boasted a light-alloy engine block with screwed-in steel cylinder liners, twin overhead camshafts driven by a vertical kingshaft, alloy pistons, dry-sump lubrication, dual ignition and four-wheel brakes. Four 1100 cc Saschas ran in the 1922 Targa Florio; one, driven in the racing class by Alfred Neubauer (later Mercedes racing manager), finished second in its class to a Grand Prix Mercedes of 4.5 litres, while two Saschas finished first and second in the touring class. That was one of 43 victories (out of 52 starts) claimed for the model that year. However, a 1.5-litre Sascha was less successful, and its failure to be finished in time for the 1922 Monza GP precipitated Pors-

che's departure from Austro-Daimler. A 2-litre version appeared at Brooklands with some success during 1926.

# Austro-Daimler ADM/ADR

In 1920, Ferdinand Porsche introduced the 4.2-litre AD 617 six-cylinder luxury car, whose light-alloy engine had a single overhead camshaft and was built in unit with gearbox, radiator and steering box to form a rigid bracing for the forward part of the chassis. Lessons learnt from the AD 617 were incorporated into the ADM I 10/50 hp of 1923, which had a single-carburettor overhead-cam 2540 cc engine and could achieve over 60 mph (97 kph), much the same performance as the larger car. A twin-carburettor version, ADM II, was built from 1925 to 1927 and a 2994 cc derivative, ADM III, appeared in 1926; its short-wheelbase sports version was the first production Austro-Daimler capable of exceeding 100 mph (161 kph). The famous German racing driver, Hans Stuck, was the works driver from 1928 to 1932, winning 43 races in that period. ADM IIIs took the team prize in the 1928 Tourist Trophy as well. In 1927 Rabe unveiled the first of his ADR series, which retained the 3-litre power unit of the ADM in a totally-new backbone chassis, in which the power unit was carried in a fork at the front of the backbone, with rear swing axles. The triple transverse springs controlling the rear

**1919 AUSTRO-DAIMLER SASCHA**

**Engine:** in-line four cylinder, overhead cam
**Bore × stroke:** 68.3 mm × 75 mm
**Capacity:** 1099 cc
**Maximum power:** 45 bhp
**Transmission:** four-speed manual
**Chassis:** pressed steel, channel
**Suspension:** non-independent with semi-elliptic leaf springs front and cantilever rear axle
**Brakes:** drums all round
**Bodywork:** two-seater sports
**Maximum speed (approx):** 90 mph (145 kph)

**1927 AUSTRO-DAIMLER ADR**

**Engine:** in-line six cylinder, overhead cam
**Bore × stroke:** 76 mm × 110 mm
**Capacity:** 2994 cc
**Maximum power:** 100 bhp
**Transmission:** four-speed
**Chassis:** tubular steel backbone
**Suspension:** non-independent front with semi-elliptic leaf springs. Independent rear with swing axles
**Brakes:** drums all round, servo assisted
**Bodywork:** to order
**Maximum speed (approx):** 100 mph (161 kph)

swing axles came into operation progressively as the load increased, giving a particularly smooth ride at speed. The long-wheelbase chassis came with engines of 70 or 100 hp; the short-wheelbase 12/100PS sports chassis had the 100 bhp engine as standard. The line was developed in 1931 into the 3614 cc Bergmeister, also known as the ADR 6, followed in 1932 by the ADR 8 with a 4624 cc eight-cylinder engine. Production – which came to around 200 – only lasted until 1933: the Bergmeister officially survived a year longer, though it was available to special order up to 1937, two years after car production had officially ended. Only 50, however, were ultimately manufactured.

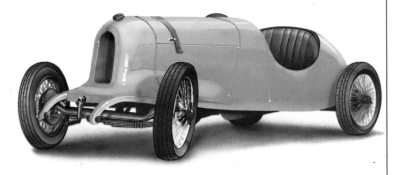

**Austro-Daimler Sascha**

# A-Z OF THE CAR

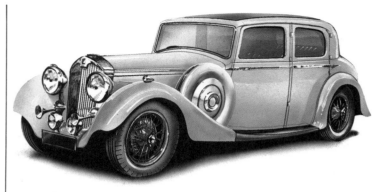
Autovia

## AUTO AVIA COSTRUZIONE
**Modena, Italy**
**1939–1941**

When in 1939 Enzo Ferrari parted company with Alfa Romeo, where he had been running the works Alfa Corse team (successors to the Scuderia Ferrari), he signed an agreement that he would not produce a competition car under his name for four years. He set up Auto Avia Costruzione in Modena, with the declared aim of producing machine tools. Nevertheless, two sports cars were built to the design of the engineer Alberto Massimino, to the order of Alberto Ascari and the Marchese Lotario Rangoni; they had 1500 cc engines with a specially-cast straight-eight block fitted with two Fiat 508 cc cylinder heads. They were called Vettura 815 (8 for the number of cylinders,

15 for the engine capacity of 1500 cc), and ran in the 1940 Brescia Grand Prix, which covered 923 miles (1486 km) and substituted for the Mille Miglia. Both Ascari and Rangoni in turn led the 1.5-litre class, but neither car lasted the distance. Further production was interrupted by Italy's entry into the war, which nicely took care of Ferrari's four-year injunction; when he resumed production post-war, it was under his own name.

## AUTOVIA
**Coventry, England**
**1937–1938**

In 1935, Victor Riley of the Riley Motor Company decided to establish a subsidiary to build a new luxury car, and called on Charles van Eugen, formerly with Lea-Francis, to head it. Van Eugen moved into the Riley factory with two Lea-Francis draftsmen, and began work on a V8 car to be called the Autovia. The original plan was to use a V8 engine which had been designed for Riley, but this proved unsuitable, and the Autovia power unit consisted of two four-cylinder Riley blocks mounted at 90 degrees on a common crankcase, although the cylinder heads were specially manufactured. The engine, of 2.8 litres swept volume, had three camshafts, one actuating the inlet valves on both banks, while the other two shafts were for the exhaust valves, no doubt inspired by the Ford V8. A pre-selector gearbox was fitted and also, surprisingly, a worm-driven rear-axle. The project died with the collapse of Riley in 1938.

### 1937 AUTOVIA
**Engine:** V8, three cam, overhead valve, overhead cam
**Bore × stroke:** 69 mm × 95.25 mm
**Capacity:** 2857 cc
**Maximum power:** 97 bhp
**Transmission:** four-speed manual
**Chassis:** fully boxed channel frame
**Suspension:** non-independent with semi-elliptic leaf springs
**Brakes:** drums all round
**Bodywork:** coupé, saloon or limousine
**Maximum speed (approx):** 89 mph (142 kph)

### 1939 AUTO AVIA CONSTRUZIONE
**Engine:** in-line eight cylinder, overhead cam
**Bore × stroke:** 63 mm × 60 mm
**Capacity:** 1496 cc
**Maximum power:** 72 bhp
**Transmission:** four-speed manual
**Chassis:** steel backbone (Fiat based)
**Suspension:** non-independent with semi-elliptic leaf springs all round
**Brakes:** drums all round
**Bodywork:** two-seater tourer
**Maximum speed (approx):** not known

**Auto Avia Construzione**

**AV Monocar**

## AV
**Teddington, England**
**1919-1926**

Ward and Avey ran AV Motors at Teddington, Middlesex and shortly after the Great War, hoping to cash in on the boom in personal transportation, they bought the rights to produce a horrific single-seat cyclecar from John Carden. Possibly the most suicidal design created in the cyclecar craze of 1912–14, the Carden consisted of a narrow hull 'stiffened' by two cross-members, with centre-pivot front steering controlled by cables

and a motorbike engine – single-cylinder or vee-twin – mounted in the tail. AV got the design because Carden was then pursuing the production of a '£100' two-seater. They originally planned to modify the design from a single-seater to a staggered two-seater, but when production eventually got under way late in 1919, it was evident that the only significant change to Carden's original concept had been the adoption of a two-speed epicyclic gearbox in lieu of direct drive only. Excessively narrow, the AV Monocar had a track of only 30 inches (76 cm); in the not unlikely instance of a front wheel dropping off, the AV could, it was said, be driven home on three wheels .... The body terminated at the front in

### 1920 AV MONOCAR
**Engine:** vee twin
**Bore × stroke:** 85 mm × 85 mm
**Capacity:** 988 cc
**Maximum power:** 8 hp
**Transmission:** two-speed
**Chassis:** wooden hull
**Suspension:** non-independent with single leaf spring front and quarter elliptic rear
**Brakes:** minimal
**Bodywork:** plywood, compressed paper or mahogany
**Maximum speed (approx):** 50 mph (80 kph)

a lethal point, behind which were the petrol and oil tanks; power was normally by JAP vee-twin, with available capacities ranging from 654 to 988 cc. These sporting power units were started like a motor mower by pulling on a cord. De luxe AV Monocars also carried a folding seat on the tail, to accommodate an unfortunate passenger who sat askew with his or her feet on the running board. Several hundred Monocars were built by a staff which at one time reached 80; bodies, supplied by the Thames Valley Pattern Works, were made of whatever materials happened to be to hand – mahogany, plywood or compressed paper ... Towards the end of production a two-seater, the AV Bicar, appeared, with JAP or Blackburne power and a three-speed Sturmey-Archer transmission. Perhaps 50 were built, but even at £160 it could not compete with the Austin Seven: and in 1924 AV production ceased.

# BALLOT

**Paris, France
1919–1932**

Though their careers as car builders only lasted from 1919–1932, the brothers Edouard and Maurice Ballot started manufacturing marine engines and proprietary engines as far back as 1905. They supplied many well-known French marques, including Delage. Their decision to build a complete car

stemmed from a desire to enhance the firm's reputation by success in motor racing. Ex-Peugeot engineer Ernest Henry was commissioned to design a 4.9-litre car for the 1919 Indianapolis 500; the car – the first really viable straight-eight – was developed in the remarkable time of 101 days. It showed great promise and broke the lap record, but failed to achieve success due to wheel and tyre problems.

A 3-litre derivative was built to meet the changed racing formula of 1920, finished second at Indianapolis and in the 1921 French Grand Prix, and took the first two places in the Italian Grand Prix at Brescia the same year. Soon after the 3-litre, Ballot evolved a 2 litre, four-cylinder racing car.

This showed its considerable potential by leading the 1925 Spa 24-hour race right into the last lap, when the rear axle broke. Perhaps a hundred of these 2-litres Sport Ballots were built between 1921 and 1924 and it was a typical Henry design, with twin bevel-driven overhead camshafts operating four valves per cylinder and a roller-bearing crank.

The 2LS was prohibitively expensive, so in 1923 a less costly touring derivative, the single-overhead-camshaft 2LT, with a three (white metal) bearing crankshaft, was developed by Henry's acolyte Vadier, who had become chief engineer on the departure of his mentor. A sport version, the 2LTS, was quickly developed to replace the 2LS; appearing in 1925, it had bigger valves – inclined in a hemi head – than the 2LT and a more rigid crankcase which was subsequently adopted for the 2LT.

In 1926 the 1991 cc six-cylinder 2LT6 was shown at the Paris Salon but, though it made the company's 1927 catalogues, it never went into production.

Its successor, however, did, in the shape of the 1928 overhead-camshaft type RH straight eight.

**Barré 10/12 hp**

The 2618 cc power unit shown at the 1927 Salon was quickly enlarged to 2874 cc and then bored out again to 3054 cc. The nine-bearing power unit was beautifully conceived but the car proved too heavy to enjoy success. It overheated on steep climbs and the weight of the power unit was too much for the steering drop-arm, prompting probably the first-ever factory recall campaign.

In the Depression, Ballot ran into financial troubles and the factory was taken over by Hispano-Suiza. The Ballot HS26, which had a pushrod six-cylinder power unit of 4580 cc designed by Birkigt and made at the Hispano Works, was launched at the Paris Show in 1930,

| **1925 BALLOT 2LTS** | |
|---|---|
| **Engine:** in-line four cylinder, twin cam | |
| **Bore × stroke:** 69.9 mm × 130 mm | |
| **Capacity:** 1991 cc | |
| **Maximum power:** not known | |
| **Transmission:** four-speed manual | |
| **Chassis:** pressed steel channel | |
| **Suspension:** non-independent with semi-elliptic leaf springs all round | |
| **Brakes:** drums all round, rod operated | |
| **Bodywork:** to order | |
| **Maximum speed (approx):** 72 mph (116 kph) | |

but soon renamed the Hispano Junior; Ballot provided only the chassis.

The Junior was a disappointment as far as Hispanos went, and the Ballot factory closed its doors for ever in 1932.

# Ballot 2LS/2LTS

When Henry left Ballot, the development of a new touring model was entrusted to the new chief engineer, F.M. Vadier. Since the aim was to produce a less prohibitively expensive model more suitable for normal road use, Vadier, though a keen disciple of Henry's, eschewed Henry's hallmark, the twin-overhead-cam layout, and produced a single-overhead-cam design known as the 2LT (*2 Litres Tourisme*), with vertical valves in a detachable cylinder head. Costing half the price of the 2LS, it was a remarkably good car (though the pre-1926 models suffered from an excessively whippy chassis) and about 2000 were built between 1923 and 1928. For 1925, the 2LS was succeeded by the 2LTS, which was identical to the 2LT except for the cylinder head, which had bigger valves, inclined in hemispherical combustion chambers, and a more rigid crankcase to cope with the extra power output. Dewandre servo brakes were optional on both models in 1925, but quickly became standard.

Up to 1925 the Ballots could be purchased in bare chassis form for the owner who wished to have a different body style.

# BARRE

**Sèvres, France
1900–1930**

A typical French provincial car factory, whose trade was largely local, Barré of Niort (Deux-Sèvres) began production in 1902 with light cars powered by De Dion, Aster or Buchet power units. A pioneering feature was the flexible mounting of the power unit on springs. In 1908 a Ballot-engined car was added to the range. An uncharacteristic move was the production of a very sporting 3 Litre which ran in the 1913 Tour de France. The vintage range,

**Ballot 2LTS**

## 1924 BARRÉ

**Engine:** in-line four cylinder, overhead valve
**Bore × stroke:** 67 mm × 120 mm
**Capacity:** 1685 cc
**Maximum power:** not known
**Transmission:** four-speed manual
**Chassis:** pressed steel channel
**Suspension:** non-independent with semi-elliptic leaf springs all round
**Brakes:** drums all round
**Bodywork:** tourer or torpedo-camionnette
**Maximum speed (approx):** 50 mph (80 kph)

**Batten Special**

announced in 1920 initially featured a car with a 1600 cc SCAP power unit; 1.1 and 1.7-litre engines were also available. The company changed its name to Barré & Lamberthon in 1923, but never regained its pre-war success, as sales continued to be confined to local customers, and could not match the new mass-producers like Citroën. A sports model was offered in the 1920s; it was said to differ from the company's light truck chassis only in the flatter set of its springs... .

## BARTLETT

**Stratford, Canada**
**1914–1917**

A Canadian millwright R.C. Bartlett was convinced that his way to a fortune lay in devising a solution to the problem of pneumatic tyres, which lasted next to no time on the rough roads of his native country. His method was to use solid tyres and two chassis, one for the engine and running gear, one for the body, with air-bag suspension units at each corner to separate them. Financed by wealthy miners, the Bartlett appeared in prototype form in 1913 with split-axle independent front suspension.

It also featured four-wheel brakes augmented by retractable spikes which dug into the road through the tyres. it was decided to

omit this feature from production vehicles after it caused a 26-car pile-up on its first test, outside Toronto's Royal Alexandra Theatre. The double chassis and independent suspension were also omitted from the 600 Bartlett cars and trucks produced in the firm's Stratford, Ontario works, although air suspension was retained.

Production was halted in 1917 when Bartlett's USA suppliers went over to war work and orders could not be fulfilled. Bartlett was then unable to pay agent's commissions on orders received or to refund deposits, and so declared bankruptcy.

## 1917 BARTLETT

**Engine:** in-line four cylinder
**Bore × stroke:** various depending on engine used
**Maximum power:** not known
**Transmission:** three-speed manual
**Chassis:** pressed steel channel
**Suspension:** air bag
**Brakes:** drums all round
**Bodywork:** roadster or tourer
**Maximum speed (approx):** not known

## 1935 BATTEN SPECIAL

**Engine:** V8
**Bore × stroke:** 77.79 mm × 95.25 mm
**Capacity:** 3622 cc
**Maximum power:** 97 bhp
**Transmission:** three-speed manual
**Chassis:** pressed steel channel
**Suspension:** non-independent with transverse semi-elliptic leaf springs front and rear
**Brakes:** drums all round
**Bodywork:** two- or four-seater sports
**Maximum speed (approx):** 120 mph (193 kph)

## BATTEN

**Beckenham, England**
**1935–1938**

Based on the Ford V8 chassis, the Batten-Special was built in Beckenham, Kent. Designed to make use of the performance inherent in the Ford chassis, the Batten was normally available with stark open two- and four-seat sporting bodywork, though a coupé version was subsequently

listed. The power unit was specially tuned, and a 120 mph (193 kph) top speed was claimed, though with the standard V8 brakes that was a speed achievable only by the very brave... . Most Battens retained the standard transverse springing of the Ford, though some were converted to split-axle independent front suspension. Production, always on a very limited scale, lasted from 1935 to 1938. The prototype Batten, in poor condition, survives in a Sussex barn... .

## BAYLISS-THOMAS

**Birmingham, England**
**1922–1929**

Like so many other manufacturers, Bayliss-Thomas had their origins in the cycle and motorcycle industry. The Birmingham-based company was renowned as the manufacturer of Excelsior cycles and motorcycles before turning to car production in 1921. The Bayliss-Thomas, despite its handsome appearance, was never more than an assembled car, which started life with a 10 hp Coventry-Climax power unit and disc wheels. One of these 10–

**Bartlett**

**Bayliss Thomas**

## 1924 BAYLISS-THOMAS 9-19 HP

**Engine:** in-line four cylinder, overhead valve
**Bore × stroke:** 60 mm × 95 mm
**Capacity:** 1074 cc
**Maximum power:** 19 hp
**Transmission:** three-speed manual
**Chassis:** pressed steel channel
**Suspension:** non-independent with quarter-elliptic leaf springs all round
**Brakes:** drums, on rear only
**Bodywork:** two or four-seater 'chummy'
**Maximum speed (approx):** 45 mph (72 kph)

20 hp Bayliss-Thomas cars, driven by Captain Ross Craddock, won a gold medal in the 1922 London–Edinburgh Trial. In 1923, a 1074 cc overhead-valve Meadows four was added to the range under the name 9–19 hp Popular. 'The power of this tiny engine,' wrote a satisfied customer, 'is a revelation'; the model enjoyed sporting success, including two gold medals in the 1924 London–Land's End Trial. A 12–22 hp, 1640 cc four was added to the Bayliss-Thomas range soon after the 9–19'hp, with a 'well-balanced and distinctive' 13-30 hp of 1795 cc appearing at the 1923 London Show. During 1924, not only did the company venture into wireless manufacture with the Excelophone receiver, but the 10–20 was replaced with the 11-22 hp, which had the well-known F-Type

Coventry-Climax engine of 1368 cc. Sports two-seater versions of the Bayliss-Thomas were also available although production was only on a limited scale after 1925 and it finally ceased in 1929.

# BEAN
### Dudley, England
### 1919–1929

A. Harper, Sons & Bean of Dudley, Worcestershire, was a long-established engineering firm which decided to enter the mass-production market with its first car, the 11.9 hp launched in 1919. To speed up the development process, Bean updated the pre-war 1174 cc Perry light car, fitting a fixed head 1794 cc power unit. The car was built in a specially-acquired factory in nearby Tipton: it had the advanced feature of a moving assembly line.

Hasty development showed in the rough engine and transmission, but nevertheless the new marque got off to a good start, with some 80 cars a week being produced. Unfortunately Bean was a member of a consortium that included ABC, Swift and Vulcan, plus a number of component manufacturers and when this British Motor Trading Corporation holding company collapsed, Bean was placed in receivership. By the time things had been sorted out and manufacture re-started later in 1922, Bean had been already been outpaced by stronger competitors like the Morris-Cowley.

At that time Bean cars were rough and unreliable, the side-valve four-cylinder engine somewhat rough-running and matched to an awkward gearchange. Its ride hardly made up for these drawbacks either, being harsh and uncomfortable. Nevertheless as Bean's better competitors could not satisfy total demand in the early '20s there was a niche in the market for Bean.

In 1923 the 2385 cc 14 hp Bean was announced. Hailed as 'a fast and fully-equipped touring car at a very moderate price, fitted with four-wheel brakes of undeniable stopping power', the new model was far more modern in conception than the old 11.9, which the press dismissed as ' a durable and well-pulling car'. The 14 hp, for instance, had unit-construction of engine and gearbox, as well as a detachable cylinder head. It was, however, distinctly overweight.

## 1928 BEAN 14/40

**Engine:** in-line four cylinder, side valve
**Bore × stroke:** 75 mm × 130 mm
**Capacity:** 2297 cc
**Maximum power:** 40 bhp
**Transmission:** four-speed manual
**Chassis:** pressed steel channel
**Suspension:** non-independent with semi-elliptic leaf springs
**Brakes:** drums all round
**Bodywork:** tourer or saloon
**Maximum speed (approx):** not known

A scaled down version of the 14, with the same power unit capacity as the old 11.9, the 12 appeared in 1924, the year in which Bean standardised front-wheel brakes. The Sheffield steel company Hadfields, which had been associated with Bean since 1919, took control of the firm in 1926 – their centenary year – and manufacture was subsequently moved to Tipton. The company proudly advertised that 'all essential component parts of Bean cars are made of Hadfield's famous Sheffield Steel'.

A six-cylinder model, the 18/50, with ohv Meadows power unit and four-speed gearbox appeared at the beginning of 1927; a special fabric-bodied 18-50 sports saloon, tuned to give 70 mph (113 kph), appeared later that year. Another 1927 debutante, the Imperial Six, was aimed at the colonial market. It had a 3.8-litre Bean engine, but, following a disastrous journey to Hindustan by the Australian explorer Francis Birtles, it never passed the prototype stage. The 14/40 Hadfield Bean appeared at the 1927 Olympia Show. It had a separate gearbox and worm-driven rear-axle, but cosmetic features like two-tone bodywork could not conceal the fact that the car was hopelessly unreliable. The old Short 14 hp lingered on for a while alongside the Hadfield. Shortly before manufacture ceased in 1929, a 14/70 hp sporting version appeared briefly. However the manufacture of commercial vehicles which was begun in 1924, lasted until 1931.

**Bean 14 hp**

# A-Z OF THE CAR

## BEARDMORE

**Glasgow, Scotland**
**1920–1928**

The first three models from the famous Scottish engineering company, Beardmore – a 1486 cc 10 hp, a 2413 cc 15 hp and a 71 cc 20 hp – appeared in 1920 and were mostly noteworthy for being built in three separate plants, at

### 1925 BEARDMORE 12-30 HP

**Engine:** in-line four cylinder, overhead cam
**Bore × stroke:** 72 mm × 114 mm
**Capacity:** 1857 cc
**Maximum power:** 30 bhp
**Transmission:** four-speed manual
**Chassis:** pressed steel channel
**Suspension:** non-independent with semi-elliptic leaf springs all round
**Brakes:** drums on rear only
**Bodywork:** two-seater sports
**Maximum speed (approx):** 60 mph (96 kph)

contributed to the car's outstanding performance. Typical of the care taken in its design was the balanced two-bearing crankshaft and the vibration damper fitted to the crankshaft. From the Eleven was developed the 1857 cc 12-30, its 2-litre Sports derivative. That boasted aluminium pistons and a 70 mph (113 kph) top speed, took the Shelsley Walsh hill-climb record in 1925. A more prosaic side-valve 16 hp six-seater, launched in late 1924, ousted the overhead-cam Beardmores at the end of 1925, but after 1928

Beck

Glasgow, Paisley and Coatbridge. The 15 hp was designed mainly as a taxicab; the other two models were rarely seen outside their native Scotland. However, the 10 hp was rapidly developed into the overhead-camshaft 1670 cc Eleven. This handsome car appeared at the end of 1921; press reports suggested that its introduction had been so protracted due to manufacturing problems. The sporting two-seater version was praised as 'particularly graceful'; its neatly-designed power unit was characterised by a carefully gas-flowed exhaust manifold, which

Beardmore abandoned cars to concentrate on taxicab construction, with which they were obviously happier . . . Building taxicabs, however, was only part of Beardmore's engineering activities.

## BECK

**Lyon, France**
**1920–1922**

The French city of Lyon always regarded itself as the true home of French automobile engineering, and this ephemeral marque

certainly had much of interest in its design. Beck showed its first car, which had coil spring independent suspension all round, at the 1920 Brussels Salon.

A second Beck was displayed at the 1921 Paris Salon; its four-cylinder overhead-camshaft power unit had a swept volume of 1495 cc, and the three-speed transmission was in unit with the final drive. Semi-streamlined coachwork was standard.

The Beck, however, failed to survive beyond 1922, and very few were built.

### 1921 BECK

**Engine:** in-line four cylinder, overhead cam
**Bore × stroke:** 65 mm × 113 mm
**Capacity:** 1495 cc
**Maximum power:** not known
**Transmission:** three speed
**Chassis:** pressed steel channel
**Suspension:** independent with sliding pillars and coil springs
**Brakes:** drums on rear only
**Bodywork:** saloon
**Maximum speed (approx):** not known

## BEDELIA

**Paris, France**
**Levallois-Perret, France**
**1910-1925**

In 1909, two young Frenchmen named Bourbeau and Devaux were on a tour by motorcycle when they wrote off their machine in an accident. Undeterred, they shipped the remains back to Paris and confected one of the very first cyclecars in the world out of them.

To underline the lack of funds, the hammock-type seats were 'upholstered' with coal sacks, and the steering wheel rim was the seat rim from a cane-bottomed chair. The resulting 'car' was known as the Bédélia, an acronym formed from the initials of the two partners, and was chiefly noteworthy for having the pilot seated at the rear and the passenger at the front, a system that had some merit since

**Beardmore 12/30hp**

**Bedelia**

## 1912 BEDELIA

**Engine:** vee twin
**Bore × stroke:** 82 mm × 100 mm
**Capacity:** 1056 cc
**Maximum power:** 10 hp
**Transmission:** two-speed
**Chassis:** wooden hull
**Suspension:** non-independent, cantilever
**Brakes:** drums on rear only
**Bodywork:** two-seat open tandem
**Maximum speed (approx):** 45 mph

the belt-drive transmission initially relied on the passenger shifting the drive belts between the high and low pulleys with a stick.

Remarkably, there was demand for replicas of the little car, which was endowed with an exciting performance thanks to its potent motor-cycle engine, and so a production company was formed, with just Fr 10,000 capital, in November 1910. Like many of the more basic cyclecars which followed, the Bédélia had a chassis hull made of wood and plywood, and had centre-pivot steering like a traction engine. Bédélias were first fitted with single-cylinder Aster power units, then with an 8/10 hp vee-twin of Bédélia manufacture. Having a three-year head-start on most of the opposition, Bédélias sold very well until the war; in 1912, the basic Bédélia cost just 56 guineas in London. The marque also enjoyed some competition success pre-war. However, in 1920 the partners sold the manufacturing rights to one M. Mahieux, who compromised the crude purity of the Bédélia concept by such sybaritic modifications as seating the passengers side-by-

side. It was perhaps hardly surprising that the Bédélia marque collapsed in 1925, since by that time the number of 'real' small cars on the market considerably outclassed the Bédélia, which had failed to progress with the times.

# BELLANGER

**Neuilly-sur-Seine, France
1912-1925**

Distinguished by a massive bull-nosed radiator, rounded at top and bottom, the Bellanger was built at Neuilly (Seine) from 1912. The first Bellangers had Daimler-Knight power units of 9/13 hp (2001 cc), 15 hp (2548 cc), 20 hp (3308 cc)

and 38 hp (6280 cc).

After the Armistice, Bellanger used American Briscoe side-valve power units – the brothers Ben and Frank Briscoe had built Ajax cars in Neuilly before the war – from 1920 to 1923 for the 3231 cc 15 hp,

## 1921 BELLANGER

**Engine:** V8, side valve
**Bore × stroke:** 90 mm × 125 mm
**Capacity:** 6362 cc
**Maximum power:** not known
**Transmission:** three-speed manual
**Chassis:** pressed steel channel
**Suspension:** non-independent, duplex semi-elliptic leaf springs front, cantilever rear
**Brakes:** drums on rear only
**Bodywork:** torpedo, coupé or landaulette
**Maximum speed (approx):** not known

**Bellanger**

available in 'Tourisme' and 'Sport' versions, and the 24 hp Sport (4253 cc). Most Bellanger cars were used as Paris taxis. In 1921 Bellanger launched a massive luxury car, the 50 hp V8 of 6361 cc.

Bellanger halted car manufacture in 1923 in favour of aero engines. There was an attempt to sell re-radiatored De Dions as Bellangers in 1928, but there were few takers, and Bellanger closed down permanently soon after.

# BELSIZE

**Manchester, England
1897-1925**

In 1896 the bicycle makers Marshall and Company, of Manchester, began work on a belt-driven car based on the French Hurtu, itself a close copy of the German Benz. The original Marshall car, completed in 1897, had tiller steering and differed from its prototype in having a front-mounted radiator.

The name Belsize was first used on a 'light, smart carriage' exhibited at the Agricultural Hall in 1901, and powered by a twin-cylinder 8.5 hp Buchet engine; it was said to be capable of 30 mph (48 khp). A more powerful Belsize with a 12 hp twin-cylinder engine appeared the following year; its makers guaranteed it 'to climb Westerham Hill with six or even seven people with ease.'

It was followed by 15/20 hp three-cylinder 'with variable lifting valve control', and a 7 hp voiturette, 'one of the best finished cars of its class'.

At the beginning of 1905, it was announced that Belsize were working on a six-cylinder car, which initially appeared in 30 hp

## 1925 BELSIZE BRADSHAW

**Engine:** vee twin
**Bore × stroke:** 85 mm × 121 mm
**Capacity:** 1370 cc
**Maximum power:** 9 hp (rated)
**Transmission:** three-speed
**Chassis:** pressed steel channel
**Suspension:** non-independent with quarter-elliptic springs
**Brakes:** drums on rear wheels and transmission
**Bodywork:** saloon
**Maximum speed (approx):** 50 mph (80 kph)

form, then in 60 hp guise and finally as a 40 hp. In 1909, a new 14/16 hp four was launched, then in 1911 a 10/12 hp of advanced design, with unit engine/gearbox, was introduced. This was built up to the outbreak of war, as was a 15.9 hp launched in 1913; Belsize production in 1914 had reached 50 cars and trucks a week.

During the war, Belsize manufactured aero engines and high explosive shells. Car manufacture resumed with a four-cylinder 15 hp of 2799 cc, which an appreciative owner described as 'a "peach" – travels faster than the driver wants her to . . .' In 1921 the Belsize-Bradshaw arrived, with a twin-cylinder 'oil-boiler' power unit designed by that erratic genius Granville Bradshaw. The marque went out in style, after producing a 1696 cc six-cylinder in 1924 and a 2.5-litre straight-eight – both with overhead valves – introduced shortly before Belsize closed down in 1925.

## Belsize Bradshaw

One of the great disadvantages of air-cooling was regarded as 'the unpleasant clatter . . . due to the metallic ring that is produced in the cylinder'; it was to eliminate this noise that Granville Bradshaw decided to adopt the system of 'oil-cooling' that he had previously used on a motorcycle engine. It involved sinking the cylinder barrels into the crankcase, so that oil was flung from the well-lubricated crankshaft and around the cylinder walls, thus cooling them. Bradshaw claimed that on test over Snake Pass (a Pennine hill not far from the Belsize works), the engines showed no sign of overheating. Belsize quickly got under way with production, which quickly accelerated to 100 cars a week. But, like many of Bradshaw's designs, the Belsize-Bradshaw and its oil-boiler power unit were prone to frustrating problems of reliability – even though it was advertised as 'a car for the busy owner-driver who has little time or inclination to tinker with his car' – and that spelt the end of Belsize in 1925.

**Belsize Bradshaw**

## BENJAMIN
**Asnières, France**
**1921-1929**

The original Benjamin cyclecar, built at Asnières (Seine), was the direct result of a taxation concession passed in 1919. This created a special fiscal class for cyclecars which, if they had only two seats, weighed less than 350 kg and had an engine of under 1100 cc, paid annual tax of only Fr. 100. Benjamin production started in 1921 with a cyclecar with a 751 cc four-cylinder Lemaitre & Gerard power unit; this diminutive car, which weighed only 270 kg in chassis form, proved a great commercial success.

It was developed in 1923 into a light car with three seats, and there was even an overhead camshaft sports version, the Bagatelle, whose boat-tailed body was in two-tone wood and had a vee-screen. Shortly after, a long-chassis version with a four-seater tourer body appeared. In 1924, Benjamin threw caution to the winds and produced an unorthodox new model with a 547 cc twin-cylinder two-stroke Duplex engine with pumping piston; then came a three-cylinder 'Triplex' version of the same design.

Benjamin quickly returned to more conventional design with a voiturette with side-valve or overhead-valve Chapuis-Dornier power units, and –surprisingly– four-wheel brakes as well as built-in electrical equipment.

However, having attempted to recapture their lost clientele, they quickly alienated them once more by presenting another eccentric design, this time with a rear-mounted twin-cylinder four-stroke of 636 cc, later of 616 cc. Hardly surprisingly, this odd little car

**Benjamin**

## 1921 BENJAMIN

**Engine:** in-line four cylinder, overhead valve
**Bore × stroke:** 54 mm × 82 mm
**Capacity:** 751 cc
**Maximum power:** 11 bhp
**Transmission:** three-speed
**Chassis:** pressed steel channel
**Suspension:** non-independent with semi-elliptic leaf springs front and quarter-elliptics rear
**Brakes:** drums on rear only
**Bodywork:** two seat cyclecar
**Maximum speed (approx):** 38 mph (60 kph)

proved a complete failure.

The inevitable financial crisis ensued in 1926, so once again the marque turned to Chapuis-Dornier-engined cars for their salvation; this, alas, was not forthcoming, and Benjamin went into liquidation, remaining in limbo until production was resumed under the name of Benova, using various proprietary power units, including a straight-eight SCAP of 1502 cc, although the last cars were Ruby-engined. Benjamin finally collapsed in 1931.

## BENTALL
**Maldon, England**
**1906-1913**

Bentall & Co had been agricultural engineers in Maldon, Essex, since 1792, and in the late 19th century also branched out into the manufacture of nuts, bolts and screw-cutting machinery. E.E. Bentall, who took over control of the company in 1889, designed a petrol engine at the turn of the century to power agricultural equipment. It was obviously not a great step to the manufacture of motor cars, and two 8 hp prototypes were built for the Bentall family in 1904. The company had the great advantage of being almost entirely self-

Bentall

### 1906 BENTALL 16/20 HP

**Engine:** in-line four cylinder, side valve
**Bore × stroke:** 100 mm × 95 mm
**Capacity:** 2985 cc
**Maximum power:** 20 bhp
**Transmission:** three-speed manual
**Chassis:** pressed steel channel
**Suspension:** non-independent with semi-elliptic leaf springs front and full elliptics rear
**Brakes:** drums on rear only
**Bodywork:** to order
**Maximum speed (approx):** 50 mph (80 kph)

sufficient, for it possessed its own foundry, and began to tool up for production the following year.

The first batch of Bentall cars were based on the prototypes, using proprietory chassis and axles, but before long the company was offering round-radiatored versions with a chassis of their own manufacture. Bentall offered cars of 8 and 11 hp (two-cylinder), 16 hp (four-cylinder) and an over-square 16/20 hp four. Ultimately, Bentall even made their own carburettor, designed by E.E. Bentall himself. In the quest for silence, Bentall built a prototype with a Silent Knight sleeve-valve engine in 1908; it was shown at Olympia but never went into production. The same fate

befell the 'Bentall Silent Piston Valve Engine' designed by C. Bingham, and shown at the 1910 Motor Show.

According to a former employee, manufacture ceased in 1912 because Bentall, being in a mainly agricultural area, only paid their engineering staff farm wages, but whatever the reason, sales were largely local. About 100 Bentalls were built, and the company invested some £60,000 on their brief foray into motoring.

## BENTLEY
**Cricklewood, Derby and Crewe, England**
**1920-**

Walter Owen Bentley had already achieved fame as the first Englishman to fit aluminium pistons in a car (the French DFP, for which he was agent) and as the designer of one of World War 1's finest rotary engines before deciding to produce a car designed for fast cruising on Continental roads. Designed by Bentley, F.T. Burgess, formerly with Humber, and Harry

*Bentley 3 Litre*

Varley (ex-Vauxhall), the first 3-litre Bentley appeared at the 1919 Motor Show but did not reach a public whose appetite had been whetted by enthusiastic press reports until September 1921, though a sizeable staff had been established in Bentley's factory in Cricklewood, North London. The Bentley 3 Litre remained in production until 1929, though a more sophisticated 6.5-litre six-cylinder car appeared in 1926.

It was so smooth by comparison with the 3 Litre that sporting customers complained of missing the 'bloody thump' of the four-cylinder Bentley. So W.O. Bentley reverted to his four-cylinder theme with the 4.5 Litre of 1927.

This model was supercharged by a separate Welwyn-based company run by racing driver Sir Henry Birkin in 1930, a development which W.O. Bentley regarded as a perversion.

Probably W.O. Bentley's most financially successful model was the

on the Derby company's 3.7-litre 20/25 model: 1936 saw this capacity increased to 4.5 litres.

The first post-war model, the Mark VI, had the same 4257 cc capacity as its pre-war counterpart, though its power unit now had overhead-inlet/side-exhaust valves.

Although 1952 saw the announcement of the 4566 cc Mulliner-bodied Continental, described as 'a very fast streamlined saloon', the marque's identity had become increasingly submerged in that of Rolls-Royce; the S-Type, with a stressed-skin four-door saloon body, was launched in 1955 and 1960 saw the disappearance of the faithful six-cylinder engine, which was supplanted by a 6.2-litre V8.

The current Bentley range, with a 6750 cc V8 power unit, consists of the Corniche convertible, the Mulsanne (announced in October 1980 to replace the T Series Bentley) and the 135 mph (217 kph) Mulsanne Turbo.

## 1923 BENTLEY 3 LITRE

**Engine:** in-line four cylinder, overhead cam
**Bore × stroke:** 80 mm × 149 mm
**Capacity:** 2996 cc
**Maximum power:** 80 bhp
**Transmission:** four-speed manual
**Chassis:** pressed steel channel
**Suspension:** non-independent with semi-elliptic leaf springs
**Brakes:** drums all round
**Bodywork:** to order
**Maximum speed (approx):** 80 mph (129 kph)

## 3½ Litre/4¼ Litre

Following the Rolls-Royce takeover, the original plan was to produce a supercharged sporting model based on a scaled down, 2.3-litre version of the Rolls-Royce 20/25, known as the Peregrine. But this proved to be a troublesome power unit, so a 20/25 engine was fitted in the Rolls-Royce Peregrine chassis and went into production as the 3½-litre 'Silent Sports Car' in 1933. Early models suffered from an excessively whippy chassis, but once this problem had been eliminated, the result was outstanding.

Unlike the Bentleys of the W.O. era, however, racing didn't form part of the programme for the new Rolls-Royce-Bentley, though E.R. Hall finished second in both the 1934 and 1935 Ulster Tourist Trophy races with a works supported 3½ litre; it was fitted with the new 4¼-litre engine in 1936 – and finished second yet again! And as late as 1950 the Hall Bentley was

from his original aim of making enough money with the 3 Litre to break into the family car market with a smaller, cheaper car bearing the Bentley nameplate. As it was, the 3 Litre was the most expensive car of its class on the British market, and its first venture into racing, a

**Bentley 3½ Litre**

8 Litre of late 1930, a further development of the 6.5-litre design.

Despite the Bentley's reputation as the epitome of the Vintage sports car, many were fitted with stately and elegant closed coachwork. However, it was the victories of the open four-seater cars at the Le Mans 24-hour race that earned the marque immortality. The company chalked up five Le Mans wins in 1924, 1927, 1928, 1929 and 1930; the last three victories went to a car driven by Woolf Barnato, who had taken on the role of the company's financial saviour in 1927. Even Barnato's diamond-based wealth, however, could not cope with the results of the crash of 1929, and he let Bentley go into receivership in 1931. In a surprise takeover, Bentley was acquired by Rolls-Royce for £125,265, when everyone thought that Napier was to be Bentley's new owner.

The first Rolls-Royce-built Bentley appeared in 1932, based

## 3 Litre

Inspired by a 1914 Grand Prix Mercedes that W.O. Bentley had seen in a cellar in London in 1915, the power unit of the Bentley 3 Litre was a long-stroke overhead-camshaft engine, with a fixed head and four valves per cylinder. Its chassis, too, had an advanced specification, and the exhibition of the prototype at the 1919 Motor Show caused great interest and attracted several orders – which Bentley turned down 'until we have something better to offer'. Sammy Davis of *The Autocar* wrote an enthusiastic road test of the first Bentley which again caused an influx of orders; again Bentley turned them down until the car was ready for production. In fact, it wasn't until September 1921 that the first production Bentley was sold.

From the start, Bentley pursued an active racing policy in the search for publicity, but already W.O. Bentley had been diverted

bold entry in the American Indianapolis 500, was a total flop. However, a few weeks later, Bentleys finished second, fourth and fifth in the Isle of Man Tourist Trophy. The largest annual production of the 3 Litre was in 1924, when 403 cars were built; that year, too, missionary's son John Duff won the 24-hour race at Le Mans (he had finished fourth in 1923, despite a punctured petrol tank). It was the first of five Le Mans victories for the marque, two of which were achieved by the 3 Litre, the 1927 victory by a car crippled in a multi-car pile-up at White House Corner passed into motoring history.

The last 3 Litres incorporated some of the modifications introduced for the newly-launched 4½ Litre. Rarest variant of the 3 Litre was the Super Sports 100 mph model, built on a 108 inch (274 cm) wheelbase with a distinctive radiator which tapered in at the foot in similar manner to the Standard 6½ Litre: just 15 were built.

## 1933 BENTLEY 3½ LITRE

**Engine:** in-line six cylinder, overhead valve
**Bore × stroke:** 82.5 mm × 114 mm
**Capacity:** 3669 cc
**Maximum power:** 110 bhp
**Transmission:** four-speed
**Chassis:** double-dropped steel channel
**Suspension:** non-independent with semi-elliptic leaf springs
**Brakes:** drums all round
**Bodywork:** to order
**Maximum speed (approx):** 90 mph (145 kph)

still competitive enough to finish eighth at Le Mans. The potential of the 4¼ Litre was shown when, in 1939, a streamlined 4¼ litre covered virtually 115 miles (185 km) in the hour at Brooklands; this car had a distinguished Le Mans history, too, finishing sixth in 1949.

# A-Z OF THE CAR

## R-type Continental

Launched in 1952, the R-type Continental carried special streamlined coachwork by H.J. Mulliner, an aerodynamic two-door saloon body in light alloy, and had a specially-tuned version of the 4566 cc six-cylinder engine fitted to the standard R-type (which took its designation from the fact that the Mk VI,

### 1952 BENTLEY R-TYPE CONTINENTAL

**Engine:** in-line six cylinder, inlet-over-exhaust valve
**Bore × stroke:** 92 mm × 114.3 mm
**Capacity:** 4556 cc
**Maximum power:** undisclosed
**Transmission:** four-speed
**Chassis:** fabricated steel
**Suspension:** independent front with coils and wishbones with anti-roll bar. Live rear axle with semi-elliptic leaf springs
**Brakes:** drums all round
**Bodywork:** two door sports or four-seat saloon
**Maximum speed (approx):** 117 mph (187 kph)

which it succeeded in June 1952, had at that point reached the letter 'R' in its chassis serials).

Unlike the standard car, which had the option of automatic transmission, the Continental only came with a four-speed, right-hand-change manual gearbox. Capable of almost two miles a minute, the Bentley Continental had a special exhaust system which, claimed its makers, gave out 'a pleasing "hubble-bubble" note'. In 1955, the 4.9-litre S-type appeared; the 4.9-litre Continental was available with alternative makes of two-door saloon and 'a drophead coupé in which lightweight construction has been given special study'. The Bentley Continental, said the Press, was aimed at 'those who wish to travel far and fast, in relaxation, with great reliability, and at reasonable mpg'.

## BENZ
### Mannheim, Germany
### 1885-1926

The first motor car to lead to sustained production was the three-wheeler built by Karl Benz of Mannheim, Germany, in 1885-86. Its power unit was mounted at the rear of the car, with its single cylinder pointing forward; final drive was by belt. Benz mounted the flywheel horizontally to avoid gyroscopic action affecting the stability of his 'Patent Motor Wagon' on bends.

Three-wheelers of similar design followed, but proved more popular in France than Germany, sales only getting under way from 1888. The 1891 Viktoria was the first four-wheeled Benz, and had a 3 hp power unit. There were also more powerful 4 hp and, later, 5 hp versions.

A smaller model, the 1.5 hp Velo, was built until 1902, and widely copied by other companies. It had a 1045 cc single-cylinder power unit. A major rift occurred in 1902 because both Benz and the French engineer Marius Barbarou were acting as chief engineer, Barbarou having been brought in to 'modernise' the company's products, which were still visibly derived from the original designs.

Barbarou's Parsifal, with its vertical engine mounted in front, won the day and Benz resigned in a huff, only returning as a director in 1904. The Parsifal range had 10, 12 and 14 hp two-cylinder and 20 and 30 hp four-cylinder power units, but were not as successful as Barbarou's backers had anticipated.

Barbarou was succeeded as chief designer by Fritz Erle, who was in turn followed by Hans Nibel. The cars built during this pre-war period ranged from 1950 cc to a potent 10,080 cc four developing 105 bhp (at 1400 rpm!);

there was even a limited run of the 200 hp model, which had the largest engine capacity ever put into production – 21,504 cc!

In 1910, Benz took over the Suddeutsche Automobilfabrik at Gaggenau, which had formerly built the Orient Express, Liliput, SAF and Gaggenau cars; the advanced 35 hp and 60 hp Gaggenaus continued in production for some months before the newly-acquired factory was turned over entirely to commercial vehicle manufacture.

After the war the Mannheim factory built a sporting overhead-camshaft 1570 cc four, the 6/18 hp; a less sporting contemporary was the side-valve 8/20 hp of 2080 cc. In 1923, a 2860 cc six-cylinder side-valve appeared as well as a sporting 4130 cc six, built until 1926. There was also a 7025 cc six.

Benz merged with Daimler (Mercedes) in 1926 to form Daimler-Benz. Benz also built many racing cars, including the 1909 200 hp Blitzen-Benz and the revolutionary aerodynamic rear-engined 1980 cc Benz 'Teardrop' racing car designed by Edmund Rumpler in 1922-24.

## Viktoria

The 1891 Viktoria – so called because it represented 'the victory of a happy idea' – was the first four-wheeler to be built by Benz: since Carl Benz had devised a proper Ackermann-type steering layout, he was no longer worried about the gyroscopic effect and therefore now permitted the flywheel to rotate vertically.

The 2.90-litre 3 hp water-cooled single-cylinder power unit had a poppet inlet-valve instead of the sliding pattern used on the three-wheelers; there were also more powerful 4 hp and 5 hp versions. A float-feed carburettor was adopted; now the driver no longer

**Bentley Continental R-type**

**Benz Victoria**

## Blitzen Benz

Developed from the 1908 Grand Prix Benz, which had an engine of a mere 15 litres or so, the 21.5-litre Blitzen Benz racer appeared in 1909. It had pushrod overhead valves and inlet ports large enough to allow the mechanic to insert his hand into the cylinder to withdraw the exhaust valve for service. A single carburettor was deemed large enough to supply the engine's gaseous needs.

The power of the Blitzen – German for lightning – was demonstrated by a series of speed records set between 1909 and 1911 which culminated in a speed of 141.7 mph (228.1 kph).

### 1892 BENZ VIKTORIA
**Engine:** single cylinder
**Capacity:** 2900 cc
**Maximum power:** 3 bhp
**Transmission:** two-speed belt and chain
**Chassis:** tubular steel
**Suspension:** non-independent with elliptic leaf springs
**Brakes:** spoon type on rear tyres, band type on rear hubs
**Bodywork:** Viktoria
**Maximum speed (approx):** 18 mph (29 kph)

### 1909 BLITZEN BENZ
**Engine:** in-line four cylinder, inlet-over-exhaust valve
**Bore × stroke:** 185 mm × 200 mm
**Capacity:** 21,504 cc
**Maximum power:** 200 bhp
**Transmission:** four-speed manual
**Chassis:** pressed steel channel
**Suspension:** non-independent with semi-elliptic leaf springs
**Brakes:** drums on rear and transmission
**Bodywork:** tourer
**Maximum speed (approx):** 142 mph (227 kph)

had to stop and refill the carburettor at frequent intervals and prolonged tours became a practical reality.

In 1894 a Viktoria, driven by the industrialist Theodore von Liebig, made Germany's first long motor tour, 'roaming through some beautiful country in a novel way' from Bavaria to Reims and back, using 140 litres of fuel and 1500 litres of cooling water .... Car Benz was so delighted with his Viktoria design that he preferred to use one of these cars for personal outings well after it had become obsolete.

In 1913 Benz introduced a touring version of the Blitzen, by far the largest-engined private car ever catalogued: it sold for £1800 in England. High-ranking German officers used the 200 hp Benz as official transportation during the Great War; the surviving 200 hp Benz tourer is said to have been so employed by Field-Marshal von Hindenburg.

## BERKELEY
**Biggleswade, England**
**1956-1961**

Designed by Laurie Bond (of Bond Minicar fame), and launched in 1956, the Berkeley was the brainchild of Charles Panter of Berkeley Caravans, who saw a market for a smaller, cheaper sports car in the wake of the Suez crisis. Panter had already developed the technique of glass-fibre body manufacture on his caravans, which were moulded like the two halves of an Easter egg and bonded together.

The Berkeley had chain drive to the front wheels from a motor cycle engine: British Anzani, Excelsior and Royal Enfield units were all used at times. The most potent Berkeley had the 692 cc Royal Enfield power unit which gave it 90 mph (145 kph) potential allied to a reputation for performance at the expense of reliability. The cars sold in steady numbers until the collapse of the caravan side of Panter's empire dragged them down.

Performance of the later versions was excellent, thanks to the more powerful power units and a weight of around 785 lb (356 kg). There was also a 325 cc three-wheeler version plus – right at the end – a more conventional model,

**Blitzen Benz**

**Berkeley Bandit**

### 1960 BERKELEY BANDIT

**Engine:** in-line four cylinder, side valve
**Bore × stroke:** 80.96 mm × 48.41 mm
**Capacity:** 997 cc
**Maximum power:** 39 bhp
**Transmission:** four-speed manual
**Chassis:** fabricated steel and glassfibre
**Suspension:** independent with MacPherson struts front and swing axles rear
**Brakes:** discs front and drums rear
**Bodywork:** two-seat sports
**Maximum speed (approx):** 85 mph (136 kph)

the Bandit, using the Ford 105E Anglia power unit and designed by John Tojeiro. At the time, it was one of the world's smallest cars with disc brakes.

Amazingly, Berkeleys powered by the three-cylinder Excelsior engine won their class in the 1959 Monza 12-hours race as well as in the Mille Miglia, in which they were the only British entry; the Mille Miglia (the rally that succeeded the famous town-to-town race) was the marque's seventh successive win in six weeks' racing in Italy! Berkeleys were also widely raced in the USA between 1958 and 1961.

## BERLIET

**Lyon, France
1895-1939**

Marius Berliet was a self-taught mechanic who assembled his first single-cylinder car in a small shed in his native city of Lyons in 1894; on one of its first journeys it ran away downhill and embedded itself in a sausage shop . . . . Undeterred, Berliet continued making cars in tiny numbers until in 1899 a local businessman put sufficient capital into the business to enable Berliet to start production in earnest.

In 1900 he also offered twin-cylinder cars, and designed a 12 hp four in conjunction with his engineer Pierre Desgouttes. The latter model proved popular, and about 100 were built. The design was also sold to Sunbeam in Wolverhampton

After taking over the large Audibert & Lavirotte works in 1901, Berliet expanded his output of two- and four-cylinder cars, and a year later introduced a completely new design on the fashionable Mercedes lines, with a honeycomb radiator and steel chassis frame (instead of the wood which had been used on all previous models).

In 1906 Berliet sold the US licence for his design to the American Locomotive Co, who built it as the Alco. Berliet gained $500,000 and the locomotive design from his radiator badge from the deal, though the Alco link was severed in 1908.

By 1907 Berliet ranked seventh in size in France, with an annual output of over 1000 vehicles. Berliet's pre-war range was complex, including a petrol-electric hybrid and cars from 8 hp to 60 hp, but production was mainly centred on three models: fours of 2412 cc and 4398 cc and a six-cylinder of 9500 cc.

A 1539 cc 12 hp model was current from 1910-12. By 1912, the big sixes were only available to special order. Berliet made cars until 1917, but developed their lorry department during the war for the needs of the French Army.

After the war they resumed production of cars with 12 hp (2613 cc), 15 hp (3308 cc) and 22 hp (4398 cc) power units, plus other minor models. The wartime emphasis on commercials seemed to have permeated the car side of Berliet's activities, for the side-valve

power units were all of pre-war design, and the cars were unexciting in concept and appearance.

In 1924 Berliet presented a range powered by new overhead valve engines, which co-existed alongside the old side-valves. The new overhead-valve 7 hp (1159 cc) was an unsuccessful attempt to create a popular car, while there were also a 2484 cc 12 hp and a 3969 cc 18 hp.

With the growth of lorry sales, Berliet's interest in making cars diminished, though the company launched two new six-cylinders of 1.8 litres and 4.0 litres in 1927.

In 1933, only two models of car were listed: 1.6- and 2.0-litre fours, available in side-valve as well as overhead-valve form.

The last Berliet model, launched in 1936, was the Dauphine, a streamlined 2 litre with independent front suspension. Towards the end of production it used the aerodynamic bodywork of the Peugeot 402.

Marius Berliet died shortly after the war; Berliet company policy had suppressed cars in favour of trucks in 1939. Berliet, still one of France's leading truck producers, was taken over by Citroën in 1967.

### 1923 BERLIET 23/70 HP

**Engine:** in-line four cylinder, side valve
**Bore × stroke:** 95 mm × 140 mm
**Capacity:** 3969 cc
**Maximum power:** 70 bhp
**Transmission:** four-speed manual
**Chassis:** pressed steel channel
**Suspension:** non-independent with semi-elliptic leaf springs
**Brakes:** drums all round
**Bodywork:** four-seat tourer
**Maximum speed (approx):** not known

**Berliet 23/70HP**

Beverley Barnes

# BEVERLEY-BARNES

**London, England**
**1924-1931**

Lenaerts and Dolphens were engineers of Belgian origin, based at Barnes in London, who made components for other manufacturers, including Bentley. The first Beverley-Barnes car, with an ambitious straight-eight overhead-camshaft power unit, appeared at the November 1923 Olympia Show. 'The Beverley-Barnes gives full value for the money,' commented *The Autocar*, adding 'in no other case does it appear possible to obtain an absolutely modern straight-eight engine in so large a chassis at so moderate a cost . . . a car of a more luxurious nature it would be difficult to find in the whole Show.'

The car, however, didn't live up to its early promise and was only made in small numbers. Engine capacity varied from 2.5 to 5 litres; at least one Beverley-Barnes was Bean-powered! Bodywork was often by Vanden Plas, also of

Belgian origin. These luxury cars did not survive the Depression; the last Beverley-Barness had twin overhead-cam power units, also fitted in the ephemeral Burney Streamline. By 1931, Beverley-Barnes was assembling Invicta cars under licence.

# BIANCHI

**Milan, Italy**
**1899–1939**

Grocer's son Edoardo Bianchi founded his Milan bicycle factory in 1885 and produced the first Italian cycle to use pneumatic tyres. The company began manufacture of motorcycles in 1897, followed by motor quadricycles in 1898. Their

Bianchi S5

first car, powered by a single cylinder De Dion engine, appeared the following year; soon after Guiseppe Merosi joined Bianchi as engineer to develop the motorcar side of the business.

In 1902, Bianchi moved into a new factory in the via Ninio Bixio, and the first Bianchi with a four-cylinder engine appeared in 1904. Most of Bianchi's output consisted of touring cars, though in 1907 a 120 hp racing car with a markedly

oversquare 7992 cc four-cylinder engine with overhead valves competed – without success – in the Coppa Florio and Kaiserpreis. A 6424 cc derivative ran in the Targa Bologna in 1908; the Bianchi competition drivers were Carlo Maserati (eldest of the six *fratelli*

Maserati) and Edoardo Bianchi's right-hand man, Gian Fernando Tomaselli. Shaft drive began to replace chain in 1909 (the year in which Merosi joined the new ALFA company), though the massive 70/80 hp of 1911, with an overhead cam 9557 cc engine, was still chain-driven. Prior to this Bianchi had built huge side-valve fours of 11,305 cc and 10,598 cc; their smallest pre-Great War machine was an 8/12 hp four of just 1244 cc.

Among their complex and confusing range, the 4390 cc Tipo C of 1912–15 was outstanding, with a sporting 'Prince Henry' variant catalogued in 1913. That was slightly uncharacteristic of a marque better known for producing staid but reliable tourers. 'We find her a splendid hill climber,' enthused an Irish lady owner in 1913, adding cryptically: 'I have also been most pleased with my chauffeur you sent to me – he is satisfactory in every way . . .'. The 1920s saw the continuation of production of cars of sound, sturdy design; a popular overhead-valve 1287 cc four-cylinder was current in 1925–7. A 2731 cc straight-eight, the V3, was built from 1928–9, with a derivative, the 2905 cc S8, current from 1930–34. The ultimate Bianchi, the S9, was a 1452 cc four, offered with streamlined "Viareggio" saloon coachwork.

Attempts to revive Bianchi production with new designs after World War II failed, partly because of the great demand for bicycles and motorcycles, partly through the high cost of developing new cars. However, the marque was revived in 1955 with Fiat and Pirelli backing, as Autobianchi.

---

## 1923 BEVERLEY-BARNES

**Engine:** in-line eight cylinder, overhead cam
**Bore × stroke:** 75 mm × 112 mm
**Capacity:** 3958 cc
**Maximum power:** 80 bhp
**Transmission:** three-speed manual
**Chassis:** pressed steel channel
**Suspension:** non-independent with semi-elliptic leaf springs
**Brakes:** drums all round
**Bodywork:** to order
**Maximum speed (approx):** not known

---

## 1927 BIANCHI S5

**Engine:** in-line four cylinder, overhead valve
**Bore × stroke:** 64 mm × 100 mm
**Capacity:** 1300 cc
**Maximum power:** 35 bhp
**Transmission:** four-speed manual
**Chassis:** pressed steel channel
**Suspension:** non independent with semi-elliptic leaf springs
**Brakes:** drums all round
**Bodywork:** saloon or torpedo
**Maximum speed (approx):** 60 mph (100 kph)

## MODEL
Aston Martin DB2/4

**UK price when announced:**
£2728  4s  2d

## ENGINE
**Location:** Front, longitudinal
**Type:** Water-cooled in-line six cylinder. Cast-iron block with removeable liners and cast-iron cylinder head. Four main bearings
**Cubic capacity:** 2580 cc
**Bore × stroke:** 78 mm × 90 mm
**Compression ratio:** 8.16:1
**Valve gear:** 2 valves per cylinder operated by twin direct-acting overhead camshafts
**Fuel supply:** 2 SU side-draught carburettors. Twin electric fuel pumps
**Ignition:** Mechanical by coil and distributor with automatic timing advance/retard
**Maximum power:** 127 bhp at 5000 rpm
**Maximum torque:** 178 lb ft at 3000 rpm

## TRANSMISSION
**Layout:** Clutch in unit with engine.
**Clutch:** Single dry plate Borg & Beck
**Gearbox:** Four-speed manual synchromesh on top three ratios
**Standard ratios:**

| | |
|---|---|
| 1st 2.92:1 | 3rd 1.33:1 |
| 2nd 1.98:1 | 4th 1.00:1 |

**Close ratios:**

| | |
|---|---|
| 1st 2.92:1 | 3rd 1.26:1 |
| 2nd 1.87:1 | 4th 1.00:1 |

**Final drive:** Hypoid bevel
**Ratio:** 3.77:1

## SUSPENSION
**Front:** Independent with trailing links, coil springs and double-acting lever arm shock absorbers
**Rear:** Live rear axle with coil springs, radius arms and Panhard rod

## STEERING
**Type:** Worm and roller

## BRAKES
**Type:** 12 in (305 mm) dia. drums all round

## WHEELS AND TYRES
**Type:** Dunlop centre-lock wire sheels with 5.75 × 16 in tyres

## BODY/CHASSIS
**Type:** Tubular steel chassis with aluminium panelled coupé body

## DIMENSIONS AND WEIGHT
**Length:** 171.5 in (4355 mm)
**Width:** 65 in (1651 mm)
**Wheelbase:** 99 in (2525 mm)
**Track – front:** 54 in (1372 mm)
**– rear:** 54 in (1372 mm)
**Weight:** 2884 lb (1308 kg)

## PERFORMANCE
**Maximum speed:** 125 mph (201 kph)
**Acceleration 0–60 mph:** 12.6 seconds
**Fuel consumption:** 18–22 mpg

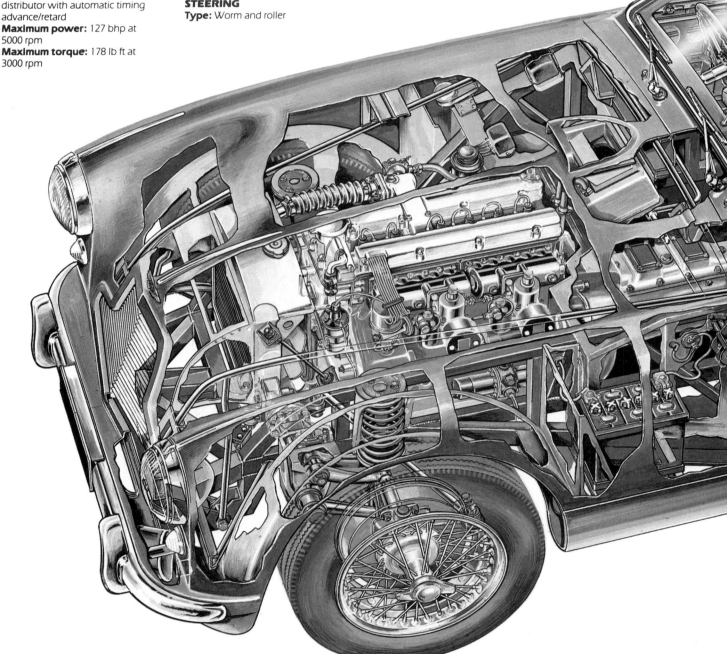

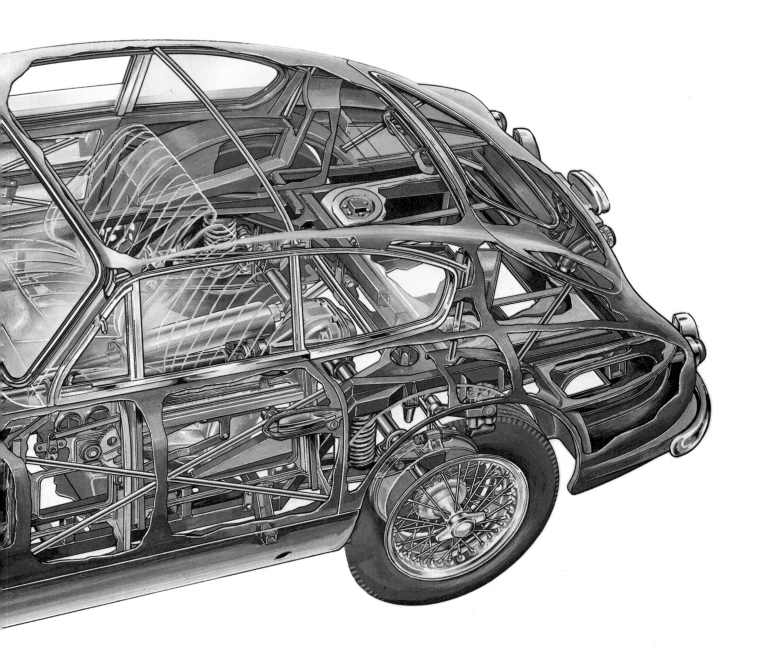

**ABOVE** The Aston Martin DB2-4, showing its twin-ovehead-camshaft straight six, independent front suspension and live rear axle. The DB2-4 was the first model in the series to offer seating for four, and thus graduated from being a sports car to a high-performance grand tourer, which has been the basis of all subsequent models. The car was an expensive one by the standards of its time, and was also engineered and finished to high standards. As its engine was developed and the performance improved, the DB2-4 naturally evolved into the DB4, introduced in 1959

# A-Z OF THE CAR

proprietary power units before the outbreak of war in 1914, assembled the first Bignan Sports in the Gregoire factory at Poissy in 1920: indeed, Malcolm Campbell sold them in the UK as Gregoire-Campbells. There were two models, with fixed-head side-valve power units of 2951 cc and 3457 cc. Bignan also made a real sports-racing car with a 16-valve 2886 cc overhead-camshaft power unit designed by Causan, formerly with La Licorne.

In 1922, in an attempt to solve the problem of hgh-speed valve-spring breakage, Bignan made a 2

won the 24 Heures du Francorchamps and established a world record by covering 3000 km (1863 miles) in 24 hours at over 80 mph (129 kph) average, as well as taking the 2-litre class at Le Mans. On the touring front, in 1922 Jacques Bignan announced an overhead-camshaft 10 hp of 1693 cc, followed in 1923 by an 11 hp.

Almost inevitably, Bignan's business failed for the first time in 1926, but quickly resumed production of a Bignan Sport with two valves per cylinder under a new board of directors. Bignan also

## BIDDLE

**Philadelphia, USA**
**1915–1923**

The Philadelphia-built Biddle was one of the finest American luxury sporting cars, and bore a vee-radiator on similar lines to the Mercedes or American Singer. It first appeared in 1915 with a Buda engine and angular Germanic 'military fenders', replaced by more aesthetically-pleasing wings in 1917, when the Biddle range was enlarged to include a raceabout on Mercer lines.

Biddle cars were, however, better known for exquisite custom coachwork on 'European' lines, and prices ranged from $2950 to over $5000. A detuned 16-valve

**Biddle**

### 1915 BIDDLE

**Engine:** in-line four cylinder, side valve
**Bore × stroke:** 101.6 mm × 152.4 mm
**Capacity:** 4941 cc
**Maximum power:** 90 bhp
**Transmission:** three-speed manual
**Chassis:** pressed steel channel
**Suspension:** non-independent with semi-elliptic leaf springs
**Brakes:** drums on rear only
**Bodywork:** to order
**Maximum speed (approx):** not known

Rochester-Duesenberg engine was used on the 1918 Model K and remained available as an option thereafter. Biddle sales were always low, and the marque disappeared in 1923.

## BIGNAN

**Courbevoie, France**
**1918–1930**

Like Hispano-Suiza, Jacques Bignan's cars carried the flying stork emblem of the World War I Escadrille des Cicognes as their emblem. Bignan, who had built

litre engine with desmodromic valves, which developed a remarkable 70 bhp but was too complex for the normal owner. So it was replaced in 1924 by a version with four valves per cylinder, which

### 1924 BIGNAN

**Engine:** in-line four cylinder, overhead cam
**Bore × stroke:** 75 mm × 112 mm
**Capacity:** 1979 cc
**Maximum power:** 75 bhp
**Transmission:** four-speed manual
**Chassis:** pressed steel channel
**Suspension:** non-independent with semi-elliptic leaf springs
**Brakes:** drums on front only. Transmission brake
**Bodywork:** sports torpedo
**Maximum speed (approx):** 96 mph (155 kph)

made 'pot-boilers' of 8 hp and 10 hp with SCAP engines and a 10 hp with a 1600 cc Ballot power unit. Bignan also practiced badge-engineering by offering Salmson cyclecars bearing Bignan radiators.

There was further sporting success the next year when a 2 litre took the Monte Carlo Rally.

Still in financial difficulties, Bignan changed the marque name to 'La Cigogne' and built a 2.5-litre six-cylinder and a SCAP-engined eight-cylinder in 1929. Between 1930 and 1931, Bignan barely kept *le loup* from *la porte* by repairing cars before finally closing.

**Bignan**

Biscuter

# BISCUTER

**Barcelona, Spain**
**1951–1958**

That French super-eccentric Gabriel Voisin had a remarkable record as pioneer aviator, maker of superbly engineered sleeve-valve automobiles, and prolific lover, but his last production vehicle was quite unlike anything that had gone before, except in its originality: it was a tiny two-seater, which originally appeared at the 1950 Paris Salon with duralumin monocoque bodywork by the Potez aircraft company and a 125 cc two-stroke Gnome & Rhône motorcycle engine driving the front wheels.

It was too unorthodox even for the French market, but car-hungry Spain was not so choosy, and in June 1953, production got under way in Barcelona. Voisin, aged 77, drove the prototype from Paris to Barcelona in one stage. The Spanish Biscuter was built by the Autonacional Sociedad Anonima, headed by Jose Maria Marcet Coll, president of the Aero Club of Sabadell, with Damien Casanova as works director.

The little car – just 8 feet (2.4 m)

long – was powered by a 197 cc Spanish-built Villiers engine. The Biscuter proved a popular solution to the problem of providing basic transport for Spaniards during the 1950s, and some 35,000 were finally built before production ended in 1958. Its promotors ultimately attempted to disguise its utilitarian design with a streamlined glass fibre coupé body reminiscent of a shrunken Pegaso; Voisin grumbled that the Spaniards had thereby managed to transform the Biscuter into 'a slow and heavy calf'.

# BIZZARRINI

**Livorno, Italy**
**1965–1969**

Giotto Bizzarrini worked for Alfa Romeo and Ferrari, then in 1962 created the Autostar company at Livorno. Working as a consultant, Bizzarrini created the Iso Grifo, and

also designed engines, notably a 3.5-litre V12 which he sold to Lamborghini. In 1964 he changed the name of his company to the 'Societa Prototipi Bizzarrini' and began to build cars of advanced design bearing his own name.

The first cars built by Bizzarrini were competition derivatives of the Iso Grifo; the degree of engine tune, it was said, 'was largely a matter of luck depending on what Bizzarrini had knocking around the workshop', though 425 bhp could be achieved. Wheels were Campagnolo cast elecktron and the first cars had lightweight aluminium bodywork, a method of

## 1964 BIZZARRINI GT 5300

**Engine:** V8, overhead valve
**Bore × stroke:** 101.6 mm × 82.5 mm
**Capacity:** 5354 cc
**Maximum power:** 365 bhp
**Transmission:** four-speed manual
**Chassis:** fabricated steel
**Suspension:** independent front with wishbones and coils. De Dion rear axle
**Brakes:** discs front and drums rear
**Bodywork:** two-door sports coupé
**Maximum speed (approx):** 175 mph (280 kph)

## 1954 BISCUTER

**Engine:** single cylinder, two stroke
**Capacity:** 197 cc
**Maximum power:** not known
**Transmission:** three-speed manual
**Chassis:** duralumin monocoque
**Suspension:** independent with coil springs
**Brakes:** drums on rear only. Transmission brake
**Bodywork:** doorless two seater
**Maximum speed (approx):** 44 mph (70 kph)

construction subsequently replaced by glassfibre.

The first Bizzarrinis had front power units, when other sporting Italian marques were already switching to rear engines. His GT Strada 5300 coupé and GT Spider 5300 were high-efficiency models powered by front-mounted Type 327 Chevrolet Corvette engines; the 538 had a similar engine at the rear. In 1966, the company was reformed as Bizzarrini SpA, and the following year showed the glass fibre-bodied GT Europa 1900, powered by an 1897 cc overhead valve four-cylinder Opel engine, at the Geneva Show. Bizzarrini ceased activity in 1969. All Bizzarrini cars were hand-built.

# BLACKHAWK

**Indianapolis, USA**
**1929–1930**

In 1928, Stutz announced their lower-priced Model B-B in an effort to boost flagging sales; a year later it was given separate marque status as the Blackhawk. Both a Stutz-built six and a Continental eight were offered. Like the larger Stutz models the Blackhawk had worm final drive, an unusual feature for an American car. This enabled it to have a noticeably dropped frame to give lower overall height. A 'silent third' gearbox was a refined feature.

Oddly enough, though the Blackhawk chassis shown at Olympia in 1930, at £685, was £250 cheaper than the Stutz eight, the Blackhawk saloon displayed (£1160) was £20 more than the Stutz. Understandably, sales were low…. However, despite the Stutz company's efforts to give the Blackhawk a distinctive marque image, it was usually regarded as just another model of Stutz, and was discontinued in 1931.

**Bizzarrini GT Strada**

## 1930 BLACKHAWK

**Engine:** in-line six cylinder, overhead valve
**Bore × stroke:** 85.7 mm × 114.3 mm
**Capacity:** 3956 cc
**Maximum power:** 27.3 hp (rated)
**Transmission:** four-speed manual
**Chassis:** pressed steel channel
**Suspension:** non-independent with semi-elliptic leaf springs
**Brakes:** drums all round with vacuum servo
**Bodywork:** coupé or sedan
**Maximum speed (approx):** 75 mph (120 kph)

# BLERIOT-WHIPPET
**Addlestone, England
1920–1927**

During the Great War, two former employees of the Zenith-Gradua motorcycle company built a cyclecar in their spare time; it incorporated the Zenith's infinitely variable transmission by belt and pulley. In 1920, the cyclecar went into production in the former Bleriot aeroplane factory at Addlestone, Surrey: thus it was known as the Blériot-Whippet.

Since the factory's owners, the Air Navigation & Engineering Company, had business dealings with Burney & Blackburne, they dictated that the power unit used in the Bleriot-Whippet should be a 965 cc Blackburne vee-twin, although after bearing trouble the bottom end of the engine was redesigned to take roller bearings. That wasn't the only problem; it was mounted fore-and aft under a dummy bonnet, and tended to overheat. The Bleriot-Whippet was originally fitted with a kick-starter; later models had a long starting handle protruding from the side of the body. When the transmission expert of the partnership went off

## 1920 BLERIOT-WHIPPET

**Engine:** vee twin
**Bore × stroke:** 85 mm × 85 mm
**Capacity:** 965 cc
**Maximum power:** not known
**Transmission:** 18-speed belt and variable pulley
**Chassis:** parallel wooden planks set on edge
**Suspension:** non-independent with quarter-elliptic leaf springs
**Brakes:** on belt pulley and countershaft
**Bodywork:** open two seater
**Maximum speed (approx):** 45 mph (72 kph)

**Blackhawk**

to help Granville Bradshaw develop the Belsize Bradshaw, the infinitely variable pulley drive was replaced by a three-speed gearbox and chain-drive for 1921. A transversely-mounted engine and shaft-drive were listed for 1924. The advent of better small cars like the Rover Eight killed off the Bleriot-Whippet, though the company survived, on paper at least, until 1927.

# BMW
**Munich, Germany
1928–**

The Bayerische Motoren Werke was founded in 1917, successor to an aero-engine company established four years earlier. After the war, BMW built airbrakes for railway rolling stock, and merged with Bayerische Flugzeug Werke in 1922: BFW had been making – unsuccessfully – motorcycles, and the design was revised and went into production bearing the BMW badge in 1923. In 1928, BMW bought the Dixi car works at Eisenach (now in East Germany), thereby acquiring the licence to build the Austin Seven. They soon announced the Wartburg sports

two-seater, with its 750 cc engine tuned to develop 18 hp; it gained the first competition successes on four wheels for the Munich company, with class prizes in the 1929 Alpine Trial and 1920 Monte Carlo Rally.

The first true BMW car was an backbone-chassis overhead-valve 788 cc four-cylinder designed by Fritz Feidler which appeared in 1931. It was soon followed by an 845 cc version and, in 1933, by the first six-cylinder BMW, an 1173 cc derivative of the four. The latter was quickly replaced by a 1490 cc six-cylinder developing 34 bhp, and

also used in a two-seater 40 bhp sports car. In 1936 it grew to a 1911 cc six, which, with a 1 mm enlargement in bore size, matured into a 1971 cc power unit used in the famous 328, which developed 80 bhp at 4500 rpm. The BMW 328 won many races for such drivers as Prince Bira, Dick Seaman and motorcycle ace Ernest Henne. The last pre-war BMW was the 3485 cc six-cylinder 355, which developed 90 bhp at 3500 rpm.

After the war, BMW's Eisenach works fell under Russian control, and began building a 'red' derivative of the prewar BMW as the EMW. Munich only had facilities for motorcycle manufacture, and had lost its chief designer, Fiedler, to Bristol in England. A limited run of the 1971 cc six-cylinder 501 was initiated in 1951; improved versions – plus a 2077 cc model – followed. A V8 appeared in 1954; it initially displaced 2580 cc, then gained a 3168 cc engine developing up to 160 bhp at 5600 rpm. From 1955, BMW built Italian Isetta bubblecars under licence, using modified

**Bleriot Whippet**

246 cc single-cylinder overhead valve motorcycle power units. There was also a 298 cc model; the 582 cc BMW-Isetta used an overhead valve BMW flat-twin. New Michelotti-designed small cars with rear-mounted 697 cc flat-twin engines appeared in 1959, saving BMW from disaster during a depression when even motorcycle sales slumped.

Larger models were launched in 1962 with four-cylinder overhead cam power units of 1499 cc, 1573 cc, 1773 cc and 1990 cc capacity; subsequently, overhead cam six-cylinder power units of 2494 cc to 3295 cc were also offered in a variety of models. BMW bought the ailing Glas automobile works at Dingolfing in 1966; some cars bearing the Glas name were built there, but in 1968 the Glas

1.3 million before it was succeeded by a new Three Series for 1983. Flagship of the range – which consisted of the Three, Five, Six and Seven series – in the early 1980s was the Motorsport division developed M635CSi, unofficially known as the M2, with a 24-valve 3.5-litre 286 bhp engine.

## BMW 328

Building on an already sound sporting reputation, the BMW 328 was developed in 1936, when pre-production models appeared in races such as the French sports car Grand Prix at Montlhéry. Launched in 1937, the 328 had an ingenious light-alloy cylinder head which achieved inclined valves in hemispherical combustion chambers while retaining the old pushrod

### 1937 BMW 328

**Engine:** in-line six cylinder, overhead valve
**Bore × stroke:** 66 mm × 96 mm
**Capacity:** 1971 cc
**Maximum power:** 80 bhp
**Transmission:** four-speed manual
**Chassis:** steel ladder frame with tubular sidemembers
**Suspension:** independent front with transverse leaf spring. Live rear axle with semi-elliptic leaf springs
**Brakes:** drums all round
**Bodywork:** two-seat sports
**Maximum speed (approx):** 100 mph (161 kph)

duction turbos.

The accent was definitely on power, not the 275 bhp of the racer but a still impressive 170 bhp at 5800 – the most powerful of the normally aspirated 2002s produced 'only' 130 bhp from its 2-litre overhead-cam four cylinder engine. A KKK turbo was used, blowing at 7.8 psi and using a low (6.9 : 1) compression ratio. The most noticeable differences between the ordinary 2002s and the Turbo were the flared wheel arches for the larger 185/70VR13 tyres and the front spoiler. Other changes included uprated brakes with ventilated discs at the front, stiffer suspension and a limited-slip diff.

It was by no means as manageable as the standard cars but was considerably quicker, able to reach 60 mph (96 kph) in an impressive

**BMW 328**

marque was discontinued. The highly successful 2002 range was launched in 1966; a derivative was the first production BMW with a turbocharger, in 1969 the model won the European Championship for saloon cars. In 1977, BMW almost went into production with a range of V8 and V12 engines, but eventually decided to stay with its range of in-line sixes, which ranged from 2 litres to 3.5 litres. During this period, too, a mid-engined car, the M1, was developed, powered by a 3.5-litre six;; it was originally intended to be produced by Lamborghini, but that company's financial crisis overruled that plan.

BMW's biggest success story was the Three Series launched in 1975 to succeed the 2002. Available with overhead-cam power units from 1573 cc to 2315 cc, the Three Series sold over

valve gear through an ingenious cross-over mechanism. The inlet valves were operated by pushrods in the normal manner, while additional horizontal pushrods worked by bell-crank rockers crossed over to actuate the exhaust valves. Power output was thus boosted from 55 bhp to 80 bhp.

The model achieved many competition successes, starting with a class win at the Nürburgring in 1936, plus fifth, seventh and ninth places at Le Mans in 1939 and victory – with a special streamlined body – at 103.6 mph in the 1940 'short' Brescia Mille Miglia. Production ended in 1940, when 400 cars and 69 chassis had been built. An updated version of the engine (taken as reparations after the defeat of Germany) powered the post-war Bristol and Frazer Nash cars.

## BMW 2002 Turbo

The Three Series car may have been BMW's greatest sales success but they never captured the imagination like the cars they replaced, the 2002s. Easily the most attention grabbing of all 2002s was the spectacular Turbo.

It was the result of a homologation exercise as BMW aimed for Group 2 saloon car racing after the pure racing 2002 Turbo had won the European Touring Car Championship in 1969. Attention soon passed to Group 1 racing instead but the road-going Turbo programme still went ahead. At the time Turbo appeared (in 1974) it was the first production turbo, beating Saab to the punch, but while every other major manufacturer eventually followed BMW's lead BMW themselves have yet to build more pro-

6.6 seconds, and 100 mph (161 kph) in only 19.1 seconds. Maximum speed was 130 mph (209 kph). The performance was certainly there, but the engine suffered from excessive turbo lag and would offer considerably less than standard 2002 performance out of its decidedly narrow powerband. However, the optional five-speed ZF gearbox helped keep the motor on the boil more than the 2002 Tii's standard four speed and helped, slightly, to mitigate the Turbo's huge thirst for fuel.

Just so the 2002 Turbo wouldn't go unnoticed, its legend was emblazoned on the chin spoiler in reverse so that it could be easily identified in rear-view mirrors. It certainly created an impression out of all proportion to its sales; just 1672 were produced between 1973 and 1974.

**BMW 2002 Turbo**

**1974 BMW 2002 TURBO**
**Engine:** in-line four cylinder, overhead cam, turbo
**Bore × stroke:** 89 mm × 80 mm
**Capacity:** 1990 cc
**Maximum power:** 170 bhpp
**Transmission:** four-speed manual
**Chassis:** steel, unitary
**Suspension:** Independent with MacPherson struts, lower wishbones and anti-roll bar front and semi-trailing arms, coil springs and anti-roll bar rear
**Brakes:** disc front, drums rear
**Bodywork:** two-door, four-seat saloon
**Maximum speed (approx):** 130 mph (209 kph)

# BMW M1

The genesis of the model was the mid-engined BMW Turbo of 1971, a gull-winged exotic rolling test laboratory. It was decided to homologate a mid-engine BMW for endurance racing, which meant that 400 'street' versions had to be produced. It was originally proposed to build a V12, but this project foundered in the wake of the energy crisis, and a more developed light-alloy 24-valve version of the 3.55-litre BMW six with dry-sump lubrication was used instead. The production version of the M1 was designed by Guigiaro: it drew on the theme of the original Turbo, but had conventional doors. The original plan was for the M1 to be produced by Lamborghini, and the necessary machinery was established at the Lambo factory-...which for financial reasons found it could not cope.

After a year's delay, production began in Ital Design's Turin plant, with suspension and powertrain added by Baur in Stuttgart. The development programme was disastrously delayed, and though the model was launched at the Paris Salon in 1978, it was not homolo-gated until 1980, with only one season of the endurance formula for which it had been built to run before new regulations came into force.

Though the model acquired almost legendary status for the precision of its handling – 'the chassis is faster than the engine', came the comment from Turin – just 450 BMW M1s were built before production ended in the summer of 1981 – far fewer than planned.

**1980 BMW MI**
**Engine:** in-line six cylinder, double overhead cam
**Bore × stroke:** 93.4 mm × 84 mm
**Capacity:** 3453 cc
**Maximum power:** 277 bhp
**Transmission:** five-speed manual
**Chassis:** fabricated sheet steel and tubular spaceframe
**Suspension:** independent with coil springs and wishbones
**Brakes:** discs all round
**Bodywork:** glassfibre two-seat coupé
**Maximum speed (approx):** 163 mph (262 kph)

# BNC

**Levallois-Perret, France
1923–1931**

In 1923, Bollack, Netter et Cie of Levallois-Perret (Seine) began production of light cars, initially derived from the Jack Muller cyclecar. The first models used SCAP and Ruby power units of 900 cc to 1100 cc in side- or overhead-valve form. A supercharged 1100 cc SCAP-engined version appeared in 1925: the heyday of BNC as a maker of sports cars really began in 1927 with the Montlhéry, Monza and Miramas models with Ruby and

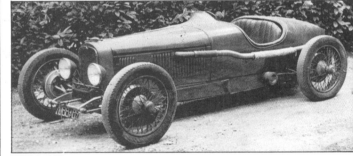
**BNC 1.5 Litre**

SCAP power units, also available in supercharged form.

BNC's small cars sold well; but their venture into the field of larger cars under the management of M de Ricoux was less successful. The ill-fated AER Aigles of 1930 had straight-eight Continental engines, Delaunay-Velleville chassis and Messier pneumatic suspension. Surprisingly, some BNC racing cars used 1500 cc British-built Meadows power units. The original firm closed its doors in the late 1930s, but the BNC marque name was taken over by their agent, M Siréjols, who continued to assemble cars in Levallois from existing parts until 1950.

**1925 BNC**
**Engine:** in-line four cylinder overhead valve
**Bore × stroke:** 69 mm × 100 mm
**Capacity:** 1496 cc
**Maximum power:** 40 bhp
**Transmission:** four-speed manual
**Chassis:** pressed steel channel
**Suspension:** non-independent with semi-elliptic leaf springs front and cantilever rear
**Brakes:** drums all round
**Bodywork:** two-seat sports convertible
**Maximum speed (approx):** 103 mph (166 kph)

**BMW MI**

# A-Z
# OF THE CAR

## BOLLEE
### Le Mans, France
### 1885–1920

Between 1873–81 Amédée Bollée, a bellfounder of Le Mans, built a number of advanced steam carriages with independent front suspension. His son, also named Amédée, built equally advanced petrol cars between 1896 and 1913; the 1896 Amédée Bollée car was the first shaft-driven car with spiral bevel gearing, though its transmission layout was unbelievably complex.

Young Amedee then designed the streamlined racing *torpilleurs*, the 1899 model featuring a 20 hp monobloc four-cylinder engine fitted with twin carburettors. Its chassis was independently sprung at the front, underslung at the rear. Bollée's designs were taken up by the long-established De Dietrich engineering works at Lunéville (Lorraine), but were quickly dropped in favour of more conventional designs.

mechanical computer, built high-performance three-wheelers from 1896; these fiery voiturettes were the first vehicles to be fitted with pneumatic tyres as standard (but then they *were* totally devoid of springs). Leon Bollee then built, in 1900, a four-wheeled voiturette with independent front suspension, rear-mounted engine and tubular backbone chassis.

Bollée's factory built large, conventional cars from 1903 to 1924, and was then taken over by Morris, whose Morris-Léon-Bollée was an unsuccessful bid to break into the French family car market.

Amédée subsequently concentrated on refined limited-production cars at Le Mans. His 1907 Type E, the first ergonomically designed car, had hydraulic tappets. He also cooperated with the Wright Brothers when they visited Europe to demonstrate flying in 1908, making their power units more reliable. The last Amédée Bollée cars were built in 1913 – but some continued to be assembled from spares until 1919.

Amédée's brother Léon, who had already devised an ingenious though rather complicated

**Bolwell Nagari**

## BOLWELL
### Melbourne, Australia
### 1963–1974

Although the Bolwell brothers started in 1963 by building glassfibre kit cars in their factory in a Melbourne suburb – one of the Bolwells had worked at Lotus in England – by 1970 they had progressed to the manufacture of the Nagari sports coupé, one of the few Australian-built high-performance cars. Powered by a Ford V8 302 engine, the Nagari

| 1896 BOLLEE VOITURETTE | |
|---|---|
| **Engine:** | single cylinder |
| **Bore × stroke:** | 75 mm × 145 mm |
| **Capacity:** | 641 cc |
| **Maximum power:** | 2 hp |
| **Transmission:** | three-speed |
| **Chassis:** | tubular steel |
| **Suspension:** | elliptic leaf springs on front only |
| **Brakes:** | wooden block against wheel rim on rear |
| **Bodywork:** | open four seater |
| **Maximum speed (approx):** | 30 mph (48 kph) |

| 1974 BOLWELL NAGARI | |
|---|---|
| **Engine:** | V8, overhead valve |
| **Bore × stroke:** | 101.6 × 76.2 mm |
| **Capacity:** | 4949 cc |
| **Maximum power:** | 230 bhp |
| **Transmission:** | three-speed manual |
| **Chassis:** | backbone fabricated steel |
| **Suspension:** | Bolwell independent all round |
| **Brakes:** | drums all round |
| **Bodywork:** | sports coupe |
| **Maximum speed (approx):** | 129 mh (208 kph) |

had a Lotus-type backbone chassis with four-wheel independent suspension of Bolwell design. Its glassfibre bodywork had attractive overtones of Ferrari, though the chassis incorporated mass-produced parts from the locally-built GM-Holden.

The firm had planned to export to the US market but that country's tough safety and emission regulations made this impossible. Despite spiralling prices (the Nagari cost $A5500 when launched, $A12,000 in its last year, 1974), nearly 100 Nagaris, plus hundreds of the earlier Mark 7 Bolwells, were sold in Australia.

## BORGWARD
### Bremen, Germany
### 1939–1961

The first car to bear the name Borgward appeared in 1939, though Carl F. Borgward had been

**Bollee**

**Borgward Isabella Coupé**

active in the industry a long while as a manufacturer of car radiators. He acquired Hansa, Goliath and Hansa-Lloyd in the early 1930s. That original Borgward was powered by a special version of the Hansa six, but Borgward didn't really come to the fore until after the war, when they caused a sensation with the Borgward Hansa, Germany's first post-war performance car with modern styling. Its four-cylinder 1498 cc power unit was also the first post-war German engine with overhead valves.

The next Borgward development was the launch of a 1758 cc engine, also available as a diesel. The popular Borgward Isabella was built from 1954 in various models powered by an overhead-valve 1493 cc four-cylinder engine. Borgward also competed in sports car events, initially with a pushrod Isabella unit modified to give 100 bhp. By 1954, fuel injection had been added to boost output to 115 bhp; these Borgward Rennsports won the 1954 Eifelrennen at the Nürburgring and took a class victory in the 1955 Mille Miglia.... For 1956, there was a new racing engine, still with the dimensions of the Isabella unit but now with a light-alloy block and twin overhead camshafts. Despite stiff Porsche opposition it powered the runner-up in the German Sports Car Championship that year. Financial problems caused Borgward's withdrawal from competition in 1958, though the twin-cam engine was subsequently lent to private entrants, most notable Stirling Moss.

A last venture was a six-cylinder

### 1956 BORGWARD ISABELLA

**Engine:** in-line four cylinder, overhead valve
**Bore × stroke:** 72 mm × 92 mm
**Capacity:** 1498 cc
**Maximum power:** 75 bhp
**Transmission:** four-speed manual
**Chassis:** steel, integral
**Suspension:** independent all round with transverse leaf springs
**Brakes:** drums all round
**Bodywork:** saloon or cabriolet
**Maximum speed (approx):** 90 mph (145 kph)

luxury car with optional air suspension. The Borgward small-car ranges were built under the Lloyd and Goliath trade marks; when the parent works collapsed, these makes also became victims. Carl Borgward was 73 when he died in 1963, having outlived his automobile works by only two years.

## BRASIER
**Ivry-Port, France
1897–1930**

One of the great racing marques of the early days of motoring – they won the Gordon-Bennet Trophy for France in 1904–05 – Richard-

### 1913 BRASIER 30/60 HP

**Engine:** in-line four cylinder, side valve
**Bore × stroke:** 120 mm × 150 mm
**Capacity:** 6786 cc
**Maximum power:** 60 bhp
**Transmission:** four-speed manual
**Chassis:** pressed steel channel
**Suspension:** non independent with semi-elliptic leaf springs front and quarter elliptic rear
**Brakes:** rear wheel and transmission
**Bodywork:** to order
**Maximum speed (approx):** not known

**Brasier 30 hp Limousine**

Brasier became simply Brasier in 1905, as one of the founding partners, Georges Richard had left to found Unic.

Brasier settled into a period of steady conservatism, offering reliable, unenterprising cars such as a 10 hp 1526 cc twin and an 1847 cc four. A 1551 cc 11 hp was introduced in 1909 and persisted until 1915. In 1911 a new range was launched, consisting of a pair-cast 4766 cc six-cylinder and a four-cylinder 3177 cc derivative, as well as other models such as a 24 hp four of 3562 cc.

In 1914, the marque's distinctive flat-fronted radiator gave way to one with rounded edges, and four new cars – a 9 hp, a 12 hp, a 16 hp and a 22 hp – were introduced. Brasier resumed production after World War I in 1919 with a 3404 cc 18 hp which had an electric starter, but it only remained in production until the end of 1920. The new 2120 cc 12 hp Brasier enjoyed better fortune, remaining current until 1926, while a 1452 cc 9 hp was introduced in 1924.

In 1926 the marque name was changed to Chaigneau-Brasier, following a reorganisation. Unfortunately, the new company went off on the wrong tack, producing a super-luxury front-wheel-drive straight-eight of 3078 cc, with the transmission mounted ahead of the front axle. The new Chaigneau-Brasier was much too advanced for the customers of the late 1920s and few left the company's Ivry-Port (Seine) factory before it closed in 1930.

## BRENNABOR
**Brandenburg
1908–1934**

Brennabor of Brandenburg/Havel (now in East Germany), founded by the Reichstein brothers, was a well-known builder of perambulators, bicycles, motorcycles and three-wheelers before turning to car manufacture in 1908.

Most Brennabor models were designed by Carl Reichstein, one of the company's founders. In the

## 1932 BRENNABOR 4/2OPS

**Engine:** in-line four cylinder, side valve
**Bore × stroke:** 62 mm × 83 mm
**Capacity:** 1002 cc
**Maximum power:** 20 bhp
**Transmission:** three-speed manual
**Chassis:** U section steel channel
**Suspension:** non independent with semi-elliptic leaf springs
**Brakes:** drums all round, servo assisted
**Bodywork:** roadster, saloon or cabriolet-limousine
**Maximum speed (approx):** 47 mph (75 kph)

Brennabor Type C

beginning, Brennabor fitted Fafnir two- and four-cylinder engines, then began making their own power units. Brennabor's pre-Great War offerings ranged from 904 cc to 3800 cc; in some export markets such as England, they were known as Brenna and noted for their good quality and advanced design. In 1919, Brennabor joined the shortlived GDA, a coalition which also included NAG, Hansa and Hansa-Lloyd. During the early 1920s, daily production was around 120 cars, which, before the rise of Opel, made Brennabor the biggest car manufacturer in Germany. The factory also built low and fast racing cars with double overhead cam 1499 cc four-cylinder power in the 1920s.

In 1927 Brennabor launched new side-valve 2090 cc four-, and 3080 cc six-cylinder models on fashionable American lines. Another six-cylinder, the Juwel,

had a 2460 cc power unit. The 3417 cc eight-cylinder Juwel was added in 1930, along with a front-wheel drive version of the Juwel 6. The last Brennabor range consisted of the rear-wheel-driven 1-litre 4/20 hp – which resembled a slightly enlarged version of the American Bantam – and two (1959 cc and 2500 cc) six-cylinder models. Brennabor, whose products competed successfully in major trials such as the Alpine trial and the Europa-Fahrt 10,000 km, ceased production in 1934.

# BREWSTER
**Long Island, USA**
**Springfield, USA**
**1915–1938**

Some 300 Brewsters were manufactured between 1915 and 1925 by the well-known

carriagebuilders Brewster & Co, of Long Island City, NY. Distinguished by an oval radiator, Brewsters were powered by a four-cylinder Knight sleeve-valve engine. Either left- or right-hand steering could be specified, and a rich choice of custom-built open or closed coachwork. Brewster cars enjoyed local polularity in the New York City area, despite prices in the $10,000 bracket, and few changes were made to the car in its ten-year production life.

The American Rolls-Royce took over Brewster & Company in 1926, then in 1934, John S. Inskip, former president of the recently defunct Rolls-Royce of America company, established the Springfield Manufacturing Company in the former Rolls-Royce works to produce a second Brewster car. There was little Brewster in the chassis however: the reincarnated marque was now mounting

Brewster bodies on lengthened Ford V8 chassis, plus the odd Buick, Oldsmobile – and even a solitary Rolls-Royce…. The Brewster featured heart-shaped radiator grilles, elaborately flared wings and styled half-bumpers. Nearly all Brewsters were town-cars priced at $3500, though a few convertible-sedans and convertible-coupés were produced. Again, some 300 of these second generation Brewsters were sold before production was ended and Mr Inskip became US distributor for Rolls-Royce.

## 1934 BREWSTER

**Engine:** V8, side valve
**Bore × stroke:** 77.7 mm × 95.25 mm
**Capacity:** 3622 cc
**Maximum power:** 88.5 bhp
**Transmission:** three-speed manual
**Chassis:** pressed steel channel
**Suspension:** non independent with transverse semi-elliptic leaf spring
**Brakes:** drums all round, mechanical
**Bodywork:** town car
**Maximum speed (approx):** not known

# BRICKLIN
**St John, Canada**
**1974–1976**

Like the DeLorean, with which it had many points of similarity, the Bricklin SV-1 – built between 1974–1976 – reflected the American Dream of the exotic sports car. Consequently, its

**Brewster Sedan**

Bricklin

## 1974 BRICKLIN SV-1

**Engine:** V8, overhead valve
**Bore × stroke:** 103.6 mm × 87.3 mm
**Capacity:** 5899 cc
**Maximum power:** 129 bhp
**Transmission:** three-speed automatic
**Chassis:** fabricated steel perimeter frame
**Suspension:** independent with coil springs and wishbones front and radius arms and coil springs rear
**Brakes:** discs front and drums rear
**Bodywork:** gullwing, glassfibre sports coupé
**Maximum speed (approx):** 110 mph (175 kph)

specification was loaded with out-of-the-ordinary features such as gull-wing doors, colour-impregnated acrylic skin bonded to a glass-fibre body, and 12 mph (19 kph) crash-resistant bumpers allied to a steel perimeter frame encircling the passenger compartment.

Malcolm Bricklin had his sights on the Corvette market and spoke grandly of a planned 12,000 units a year. Despite an enthusiastic reception by the press, the SV-1 was never produced in significant numbers. AMC suspension, brakes and 5899 cc V8 were used initially, with a switch of power unit to a 5161 cc Ford engine in 1975.

Despite reports of orders for 4000 cars, total production was 2875.

## BRISCOE

Jackson, USA
1914–1921

Benjamin Briscoe, former haed of Maxwell, moved to France with grandiose ideas of large-scale production of a cyclecar called the Ajax. Manufacture of these cyclecars at Neuilly (Seine) lasted only from 1913 to 1914 before it was interrupted by the outbreak of war and Ben Briscoe returned to his native America, carrying with him designs for a more substantial mass-production car, which was built in Jackson, Michigan.

Known as 'the car with the half-million-dollar motor', the Briscoe initially had a distinctive 'cyclops'

## 1915 BRISCOE

**Engine:** in-line four cylinder, side valve
**Bore × stroke:** 81 mm × 127 mm
**Capacity:** 2680 cc
**Maximum power:** 24 bhp
**Transmission:** three-speed
**Chassis:** pressed steel channel
**Suspension:** non-independent with semi-elliptic leaf springs
**Brakes:** drums on rear only
**Bodywork:** runabout or tourer
**Maximum speed (approx):** not·known

headlamp built into the radiator header tank; however, later models had conventional lighting. Briscoe built a few V8s in 1916; production of cars under the Briscoe name ended in 1921, but between 1921 and 1923 the same four-cylinder car continued to be built under the name Earl. Total Briscoe and Earl production was approximately 75,000.

## BRISTOL

Bristol, England
1945–

The car division of the Bristol Aeroplane company was formed in 1945 to build high performance quality cars, initially Anglicised versions of the 2-litre six-cylinder BMW. Since both companies had their roots in the aeronautical industry, the 400 Series, unveiled at the 1947 Geneva Salon, carried distinctive strealined coachwork.

Briscoe

**Bristol 401**

though its BMW ancestry was clearly recognisable. However, the marque soon found its own individuality with the 401, which carried aerodynamic bodywork developed in the Bristol wind tunnel at Filton from a theme proposed by Touring of Milan.

The Bristol crossover-pushrod 2-litre engine also powered many racing cars in the 1950s, not least the Formula 2 Cooper-Bristol with which Mike Hawthorn first achieved stardom. The Bristol 402 was a limited production drophead coupé, the 403 a revised version of the 401. The 450 was a two-seat endurance racer which won class and team awards at Reims and Le Mans; the 404 coupé was the first Bristol production model to shed all traces of BMW influence from its styling, adopting a radiator intake derived from that of the Bristol Brabazon. The 405 marked Bristol's sole venture into four-door bodywork, built from 1954 to 1958. By 1961, it was apparent that the old straight-six had reached the limit of its development, so a special version of the Chrysler 5.2-litre V8 was adopted. Production continues at Filton, though Bristol Cars Ltd now has no direct links with the aircraft industry, being owned by former racing driver Anthony Crook.

Current production models are the Beaufighter, Britannia and the turbocharged V8 Brigand.

---

### 1950 BRISTOL 401

**Engine:** in-line six cylinder, overhead valve
**Bore × stroke:** 66 mm × 96 mm
**Capacity:** 1971 cc
**Maximum power:** 100 bhp
**Transmission:** four-speed manual
**Chassis:** fabricated steel box section
**Suspension:** independent front with transverse leaf spring and wishbones. Live rear axle with torsion bar
**Brakes:** drums all round
**Bodywork:** aerodynamic saloon in aluminium
**Maximum speed (approx):** 107 mph (172 kph)

---

## Bristol 401

Designed by Touring of Milan and styled in the Filton wind-tunnel, the body of the Bristol 401 had a satisfying aerodynamic sleekness that materially contributed to the car's outstanding performance. It had, of course, the BMW-derived Bristol six-cylinder engine, which featured an ingenious way of obtaining inclined valves in a hemispherical combustion chamber without the complication of overhead camshafts. Panelled in aluminium over a tubular steel framework, the 401 was designed

as a fast touring car, which it amply demonstrated by covering 104 miles (167 km) in an hour at Mont-lhéry. Bristol specified radial ply tyres as original equipment on the 401, making it one of the very first manufacturers to move out of crossply rubberwear.

The 401's weight was only 1.2 tons (1016 kg), although it had room for five adults and plenty of luggage. A rare drophead version was offered in 1949, designated the 402, while the 403, announced in 1953, retained the efficient bodyshell, and featured improvements to engine and suspension.

**British Salmson**

---

### 1936 BRITISH SALMSON 20/90

**Engine:** in-line six cylinder, twin cam
**Bore × stroke:** 75 mm × 98 mm
**Capacity:** 2590 cc
**Maximum power:** 90 bhp
**Transmission:** four-speed manual
**Chassis:** pressed steel channel
**Suspension:** independent front with transverse leaf spring. Live rear axle with quarter elliptic leaf springs
**Brakes:** drums all round
**Bodywork:** saloon or coupé
**Maximum speed (approx):** 90 mph (145 kph)

---

## BRITISH SALMSON

London, England
1934–1939

The British Salmson Aero Engines Ltd, of Raynes Park, was an offshoot of the French Salmson company, so it was hardly surprising that the first British Salmsons of 1934 were Anglicised versions of the twin-overhead-camshaft 1.5-litre French Salmson S4C model. However, the company moved in a more original direction with the 20-90 British Salmson of 1936, which was a wholly British design with a twin-overhead-camshaft 2.6-litre engine.

The 14 hp model of 1937-38 was less agile, but could nevertheless cruise at 60 mph (96 kph), with 'remarkable road holding qualities'. The company also imported French four-cylinder Salmsons for sale under the British Salmson banner. UK Production ceased at the outbreak of World War II, although the parent company continued producing twin-overhead-cam saloons after the war until 1956, when the company was taken over by Renault.

# A-Z OF THE CAR

## BRITON

**Wolverhampton, England**
**1914–1921**

The Star Cycle Company of Wolverhampton, was a sister company to Edward Lisle's Star Engineering Company, which built the Star cars: Star Cycles was run by Lisle's son, also Edward, and made cycles and motor cycles before also entering the car field in 1905 with the Starling car. The Starling was followed in 1906 by the more modern Stuart car. In 1908, a new model, the 10 hp 'Little Briton' semi-racer was added to the range; a year later the Star Cycle Company changed its name to the Briton Motor Company 1909 and moved into a new factory with the intention of building a lower-priced companion model to the Star.

The range was soon enlarged to include a 14 hp four-cylinder model, available with tourer, landaulette or racer bodywork. In 1913, Britons were endowed with handsome bullnosed radiators like those fitted to the Star. The 1914 10/12 hp Briton formed the basis of post/Armistice production, but the original company ran into trouble in 1922, and went into liquidation. It was purchased by C.A. Weight, who resumed production with a 1372 cc side-valve four-cylinder model, of which 1000 were built before production ceased in 1928.

The last four Britons built were shipped to Australia. By the late '20s Mr Weight was already making spares for Caterpillar tractors, in which guise Briton continued operation.

**Briton 10/12 HP**

### 1914 BRITON 10/12 HP

**Engine:** in-line four cylinder, side valve
**Bore × stroke:** 68 mm × 120 mm
**Capacity:** 1743 cc
**Maximum power:** 12 bhp
**Transmission:** three-speed manual
**Chassis:** pressed steel channel
**Suspension:** non independent with semi-elliptic leaf springs front and three-quarter elliptic leafs springs rear
**Brakes:** drums on rear only
**Bodywork:** two or four seater
**Maximum speed (approx):** not known

## BROOKE

**Lowestoft, England**
**1901–1913**

The Lowestoft-based marine engineering company J.W. Brooke was 'quite notorious for the excellence of its motorboats', and had a six-cylinder engine running a motor launch in 1903, before the first Napier six-cylinder car was on the road. However, the early Brooke cars – the first appeared in 1900 – had transversely-mounted three-cylinder horizontal engines. They were also distinguished by all-chain transmissions and a steering wheel with a deeply dished centre intended as storage for gloves, maps or tools (although it looked as though Brooke were catering for drivers prone to car sickness...).

Brooke's first six-cylinder car appeared late in 1903, followed closely by a 15/20 hp vertical four. A 25/30 hp six was standardised in 1906 during a brief one-model policy, which ended with the introduction of a similar 40/60 hp model in 1907. Nevertheless, though they had acquired a sound reputation for the manufacture of quality cars, Brooke gradually ran down the automotive side of their business, which ceased in 1913.

### 1907 BROOKE 40 HP

**Engine:** in-line six cylinder, side valve
**Bore × stroke:** 108 mm × 120 mm
**Capacity:** 6596 cc
**Maximum power:** 40 hp (rated)
**Transmission:** four-speed manual
**Chassis:** pressed steel channel
**Suspension:** non independent with semi-elliptic leaf springs
**Brakes:** drums on rear only
**Bodywork:** to order
**Maximum speed (approx):** 36 mph (58 kph)

## BROUGH SUPERIOR

**Nottingham, England**
**1935–1939**

'Known for his remarkable motorcycles', which, built in Nottingham since 1921, were rightly called 'the Rolls-Royce of Motor Cycles', George Brough built a prototype Dorman-engined car in 1932. However, when he eventually moved into production of a car under his Brough Superior name-plate, it was Hudson-engined. Six- and eight-cylinder versions of this American power unit were available, while supercharging was an option on the later Brough Superior, which was promoted as 'offering noteworthy performance with perfect road holding and controlled steering even at the high speeds of which it was capable'.

Standard bodywork was a patent Dual Purpose cabriolet built by Atcherley of Birmingham, though the 1936 Alpine Grand Sports was a fast supercharged two-seater. In 1939, components were laid down for three Brough Superiors fitted with V12 Lincoln-Zephyr engines, but only one was eventually built before car production ended with the outbreak of war.

**Brooke**

**Brough Superior**

steel open bodywork in 1912.

A change of policy followed the Great War with the launch of the vee-twin BSA Ten, which only lasted until 1924; the sleeve-valve cars continued until 1926. In 1929, the group's motorcycle division, BSA Cycles Ltd, produced a front-wheel-driven three-wheeler with an air-cooled 1000 cc vee-twin engine. A fourth wheel was added in 1932 and an 1100 cc four-cylinder was introduced the following year, remaining in production until 1940. There was an interruption in production in 1934, and the car was then re-named the Scout for 1935.

The main BSA company had reappeared in 1933 with a car similar to the 10 hp model built by Lanchester (taken over by BSA in 1931). This and the Light Six – also Lanchester based – only lasted until 1936.

## 1935 BROUGH SUPERIOR

**Engine:** in-line six cylinder, side valve
**Bore × stroke:** 76.2 mm × 127 mm
**Capacity:** 3455 cc
**Maximum power:** 93 bhp
**Transmission:** three-speed manual
**Chassis:** pressed steel channel
**Suspension:** non independent with semi-elliptic leaf springs
**Brakes:** drums all round, hydraulic
**Bodywork:** sports, coupé or saloon
**Maximum speed (approx):** 97 mph (156 kph)

## BSA

**Birmingham, England**
**1907–1940**

The Birmingham Small Arms company had a long history of cycle production – it had built the unstable two-wheels-in-parallel Otto Dicycle in the 1880s – and only began car production in 1907. Originality was not a strong point of early BSA design policy since their 1908 model was an unabashed copy of the 40 hp Itala. Once BSA took over Daimler in 1911, their cars became scaled-down versions of the sleeve-valve Daimlers, though a pioneering step was the adoption of all-pressed-

## 1935 BSA SCOUT

**Engine:** in-line four cylinder, side valve
**Bore × stroke:** 63 mm × 95 mm
**Capacity:** 1185 cc
**Maximum power:** not known
**Transmission:** three-speed manual
**Chassis:** pressed steel channel
**Suspension:** independent front with coil springs. Live rear axle with semi-elliptic leaf springs
**Brakes:** drums all round
**Bodywork:** two or four-seater tourer or coupé de luxe
**Maximum speed (approx):** not known

## BUCCIALI

**Courbevoie, France**
**1923–1932**

The brothers Angelo and Paul-Albert Bucciali began by building twin-cylinder two-stroke 1340 cc Buc cyclecars at Courbevoie in 1922. Under the Buc name, they also built a 1600 cc SCAP-engined car in 1925 – which was available in Tourisme and supercharged Quatre Spéciale versions – and a 1500 cc overhead – camshaft six-cylinder model. The Bucciales then turned to front-wheel-drive, and both four- and eight-cylinder models were catalogued.

Then in 1928 came the first cars

**BSA Scout**

**Bucciali TAV**

---

### 1932 BUCCIALI DOUBLE HUIT

**Engine:** U16, side valve
**Bore × stroke:** 72 mm × 120 mm
**Capacity:** 7817 cc
**Maximum power:** 155 bhp
**Transmission:** four-speed manual
**Chassis:** boxed steel channel
**Suspension:** independent with rubber in compression as spring
**Brakes:** Eclair electrical front, servo mechanical drums rear
**Bodywork:** to order
**Maximum speed (approx):** not known

---

produced under the Bucciali name, the sensational front-wheel-driven TAV (from Traction AVant), with six- and eight-cylinder Continental power units. It had originally been proposed that the Sensaud de Lavaud automatic gearbox would be used, but in the event, a sliding gearbox of Bucciali design was fitted to the few TAVs sold. TAVs were distinguished by their flamboyant, ultra-low styling and huge cast-aluminium wheels.

There was an unsuccessful liaison with Peerless in America, which possibly inspired the legendary front-wheel-drive Double Huit of 1932, reputedly powered by two straight-eight Continental engines mounted side by side (but when the car was ultimately dismantled for restoration 40 years later, the sheet-metal engine casing was found to be stuffed with newspaper…). The last Bucciali was a prototype with a Voisin 12-cylinder engine.

## BUCKLER

**Reading, England
1949-1962**

Derek Buckler built his first tubular-framed Buckler Special in 1947, and began serious production at Reading, Berkshire, in 1949 with the streamlined Mark V Airflow, available fully built-up or as a kit to which Ford mechanicals could be fitted. The business was small enough for Buckler personally to

road-test each car built and provide it with a signed report.

Later Bucklers used a variety of engines up to 2 litres, including a Buckler-modified Ford 1172 cc unit and the Coventry-Climax FWA. The most successful car, the Buckler 90, had an all-enveloping body and weighed under 1000 lb (454 kg). Shown at the 1960 Racing Car Show was the Buckler BB (Backbone) which had a tubular backbone chassis, weighed only 840 lb (381 kg) and stood just 22 inches (55.8 cm) high at the scuttle. Production ceased in 1962, and sales had totalled over 500 chassis. Malcolm Buckler outlived the company that bore his name by only two years.

---

### 1955 BUCKLER

**Engine:** in-line four cylinder, side valve
**Bore × stroke:** 63.5 mm × 92.5 mm
**Capacity:** 1172 cc
**Maximum power:** 30 bhp
**Transmission:** three-speed manual
**Chassis:** multitube space frame
**Suspension:** independent front with split beam axle and transverse leaf spring. Transverse leaf spring rear
**Brakes:** drums all round
**Bodywork:** two-seater sports
**Maximum speed (approx):** not known

---

## BUGATTI

**Molsheim, Alsace
1909-1956**

After a decade of designing cars for others, including De Dietrich, Mathis and Deutz, Ettore Bugatti set up his own factory at Molsheim, near Strasbourg (then in German-held Alsace) in 1909 to produce small cars based on his private venture Type 10, built while he was working for Deutz in Cologne.

Bugatti production started with the 1327 cc overhead-camshaft four-cylinder Type 13. He also designed the *Bébé* Peugeot. Pre-war, Bugatti built fours of 1327 cc and 5027 cc, the latter known as the Type Garros after the first customer, the famous aviator. In 1913 two four-cylinder Bugatti engines were mounted in tandem in a chassis to create a 2655 cc straight-eight, though the first production eight-cylinder Bugatti, the 1991 cc Type 30, didn't appear until 1922.

At the 1924 Lyon Grand Prix, Ettore unveiled the archetypal Bugatti, the 1991 cc eight-cylinder

Type 35, subsequently developed into the 1991 cc 35A, the 2261 cc 35T and supercharged 35B, as well as the 1492 cc 39 and 39A, the latter also supercharged. On the sports car front, Bugatti's four-cylinder Type 40 (nicknamed the Molsheim Morris-Cowley as it was the nearest thing Bugatti ever made to a popular car) and eight-cylinder Type 43 were outstanding, while touring Bugattis included the 3-litre Type 44 and the 5.3-litre Type 46.

Only half-a-dozen of the gigantic 12,762 cc eight-cylinder Royales were built; the Royale engine subsequently found a more successful application in high-speed European railcars.

Bugatti's first twin-overhead-camshaft engine appeared in 1931 on the eight-cylinder 2261 cc Type 51 racing car. The last great racing Bugatti was the Type 59, made in 2.8-litre, 2.9-litre and 3.3-litre forms. The Type 55 2.3-litre twin overhead camshaft sports car paved the way for the Type 57, built from 1934 until the outbreak of World War II.

This outstanding 3257 cc sports/racer, also available in supercharged form as the 57S and 57SC, was the last production Bugatti, though a few Type 57-derived Type 101s were built post-war although very few were built after Ettore Bugatti died in 1947. Subsequently Hispano-Suiza took over the Molsheim factory to make aircraft components.

## Bugatti Type 13

The Type 13 Bugatti was directly derived from the first prototype Type 10 Petit Pur Sang built in Ettore Bugatti's cellar in Cologne. Inspired by the Tipo FE Isotta-Fraschini designed by Stefanini, the little Bugatti was one of the first small cars to offer an acceptably lively performance without the crudity and danger associated with unpredictable cyclecars.

Production was initally slow get-

**Buckler**

ting under way – only five cars were built during 1910 – but the astounding performance of a standard Type 13 which came second in the Le Mans Grand Prix in 1911 behind a Fiat of similar engine design but over 10 litres in swept volume, established the name of Bugatti among a relatively exclusive clientele, and sales became steady.

Alongside the Type 13, Bugatti built two derivatives, Types 15 and 17, which had longer chassis. The Type 17 also had twin semi-elliptic springs to cope with the weight of heavier coachwork. For 1914, the 15 and 17 became the Types 22 and 23, while the Type 13 acquired Bugatti's distinctive reversed quarter-elliptic rear suspension, inspired, according to legend, by the springs on Covent Garden costermongers' barrows....

A 16-valve engine originally designed for the abortive 1914 Coupe des Voiturettes was fitted in the Type 13 chassis, and when this model swept the board in the voiturette race at the 1921 Italian Grand Prix, it was christened Brescia after the race's venue. In this guise, with a ball- (as opposed to the standard plain-) bearing engine, the

**Bugatti Type 13**

---

## 1921 BUGATTI BRESCIA

**Engine:** in-line four cylinder, overhead cam
**Bore × stroke:** 69 mm × 100 mm
**Capacity:** 1496 cc
**Maximum power:** 40 bhp
**Transmission:** four-speed manual
**Chassis:** pressed steel channel
**Suspension:** non independent with semi-elliptic leaf springs front and reversed quarter-elliptic leaf springs rear
**Brakes:** on rear (hand) and transmission (foot)
**Bodywork:** two-seater sports
**Maximum speed (approx):** 100 mph (161 kph)

---

16-valve Bugatti had a distinguished post-war competition career, the cars modified by Amherst Villiers for Raymond Mays and christened Cordon Rouge and Cordon Bleu proving capable of revving in the upper 6000s (standard peak revs were about 4500). The Type 23 touring version of the Brescia was produced under licence in Britain, Germany and Italy.

## Bugatti Type 35B

The 1924 French Grand Prix at Lyon saw the public debut of Bugatti's Type 35, regarded by many people as the typical Bugatti, remarkable for its purity of line and advanced styling, a unique blend of form and function in which all the elements of coachwork and chassis were united in a purposeful, yet

aesthetically-pleasing whole. The body was fronted by Bugatti's traditional 'horse-shoe' radiator and, apart from the front dumb irons and springs, the chassis was entirely concealed within the bodywork, and varied in depth from 0.75 inches (1.9 cm) at the front dumb irons to 6.75 inches (17.1 cm) at the centre, concentrating strength where it was most needed.

The Type 35 was quite remarkable: its original engine displaced 1991 cc – a 2292 cc version was created for the 1926 Targa Florio (which it won) – and was a bi-block straight–eight with five roller main bearings. The 1991 cc model gained a supercharger in 1926 as the Type 35C. The supercharged 2292 cc version of 1927, was known as the Type 35B. There was also the Type 35A, with a three-bearing crank,

---

## 1935 BUGATTI TYPE 35B

**Engine:** in-line eight cylinder, overhead cam
**Bore × stroke:** 60 mm × 100 mm
**Capacity:** 2262 cc
**Maximum power:** 135 bhp
**Transmission:** four-speed manual
**Chassis:** pressed steel channel
**Suspension:** non independent with semi-elliptic leaf springs front and reversed quarter-elliptic leaf springs rear
**Brakes:** drums all round, cable operated
**Bodywork:** open two-seater sports
**Maximum speed (approx):** 125 mph (200 kph)

---

**Bugatti Type 35B**

wire wheels and coil ignition. This 'base' model was nicknamed the Thécla after a well-known brand of imitation jewellery.

In unblown form, the 2-litre Type 35 engine developed some 90 bhp, the 2.3-litre 35T around 120 bhp, the blown derivatives probably 135 bhp.

In their day, the Type 35 and its derivatives won a remarkable 1800 racing victories – against little effective opposition – before the Type 35 was superseded by the double-overhead-cam Type 51 Grand Prix car in 1930.

# Bugatti Royale

Having made his name originally as a manufacturer of very small high-performance cars, so Bugatti reached the opposite end of the scale with the vast Royale, which first appeared at the end of 1926: in prototype form it displaced the 14.7 litres, making it the biggest production car of the 1920s.

Its straight-eight engine was a gigantic version of the typical Bugatti power unit, straight-cut and with a single overhead camshaft operating three valves per cylinder. Valve grinding, however, required the engine to be removed.

The three-speed gearbox (third was an overdrive) was mounted in unit with the rear axle, and on the prototype the ultra-light clutch was fitted under the front seat.

Bugatti spoke of a production run of 25 cars, and claimed that King Alfonso XIII of Spain had ordered a Royale: neither came to pass, and only six Royales were actually sold after the construction of the prototype. So Bugatti adapted the Royale engine to power (in sets of two or four) ultra-fast streamlined railcars capable of over 125 mph (201 kph), which went into production in 1933.

**Bugatti Type 57**

### 1927 BUGATTI ROYALE
**Engine:** in-line eight cylinder, overhead cam
**Bore × stroke:** 125 mm × 130 mm
**Capacity:** 12,763 cc
**Maximum power:** 200 bhp
**Transmission:** three-speed manual
**Chassis:** pressed steel channel
**Suspension:** non independent with semi-elliptic leaf springs front and reversed quarter-elliptic leaf springs rear with supplementary cantilever springs
**Brakes:** drums all round
**Bodywork:** to order
**Maximum speed (approx):** 112 mph (180 kph)

# Bugatti Type 57

Launched at the 1933 Paris Salon, the Type 57 was the ultimate Bugatti produced in series, and probably the most brilliant in concept, in which Jean Bugatti, Ettore's eldest son, had a major role. With a 3.3-litre twin-cam engine mounted in a chassis of advanced design, the first of the Type 57s had a curious split front beam axle in which the two halves were united by a screwed-on collar and could twist independently under braking torque: it didn't work, and those early Type 57s had to return to the works to have the collar brazed to the axle....

About 725 Type 57 Bugattis were produced, a significant proportion of Bugatti's total output of some 6000 cars, and of those approx-

### 1933 BUGATTI TYPE 57
**Engine:** in-line eight cylinder, twin cam
**Bore × stroke:** 72 mm × 100 mm
**Capacity:** 3257 cc
**Maximum power:** 135 bhp
**Transmission:** four-speed manual
**Chassis:** pressed steel channel
**Suspension:** non independent with semi-elliptic leaf springs front and reversed quarter-elliptic leafs springs rear
**Brakes:** drums all round
**Bodywork:** to order
**Maximum speed (approx):** 100 mph (161 kph)

imately 40 were the short-chassis Type 57S sports and a further 100 the supercharged Type 57C, launched in October 1936. There was also a supercharged sports chassis, Type 57SC.

While the Type 57 was fitted with a wide variety of bespoke coachwork, there were also several catalogue bodystyles, including the bizarre but beautiful Atlantic two-seater coupé whose body panels were riveted together down the centre spine of the body. The Atlantic was not only odd but rare too, only three being built.

Type 57 also enjoyed sporting success, and a 'tank' bodied Type 57 won the 1937 Le Mans 24 Hours. An improved 'Tank' Type 57 was built in 1939, and it was while testing this car that Jean Bugatti swerved to avoid a cyclist, crashed and was killed.

With Jean and Ettore (who died in 1947) gone, post-war Bugatti production was sporadic. The last left Molsheim as late as 1960 and was fitted with a roadster body designed by Virgil Exner.

**Bugatti Royale**

# A-Z OF THE CAR

## BUICK
**Flint, USA**
**1903-**

Buick has never built a side-valve-engined car, even when Scots-born plumber David Dunbar Buick, having amassed sufficient capital from his invention of the enamelled bathtub, built his first prototype in 1903. That car used his own design of overhead-valve flat-twin engine. Buick started production in 1904 backed by the Briscoe brothers, who later built Ajax, Briscoe and Earl cars.

William Crapo Durant took over in 1908 when the company ran out of finance, and Buick was elbowed out. Buick, already one of the Big Four, was the cornerstone of Durant's 1908 formation of General Motors. At the time of the takeover, the Buick twin had been joined by three four-cylinder models of 2.7, 4.2 and 5.5 litres.

Buick was a training ground for two of the great names of the American motor industry: from 1910 to 1912 it was managed by Charles Nash and from 1912 to 1920 by Walter Chrysler. Between 1919 and 1926, Buick led the US automotive industry terms of sales income.

Between 1925 and 1930, Buick offered a range of six cylinder models of between 3.1 and 5.4 litres. In 1929, Buick launched a new car line, the Marquette: the name concealed the fact that the car had side valves....

The styling of the 1929 'pregnant Buick' inspired a fall in sales, which was not halted by the introduction in 1931 of 3.6-, 4.5- and 5.7-litre straight-eights. Despite new styling and independent front suspension on 1934 models, Buick's fortunes did not pick up until 1936, and the

advent of a new general manager, Harlow H. Curtice. In conjunction with stylist Harley Earl, Curtice produced new Special, Century, Roadmaster and Limited Bucks with hydraulic brakes and more powerful engines fitted with aluminium pistons.

A further model line, the Super, appeared in 1940. Earl's influence was further emphasised by the controversial styling of the 1942 range, which had full-width front wings whose line continued into the rear wings; this style continued after the war, as did Buick's flamboyant 'toothy' grille design.

The 1948 Buick Roadmaster was the first American car fitted with automatic torque-converter drive; the transmission was known as Dynaflow. Buick's first hardtop coupe was the 1949 Riviera. A short-stroke 5277 cc six-cylinder Buick was announced in 1953, breaking a long succession of straight-eights; this power unit was used in the limited edition Skylark produced to mark Buick's golden jubilee.

In 1953, too, Buick produced its 7 millionth car. The V8 Buick Century of 1954 could achieve 110 mph (177 kph); that same year, over 200 colour schemes – single and two-tone – were available. Buick wrested third place in the sales league from its rival, the Plymouth, from 1955 to 1957, but by 1960 had fallen to ninth position.

Vulgar names like LeSabre, Invicta, Electra and Electra 225 were applied to the 1959 models, matched by bad-taste styling with drooping fins fore and aft. A new 6571 cc engine was specified for the entire Buick range save for the LeSabre.

The all-alloy 3359 cc V8 of the 1961 Special compact model was overly expensive to produce, and was sold to British Leyland for the Rover 3500 in 1964. The 1964 Riviera Sport Coupe had V8 engines of 6571 cc or 6965 cc, with the 6965 cc Skylark Gran Sport added – briefly – to the range in 1966, but supplanted in 1967 by the 6555 cc GS400.

The Riviera was restyled for the third time in 1971; its raked-

forward front and boat-tail rear end were an alteration of questionable value. Nader-mania killed off Buick's convertible models – only two were built in 1972, followed by single cars in 1973 and 1974 – electric sunroofs were a poor substitute. Amid myriad model changes that decade, an interesting move was the fitting of a turbocharged V6 in the 1977 Regal, while the 1979 Riviera, with V6 or V8 engines, shared the front-wheel-drive all-independent suspension layout of the Olds Toronado and Cadillac Eldorado.

During the '80s engine sizes

### 1914 BUICK B55

**Engine:** in-line six cylinder, overhead valve
**Bore × stroke:** 95.25 mm × 127 mm
**Capacity:** 5429 cc
**Maximum power:** 33.7 bhp
**Transmission:** three-speed
**Chassis:** pressed steel channel
**Suspension:** non indepdendent with semi-elliptic leaf springs
**Brakes:** rear only
**Bodywork:** five-seater tourer
**Maximum speed (approx):** not known

Buick B55

have been further reduced, ranging between the turbocharged 1.8-litre overhead-cam four-cylinder of the compact Skyhawk to the V6 options of between 2.8 and 4.1 litres for the rest of the range. Today it consists of the Riviera, Century, Skyhawk, Skylark and LeSabre, all with restrained styling and available as sedans or coupés. Top of the range are the 4.1-litre Electra Limited Coupé and Park Avenue Sedan, about which Buick say: 'Traditional full-size luxury is alive and very well, thank you.'

## Buick B55

The first Buick Six, designed by Walter Marr, appeared in 1914. It was the first Buick to weigh over 3000 lb (1361 kg), and rode on a 130 inch (330 cm) wheelbase. To suit the different gauges of rut on rural American road (horse-drawn carriages in the south had the wheels set further apart than in the north), two different track widths were available, 56 inches (142 cm) or 60 inches (152 cm). By the standards of the day, the B55 six-cylinder was an advanced machine, with Delco coil ignition, electric lighting and starting and left-hand drive.

## Buick Six

The 1924 Buicks were distinguished by a Packard-like radiator and the company's first four-wheel brakes. Four- and six-cylinder models were listed: top of the range was the Master Six, whose 'equipment was remarkably complete, including electric lighting and starting, spare set of bulbs, windscreen wiper, rear vision mirror, radiator

### 1924 BUICK SIX

**Engine:** in-line six cylinder, overhead valve
**Bore × stroke:** 89 mm × 120 mm
**Capacity:** 4493 cc
**Maximum power:** 77 bhp
**Transmission:** three-speed manual
**Chassis:** pressed steel channel
**Suspension:** non independent with semi-elliptic leaf springs front and reversed quarter-elliptic leafs springs rear
**Brakes:** four wheel, contracting
**Bodywork:** roadster, saloon or coupé
**Maximum speed (approx):** not known

**Buick Six**

thermometer and all necessary instruments', which puts a suitable period complexion on the definition of luxury equipment. And as if that wasn't enough, the closed Master Sixes had floor heaters as well, and the tool kit included a hydrometer for testing the condition of the batteries.

## Buick Riviera T-type

Buick are nicely positioned in the GM hierarchy between Oldsmobile and Cadillac and make the kind of luxurious middle class sedans that implies. For 1984, however, the division decided to show what it could do in the way of advanced electronic engine control systems, fuel injection and turbocharging. The result was a comprehensive revamp-

ing of the trusty 3.8-litre V6.

The traditional distributor ignition was discarded in favour of a three-coil system feeding voltage direct to the spark plugs. Fuel injection was fitted, along with a turbocharger, to produce 200 bhp and 300 lb ft of torque – impressive totals for a 1980's American engine.

It was fitted to versions of the Regal and Riviera, the Riviera being best known as Buick's top-of-the-line convertible. Given its reputation for minimal torsional rigidity, however, the turbo was only fitted to the T-type coupé with a roof to stiffen proceedings. Buick's T-type range was designed to be more European in feel, ie with stiffer suspensions and far less chrome. Nevertheless the Riviera is still hardly European in feel, although its performance is good for a car weighing a substantial 3600 lb (1633 kg), with

---

### 1984 BUICK RIVIERA T TYPE

**Engine:** V6, overhead valve, turbo
**Bore × stroke:** 96.5 mm × 86.4 mm
**Capacity:** 3785 cc
**Maximum power:** 190 bhp
**Transmission:** four-speed automatic
**Chassis:** perimeter steel frame with cross members
**Suspension:** independent with wishbones and torsion bars front and trailing arms and coil springs rear
**Brakes:** discs front, drums rear, power assisted
**Bodywork:** two-door, four-seater coupé
**Maximum speed (approx):** 117 mph (189 kph)

---

a top speed of 117 mph (188 kph).

The front-wheel drive Riviera is luxuriously appointed by European standards, fitted with air-conditioning, electronic cruise control, six-way power driver's seat, power steering and electric locking. Personal comfort remains a Buick priority, but the body styling remains restrained, little changed during the last five years.

## LA BUIRE
**Lyon, France**
**1902-1930**

Founded in Lyon in 1847, La Societe de L'Horme et de La Buire specialised in the manufacture of railway and tramway rolling stock, as well as road locomotives. Their first cars appeared in 1902, and

**Buick Riviera Coupé**

then a four on Mercedes lines two years later. By 1907 there was a 9500 cc six in the range, which sold at 1200 in chassis form in Britain. Smaller sixes – 16 hp (3619 cc), 24 hp (4786 cc) and 30 hp (6374 cc) – were added for 1909, the complicated range also including five four-cylinder models from 12 hp to 28/35 hp. Wealthy Stockport businessman J. A. Higginson competed in British sprints and hillclimbs with the more powerful La Buires but the marque was not seriously involved in racing.

The 1914 range was notable for its long-stroke engines, and included an 8/10 hp four of 1726 cc to a 24 hp six of 4767 cc (the 4071 cc 20 hp four had bore and stroke measurements of 90 mm × 160 mm). Like so many famous French marques, La Buire went downhill in the 1920s, producing nothing except undistinguished medium-sized four-cylinder models, the only advanced feature of which was the addition of four-wheel brakes in 1922.

## La Buire Type Fraignac

Real success for La Buire was first attained with the Mercedes-like 20 hp four-cylinder Type Fraignac, introduced at the 1904 Paris Salon and named for their most energetic agent, the engineer Fraignac, whose idea it had been. The pair-cast power unit had drop-feed lubrication; the Dubrulle automatic drip-feed unit was 'armed with an oil pump permitting the lubrication to be forced in the moments of

La Buire Type Fraignac

fatigue of the motor'.

The 20 CV Type Fraignac, concluded *La Vie Automobile*, 'didn't claim to overturn the motor industry by bold and dangerous concepts, but, on the contrary, to combine all the processes and all the systems that have been perfectly proved by experience'. Among these was the ability to dismount the gearbox without removing the coachwork. There was also a 30 CV version which had direct drive in third and fourth gears.

# BURNEY
**Maidenhead, England
1930-1933**

The brilliant Sir Dennistoun Burney was the highest paid inventor of World War I. His paravane a was a device used for the destruction of

mines and submarines, and he was said to have received £400,000 from the British government for his work, which, it was estimated had preserved £100,000,000's worth of shipping from enemy action. In the 1920s Burney designed the airship R100, and unveiled his R101 on wheels in 1930.

Super-streamlined, the rear-engined Burney car had independent suspension on all four wheels, but its concept was far in advance of its execution, since the power unit overheated and filled the passenger compartment with fumes. The car was not a commercial success, despite a much-publicised order from the Prince of Wales, and only twelve Burney Streamlines were built between 1930 and 1933, in addition to the original 1929 prototypes, which had been based on a front-wheel-drive Alvis chassis turned back-to-front.

Production Burneys used a variety of engines, including Beverley-Barnes, Lycoming and Armstrong-Siddeley. The design was later acquired by Crossley.

**Burney Streamliner**

# A-Z OF THE CAR

## CADILLAC
**Detroit, USA**
**1902 to date**

This firm started life as the Henry Ford Company, but when Ford resigned after a few months to found the Ford Motor Company and was replaced as chief engineer by Henry Leland, the name of Antoine de la Mothe Cadillac, founder of Detroit in 1701, was adopted instead.

Leland, the 'master of precision', had originally learnt his trade in the arms industry, so believed in rigorous interchangeability of parts, for which Cadillac won the Dewar Trophy in 1908.

Cadillac was absorbed into the new General Motors group in 1909; the firm had recently dropped their original single-cylinder model and was only making four-cylinder cars.

In 1912, Cadillac won a second Dewar Trophy for the first practical automotive electric lighting, starting and ignition system.

The company adopted a one-model policy with the 5150 cc V8 in 1914; Leland and his son Wilfred resigned in 1917 to found the Lincoln Motor Company.

During the 1920s Cadillac produced well-engineered cars of unexciting appearance; mechanical improvements included a dynamically-balanced crankshaft (1924), four wheel brakes (1925), chromium plating and synchromesh gearchange (1928). A LaSalle-based 5.6-litre V8 engine was adopted in the latter year.

The world's first production V16 was announced in January 1930; a total of 3863 of this overhead-valve 7.4-litre luxury car were built up to 1938, when it was replaced by a side-valve V16 (511 of which were built by 1940). A V12 sharing the V8 chassis was listed until 1937; otherwise Cadillac produced only V8s for the next four decades.

Styling chief Harley Earl introduced his bold 'egg-crate' grille on 1941 Cadillacs, while in 1948 he created tailfins, inspired by the P-38 Lightning fighter plane, and started a styling trend that reverberated round the motor industry for almost 20 years....

Cadillac's new 5.4-litre short-stroke V8 appeared in 1949, followed in 1950 by the standardisation of Hydramatic three-speed automatic transmission (previously optional) on the 60 special and 62, and on all Cadillacs – except the 75 – from 1952.

Air conditioning was available in 1953, and the Eldorado limited edition convertible was launched; it was succeeded by the hand-built 1957 Eldorado Brougham, with quadruple headlamps and self-levelling air suspension, of which 904 were made between 1957–60.

Tailfins reached their evolutionary peak on the supremely vulgar 1959 Cadillac range, then faded away until they had almost vanished by 1965.

In 1967 came the razor-edged, front-wheel-drive Cadillac Eldorado, which by 1970 had become the world's biggest production car, with an 8.2-litre V8. US President Richard Nixon presented a 1972 Eldorado to that well-known luxury car enthusiast, Soviet leader Leonid Brezhnev.

Cadillac introduced the 5.7-litre Chevy Nova-based Seville in the wake of the energy crisis to combat European luxury car imports, while 'full-size' Cadillacs had their engine displacement trimmed to 7 litres in 1978 (when Sevilles were first fitted with on-board computers).

A totally new and shorter Eldorado appeared in 1979, with improved handling and the same engine as the Seville (but still retaining front-wheel drive).

The early 1980s saw an ill-starred attempt to produce a variable-displacement Cadillac, with one bank of cylinders disabled by electronically controlled solenoid valve actuation.

The early '80s also saw GM force Cadillac to produce the first four-cylinder Cadillac for many decades, in the form of the Cimarron. That was merely a luxury version of GM's four-cylinder J-car, the brother of the Vauxhall Cavalier in Britain. Although it was improved year by year it was hard to convince anyone it was a real Cadillac. In 1984 Cadillac introduced a new range of front-drive Fleetwoods thus making all the range front-wheel drive.

## Cadillac V8

The V8 Cadillac was developed in great secrecy by a team led by ex-Napier engineer D. McCall White, and, though the V8 De Dion had been an element in its inspiration, the design proved to be one of great originality and refinement. The chassis was exceptionally rigid, and the adoption of coil ignition and electric starting was a distinct advance over contemporary luxury cars.

It was also the first American luxury car to be produced in relatively large numbers (15,000 cars a year) at affordable ($1975-$3600) prices. Cadillac, it was said, 'did for the rich what Ford had done for the poor'.

---

### 1915 CADILLAC V8

**Engine:** V8, side valve
**Bore × stroke:** 79.4 mm × 130 mm
**Capacity:** 5152 cc
**Maximum power:** 70 bhp
**Transmission:** three-speed manual
**Chassis:** carbon steel channel section
**Suspension:** non independent with semi-elliptic leaf springs front and three-quarter elliptic rear
**Brakes:** internal and external drums on rear only
**Bodywork:** choice of seven styles
**Maximum speed (approx):** 72 mph (116 kph)

---

**Cadillac V8**

By 1917, production was already approaching the 50,000 mark, and rival marques were beginning to emulate the Cadillac's V8 power unit. It even impressed W. O. Bentley, then a prominent aero-engine designer: 'A very remarkable machine in many ways . . . one of the most flexible cars in top gear I have ever driven, and astonishingly quiet . . .'

The original Cadillac V8 design survived until 1923, when the new chief engineer, Ernest Seaholm, produced an improved power unit with a balanced crankshaft which eliminated the annoying vibration period that had characterised the earlier V8 at certain speeds.

## Cadillac V16

In January 1930, Seaholm announced his greatest Cadillac, the Model 452, the world's first production V16. Among the outstanding features were hydraulically-operated overhead valves, which made the Model 452 remarkably silent. The range was exclusively bodied by Fleetwood,

and the car acquired an excellent reputation for the ability to cruise fast – 70 mph (113 kph) was a comfortable speed – with a degree of smoothness unmatched by any other American luxury car.

In August 1930, a V12 derived from the V16 was announced, using the chassis of the V8. V12 and V16s were produced until 1937 when they were replaced by a new wide-angle V16 with side valves, built until 1940.

## Cadillac Eldorado Biarritz

There has been an Eldorado in the Cadillac range for decades, usually available in open-top form. Although the spectre of US Federal safety regulations led GM to discontinue such cars in 1976, they were never actually banned, and in the early '80s the open Cadillac made a welcome reappearance as the Biarritz, built on the same separate ladder chassis as the Eldorados and Sevilles – a design that requires little extra body stiffening.

Although huge V8s are a thing of the past, its 4.1-litre V8 makes it one of the largest displacement front-wheel-drive cars. Naturally the emphasis is on luxury with power steering, brakes, windows, seats and roof. A five-seater, the Eldorado can cruise effortlessly all day at freeway speeds.

### 1984 CADILLAC ELDORADO BIARRITZ

**Engine:** V8, overhead valve
**Bore × stroke:** 88 mm × 84 mm
**Capacity:** 4097 cc
**Maximum power:** 135 bhp
**Transmission:** four-speed automatic
**Chassis:** box type ladder frame
**Suspension:** independent with wishbones and torsion bars front and swinging arms and coil springs rear
**Brakes:** discs all round
**Bodywork:** convertible
**Maximum speed (approx):** 102 mph (165 kph)

## CALCOTT
### Coventry, England
### 1913-1926

The classic Calcott was built by a Coventry company which had made its name in the manufacture of cycles and motorcycles. Launched just before the Great War, the Calcott had a shouldered radiator shell almost indistinguishable from the contemporary Standard.

The pre-war Calcott 10 had a power unit of 1460 cc: the post-war 10/15 model launched in 1924 was basically similar, but had a detachable cylinder head. A 12/24 hp model with a 2-litre engine was launched at the 1924 Olympia Show: 'The appearance of the car is

### 1930 CADILLAC 452

**Engine:** V16, overhead valve
**Bore × stroke:** 76.2 mm × 101.6 mm
**Capacity:** 7407 cc
**Maximum power:** 165 bhp
**Transmission:** three-speed manual
**Chassis:** pressed steel channel
**Suspension:** non independent with semi-elliptic leaf springs (underslung at rear)
**Brakes:** drums all round
**Bodywork:** choice of 15 styles
**Maximum speed (approx):** 100 mph (161 kph)

**Cadillac Eldorado Biarritz**

**Cadillac V16**

**Calcott 12/24**

Voiturettes, the Coupe des Voitures Legeres in 1911 and the Coupe de l'Auto in 1912.

Calthorpe fitted White and Poppe power units to their more conventional products: at the 1913 Olympia Show appeared the 1094 cc Calthorpe Minor, a well-made light car that was produced well into the 1920s. It was produced in two- and four-seater variants, often with polished aluminium bodies by Mulliner of Birmingham (whose works were next door to Calthorpe). Hands resigned in 1922 to produced the Hands light car, built in the Calthorpe motorcycle factory; Calthorpe's next model was the 12/20 of 1923, which had the somewhat retrograde feature of a fixed cylinder head.

In 1925 Hands returned to the Calthorpe fold, bringing the design of the 15/45 Hands Six with him. However, the Calthorpe factory closed down in 1927, and was converted into a service centre for Morris cars. Apparently, a few more Calthorpe cars were assembled in the motorcycle works, where the latter were built until 1939.

---

### 1924 CALCOTT 12/24

**Engine:** in-line four cylinder, side valve

**Bore × stroke:** 72 mm × 120 mm

**Capacity:** 1954 cc

**Maximum power:** 24 hp (rated)

**Transmission:** four-speed manual

**Chassis:** pressed steel channel

**Suspension:** non independent with semi-elliptic leaf springs (underslung at rear)

**Brakes:** drums all round

**Bodywork:** three or five-seat tourer or saloon

**Maximum speed (approx):** 55 mph (88 kph)

---

all that can be desired, for a tall radiator allows the bonnet line to blend with that of the scuttle, and thus lends the vehicle a comfortable and snug appearance.

Calcott attempted to break into a new market sector with the 16/50 hp model launched during 1925, but this did not prevent their being taken over by Singer in 1926.

## CALTHORPE

**Birmingham, England 1904-1932**

Bicycle manufacturer G. W. Hands' first Calthorpe car was a shaft-driven 10 hp with a Fafnir four-cylinder engine: by 1906, the model had developed into the 12/14 hp Calthorpe, and a 28/40 costing twice the price was also listed. The 1907 16/20 was a 2.8-litre car driven by Hands in the 1908 Irish Trials: a Calthorpe also came fourth that year in the famous 'Four-Inch' Tourist Trophy in the Isle of Man.

Less successful was the company's entry for the 1909 Coupe des Voiturettes, where two cars with 1775 cc Alpha engines finished 8th and 9th. There were also entries in the 1910 Coupe des

---

### 1920 CALTHORPE MINOR

**Engine:** in-line four cylinder, side valve

**Bore × stroke:** 62 mm × 90 mm

**Capacity:** 1087 cc

**Maximum power:** not known

**Transmission:** three-speed manual

**Chassis:** pressed steel channel

**Suspension:** non independent with semi-elliptic leaf springs

**Brakes:** drums on rear only

**Bodywork:** two or four-seat tourer

**Maximum speed (approx):** 60 mph (97 kph)

---

## CARDEN

**Teddington & Ascot, England 1912-1925**

Carden began production at Teddington with a crude and lethal monocar which combined unstable centre-pivot steering with a rear-mounted motorcycle engine – single or vee-twin power units up to 5 hp were employed.

Post-war, this horrific design was sold to AV and Carden manufacture shifted to Ascot. The Carden reappeared in 1919 as a two-seater with a 707 cc two-stroke flat-twin engine built in unit with the back axle, which it drove direct by gears. King Alfonso of Spain was rash enough to buy one.

In 1923, the marque was updated by its new owners, Arnott & Harrison of Willesden, given the

**Calthorpe Minor**

name New Carden and endowed with slightly more civilised two- and four-seat bodies – 'evokes admiration wherever she goes' – at prices starting from £90: in 1924-25 there was also a £130 three-seat variant sold as the Sheret.

## 1914 CARDEN MONOCAR

**Engine:** vee twin
**Bore × stroke:** 70 mm × 84 mm
**Capacity:** 646 cc
**Maximum power:** 6.1 hp (rated)
**Transmission:** two-speed manual
**Chassis:** wooden planks on edge
**Suspension:** non independent with quarter-elliptic leaf springs
**Brakes:** rear wheel only
**Bodywork:** sports monocar
**Maximum speed (approx):** not known

**Carden Monocar**

# CARTERCAR
**Pontiac, USA**
**1906-1919**

The Cartercar was one of the more successful friction-drive cars, which began life with a flat-twin power unit. In 1908, the original manufacturers, the Motor Car Company, combined with the makers of the Pontiac high-wheeler to form the Cartercar Company, which was absorbed into the newly-formed General Motors group the following year. The twin-cylinder model was still being

offered alongside vertical fours in the 1909 range.

In 1912, there were two models, both pair-cast fours – the 4160 cc Model R and the 5473 cc Model S – with single central chain final drive to the back axle.

The company's progenitor, Byron Carter, came to an unfortunate end in the winter of 1910 when he tried to start a lady's stalled Cadillac car. The car backfired, its crankhandle flying out and breaking Carter's jaw. The injury caused gangrene from which Carter died.

To avoid the recurrence of such tragedies – 'the Cadillac will kill no

## 1909 CARTERCAR

**Engine:** flat twin
**Bore × stroke:** not known
**Capacity:** 3506 cc
**Maximum power:** 24 bhp
**Transmission:** infinitely variable friction drive
**Chassis:** pressed steel channel
**Suspension:** non independent with semi-elliptic leaf springs front and three-quarter elliptic rear
**Brakes:** rear wheel only
**Bodywork:** tourer
**Maximum speed (approx):** not known

more men if we can help it' – Carter's friend Henry Leland fitted Cadillac cars with perhaps the first practical electric starting system.

# CASE
**Racine, USA**
**1910-1927**

One of America's best-known agricultural machinery manufacturers, the J. I. Case Threshing Machine Company took over Pierce-Racine, which had built its first prototype as early as 1894, and launched a three-car range – 25 (3439 cc), 35 (5114 cc) and 40 (5473 cc). The 25 and 35 models were unusual for the period in having left-hand drive.

In 1918, Case offered their first six-cylinder car, the 4957 cc Continental-engined Model U. It was available with Touring Family, All-Seasons Sedan or Sport bodies.

The 1922 Case Model X had a 3958 cc six-cylinder side-valve engine: the contemporary Model Y was a large-bore development displacing 5328 cc: both power units were proprietory units supplied by Continental.

Case's ultimate model was called the Jay-Eye-See, a nomenclature previously used on the firm's racing and sports cars. It had the 3958 cc engine, in conjunction with hydraulic four-wheel brakes.

After 1927 Case gave up car manufacture to concentrate on tractors and agricultural machinery.

The company still prospers, the products bearing the same 'Old Abe' eagle badge as the cars – a 19th century military mascot.

**Cartercar 24 hp**

**Case Jay-Eye-See**

### 1927 CASE JAY-EYE-SEE

**Engine:** in-line six cylinder, side valve
**Bore × stroke:** 85.7 mm × 114.3 mm
**Capacity:** 3958 cc
**Maximum power:** 27.3 hp
**Transmission:** three-speed.
**Chassis:** pressed steel channel
**Suspension:** non independent with semi-elliptic leaf springs
**Brakes:** drums all round
**Bodywork:** tourer, brougham or sedan
**Maximum speed (approx):** not known

**Castle Three**

## CASTLE THREE

Kidderminster, England
1919-1922

The Goodwin Brothers, in order to keep their engineering works busy after World War I, decided to produce a light car that would 'Rolls-Royce the Morgan Three-wheeler.' Their Castle Three prototype used a 1094 cc four-cylinder Dorman engine driving through a patented pedal-operated two-speed epicyclic gearbox.

Production models of the Castle Three used the more powerful 1208 cc Belgian-built Peters engine. A rear disc brake was used on early Castle Threes, but proved insufficiently powerful, so was replaced by a conventional drum.

The prototype Castle Three proved successful in trials and rallies, and over 3300 orders were taken at the Motor Cycle Show. Several hundred Castle Threes were built, but, seeking extra production space, the Goodwins approached a local carpet makers

### 1920 CASTLE THREE

**Engine:** in-line four cylinder, side valve
**Bore × stroke:** 62 mm × 100 mm
**Capacity:** 1208 cc
**Maximum power:** not known
**Transmission:** two-speed epicyclic
**Chassis:** vee-shaped channel steel
**Suspension:** non independent with quarter-elliptic springs front and semi-elliptic rear
**Brakes:** rear wheel only
**Bodywork:** open two-seater
**Maximum speed (approx):** not known

for financial assistance. He guaranteed the loan, then ordered all the remaining cars and parts to be sold for scrap and took over the works to extend his carpet business. . . . A four-wheeler was built in prototype form in the last year of production, and still survives, the only Castle Four.

## CEIRANO

Turin, Italy
1919-1928

The four Ceirano brothers played a crucial role in the foundation of the Turinese automobile industry. Giovanni Ceirano founded the SCAT company before World War I, but resigned to set up the Ceirano company in 1919. Its President was the Count Belli di Carpenea, with Ceirano as chief executive.

Despite spiteful attempts by SCAT to hinder production, Ceirano was a success from the start, since the clientele approved of the return of Giovanni Ceirano to independent manufacture. Moreover, the Ceirano car was a post-war design, unlike the SCAT, basically a 1914 design.

Most Ceiranos had four-cylinder side-valve engines of between 2 and 3 litres: a sporting derivative, the CS appeared in 1922, and there was also a racing model, the CS2 H.

In 1923, Giovanni Ceirano succeeded in acquiring the majority shareholding in SCAT, and there followed a complex financial transaction which ended in Ceirano first merging with SCAT, then being liquidated in December 1924, the trademark passing to SCAT. The latter company launched the SCAT-Ceirano, a 1458 cc light car resembling the Lancia Lambda in 1925. Its coachwork was designed by Candido Viberti, and it was nicknamed Ceiranina. Production ceased in '28 when Fiat took over.

In England, the Ceirano was modified by the importers, Newton & Bennett, and known as the Newton-Ceirano.

**Ceirano 150S**

### 1925 CEIRANO 150S

**Engine:** in-line four cylinder, overhead-valve
**Bore × stroke:** 65 mm × 110 mm
**Capacity:** 1458 cc
**Maximum power:** 35 bhp
**Transmission:** four-speed manual
**Chassis:** pressed steel channel
**Suspension:** non independent with semi-elliptic leaf springs
**Brakes:** drums all round
**Bodywork:** four-seater torpedo
**Maximum speed (approx):** 59 mph (95 kph)

— its boxed steel chassis with all-round independent suspension, its flat-four engine — but few were built before the Caproni company failed. The handful of cars were sold as part of the liquidation.

Surprisingly, the F11 resurfaced in 1953 on the Minerva stand at the Brussels Motor Show as that company made a forlorn attempt to return to car manufacture. In 1960, the basic design of the F11 was produced as the Lancia Flavia.

### 1948 CEMSA

**Engine:** flat four, overhead valve
**Bore × stroke:** 72 mm × 67.5 mm
**Capacity:** 1099 cc
**Maximum power:** 46 bhp
**Transmission:** four-speed manual
**Chassis:** fabricated steel
**Suspension:** independent all round
**Brakes:** drums all round
**Bodywork:** saloon
**Maximum speed (approx):** 75 mph (120 kph)

# CEMSA

**Saronno, Italy**
**1946-1950**

This 1100 cc front-wheel drive saloon was designed by Professor Antonio Fessa to be produced as a joint venture between the Costruzioni Elettromeccaniche SA of Saronno (who built the mechanics) and the Caproni aircraft company of Taliedo (who made the bodywork).

Exhibited at the 1947 Paris Show, the Cemsa Caproni F11 caused a sensation due to its advanced mechanical specification

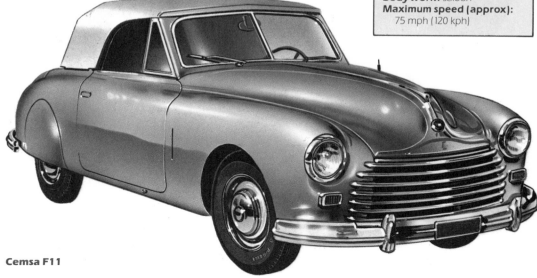

**Cemsa F11**

## MODEL
BMW 328 (1937)
**UK price when announced:** £695

## ENGINE
**Location:** Front, longitudinal
**Type:** Water-cooled in-line six-cylinder with cast-iron block and light-alloy head. Four main bearings
**Cubic capacity:** 1971 cc
**Bore × stroke:** 66 mm × 96 mm
**Compression ratio:** 7.5:1
**Valve gear:** 2 valves per cylinder operating in hemispherical combustion chambers. Inlet valves operated by pushrods and rockers from single block-mounted camshaft. Exhaust valves operated by horizontal pushrods from inlet side
**Fuel supply:** 3 Solex downdraught carburettors
**Ignition:** Mechanical by coil and distributor. Six-volt electrics
**Maximum power:** 80 bhp at 5000 rpm
**Maximum torque:** 93 lb ft (approx) at 4000 rpm

## TRANSMISSION
**Layout:** Gearbox and clutch in unit with engine
**Clutch:** Single dry plate
**Gearbox:** Four-speed manual with synchromesh on top two gears. Gearboxes were supplied by Hirth or ZF and two sets of ratios were available

| | |
|---|---|
| 1st 3.64:1 | 3rd 1.487:1 |
| 2nd 2.05:1 | 4th 1.00:1 |

**Final drive:** Hypoid bevel
**Ratio:** 3.90:1

## SUSPENSION
**Front:** Independent with lower wishbones, transverse semi-elliptic leaf spring and lever-arm dampers
**Rear:** Non independent with live rear axle, semi-elliptic leaf springs and lever arm dampers

## STEERING
**Type:** Rack and pinion

## BRAKES
**Type:** Hydraulically operated drums all round, 11 inches (28 cm) in diameter

## WHEELS AND TYRES
**Type:** Steel disc wheels with peg-drive hubs and 5.25 × 16 in low-pressure tyres

## BODY/CHASSIS
**Type:** Tubular steel chassis with cross members in form of a capital 'A' with the apex to the front. Two-seat, two-door convertible sports body

## DIMENSIONS AND WEIGHT
**Length:** 153.5 in (390 cm)
**Width:** 61 in (155 cm)
**Wheelbase:** 93 in (236 cm)
**Track – front:** 45.5 in (115 cm)
– rear: 48 in (122 cm)
**Weight:** 1638 lb (743 kg)

## PERFORMANCE
**Maximum speed:** 103 mph (166 kph)
**Acceleration 0–60 mph:** 9.5 seconds
**Fuel consumption (approx):** 23 mpg

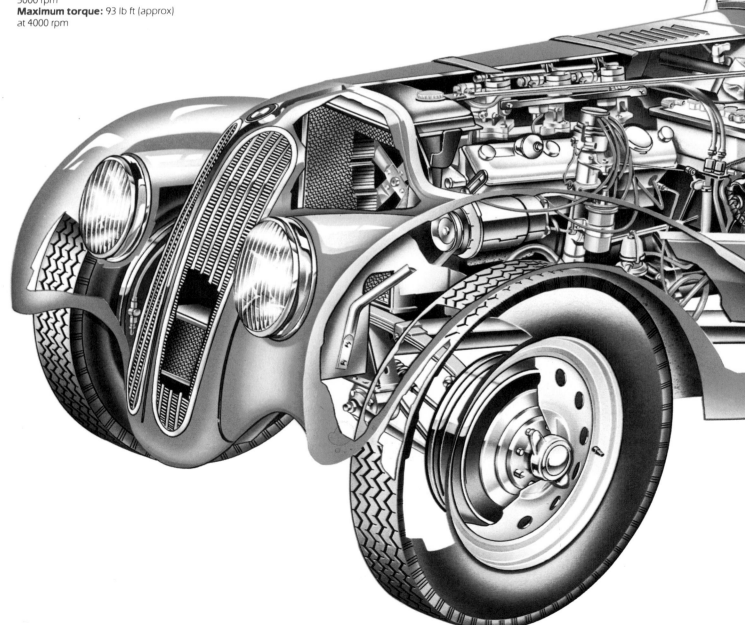

The BMW 328 was one of those rare designs that seemed to be exactly right in every respect, yet there was little completely original in it apart from the stylish semi-streamlined bodywork. Although the front suspension was independent it was a simple system using a transverse semi-elliptic leaf spring. The live axle was also simply located by semi-elliptic leaf springs, but the car still handled extremely well. Its performance matched its handling thanks to the superb straight-six engine which enjoyed the advantages of hemispherical combustion chambers without the need for twin-overhead camshafts. That was made possible by the use of an ingenious cross-over pushrod system (shown right) which was activated by a single block-mounted camshaft

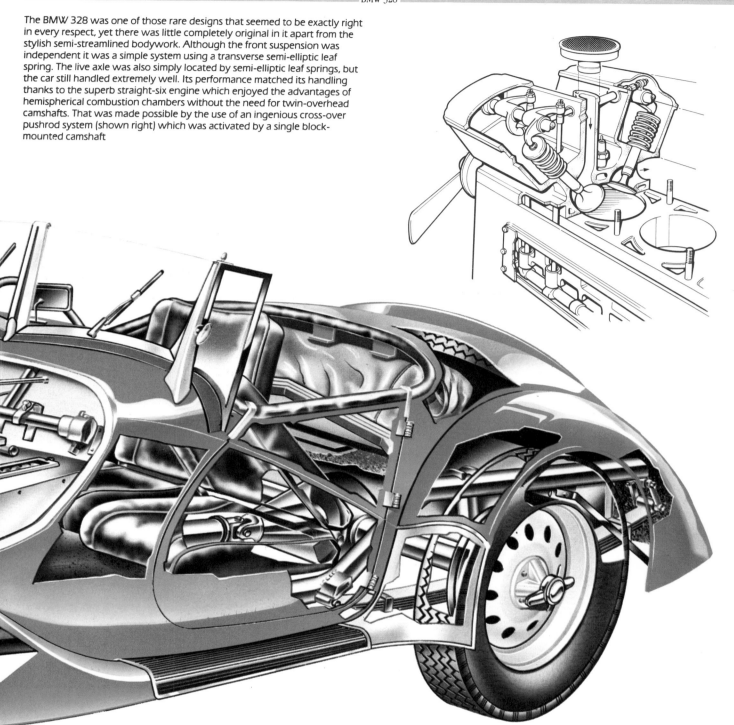

# A-Z
## OF THE CAR

Charron design was notably conservative: a major redesign in 1909 placed the radiator behind the engine, close to the petrol tank. Bigger models retained the flitch-plated wooden chassis and chain final drive.

Fernand Charron left the company in 1912 to establish Alda.

Just before the outbreak of war in 1914, Charron introduced a new 6 hp of 1056 cc, named Charronette.

Charron was one of the few French manufacturers who continued to make cars during the Great War, for the French Army.

## 1909 CHADWICK 60HP

**Engine:** in-line six cylinder T head
**Bore × stroke:** 127 mm × 152.4 mm
**Capacity:** 11,581 cc
**Maximum power:** 60 hp
**Transmission:** four-speed
**Chassis:** pressed steel channel
**Suspension:** non independent with semi-elliptic leaf springs
**Brakes:** rear wheel and transmission
**Bodywork:** runabout
**Maximum speed (approx):** 65 mph (105 kph)

## CGV, CHARRON

**Puteaux, France
1901-1930**

Three famous former racing cylists, Charron, Girardot and Voigt, began production in 1901 with a four-cylinder 3300 cc chain-driven car. In 1903, the partners constructed one of the very first straight-eights in the world, a single-speed 7.2-litre model; at that time, the licence to build CGVs in the USA was sold to Smith and Mabley, later to achieve fame as makers of the Simplex.

As early as 1905, the famous journalist, L. Baudry de Saunier, wrote of the newly-introduced 15CV CGV: 'It's by such carefully-

**Chadwick Great Six**

## 1913 CGV 10 HP

**Engine:** in-line four cylinder, side valve
**Bore × stroke:** 65 mm × 120 mm
**Capacity:** 1593 cc
**Maximum power:** 10 hp (rated)
**Transmission:** three-speed manual
**Chassis:** pressed steel channel
**Suspension:** non independent with semi-elliptic leaf springs
**Brakes:** rear wheel only
**Bodywork:** two-seater or coupé
**Maximum speed (approx):** not known

designed mechanism that the progress of the automobile will henceforth be realised . . . It is in neat attention to detail, executed with "chic", that effort will be apparent. There's no denying that the young CGV marque, whose products I've often admired, is a class leader in this respect.'

Most CGVs were chain driven; it was as late as 1906 that the company's first shaft-drive model appeared. At that time, Leonce Girardot resigned from CGV, whose name was changed into Charron Ltd, the company being re-formed in London, since British company law on limited companies was kinder than French.

Like so many great French marques, Charron went into decline during the 1920s; though they introduced a line-up of seven models in 1919. Most significant of these was the Charronette. This impressive line-up gradually atrophied to three models. In 1925, a new 12/14 hp six of 2770 cc appeared. The Charronette remained in production right to the end; the ultimate Charronette was bodied as a small van which could be quickly and easily converted into a family tourer.

## CHADWICK

**Philadelphia, USA
1905-1916**

Lee Sherman Chadwick's first production model was a pair-cast four. The Chadwick — one of the great sporting marques — originated from Chester, Pennsylvania. Production was transferred to Philadelphia in 1906 and then to Pittsburgh in 1907.

That season, Chadwick introduced their first Great Six; it had a copper-jacketed power unit which boasted 'general simplicity of construction' and its massive engine displaced 11,581 cc.

The 1909 60 hp 'Semi-racer runabout' had stub exhausts fitted with cutouts protruding through

the bonnet sides for 'speeding'.

In 1911, the engine configuration was changed from T-head to F-head, with the overhead inlet valve in the centre of the combustion chamber. Perhaps half a dozen 1908 racing Chadwicks had forced induction by centrifugal supercharger, but this did not find its way into production. Total Chadwick output was just 235.

## CHALMERS

**Detroit, USA
1908–1924**

Hugh Chalmers, who had risen to the post of vice-president of the National Cash Register company before he was 30, was appointed president of the Thomas-Detroit company (which had been founded by E. R. Thomas, Howard Coffin and Roy Chapin in 1906) in June 1908. His salary was the then fabulous sum of $50,000 per annum.

Apart from changing the company's name, Chalmers launched a new F-head 30 hp model on European lines. It was joined — briefly — by a 20 hp in 1909, but the design for the latter car was ceded to the Hudson Motor Car Company, newly formed by Roy Chapin.

In 1911 the Detroit part of the

**CGV 10 hp**

**Chalmers Six**

### 1914 CHALMERS SIX

**Engine:** in-line six cylinder, side valve

**Bore × stroke:** 101.6 mm × 139.7 mm

**Capacity:** 6974 cc

**Maximum power:** 38.4 bhp

**Transmission:** four-speed manual

**Chassis:** pressed steel channel

**Suspension:** non independent with semi-elliptic leaf springs front and three-quarter elliptic rear

**Brakes:** rear wheel, expanding and contracting

**Bodywork:** roadster, tourer, coupé or limousine

**Maximum speed (approx):** not known

---

name was dropped, and cars and company became known as plain Chalmers. A 36 hp four was launched in 1912.

It was joined in 1913 by the Chalmers Six, a bi-block 38 hp with electric lighting and starting.

A new chief engineer, C. C. Hinkley, produced the six-cylinder overhead camshaft 6/40 hp Model 32 in 1915; it replaced the four-cylinder 4/36. The similar, but slightly smaller, 6/30 was launched in 1916. That year, Chalmers recorded their all-time best year, with 21,000 cars leaving the works.

Output plummeted to 12,000 cars in 1917, and Chalmers was taken over by Maxwell (which was

now run by Walter Chrysler). By 1921, Chalmers had become a wholly-owned subsidiary of Maxwell. Hydraulic band brakes on all four wheels were added for 1924 – then in January of that year, the Chalmers marque was ousted by the new Chrysler four designed by Fred Zeder, Owen Skilton and Carl Breer.

## CHANDLER

**Cleveland, USA**
**1913–1929**

'The Marvelous Motor' was one of the better American independent makes, which, for most of its production span, used a 4736 cc bi-block six; unusually for such a

relatively small company, this was of Chandler's own make. From 1923, Chandler fitted an easy-change constant-mesh 'Traffic Transmission' to this model.

By 1925, *The Autocar* was remarking that 'the engine is large as engines go nowadays', though the magazine had earlier commented on the car's outstanding hill-climbing performance allied to smoothness and silence equivalent to much more expensive vehicles.

Chandler already had another string to their bow in the 3529 cc Cleveland Six, which they built between 1919 and 1926, but widened their normal model range in 1927 with the monobloc Standard Six of 2954 cc. Two straight-eight models were offered the following year, but as sales fell the company was absorbed by Hupmobile in 1929 and Chandler production came to an end.

## CHARRON-LAYCOCK

**Sheffield, England**
**1920–1926**

Charron Ltd had been formed in 1906 by the financier Davison Dalziel to buy out CGV; after the Great War, Dalziel predicted that Britain would not return to free trade in cars so, in order to protect his British market, he acquired a controlling interest in the railway equipment manufacturer W. S. Laycock of Sheffield, and began to produce a 1460 cc four-cylinder car of British design called the Charron-Laycock.

This 10/25 model was, claimed its makers, the result of 'meticulous care in the translation of a design only reached through long and patient research'; inevitably, that also meant that it was disproportionately expensive. The 1922 prices ranged from £525 for the two-seater to £625 for the coupé. Though the marque boasted of its 'gratified owners', there were not sufficient of these to prevent the firm from closing down in 1926.

### 1925 CHANDLER SIX

**Engine:** in-line six cylinder, side valve

**Bore × stroke:** 89 mm × 127 mm

**Capacity:** 4736 cc

**Maximum power:** 30 hp (rated)

**Transmission:** three-speed manual

**Chassis:** pressed steel channel

**Suspension:** non independent with semi-elliptic leaf springs front and rear

**Brakes:** four-wheel, contracting band

**Bodywork:** sports, brougham, saloon or Imperial saloon

**Maximum speed (approx):** not known

**Chandler Six**

**Charron-Laycock 10/25**

1965, with the adoption of Chevrolet's 3769 cc six. V8s of 4.6 and 5.3 litres were also offered.

In 1970, Ghia of Turin designed a more up-to-date prototype Checker which had failed to reach production by the time the decision was taken to end production 12 years later: indeed, the last Checkers still used the uncompromising 1956 bodyshell, though the standard power unit was now the 4097 cc Chevrolet six.

## 1924 CHARRON-LAYCOCK 10/25

**Engine:** in-line four cylinder, side valve
**Bore × stroke:** 69 mm × 100 mm
**Capacity:** 1496 cc
**Maximum power:** 25 bhp
**Transmission:** three-speed manual
**Chassis:** pressed steel channel
**Suspension:** non independent with semi-elliptic leaf springs
**Brakes:** rear wheel only
**Bodywork:** two-seater or four-seater, coupé
**Maximum speed (approx):** not known

# CHECKER

**Kalamazoo, USA**
**1923–1982**

Checker produced nothing but taxicabs until 1948, when their first 'pleasure car' was introduced, though as it was closely based on the standard cab, the 'pleasure' can only have been relative. Like the immediately pre-war models, the post-war Checkers were powered by a sidevalve 3704 cc Continental six until 1965.

The totally new 1956 A8 had a slab-sided modern appearance which was strictly utilitarian; however, a sign of more committed modernity was that independent front suspension replaced the old beam axle. Yet more progress was made in 1958, when an overhead-valve six was offered on the new 12-seater A9 'Airport Limousine' on a 189-inch wheelbase.

In 1960, Checker unexpectedly produced the Superba, their first model seriously intended for general public sale, available as sedan or station wagon.

Checker attempted to move upmarket – a relative term when talking of this proletarian marque – with the 1963 Town Custom Limousine which had optional air-conditioning and centre division.

Upstairs valves were standardised across the range in

## 1980 CHECKER

**Engine:** in-line six cylinder, overhead valve
**Bore × stroke:** 98.2 mm × 89.6 mm
**Capacity:** 4097 cc
**Maximum power:** 110 bhp
**Transmission:** three-speed automatic Turbo-Hydramatic
**Chassis:** box-type ladder frame
**Suspension:** independent front with wishbones and coil springs. Live rear axle with semi-elliptic leaf springs
**Brakes:** discs front, drums rear
**Bodywork:** sedan
**Maximum speed (approx):** 90 mph (145 kph)

**Checker Marathon**

# A-Z
## OF THE CAR

## CHENARD & WALCKER

**Asnieres/Gennevilliers, France**
**1901–1946**

Ernest Chenard began making bicycles in 1888, and was joined by young Henry Walcker at the end of the 1890s. The partners began by making tricycles and built their first car in 1900: it was unsuccessful, so they tried again in 1901 with a more modern design which won a fuel consumption contest.

By the end of 1902, they were building a 10 hp and a 14 hp, the latter with the transmission that would become a characteristic of the marque, with the rear hubs carried on a dead beam axle and independent drive shafts transmitting the power to internally-toothed drums on the wheels.

Annual production was soon in the region of 400 cars, then in 1906 the company was reformed as the Société Anonyme des Anciens Etablissements Chenard et Walcker and moved to new premises in Gennevilliers, where a popular single-cylinder voiturette was launched later that year.

In 1908, Chenard & Walcker launched a 14/16 CV of 3020 cc and a 30/40 CV of 5881 cc, and, in order to weather the slump, established a taxicab and car rental agency, the Comptoir Automobile, which ordered several hundred Chenard & Walcker taxicabs to boost production at Gennevilliers.

In 1912, the year that Walcker died, the range consisted of five models, from 7/9 CV (1592 cc) to 20 CV (5881 cc). The following year, a new six-cylinder 20 CV of 4523 cc was added to the line-up.

After the war, Chenard & Walcker quickly resumed production with a 3015 cc 14 CV, which remained in production for

several years; this was followed in 1920 by a 2650 cc 12 CV and in 1921 by a 10 CV model.

In 1922 Chenard & Walcker launched their famous 2978 cc 3-litre, as well as an overhead-camshaft 2-litre, which won the very first Le Mans 24 Hours race in 1923 at over 57 mph (92 kph), driven by Lagache and Leonard,

A 22 hp straight-eight of 3945 cc was introduced in 1924, in which year Chenard & Walcker absorbed the Senechal company.

One of the most famous vintage Chenard & Walcker models appeared in 1925 in the shape of the 1095 cc four-cylinder sports car with streamlined 'tank' bodywork.

Chenard & Walcker followed this technically-advanced model with some mediocre cars of 1286 cc and 1495 cc.

In 1934 came a 20 CV V8, available with odd aerodynamic coachwork; 1935 models were offered with Cotal electric gearboxes, and there was a front-wheel-drive 14 CV.

By the end of the 1930s, Chenard & Walcker were struggling desperately to survive, producing front-wheel-drive Aigles with Citroën four-cylinder or Ford V8 engines, and Matford bodywork. They also offered rear-wheel-driven cars with – bizarrely – 11 CV Citroën Traction Avant power units. Chenard & Walcker was taken over by Peugeot in 1946, and for the next few years produced forward-control light vans.

## Chenard & Walcker Tank

Toutée, who later went to Aries, designed the original Chenard & Walcker 'Tank' of 1925, which was inspired by the marque's 1923 victory at Le Mans and the wish to succeed in a smaller engine category. The engine was of curious design, with very large inlet valves and very small exhaust valves supplemented by auxiliary exhaust ports opened by a rotary valve turning at quarter engine speed. Oversize brakes were a tribute to the speed potential of this car; in racing trim, it was capable of attaining

150 kph (94 mph) unsupercharged and 170 kph (106 mph) supercharged.

The first outing for the Tanks was at the 1925 Le Mans, where they finished 10th and 13th overall, winning the Biennial and Triennial Cups.

The Tanks were still competitive over a decade later, for Rigoulot won the Bol d'Or in one in 1937 but that was a cheaply gained victory of little merit.

In production form, the Tank two-seater sold in Britain at £245, and there was also an aerodynamic coupé, costing £345.

**1928 Chenard & Walcker Tank**

### 1928 CHENARD & WALCKER TANK

**Engine:** in-line four cylinder, F head
**Bore × stroke:** 69 mm × 100 mm
**Capacity:** 1496 cc
**Maximum power:** 12 hp (rated)
**Transmission:** four-speed manual
**Chassis:** pressed steel channel
**Suspension:** non independent with semi-elliptic leaf springs
**Brakes:** drums all round
**Bodywork:** aerodynamic two seater and coupé
**Maximum speed (approx):** 75 mph (120 kph)

## CHEVROLET

**Detroit, USA**
**1911–**

Racing driver Louis Chevrolet joined with Billy Durant, who had recently lost control of his General Motors group, to produce four- and six-cylinder prototypes designed by Etienne Planche in a Detroit garage. The six was adopted for production, and was launched in 1912, when 2999 units were sold.

In 1913, manufacture was transferred to Flint, Michigan, where Chevrolet's sister marque, the Little Four, had recently started production; Louis Chevrolet resigned as a result of this tie-up with Little later that year. The Little was phased out in 1915, but a

similar design persisted in the shape of the new Model H Chevrolet, which had an overhead-valve 2.4-litre four-cylinder Mason engine.

By that time, Chevrolet had become so successful that Durant was able to exchange its shares for those of GM (which had become moribund since his departure) and regain control of the group.

The next major step forward for the marque was the launch in 1915 of the Chevrolet 490 (it cost $490), which put Chevrolet in head-on confrontation with Ford; sales instantly soared from 13,600 to 70,701 in 1917, and by 1920 had

reached 150,226.

Late that year, a financial crisis forced Durant out of GM for a second – and final – time, the group being rescued by the money of the Du Pont family. The conscious decision was taken to challenge Ford head-on, and the 1923 Superior, which followed the 490, offered better equipment than Ford at a slightly higher price; the result was that 480,737 Superiors were sold in its first year. On the debit side, the 1923 'copper-cooled' Chevrolet was an unmitigated disaster; only 100 of the 759 cars produced ever reached the public, and most of those were recalled and destroyed.

In 1927, the year in which Ford's Model T ceased production, Chevrolet became America's best-selling marque; the company produced over a million cars for the first time. Chevrolet made sure it hung on to the newly-won sales lead by introducing the overhead-valve 3.2-litre International Six, in 1928.

While Ford regained the lead in 1929–30, Chevrolet re-established leadership in 1931, since when it has taken 'No. 1' position in the US sales league virtually uninterrupted ever since.

Chevrolet introduced its Master and Standard ranges in 1933; they were endowed with 'knee-action' independent front suspension from 1934 (though a solid beam front axle was still available for the unadventurous).

The range was extensively redesigned in 1937, and the 3.5-litre Blue Flame six made its debut.

Post-war plans to build a new Chevrolet light car were shelved at a fairly advanced stage, and the pre-war designs had to soldier on until 1949, when the Special and the De Luxe model lines were introduced. Under their new styling, the 1949 Chevrolets were still powered by the old 'stove bolt six' dating back to 1929.

In 1950 Chevrolet became the first low-priced marque to be offered with a fully-automatic transmission, the two-speed Powerglide; some 300,000 of the record 1950 Chevrolet sales of 2.1 million cars being automatics.

A totally new trend was started by the 1953 Corvette sports car, with its two-seater glassfibre body and 3.8-litre Blue Flame six; Powerglide automatic transmission was fitted.

New from the ground up, the 1955 Chevrolets were equipped with the marque's first V8 engine since 1919. Fitted with fuel injection, the 1957 version of the 4637 cc V8 became America's first production engine to develop 1 hp/cu in.

Chevrolet sales slumped that year in the face of restyled Plymouth and Ford ranges, but all-new cars in 1958 – five different series were available – put Chevrolet back on top again.

In line with other divisions of GM, Chevrolet offered all-new bodies and frames for 1959, featuring a 'gullwing' rear deck with huge peardrop-shaped tail-lights, but this dramatic styling was toned down at the end of the year.

Chevrolet's first unit-construction model, the compact Corvair, powered by a rear-mounted 2294 cc flat-six, and with all round independent suspension, was a 1960 model, with sales of over 250,000 in the first year. Ultimately, however, condemned as 'unsafe at any speed' by consumers' champion Ralph Nader, the Corvair was dropped in 1969.

A totally new economy line, the Chevy II, appeared in 1962; it had 2507 cc four-cylinder or 3179 cc six-cylinder power units. A new 6702 cc V8 was listed, and the new Monza Spyder performance version of the Corvair boasted a turbo.

In 1963 the Corvette was transformed into the Corvette Sting Ray; and in 1967 came the Camaro, Chevrolet's belated response to the Ford Mustang, with 3769 cc six-cylinder or 5359 cc V8 power.

The 1971 'sub-compact' Vega, with all-aluminium overhead-camshaft four, led to the 1975 Monza 2+2 hatchback.

The 1971 Chevette rapidly became a best-seller; overseas GM subsidiaries had unique versions of this overhead-camshaft 1393 cc small car.

The Vega, which in 1974 had even featured a twin-cam Cosworth four, was killed off in '77.

The Corvette and Camaro carried their 1968 styling into 1979 – except for a new Camaro Berlinetta, with a six or two V8s available.

In April 1979, Chevrolet unveiled the 1980 Citation X-car, with a transverse four-cylinder power unit driving the front wheels.

Noteworthy among Chevrolet's 1984 product offerings was the Celebrity Eurosport, with uprated suspension and a 'European flavour', while the Camaro Berlinetta gained an electronic instrument panel 'that would make an astronaut feel at home'.

## 1912 Chevrolet

In 1910, Billy Durant, having lost control of General Motors, employed Louis Chevrolet (the French-Swiss racing driver whom he had brought into Buick two years earlier) in a small garage on Grand River Avenue, Detroit, to develop a new car to be marketed under the Chevrolet name.

Design was by a brilliant and under-rated French engineer, Etienne Planche. Designs for both four- and six-cylinder cars were prepared, but it was the six which went into production when the Chevrolet company was organised in November 1911. The Chevrolet Classic Six was a large and expensive car with a 4.9-litre T-head engine, but sales of 2999 in the first year were distinctly encouraging.

However, when Louis Chevrolet felt that Durant's future plans for Chevrolet would cheapen the marque's image, he resigned to found his own company, first to design and build racing cars, then to make tuning equipment. Having lost all his money during the Depression, Louis rejoined the Chevrolet company as a mechanic.

**1912 Chevrolet Six**

### 1912 CHEVROLET SIX

**Engine:** in-line six cylinder T head
**Bore × stroke:** not known
**Capacity:** 4900 cc
**Maximum power:** 50 bhp
**Transmission:** three-speed manual
**Chassis:** pressed steel channel
**Suspension:** non independent with semi-elliptic leaf springs
**Brakes:** rear wheel only
**Bodywork:** five-seater tourer
**Maximum speed (approx):** not known

## Chevrolet Master Six

The Master Six line first appeared in 1933, the result of major restyling by Harley Earl and his staff which dramatically updated the car's appearance. Dubonnet 'knee-action' independent front suspension appeared in 1934.

In 1937, the Blue Flame power unit was redeveloped to produce 85 bhp: it was one of these power units, installed in a 1939 master 85 coupé, which powered 29-year-old Juan Manuel Fangio to his first major victory, in the 5900 mile (9500 km) road race from Buenos Aires to Lima, Peru and back, in 1940, at an average speed of 53.6 mph (86.3 kph).

### 1933 CHEVROLET MASTER SIX

**Engine:** in-line six cylinder, overhead valve
**Bore × stroke:** 88.9 mm × 95.25 mm
**Capacity:** 3548 cc
**Maximum power:** 80 bhp
**Transmission:** three-speed manual
**Chassis:** X-braced steel ladder frame
**Suspension:** independent front with 'knee action'. Live rear axle with semi-elliptic leaf springs
**Brakes:** drums all round, hydraulically operated
**Bodywork:** 'turret top' saloon or coupé
**Maximum speed (approx):** 80 mph (129 kph)

**1935 Chevrolet Master Six**

# Chevrolet Corvette

'America's only true sports car' first appeared in 1953, with a 160 bhp version of the six-cylinder engine. Remarkably, its swoopy glassfibre bodywork remained essentially the same in concept for three decades, though of course the car became increasingly powerful. It was developed, by Chevrolet chief engineer Ed Cole and Zora Arkus-Duntov, into an outstanding muscle car, and even survived the energy crisis with only the loss of a couple of litres of displacement – from 7.4 litres to 5.7 litres – to show for it.

There were rumours in 1974 that a Wankel-engined version was going into production, but this remained a prototype only.

By the early 1980s, the Corvette was really beginning to show its age, so, after a 'Collector's Edition' 'Vette had signalled the end of an era in the 1982 model line, there was a 12-month hiatus before an all-new Corvette appeared as a 1984 model.

While the glass-fibre body of the new 'Vette bore a family resemblance to its predecessor, underneath the car was all new, with an ingenious 'backbone drivetrain' in which engine and transmission were rigidly attached to the differential by an aluminium C-section beam. Other advanced features were graphite springs and outstanding roadholding due, in large part, to specially-developed Goodyear tyres which were not only a different size on front and rear wheels, but also 'handed' for the left and right sides of the car.

# CHIRIBIRI

**Turin, Italy**
**1914–1929**

Antonio Chiribiri was a Venetian engineer who, after working with Florentia, Züst and Isotta-Fraschini, established his own factory in Turin to manufacture aeroengines. Around 1914, Count Gustavo Brunetta d'Usseaux commissioned the production of an 8/10 hp voiturette called the Siva, after the Hindu supreme deity. About 100 were built before economic problems caused the count to withdraw from the venture; the Chiribiri II of 1915 was only a slightly modified Siva.

At the 1919 Paris Salon, Chiribiri exhibited a new 12 hp model which in 1922 became known as the Roma 5000 to cash in on the anniversary of the founding of that city.

Three double-overhead-cam 1.5-litre racing Chiribiris on GP Fiat lines were built in 1922, and enjoyed some success in local competitions over the next few seasons. Among the works drivers were Englishman Jack Scales, Chiribiri's son Deo and a young racing motorcyclist called Tazio Nuvolari, who was just making the transition to four wheels, and enjoyed his first competition successes with Chiribiri. The racing Chiribiri provided the basis for the Tipo Monza (*la piccola aristocrata*) of 1923, developed into the Monza Tipo Spinto in 1925; there was also a supercharged version capable of 112 mph (180 kph), known as the Chiribiri Monza Corsa.

Chiribiri was reformed in 1925, but this reorganisation failed to stave off the incipient financial crisis for long, and production ceased in 1927. In 1928, Chiribiri went into liquidation and the works were acquired by Lancia.

## 1923 CHIRIBIRI MONZA

**Engine:** in-line six cylinder, twin cam
**Bore × stroke:** 65 mm × 112 mm
**Capacity:** 1486 cc
**Maximum power:** 45 bhp
**Transmission:** four-speed manual
**Chassis:** pressed steel channel
**Suspension:** non independent with semi-elliptic leaf springs
**Brakes:** drums all round
**Bodywork:** sports tourer
**Maximum speed (approx):** 75 mph (120 kph)

## 1984 CHEVROLET CORVETTE

**Engine:** V8, overhead valve
**Bore × stroke:** 101.6 mm × 88.4 mm
**Capacity:** 5736 cc
**Maximum power:** 205 bhp
**Transmission:** four-speed overdrive
**Chassis:** perimeter steel frame
**Suspension:** independent with coils and wishbones front and four trailing arms, track rods and transverse leaf spring rear. Anti-roll bars back and front
**Brakes:** discs all round
**Bodywork:** glassfibre two-seater sports coupé
**Maximum speed (approx):** 124 mph (198 kph)

**1923 Chiribiri Monza**

**1984 Chevrolet Corvette**

# CHRISTIE

**New York, USA**
**1904–1910**

Though his output was small and spasmodic, John Walter Christie is significant in motoring history as having pioneered the transverse engine front-wheel-drive layout more than 50 years before the Mini popularised it.

Christie first came to public notice in January 1904 with a racer which had a transverse four-cylinder power unit whose crankshaft took the place of a front axle. A subsequent racing car was built for the 1907 French Grand Prix; it was the biggest-engined car ever to run in a Grand Prix, but retired with a jammed exhaust valve.

Standardisation was not a fault that Mr Christie could ever have

**1906 Christie Grand Prix**

### 1907 CHRISTIE GRAND PRIX

**Engine:** V4 transversely
  mounted
**Bore × stroke:** 185 mm ×
  185 mm
**Capacity:** 19,981 cc
**Maximum power:** 135 bhp
**Transmission:** two-speed
  manual
**Chassis:** fabricated steel
**Suspension:** non independent
  with coil springs front and
  beam rear axle with semi-
  elliptic leaf springs
**Brakes:** rear wheel only
**Bodywork:** two-seater open
  racer
**Maximum speed (approx):**
  120 mph (193 kph)

been accused of, and though he
built very few road cars, all were
different from one another.

Christie built two or three
touring cars in 1905 – one of them
a handsome 50 hp touring car
bodied by Healey – and in 1909
built a transverse-engined taxicab.

In 1911 Christie turned to the
production of front-wheel-drive
tractor conversions for horsedrawn
fire engines, and later
manufactured high-speed tanks.

# CHRYSLER

**Detroit, USA**
**1924–**

Walter Chrysler, having previously
worked for Buick and Willys, took
over Maxwell-Chalmers in 1923,
and commissioned his three brilliant
engineers – Breer, Skelton and
Zeder – to create a car worthy of

carrying the name Chrysler. The
resulting Chrysler 75 was an
instant success and orders worth
$50 million were taken in the first
twelve months. A Chrysler four
appeared in 1925 to replace the old
Maxwell marque, and a luxury
Chrysler Imperial Six was added to
the line-up.

Chrysler expanded rapidly: in
1928 the De Soto and Plymouth
marques were created and Dodge
was taken over. The company set a
styling trend in 1929 with the
widely-copied 'ribbon' radiator
shell.

The 1931 Chryslers had a
radiator like that of the Cord L29;
two new straight-eights – the 3.9-
litre 29-80 hp and the 6.3-litre
Imperial 40-125 hp – were
announced. Chrysler enhanced
their reputation for innovation with
the 1932 models, which had
automatic clutches and freewheels.
Synchromesh came in 1933,
followed in 1934 by automatic
overdrive.

The 1934 Airflow attempted to
popularise streamline design, but
was a commercial failure and only
survived until 1937. Some of the
Airflow's advanced features were
used on conventional Chryslers,
which had weathered the Airflow's

problems to move Chrysler into
second place in the American
market. There was a radical facelift
for 1942 models, which had full-
width wraparound grilles; the
limited-production Town and
Country had external wood
framing.

The three 1946 Chrysler series –
the C38 side-valve six, and the
straight-eight C39 and C40
Imperial – differed only in grilles
and trim from the prewar models.
The Town and Country was
reintroduced, and standard
transmission was Chrysler's 1938-
introduced clutchless FluiDrive.

Chrysler's 1949 Silver Jubilee
was celebrated with new models,
while in 1951 the marque
introduced its first V8. This was the
famous 5424 cc overhead-valve
'Hemi', which appeared in the New
Yorker, Saratoga and Imperial
series; it also powered Briggs
Cunningham's racers.

PowerFlite – Chrysler's first fully
automatic transmission – and
AirTemp recirculating air-
conditioning appeared in 1953
models, which had been restyled
with a curved one-piece
windscreen.

Virgil Exner's 'Flight Sweep'
styling of the 1955 models revived
flagging sales, and two series –
Windsor and New Yorker, both
powered by the hemi V8 – were
offered.

The limited edition 300 series
was based on the New Yorker,
which was said to be America's
fastest and most powerful stock
production car. In 1956 a Chrysler
300B established a world
passenger car speed record of
139.9 mph (225 kph).

The most flamboyant tailfins
were seen on 1957 models, which

were equipped with TorqueFlite
pushbutton automatic
transmission. The hemi was
replaced in 1959 by new wedge-
head power units of 6276 cc and
6768 cc, while 1960 saw the
introduction of new unitary bodies.
That year, too, a Chrysler 300C set
a new stock car speed record of
176.6 mph (283.4 kph).

The slab-sided look of 1965
models persisted until 1969, when
bulbous 'fuselage styling', with
narrow curved windows appeared.

In 1971, the Imperial ceased to
be regarded as a separate marque,
and flagging sales caused the end
of this luxury car line in 1975,
although it was reintroduced for a
few years after the energy crisis.

Aimed at the 'personal luxury'
market, the 1975 Cordoba was the
smallest Chrysler for many years; in
1978, it was equipped with a new
5211 cc 'Lean Burn' engine and a
power sunroof.

In 1978, too, the LeBaron model
name, dating back well before the
war, was revived for a luxury
compact line; optional power units
were a 3687 cc six or V8s of
5211 cc and 5899 cc.

For 1979, the New Yorker/
Newport series was lightened by
790 lb (360 kg) and gained
electronic spark control instead of
Lean Burn, plus an electronic
feedback carburettor and catalytic
convertor to reduce emissions.

That year, Chrysler lost over a
billion dollars, and was teetering on
the edge of financial disaster; it had
to be bailed out by the US
Government and its troublesome
European subsidiaries in Britain and
France were swallowed by the
Peugeot Citroën Group – which
was to find them almost
indigestible....

**1924 Chrysler 65 Roadster**

The slimmed-down Chrysler Corporation launched a new front-wheel-driven K-car line for 1981, initially only available in Plymouth and Dodge guise, but subsequently appearing as the Chrysler LeBaron (the old LeBaron line was taking over the role played by Chrysler's discontinued 'full-size' models).

Also for 1981, Chrysler revived the Imperial, though in only one model – a two-door 5211 cc V8 – with one option – a sunroof.

Chrysler production was 25 per cent down in 1982 compared with the year before, but the corporation led a return to convertible production with the Chrysler LeBaron and Dodge 400, which attracted considerable demand; the 1983 E-Class Chryslers were a larger, more luxurious derivative of the successful K-car line. Chrysler also announced that they would be moving into the sporty end of the market with an association with Carroll Shelby, and the signs that their new image was reviving the corporation's fortunes came when Chrysler not only reported its return to profitability in 1983, but actually paid off the huge Government loan ahead of time.

The company's continuing interest in performance cars was seen by the launch for 1984 of the Laser hatchback sports coupé with a 2.2-litre power unit, available either naturally-aspirated or with a turbocharger.

## Chrysler Six

The six-cylinder power unit of the 1924 Chrysler took advantage of wartime developments in engine design, and incorporated a high-compression Ricardo-type head; to match this 70 mph (113 kph) power unit, the Chrysler Six had four-wheel hydraulic brakes – though they had the disadvantage of being the external-contracting pattern.

A special exhibit of a prototype Chrysler in the lobby of the Hotel Commodore in New York at the time of the 1924 New York Motor Show attracted sufficient financial backing for Chrysler to go into full

production with the new model. At a basic price of $1565, the Chrysler Six was outstanding value for money, and in the first 12 months, nearly 32,000 Chryslers were sold, generating $50 million worth of business and creating an industry sales record for a new car.

The Six was good enough to go to Le Mans and finish a fine third and fourth in 1928.

---

### 1924 CHRYSLER SIX

**Engine:** in-line six cylinder, side valve
**Bore × stroke:** 76 mm × 121 mm
**Capacity:** 3293 cc
**Maximum power:** 75 bhp
**Transmission:** three-speed manual
**Chassis:** pressed steel channel
**Suspension:** non independent with semi-elliptic leaf springs
**Brakes:** contracting type all round, hydraulically operated
**Bodywork:** roadster, tourer or sedan
**Maximum speed (approx):** 70 mph (113 kph)

---

## Chrysler Airflow

When the Great Depression was at its worst, Walter Chrysler proposed closing down the company's research department as an economy measure. Engineer Harold Hicks, who had come to Chrysler from Ford, where they were already experimenting with scale model cars in wind tunnels to study the behaviour of the airflow, produced the results of tests he had carried out which proved that modifying the bodywork of a car to give a smoother airflow could raise its top speed from 83 to 98 mph (134 to 158 kph) *and* cut fuel consumption.

'Well,' said Chrysler, 'if that's what research will do, we must always have research!'

This interest in wind tunnel work led Carl Breer to the conclusion that the average car of the 1930s was more efficient aerodynamically going backwards; so he set out to design a car which put that principle into practice.

The result was the controversial Airflow range launched in 1934, which had a wide, fully-streamlined body mounted on a frame of steel

tubing welded to the chassis members, with its engine mounted well forward over the front axle, putting 55 per cent of the weight on the front axle. Long springs gave a 'floating' ride.

Unfortunately the Airflow proved to be a trend-setter that was running too far ahead of the pack. The industry liked many of its advanced features, many of which began to creep into use on rival marques, but the streamlined totality was too much for the public to take.

So, instead of the 'waterfall' front end, a dummy vee-bonnet was fitted to the 1936 models, but sales continued to be disappointing, and the Airflow was discontinued after 1937.

The British Singer company, who had attempted to market a similarly styled Airstream range, found customer resistance just as strong. But Chrysler's conventional models, many of which were identical in styling to the Airflow from the scuttle back, continued to sell very strongly.

---

### 1934 CHRYSLER AIRFLOW

**Engine:** in-line six cylinder, side valve
**Bore × stroke:** 85.7 mm × 114.3 mm
**Capacity:** 3956 cc
**Maximum power:** 87 bhp
**Transmission:** three-speed manual with overdrive
**Chassis:** pressed steel channel with integral tubular body frame
**Suspension:** non independent with semi-elliptic leaf springs
**Brakes:** drums all round
**Bodywork:** streamlined saloon
**Maximum speed (approx):** 90 mph (145 kph)

---

**1935 Chrysler Airflow**

# A-Z
## OF THE CAR

Cisitalia 202

## Chrysler Laser/ Daytona

In the early 1980s Chrysler had emerged from the doldrums and were profitable enough to think of producing sports cars, reviving the old Charger name but now with a 2.2-litre four instead of the powerful V8s of a few years ago. The Charger 2.2 was an obvious development of the K-car sedans that rescued Chrysler, but although the '84 Daytona/Laser (different names but essentially the same car) were visually similar to the Charger they were claimed to be completely new designs. Like all of Chrysler's current range they are front-wheel drive and still share a good number of the K-car's parts, like the 2.2-litre overhead-cam four.

That engine is fast becoming as respected in North America as Chrysler's old slant-six was before it. In the top-of-the-range Laser and Daytona models it is turbocharged (as it is in the top models in almost all Chrysler's current range) by a Garret AiResearch turbo to produce 142 bhp (SAE) at 5600 rpm. The turbo installation is designed to produce more torque than power and in fact torque output at 160 lb ft at 3600 rpm is quite impressive and gives the car good

acceleration and lots of low-engine speed performance. Overall top speed, however, is disappointing by European standards as the cars can only just exceed 100 mph (161 kph). From the point of view of handling and roadholding however these new front-drive sports cars are a world away from the old muscle car approach and precise and rewarding to drive.

### 1984 CHRYSLER DAYTONA TURBO

**Engine:** in-line four cylinder, overhead cam
**Bore × stroke:** 87.5 mm × 92 mm
**Capacity:** 2213 cc
**Maximum power:** 142 bhp
**Transmission:** five-speed manual
**Chassis:** integral, steel
**Suspension:** independent front with lower wishbones, struts and anti-roll bar. Beam rear axle with trailing arms panhard rod, coil springs and dampers
**Brakes:** discs front, drums rear
**Bodywork:** 2 door hatchback coupé
**Maximum speed (approx):** 100 mph (161 kph)

## CISITALIA
Turin, Italy
1946–1965

Ex-racing drive Piero Dusio's Compagnia Industriale Sportiva Italia began production of single-seater racing cars in 1946. Powered by highly tuned four-cylinder 1098 cc Fiat engines developing around 60 bhp, these Cisitalia D46 racers achieved their first notable success in the 1946 Coppa Brezzi in Turin, won by Dusio himself.

In 1947, Dusio brought out the 202 two-seater, 'for sporty types who want a car that is light, roomy, manageable and exuberant for fast touring, with, at the same time, the

### 1947 CISITALIA

**Engine:** in-line four cylinder, overhead valve
**Bore × stroke:** 68 mm × 75 mm
**Capacity:** 1098 cc
**Maximum power:** 55 bhp
**Transmission:** four-speed
**Chassis:** chrome molybdenum steel tube
**Suspension:** independent front with transverse leaf spring. Live rear axle with transverse leaf spring
**Brakes:** drums all round
**Bodywork:** coupé
**Maximum speed (approx):** 97 mph (155 kph)

best possibility of success in national and international sports car competition'. Various types of coachwork were available, but the real trendsetter was Pinin Farina's Coupé Gran Sport, which not only established a style that was widely copied by other sports car manufacturers, but which was also chosen by the Metropolitan Museum of Modern Art in New York as one of the ten outstanding designs of all time. The Cabriolet Gran Sport was equally handsome; in 1948 Henry Ford II bought one

**Chrysler Daytona Turbo**

of these open Cisitalias from the New York importers.

The following year, Cisitalia were working on a Porsche-designed 1492 cc Grand Prix car, whose twin supercharger twelve-cylinder power unit was mounted at the rear of the tubular chassis, when Dusio ran out of money and transferred operations to Argentina. Though Cisitalia-badged cars were built in Argentina, their basis was the Willys Jeep.

In 1950, another sponsor attempted to resume Cisitalia production in Italy, but without much success. Dusio was back in Italy in 1952, but the great days of Cisitalia were over, and production was henceforth only intermittent. Early attempts to revive the Cisitalia included the production of 1095 cc, 1248 cc and even 2760 cc coupés. Following a break between 1958–61, the last Cisitalias had 847 cc Fiat-based power units.

# CITROËN

**Paris, France
1919–**

Andre Citroën had first achieved fame for his 'double chevron' gears, which he supplied not only to the automotive industry but also to ships (including the *Titanic*); then he reorganised the ailing Mors company and during the war introduced American ideas of mass-production to the manufacture of munitions, and applied the same techniques to car manufacture after the war.

Citroën's first car, the side-valve 1327 cc Type A of 1919, was joined by the 1453 cc Type B and the popular 855 cc Cloverleaf in 1922; that year also saw the first of Citroën's famous expeditions with Citroën-Kégresse half-tracks, across the Sahara.

With the B10 in 1925, Citroën introduced France's first all-steel body. The C-Series followed, of which the most notable was the six-cylinder C6, offered with a choice of engine capacity (2442 cc or 2650 cc).

In 1934, Citroën presented his revolutionary 7 CV 'Traction Avant'; its huge development costs bankrupted him, and the Citroën company was taken over by Michelin. Between 1934 and 1940, Citroën offered 21 different versions of the Traction Avant, with engines of 7 CV and 11 CV (four-cylinders) and the 15 CV six.

A 22 CV V8-engined front-wheel-drive Traction never reached production.

After the Second World War, Citroën resumed production of the 11 CV and 15 CV Tractions, then at the 1949 Paris Salon, launched the amazing 2 CV, a spartan car with front-wheel drive and a 375 cc air-cooled flat-twin power unit.

In 1954, Citroën fitted the 15 CV with hydropneumatic suspension, a prelude to the introduction the following year of the immortal DS 19, though the old Traction soldiered on until 1957.

A simplified version of the DS, the ID 19, appeared in 1956, while 1961 saw the launch of the Ami 6, a 'super 2 CV'.

The DS 21 followed the DS 19 in 1967, and in 1968 came the Dyane, still with the air-cooled flat-twin.

In 1968, the first plastics-bodied Mehari off-road and recreational vehicle left the works.

However, the most significant 1968 car was the flat-four GS; that same year, Citroën acquired a controlling interest in Maserati which led in 1969 to the luxurious SM with its 2675 cc twin-overhead-camshaft Maserati V6.

In 1975, the DS was replaced by the CX 2000, later enlarged to 2200 cc, 2400 cc and 2500 cc. Control of Citroën passed to Peugeot in the mid-1970s, initially resulting in the Citroën LN, which combined a Peugeot body with a Citroën power unit.

In 1982, Citroën launched a new mid-range model, the Bertone-styled BX, which made remarkable use of modern lightweight materials in its body construction.

Today's extensive range includes the very quick CX 25 GTI Turbo saloon, their first petrol car to have this technology.

# Citroën 5 CV Cloverleaf

Though Jules Salomon had largely designed the first Citroëns, the little 5 CV, launched at the beginning of 1922, was very largely the work of Edmond Moyet.

While the A and B2 Citroëns had been conventional cars which achieved popularity because of their utilitarian nature, the 5 CV plugged a gap in the existing market, neatly slotting in between the basic cyclecar and the true light car.

Most 5 CVs – and 80,232 of them were built between the start of production and May 1926, when the last one left the line – carried the characteristic cheeky 'cul de poule' pointed-tail bodywork. The third passenger sat in cloverleaf formation with the front seats, thus giving the 5 CV its Cloverleaf nickname.

## 1923 CITROËN CLOVERLEAF

**Engine:** in-line four cylinder, side valve
**Bore × stroke:** 55 mm × 90 mm
**Capacity:** 856 cc
**Maximum power:** 11 bhp
**Transmission:** three-speed
**Chassis:** pressed steel channel
**Suspension:** non independent with quarter-elliptic leaf springs
**Brakes:** rear wheels only
**Bodywork:** three-seater torpedo
**Maximum speed (approx):** 37 mph (60 kph)

**Citroën 5CV Cloverleaf**

**Citroën Traction Avant**

The 5 CV's remarkable combination of low price and high reliability ensured its popularity; the design also established Opel as a mass-producer, for they borrowed it, without benefit of licence, and built it in Germany, where its standard green finish earned it the title of *Laubfrosch* (tree frog).

# Citroën Traction Avant

In May 1924, André Citroën unveiled his master-stroke, the 7CV Traction Avant, which combined for the first time front-wheel drive, monocoque chassis/body construction, torsion-bar suspension and an overhead-valve engine with removable cylinder sleeves. It had also been proposed to launch the car with a Sensaud de Lavaud automatic transmission but this was abandoned due to technical problems at the eleventh hour and replaced by a conventional gearbox.

Equally, the original 7CV engine was judged to be lacking in power, and was quickly replaced by a 9CV unit, bored out to 1628 cc, followed by the 7S (for 'sport') of 1911 cc; at the 1934 Salon, Citroën announced the 1911 cc 11, while the engine of the 7 was brought into line with that of the 11 with an identical stroke measurement but smaller bore to create a swept volume of 1628 cc.

Also shown at the 1934 Salon had been a prototype 22CV V8 Traction that failed to reach production. The development costs of the Traction had been so immense that André Citroën lost control of his firm to the Michelin tyre company, and died a broken man in 1935.

But the Traction continued to progress; a six-cylinder version, the 15/6 appeared in 1938, and by the outbreak of war some 250,000 Tractions had been built.

---

### 1934 CITROËN TRACTION AVANT

**Engine:** in-line four cylinder, overhead valve
**Bore × stroke:** 72 mm × 80 mm
**Capacity:** 1298 cc
**Maximum power:** 30 bhp
**Transmission:** three-speed manual
**Chassis:** steel monocoque
**Suspension:** independent with torsion bars
**Brakes:** drums all round, hydraulically operated
**Bodywork:** saloon
**Maximum speed (approx):** 60 mph (95 kph)

---

In 1948, the first commercially-available radial tyre, the Michelin X, appeared on the Traction and this remarkable car, which epitomised a whole French era, remained in production until 1957. It finally gave way to the no less revolutionary DS19, which had first appeared two years earlier.

# Citroën 2CV

The first design studies for what would become the 2CV Citroën were made as early as 1936; the company's Director General, Pierre Boulanger, had called for a car with 'four wheels under an umbrella …that can cross a field, loaded with eggs, without breaking one…'

---

### 1949 CITROËN 2CV

**Engine:** flat twin, overhead valve
**Bore × stroke:** 62 mm × 62 mm
**Capacity:** 375 cc
**Maximum power:** 9 bhp
**Transmission:** four-speed manual
**Chassis:** tubular steel
**Suspension:** independent with coil springs
**Brakes:** drums all round
**Bodywork:** four-seater saloon
**Maximum speed (approx):** 35 mph (55 kph)

---

Aimed right at the lower end of the market, the 2CV as originally conceived had no electric starter but a pull-cord like an outboard, a solution that was abandoned in favour of a crankhandle when it was pointed out that the factory typists were ruining their fingernails trying to start a prototype.

Some 250 prototypes had been built by mid-1939, and it was proposed to launch the car at the 1939 Salon; the outbreak of war caused these plans to be abandoned, and development continued in secret in the Auvergne mountains during the occupation, which resulted in water-cooling being replaced by air-cooling and the development of Citroën's famous interconnected suspension.

Finally launched at the 1948 Salon, the 2CV provoked both hilarity and keen interest, and succeeded in creating a new class of motorist.

By the early 1980s, production of the 2CV was based in the world's oldest car factory, the 1902-built former Clément works at Levallois. It was said that production would cease late in 1984, though the proposed replacement for the 2CV seemed to be a car in an entirely different social bracket, without the practical virtues that had made the 2CV almost indispensible to rural France.

# Citroën SM

Offspring of the union between Citroën and Maserati, the SM was launched in 1970, and claimed to be the most technically advanced car in the world. Typically Citroën was the hydropneumatic suspension, five-speed gearbox and front-wheel drive: typically Maserati was the fuel-injected 2.7-litre V6 power unit, with twin overhead camshafts on each cylinder block.

For its day, the SM was extremely luxurious, with electric windows, heated rear windscreen and energy-absorbing steering column as part of its standard specification.

**Citroën 2CV**

**Citroën SM**

## 1970 CITROËN SM

**Engine:** V6, twin cam
**Bore × stroke:** 87 mm × 75 mm
**Capacity:** 2670 cc
**Maximum power:** 178 bhp
**Transmission:** five-speed manual
**Chassis:** steel monocoque
**Suspension:** self levelling hydropneumatic with front transverse arms and rear trailing arms
**Brakes:** discs all round
**Bodywork:** coupé
**Maximum speed (approx):** 142 mph (229 kph)

A 3-litre version with automatic transmission was subsequently created for the French market.

Most SMs were built with two-door saloon bodywork: there was, however, also a very rare four-door version of which one or two examples survive.

# CLAN

### Washington, England
### 1971–1974

The Clan Motor Company was founded by an ex-Lotus engineer, Paul Haussauer, and hardly surprisingly he followed Lotus in making his Clan Crusader in glassfibre. Apart from its angular and rather awkward looks it echoed the Lotus Elite of the '50s in having a glassfibre monocoque body with good aerodynamics.

The small car's aerodynamic efficiency coupled with its light weight gave it good performance despite its rather small engine. The Clan Crusader, like one of its chief rivals of the time the Ginetta G15, used the running gear from the Hillman/Sunbeam Imp Sports and that meant a rear-mounted alloy overhead-cam four-cylinder engine of just 875 cc which produced 51 bhp at 6100 rpm. That gave the small coupé a top speed approaching 100 mph (161 kph) with the capacity to reach 60 mph in under 13 seconds.

Unlike the Ginetta G15 which used Triumph Spitfire front suspension and steering, the

## 1972 CLAN CRUSADER

**Engine:** rear-mounted in-line four cylinder, overhead cam
**Bore × stroke:** 68 mm × 60.4 mm
**Capacity:** 875 cc
**Maximum power:** 51 bhp
**Transmission:** four-speed manual
**Chassis:** glassfibre monocoque
**Suspension:** independent with lower wishbones and coil springs front and semi-trailing arms rear
**Brakes:** drums all round
**Bodywork:** glassfibre two-seater coupé
**Maximum speed (approx):** 100 mph (161 kph)

Crusader used the rather less sophisticated Imp front suspension. Nevertheless the Crusader still handled very well indeed and became popular in group 4 racing until the RAC rescinded its homolgation because the necessary 500 had not been built....

The company foundered due to tax changes and the problems of economies of scale. When the car was introduced and sold in component form it was not subject to purchase tax but when VAT was introduced in April 1973 its price climbed dramatically making it far less of a bargain than the larger mass-produced British sports cars of the time. The end came in late '73 as the company went into voluntary liquidation. The Crusader design, however, was too good to die and in the early '80s production began once more – this time in Northern Ireland and with an Alfa Romeo Alfasud flat four rather than the original in-line four which was no longer in production.

**Clan Crusader**

# A-Z OF THE CAR

## CLAVEAU
**Paris, France**
**1923–1950**

Emile Claveau was a brilliant engineer but a totally impossible businessman who found it difficult to work with others whom he felt might compromise the integrity of his unorthodox designs. As he had the handicap of designing cars that were far in advance of what the market found acceptable, Claveau production was intermittent, consisting mainly of prototypes, though he did exhibit regularly at the Paris Salon.

Claveau's first cars had rear engines, streamline bodywork and independent suspension all round. The power units were an air-cooled 1478 cc 9 hp flat-four using much Alpax alloy in its construction and a

7 hp flat-twin of 739 cc.

Claveau's 1927 Paris Salon exhibit was an ultra-streamlined saloon of monocoque construction with a long 'teardrop' tail.

The 1930 Claveau had 'tank' bodywork and front-wheel drive. A post-war prototype with 2.3-litre V8 power and five-speed front-wheel-drive never went into production.

### 1927 CLAVEAU

**Engine:** flat four
**Bore × stroke:** 70 mm × 96 mm
**Capacity:** 1478 cc
**Maximum power:** 9 hp (rated)
**Transmission:** four-speed manual
**Chassis:** steel monocoque
**Suspension:** independent all round
**Brakes:** drums all round
**Bodywork:** aerodynamic saloon
**Maximum speed (approx):** not known

## CLÉMENT-BAYARD
**Levallois Perret, Mézières, France**
**1903–1922**

Before he began car manufacture, Adolphe Clément had already become rich through marketing bicycles and pneumatic tyres. The first cars bearing his name were Clément-Gladiators, after he amalgamated with Gladiator.

By 1899 the company were producing tricycles and quads, but at the turn of the century they were offering two cars, a light voiturette with a 2.5 bhp De Dion engine at the rear, and a Clément-Panhard, with a 3.5 bhp single-cylinder at the rear and a steering system which involved turning the entire front axle. This latter model was designed by Commandent Krebs of Panhard-Levassor, where Clément was a director, and was made in Scotland by Stirlings.

During 1901 the company produced light, front-engined cars with 7 bhp single cylinder or 12 bhp twin cylinder motors. Two years later they offered 9, 12 and 16 bhp cars, the latter two with four-cylinder engines. Built at the

### 1909 CLÉMENT-BAYARD 7 CV

**Engine:** longitudinal twin-cylinder
**Bore × stroke:** 73 mm × 110 mm
**Capacity:** 2930 cc
**Maximum power:** 7 hp (rated)
**Transmission:** three-speed manual
**Chassis:** pressed steel channel
**Suspension:** front, semi-elliptic leaf springs; rear, transverse leaf spring
**Brakes:** rear-wheel drums
**Bodywork:** torpedo, saloon, delivery van
**Maximum speed (approx):** not known

Clément-Bayard 7CV

same factory as the Gladiators the main difference was that the Gladiators used chain drive.

In 1903 when Clément resigned from Gladiator he could no longer call his products Cléments, and chose the name Clément-Bayard, the latter the name of a 16th Century knight who had once saved the town of Mézières, where Clément had a factory. Clément's admiration for this hero was such that he changed his own name to Clément-Bayard.

In 1904 five Clément-Bayards were available, ranging between a six hp single-cylinder to 14, 20 and

Claveau Torpedo Sport

**Clénet**

27 bhp four-cylinder models.

1907's range extended between 7/10 hp twin-cylinder and a 50/60 hp four, the larger models featuring chain-drive. A 10/12 model had a monobloc four-cylinder engine and a dashboard radiator, the latter featured on the smaller models until 1914. In 1911 the big chain-drive cars were discontinued and three six-cylinder models offered, of 15, 20 and 30 bhp. By now they were quite distinct from the English Talbots, and were imported to Britain as Clement-Talbots. At the outbreak of World War I, when M. Clément-Bayard retired, the catalogue contained 12 models, ranging between a 7 bhp twin to the 30 bhp six-cylinder car.

After the war the company produced a new 8 hp four-cylinder light car until 1922, when the factory was taken over by Citroën.

## CLÉNET

**Santa Barbara, USA**
**1976–1982**

Designed by French-born Alain Clénet, the car bearing his name was one of the first of the modern 'replicars' which ape the features of Jaguar and Mercedes sports cars of the 1930s, yet totally fail to capture the essential style of the period. Each Clénet, with oversized external exhaust pipes and wire wheels, took 1600 man-hours to build and cost $75,000 in 1982. The all-steel bodies — open two- or four-seaters with MG doors and windscreen — were mounted on modified Lincoln Continental MkV chassis. Production was around 125 cars a year, each one carrying an individual limited edition

| **1982 CLÉNET** |
| --- |
| **Engine:** V8, overhead valve |
| **Bore × stroke:** 101.6 mm × 88.8 mm |
| **Capacity:** 5732 cc |
| **Maximum power:** 151 bhp |
| **Transmission:** three-speed automatic |
| **Chassis:** box-type perimeter steel frame |
| **Suspension:** independent front with wishbones and coil springs. Live rear axle |
| **Brakes:** discs front, drums rear |
| **Bodywork:** convertible |
| **Maximum speed (approx):** 121 mph (194 kph) |

number on an engraved plate fitted to the bodywork. The dashboard was made from hand-rubbed walnut taken, it was claimed, from 1200-year-old trees.

## CLULEY

**Coventry, England**
**1922–1928**

Clarke, Cluley & Company were well-known in the bicycle trade long before they moved into car manufacture. Their first cars used proprietory sidevalve four-cylinder 10 hp and 11.9 hp engines, to which was added a six-cylinder 16/40 in 1924.

'Everything about the Cluley is solid and reassuring,' commented

*The Light Car & Cyclecar.*

Cluley's final model was to have been an overhead-valve 14/50, but this model never passed the prototype stage.

| **1924 CLULEY 10/20HP** |
| --- |
| **Engine:** in-line four cylinder, side valve |
| **Bore × stroke:** 65 mm × 110 mm |
| **Capacity:** 1460 cc |
| **Maximum power:** 20 bhp |
| **Transmission:** three-speed manual |
| **Chassis:** pressed steel channel |
| **Suspension:** non independent with semi-elliptic leaf springs |
| **Brakes:** rear wheel only |
| **Bodywork:** two or four-seater tourer |
| **Maximum speed (approx):** 46 mph (74 kph) |

**Cluley 10/20 hp**

Clyno 10.8 hp

# CLYNO

Wolverhampton, England
1922–1929

Frank and Allwyn Smith were well-known motorcycle manufacturers well before the Great War, and the company name came from their variable-ratio 'Clyno' belt-pulley. The Smith family came from Thrapston in Northamptonshire, where they were industrial pulley makers, but the young cousins had been established in Wolverhampton since 1910, having begun motorcycle manufacture the year before.

Intending to enter the car market after the Armistice, Clyno built three prototype 10 hp overhead-valve sports cars in 1920, but ran into financial troubles during the post-war slump, which killed the project.

The company was re-organised

in 1922, and took a diametrically-opposed approach to car manufacture by launching a low-priced light car intended to compete head-on with the Morris Cowley; though it matched Morris price for price, the Clyno had a more up-market image, and proved an instant success.

The initial model had a 10.8 hp Coventry Climax engine, and early in 1924 a wide-track Colonial model and a short-lived Sports Clyno, with four-wheel brakes and external exhaust, were launched; it seems as though total output of Sports Clynos was 25.

At the 1924 Olympia Show, the Clyno range was widened to encompass the better-finished Royal models – tourer, two-seater and saloon, with right-hand gear change and balloon tyres as standard; four-wheel brakes were available, but were standardised shortly afterwards.

For 1926, Clyno added an 11.9 hp four of their own make, though the first examples of this new, larger car, had Coventry-Climax power.

Production reached an all-time record of over 12,000 in 1926, making Clyno Britain's third-biggest car manufacturer; to cope with anticipated demand, construction of a vast new factory

## 1927 CLYNO 10.8 HP

**Engine:** in-line four cylinder, side valve
**Bore × stroke:** 66 mm × 100 mm
**Capacity:** 1368 cc
**Maximum power:** 23 bhp
**Transmission:** three-speed manual
**Chassis:** pressed steel channel
**Suspension:** non independent with semi-elliptic leaf springs front and quarter-elliptic rear
**Brakes:** drums all round
**Bodywork:** two-seater, tourer or saloon
**Maximum speed (approx):** not known

in the Wolverhampton suburb of Bushbury began.

In September 1927, Clyno launched a new 8.3 hp Clyno Nine designed by A. G. 'General' Booth, (later responsible for the AJS Nine and the Hillman Minx). By February 1928, Bushbury was turning out 70 Nines a week, but a misguided attempt to pre-empt the anticipated Morris Eight led to Clyno launching the £112 Century Nine during 1928 (it had originally been planned as a £100 car, hence the name).

The 1928 range was restyled to

look more imposing, with a new, square-cut radiator, though the new look did little to boost sales. Nor did the launch in May 1928 of the luxury 12/35 hp, with wire wheels and Olympic saloon coachwork.

By now, the Century was proving so unpopular with agents and public, that it was affecting the company's financial viability, already burdened with the cost of building Bushbury, and when their creditors called in their money in 1929, Clyno collapsed, though their agents, Rootes, were offered the chance to buy the company cheaply, but decided against it. The company deficit was just £173,454.

The failure of Clyno meant that their prototype monobloc straight-eight (derived from two Nine engines) got no further; however, this unique car is still in existence.

R. H. Collier of Birmingham bought up the remnants of Clyno, and built a further six 12/35s from the vast pile of spares they had acquired. Engine manufacturer Henry Meadows had ambitious ideas to revive the Clyno marque in the mid-1930s, but Meadows became heavily involved in rearmament, and the project was finally abandoned.

# A-Z
## OF THE CAR

**1909 CORBIN**

**Engine:** in-line four cylinder (air or water cooled)
**Bore × stroke:** 114.3 mm × 107.9 mm
**Capacity:** 4430 cc
**Maximum power:** 32 hp
**Transmission:** three-speed
**Chassis:** pressed steel channel
**Suspension:** non independent with semi-elliptic leaf springs
**Brakes:** rear wheels only
**Bodywork:** tonneau, runabout,
**Maximum speed (approx):** not known

## CORD

**Auburn, Indiana, USA**
**1929–1932, 1936–1937**

Erret Lobban Cord announced America's first series production front-wheel-drive car in November 1929. An offshoot of his Auburn Automobile Co, the car bearing his name was designed to occupy a sales position between his Auburn and Duesenberg car lines. The advanced Cord L-29 was powered by a 4894 cc Lycoming straight-eight engine (built by another

## COLE

**Indianapolis, USA**
**1909–1925**

J. J. Cole's carriage-works began automobile manufacture with a 14 hp flat-twin high-wheeled buggy, but quickly turned to making big four- and six-cylinder models of conventional design. In 1913, Cole began fitting electric starting and lighting, and in 1915 announced their first V8, with a proprietory Northway engine.

The 1916 range was basic in the extreme, consisting of Roadster, Sportster and Touring, offered in a single colour – 'dustproof grey', but a more expansive mood prevailed in the early 1920s, when the Aero-Eight range included the curiously-named Sportsedan, Sportcoupe, Sportosine, Tourosine and Toursedan. These had unusual closed bodies featuring octagonal rear quarter windows.

In 1924 the company adopted baloon tyres, for which they claimed to be pioneers, and Westinghouse air springs.

Right at the end of production, Cole created its most appalling model names, with one model entitled the Aero-Volante, and another called, for some reason, Brouette (the French word for wheelbarrow).

**Corbin Cannonball**

## CORBIN

**New Britain, Connecticut, USA**
**1904–1912**

The first Corbins, built by an offshoot of a major hardware company, had air-cooled engines – the 1906 Model G 'High Powered Runabout', which sold for $1800, had a four-cylinder 24 hp power unit cooled by twin fans rotating

above the cylinders – though water-cooling was offered as an option from 1908. This was apparently because there was perceptible customer resistance to air-cooling. Curiously enough, the 1908 30 hp six cost $2650 if air-cooled, $2500 water-cooled.

Though its cars were of considerable quality, Corbin ceased manufacture in 1912, though the name continued to be seen on brass hardware like padlocks.

Cord-controlled company) developing 125 bhp.

The rakish styling of the L-29 was well matched to the car's height of only 61 inches (155 cm); the L-29 rode on a 137-inch (348 cm) wheelbase. Four standard models were offered: Sedan, Brougham, Cabriolet and Phaeton; prices ranged from $3095 to $3295.

Two L-29 town-cars were additionally built to special order, as were a handful of boat-tailed speedsters, and open and closed cars were also built in America by Murphy and Hayes, and in England by Freestone and Webb.

But no matter how advanced and appealing the Cord L-29 may have been, its introduction coincided with the Wall Street

**1921 COLE AERO-EIGHT**

**Engine:** V8, side valve
**Bore × stroke:** 88.9 mm × 114.3 mm
**Capacity:** 5677 cc
**Maximum power:** 39.2 hp (SAE)
**Transmission:** three-speed manual
**Chassis:** pressed steel channel
**Suspension:** non independent with semi-elliptic leaf springs
**Brakes:** rear wheels only
**Bodywork:** Tourster, Roadster, Sportster, Sportsedan, Sportosine, Sportcoupe, Toursedan
**Maximum speed (approx):** not known

**Cole Aero-Eight**

**Cord L-29**

## 1929 CORD L-29

**Engine:** in-line eight-cylinder
**Bore × stroke:** 83 mm × 114 mm
**Capacity:** 5175 cc
**Maximum power:** 125 hp
**Transmission:** three-speed
**Chassis:** pressed steel channel
**Suspension:** independent front with quarter-elliptic leaf springs. Beam rear axle with semi-elliptic leaf springs
**Brakes:** drums all round, inboard at front
**Bodywork:** to order
**Maximum speed (approx):** 80 mph (129 kph)

Crash, with the result that sales, though consistent, remained small.

In an effort to 'move the metal', prices were reduced in early 1931 to between $2395 and $2595, though this had little effect, and the L-29 ceased production early in 1932. Total output had been 4429 cars.

Late in 1935, the Cord name was revived for the futuristic Model 810 designed by Gordon Buehrig.

## Cord 810/812

Buehrig's advanced front-wheel-driven Cord was originally intended to be built as a smaller Duesenberg model. However, an eleventh-hour decision was taken to call it Cord.

The car's unique modern 'coffin-nose' bonnet had no radiator shell; instead, it possessed wrap-around chrome louvres reminiscent, in some ways, of the cooling tubes that made up the bonnet sides of

the Edwardian racing Napier Samson.

The wing-mounted headlights, adapted from the landing lights of Stinson aeroplanes (another Cord Company) were retractable by hand-crank. The 3547 cc Lycoming V8 engine developed 125 bhp at 3500 rpm. The ultra-modern 810 came in four body styles – two sedans, the two-seater Sportsman

## 1937 CORD 812

**Engine:** V8, side valve, supercharged
**Bore × stroke:** 88.9 mm × 95.2 mm
**Capacity:** 4730 cc
**Maximum power:** 195 bhp
**Transmission:** four-speed preselector
**Chassis:** pressed steel channel
**Suspension:** independent front with coil springs. Beam rear axle with semi-elliptic leaf springs
**Brakes:** drums all round
**Bodywork:** phaeton, cabriolet, sedan
**Maximum speed (approx):** 100 mph (160 kph)

and the four-seater convertible sedan-phaeton.

In 1937, the 810 was replaced by the supercharged 812, which developed 195 bhp, and a custom berline with glass division and lengthened wheelbase was added to the range. It cost $3575 compared with the $1995 of the 1936 sedan.

Only 2320 810 and 812 Cords were made, though the design was praised for its beauty by the New York Museum of Modern Art. The body dies were subseauently sold to Hupp, then to Graham, the last models of these two marques closely resembling the Cord in appearance, if not in mechanical specification.

In recent years, at least three separate companies have built replica Cords with modern running-gear.

## CORRE-LA LICORNE

**Levallois, Neuilly and Courbevoie, France**
**1899–1950**

The Societe Française des Automobiles Corré began manufacture with motor tricycles and quadricycles, then put cars with proprietary power units into production. In 1906, when the range consisted of a single-cylinder 942 cc De Dion-engined 8 hp, a 1727 cc twin-cylinder and a 2544 cc 15/20 hp four, the company name was changed to 'Corré-La Licorne' on the departure of M. Corré.

The 8 hp single was manufactured until 1912, after which all Corrés had four-cylinder power units.

Nine models, from 7 hp to 25 hp, were available in 1914. After the Great War, Corré-La Licorne moved to Neuilly, and their products were now simply known as La Licorne. Their first post-war model, launched in 1919, had a side-valve 1244 cc Ballot engine, and was

**Cord 812**

followed by the Ballot-engined 9/12CV (1692 cc) and 12/15CV (2997 cc), plus the SCAP-engined 8/10CV (1393 cc).

In 1927, the company launched a double-overhead camshaft 1492 cc six, which enjoyed some racing success – it lapped Montlhéry at an average of 80.23 mph (129.1 kph), a class record – but the company's fortunes were now in full decline. The ailing firm staggered along with the 905 cc 5CV (launched in 1928) and the 1450 cc 8CV, then moved to Courbevoie and made some conventional front-engined, rear-wheel-drive cars which bore the front-wheel-drive Citroën body.

At the outbreak of the war, two new cars, a 6CV and 8CV, were introduced, with unusual Y-shaped chassis, but they came too late to save the company.

A prototype 14CV appeared at the Paris Show in 1949, but the company closed the following year.

**Corre-La Licorne**

## 1925 CORRE-LA LICORNE SPORTS

**Engine:** in-line four cylinder, overhead valve
**Bore × stroke:** 70 mm × 105 mm
**Capacity:** 1614 cc
**Maximum power:** not known
**Transmission:** four-speed manual
**Chassis:** pressed steel channel
**Suspension:** non independent with semi-elliptic leaf springs
**Brakes:** rear wheels only
**Bodywork:** two- or four-seater sports
**Maximum speed (approx):** not known

Only two of these were built, and the company came to a wider notice at the 1905 Paris Salon, with a range marketed through *le sportsman bien connu* Fraignac.

The four-cylinder series was current from 1906 to 1914, and consisted of two models with 3770 cc power units, and two longer-stroke derivatives of 4398 cc and 5027 cc respectively, the latter also available in sporting guise.

A 50 hp four of 8620 cc and a 45/70 hp of 10,619 cc were built in small numbers from 1907–1909, while a six of 3619 cc was available from 1908 to 1910. A four-cylinder version was built up to 1915, along with updated developments of the 1906 four-cylinder models.

After the war, Cottin-Desgouttes did not recommence manufacture until 1921 with the Type K, derived from the Type DF of 1912–1915. This 14/16CV model of 3216 cc was quickly followed by longer-stroke 18/20CV (4072 cc) and 23/25CV (5026 cc) derivatives.

In 1924, Cottin-Desgouttes announced a new range with pushrod, overhead-valve power units of 2614 cc, as well as the famous 2987 cc three-valves-per-cylinder model. The latter appeared in racing guise for the Grand Prix du Tourisme, and its success ensured the appearance of a production version of the Grand Prix model.

The 1926 2614 cc 'Sans Secousses' model boasted independent suspension all round.

The last Cottin-Desgouttes was an entirely conventional 3813 cc side-valve six: having always made luxury cars, Cottin-Desgouttes soon succumbed to the Depression.

# COTTIN-DESGOUTTES

Lyon, France
1904–1933

Cottin-Desgouttes were one of the better makes of car built in Lyon, a city which had a stronger tradition of quality engineering than Paris.

Their first cars were known simply as Desgouttes, and production began in 1904 with a 9500 cc six, the 45 bhp Type A.

## 1926 COTTIN-DESGOUTTES SANS SECOUSSE

**Engine:** in-line four cylinder, overhead valve
**Bore × stroke:** 80 mm × 130 mm
**Capacity:** 2614 cc
**Maximum power:** not known
**Transmission:** four-speed manual
**Chassis:** pressed steel channel
**Suspension:** independent all round with sliding king pins and transverse leaf spring front and four transverse leaf springs rear
**Brakes:** drums all round, hydraulically operated
**Bodywork:** tourer
**Maximum speed (approx):** not known

**Cottin-Desgouttes Sans Secousse**

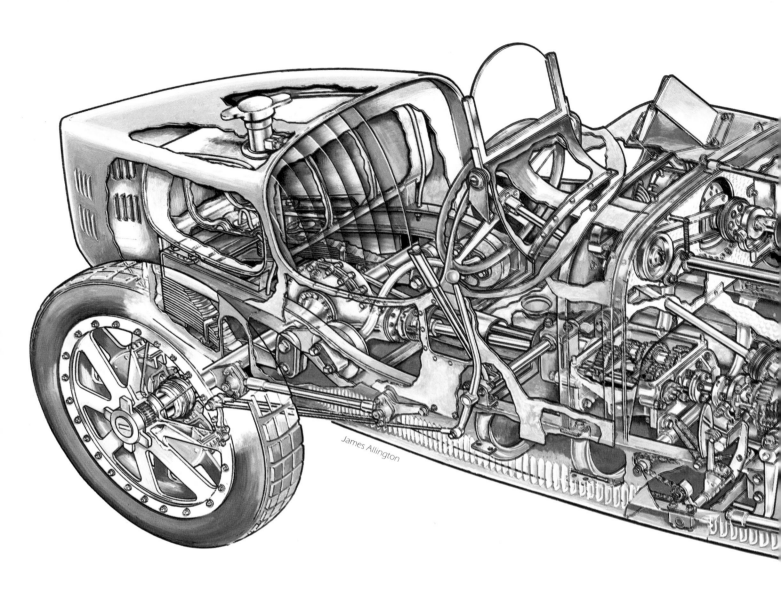

James Allington

## MODEL

Bugatti Type 35B (1927)

**UK price when announced:** £630

### ENGINE

**Location:** Front longitudinal
**Type:** Water-cooled straight eight made up from two monobloc fours with roller bearing crankshaft
**Cubic capacity:** 2262 cc
**Bore × stroke:** 60 mm × 100 mm
**Compression ratio:**
**Valve Gear:** 3 vertical valves per cylinder (2 inlet, 1 exhaust) operated by single overhead camshaft
**Fuel supply:** Zenith or Solex carburettor with three lobe roots-type supercharger
**Ignition:** Mechanical, with magneto
**Maximum power:** 130 to 150 bhp

### TRANSMISSION

**Layout:** Separate gearbox and engine
**Clutch:** Multi-plate, wet with centrifugal servo assistance
**Gearbox:** Four-speed manual with straight-cut gears

| | | | |
|---|---|---|---|
| 1st | 2.42 : 1 | 3rd | 1.31 : 1 |
| 2nd | 1.85 : 1 | 4th | 1.00 : 1 |

**Final drive:** Spiral bevel
**Ratio:** Various, ranging from 3.37 : 1 to 4.5 : 1

### SUSPENSION

**Front:** Non-independent with hollow axle and semi-elliptic leaf springs
**Rear:** Live rear axle with reversed quarter-elliptic leaf springs

### STEERING

**Type:** Worm and wheel with one turn lock to lock

### BRAKES

**Type:** Drums all round, cable operated

### WHEELS AND TYRES

**Type:** Cast alloy wheels with integral brake drum 710 mm × 90 mm

### BODY/CHASSIS

**Type:** Tapered channel steel outer longitudinal chassis members with cross members. Two seater racing body.

### DIMENSIONS AND WEIGHT

**Length:** 145 in (3683 mm)
**Width:** 52 in (1321 mm)
**Wheelbase:** 94.5 in (2400 mm)
**Track – front:** 45 in (1143 mm)
**– rear:** 47 in (1194 mm)
**Weight:** 1653 lb (750 kg)

### PERFORMANCE

**Maximum speed:** 120 mph (193 kph)
**Acceleration 0-60 mph:** 7 seconds (approx)

The 35B revealed. Clearly shown
are the shaft drive from the
crankshaft to the overhead
camshaft, the typical Bugatti three-
valve-per-cylinder layout and the
ribbed housing for the Roots type
supercharger. The chain of gears at
the bottom of the radiator is the
gear drive to the supercharger.
Another typical Bugatti feature is
the use of reversed quarter elliptic
leaf springs at the rear. Bugatti's
attention to detail shows in things
like the brake pedal with its
compensator to ensure that the
brake balance was equal on both
sides of the car.

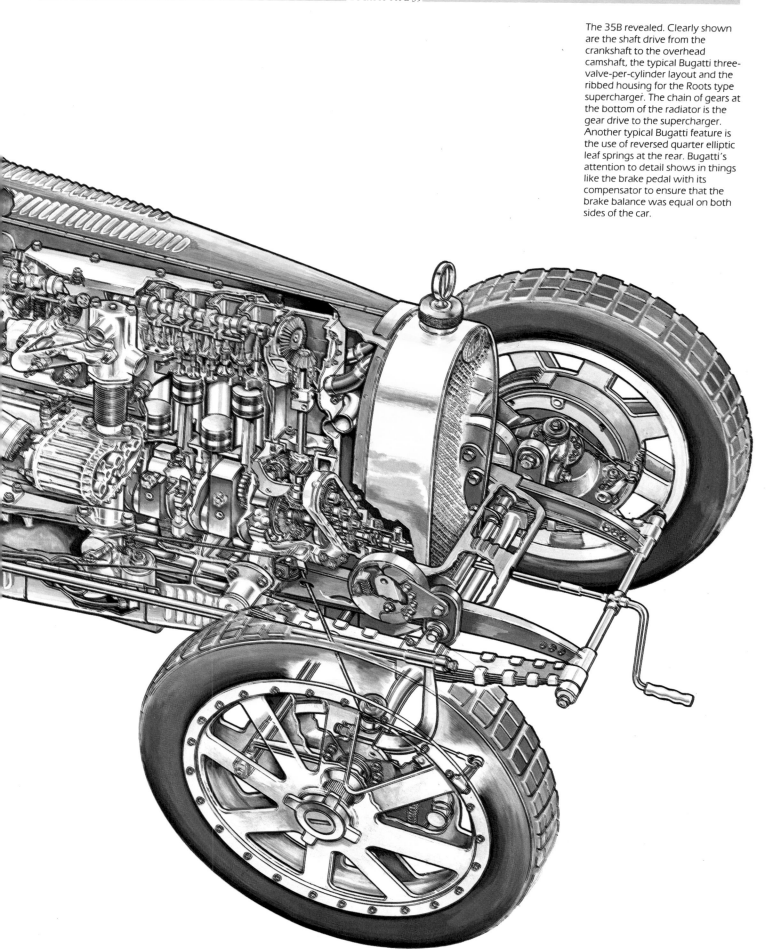

# A-Z
## OF THE CAR

## CROSLEY

**Marion, Indiana, USA**
**1939–1952**

'Famous for his daring and vision in pioneering the developments of many conveniences now commonplace in America', radio pioneer Powel Crosley Jr.'s first small cars had 580 cc twin-cylinder power units, but when manufacture recommenced in 1946, Crosley adopted the Cobra (COpper BRAzed) sheet-steel engine, a 721 cc four originally developed to power Navy generators.

Technically advanced, 'full of pep and sparkle', the Cobra was insufficiently reliable, and in 1949 was replaced by the CIBA cast-iron unit. Perversely, sales never regained the 1948 peak of 24,871, and quickly began to taper off.

The 1949 Crosleys were America's first production cars with disc brakes, but the discs were susceptible to damage by road salt, and the company reverted to drums in 1950.

Crosley's immediate post-war range was complex – four-passenger sedan, convertible sedan, station wagon, panel delivery, pick-up and sports-utility – and by 1950 it had been simplified to sedan, station wagon, convertible and the nippy Hotshot roadster. The Hotshot won the

Performance Index at Sebring in 1950, but failed to win its class in the 1951 Le Mans 24 Hour Race when the electrics failed.

A Super Sports Roadster appeared in 1951, but annual sales had dropped to a paltry 4839; the following year, just 1522 Crosleys were sold. Powel Crosley, having invested $3 million in the venture, called it a day at that point, and the company was sold to General Tire & Rubber, who built no more cars.

### 1946 CROSLEY

**Engine:** in-line four cylinder, overhead valve
**Bore × stroke:** 63.5 mm × 63.5 mm
**Capacity:** 721 cc
**Maximum power:** 26.5 bhp
**Transmission:** three-speed manual
**Chassis:** ladder-type
**Suspension:** non independent with semi-elliptic leaf springs front and rigid axle with coil springs
**Brakes:** drums all round, hydraulically operated
**Bodywork:** convertible, sedan, pickup, sports-utility, wagon
**Maximum speed (approx):** 70 mph (113 kph)

## CROSSLEY

**Manchester, England**
**1904-1937**

The Crossley brothers of Gorton, Manchester, were the first British engineers to build four-stroke power units, for they acquired the licence to build Otto & Langen gas engines in the 1860s. The reputation of these stationary power units was such that when the motor agents Jarrott & Letts were looking for a company to produce a quality British car for

them to sell alongside imported De Dietrich and Oldsmobile cars, they chose Crossley even though the company had no previous experience of car manufacture.

Crossley's first model was a 22 hp four-cylinder car designed by J.S. Critchley, formerly with Daimler; it was largely assembled from imported components. Nevertheless, it received an enthusiastic Press, and was joined in 1906 by a 40 hp four designed by Walter Iden. Jarrot managed to drive one of these cars from London to Monte Carlo in 37 hours 30 minutes.

All these early Crossleys were chain-driven; the company's first live axle car was the 20/26 hp of 1906, and chains were phased out

over the next two years.

Crossley had a reputation for advanced engineering; their 1909 models had four-wheel brakes, making them the first English company to standardise this feature (but it was relegated to being an option when too many unskilled customers skidded or broke the front axles of front-braked Crossleys).

The 12 hp model launched in 1909 was soon uprated to 15 hp, and a sporting variant, the Shelsley, introduced.

During the First World War, the 20/25 hp was adopted as the standard transport of the Royal Flying Corps, and was produced as staff car, light truck, tender and ambulance, enabling the firm to continue manufacture throughout the hostilities.

Uprated to 25/30 hp and endowed with the bullnosed radiator first devised for the Shelsley, the model continued in production until 1926, and achieved Royal patronage, the Prince of Wales (later King Edward VIII) being a particularly enthusiastic owner.

Designed, like all subsequent Crossleys, by T. Wishart, the first new Crossley to appear post-war was the 3.8-litre 19.6 hp of 1920, which was available until 1925, and also appeared in sporting guise as the 20/70.

Crossley even tried to build Bugattis under licence at Gorton in 1921-22, but the project was abandoned after a couple of dozen Type 13s had been completed. Another, longer-lived offshoot was the assembly of American Overland cars at Heaton Chapel after 1920.

The company's first six, the 18/50, replaced the 25/30 in 1925; two years later its engine capacity was increased from 2.2 to 3.2 litres. Further six-cylinder models followed, the 2-litre 15.7 hp in 1928 and 20.9 hp Super Six in 1931.

With the onset of the Depression, Crossley decided to enter the mass-production field with the dreary Ten of 1932, powered by a Coventry-Climax overhead-inlet/side-exhaust engine of 1100 cc; three years later the stylist C.F. Beauvais revamped the Ten as the Regis, available with 1122 cc and 1476 cc Coventry-Climax engines. Despite such features as double-dropped chassis for low build and Wilson preselector gearboxes with centrifugal clutches, they failed to boost the company's fortunes.

There was a curious venture into advanced design with the awful rear-engined semi-streamlined Crossley-Burney of 1934, but a year later the range had shrunk to Regis saloons and coupés plus the 20.9 hp saloon. Private car manufacture finally stopped in 1937, though trucks were produced until 1956.

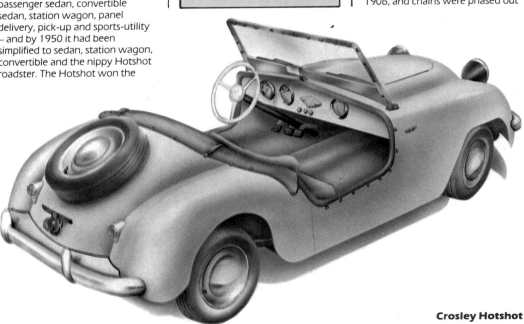

**Crosley Hotshot**

**Crossley 15 HP**

# Crossley Shelsley

One of the finest Edwardian sporting cars, the Shelsley Crossley was a longstroke derivative of the 15 hp model which appeared in 1913, distinguished by a handsome bull-nosed radiator, 'quite one of the most presentable of its kind', designed to harmonise with the new torpedo coachwork. Though Crossley had little sporting history, the Shelsley was capable of achieving good results in reliability trials and hillclimbs; however, an entry for the 1914 Swedish Winter Trials was aborted after the car became bogged down in axle-deep mud.

In 1914, too, a mildly-modified Shelsley fitted with hydraulic shock-absorbers and an oil-cooler mounted between the dumb-irons competed in the Isle of Man Tourist Trophy. It failed to finish.

Considering that the original 15 hp Crossley had been by no stretch of the imagination a sporting car, the Shelsley — 'smart, racy and wind-cutting' — represented a remarkable step forward for the company. Moreover, its performance was achieved in a refined manner, the car being noted for its power, flexibility and silence.

Nevertheless, the Shelsley was available with the old pattern flat radiator for owners who wished to camouflage its speed potential — one of the first 'Q-cars', in fact!

Handling was especially good — *The Autocar* ran one of the first Shelsleys for six months and was moved to comment: 'We are fain to say we have never possessed or handled a sweeter-steering vehicle.'

Another accolade came when S.F. Edge, who had not long before parted from Napier, ordered a Shels-

### 1913 CROSSLEY SHELSLEY

**Engine:** in-line four-cylinder, side-valve
**Bore × stroke:** 80 mm × 130 mm
**Capacity:** 2613 cc
**Maximum power:** 15 hp (rated)
**Transmission:** four-speed manual
**Chassis:** tapered steel channel, ladder frame
**Suspension:** non independent with semi elliptic leaf springs front and three-quarter elliptics rear
**Brakes:** rear wheel and transmission
**Bodywork:** torpedo tourer, four-seater tourer
**Maximum speed (approx):** 60 mph (100 kph)

ley Crossley with an Alford & Alder drophead coupé of his own design.

The Shelsley's handsome radiator was adapted as standard for the post-war Crossleys, but oddly enough the Shelsley itself was not reintroduced after the Armistice.

# CROUCH
### Coventry, England
### 1912–1928

John Crouch was an engineer who had served with Daimler and Siddeley-Deasy before deciding, in the early days of the cyclecar boom, to produce a simple light car. His first offering was the chain-driven Crouch Carette three-wheeler with an own-make 8 hp vee-twin engine mounted amidships.

A fourth wheel was added in

1913; the vee-twin four-wheeler was successfully raced at Brooklands in the early 1920s by garage-owner J.W. Tollady.

In 1922, a more conventional model with a front-mounted vee-twin and shaft final drive made its

### 1912 CROUCH

**Engine:** vee twin
**Capacity:** 1018 cc
**Maximum power:** 8 hp
**Transmission:** three-speed manual
**Chassis:** pressed steel channel
**Suspension:** non independent with semi-elliptic leaf springs
**Brakes:** drums on rear
**Bodywork:** two-seater light car
**Maximum speed (approx):** not known

**Crouch Carette**

appearance, though the vee-twin was quickly superseded as four-cylinder power units by Anzani and Coventry Climax were offered; probably fifty per cent of total Crouch production – some 3000 cars – was Anzani-engined. This included a handsome boat-tailed sports two-seater, which was raced at Brooklands by Dagenham dentist Alfred Moss (father of Stirling). And in 1922 B.S. Marshal drove a four-cylinder Crouch to fourth place in the Coupe des Voiturettes at Le Mans.

# CUNNINGHAM

**Rochester, New York, USA**
**1907–1937**

One of the America's most prestigious automobiles, the Cunningham car was manufactured by the famous carriage-building firm of James Cunningham Son & Co, established in 1842.

The first Cunningham cars were electrics, which appeared in 1908, but were quickly succeeded by petrol cars assembled from proprietory components, with four- and six-cylinder power units by Continental as well as Cunningham's own four.

After 1910, Cunningham used components of its own manufacture; cars and horse-drawn carriages were built side-by side in the same plant until the latter were discontinued in 1915.

For 1916, Cunningham cars became larger, more powerful – and considerably more expensive; Cunningham's new V8 engine was one of the first of its type to be built in America. In its heyday – 1917 to 1927 – the Cunningham car occupied a prestigious niche in the American luxury car market, competing with marques such as Rolls-Royce, McFarlan, Stevens-Duryea, Pierce-Arrow, Locomobile and Packard, with prices of Cunningham limousines frequently exceeding $10,000

The majority of Cunninghams bore the company's own

**Cunningham Boat-tail Speedster**

---

### 1916 CUNNINGHAM

**Engine:** V8, side valve
**Bore × stroke:** 95.25 mm × 127 mm
**Capacity:** 7238 cc
**Maximum power:** 45 hp (rated)
**Transmission:** three-speed manual
**Chassis:** channel steel
**Suspension:** non independent with semi-elliptic leaf springs
**Brakes:** rear wheel
**Bodywork:** roadster, tourer, limousine, landaulet
**Maximum speed (approx):** not known

---

coachwork, which maintained its high standards of quality right to the end of manufacture.

By 1931, the Cunningham had become a snobbish anachronism, but though production actually ceased that year, a number of cars were sold in 1932 as 'new' models. Cunningham then concentrated on its well-established hearse and ambulance business, but continued to build an increasing number of bespoke bodies for other chassis.

The company also built a number of Cunningham-badged town-car versions of the Ford V8, the last being made in 1937.

# CUNNINGHAM

**West Palm Beach, USA**
**1951–1955**

Wealthy sportsman Briggs Swift Cunningham began racing with the Bu-Merc – a Buick straight-eight with an SSK Mercedes body – in 1940, and after an attempt on the Le Mans 24 Hours in 1950 with a two-car team of Cadillacs, Cunningham built his prototype C1 sports car in 1951.

Fully independently sprung, the car had a tubular chassis and was powered by Chrysler's new hemi-head V8. It was clothed in a sleek two-seater body formed from aluminium.

Hard on its heels came the C2, with Chrysler's new 5426 cc Firepower V8 engine; open and closed body styles were offered. For the C2Rs destined for Le Mans, the power output was boosted from the standard 180 to 220 bhp. Three C2Rs competed at Le Mans in 1951; two crashed and engine trouble put paid to the chances of

the third, though it lay second for six hours.

The C3 was derived from the C2, but had a Chrysler live rear axle instead of the complex De Dion arrangement; approximately ten each of the coupé and convertibles were built in 1952–53.

The vastly improved C4R of 1952 had a rigid chassis formed from two pairs of large superimposed tubes linked by vertical sheet steel spacers; smaller, lighter and more powerful than the C3, the C4, driven by Cunningham himself, achieved fourth place in the 1952 Le Mans.

The following year, the big C5R, with torsion bar suspension, came third overall; C4Rs were seventh and tenth. The unsuccessful 1955 Le Mans contender, the C6R, was powered by a 16-valve Offenhauser four. After that, Cunningham, who was spending $50,000 annually on his Le Mans attempts, suspended production, though he subsequently competed at Le Mans with cars of other makes. Apart from the Michelotti-designed C3 coupé, with automatic transmission and a 220 bhp hemi engine, there was also a 200 bhp road-going version of the C4.

In 1955 Briggs Cunningham gave up his five-year enterprise which, due to its unprofitability, had been classed as a 'hobby' by his tax man.

---

### 1952 CUNNINGHAM

**Engine:** V8
**Bore × stroke:** 96.8 mm × 92 mm
**Capacity:** 5426 cc
**Maximum power:** 220 bhp
**Transmission:** four-speed automatic
**Chassis:** tubular
**Suspension:** front independent coil and wishbone, rear semi-elliptic
**Brakes:** four-wheel drums
**Bodywork:** Vignale coupé or convertible
**Maximum speed (approx):** 145 mph (233 kph)

---

**Cunningham C4**

## DAF

**Eindhoven, Holland**
**1958–1975**

Founded in the early '20s by the brothers Wim and Hub Van Doorne, the company initially produced trailers for lorries. Many years later, in 1950, with an extensive sales and service network in Europe, they began to produce their own lorries, and these too sold very well.

In 1958 at the Amsterdam Motor Show there was a surprise as DAF unveiled their first car, the Daffodil, a small two-door saloon with a front-mounted air-cooled 600 cc twin-cylinder engine and all independent suspension. Its most unusual feature was the Variomatic transmission, designed by Hub Van Doorne, whereby an arrangement of rubber belts and variable diameter pulleys (altered by centrifugal force, bob weights and vacuum chambers) allowed an infinitely variable drive ratio. The gear lever simply selected forward

or reverse, and acceleration and deceleration were completely smooth. The car was easy to drive and very popular, and in 1962 the engine was enlarged to 750 cc and 30 bhp. Sales had by then totalled 60,000, and in 1964 production was running at 20,000 per year. In the following year the transmission was successfully built into a military four-wheel-drive vehicle and an interesting but unsuccessful Brabham-engined Formula 3 car.

---

### 1973 DAF 66

**Engine:** front-mounted in-line four-cylinder, water-cooled
**Bore × stroke:** 70 mm × 72 mm
**Capacity:** 1108 cc
**Maximum power:** 47 bhp
**Transmission:** Variomatic transmission driving rear wheels
**Chassis:** integral
**Suspension:** front, independent with longitudinal torsion bars, wishbones and anti-roll bar; rear, non independent with de Dion axle and semi-elliptic leaf springs.
**Brakes:** discs, front, and drums, rear
**Bodywork:** 2-door saloon, 2-door coupé and 3-door estate
**Maximum speed (approx):** 85 mph (137 kph)

---

In 1967 the DAF Daffodil was joined by the larger type 44, styled by Michelotti and, with its 850 cc engine, capable of 75 mph (121 kph).

In 1968 the type 55 appeared with an 1100 cc Renault engine, the marque's first use of a four-cylinder unit. In 1970 a racing version became available, with 1440 cc and 140 bhp, and the Variomatic transmission was strong enough to take it to 115 mph (185 kph).

In 1973 the Type 66 featured a de Dion rear axle, and was available as a saloon, coupé or estate, with an engine size of 1108 cc or 1289 cc for the Marathon 1300 and top speeds of 80 and 85 mph (129 and 137 kph) respectively.

The last DAF (apart from the trucks, which are still in production) was the 46, based on the 44, with de Dion axle and a single-belt Variomatic unit. On 1 January 1975 Volvo, keen to enter the small car market, raised their shareholding in the car division from 33 to 75 per cent, and it was subsequently known as Volvo Cars BV, Netherlands.

When it appeared later that year the Volvo 66 was an upmarket version of the DAF, and featured the Variomatic drive, as did the subsequent Volvo 343. Today, further refined and with a new control mechanism, Continuously Variable Transmission, as it is now known, is only used on the Volvo 340 Automatic.

## DAIMLER

**Coventry, England**
**1897 –**

Though F.R. Simms acquired the Daimler engine patent rights for the United Kingdom and colonies (excepting Canada) as early as 1891, it wasn't until January 1896 that Harry J. Lawson, a member of the syndicate which had bought

the engine rights the previous year, decided to exploit the patent and floated the Daimler Motor Co Ltd.

The new company took over a disused cotton mill in Coventry and, after having imported cars from the Continent, began production in 1897 of a 4 hp two-cylinder car based on the Panhard. An early Coventry Daimler was the first car to travel from John O'Groats to Land's End.

Over the next five years, the 'Motor Mills' produced a complex range of cars using 12 different two- and four-cylinder engines. Daimler's first works manager was J.S. Critchley.

Things were simplified in 1902, when a three-car line-up designed by Edmund Lewis was introduced, including a 22 hp model, one of the first of which was bought by King Edward VII; his purchase of a 6 hp Daimler in 1900 when Prince of Wales marked the start of a long Royal patronage for the firm.

Up to 1908, Daimler built large and luxurious poppet-valve fours and sixes of 3.3 to 10.4 litres: then the company acquired exclusive British rights to the Knight sleeve-valve engine, which gave smooth, silent running, though at the cost of out-and-out performance. After about a year, the Knight engine became standard in Daimlers.

In 1910 Daimler was absorbed into the profitable Birmingham Small Arms group, with the result that there was some rationalisation of the ranges produced by the two companies.

Daimler's war-time production was particularly varied – staff cars, lorries, ambulances, aero engines, aircraft, tractors, tanks and shells were all built, then in November 1919 the first post-war Daimlers, two 30 hp models and a 'special' 45 hp, were launched; four-wheel brakes were standardised in 1924, along with thinner sleeve-valves for greater power. Four special 57 hp Daimlers were also built for King George V during 1924.

In 1926, Daimler chief engineer Laurence Pomeroy designed the complex sleeve-valve V12 Double-Six, then, in 1930, brought out the Fluid Flywheel. In conjunction with the Wilson preselector gearbox, this hydraulic coupling gave a simplicity of control unrivalled at the time.

The Lanchester company, which had built the first all-British four-wheeled car in 1895, was acquired in 1931, and its products henceforward mirrored the current Daimler range.

The development of more refined poppet-valve power units resulted in the phasing out of

**Daf 66**

**Daimler Double-Six**

sleeve valves in the mid-1930s, when Pomeroy introduced a 4.6-litre poppet-valve straight-eight. That was in 1936; soon after he also brought out three straight-sixes. A few poppet-valve V12s were also built for prestige purposes.

Coil-spring independent front suspension appeared in the late 1930s on Daimlers and Lanchesters; the introduction of more up-to-date and stylish Daimler models was referred to as 'lifting the old lady's skirts'.

The post-war Daimler range – DB18 2.5-litre and DE27 4.1-litre sixes and 5.5-litre eights – was derived from pre-war designs.

A 3-litre six-cylinder power unit appeared in 1950, while a four-cylinder variant, first seen in the new Lanchester 14, was used in the 1953 Daimler Conquest, of which a performance version, the 100 bhp Conquest Century, was current from 1954 to 1958.

Another 1953 model was the 3-litre Regency, which progressed through a 3.5-litre version into the 3.8-litre Majestic of 1958, and Majestic Major 4.5 litre of 1960.

In 1960, Daimler was taken over by Jaguar, and since then – apart from specialist models like the glassfibre-bodied SP250 sports designed by Edward Turner – the bulk of Daimler production has been based on contemporary Jaguars, though the pre-merger engines were used for a number of years.

A V12 Jaguar engine powers the modern Daimler's 1973 Double-Six, while the Sovereign 4.2 and the limited-production limousine use the 4.2-litre XK engine.

## Daimler Double-Six

The epitome of complexity in the cause of refinement, the Double-Six was Britain's first production 12-cylinder car, announced in 1926 and designed by Laurence Pomeroy, the company's chief engineer. Launched with a capacity of 7136 cc, the Double-Six was built in a variety of engine sizes from 3.7 litres upwards. Cars produced ranged from the excessively tall limousines supplied to King George V in 1931 to a brace of lowered chassis sports Double-Sixes created by Thomson & Taylor of Brooklands, which still survive. For 1931, when a new 40–50 hp Double-Six of 6511 cc was launched, the Daimler range was available with the revolutionary new fluid flywheel transmission in conjunction with a preselector gearbox,

### 1931 DAIMLER DOUBLE-SIX

**Engine:** V12 sleeve-valve
**Bore × stroke:** 73.55 mm × 104 mm
**Capacity:** 6511 cc
**Maximum power:** 50 hp
**Transmission:** fluid flywheel coupling, four-speed preselector
**Chassis:** pressed steel channel
**Suspension:** non-independent with semi-elliptic leaf springs
**Brakes:** drums all round
**Bodywork:** coupé de ville, saloon
**Maximum speed (approx):** not known

giving an ease of control unrivalled till the advent of automatic transmissions many years later introduced similar convenience to the masses.

## Daimler Limousine

Daimler's limousine is a unique anachronism, a limited-production luxury car built in a special workshop in the Jaguar plant at Brown's

### 1984 DAIMLER LIMOUSINE

**Engine:** in-line six-cylinder
**Bore × stroke:** 92.1 mm × 106 mm
**Capacity:** 4235 cc
**Maximum power:** 165 bhp
**Transmission:** three-speed automatic
**Chassis:** integral, with auxiliary frames front and rear
**Suspension:** all independent
**Brakes:** discs all round
**Bodywork:** limousine
**Maximum speed (approx):** 115 mph (185 kph)

**Daimler Limousine**

**Daniels V8**

Lane. Originally launched in 1968, the Limousine uses Jaguar running gear under Vanden Plas coachwork and can, if the occasion arises, move at a surprisingly rapid speed, despite its weight of 4480 lbs (2032 kgs). Though its basic design is over 15 years old, there is still a brisk demand for this bespoke motor car, and it is particularly favoured as today's mayoral carriage. Utterly traditional, its small market niche, under that of Rolls-Royce seems assured.

# DANIELS

**Reading, Pa, USA**
**1915–1924**

One of America's most highly-regarded luxury cars of its day, the Daniels was the product of a company headed by G.C. Daniels, who had been president of Oakland before striking out solo.

Though the company used nothing but V8 engines, up to 1919 the Daniels was powered by

### 1915 DANIELS

**Engine:** side-valve V8
**Bore × stroke:** 88.9 mm × 133.4 mm
**Capacity:** 6621 cc
**Maximum power:** 39.2 hp (rated)
**Transmission:** three-speed manual
**Chassis:** pressed steel channel
**Suspension:** non-independent with semi-elliptic leaf springs
**Brakes:** rear-wheel drums
**Bodywork:** touring, coupé, sedan, brougham, limousine
**Maximum speed (approx):** not known

a Herschell-Spillman engine. After that, power units of Daniel's own make were adopted.

The Daniels' high rounded radiator bore no identification; the marque was distinguishable to the cogniscenti only by the letter 'D' on the hubcaps. Among the highly individualistic body styles were the

sporting 'Submarine Speedster' and 'Submarine Roadster'.

In 1923, ownership of the marque passed to a Philadelphia motor combine. The new owners assembled a handful of Daniels sedans which they offered at $10,000, a price which represented a considerable increase on the earlier Daniels models. These later cars were not of the quality formerly associated with the marque, and the rapid demise of the Daniels was inevitable; production ceased in 1924.

Many of the closed bodies fitted to the Daniels were built by Fleetwood, more commonly associated with Cadillac.

# DARL'MAT

**Paris, France**
**1936–1950**

Emile Darl'Mat was a leading Peugeot agent who, with works backing, constructed sports cars

based on a strengthened Peugeot 302 chassis fitted with the larger 402 engine and axles.

Streamlined bodywork designed in his spare time by a dentist named Paulin (killed by the Gestapo during the war) was built at Rueil-Malmaison by Pourtout, and included a roadster whose windscreen could be cranked down into the scuttle, as well as a 'competition' doorless two-seater made from aluminium.

Darl'Mats enjoyed sporting success at Le Mans, finishing 7th, 8th and 10th overall in 1937, and 5th in 1938, when the marque took the under-2-litre class at an average of some 75 mph (121 kph).

Darl'Mat built around 105 cars in 1937-38, then, after the war, produced a small number of cars based on the very popular Peugeot 203. Under the sports bodywork was a 42 bhp 1.3-litre engine with hemispherical heads, hydraulic brakes, coil suspension all round and, an echo of pre-war practice, a high top gear ratio.

**Darl'Mat 402**

### 1937 DARL'MAT

**Engine:** in-line overhead-valve four-cylinder
**Bore × stroke:** 83 mm × 92 mm
**Capacity:** 1991 cc
**Maximum power:** 70 bhp
**Transmission:** three-speed
**Chassis:** 'Bloctube' boxed steel channel
**Suspension:** front, independent by transverse spring and wishbones; rear, cantilever
**Brakes:** hydraulic drum
**Bodywork:** roadster, coupé, drop-head coupé
**Maximum speed (approx):** 87 mph (140 kph)

# A-Z OF THE CAR

## DARMONT
**Courbevoie, France**
**1920–1939**

R. Darmont was French agent for the Morgan three-wheeler, and had also raced these speedy tricycles from Malvern. Following World War I, he decided to build replicas under his own name.

These followed the original pattern pretty closely, with two-speed chain-and-dog transmission; they were mostly powered by British-built air- or water-cooled vee-twins from Blackburne or JAP.

Darmonts achieved a number of sporting successes, in hillclimbs at Gaillon, La Turbie and Mont Ventoux as well as the 1921 Paris-Nice trial, in which Darmonts finished 1–2–3.

Although production of the three-wheelers ended in 1930, the company built a few vee-twin-engined four-wheeled cars which were marketed under the name of 'Etoile de France'.

### 1920 DARMONT

**Engine:** overhead-valve vee-twin
**Bore × stroke:** 83.5 mm × 99 mm
**Capacity:** 1084 cc
**Maximum power:** 40 bhp
**Transmission:** two-speed manual (no reverse)
**Chassis:** tubular steel
**Suspension:** front independent sliding pillar; rear, quarter elliptic
**Brakes:** rear wheel drum
**Bodywork:** sports two-seater
**Maximum speed (approx):** 78 mph (125 kph)

## DARRACQ
**Suresnes, France**
**1896–1920**

Alexandre Darracq founded the Gladiator cycle company in the early 1890s and sold out to a British combine five years later; he began building electric cabs in 1896, but the design proved 'worthless', and he turned to the manufacture of petrol-engined tricycles and quadricycles.

Darracq was rash enough to spend £10,000 on the acquisition of Léon Bollée's patents, which resulted in the appearance in 1898 of an unsuccessful 5 hp belt-driven voiturette called the Darracq-Bollée.

Darracq's 6.5 hp single-cylinder light car of 1900 really made the company's name, and was quickly followed by two- and four-cylinder models.

In 1904 Darracq introduced a distinctive design of chassis, pressed from a single sheet of steel in unit with its undershield.

In 1905, like so many French companies, Darracq was reformed

**Darracq Torpedo**

### 1913 CLEGG-DARRACQ

**Engine:** in-line monobloc four-cylinder, side valve
**Bore x stroke:** 75 mm x 120 mm
**Capacity:** 2121 cc
**Maximum power:** 12 hp (rated)
**Transmission:** four-speed manual
**Chassis:** pressed steel channel
**Suspension:** non-independent with semi-elliptic leaf springs
**Brakes:** drums on rear wheels
**Bodywork:** tourer
**Maximum speed (approx):** 50 mph (80 kph)

with British capital. A complex range was offered subsequently; all types of car from a 1039 cc 8 hp single to an 8143 cc 50/60 hp six were listed, and in 1907 it was even possible to order an 11.5-litre 'Vanderbilt Cup' racer.

A disastrous range of four-cylinder cars equipped with Henriod rotary valves appeared in

**Darmont Three-Wheeler**

**David**

1912; these consisted of a 2613 cc 15 hp (uprated to 2951 cc for 1913) and a 3969 cc 20 hp. These cars were so unreliable that profits virtually vanished overnight, and Alexandre Darracq took the opportunity to retire (he never liked cars, could not drive and did not even like to be driven) to take an interest in running the Casino at Deauville…

The management of the Darracq company was taken over by a Briton, Owen Clegg, who quickly brought out a 1913 range based on the design of his well-proven Rover Twelve. These Clegg-Darracqs had monobloc four-cylinder L-head engines of 2121 cc and 2971 cc, and healthy sales soon restored company funds.

A 4084 cc Darracq launched in 1914 became regular French Army transport during World War I; it was joined in 1919 by an advanced side-valve 4595 cc V8, but only a year later there was a merger with the British Sunbeam-Talbot company. The Darracq marque ceased to exist in France, where the cars became known as 'Talbots'. Confusingly, they were still sold as 'Darracqs' or 'Talbot-Darracqs' in England until 1939.

## DAVID

**Barcelona, Spain
1914–1922, 1951–1957**

When a lack of snow prevented Jose Maria Armangué from representing Barcelona in a bobsleigh contest, he fitted the sleigh with cycle wheels… This started a dangerous craze for engineless 'down cars' among the young men of Barcelona, resulting in the founding of a club.

Armangué and his three brothers then fitted a JAP motorcycle engine and belt drive to a 'down car' in order to get up the hills, the resulting cyclecar being christened the 'David'.

The Fabrica Nacional de Cyclecars David was incorporated on 14 July 1914, and began production using vee-twin MAG engines; later Davids also used four-cylinder Ballot power units.

### 1918 DAVID

**Engine:** in-line water-cooled four-cylinder
**Bore x stroke:** 60 mm x 100 mm
**Capacity:** 1131 cc
**Maximum power:** not known
**Transmission:** variable-ratio pulley and belt
**Chassis:** pressed steel channel
**Suspension:** front, independent, parallel transverse leaf springs; rear, cantilever
**Brakes:** drums on rear wheels
**Bodywork:** two-, three- or four-seater sports
**Maximum speed (approx):** 50 mph (80 kph)

An advanced feature of the David, which enjoyed many sporting successes, was independent front suspension.

When Jose Mare Armangué was killed in a flying accident in 1917 the control of his company passed to his collaborators Jose Maria and Ramon More.

After all these sporting vehicles, it's curious to note that the last production David cyclecars were taxicabs which saw service in Barcelona, the company subsequently operating taxis and hire cars – mostly Citroëns.

During the Spanish Civil War, David built a number of electric cars, while from 1951–57 a few three-wheelers with single-cylinder 345 cc two-stroke engines were produced.

## DB

**Champigny-sur-Marne, France
1938–1961**

Charles Deutsch and René Bonnet began production of specials with Citroën traction avant engines just before World War II. Beginning again in 1947, DB made a few more Citroën-engined cars but quickly turned to the manufacture of Panhard-engined 'Racer 500s'. These proved successful, and were soon joined by a larger version, the 'Monomille' 750 cc; this was built in sufficient numbers to justify the creation of its own junior formula.

DB also built Panhard-engined sports-touring coupés, first with light-alloy, then (from 1955)

### 1954 DB

**Engine:** overhead-valve flat-twin
**Bore × stroke:** 85 mm × 75 mm
**Capacity:** 850 cc
**Maximum power:** 55 bhp
**Transmission:** four-speed manual
**Chassis:** fabricated
**Suspension:** front, independent; rear, transverse springs, torsion bar
**Brakes:** hydraulic drums all round
**Bodywork:** sports coupé
**Maximum speed (approx):** not known

glassfibre bodies; engines ranged from 610 cc to 1300 cc. Superchargers were an optional extra from 1954, and disc brakes became available a year later.

There were experiments with twin engines and four-wheel-drive in 1951, and with rear-mounted Renault engines and five-speed transmissions the following year.

DBs won the Index of Performance at Le Mans five times, and also took the 1954 Tourist Trophy outright. After their association was dissolved in 1961, the two partners made cars under their own names.

## DEASY, SIDDELEY-DEASY

**Coventry, England
1906–1919**

This marque took its name from its sponsor, Captain J.D. Deasy, and the original Deasy was a 4.5-litre four designed by E.W. Lewis, formerly with Rover. Unusual features included adjustable steering column, armoured wood chassis and huge brakes.

By 1908, Deasy was offering two huge fours, of 8621 cc and 11,947 cc, joined the following year by a '15' of 2.9 litres.

J.D. Siddeley joined Deasy during 1909, and immediately introduced his JDS, whose 4084 cc four-cylinder engine was housed under a coffin-nosed bonnet. Lanchester worm-drive and cantilever rear springs were also part of the specification.

On 7 November 1912, the company name was altered to 'Siddeley-Deasy'; two Knight sleeve-valve-engined models – a 3308 cc 18/24 hp four and a 24/30 hp 4694 cc six – as well as two 1944 cc and 3308 cc poppet-valve

**DB Rallye Coupé**

## 1913 SIDDELEY-DEASY

**Engine:** in-line sleeve-valve four-cylinder
**Bore X stroke:** 80 mm × 130 mm
**Capacity:** 2614 cc
**Maximum power:** 20 bhp
**Transmission:** four-speed manual
**Chassis:** pressed steel channel
**Suspension:** front, semi-elliptic leaf springs; rear, cantilever
**Brakes:** rear wheels only
**Bodywork:** tourer, limousine, landaulette
**Mximum speed (approx):** not known

models, formed the new line-up.

Siddeley-Deasy announced a poppet-valve 4962 cc six for 1914; after the war, the marque merged with Armstrong-Whitworth to form Armstrong Siddeley.

Siddeley-Deasy

# DE DION BOUTON

**Puteaux (Seine), France
1883–1932**

The rumbustious Comte Albert de Dion backed two brother-in-law mechanics named Bouton and Trepardoux in the manufacture of steam carriages during the 1880s and early 1890s.

The mechanical feature pioneered by the marque, the de Dion axle, was actually designed by Trepardoux to transmit the power of their heavy steam brakes. Trepardoux resigned in 1894

because de Dion and Bouton were experimenting with petrol engines, which he thought were a waste of time.

However, Bouton's 1895 single-cylinder petrol engine ran at up to 3500 rpm on test, and powered the fast sporting tricycles that De Dion Bouton built until 1901.

Though a quadricycle appeared in 1899, it was quickly replaced by a rear-engined 3.5 hp voiturette, the 402 cc model D.

De Dion Bouton also produced huge quantities of engines to sell to other manufacturers, and by 1904 over 40,000 engines had been built at Puteaux.

By 1902, the rear-engined model, distinguished by a neat two-speed expanding clutch transmission, was powered by a 6 hp engine; then came the famous Model K, with a front-mounted

## 1906 DE DION BOUTON

**Engine:** twin-cylinder, water-cooled
**Bore × stroke:** 80 mm × 120 mm
**Capacity:** 1206 cc
**Maximum power:** 8 hp
**Transmission:** three speed
**Chassis:** tubular
**Suspension:** non-independent, with semi-elliptic leaf springs all round
**Brakes:** rear wheels and transmission
**Bodywork:** coupé
**Maximum speed (approx):** 28 mph (45 kph)

8 hp engine under a crocodile bonnet.

Until the end of 1914, all De Dions were fitted with *decelerator* pedals.

The firm's first twin-cylinder car, the 12 hp Model S, appeared in 1903; fours of 15 and 24 hp were added two years later, and all De Dion Boutons had conventional sliding gearboxes by the end of 1906.

De Dion Bouton introduced the first significant production V8 in 1910 but abandoned the de Dion axle in 1911, and the last single-cylinder De Dion Bouton, the DE1, was built in 1913.

The V8 continued in production until 1923, alongside fours of obsolescent design; in 1923 De Dion Bouton introduced the overhead valve 12/28 hp, which had aluminium pistons and the option of front wheel brakes. The factory struggled on until 1927, when it temporarily closed, to reopen with the introduction of a 2.5-litre straight-eight.

A 2-litre four was also offered, but few examples of either model were sold. The eight was increased in capacity to 3 litres in 1930, but

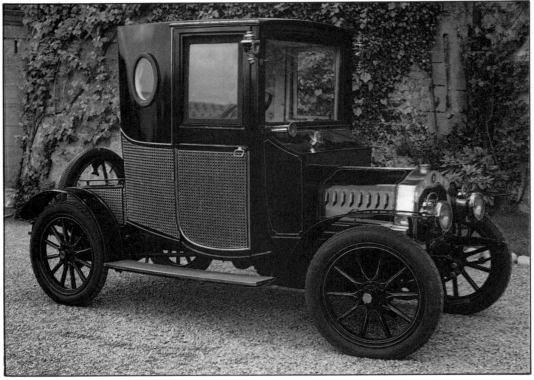

De Dion 8 hp

proved no more popular in its new guise. De Dion Bouton delivered its last car, an 11 hp, in 1932, but built trucks until the late 1940s when it was transformed into a service garage. The De Dion Bouton name was last used on lightweight motorcycles in the 1950s, while the old factory is now used to sell houseplants.

# DELAGE

**Courbevoie, France**
**1905–1954**

One-eyed engineer Louis Delage, born in Cognac in 1874, started his career in the motor industry with Turgan-Foy in Levallois, then moved over to Peugeot's Paris branch. Wanting to be his own boss, he borrowed Fr 35,000 and set up his own little workshop at Courbevoie in 1906. At first, Delage made parts for other manufacturers, then in December 1905 brought out his first complete car, a voiturette powered by a single-cylinder De Dion engine.

The company sprang to fame with victory in the 1908 Coupe des Voiturettes, which was won by a Delage powered by a 1257 cc single cylinder Causan engine, which had four valves and two sparking plugs (but De Dion bribed Delage to say that the winning car had a De Dion engine…).

In 1908, Delage sold over 300 cars, then, in 1909 introduced a 1460 cc four-cylinder 9 hp model. The following year, the company moved to a new factory on the Boulevard de Verdun, and by 1912 its 300 workmen were turning out a range of 12 hp fours and a six-cylinder of 2588 cc; the company also made its mark in racing with fast and powerful cars of advanced design.

Delage changed their image after the war, producing large luxury cars rather than the small and medium sized models that had established their reputation. The first of these much-admired vintage Delage cars was the 1918 CO, which had a 4532 cc six-cylinder 20 hp engine, and was developed into the CO2 in 1921.

Delage enjoyed many racing successes during the 1920s: the most notable touring cars of the period were the 2120 cc DI and the overhead camshaft GL with a 30 hp engine of 5945 cc. These were followed by a long line of six-cylinder Delages, including the

**Delage D8**

3174 cc overhead-valve DM (derived from the DI, and one of the best vintage Delage models) and its sporting DMS version: there were also ephemeral side-valve sixes, the DR models of 2.2 and 2.5 litres.

Delage had already achieved many racing successes with racing cars powered by V12 and straight-eight engines, but it wasn't until 1929 that they introduced their first production straight-eight, the 4060 cc D8. This was developed into the sporting D8S model.

In 1932 Delage launched their D6/11 of 2100 cc; followed two years later by the eight-cylinder D8/15 of 2700 cc.

Financial problems forced Delage to sell out to Delahaye in 1935, but cars continued to be produced bearing the Delage badge. These included the 4300 cc D8/100, the D8/120 and the 2700 cc D6/70.

After the war six-cylinder Delahayes were sold at Delages, but the name finally disappeared when both companies were absorbed by Hotchkiss in 1954, car manufacture ending in '55.

## Delage D8

Launched at the Paris Salon in October 1929, the Delage D8 was designed by the company's engineering chief, Maurice Gaultier. It was a car worthy to be placed in the same exclusive bracket as the Hispano Suiza, but the timing of its introduction unfortunately coincided all too neatly with the start of the Depression in 1930.

Despite its sound finish, it sold for about one-third of the price of the Hispano in chassis form – £685 against £1950. Gabriel Voisin said that he could not explain how Delage could sell such fine cars at such low prices. Nevertheless, Delage managed to produce over 1900 D8 chassis before the inevitable bank-

**1930 DELAGE D8**

**Engine:** in-line eight-cylinder, overhead-valve
**Bore × stroke:** 77 mm × 109 mm
**Capacity:** 4061 cc
**Maximum power:** 105 bhp
**Transmission:** four-speed
**Chassis:** pressed steel channel
**Suspension:** non independent with semi-elliptic leaf springs
**Brakes:** drums front and rear
**Bodywork:** to order
**Maximum speed (approx):** 80 mph (129 kph)

ruptcy which came in 1935.

Needless to say, there was also a sports version, the D8S, which has been described as 'the best road car Delage ever built'. With a tuned engine, it was capable of 100 mph (161 kph): an excellent performance at the period for a 4-litre pushrod engine. It achieved its International class 12-hour record at an average of 112 mph (180 kph).

# DELAHAYE

**Tours/Paris, France**
**1894–1954**

Emile Delahaye had been chief engineer of a company building railway rolling stock before taking over a little machine shop in Tours around 1890. Some four years later, his company started production of belt-driven single- and twin-cylinder cars. A second factory was opened in Paris in 1898, but Emile Delahaye resigned from his

company three years later, leaving the running of the firm to his partners Desmarais and Morane. A new works manager, Charles Weiffenbach, was appointed at this time, and took over the company from 1906, from which date the great days of Delahaye really started, although the chain-driven 8 litre of 1905 was interesting enough to secure an order from that royal enthusiast, Alfonso XIII of Spain. 'Monsieur Charles' was to head Delahaye for over three decades.

In 1908 Delahaye introduced their first monobloc four-cylinder model, the 1460 cc 9 hp, followed by a 12 hp of 2120 cc. These models were continued until the outbreak of the Great War in 1914, along with perhaps the first production car with a V6 power unit, the not entirely successful 2565 cc Type 44.

Delahaye cars were exported to England from 1909, and built under licence by Protos in Germany (and without benefit of licence by White in America). After the war, Delahaye were preoccupied with making lorries, motor ploughs and fire engines, and the company's private cars were stodgy models on American lines with four-cylinder engines of 1847 cc and 2950 cc and six-cylinders of 4426 cc.

There was a brief collaboration with Chenard-Walcker, then for 1934, Delahaye blossomed forth with two new cars, the four-cylinder 12CV (2150 cc) and the six-cylinder 18CV (3200 cc) Superluxe, also available as a sports model.

In 1935 Delahaye bought Delage, perpetuating that marque with cars constructed from Delahaye components; that same year, the most famous Delahayes, the six-cylinder overhead valve 3.2 Coupe des Alpes and the 3557 cc 135, were launched. A V12 designed by Jean Francois, and available with exaggeratedly 'swoopy' roadster coachwork, appeared in 1937.

Such famous coachbuilders as Figoni, Chapron and Letourneur et Marchand were commissioned to build elegant bespoke bodies for the Delahayes of the 1930s. Meantime, Delahaye continued to build lorries and armoured vehicles.

The 135 was revived after the war, then in 1947, factory styling by Phillipe Charbonneux was adopted.

The 4.5-litre 175 was launched in 1948, then in 1951 the last new Delahayes appeared in the guise of the Jeep-Delahaye and the 3.5-litre Delahaye 235.

Hotchkiss acquired Delahaye in 1954, and only built lorries, known as Hotchkiss-Delahaye for a few months, and thereafter called simply Hotchkiss.

## Delahaye 135

The 3.5-litre engine of the Delahaye 135 was derived from the unit fitted to the company's lorries – but that didn't stop it from being one of the great classic power units designed before World War II.

### 1935 DELAHAYE 135

**Engine:** in-line six-cylinder, overhead-valve
**Bore × stroke:** 84 mm × 107 mm
**Capacity:** 3558 cc
**Maximum power:** 120 bhp
**Transmission:** four-speed manual
**Chassis:** pressed steel channel
**Suspension:** independent front with transverse leaf spring. Live rear axle with semi-elliptic leaf springs
**Brakes:** drums front and rear
**Bodywork:** sports roadster
**Maximum speed (approx):** 100 mph (161 kph)

Delaunay-Belleville SMT

Delahaye 135s finished 2–3–4–5 in the 1936 French Sports Car Grand Prix, and won the event in the 1937 and 1939 Monte Carlo Rallies, the 24 Heures du Mans in 1938, and the 'Fastest Sports Car' challenge race at Brooklands in 1939, against a 2.9-litre Alfa Romeo and a 4-litre Darracq.

The 135 had very effective independent front suspension using an interesting arrangement whereby a transverse leaf spring was connected to the bottom of the king pins, with single transverse links to the top ends while extra location was by two longitudinal radius rods. Another notable Delahaye feature was the use of an electrically-operated Cotal epicyclic gearbox.

The 4.5-litre V12 derivative of 1937 was derived by Jean Francois, and had a de Dion rear axle. 'It is,' claimed Delahaye advertising, 'the car that is missing from the French market... its performance is limitless. It doesn't depend on the mechanism, nor on the driver. It only depends on the road conditions... it's the incomparable competition car which gives its drivers all the joys of the struggle crowned with the immense satisfaction of speed and victory....

## DELAUNAY-BELLEVILLE

**St Denis, France 1904–1950**

This engineering firm, renowned for its steam engines and marine boilers, was one of the great names of French industry, and began by building a range of 16, 24 and 40 hp four-cylinder cars designed by former Benz engineer Marius Barbarou. But before long, the six-cylinder engine had become a hallmark of Delaunay-Belleville.

'The Car Magnificent' was considered in France as the ultimate motor-car; its round radiator, which recalled the famous Belleville marine boilers, was well known.

Their standard range of six-cylinder cars built before World War I ranged from the 12 hp of 2913 cc to the 45 hp of 7998 cc, with a gargantuan 70 hp, the SMT, available to special order.

After the war, Delaunay-Belleville initially resumed production with pre-war models.

In 1922, the 2613 cc 12 hp four acquired an overhead camshaft, while new 14/40 and 16/60 models appeared in 1926.

These had nondescript radiators rather than the traditional circular pattern, symptomatic of the fact that by the late 1920s the Delaunay-Belleville had lost its prestige. Some 1931 models even used American power units like the Continental straight-eight, which were said to be cheaper and quieter than the French product.

At the very end, after World War II, Delaunay-Belleville briefly revived the 2.3-litre six of the late 1930s, updated with a new radiator grille and Cotal electrically-operated gearbox.

## Delaunay Belleville SMT

The model designation of this biggest of all the Delaunay-Bellevilles was chosen in honour of the marque's most prestigious customer, the Tsar of Russia (SMT standing for *Sa Majesté le Tsar*).

The original SMT was delivered to the Imperial Garages in 1909, a colossal limousine by Kellner painted dark blue lined in cream and gold: its wheelbase was 13 feet 6 inches, and the length overall was some 17 feet 6 inches. It stood nearly 8 feet high, and the engine was equipped with a special compressed air starter.

Quite apart from the sheer size of the car, the remarkable feature of the SMT was the complexity of its controls: the chauffeur – a Russian Prince – was faced with operating no fewer than *nine* pedals – right-hand differential brake, left-hand differential brake sprag to prevent the car rolling backwards, clutch pedal, engine brake, accelerator, extra engine oil pump, compressed air whistle, even a carburettor float agitator...

No wonder the chief mechanic of the Tsar's garage held the rank of General!

### 1909 DELAUNEY BELLEVILLE SMT

**Engine:** in-line six-cylinder, side-valve
**Bore × stroke:** 134 mm × 140 mm
**Capacity:** 11,846 cc
**Maximum power:** 70 bhp
**Transmission:** four-speed manual
**Chassis:** pressed steel channel
**Suspension:** non independent with semi-elliptic leaf springs and additional single transverse platform spring at rear
**Brakes:** rear wheel and transmission
**Bodywork:** limousine
**Maximum speed (approx):** not known

Delahaye 135

# A-Z OF THE CAR

## DELLOW

**Birmingham, England**
**1947–1959**

The name Dellow was derived from the surnames of the partners who created these sturdy road-going competition cars, K.C. Delingpole and R.C. Lowe. The original Dellow was a trials special, and the early production cars followed its example in dispensing with such unnecessary frivolities as doors. Powered by a Ford Ten engine in a purpose-built chassis, the Dellow was available with a Wade supercharger as an optional extra.

Later versions included a four-seater MkIII Dellow and the MkV, which had coil front suspension.

The MkVI, offered by a re-formed Dellow company in 1956, had enveloping glassfibre bodywork, which took away all the primitive charm of the original alloy-bodied Dellows; consequently, few were sold.

### 1947 DELLOW

**Engine:** in-line four-cylinder, side valve
**Bore × stroke:** 63.5 mm × 92.5 mm
**Capacity:** 1172 cc
**Maximum power:** 36 bhp
**Transmission:** three-speed manual
**Chassis:** tubular steel
**Suspension:** independent with transverse leaf springs
**Brakes:** drums front and rear
**Bodywork:** open two seater
**Maximum speed (approx):** 60 mph (97 kph)

purpose-built complex at Dunmurry in West Belfast, which began limited production during 1979. It took the engineering skills of Lotus to sort out the handling of the DeLorean, but the plans for the car were over-optimistic from the start. The success of the car always depended on sales in America, and the company's forecasts of the potential market were wildly optimistic. At first, demand was strong, but once the novelty had worn off the myriad quality problems sometimes called for the irate customer to be given a new car in replacement for the

De Lorean DMC

## DE LOREAN

**Belfast, Northern Ireland**
**1979–1982**

'Drive the dream' exhorted the advertising for John Zachary DeLorean's exotic DMC-12 sports car, with its brushed stainless steel body panelling. It was a dream that quickly turned to nightmare. Gulled by the promise of new jobs in an area of chronic unemployment, the British Labour government put an initial investment of more than £40 million into the construction of a

### 1980 DE LOREAN DMC

**Engine:** V6, overhead-cam
**Bore × stroke:** 91 mm × 73 mm
**Capacity:** 2850 cc
**Maximum power:** 145 bhp
**Transmission:** five-speed
**Chassis:** steel backbone
**Suspension:** independent with unequal length parallel arms and trailing arms rear
**Brakes:** discs front and rear
**Bodywork:** two-door coupé
**Maximum speed (approx):** 125 mph (201 kph)

Dellow Mk III

unsatisfactory one. Among the early faults were totally inadequate electrical systems, power windows that dropped out of their tracks, inaccurate fuel gauges and leaking cooling systems… The DMC was not a bad car but it felt a little underdeveloped and old fashioned.

Moreover, many of the reported sales were based on potential customers who had put down deposits on cars, only to renege when the time came actually to take delivery. In February 1982, when Government grants had reached £67 million, it was revealed that DeLorean needed to raise £25 million just to meet outstanding bills.

The 2600 workforce were handed their redundancy notices, and before long the company had closed its doors and DeLorean was involved in a court case which accused him of trafficking in drugs to raise finance to keep his company afloat although he was eventually acquitted.

## DE SOTO

**Detroit, USA**
**1928–1960**

By 1928, after only four years in existence, Chrysler had become the third biggest car company in the United States. In order to break into a new market sector, the Chrysler Corporation announced in 1928 that they were to build a lower-priced 3.2-litre side-valve six running under the name De Soto. With rubber-mounted engine to reduce vibration, four-wheel hydraulic brakes and ribbon radiator, the De Soto may have been cheaper than the Chrysler, but it still represented up-to-date engineering practice.

A 3.5-litre straight-eight appeared in 1930, with four-wheel

**De Soto Fireflight Convertible**

Lockheed hydraulic brakes and a downdraught carburettor; from about 1931, the marque was sold in Britain under the Chrysler name.

De Soto's 1933 models incorporated all the Chrysler innovations such as 'floating power' engine mountings and double-drop girder truss chassis, while the 1934 models followed the corporate Airflow line; the 4-litre De Soto Airflow six, with optional overdrive, was sold in Britain as the Chrysler Croydon.

To soften the Airflow look, which was not too successful in sales terms, vee-bonnets were adopted in 1936; a dummy radiator grille and rear-hinged bonnet were featured on 1937 De Sotos.

The 1939 De Sotos incorporated independent front suspension, a choice of two six-cylinder engines and steering-column gearchange; Vacumatic semi-automatic transmission became available on 1941 models.

Most post-war models had the same bodyshells as the

---

**1958 DE SOTO FIREFLIGHT**

**Engine:** V8, overhead-valve
**Bore × stroke:** 92.1 mm × 84.9 mm
**Capacity:** 4769 cc
**Maximum power:** 200 bhp
**Transmission:** three-speed
**Chassis:** steel boxed side members with cruciform bracing
**Suspension:** independent front with coil springs. Live rear axle with semi-elliptic leaf springs
**Brakes:** Lockheed hydraulic drums front and rear
**Bodywork:** convertible
**Maximum speed (approx):** 100 mph (161 kph)

---

contemporary Chryslers, though the 1949 Carryall car-cum-station wagon was unique to De Soto.

The L-head side-valve six was joined in 1952 by the 4525 cc Firedome V8; 45,800 Firedomes were sold in the model's first year, and the V8 was soon outselling the six by two units to one.

The 1955 FireFlyte series was powered by a 200 hp V8 displacing 4769 cc: thereafter, all De Sotos were powered by V8 engines, save for the export-only Diploma (which was, in fact, a thinly disguised Plymouth).

In 1956 De Soto launched its limited-production Adventurer (named for one of the Chrysler Corporation's outstanding Ghia-built show cars), which featured a gold-on-white paint scheme, gold trim and a 5595 cc hemi-head V8

Chrysler Corporation's striking new FlightSweep styling, combined with the launch of the low-priced FireSweep series with a new 5326 cc V8, boosted De Soto sales to a record 117,747 in 1957.

This, however, was not a harbinger of good times coming, for appalling quality control slashed the following year's sales to 35,556, which was hardly redeemed for 1959 by the introduction of new wedge-head V8s of 5916 cc and 6276 cc, which only just lifted sales. It was not enough.

De Soto's 1961 models, with slanted fins, 'double layer' grille and 5916 cc engine, had only been on the market for four months before De Soto finally ceased building cars on 18 December, 1960, after merging with Plymouth the year before.

## DE TOMASO

**Modena, Italy**
**1959–**

Argentinian racing driver and entrepreneur Alejandro de Tomaso, and his wife, American ex-racing driver Isabelle Haskell, moved to Italy in the late 1950s, where De Tomaso built a number of prototypes – including racing cars – which incorporated bright ideas but never seemed to be fully developed.

In 1964, De Tomaso brought out the Vallelunga, a sporting mid-engined two-seater with a backbone chassis and Lotus Cortina power. A Giugiaro-designed coupé appeared in 1965, but the Vallelunga's chassis was too whippy.

Nevertheless, De Tomaso persisted with the backbone layout, which resulted in the 1966 launch of the Giugiaro-styled Mangusta, with a 4728 cc V8 Ford engine and a Ghia coupé body.

Production of Mangustas in the Ghia factory, which De Tomaso took over in 1967, totalled 401.

In 1970, De Tomaso launched the Tjaarda-styled Pantera powered by a 5796 cc Ford V8; it was a sports coupé with a claimed top speed of 162 mph (261 kph). The 5796 cc Deauville, an XJ6 look-alike with luxurious limousine bodywork was also introduced.

At the end of 1970, Ford acquired 84 per cent of the De Tomaso group shares, and the company became a Ford subsidiary, wholly owned from 1973.

New in 1972 was the Longchamp luxury coupé derived from the Deauville.

Ford decided to stop building the Pantera in 1974, and the rights were re-acquired by De Tomaso, who owned the Moto Guzzi and

**De Tomaso Pantera GP IV**

Benelli motorcycle factories as well as his Modena-based De Tomaso car works. Today, his many other industrial interests also include Innocenti and Maserati.

The De Tomaso range today includes variants on the Pantera as well as the 300 bhp Longchamp and Deauville. The Longchamp is also available as a Spyder.

## De Tomaso Pantera

One of the great survivors in the exoticar field, the Pantera was designed in the late 1960s to overcome the notable shortcomings of the Mangusta, which had poor weight distribution and unpredictable handling. Styling of the Pantera was by American-born Tom Tjaarda, who had succeeded Giorgetto Giugiaro as chief designer at Ghia,

---

### 1974 DE TOMASO PANTERA

**Engine:** V8, overhead-valve
**Bore × stroke:** 101.6 mm × 89 mm
**Capacity:** 5763 cc
**Maximum power:** 330 bhp
**Transmission:** ZF five-speed manual
**Chassis:** steel monocoque
**Suspension:** independent with coils and wishbones all round
**Brakes:** discs front and rear
**Bodywork:** two-seater coupé
**Maximum speed (approx):** 162 mph (260 kph)

---

where the first Panteras were built. Production then shifted to the more spacious Vignale factory, acquired by De Tomaso at the end of 1969.

Offering virtually the same performance as a Ferrari at half the price, the Pantera was eventually launched on the American market in 1971, but suffered from annoying teething troubles: a combination of the energy crisis and American emissions regulations prompted Ford to cease production of the Pantera in 1974, whereupon Alejandro de Tomaso, who still had distribution rights for Europe, reacquired the rights to assemble and sell the Pantera, so that today the car is produced in De Tomaso's factory in Modena which he retained after Ford had bought Ghia and Vignale.

The car is available in three versions, the L, GTS and GT5, the latter two with distinctive front and rear spoilers and more highly tuned engines. Top speed for the GTS is claimed to be 174 mph (208 kph) with 60 mph (97 kph) coming up in just under 6 seconds. Performance is combined with luxury with air conditioning standard.

## DETROIT ELECTRIC

Detroit, USA
1907–1938

Probably America's best-known and most popular electric car, the Detroit Electric was selling at the rate of 1000 cars annually in the period from 1912 to 1915. Because the original Detroit Electrics looked more like preambulating china closets, a dummy bonnet was offered as an option from 1920.

Although electric cars had become obsolete by the 1920s, nevertheless Detroit Electrics continued to be purchased by a loyal but diminishing band of enthusiastic owners.

The ultimate Detroit Electrics were fitted with Willy-Overland bodywork as a concession to modern design; nevertheless, the ultra-conservative element among the company's clientele continued to be catered for, since the antique pattern Detroit Electric with baroque battery covers fore and aft continued to be offered. The sole visible gesture to the twentieth century lay in the provision of safety glass and balloon tyres.

---

### 1922 DETROIT ELECTRIC

**Engine:** electric
**Maximum power:** not known
**Transmission:** five-speed
**Chassis:** channel steel
**Suspension:** non independent with semi-elliptic leaf springs
**Brakes:** expanding on rear wheels, electric brake on motor
**Bodywork:** brougham
**Maximum speed (approx):** 25 mph (40 kph)

---

**Detroit Electric**

# A-Z OF THE CAR

## 1910 DEUTZ PRINCE HENRY

**Engine:** in-line four-cylinder
**Bore × stroke:** 92 mm × 120 mm
**Capacity:** 3192 cc
**Maximum power:** not known
**Transmission:** four-speed
**Chassis:** channel steel
**Suspension:** non independent with semi-elliptic leaf springs
**Brakes:** rear wheels only
**Bodywork:** Torpedo
**Maximum speed (approx):** 93 mph (150 kph)

## DFP
### Courbevoie, France
### 1906–1926

Auguste Doriot and Ludovic Flandrin had worked at Peugeot for several years before setting up their own company in 1906. They were joined two years later by the Parant brothers, Alexandre and Jules-René, at which point the Doriot-Flandrin car became known as the DFP. The company built 1100 cc single-cylinder cars up to 1910, but from 1909 they also produced an 1874 cc 8/10cv four.

In 1911, DFP decided to abandon proprietary engines in

## 1913 DFP 12/15

**Engine:** in-line four-cylinder, side-valve
**Bore × stroke:** 70 mm × 130 mm
**Capacity:** 2001 cc
**Maximum power:** not known
**Transmission:** four-speed
**Chassis:** pressed steel channel
**Suspension:** non independent with semi-elliptic leaf springs
**Brakes:** rear wheel and transmission
**Bodywork:** torpedo two- or four-seater
**Maximum speed (approx):** 65 mph (105 kph)

*Deutz Prince Henry*

## DEUTZ
### Köln-Deutz, Germany
### 1907–1911

Deutz produced big chain-driven cars with ohc engines of 4960 cc, 6400 cc, 9900 cc and even 10,500 cc which were built at Cologne in Gustav Langen's Deutz factory (where the first production four-stroke engines had appeared in the 1870s). They were notable in being designed by a young Italian named Ettore Bugatti.

While producing these big cars, Bugatti built a little 1327 cc four-cylinder car in the cellar of his house. The car was never adopted for production.

Instead, Bugatti used the little Type 10 to found his own factory at Molsheim (Alsace); nevertheless, he continued to carry out design and development work for Deutz, and his 5 litre Type Garros was, it seems, originally built as a version of the Deutz Prince Henry.

The last Deutz cars were built in small numbers only.

**DFP 12/15 CV**

favour of power units of their own manufacture. Their first power units were 2950 cc and 2001 cc four-cylinder models, followed the following year by fours of 1592 cc, 1847 cc and 2412 cc, plus a short-lived six of 3619 cc.

The company's reputation was really made by their London agent, a young man named W.O. Bentley, who raced the 2001 cc model with some success, and by the 1913 London Motor Show was offering a vee-radiatored speed model, which was fitted with aluminium pistons.

DFP restarted production with the latter model after the war.

However, financial problems soon forced a return to proprietary power units; thereafter, DFP built cars with 1098 cc CIME, 1847 cc Sergant and 2001 cc overhead-camshaft Altos power units.

In 1926, DFP ceased production and their factory was acquired by Théophile Lafitte, who built an improbable friction-drive cyclecar.

# DIANA

**St Louis, USA**
**1925–1928**

In mid-1925 the Moon Motor Car Company introduced the Diana, powered by an eight-cylinder Continental engine and promoted as 'Queen of the Eights' as a running mate to the Moon range.

The Diana's radiator was closely modelled on that of the Belgian Minerva. The sporting Diana model had roadster bodywork, and featured a bronze radiator, with matching wire wheels.

*Diana*

## 1925 DIANA

**Engine:** in-line eight-cylinder
**Bore × stroke:** 76.2 mm × 108 mm
**Capacity:** 3938 cc
**Maximum power:** 28.8 hp
**Transmission:** three-speed
**Chassis:** pressed steel channel
**Suspension:** non independent with semi-elliptic leaf springs
**Brakes:** four-wheel hydraulic
**Bodywork:** roadster, phaeton, sedan and brougham
**Maximum speed (approx):** not known

Prices of the Diana range were between $1595 and $2895, though there was a rare town car Diana, available to special order only at $5000!

# DIATTO

**Turin, Italy**
**1905–1927**

Diatto started as coachbuilders as early as 1835, and later diversified into tram manufacture. In 1905 they began building cars based on the French Clément under the marque name Torino; these were two- and four-cylinder models.

Adolphe Clément severed his connection with the company in 1909, and the firm was reorganised financially.

The firm took over two other makes, John Newton and Scacchi in 1915, and a year later also acquired the Italian subsidiary of the Gnome and Rhone aero-engine company, which attempted to build Bugatti aero engines under licence.

In 1919, Diatto acquired the licence to build the Type 13 Bugatti under licence, though the Diatto Tipo 30 which resulted bore little external resemblance to its Molsheim counterpart. That same year, Diatto achieved sporting fame with a victory in the Targo Florio by a 2.7 litre Diatto 4DA driven by Gamboni.

Several of the famous Diattos of the 1920s were designed by the famous Alfieri Maserati, who, working with his four brothers, created a supercharged eight-cylinder overhead camshaft racing car, which became the basis for the first Maserati when the brothers established their own factory in

## 1922 DIATTO TIPO 20S

**Engine:** in-line four cylinder, overhead cam
**Bore × stroke:** 79.7 mm × 100 mm
**Capacity:** 1996 cc
**Maximum power:** 75 bhp
**Transmission:** four-speed manual
**Chassis:** pressed steel channel
**Suspension:** non independent with semi-elliptic leaf springs
**Brakes:** drums all round
**Bodywork:** sports two seater
**Maximum speed (approx):** 75 mph (120 kph)

*Diatto Tipo 20A*

1926. As early as 1922, production Diatto Tipo 20 models had overhead camshaft 1990 cc four-cylinder engines of advanced design and were equipped with four-wheel brakes and four-speed gearboxes.

A 2952 cc four-cylinder Diatto appeared in 1926, but the company's new owners, the Musso brothers, ran into difficulties the following year and production halted in 1927, though the manufacture of spares and motorised generators continued for some time after that.

## DIXI
### Eisenach, Germany
### 1904–1928

The Fahrzeugfabrik Eisenach built Wartburg cars (based on the French Decauville voiturelle from 1898, but in 1903 they split from their parent company, Ehrhardt, and launched the Dixi ('I have spoken') cars in 1904, introducing a 2815 cc four-cylinder model, quickly followed by a single-cylinder of 1240 cc and a twin-cylinder of 2468 cc.

The company's pre-Great War models ranged from 1320 cc to 7300 cc, two of the latter models appearing in the 1907 Kaiserpreis race, with little success.

### 1927 DIXI 3/15PS WARTBURG

**Engine:** in-line four cylinder, side-valve
**Bore × stroke:** 56 mm × 76 mm
**Capacity:** 743 cc
**Maximum power:** 15 bhp
**Transmission:** three-speed
**Chassis:** A-frame channel steel
**Suspension:** non independent with transverse leaf spring front and quarter-elliptic leaf springs rear
**Brakes:** drums all round
**Bodywork:** sports two-seater
**Maximum speed (approx):** 60 mph (100 kph)

**Dixi Roadster**

The 1920 6/24PS model was an improved 1568 cc version of the pre-war 1320 cc side-valve; that year the company was taken over by a manufacturer of rolling-stock, the Gothaer Waggonfabrik.

In 1922, tuned 6/24PS cars came 1, 2 and 4 in the second AVUS race.

Two six-cylinder models of 2330 cc and 3557 cc were launched in the mid-1920s, then, in 1927 the factory acquired the licence to manufacture the Austin Seven at Eisenach but ran out of money. BMW of Munich took over the design and the works in 1928, initially building it as the BMW-Dixi.

## DKW
### Berlin-Spandau, Germany
### 1928–1966

Jörge-Skafte Rasmussen's DKW factory (the initials stood for 'Das Kleine Wunder' – 'the little wonder') built its two-stroke motorcycles from 1919; then, after building Slaby & Behringer and DEW electrics in the mid-1920s, used a similar wood-framed chassis-less construction to the latter marque, with bodies built by the former (!) on its first petrol-powered two-stroke cars of 1928.

In 1928, Rasmussen bought engine tooling and equipment from the defunct Rickenbacker plant in the USA and used it to produce big six- and eight-cylinder engines for Audi and other firms.

The first complete DKW cars had 584 cc twin-cylinder engines, followed in 1930 by water-cooled V4 models with two-stroke engines of 780 cc. A 992 cc engine appeared later.

DKW pioneered front-wheel drive with its two-stroke 490 cc and 584 cc two-cylinder models of 1931; the factory subsequently produced two-stroke cars in 684 cc and V4 1047 cc guise. These cars were good, but rarely economical.

After 1945, the group's factories were nationalised, for they were located in the area which became the DDR, and new Auto Union factories in West Germany at Ingolstadt and Dusseldorf were opened in 1949 to build DKW cars with 684 cc twin-cylinder – and then three-cylinder 896 cc – water-cooled two-stroke power units.

The Auto Union DKW 1000 of 1957 had a new three-cylinder two-stroke 980 cc engine which developed 44 bhp, and there was also a Special version developing 55 bhp. The chassis was made by DKW but the bodies were specially built in glassfibre. The sports model was known as the Monza after gaining five world records at that circuit, and was also successful in international competitions. Tuned

**DKW Front**

### 1937 DKW FRONT

**Engine:** two-cylinder-two stroke
**Bore × stroke:** 76 × 76 mm
**Capacity:** 684 cc
**Maximum power:** 20 bhp
**Transmission:** three-speed
**Chassis:** steel backbone
**Suspension:** independent front with swing axles and transverse leaf spring. Live rear axle
**Brakes:** drums all round
**Bodywork:** cabriolet, limousine
**Maximum speed (approx):** 56 mph (90 kph)

engines were also used in Formula Junior racing.

These power units were not particularly economical, a trend which led to the introduction of four-stroke engines and to the first 'new' Audi.

Daimler-Benz bought the works in 1958, but sold it to VW in 1965, and the last two-stroke DKW was produced very soon after that in February 1966.

## DOBLE
### Emeryville, USA
### 1914–1932

Abner Doble's first production steam car, the Doble-Detroit, appeared in 1915–17, but the war promptly halted the project, and production was not resumed until 1924, in Emeryville, California.

Doble was a perfectionist, and as a consequence, production never attained anything like the anticipated rhythm, and only some 45 Doble steamers were ever built.

In its final form, the Doble could reach a full head of steam in less than 90 seconds from cold, and run for 1500 miles on 24 gallons of water, thanks to an efficient condenser. Though its 75 bhp four-cylinder engine gave exceptional acceleration and hill-climbing powers, the Doble was really only a magnificent might-have-been…

## 1930 DOBLE STEAMER

**Engine:** four-cylinder, double-acting balanced compound steam
**Bore × stroke:** 66.7 mm × 127 mm (low pressure) 114.3 mm × 127 mm (high pressure)
**Maximum power:** 75 bhp
**Transmission:** engine geared direct to back axle
**Chassis:** pressed-steel channel
**Suspension:** non independent with semi-elliptic leaf springs
**Brakes:** rear-wheel only
**Bodywork:** phaeton or limousine
**Maximum speed (approx):** 75 mph (120 kph)

**Doble Steamer**

# DODGE

Hamtramck, Detroit, USA
1914–

Founded by the rumbustious Dodge brothers, who had made their name – and fortune – as suppliers of engines and transmissions to Henry Ford, the 'Dependable Dodge' car was a 3.5-litre four with the advanced touch of a 'North-East' dynastarter which operated automatically to restart the engine if it stalled.

By 1916, when Dodge was America's first company to adopt Budd all-steel coachwork, the marque had become the country's fourth-biggest seller: by 1920 it was second only to Ford.

The Dodge brothers died of pneumonia in 1920, when ownership of the company passed to their widows, and day-to-day management to Frederick J. Haynes, former Vice-President and General Manager. Dodge was now building 1000 cars a day.

Bankers took over the company for some $146 million in 1925, of which $50 million represented goodwill (down in the books as worth a dollar!).

Dodge's first new model in over 10 years, the Senior Six (which boasted hydraulic brakes), appeared in 1927; the following year, the cautious marketing approach of the bankers had brought Dodge to the brink of disaster, so rising star of the motor industry Walter Chrysler bought the company for $126 million.

The same year, the old Dodge four was replaced by a cheaper Victory Six. A Chrysler-based straight-eight appeared in 1930, along with a 2.6-litre six.

The first truly new post-war models – the Wayfarer, Meadowbrook and top-of-the-line Coronet – were launched for 1949; the old 3769 cc six-cylinder was now either linked to FluiDrive transmission or to the new GyroMatic semi-automatic.

In 1953, Dodge launched its version of the Chrysler hemi-head V8, the 3949 cc Red Ram, initially only available in the Coronet.

Unitary construction arrived on the 1960 range, which featured a standard range, whose models were renamed Matador and Polara, and a new intermediate Dart range.

The 'Swept-Wing' styling of the 1959 range had featured huge tailfins, but these had vanished completely by 1962, when the 2785 cc Lancer compact (derived from the Plymouth Valiant) appeared, but only lasted two seasons. The Dart took over as Dodge's compact in 1963.

In 1966 came the Charger performance model, which had a 5211 cc V8 engine as standard, and optional power units up to a 425 bhp V8 displacing 6891 cc;

these engines were also used in the handsome 1968 Charger, which could accelerate from 0–60 mph in 4.75 seconds.

With the Dart series as their bread-and-butter line for the 1970s, Dodge added the Challenger to their performance models; it had the slant six as standard and V8s up to 425 bhp as options.

New for 1978 were the Colt-based 2540 cc Challenger, with

## 1953 DODGE CORONET D44

**Engine:** V8, overhead-valve
**Bore × stroke:** 87.3 mm × 82.5 mm
**Capacity:** 3949 cc
**Maximum power:** 140 bhp
**Transmission:** three-speed manual or automatic
**Chassis:** X-frame with box-section side members
**Suspension:** independent front with coil springs and wishbones. Live rear axle with semi-elliptic leaf springs
**Brakes:** drums all round
**Bodywork:** four-door sedan
**Maximum speed (approx):** 90 mph (145 kph)

four-wheel disc brakes and five-speed manual transmission, the Diplomat (based on Chrysler's LeBaron) the luxury Magnum XE (derived from the Charger SE) and the Omni front-drive compact.

Helping Chrysler weather its economic problems was the Aries K-car, the result of a massive investment in new manufacturing equipment aimed at bringing Chrysler Corporation quality up to Japanese fit-and-finish levels.

# Dodge Coronet

The 1953 Dodge Coronet D44 was the top of the Dodge range, and was equipped with the new V8 power unit, with hemispherical combustion chambers – the legendary 'Hemi'.

It broke new ground in terms of transmission, too, for it had PowerFlite automatic transmission which was claimed to be 'one of the simplest yet produced, having a fairly small number of moving parts'.

But technically advanced though the Chryslers of the early 1950s were, they lost sales through their dowdy styling, to counter which chief stylist Virgil Exner inaugurated a series of exciting concept cars built with Ghia of Turin.

**Dodge Coronet D44**

**RIGHT** The 1984 Corvette is notable for its use of plastic monofilament transverse leaf springs for both front and rear suspension and for its superbly forged aluminium alloy suspension arms

**BOTTOM RIGHT** The '84 Corvette has moved away from the traditional ladder frame to the perimeter steel chassis built of galvanised high strength steel. The subframes front and rear are in aluminised steel

## MODEL
Chevrolet Corvette
**UK price (1984):** £28,600

## ENGINE
**Location:** Front, longitudinal
**Type:** Water cooled V8 with cast iron block and heads
**Cubic capacity:** 5736 cc
**Bore × stroke:** 101.6 mm × 88.4 mm
**Valve gear:** 2 valves per cylinder in line operated via single block-mounted camshaft, pushrods and hydraulic tappets
**Fuel supply:** 'Cross Fire' throttle body fuel injection
**Ignition:** Delco Remy high energy electronic with engine management control
**Maximum power:** 205 bhp at 4200 rpm (SAE net)
**Maximum torque:** 290 lb ft at 2800 rpm (SAE net)

## TRANSMISSION
**Layout:** Clutch and gearbox in unit with engine
**Clutch:** Single dry plate
**Gearbox:** Four-speed manual with computer-controlled overdrive on top three ratios or Turbo-Hydramatic four-speed automatic with following ratios
| | |
|---|---|
| 1st 3.060:1 | 3rd 1.00:1 |
| 2nd 1.630:1 | 4th 0.70:1 |
**Final drive:** Hypoid bevel with limited slip differential
**Ratio:** 2.730:1

## SUSPENSION
**Front:** Independent with wishbones, anti-roll bar and transverse monofilament plastic leaf spring
**Rear:** Independent with five links – upper and lower control arms per side with lateral Panhard rod, transverse monofilament leaf spring

## STEERING
**Type:** Rack and pinion, servo assisted with 2.36 turns lock to lock

## BRAKES
**Type:** Discs front and rear with 329.9 sq in (2128 sq cm) swept area

## WHEELS AND TYRES
**Type:** Alloy 16 in × 8 in with Goodyear 225/50VR16 radial tyres

## BODY/CHASSIS
**Type:** High-strength steel perimeter frame with glassfibre and SMC 2-door, 2-seat coupè body

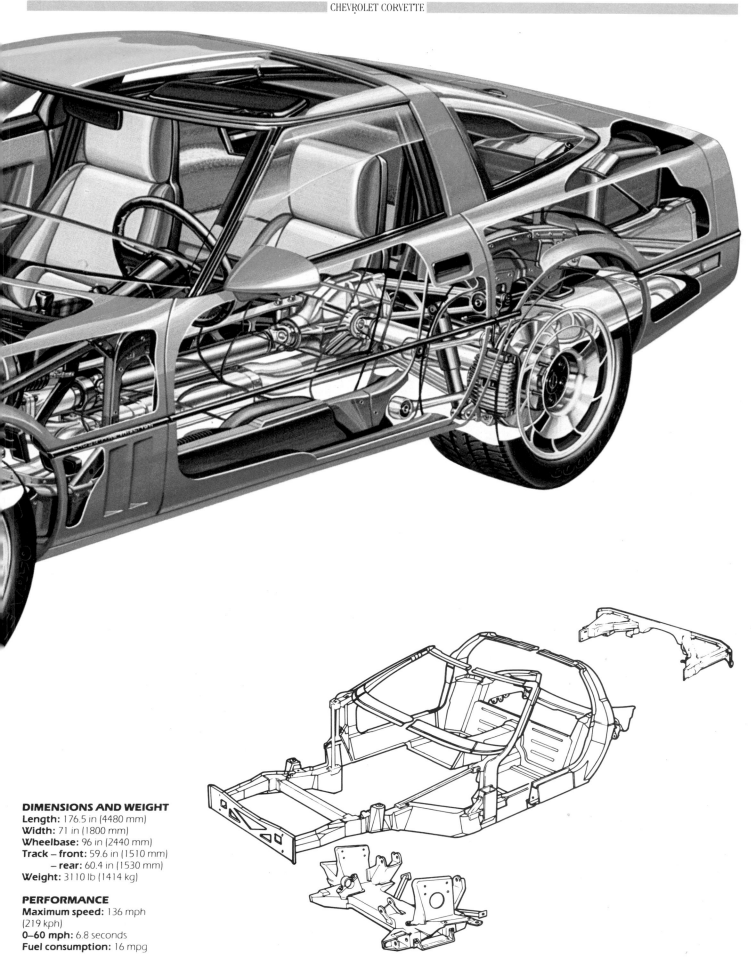

**DIMENSIONS AND WEIGHT**
**Length:** 176.5 in (4480 mm)
**Width:** 71 in (1800 mm)
**Wheelbase:** 96 in (2440 mm)
**Track – front:** 59.6 in (1510 mm)
    **– rear:** 60.4 in (1530 mm)
**Weight:** 3110 lb (1414 kg)

**PERFORMANCE**
**Maximum speed:** 136 mph
(219 kph)
**0–60 mph:** 6.8 seconds
**Fuel consumption:** 16 mpg

# A-Z OF THE CAR

## Dodge Charger

Aimed at capturing some of the medium-price performance market from General Motors by 'biting deep into the Pontiac GTO belt', the Dodge Charger built on the marque's competition record.

'The Charger', said the press,' was a way of letting the potential buyer recognise the Chrysler-Dodge speed image'. Launched in 1966, for 1967-68 the Charger had acquired notchback 'sport-oriented' styling that meant a recessed rear window, spoiler formed in the bootlid and retractable headlamps.

Its styling features were adopted for 1968 models from both Chrysler and Plymouth.

Both wedge-head and hemi-head engines were offered. with a choice of capacities ranging from 5211 cc to 7210 cc and , with a choice of manual and automatic transmissions allied to 'go-go looks', the Charger was designed for rapid straightline performance, something for which it quickly became famous. The Charger was most sought after with the legendary 426 cu in hemi but the 440 cu in (7.2-litre) V8 with conventional wedge-shape com-

bustion chambers gave even more torque. It was offered only in the R/T (Road and Track) version, making it one of the fastest cars of the era.

But the writing was on the wall for 'muscle cars' like the Charger, for America's motor industry was already beginning to wrestle with the problem of meeting increasingly strict Federal limits on engine emissions.

### 1967 DODGE CHARGER

**Engine:** V8, overhead-valve
**Bore × stroke:** 109.7 mm × 95.2 mm.
**Capacity:** 7210 cc
**Maximum power:** 375 bhp
**Transmission:** three or four-speed manual or three-speed automatic
**Chassis:** steel, integral
**Suspension:** independent front with wishbones and torsion bars. Live rear axle with semi-elliptic leaf springs
**Brakes:** drums all round
**Bodywork:** coupé
**Maximum speed (approx):** 120 mph (193 kph)

## DORT

Flint, Michigan, USA
1915–1924

J. Dallas Dort was working as a clerk in a hardware store when in 1886 he was persuaded to invest $1000 as a half-share in a new carriage company, along with a persuasive entrepreneur named William Crapo Durant. His bold investment was amply rewarded when the Durant-Dort company rapidly became America's biggest carriage-builder, with 15 plants producing some 150,000 vehicles annually.

The Durant-Dort company was slow entering the motor business, but eventually took the plunge in 1903, and began manufacturing a car designed by Scottish plumber David Dunbar Buick.

Though that marked the start of Durant's inexorable progress towards forming General Motors,

Dort remained staunchly in the carriage trade until 1915, when he began manufacturing cars under his own name.

Those initial Dorts had four-cylinder 2720 cc power units supplied by Lycoming; in 1918 Dort brought out the Model 11, with a 3146 cc Lycoming engine. It had a curious two-pedal control: one pedal operated the clutch and parking brake, while the other pedal applied the 'emergency' brake. In 1920 conventional controls were adopted, and sales reached a peak of 30,000.

Dort cars were totally restyled for 1921, with angular radiator shells: two years later, a softer line was adopted, featuring rounded nickel-plated radiators.

That year, too, an overhead-valve 3205 cc six was added to the range; it became the sole chassis offered by Dort the following year, which was also Dort's last season.

Dort had an alter ego, the Canadian-built Gray-Dort, licence-

Dort

**Dodge Charger**

**Duesenberg Model J**

## 1918 DORT MODEL 11

**Engine:** in-line four-cylinder, side-valve
**Bore × stroke:** 90 mm × 127 mm
**Capacity:** 3153 cc
**Maximum power:** 19.6 hp (rated)
**Transmission:** three-speed manual
**Chassis:** pressed steel channel
**Suspension:** non-independent with semi-elliptic leaf springs
**Brakes:** drums on rear only
**Bodywork:** roadster, tourer, sedan, coupé or sedanet
**Maximum speed (approx):** not known

built by a carriage and sleigh manufacturer in Chatham, Ontario: oddly enough, the Canadian-built version of the Dort proved much more successful than the original, and only went out of business in 1925, after the failure of Dort cars. Not only did Gray-Dort export some sports models to the United States, but the marque was also the first to fit a reversing light.

## DUESENBERG

**Indianapolis, USA**
**1920–1937**

Fred Duesenberg and his brother August began production under their own name in 1913 with engines and racing cars, and were involved in the building of the unsuccessful U-16 Bugatti aero-

engine during the war.

Towards the end of 1916, the Duesenbergs brought out their Model A, America's first production straight-eight, which also pioneered hydraulic four-wheel brakes.

It remained in production until 1926, when E.L. Cord took over control of the company, though Fred and Augie stayed on. Cord replaced the Model A (which was a designation given the Duesenberg by the public, not the factory) with the Model X (again, not an official designation).

The Model X was very similar to the Model A, but had much more striking styling. It was intended as a stop-gap while the brothers developed 'The World's Finest Motor Car' – the Duesenberg Model J, announced in December 1928 (and this time the designation was official). It had a 6876 cc straight eight (built by another of Cord's companies, Lycoming, to Duesenberg design).

This very un-American engine had twin overhead cams and four valves per cylinder, with fully-machined hemispherical combustion chambers. Every Model J chassis was tested for 500 miles on the Indianapolis Speedway before being handed over to a leading bodybuilder for custom coachwork. Most cars were sold complete with bodywork approved by the company and built by companies like Le Baron, Murphy and Bohmann & Schwartz. Catalogued models could cost up to $17,950, more than a Rolls-Royce or Hispano-Suiza, while those clothed by the European houses – Letourneur et Marchand, Gurney Nutting, Barker and Weymann – cost nearer $20,000.

Unashamedly luxurious, it offered performance unheard of in

## 1928 DUESENBERG MODEL J

**Engine:** in-line straight-eight double overhead-cam
**Bore × stroke:** 95 mm × 121 mm
**Capacity:** 6876 cc
**Maximum power:** 265 bhp
**Transmission:** three-speed manual
**Chassis:** pressed steel channel
**Suspension:** non-independent with semi-elliptic leaf springs
**Brakes:** drums all round hydraulically operated
**Bodywork:** to order
**Maximum speed (approx)::** 116 mph (187 kph)

such a car, with a top speed of 116 mph (187 kph).

Model Js were purchased by Greta Garbo, Mae West and William Randolph Hearst. Prince Nicholas of Romania bought three and raced one unsuccessfully at Le Mans. Other royal owners included King Alfonso XIII of Spain, Queen Marie of Yugoslavia and the King of Italy.

Included in the comprehensive instrumentation was the world's first on-board computer, the timing box. Driven by the fuel pump shaft, this was a complex unit containing 24 sets of planetary gears which actuated warning lights. One came on every 700 miles to tell the driver to change his engine oil, another came on at 1400 miles to warn that the battery level needed checking. Every 75 miles the timing box operated a Bijur pump to lubricate all the chassis greasing points.

Duesenberg weathered the Depression well, and was confident enough to launch the SJ in 1932; with a centrifugal supercharger, it developed a claimed 320 bhp, and

had a top speed in the region of 130 mph (210 kph). In addition, two short-wheelbase SSJ speedsters were built, one for Clark Gable, the other for Gary Cooper.

But Duesenberg's high noon came when Cord's empire collapsed in 1937, and the purchasers of the wreckage decided to stop car production.

There have been two or three unsuccessful attempts to revive the marque, most notably in 1947 and 1966, but these ventures only resulted in prototypes.

## DUPONT

**Moore, Pennsylvania, USA**
**1920-1932**

E. Paul DuPont was a wealthy industrialist whose company's rationale was the building of quality cars in limited numbers. In its 12 years of existence, DuPont built just 537 luxury cars, starting in 1920 with Model B, a four-cylinder model powered by a 4.1-litre side-valve unit of DuPont's own make; it retailed at $2,600.

That model was followed by a six-cylinder DuPont with a proprietary Herschell-Spillman power unit; a later DuPont, the 1925 Model D, used the Wisconsin six.

Best-known of all the DuPonts was the 1929 Model G Speedster, powered by a 5.3-litre Continental straight-eight. Its radiator was enclosed in a distinctive bullnosed cowling, while the odd Woodlite headlamps were standard: the engine developed 114 bhp in standard form, but could be modified to produce 140 bhp. One of these cars was the fastest American-built car at Le Mans in 1929, but retired.

119

**DuPont Model G**

## 1929 DUPONT MODEL G

**Engine:** in-line eight-cylinder, side-valve
**Bore × stroke:** 85.7 mm × 114.3 mm
**Capacity:** 5275 cc
**Maximum power:** 140 bhp
**Transmission:** four-speed manual
**Chassis:** pressed steel channel
**Suspension:** non-independent with semi-elliptic leaf springs
**Brakes:** drums all round
**Bodywork:** sedan or speedster
**Maximum speed (approx):** 114 mph (184 kph)

# DURKOPP

**Bielefeld, Germany**
**1898-1927**

Durkopp were makers of bicycles, ball-bearings, motorcycles and sewing machines as well as motor cars, and began production with twin-cylinder Panhard-inspired models.

Four-cylinder models were added to the range in 1902, and the marque was sold in export markets as the Canello-Durkopp, though in Britain the less Germanic name of 'Watsonia' was used.

Durkopp were early on the scene with a six-cylinder, which was running in 1904, and there was even an eight-cylinder prototype in 1905, but in Edwardian days the firm was better known for its massive fours, which were based on the 70 bhp, 7.2-litre racing car developed for the Kaiserpreis race of 1907. Biggest of all was the Type DG43 100 hp model of 13 litres.

At the other end of the scale was the Knipperdolling light car, of which the Type EK6 was produced into the 1920s.

In 1909 Durkopp had taken over

## 1901 DURKOPP

**Engine:** vertical twin-cylinder, automatic inlet valves
**Bore × stroke:** 82 mm × 100 mm
**Capacity:** 1056 cc
**Maximum power:** 10 hp
**Transmission:** four-speed
**Chassis:** armoured wood and pressed steel
**Suspension:** non-independent with semi-elliptic leaf springs
**Brakes:** rear wheels and transmission
**Bodywork:** open four-seater
**Maximum speed (approx):** not known

the Oryx company, which continued to produce its own small cars until World War I.

The Durkopp 8/40/60PS was a 2-litre sports of the 1920s, available blown or unblown, and it was with a P8A supercharged version that Hans Stuck first achieved success: indeed, challenged to climb a mountain road faster in reverse than his rivals could going forwards, he reversed the differential of his car to give four reverse speeds and spent a week practising to ensure victory!

Though car production ceased in 1927, lorries were built for a few more years, while motorcycles reappeared after World War II.

**Durkopp**

# A-Z OF THE CAR

## D'YRSAN
**Asnieres, France**
**1923-1930**

One of the great sporting three-wheelers, the D'Yrsan was rare in that it was not a derivative of the British Morgan; instead it was completely French in design, and took its name from its constructor, the Marquis Raymond Siran de Cavanac. Consequently, it never used a vee-twin motorcycle power

unit, relying instead on proprietary French four-cylinder engines of 750 cc and 1100 cc, made by Ruby and SCAP.

From 1928, four-wheeled D'Yrsans were also listed, with underslung rear suspension, a Cozette-blown Ruby 'Kappa' 1098 cc power unit and external exhaust pipe.

Some D'Yrsan four-wheelers also had special 1455 cc and 1645 cc supercharged six-cylinder engines made by Michel-Aviation, with overhead valves operated by short pushrods, similar in design to those of the British Riley. D'Yrsan also made motorcycles, but went out of business at the onset of the Depression.

### 1929 D'YRSAN K SPORT
**Engine:** in-line four-cylinder overhead-valve, supercharged
**Bore × stroke:** 62 mm × 90 mm
**Capacity:** 1088 cc
**Maximum power:** 55 bhp
**Transmission:** three-speed manual
**Chassis:** pressed steel channel
**Suspension:** front independent with leaf springs; rear quarter-elliptic leaf springs
**Brakes:** drums all round
**Bodywork:** open sports two-seater
**Maximum speed (approx):** 90 mph (145 kph)

## EDSEL
**Detroit, USA**
**1958-1960**

Ford's new marque, the Edsel, was launched with a fanfare of publicity to plug what the company's marketing department had identified as a gap between the Lincoln and Mercury ranges.

Unfortunately, the complexion of the market completely changed between the time of the market survey and the launch, and the unfortunately-styled Edsel proved to be an immensely costly mistake; Ford lost a reported $250-350 million on the Edsel during the marque's short lifespan.

There was certainly no shortage of choice with Edsel, as four series were available with no less than 18 models, from the low-priced Ranger and Pacer, both powered by a 5916 cc V8, to the 'upper-medium-priced' Corsair and Citation ranges with 6719 cc V8s.

The Edsel's front-end styling, with a vertical grille that polite critics referred to as a 'horsecollar', others in baser anatomical terms, was controversial, while the rest of the design, by ex-dance band crooner Roy Brown, was a visual affront that defied description.

The automatic transmission – standard on more expensive models – was controlled by push-buttons mounted in the hub of the steering wheel.

The post-Korean War boom had evaporated by the time that the Edsel was launched, and only 35,000 were sold in the first six months, 60,000 in the first year; the figure plunged to 44,000 in 1959.

### 1958 EDSEL CITATION
**Engine:** V8
**Bore × Stroke:** 102.8 mm × 88.9 mm
**Capacity:** 6719 cc
**Maximum power:** 303 bhp
**Transmission:** push-button automatic
**Chassis:** perimeter frame
**Suspension:** front independent, with coil and wishbone. Live rear axle with semi-elliptic leaf springs
**Brakes:** drums all round, self-adjusting
**Bodywork:** sedan
**Maximum speed (approx):** 100 mph (161 kph)

**Edsel Citation**

**D'Yrsan Sport K**

There was a hasty restyling for 1960, with that generous model lineup reduced to just the Ranger Series; the Edsel was now no more than a Ford with a grille that made it look like a Pontiac, and sales of the new models were only 2846 when, within weeks of the launch of the 1960 range in November 1959, the Edsel division ceased operation altogether. Sales were at this time rising dramatically for the relatively new 'compact' cars.

Roy Brown was sent to England, where, among other models, he created the amazingly successful Cortina Mark I of 1962.

# EHP

**Courbevoie, France**
**1921-1929**

Les Etablissements Henri Precloux started by making a sporting 903 cc Ruby-engined cyclecar with transverse front suspension: subsequently, proprietary engines of 959 cc and 1094 cc were employed. They were similar in construction to the contemporary

**Ehrhardt**

## 1926 EHP 1200 cc

**Engine:** in-line overhead-valve four-cylinder
**Bore × stroke:** 64 mm × 93.5 mm
**Capacity:** 1200 cc
**Maximum power:** not known
**Transmission:** three-speed manual
**Chassis:** pressed steel channel
**Suspension:** non-independent with semi-elliptic leaf springs front and quarter-elliptic leaf springs rear
**Brakes:** rear-wheel drums
**Bodywork:** open two/three-seater sports, coupé
**Maximum speed (approx):** 56 mph (90 kph)

Salmson, Amilcar and Derby products, conventional voiturettes, but were unusual in also being offered as saloons and coupés.

These early EHP models were also built in Majorca under the name LORYC by Lacy, Ribas of Palma de Mallorca.

After 1924, EHP offered a more substantial 1203 cc CIME-engined model, which could be specified with semi-elliptic front springs.

A popular marque, EHP appeared regularly at Le Mans between 1925 and 1928. For their occasional forays into racing, EHP built a model with an overhead-camshaft 1500 cc engine for that purpose, but their last models incorporated side-valve 1792 cc CIME six-cylinder engines.

# EHRHARDT, EHRHARDT-SZAWE

**Zella-St Blasii/Dusseldorf, Germany**
**1905-1925**

After Heinrich Ehrhardt resigned from Wartburg (which then became Dixi), his son Gustav began independent manufacture of high quality two- and four-cylinder cars, initially on Decauville lines, at proportionately elevated prices.

Ehrhardt's biggest model was a 7956 cc four-cylinder based on their 1907 Kaiserpreis racer; in 1913 this car became Germany's

## 1920 EHRHARDT-SZAWE

**Engine:** in-line six-cylinder, overhead cam
**Bore × stroke:** 83 mm x 118 mm
**Capacity:** 2570 cc
**Maximum power:** 50 bhp
**Transmission:** four-speed preselector
**Chassis:** pressed steel channel, ladder-frame
**Suspension:** non-independent with semi-elliptic leaf springs all round
**Brakes:** drums all round
**Bodywork:** to order
**Maximum speed (approx):** 70 mph (113 kph)

first to be equipped with four-wheel brakes.

From 1918, Ehrhardt built 40hp four- and 55hp six-cylinder luxury cars with overhead-cam engines.

When Szabo & Wechselmann closed their Berlin-Reinickendorf factory, which had built one of Germany's most luxurious cars, the Szawe, Ehrhardt took over the (limited) manufacture of the 2570 cc overhead-camshaft six-cylinder Szawe 10/50 hp, which was built without regard for cost; its radiator, for example, was hand-beaten from German silver.

The aviation background of its designer, Dr Georg Bergmann, was reflected in the polished wood 'aircraft propeller' used as a radiator fan and mounted on the nose of the camshaft.

Low sales prompted the company to switch to building Amilcars until 1927.

**EHP**

# ELIZALDE

**Barcelona, Spain
1914-1928**

In 1909, Arturo Elizalde Rouvier opened a garage in Barcelona where cars were repaired and French Delahaye cars sold; he also operated a workshop for the manufacture of automobile components, such as valves, gears, half-shafts and shock absorbers. Then, with financial backing from his brothers-in-law, the Biadas, who had been involved in the garage since 1910, he began developing an all-Spanish car of the highest quality.

After a year's work, the first series of Elizalde cars went on sale in 1914, and the marque first distinguished itself when a Biada-Elizalde drove from Barcelona to Madrid, via Zaragoza and Guadalajara in 13 hours – 'much faster than an express train!'

A year later, King Alfonso XIII, after a test run to La Coruna and back, bought a 20 hp Biada-Elizalde cabriolet, and granted the company the prestigious title of *Proveedora de la Real Casa*.

Following the premature death of Arturo Elizalde in 1914, his widow, Carmen, took over the running of the company.

A 25 hp sports version of this car was subsequently developed and marketed as the Reina Victoria, which, apart from the provision of an electric lighting set, was also the first Spanish car to be equipped with four-wheel brakes – 'a notable technical precedent'.

The original Elizalde model, the 15/20 hp Tipo 26 remained in production for three years, then in 1917 the engine capacity was increased from 2297 cc to 2676 cc. In 1920 Elizalde announced the 19/30 hp Model 29, powered by an overhead-valve 3817 cc four-cylinder engine; similar models, which included the 3405 cc 18/25 hp, were built until 1927.

But these models were overshadowed by the introduction at the end of 1920 by the magnificent 50/60 Tipo 48, one of

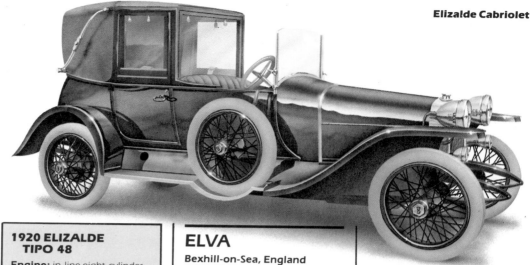

*Elizalde Cabriolet*

## 1920 ELIZALDE TIPO 48

**Engine:** in-line eight-cylinder with four overhead valves per cylinder
**Bore × stroke:** 90 mm × 160 mm
**Capacity:** 8143 cc
**Maximum power:** 60 bhp
**Transmission:** four-speed manual
**Chassis:** pressed steel channel
**Suspension:** non-independent with semi-elliptic leaf springs front and cantilever rear
**Brakes:** servo-assisted drums all round
**Bodywork:** to order
**Maximum speed: (approx):** 80 mph (129 kph)

the first straight-eight cars to go into production. It had an 8143 cc 32-valve, twin-carburettor power unit and rode on a massive 147 in (3528 mm) wheelbase. Integral with the engine was a tyre pump which could also be used for vacuum-cleaning the interior of the car.

Commented the press: 'This is the largest car ever produced. . . the bonnet of the Elizalde limousine is so high that people of normal stature can't see over it. . .'

Between 1924-27, Elizalde built a 5181 cc straight-eight Gran Sport capable of 100 mph (161 kph). Elizalde also built lorries and aero engines.

# ELVA

**Bexhill-on-Sea, England
1955-1968**

Elva – the name is a phonetic rendering of the French *elle va!* (she goes) – was an engineering company formed by garage owner Frank Nichols to build competition cars, following the construction of a successful Ford Ten special called the CSM Special. Between 1955-58, Elva built a number of sports-racing cars, initially with a Weslake-designed overhead-valve conversion of the side-valve Ford Ten engine, later with 1100 cc Coventry-Climax power units and, as a result, received a constant stream of enquiries about the possibility of building a road-going version.

Consequently, Nichols designed the Elva Courier in a remarkably short space of time; the prototype had a BMC B-series engine in a space frame chassis clothed in

aluminium bodywork, though production versions had glassfibre bodywork.

The company underwent its first financial crisis in 1961, and was reformed, then in 1964 the Trojan Group (which had been building the Courier under licence since 1962) took over the entire Elva business. By then the impetus of the Elva marque was failing anyway, and, despite the introduction of a redesigned chassis plus new sports bodywork in 1964, when a sports/racer called the Sebring was also announced, Trojan disposed of the Elva Courier to Ken Sheppard Customised Sports Cars of Radlett, Herts, in 1966. They produced a few cars at spasmodic intervals until 1969, when the remaining spares were sold to Tony Ellis of Windsor. He attempted to revise the marque with a Ford 3-litre V6 sports coupé, the 130 mph (209 kph) Cougar, but it failed to sell, and production finally ground to a halt in 1968. Its early-'50s, Bristol-like styling may have been partly to blame.

Over 2000 Elvas of all types were eventually made. The most famous of these were obviously the Courier and the stillborn 160XS road-going coupé version of the Elva Mk 8 racer, powered by a 2-litre BMW engine and styled by Trevor Fiore. Only three prototypes were built.

## 1960 ELVA COURIER

**Engine:** in-line four-cylinder
**Bore × stroke:** 73 mm × 89 mm
**Capacity:** 1489 cc
**Maximum power:** 70 bhp
**Transmission:** four-speed
**Chassis:** tubular steel frame
**Suspension:** independent front with double wishbones and live rear axle with twin trailing arms and Panhard rod
**Brakes:** drums all round
**Bodywork:** two-seater sports
**Maximum speed (approx):** 110 mph (177 kph)

*Elva Courier*

# A-Z OF THE CAR

cylinder doesn't seem to have passed the artist's impression stage.

Bertelli hurriedly had to design an orthodox 1.5-litre water-cooled four-cylinder, which was marketed as the 10/20; maybe a hundred examples of this and the broadly similar 12/30 were built in 1921-25.

Bertelli drove a racing 10/20 in the 1500 cc race run as part of the 1922 Isle of Man Tourist Trophy.

When the Enfield-Allday factory closed down, Bertelli developed the Renwick & Bertelli sports car, with an Enfield-Allday chassis, which became the basis of post-1925 Aston-Martin cars.

and an electric fuel pump. The model that went on sale had wood-spoked wheels and a vacuum fuel feed.

In 1928 the capacity of the power unit was increased to 2619 cc to create the Erskine 'Royal' model; the car was restyled the following year. By 1930, the Erskine was bigger, with a 3.4-litre engine; with a price of nearly $1000 it was now no more than a slightly smaller, slightly cheaper Studebaker. The fact was recognised when the Erskine was re-christened the 'Studebaker Six' in May 1930.

## ENFIELD-ALLDAY
**Sparkbrook, England**
**1919-1925**

The Enfield Cycle Company of Redditch was a well-known manufacturer of bicycles and armaments – their slogan was 'built like a gun' – who had built motorcycles and quadricycles from 1900 before manufacturing their first cars in 1904; the Alldays & Onions Pneumatic Engineering Company of Birmingham, which had originally been founded in the 1600s and produced its first motor vehicle in 1898, took over Enfield in 1908, when the latter company was in a parlous financial situation.

Erskine Sedan

### 1922 ENFIELD-ALLDAY 10/20

**Engine:** in-line four-cylinder, overhead-valve
**Bore × stroke:** 69 mm × 100 mm
**Capacity:** 1496 cc
**Maximum power:** not known
**Transmission:** four-speed manual
**Chassis:** pressed steel channel
**Suspension:** non-independent with semi-elliptic leaf springs front and cantilever rear
**Brakes:** four-wheel drums plus transmission brake
**Bodywork:** tourer or saloon
**Maximum speed (approx):** 94 mph (151 kph)

Though the products of the two companies were thereafter similar, the two factories weren't merged until after the Great War, when the first Enfield-Allday appeared.

The car was a bold attempt to translate the technological experiences gained during the war into road-going terms; designed by A.W. Reeves and A.C. Bertelli, the Enfield-Allday was totally unconventional, with a tubular backbone chassis in which was mounted a radial five-cylinder side-valve 1.5-litre engine. Entitled the Bullet, the car featured a three-seat body mounted on outriggers, and its quality was matched by the price.

It was a total failure: perhaps four cars were built, and a proposed sleeve-valve 15 hp six-

## ERSKINE
**South Bend, Ind., USA**
**1926–1930**

The Erskine car took its name from the president of Studebaker, Albert R. Erskine. A small car by American standards, with a 2394 cc six-cylinder sidevalve power unit, the Erskine was promoted as a 'European motor car': unfortunately for its makers, that's what it turned out to be, with export sales markedly ahead of those made in America.

Prototypes shown in Europe in 1926 had two features not continued into production; fixed wire wheels with detachable rims

### 1927 ERSKINE CUSTOM SEDAN

**Engine:** in-line side-valve six-cylinder
**Bore × stroke:** 66.7 mm × 114.3 mm
**Capacity:** 2394 cc
**Maximum power:** 17 hp (rated)
**Transmission:** three-speed manual
**Chassis:** pressed steel channel
**Suspension:** non-independent, with semi-elliptic leaf springs
**Brakes:** expanding drums all round
**Bodywork:** tourer or sedan
**Maximum speed (approx):** 65 mph (104 kph)

## ESPAÑA
**Barcelona, Spain**
**1917–1928**

Textile engineer Felipe Battlo y Godo had, they said, 'an irresistible vocation for automobilism', and finally his family decided to back him in the manufacture of a car.

The prototype 8-10CV was put into production under the illogical title of España 2: it had a four-cylinder French-built Altos engine of 1847 cc. Several hundred of these 8-10CV models were build, 'in 34 series of 25 chassis'. Many

Enfield-Allday

**Essex Super Six**

were bought by the Spanish Military Aviation Service and equipped with four-seater tourer bodies; others were sold as taxis.

Apart from this model, España built a number of 'one off' models with four and six cylinders. Among these was the España 3 with a four-cylinder 3690 cc overhead-valve engine and four speeds forward, of which two prototypes were built. One was supplied to Battlo y Godo's father, the other was delivered to King Alfonso XIII, who ultimately passed it to his son, the Infante Don Juan de Bourbon. España 4 was another prototype with a 4.5-litre 16-valve engine; a six-cylinder España was also built.

In 1928 the company ran into financial difficulties: in order to sell new cars it found itself obliged to take the clients' old cars in part exchange, and had thereby contrived to acquire 'more than 300 cars which were practically unsaleable'. The España company therefore merged with another quality car manufacturer, Ricart y Perez, whose chief engineer, Wifredo Pelayo Ricart y Medina,

would achieve his greatest glory over 20 years later as the designer of the Pegaso

The Ricart-España was a 2.4-litre car of high quality particularly favoured by bishops; though it found a number of influential clients the new company lacked sufficient finance to survive beyond the hard times of 1929.

# ESSEX
**Detroit, USA**
**1918–1932**

The outstanding success of Hudson's low-priced Essex line wasn't attributable solely to its basic cost of $1595 but to the fact that in 1922 it became the first marque to offer a mass-produced, and therefore cheap ($1295), two-door sedan. The angular Essex

---

### 1920 ESPAÑA 2 8/10CV

**Engine:** in-line four-cylinder
**Bore × stroke:** 70 mm ×
  120 mm
**Capacity:** 1847 cc
**Maximum power:** 30 bhp
**Transmission:** four-speed
**Chassis:** pressed steel channel
**Suspension:** non-independent
  with semi-elliptic leaf springs
  front, double-cantilever leaf
  springs rear
**Brakes:** rear-wheel only
**Bodywork:** torpedo
**Maximum speed (approx):**
  47 mph (75 kph)

---

### 1929 ESSEX SUPER SIX

**Engine:** in-line six-cylinder,
  side-valve
**Capacity:** 2500 cc
**Maximum power:** 55 bhp
**Transmission:** three-speed
  manual
**Chassis:** pressed steel channel
**Suspension:** non-independent
  with semi-elliptic leaf springs
**Brakes:** rear-wheel only
**Bodywork:** tourer or sedan
**Maximum speed (approx):**
  60 mph (96 kph)

became a best-seller.

The original power unit was a 2.9-litre inlet-over-exhaust four-cylinder: a 2.1-litre six supplanted the four in 1924. This was later uprated to 2.5 litres and became the Super Six.

In 1930, Essex introduced a

new 18.2 hp six, the Challenger which reinforced the popularity of the marque.

In 1932 Essex introduced a new vee-radiatored model with a 3.2-litre six-cylinder engine and Startix automatic starting, but the marque name Essex was replaced the following year by the new Hudson Terraplane.

# EXCALIBUR
**Milwaukee, Wisconsin, USA**
**1964–**

Automotive stylist Brooks Stevens had been pondering the building of a car with classic styling for a dozen years before production began in 1964. His Excalibur SS was loosely based on the 1930 Mercedes SSK, but used a modern Studebaker Lark chassis, the beauty of which was

**España**

Excalibur Roadster

**1984 EXCALIBUR
SERIES IV**

**Engine:** V8, overhead-valve
**Bore × stroke:** 94.9 mm ×
88.4 mm
**Capacity:** 4999 cc
**Maximum power:** 155 bhp
**Transmission:** four-speed
automatic
**Chassis:** box-type ladder frame
**Suspension:** independent with
coils and wishbones front
and semi-axle and pivoting
arm with transverse leaf
spring rear
**Brakes:** discs all round
**Bodywork:** roadster or
phaeton
**Maximum speed (approx):**
110 mph (177 kph)

that, since Studebaker had just
gone out of business, new
components were cheap.

The Studebaker chassis proved
not to be strong enough, so
Stevens designed his own chassis,
intended to take Chevrolet parts.

The Excalibur, one of the first
replicars, has outlasted many other
competitors and is now in its fourth
series. It is less stark now than
originally, and its 5-litre engine,
with the emission control
equipment that 1985 demands, has
a top speed of 110 mph (177 kph) –
in 1970 Excalibur were claiming a
maximum of 160 mph (257 kph)!

Two models have been
available throughout, a two-seater
roadster (a 2+2 with rumble seat)
and a four-passenger phaeton.
Approximately 200 are produced in
a year, costing nearly $60,000
each, the roadster marginally more
expensive than the phaeton. Purists
rightly argue that their styling falls
far short of the original Mercedes,
but both models, in a very
competitive market, never fail to
attract attention; and sales to those
who seek it.

Excelsior Adex C

# EXCELSIOR

**Brussels, Belgium
1903–1932**

Arthur de Coninck founded his
Compagnie Nationale Excelsior in a
modest Brussels garage in late
1903, and starting in January 1904
began small-scale production of
light cars with Aster engines.

In 1905 three new models were
introduced, with Arbel pressed-
steel chassis and four-cylinder
engines of 16, 22 and 30 hp.

By 1907, the company was
reformed and moved into new
premises, where production began
of the first 'all-Excelsior' car, a four-
cylinder 14/20 hp.

By 1910, this model was
available with automatic
lubrication of all the moving parts,
the reservoir only needing topping

**1922 EXCELSIOR
ADEX C**

**Engine:** in-line six-cylinder,
overhead-cam
**Bore × stroke:** 90 mm ×
140 mm
**Capacity:** 5332 cc
**Maximum power:** 110 bhp
**Transmission:** four-speed
manual
**Chassis:** pressed steel channel
**Suspension:** non independent
with semi-elliptic leaf springs
**Brakes:** drums all round
**Bodywork:** to order
**Maximum speed (approx):**
87 mph (140 kph)

up once every six months.

In 1911 Excelsior introduced
their classic Edwardian model, the
bi-block six-cylinder 4426 cc Adex
D-6, which from the beginning was
praised for its flexibility of running,

its durability and its exceptional
road-holding.

The Belgian Royal Family
bought its first Excelsior before the
Great War, and the 1914 bi-bloc
Type F 5344 cc six was christened
Roi des Belges in honour of the
royal connection; King Albert
became a regular client.

That original six was produced
until 1920, when de Coninck
launched a new model, derived
from the D-6 but with an increased
stroke to bring the swept volume
to 4766 cc; it was fitted with his
'Adex' diagonally compensated
four-wheel braking system and
stabilised rear suspension.

The launch of the new car had
been delayed by the fact that, in
abandoning the occupied factory in
1918, the Germans had taken most
of the production machinery.

In 1922 Excelsior launched the
magnificent overhead-camshaft
Adex C, a 5350 cc six with triple
Zenith carburettors.

A three-model policy was
adopted in 1925; all were equipped
with the 5350 cc engine, but in
three stages of tune.

An improved version of the
Adex C appeared at the end of
1926 in two forms, the single
carburettor Tourisme and the triple
carburettor Sport, and in normal or
long chassis form.

The growing imports of
American cars into Belgium proved
too competitive for Excelsior, which
was both expensive and built in
limited numbers. The company was
acquired at the end of 1927 by
Imperia, whose proprietor, Van
Roggen, was attempting to create a
Belgian General Motors.
Production ceased soon after
although a few Albert Premiers
were assembled from spare parts to
special order in Liege.

# A-Z OF THE CAR

## FACEL VEGA

**Paris, France**
**1954–1964**

Jean Daninos founded *les Forges et Ateliers de Construction de L'Eure et Loire* before the war to carry out general engineering work, and entered the motor industry as a body builder for Simca, Ford and Panhard, while still making office furniture, jet engine components and panels for military vehicles.

When Panhard started to make their own bodywork Daninos decided to build complete luxury cars, and unveiled the first Facel Vega in July 1954 at their Paris plant. A Chrysler V8 engine of 4.5 litres powered the first Vegas; subsequently 5.8 and 6.3 litre Chrysler engines were used.

In 1957 Facel announced a long wheelbase *voiture de prestige*, the

'Excellence'. Its pillarless four-door looked splendid but lacked rigidity, so that problems with door closing persisted throughout the model's spasmodic existence.

The original model, the FV, was replaced by a redesigned and stretched model, the HK500, in 1958; a higher-compression engine gave it a 146 mph (235 kph) top speed and fast acceleration.

In an attempt to build a more popular car, a smaller model – the Facellia – was launched in 1960 with a Facel-designed twin-overhead-camshaft four-cylinder 1600 cc engine. This engine, built largely by Pont-a-Mousson, who also supplied Facel's transmissions,

proved hopelessly unreliable.

It took two years to sort out the worst of the problems but the engine had caused a great loss of confidence among Facel's customers, and was mainly responsible for the failure of Facel Vega. The replacement of the 1600 cc engine by the Volvo 1800 unit in 1962 came too late to save Facel; the company went into receivership that year and was taken over by a company called SFERMA, which attempted to market a Healey 3000-engined Facel 6. In September 1964 Facel ceased production.

## FAFNIR

**Aachen, Germany**
**1908–1926**

Fafnir was a leading manufacturer of power units for motorcycles and cars long before it built cars under its own name. And from 1904 to 1910 Fafnir also supplied 'Omnimobil' kits – engine, chassis and transmission – to companies

who wanted to enter the motor industry without investing in production machinery.
The successful sales of cars fitted with these kits prompted the company to embark upon designing its own models.

Fafnir launched a range of four-cylinder cars, naturally using its own make of inlet-over-exhaust engines of 1520–2496 cc, and with such refinements as automatic lubrication, interior gear-leaver and low centre of gravity.

Their cars were always of advanced design, and in the early 1920s Fafnirs enjoyed racing success; the cars were driven by Caracciola, Uren, Muller, Hirth and Utermohle.

The 471 was the ultimate Fafnir, built from 1923 to 1926; it had striking styling, with an airship tail and flat wings to minimise wind resistance. Some of these sporting Fafnirs had a curious face stamped out of the radiator cowling. In standard form, the 471 developed 50 bhp at 2500 rpm, but the supercharged 471K racing cars developed 80 bhp.

---

**1954 FACEL VEGA**

**Engine:** Chrysler Firedome V8
**Bore × stroke:** 92 mm × 85 mm
**Capacity:** 4528 cc
**Maximum power:** 180 bhp
**Transmission:** four-speed manual
**Chassis:** tubular steel
**Suspension:** independent front with coils and wishbones; non-independent rear with semi-elliptic leaf springs
**Brakes:** hydraulic drums all round
**Bodywork:** coupé
**Maximum speed (approx):** 125 mph (200 kph)

---

**Fafnir 471**

---

**Facel Vega Facel II**

---

**1923 FAFNIR 471**

**Engine:** in-line four-cylinder, overhead-valve
**Bore × stroke:** 71 mm × 125 mm
**Capacity:** 1980 cc
**Maximum power:** 50 bhp (80 bhp supercharged)
**Transmission:** four-speed manual
**Chassis:** pressed steel channel
**Suspension:** non-independent with semi-elliptic leaf springs front and rear
**Brakes:** drums all round
**Bodywork:** two-seater sports
**Maximum speed (approx):** 87 mph (140 kph)

# FAIRTHORPE
**Denham, England**
**1954–1981**

Founded by wartime bomber ace Donald Bennett, Fairthorpe began production in Chalfont St Peter with the plastic-bodied Atom, powered by rear-mounted BSA motorcycle engines of 250–650 cc.

This curiously-styled model was followed by the 650 cc front-engined Atomota, which was succeeded in 1957 by the Standard 8-powered Electron Minor, capable of 75 mph (121 kph).

An 1100 cc Coventry-Climax engine was adopted in 1958, but the search for more power went too far when the 2½-litre Ford Zephyr engine was dropped into the Electron chassis to create the Zeta, and only 14 were built.

The Rockette proved more successful, fitted with a 1596 cc Triumph Vitesse engine.

Fairthorpe moved first to Gerrards Cross, then to Denham, where it began manufacture of grand touring cars designed by Air Vice Marshal Bennett's son Torix. Designated 'TX', they incorporated Torix Bennett's ingenious parallel-motion rear suspension. The TX-GT of 1968 was, like all the TX series,
bodied in glassfibre; it was a hatchback coupé powered by the 2-litre Triumph GT6 engine.

A lighter two-door derivative, the TX-S was also available with fuel injection as the TX-SS.

The Electrons lasted into the 1970s, but the ultimate Fairthorpes were the Triumph Spitfire-engined TX-S 1500, and the TR7-engined – and rather fast – TX-S 2000.

# FARMAN
**Billancourt, France**
**1920–1931**

Born in Paris of an English father, the three Farman brothers – Dick, Maurice and Henry – were champion cyclists before they went into motor manufacture, specialising in the supply of proprietary engines. Maurice and Henry were also racing drivers of note. Next the Farmans moved into aviation; Henry Farman was the first man in the world to fly around a marked kilometre course.

After the war the Farmans
continued to build aeroplanes and aeroengines and also operated one of Europe's first airlines, the General Air Transport Company.

The brothers, in expansive mood, decided to build a luxury car, 'absolutely perfect in every detail', in their aeroplane works.

Its engine was an overhead-camshaft straight-six of 6597 cc which revealed the influence of aeroengine practice in its layout. Early Farman engines had steel cylinders welded into a steel water jacket, but aluminium was later used for the block and crankcase.

The Grand Sport Farman shown at Olympia in 1923 was a pointed-tail tourer with a fully-faired underside: 'the beautifully-finished instrument board, with its many dials and gauges, puts the last touch to an engineering work of art' said *The Autocar*.

The car had a four-speed gearbox, a double steering mechanism and an unusual, though effective, cantilever suspension.

One of the earliest Farman town cars was ordered by silent-film star Pearl White.

A larger Farman, the NF, was introduced alongside the original A6 in 1927; it had an engine of 7069 cc.

Farman, who limited production to keep quality up, built very few examples of either model; in the mid-1920s an A6B limousine cost around 170,000 francs in the company's Champs-Elysees showroom.

---

**1923 FARMAN A6B**

**Engine:** in-line overhead-camshaft six-cylinder
**Bore × stroke:** 100 mm × 140 mm
**Capacity:** 6597 cc
**Maximum power:** 40 hp
**Transmission:** four-speed
**Chassis:** pressed steel channel
**Suspension:** non-independent with semi-elliptic transverse and cantilever leaf springs front and rear
**Brakes:** drums all round
**Bodywork:** to order
**Maximum speed (approx):** 80 mph (130 kph)

---

**1968 FAIRTHORPE TX-S 2000**

**Engine:** in-line six-cylinder, overhead-valve
**Bore × stroke:** 90.3 mm × 78 mm
**Capacity:** 1998 cc
**Maximum power:** 127 bhp
**Transmission:** four-speed
**Chassis:** box section double backbone with outriggers
**Suspension:** independent with coils and wishbones front, transverse leaf spring rear
**Brakes:** front discs, rear drums
**Bodywork:** glassfibre coupé
**Maximum speed (approx):** 118 mph (190 kph)

**Farman A6B**

**Fairthorpe TX-S 2000**

# FAST

Turin, Italy
1919–1925

At one time, Italian makers had a craze for christening their cars with acronyms – there was the FLAG, the FLIRT and, of course, the FIAT – but although its life was short and its production small, the FAST (its name came from the company that built it, the Fabbrica Automobili Sport Torino) was a classic sporting car with a lively 2.9-litre overhead-camshaft engine.

The aim of Arturo Concaris, who created FAST out of his former Fabbrica Italiana Motori Aviazione, was to build a sporting car that could also be used for touring. His Tipo Uno was a wire-wheeled two-seater with a vast external exhaust.

Driven by Caberto Conelli and Beria d'Argentina, Tipo Unos took part in the Parma-Poggia di Berceto hillclimb in 1920, and in the Susa-

### 1922 FAST 2S

**Engine:** in-line overhead-camshaft four-cylinder
**Bore × stroke:** 84 mm × 135 mm
**Capacity:** 2891 cc
**Maximum power:** not known
**Transmission:** four-speed manual
**Chassis:** pressed steel channel
**Suspension:** non-independent with semi-elliptic leaf springs
**Brakes:** drums all round
**Bodywork:** sports two-seater
**Maximum speed (approx):** 75 mph (120 kph)

Fejes 9 hp

Moncenisio and Aosta-Gran San Bernado climbs the following year.

A financial crisis in 1922 saw FAST acquired by Ing. Alberto Orasi the following year; he used the same power unit in a new chassis to create the sporting 2S and the long wheelbase 2T; a team of 2S FASTs competed in the 1924 Targa Florio, driven by Tarabusi (he came 20th) Tagliavia and Gastaldetti.

# FEJES

Budapest, Hungary
1923–1928

Eugene Fejes designed his car to be built as cheaply as possible by unskilled labour, so the entire car was manufactured from pressed and welded sheet iron – even its overhead-valve engine. The only two castings in the car were said to be the timing gear case and the gearbox lid.

This made the car considerably lighter than a conventionally constructed vehicle, and its performance was said to be 'extremely lively'.

Cyril Pullin – of Ascot-Pullin motorcycle fame – planned to produce a more elegant version of this Hungarian utility car (the original Fejes was intended as a military or postal car, so its appearance was secondary – and it showed!) in England under the name 'Ascot', but though several prototypes were built, the project came to nothing. The company was still short of money, and in 1925 it

### 1923 FEJES

**Engine:** in-line four-cylinder, overhead-valve
**Bore × stroke:** 63 mm × 110 mm
**Capacity:** 1371 cc
**Maximum power:** 9 hp
**Transmission:** three-speed manual
**Chassis:** pressed steel channel
**Suspension:** non-independent with semi-elliptic leaf springs
**Brakes:** rear-wheel drums
**Bodywork:** pressed steel tourer
**Maximum speed (approx):** 40 mph (65 kph)

was declared bankrupt. Had Pullin succeeded, the Ascot would have sold for only £130.

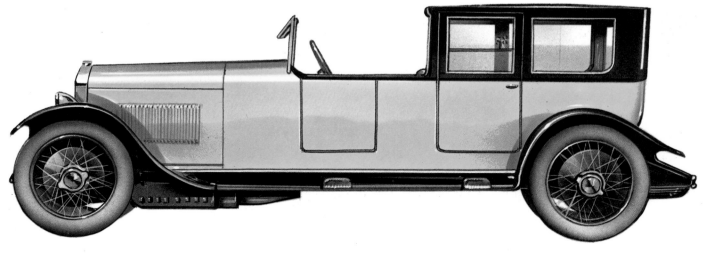

# A-Z OF THE CAR

## FERRARI

**Maranello, Italy**
**1946–**

Enzo Ferrari, born in Modena in 1898, made his name as a racing driver, a career he began when he joined CMN just after the Great War. In 1920, he moved to Alfa Romeo as a driver and tester, and then in 1929 he established his own team, the *Scuderia Ferrari*. However, he retained his connection with Alfa Romeo until the end of 1938.

The terms under which he had severed the link with Alfa stipulated that he was not able to build or race cars under his own name, and he therefore set up the Societa Auto Avio Costruzioni to manufacture machine tools.

He couldn't stay away from motor racing, though, and built two sports cars, known as the 815 from the number of cylinders and the swept volume, with a power unit that employed Fiat blocks on a special crankcase. They were driven by Ascari and the Marchese Rangoni in the 1940 Mille Miglia.

During the war, the Italian decentralisation laws compelled Ferrari to move his company from Modena to Maranello, 12 miles further south. There he began production of cars bearing his own name and the *Cavallino Rampante* prancing horse badge, which had been presented to him after a notable race victory in 1923 by the Contessa Paolina Baracca, mother of World War I air ace Francesco Baracca, another native of Modena, who had borne the emblem on the fuselage of his fighter plane.

That first series of Ferrari cars was designed by Colombo; first to appear was the 1947 125C sports racer, followed by the 166 sports car. Colombo's power unit was a V12 – a configuration admired by Enzo Ferrari ever since he had seen a racing Packard Twin-Six after the Great War – with a single overhead camshaft per bank.

The nomenclature of those cars, like that of most classic Ferraris, simply represented the capacity of a single cylinder. In 1950, the 2.3-litre 195 and 2.6-litre 212 appeared, followed in 1952 by the 2.7-litre 225.

Aurelio Lampredi succeeded Colombo as engine design consultant and developed a 4.5-litre V12 Grand Prix engine, then created a four-cylinder 2-litre power unit, easier to maintain and possessing superior acceleration to the V12; it subsequently appeared in 2.5- and 3-litre forms.

The Lampredi V12 first appeared in the 3.2-litre 265S sports car of 1950 and later that year was fitted, in 4.1-litre guise, to the 340 series, an early example of which won the Mille Miglia in 1951, driven by Luigi Villoresi.

Aimed at the US market, the Tipo 342 was known as the America; it was followed by the 4.5-litre Tipo 375 and the 4.9-litre Tipo 342 SuperAmerica.

A development prototype of a new model, the 250 Sport, won the 1952 Mille Miglia, and at the 1953 Paris Salon the road-going 250 Europa was unveiled

At the end of 1954 Ferrari introduced a new four-cylinder 2-litre model, the 500 Mondial.

In 1955 Ferrari, whose Squalo and Super Squalo F1 cars had been outclassed by the opposition, took over the 2.5-litre F1 Lancia D50 cars and the services of designer Vittorio Jano; the Ferrari-modified Lancias won the 1956 World Championship.

From 1961, Ferrari competition cars were rear engined, while road cars continued to have front engines, such as the 275GTB with a 300 bhp, 3.3-litre V12 and the 300 bhp, 4-litre V12 330GT and GTC.

The mid-engined Dino, named after Ferrari's only son, who had died in 1956, was fitted with the 2-litre V6 that Dino had helped to develop.

A classic Ferrari was the 365 GTB/4, with twin-overhead-cam, 4.4-litre, 352 bhp V12; this was the last great front-engined model and had a top speed of 174 mph (280 kph). This was succeeded by the mid-engined twin-overhead-cam, 2.9-litre 308 GTB/GTS and the 4.8-litre V12 400 and 400GT, which, like most modern Ferraris, were coupés with Pininfarina bodywork. In 1969, the company became part of the Fiat empire and Enzo stayed on as head of the works.

The Ferrari Boxer went into production in 1973, with a mid-mounted overhead-cam, 4.4-litre flat-12, replaced in 1984 by the 5-litre, 181mph (291 kph) BB512, named after the outstanding 1956 sports-racer.

The Mondial 2 + 2, with 3-litre V8, had been launched at the 1980 Geneva motor show and a drophead version appeared in 1984, as did the new GTO, with a twin-turbo 3-litre V8 of 400 bhp, capable of 190 mph (306 kph). In 1987, the F40 was launched, intended to be as near as possible a racing car for road use, and with the V8 tuned to 478 bhp, enough for a genuine 200 mph (322 kph). Enzo died in 1988, after which Fiat took complete control of the company. A front-engined replacement for the 400 series, with 48-valve, four-cam, 5.6-litre, 442 bhp V12, was launched in 1993, called the 456 GT.

## Ferrari 166

Introduced in 1948, the Ferrari 166 was described by *The Autocar* as 'the most advanced unsupercharged sports car in the world today'.

The aluminium bodywork, by Ghia, Touring and Farina among others, was built over a light space frame.

In its first two seasons, the Ferrari 166 amassed an outstanding record of success, including two successive wins in both the Mille Miglia and the Targa Florio as well as sports car races and Formula B racing.

In 1949 the 166 achieved Ferrari's first win in the Le Mans 24-Hour race, driven by Luigi Chinetti.

The engine was available in four stages of tune – Sport (89 bhp), Inter (108 bhp), Mille Miglia (140 bhp) and F2 (155 bhp), the latter two equipped with triple carburettors.

While the Sport and Inter engines ran on 80 octane petrol, the 166MM operated on a mixture of petrol, benzole and ethyl alcohol.

**Ferrari 166**

---

**1948 FERRARI 166**

**Engine:** V12, overhead-cam
**Bore × stroke:** 60 mm × 58.8 mm
**Capacity:** 1995 cc
**Maximum power:** 140 bhp (Mille Miglia)
**Transmission:** five-speed
**Chassis:** tubular steel
**Suspension:** independent front with wishbones and transverse leaf spring. Live rear axle and underslung semi-elliptic leaf spring
**Brakes:** drums all round
**Bodywork:** two-seater sports
**Maximum speed (approx):** 112 mph (180 kph)

Ferrari 250GT

# Ferrari 250 GT

The first Ferrari 250 GT appeared in 1954, spawning a line that descended all the way to the Daytona of 1968, which was the last of the V12, front-engined cars. In 1956 the Colombo-designed V12 displaced just 3 litres and had but a single overhead cam per bank of cylinders. Nevertheless a great deal of power was still possible, the most from the racing GTO (the O stood for Omologata, or homologation and was adopted by Pontiac for their high-performance GTO). The 250 GTO was a rather stark alloy-bodied racing version of the short-wheelbase GT Berlinetta of 1960–61 and produced 300 bhp.

The road version of the GTO was the extremely attractive Pininfarina-bodied Berlinetta Lusso which was introduced at the 1962 Paris Salon. It produced rather less power than the GTO, 250 bhp rather than 300, and weighed a substantial 3000 lb (1360 kg). Nevertheless it could still just exceed 150 mph (240 kph) and cover the standing quarter mile in 16 seconds with consummate ease.

It was a very traditional piece of engineering with a four-speed manual transmission in unit with the engine and a live rear axle, all built on a separate chassis as are Ferraris to this day.

In addition to the Lusso there was a bewildering number of other styles – coupé, cabriolet, Spyder California, short-wheelbase Berlinetta and so forth, built by coachbuilders other than Pininfarina.

The 250 GT line lasted until 1963 and was then superceded by the 275 GTB which was then introduced with the much more modern layout of independent suspension all round and a rear mounted transmission.

## 1964 FERRARI 250 GT LUSSO

**Engine:** V12, overhead-cam
**Bore × stroke:** 73 mm × 58.8 mm
**Capacity:** 2953 cc
**Maximum power:** 250 bhp
**Transmission:** four-speed manual
**Suspension:** independent front with unequal length wishbones and coil springs. Live rear axle with semi-elliptic leaf springs
**Brakes:** discs all round
**Bodywork:** steel and alloy panelled coupé
**Maximum speed (approx):** 150 mph (242 kph)

# Ferrari 365 GTB Daytona

The Daytona was introduced at the Paris Salon in 1968, named after the company's famous victory at the Florida racetrack. It was the culmination of the 275GTB line, retaining that car's all-independent suspension layout and rear transaxle but having a much larger 4390 cc four-cam version of the V12 engine.

The engine, with a block sand-cast in Silumin, breathed through six twin-choke Weber carburettors; its twin-overhead camshafts were chain driven from the crankshaft and actuated the valves via gears. The rigid torque-tube connection of engine to rear transmission had been introduced to cure a vibration problem. Stressed steel bodywork also contributed to rigidity.

That alloy V12 produced 352 bhp, or enough to power the Daytona to a top speed of 175 mph (282 kph), to 60 mph (96 kph) in 5.4 seconds and over the standing quarter mile in a mere 13.7 seconds. Its performance is put into perspective when one realises that the Daytona could exceed the UK's current maximum speed limit in second gear.... For the right driver the Daytona's chassis matched the power, as one understated road test put it, '...the limits of adhesion are well beyond what is sane and rational on public roads'. The same writer felt that the 365GTB would cope '...easily with a trip from the Channel to the South of France and back in a day', the measure of a true GT. Far rarer than the 'ordinary' Daytona was the Spyder, just 127 of which were commissioned by Ferrari and built by Scaglietti. Most were exported to North America and their rarity has led to a considerable number of the coupés being converted.

## 1971 FERRARI 365 GTB/4 DAYTONA

**Engine:** V12, four-overhead-cam
**Bore × stroke:** 81 mm × 71 mm
**Capacity:** 4390 cc
**Maximum power:** 352 bhp
**Transmission:** five-speed manual rear transaxle
**Chassis:** tubular steel
**Suspension:** independent with unequal length wishbones, telescopic dampers, coil springs and anti-roll bars
**Brakes:** discs all round
**Bodywork:** steel coupé
**Maximum speed (approx):** 174 mph (280 kph)

Ferrari 365 GTB Daytona

## MODEL
Delage D8 (1929)
**UK price when introduced:** £685 (chassis only); £945 (saloon)

## ENGINE
**Location:** Front, longitundinal
**Type:** Water-cooled straight-eight, cast iron, with detachable block and cylinder head and five main bearings
**Cubic capacity:** 4050 cc
**Bore × stroke:** 77 mm × 109 mm
**Compression ratio:** 6.8:1
**Valve gear:** Two valves per cylinder operated by single block-mounted camshaft, pushrods and rockers
**Fuel supply:** Single Smith-Barriquand five-jet carburettor
**Ignition:** Delco-Remy coil and distributor
**Maximum power:** ·102 bhp at 3500 rpm

## TRANSMISSION
**Layout:** Gearbox and clutch in unit with engine, driving rear wheels
**Clutch:** Single dry plate
**Gearbox:** Four-speed manual
| | | | |
|---|---|---|---|
| 1st | 3.5:1 | 3rd | 1.36:1 |
| 2nd | 2.1:1 | 4th | 1.00:1 |
**Final drive:** Spiral bevel
**Ratio:** 3.6:1

## SUSPENSION
**Front:** Non-independent, with beam axle, semi-elliptic leaf springs and friction dampers
**Rear:** Non-independent, with live axle, semi-elliptic leaf springs and friction dampers

## STEERING
**Type:** Worm and nut

## BRAKES
**Type:** Finned drum brakes all round, cable-operated and assisted by Dewandre vacuum servo

## WHEELS AND TYRES
**Type:** 18 in (46 cm) wire wheels fitted with 7.00/18 crossply tyres

## BODY/CHASSIS
**Type:** Ladder-frame pressed steel chassis with cross-members, supporting coachbuilt fabric-covered four-seat tourer

## DIMENSIONS AND WEIGHT
**Length:** 192 in (4876 mm)
**Width:** 66 in (1776 mm)
**Wheelbase:** 122 in (3098 mm)
**Track – front:** 56 in (1422 mm)
**– rear:** 56 in (1422 mm)
**Weight:** 3360 lb (1524 mm)

## PERFORMANCE
**Maximum speed:** 80 mph (129 kph)
**Acceleration 0-60 mph:** 23 seconds
**Fuel consumption:** 12 mpg

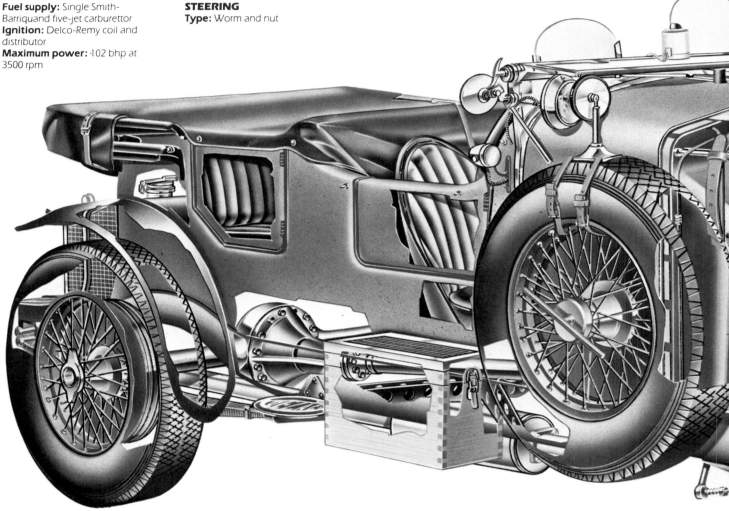

**BELOW** The cutaway reveals the mechanical simplicity of the D8's drivetrain, suspension and chassis. The tall, cast-iron engine featured an unusual valve arrangement wherein the valve spring actually acted directly on the rocker rather than the valve. The engine's weight was partly responsible for the fitting of twin friction dampers to the front beam axle, for the suspension on these cars had been designed with comfort very much in mind, so that the springs were not particularly stiff. The straight-eight had a high torque output and the D8 series cars were all admired for their acceleration and ability to be driven practically everywhere in third and top gears, despite their high ratios. The car shown is a D8 from the first year of production, and its coachwork is far more a workable '20s creation than some of the more flamboyant saloons, coupés, roadsters and Continental tourers which were later featured on D8 chassis and which made the marque so popular with motoring journalists, the nouveaux riches, show people and all who aspired to buy class with style

**Ferrari Berlinetta Boxer**

# Ferrari Berlinetta Boxer

The Boxer was first shown at the Turin Show in 1971 before going into production in 1973. It was a break in Ferrari supercar tradition in dispensing with the front-mounted V12 in favour of a mid-mounted flat 12. Although the new engine shared the same 4.4-litre displacement as the Daytona's V12 (and naturally a number of the same components) it again broke tradition in having four belt- rather than chain-driven overhead cams.

Its five-speed transmission was mounted below the engine, giving the Berlinetta Boxer an unusually high centre of gravity for such a car and the overall weight distribution was biased towards the rear despite the mid engine location. A revised Boxer, the BB512, was introduced in 1976 with a longer stroke to the engine to give a displacement of 5 litres. At the same time track, overall and rear tyre width were all increased. In 1981 the Boxer was furth-

er modified with the switch from triple Weber carburettors to Bosch K Jetronic fuel injection to form the BB512i and Michelin TRX low profile tyres became standard equipment.

The Boxer was perhaps a more civilized car than the Daytona, but did not earn the same affection.

---

**1984 FERRARI BB512i BOXER**

**Engine:** flat 12, four-overhead-cam
**Bore × stroke:** 82 mm × 78 mm
**Capacity:** 4942 cc
**Maximum power:** 340 bhp
**Transmission:** five-speed manual
**Chassis:** tubular steel
**Suspension;** independent with unequal length wishbones, coil springs and anti-roll bars
**Brakes:** discs all round
**Bodywork:** steel, coupé
**Maximum speed (approx):** 170 mph (274 kph)

---

# Ferrari F40

The F40 was created to celebrate 40 years of Ferrari production and to counter Porsche's claim to produce the fastest road-going car, in the shape of the 959. As a result, it was not four-wheel-driven and did not even have ABS braking. It was, however, an almost purely race-inspired road car, with prodigious power in a light car. It was developed in a short time, and based on the 288 GTO, the marque's first real limited-edition supercar; power was courtesy of a longitudinally mid-mounted 3-litre quad-cam V8, which gave 478 bhp at 7000 rpm and 425 lb ft at 4000 rpm. This four-valve-per-cylinder unit had twin IHI turbochargers and was powerful enough to propel the 2425 lb (1100 kg) car to 60 mph (97 kph) in 4.5 seconds and on the 201 mph (323 kph). Weight had been a primary consideration and the F40's body, only 44.3 in (1124 mm) high, was made from 12 sections of Kevlar/carbon fibre/glassfibre

composite, in which the entire tail section lifted up to reveal the engine. The chassis was a steel spaceframe with bonded composite panels to give additional strength.

---

**1987 FERRARI F40**

**Engine:** V8, 32-valve, quad-cam, twin turbo
**Bore x stroke:** 82 mm x 69.5 mm
**Capacity:** 2936 cc
**Maximum power:** 478 bhp
**Transmission:** five-speed manual
**Chassis:** tubular-steel spaceframe
**Suspension:** all independent, with wishbones, coil spring/damper units and anti-roll bars front and rear
**Brakes:** ventilated discs
**Bodywork:** two-seat composite body
**Maximum speed (approx):** 201 mph (323 kph)

---

**Ferrari F40**

# FIAT

**Turin, Italy**
**1899–**

The roots of Fiat date back to 1898, when Giovanni Battista Ceirano, who built Welleyes bicycles in a little workshop attached to the house of wealthy soup manufacturer Giuseppe Lancia, signed an agreement with a group of Torinese businessmen to construct a prototype car.

The first Welleyes car, designed by Aristide Faccioli, appeared in March 1899; it had a twin-cylinder engine of 663 cc and two gears.

Four months later Ceirano's company was taken over by the Fabbrica Italiana di Automobili Torino, headed by Giovanni Agnelli, Count Carlo Biscaretti di Ruffia and Emanuele Bricherasio. F.I.A.T. also took over some of the Welleyes staff, including the soup-maker's son Vincenzo Lancia, Felice Nazzaro and designer Faccioli, who created the first F.I.A.T. car on similar lines to the Welleyes, though its 3½ hp engine had horizontal cylinders.

In 1901 the directors insisted on Faccioli's designing a new model with the engine at the front; he resigned and was replaced by Ing. Enrico, who in 1902 brought out a Mercedes-inspired 4.2-litre four-cylinder model.

Armoured wood chassis were only replaced by pressed steel in 1904, in which year the Mercedes-pattern scroll clutch was also adopted. The company was manufacturing luxury cars in small numbers; its 1905 60 hp model had a 10,082 cc four-cylinder engine

and water-cooling of the transmission brake.

At the end of 1906 F.I.A.T. dropped the full stops and became known by the acronym 'Fiat' (Latin for 'let it be').

The following year saw the company's first six-cylinder model, of 11,034 cc, equipped with compressed-air starting. Their first popular mass-produced model was the 1846 cc Tipo Zero of 1912.

Post-war came the Tipo 501, designed by Cavalli; it had a four-cylinder 1.5-litre engine and over 45,000 had been built by the time production ended in 1926.

Alongside this outstanding success Fiat offered the hyper-luxury V12 6.8-litre SuperFiat, which proved one of the company's few flops, and only about 30 examples were sold between 1921 and 1923. A smaller luxury model, the 4.8-litre six-cylinder Tipo 519, possessed hydro-mechanical servo brakes and was still listed in 1929.

In 1925 Fiat introduced a more modern light car, the flat-radiatored 509, with an overhead-camshaft 990 cc engine; it was replaced in 1929 by the dismal 1440 cc Tipo 514, which was a total disaster in comparison (although the licence to build it was taken up by NSU.)

Other Fiats of the late 1920s were the 2516 cc Tipo 521 and 3740 cc Tipo 525 six-cylinder models, the former the first Fiat with hydraulic brakes.

Fiat made a major step forward in 1932 when they introduced the Tipo 508 Ballila, which took its name from a Fascist youth organisation. Its 995 cc four-cylinder engine developed 25 bhp in touring form and 36 bhp in its rare overhead-valve sporting form, in which it normally wore elegant Ghia bodywork. The Ballila was licence-built in Germany by NSU, in Czechoslovakia by Walter, in Warsaw as the Polski-Fiat and in France by Simca (who also offered a very fast version tuned by Gordini).

Fiat's backbone-framed 1500 of 1936 combined aerodynamic bodywork and Dubonnet-type independent front suspension; later that year the company unveiled the immortal Tipo 500 Topolino

(Mickey Mouse), with a tiny 570 cc four-cylinder engine mounted ahead of the radiator.

Capable of 55 mph (88 kph) and 55 mpg, this remarkable well-equipped economy two-seater (it had independent front suspension, hydraulic brakes and synchromesh) continued almost unchanged until 1948. It quickly became a best-seller; the 1100 Millecento, introduced in 1937, was a development of the 508, and had independent front suspension and combined excellent handling and performance, with a top speed of 70 mph (113 kph).

Alongside these admirable small cars the biggest model in the Fiat range was the 2852 cc six, which cost £795 in Britain.

After World War II Fiat produced little of novelty for several years; an over-square 1400 cc four-cylinder was the first development of note, in 1950.

An excellent limited production 2-litre V8, the 8V appeared in 1952 and was endowed with coachwork by the leading coachbuilders of Turin; Ghia, for instance, built about 50 8V bodies.

A Nuova 1100 appeared in 1953, with integral body/chassis construction. In 1955 the last development of the Topolino, the overhead-valve 500C, was replaced by a new unit-construction rear-engined 600; by 1960 more than a million of these 633 cc saloons had been sold.

A twin-cylinder Nuova 500 was launched in 1957; it had a 499 cc overhead-valve power unit and more than 3 million were built before it was succeeded by the derivative 126 in 1972. Designed along the same lines as the 500 and 600, the 850 had a rear-mounted four-cylinder in-line engine.

The popular 124 of 1966, with engines of 1197 cc and 1438 cc, formed the basis for big licence-production deals, particularly with Eastern bloc countries.

In complete contrast, that same year saw Fiat introduce the Dino Spyder and Coupé with the 1987 cc Ferrari-designed twin-overhead-cam Dino V6.

In 1967 Fiat introduced the 125, with a twin-overhead-camshaft 1608 cc four-cylinder engine, alongside the 1481 cc 1500L, the six-cylinder 1795 cc 1800B and 2279 cc 2300.

Fiat took over Lancia and Ferrari in 1969, and Abarth in 1971.

In 1971 Fiat also introduced the front-wheel drive 127, with transverse four-cylinder overhead-valve engines of 903 cc and 1049 cc. The 128 was another front-wheel drive model, available in 1116 cc and 1290 cc forms. Named after the main Fiat production plane, the 131 Mirafiori succeeded the 124 and was offered with 1297 cc or 1585 cc engines in various stages of tune, plus a

140 bhp twin-overhead-camshaft 1995 cc Abarth version, with independent rear suspension and a five-speed gearbox. The latter was capable of almost 145 mph (233 kph) in racing guise.

Underlining the way the concept of the popular car had changed, Fiat's new 132 had twin-overhead-camshaft, four-cylinder engines, of 1585 cc and 1995 cc.

Introduced in 1973, the X1/9 was a mid-engined two-seater sports car with a 1290 cc power unit. For 1978, this was replaced by a 1498 cc engine. A new small Fiat, the Ritmo, was also introduced then, with idiosyncratic Giugiaro styling. There was also a 1756 cc Supermirafiori.

In 1980 Fiat announced a boxy new front-engined small car, the Panda, available with either an air-cooled twin of 652 cc or a 903 cc four. Subsequent developments included a 4WD variant.

Revealed in January 1983, the Fiat Uno represented the largest investment – a million million lire – in the company's long history. An outstanding entry in its class, the Uno was available with power units of 903 cc, 1116 cc and 1301 cc, the latter model capable of 100 mph (161 kph).

1984 saw the introduction of the Regata, a booted variant of the Ritmo, to replace the Mirafiori.

For many years Fiat has been far more than just a motor manufacturer; its interests range as wide as hotels, railway rolling stock, aircraft, publishing, shipbuilding, tourism, roadbuilding and machinery.

It has provided car manufacturing knowledge to many developing and Iron Curtain countries; it operates well over 200 manufacturing facilities, including 35 car plants, in over 20 countries.

# Fiat 501

Designed by former lawyer Carlo Cavalli, the Tipo 501 was Italy's first truly mass-produced car; it was claimed that there were only 51 ball-bearings in the entire chassis, as against over 1000 in a comparable pre-war chassis.

The 501 was otherwise a conventional side-valve economy model with a three-bearing engine: its four-speed gearbox was endowed with a super-low bottom gear and the power unit was over-cooled, both resulting from the proximity of Turin to the Alps.

The 501 was little changed throughout its five-year production life; a sporting variant, the 501S, appeared in 1921 and four-wheel brakes became available in 1923. A long-wheelbase variant, the 502, announced in 1924, was normally seen as a taxicab.

When production of this robust and durable light car ended in 1926, total sales were in excess of 45,000

**Fiat 501**

## 1919 FIAT 501

**Engine:** in-line four-cylinder, side-valve
**Bore × stroke:** 65 mm × 110 mm
**Capacity:** 1460 cc
**Maximum power:** 23 bhp
**Transmission:** four-speed manual
**Chassis:** pressed steel channel
**Suspension:** non-independent with semi-elliptic leaf springs all round
**Brakes:** drums on rear only
**Bodywork:** sports, tourer or saloon
**Maximum speed (approx):** 50 mph (80 kph)

# Fiat 509

Launched at the end of 1924, the Tipo 509 baby car was hailed by motoring journalist W.F. Bradley as 'quite a national event'; its 990 cc engine boasted an overhead camshaft, and the four-wheel brakes were powerful.

Well-made, the little Fiat nevertheless attracted an illustrious clientele; the heir to the Italian throne owned two, and his sister Princess Giovanna and the Queen of Yugoslavia also drove Fiat 509s.

The two-bearing crank proved something of an Achilles heel and was prone to break, and consequently the 509A of 1926 had improved lubrication. A sport variant,

## 1925 FIAT 509

**Engine:** in-line four-cylinder overhead-camshaft
**Bore × stroke:** 57 mm × 97 mm
**Capacity:** 990 cc
**Maximum power:** 20 bhp
**Transmission:** three speed manual
**Chassis:** pressed steel channel
**Suspension:** non-independent with semi-elliptic leaf springs
**Brakes:** four-wheel semi-servo-assisted
**Bodywork:** sports, roadster, tourer, cabriolet or saloon
**Maximum speed (approx):** 50 mph (80 kph)

the 509S, was mildly tuned and endowed with smart pointed-tail two-seater bodywork, although top speed was less than 60 mph (96 kph). There were also more potent versions: the 509 Sport Monza, capable of 65 mph (105 kph) and the rare low-chassis 509MM, equipped with a supercharger and capable of 80 mph (129 kph).

In Britain, Swallow (which later became Jaguar) built 100 elegant little saloon cars on the 509 chassis.

More then 90,000 examples of this lively lightweight were sold until production ended in 1929.

# Fiat 508S Ballila Sport

Before 1933, Fiat had rarely ventured into sports car manufacture, and then the sports element related mainly to the bodywork.

But then they launched a delightful little two-seater Tipo 508S sporting version of the popular Ballila model (named for the Fascist youth organisation), with flowing wings and a 'spine' down the tail.

The glamorous appearance of the standard two-seater made the 508S deservedly popular, and its good performance meant that the model was raced in Britain, France, Germany and Poland.

The first 508S cars had side-valve engines, though in 1933 a 508S fitted with an overhead valve conversion by Siata came third in the 1100 cc class of the Mille Miglia, and overhead valves were provided on production cars in 1934.

Variants of the 508S were the Spyder Normale with long, flowing wings, the Spyder Corso with cycle wings and the Berlinetta Aerodinamica fast-back coupé.

**Fiat 509 Spider**

**Fiat 508S Ballila Sport**

## 1933 FIAT 508S BALLILA SPORT

**Engine:** in line four-cylinder, overhead-valve
**Bore × stroke:** 65 mm × 75 mm
**Capacity:** 995 cc
**Maximum power:** 35 bhp
**Transmission:** four-speed manual
**Chassis:** pressed steel
**Suspension:** non-independent with semi-elliptic leaf springs all round
**Brakes:** drums all round
**Bodywork:** two-seat sports
**Maximum speed (approx):** 73 mph (118 kph)

## Fiat Topolino

Designed by Franco Fessia, the Fiat 500 was a remarkable little car, which combined extreme economy – it would return 50 mpg even when driven hard – with advanced engineering. Front suspension was independent, and the cross-braced chassis was drilled for lightness.

The tiny four-cylinder engine was mounted at the forward end of the chassis, with the radiator behind; engine, clutch and gearbox were supported in the frame by a massive pressed steel collar, which doubled as a cross-bracing between the side members. Accessibility was excellent, with a lift off bonnet.

Because of its cheeky appearance, Italians called the Fiat 500 Topolino (Mickey Mouse), while in Denmark it was known as the Mariehone or Maybug.

Sliding windows increased the internal room, and there was ample luggage (or child!) space behind the two seats.

Post-war, Fiat introduced the 500B, which gained overhead valves, another 3.5 bhp and some extra performance, and survived in production until 1955. The 500 was also built in France by Simca.

## 1936 FIAT TOPOLINO

**Engine:** in-line four-cylinder, overhead-valve
**Bore × stroke:** 52 mm × 67 mm
**Capacity:** 569 cc
**Maximum power:** 13 bhp
**Transmission:** four-speed
**Chassis:** X-braced pressed steel
**Suspension:** independent front with wishbones and transverse leaf spring. Live rear axle with semi-elliptic leaf springs
**Brakes:** drums all round
**Bodywork:** two seat coupé
**Maximum speed (approx):** 55 mph (88 kph)

**Fiat Topolino**

# A-Z OF THE CAR

## Fiat Spider

The present Fiat Spider can trace its history back to the 124 Sport Spider of 1966 which was mechanically similar to the 124 saloon except for a shorter wheelbase. Pinnifarina's design was apparently inspired by the 1963 Corvette Rondine, of all things.... It was aimed at the US market, made only in left-hand-drive form and never exported to the UK where its natural rival would have been the frankly inferior and cruder MGB. Back in 1966, the 124 Sport Spider was powered by the 1.4-litre version of the Fiat belt-driven twin-cam four which produced a very respectable 90 bhp at 6000 rpm.

It was an instant and huge success and over the years the engine's displacement was increased to compensate for the power-sapping emission-control regulations, first to 1.6 and then 1.8 litres, until finally a 2-litre engine appeared. The car is still sold in 2-litre form in North America but even with fuel injection the twin-cam only produces 103 bhp, limiting the car to less than sporting performance with a top speed of only 102 mph (164 kph) and a 0–60 time of 10.6 seconds.

In an effort to boost performance, some American spec Spiders were fitted with small Japanese IHI turbochargers which helped produce a further 20 bhp. By 1985 the Spider was beginning to feel a little old fashioned but its appeal seemed almost as strong as ever.

## Fiat X1/9

The X1/9 was a bold attempt by Fiat to bring the mid-engined layout within the sphere of mass-production.

The power unit of the X1/9 was taken from the 128 1300 cc coupé, and it gave excellent performance in the little Bertone-bodied two-seater. With its neat wedge-shaped profile and pop-up headlights the car has already become a modern classic.

With a removable Targa top, the X1/9 was designed as an enthusiastic drivers' car, with a high standard of road-holding.

In the 1980s, Fiat decided to cease production of the X1/9, continuing demand saw production of the entire car taken over by coach-builders Bertone just as Pininfarina took over Spider manufacture.

### 1984 FIAT SPIDER TURBO

**Engine:** in-line, four-cylinder, twin-overhead-cam, turbocharged
**Bore × stroke:** 84 mm × 90 mm
**Capacity:** 1995 cc
**Maximum power:** 120 bhp
**Transmission:** five-speed manual
**Chassis:** integral, steel
**Suspension:** independent front with coil springs, wishbones and anti-roll bar. Live rear axle with radius arms, Panhard rod coil springs and anti-roll bar
**Brakes:** discs all round
**Bodywork:** two-seater sports
**Maximum speed (approx):** 107 mph (173 kph)

### 1973 FIAT X1/9

**Engine:** tranversely-mounted four-cylinder, overhead-cam
**Bore × stroke:** 86 mm × 55.5 mm
**Capacity:** 1290 cc
**Maximum power:** 75 bhp
**Transmission:** four-speed
**Chassis:** integral
**Suspension:** independent with MacPherson struts and wishbones all round
**Brakes:** four-wheel discs
**Bodywork:** two-seater sports
**Maximum speed (approx):** 105 mph (169 kph)

**Fiat X1/9**

**Fiat Spider**

**Fischer**

# FISCHER

**Zurich, Switzerland
1909–1919**

Martin Fischer, who had created the unorthodox friction-drive Turicum car in 1904, resigned at the end of 1908 to begin development of a four-cylinder voiturette, which retained the distinctive feature of friction drive.

Production began late in 1909 in a former tinsmith's works in Zurich, but the little cars sold slowly; a Zurich industrialist later put some financial backing into the venture and production was transferred to the former Weidmann factory at Brunau, on the outskirts of Zurich, where a staff of 90 workmen built a first series of 70 cars.

Fischer then adopted an ingenious four-speed gearbox in which direct drive in every ratio was obtained by using internally-toothed gears in conjunction with a pinion on the cardan shaft.

In 1911, Fischer launched a 33 hp five-bearing sleeve-valve 2724 cc four-cylinder model with oval bores 'rounded off' by half-moon-shaped sleeves.

By 1913, production had reached some 180 cars, with vehicles sold to Germany, Brazil and England.

Fischer introduced a handsome sleeve-valve six-cylinder of 4086 cc in 1914, but the outbreak of war meant that only two examples of this SS model were built in Switzerland before the Fischer plant closed down.

However, Fischer sold the licence to produce the SS to a Dr Lewis in the USA, and a number of

---

**1914 FISCHER SS**

**Engine:** in-line six-cylinder, sleeve-valve
**Bore × stroke:** 85 mm × 120 mm
**Capacity:** 4086 cc
**Maximum power:** 40 bhp
**Transmission:** three-speed
**Chassis:** pressed steel channel
**Suspension:** non-independent with semi-elliptic leaf springs front and quarter-elliptics rear
**Brakes:** rear wheel
**Bodywork:** saloon
**Maximum speed (approx):** 50 mph (80 kph)

---

Fischer cars was built in America; the oval-bore sleeve-valve engine was also used by Mondex-Magic and Palmer-Singer in the USA and by Delaugere-Clayette in France.

In 1919, Fischer built a prototype cyclecar with a vee-twin MAG engine and, again, friction drive, but despite the interest of a major metalworking company, SIF, the venture proved short-lived, and only a few cyclecars were built.

A German company bought the rights to a new Fischer sleeve-valve engine in 1922, but failed to exploit the design.

# FN

**Liège, Belgium
1899–1939**

FN was a famous armaments producer before its entry into the motor industry, and the decision to diversify was made after the company was taken over in 1896 by a German combine.

After testing a French

quadricycle and an American electric car, FN showed an air-cooled 2½ hp twin-cylinder, two-speed voiturette in March 1899; a series of 100, with the engine increased to 3½ hp, was constructed in the spring of 1900. It proved so successful that a 4½ hp version was put into production from the end of 1900 until 1902, and a total of 280 was built.

During 1901, FN also constructed a monstrous '100 hp' petrol-electric car for Baron Pierre du Caters.

The following year FN took on the agency for the French De Dion Bouton car and suspended production of its own cars.

In November 1905 an agreement was signed for FN to take over licence production of the French Rochet-Schneider marque from La Locomotrice.

In 1908 FN cars were once again taking on an individual character, with a range which included an impressive 6.9-litre 30/40 hp four which was sold to such exalted customers as the Crown Prince of Germany, King Peter of Serbia and the Shah of Persia. 125 examples were built before production ended in 1913.

A lower-priced 2-litre 14/18 hp four, introduced in 1906, was progressively developed into the 2100 of 1909. Alongside this model FN also marketed a range of well-engineered light cars of 8/10 hp and 8/12 hp, plus larger cars of 14/18 hp and 16/24 hp.

After the Great War, car

---

production was resumed in 1920 with a range derived from the 1914 models; the 25 hp of 3800 cc was the first new post-war FN, introduced at the October 1920 London Motor Show.

The best-known FN of the 1920s was the overhead-valve 1300 cc; this model, and its 1400 cc and 1625 cc derivatives, remained in production until 1933.

A 3.2-litre straight-eight on American lines, the 832 was marketed between 1930 and 1935; it had a four-speed gearbox and a choice of right- or left-hand drive.

In 1933 the 2-litre Prince Baudouin replaced the old 1625 cc models, and was the first FN with all-steel bodywork. In December 1934 the Prince Albert appeared, with a choice of 2.2-litre or 3.8-litre engines. It was available with aerodynamic saloon bodywork, the Surprofile, built by the Liège coachbuilder Pritchard-Dumoulin.

Production of FN cars ceased in 1935, when Belgium signed an agreement with the United States which drastically reduced import duties on spare parts in order to encourage the construction of assembly plants for American cars.

# FN 1300

A new model, the 1300, replaced the old FN 1250 in September 1923. It had been designed by Perrier, chief engineer of FN's car department, and had a three-bearing crankshaft and, right from the start, four-wheel brakes to match its lively performance.

Of the 2700 FN 1300s built, 200 were the Type Sport, which enabled FN to compete for the first time in international motor sport; 1300 Sports were particularly successful in the 24-hour race at Francorchamps, where in 1925 and 1926 the FN team won the team prize, the Coupe du Roi. In 1925 an FN 1300 took third place in the Monte Carlo Rally.

In 1927 the 1300 was replaced by the larger and heavier 1400; again there was a sports version, equipped with twin carburettors.

---

**1923 FN 1300**

**Engine:** in-line four-cylinder, overhead-valve
**Bore × stroke:** 65 mm × 100 mm
**Capacity:** 1327 cc
**Maximum power:** 35 bhp
**Transmission:** three-speed manual
**Chassis:** pressed steel channel
**Suspension:** non-independent, with semi-elliptic leaf springs front and rear
**Brakes:** drums all round
**Bodywork:** sport, tourer or saloon
**Maximum speed (approx):** 70 mph (15 kph)

**FN 1300 Sport**

# FORD

Detroit, USA/Dagenham,
England/Cologne, Germany/
1903–

Farmer's son Henry Ford decided at an early age that he would 'invent a machine that would 'take the drudgery out of the farm'. While working with the Edison Illuminating Company in Detroit, Ford constructed a primitive internal combustion engine in 1893 working solely from reports published in magazines. Then, in June 1896, he rolled a little experimental Quadricycle out of the shed behind his house, pausing only to widen the door with an axe (thereby creating America's first garage).

After a couple of ultimately unsuccessful attempts to establish car companies – his 1902 Henry Ford Company became Cadillac after his departure – Ford made it third time lucky with the Ford Motor Company, incorporated on 24 June, 1903.

His aim was to 'build a car for the great multitude', represented by his early twin-cylinder A, C and F models; his backers, particularly the coal merchant Alexander Malcomson, forced him against his will to build higher-priced, less-successful models – the four-cylinder B and the six-cylinder K – which reinforced Ford in the view that the sooner he could break free from the pernicious influence of

outside finance, the better.

Ford's first major success came in 1906 with the launch of his modestly priced 15 hp four-cylinder Model N: this spidery economy car (Models R and S were better-bodied, costlier derivatives) led to the immortal Model T, which made its debut in October 1908. Right up to its demise in 1927, the eccentric T retained a pedal-operated two-speed epicyclic transmission and rear-wheel brakes. Nevertheless, the Model T achieved unprecedented sales, fully justifying its nickname of 'the car that put the world on wheels'.

At the peak of its popularity in the early 1920s, half the cars in the world were Model Ts. Its success enabled Ford to buy out all his shareholders. Ultimately, over 16 million Model Ts were built worldwide, for Ford had seen the advantages of worldwide expansion right from the beginning.

The successor to the Model T represented a new beginning for Ford, so it was called 'Model A': the Model A was thoroughly up to date, with four-wheel brakes and a three-speed sliding gearbox, and established some notable firsts among mass-production cars. For example, it was the first mass-production car with a safety glass windscreen, the first to feature hydraulic shock-absorbers and, in 1929, offered the first production-line station wagon derivative.

The Model A was an instant success: a million were sold in its first 16 months, a record which remained unbroken until Ford launched its Escort 57 years later.

In the spring of 1932 the Model A was succeeded by the four-cylinder AB (which took the unofficial title Model B) and, more

significantly, by the 18F V8, 'Ford's last mechanical triumph', which shared the chassis of the Model B, thereby revealing the inadequacy of its brakes. Despite the sort of annoying teething troubles that were inevitable given its rapid development programme, the flathead V8, now prey to the annual styling changeabout that had for so long been anathema to old Henry, proved to be Ford's American mainstay throughout the difficult period of the 1930s.

By the '30s cars designed for the roads of America were out of tune with the highly-taxed highways of Europe, so Ford had to develop a new small car to save the newly-opened British factory at Dagenham, Essex (which succeeded a pioneering operation in Trafford Park, Manchester, opened in 1911).

The 933 cc Model Y went from drawing board to prototype between October 1931 and February 1932, was redesigned in line with comments from dealers and public, and put into production at Dagenham in August 1932. With the 1172 cc Model C launched in 1934, the Model Y was the cornerstone of Ford's European production for nearly three decades. And though the 3.2-litre V8 was offered in Europe, there was also a 22 hp, 2.2-litre version for the old world, produced in Dagenhem as well as in a joint-venture plant at Strasbourg, under the name Matford.

However, the 3.6-litre V8 was the mainstay of American production throughout the 1930s; the 1942 design was resumed for post-war production, though with the Mercury 3916 cc V8 instead of the pre-war unit. (That engine lived

on in Europe, where it was featured in the 1947 V8 Pilot from Dagenham.)

A major breakthrough came with the 1949 American line, styled by George Walker. These good-looking cars were the first Fords with independent front suspension; rear suspension was semi-elliptic, another break with Ford tradition. Since old Henry had died in 1947, his personal idiosyncracies could now be ignored....

Britain broke new ground in 1950 with the Consul four and Zephyr six, which combined integral construction with the first application anywhere of MacPherson strut independent front suspension.

In 1952 Ford's basic American power unit became the new 3654 cc short-stroke six-cylinder, produced until 1964; a 3917 cc Y-block overhead-valve V8 followed soon after in 1954.

The 1955 range had all-new styling with wraparound windscreens and two-tone paint; it included the instantly successful two-passenger Thunderbird.

Other notable models in the 1955 line-up were the Fairlane Sunliner Convertible and the Crown Victoria, available with the Skyliner hardtop, a transparent plexiglass roof over the front seat.

This gave way to the Skyliner retractable hardtop, of which 48,000 were sold from 1957–59.

If the restyled 1957 American Ford range – Custom and Custom 300, Fairlane and Fairlane 500 – was bewilderingly complex, with engines from 4457 cc to 5113 cc in a 21-model line-up – Europe's offerings were easier to comprehend.

**continued in issue 33**

# A-Z OF THE CAR

## FORD continued

A 'small' 2.2-litre V8 called the Vedette had gone into production in France after the war, but both design and factory had been sold to Simca in 1954: otherwise Europe's model lines were well-rooted in tradition, with the 1172 cc side-valve 10 hp engine powering both English and German small Fords in the 1950s. Indeed, the cheapest British saloon car of the 1950s was the 103E Popular, which in styling and chassis design went back to the 1930s. In larger cars, however, the common thread of development had been broken by the war, and the British and German companies would pursue separate paths of development until the formation of Ford of Europe in 1967.

Notable models of this period were the various German Taunuses, and, from Britain, the overhead-valve four-speed 105E Anglia, with its reverse-rake rear window, the Cortina and the ultra-limited edition GT40 supercar.

As far as America was concerned, one of the most successful Ford models, the Mustang 'personal sports car', appeared in 1964, this 2+2 model was powered by a 2786 cc six as standard, with the option of three V8s up to 4736 cc. The millionth Mustang was sold in 1966.

Europe's common model range started with the 1968 Escort, joined in 1969 by the 'car you always promised yourself', the Capri, inspired by the Mustang.

The Fiesta of 1976 was a new step for Ford, a front-wheel-drive minicar, and the first produced in Ford's Spanish factory in Valencia.

From 1974, all US Fords had disc brakes and by 1976 the line-up comprised the Pinto, Maverick, Torino, Granada, Bronco, Mustang II, Thunderbird, Elite and mighty LTD, 18 ft 7 in (5664 mm) long and with engines of up to 7.5 litres. In 1978, the European-style Fairmont replaced the Maverick and the Fiesta 1600 hatchback was imported from Europe.

During the 1980s, there was an increasing convergence between European and American Ford.

The front-drive Escort of 1980 broke sales records and the 1982 European Sierra and the American Tempo evinced Ford's commitment to aerodynamic styling. In 1985, the European Sierra XR4 was built for export to America, Fords sold in the USA were sometimes built overseas, such as in the 1980s Probes and Capris, and new styling themes led to the smooth Taurus range. The European range, by the early 1990s, comprised the Fiesta, the Escort, including the ultra-fast RS Cosworth model, the Granada saloons and estates and Ford's much vaunted new family car, the Mondeo, with 1.8 and 2-litre engines.

## Ford Model T

The 'Universal Car' made its first public appearance in October 1908, created to Henry Ford's specifications by the Hungarian engineer

### 1926 FORD MODEL T

**Engine:** in-line four-cylinder, side-valve
**Bore × stroke:** 95 mm × 101 mm
**Capacity:** 2864 cc
**Maximum power:** 22 bhp
**Transmission:** pedal-controlled two-speed epicyclic
**Chassis:** pressed steel channel
**Suspension:** non-independent with semi-elliptic transverse leaf springs
**Brakes:** rear wheel
**Bodywork:** roadster, tourer, coupé, town car, sedan
**Maximum speed (approx):** 45 mph (72 kph)

Joseph Galamb and the brilliant metallurgist Childe Harold Wills (who also designed the Ford script trademark).

Tall and spidery, the Model T was designed for the roads of rural America; but though it was cheap it was made of the best materials, the use of vanadium steel endowing its chassis with great strength.

It was also designed to be simple to drive – hence the two-speed epicyclic transmission, which remained a feature of the Model T throughout its 19-year production life.

In 1913, the Model T became the first-ever car to be built on a moving production line; output between 1908–1927 totalled 16 million.

## Ford Model A

When Henry Ford decided to kill off the Model T in the summer of 1927, he had no clear idea of the form its successor would take: his previous experiments with possible successors had led him to investigate such unorthodox power units as the X8 layout.

His son Edsel played a considerable part in the development of the new Model A, which was as modern as the Model T had become antique. Four-wheel brakes were at last adopted, while a crash during the test programme led Ford to take the bold step of standardising safety glass in the windscreen. Another first was the adoption of hydraulic shock absorbers.

The Model A proved to be every bit as tough as its predecessor, despite its accelerated development cycle, and a million were sold in the 16 months following its eagerly-awaited launch in December 1927.

**Ford Model T**

**Ford Model A**

### 1930 FORD MODEL A

**Engine:** in-line four-cylinder, side-valve
**Bore × stroke:** 98.4 mm × 108 mm
**Capacity:** 3285 cc
**Maximum power:** 40 bhp
**Transmission:** three-speed
**Chassis:** pressed steel channel
**Suspension:** non-independent with transverse semi-elliptic leaf springs
**Brakes:** drums all round, mechanically operated
**Bodywork:** roadster, coupé, tourer, sedan
**Maximum speed (approx):** 60 mph (97 kph)

But the very different commercial conditions of the depression years meant that Model A could not expect the longevity of Model T, and production ceased in the spring of 1932 to make way for the new V8 (whose four-cylinder derivative, Model AB, was known within Ford as the improved Model A). Some 5 million Model As were built.

## Ford Model Y

The adoption of horsepower tax in the 1920s had proved a bitter blow for the Model T in Britain; and even the adoption for Model A of a special 'European' optional power unit of 14.9 hp (against the normal 24 hp) could not alleviate the disadvantage that this model laboured under in Britain.

Things became so bad during the Depression that the new Dagenham plant, built in 1929–31 at a cost of £5 million, produced only five Model As during its first three months in operation. So Sir Percival Perry, who headed Ford's British operation, appealed as a matter of urgency to Henry Ford for a small car to be built there.

Chief engineer Lawrence Sheldrick began drawing up the new small Ford, Model 19-Y, in October 1931: by February 1932, the first prototypes had been built and shipped to Europe for exhibition.

The original plan had been to create a new marque called Mercury. In the event, that marque name didn't appear until a few years later on a full-sized car for North America, but the little Model Y was an instant success when it went into production in 1932, and gave Ford 44 per cent of the small car market.

Its advanced styling was copied by Morris and Singer, and the 8hp Model Y was the prototype for Ford's European small cars until 1959.

### 1933 FORD MODEL Y

**Engine:** in-line four-cylinder, side-valve
**Bore × stroke:** 56.6 mm × 92.5 mm
**Capacity:** 933 cc
**Maximum power:** 23 bhp
**Transmission:** three-speed manual
**Chassis:** pressed steel channel
**Suspension:** non-independent with transverse leaf springs front and rear
**Brakes:** four-wheel mechanical drum
**Bodywork:** saloon
**Maximum speed (approx):** 50 mph (80 kph)

## Ford V8

'Henry Ford's last mechanical triumph' was the result of a long-term obsession of old Henry's to produce an eight-cylinder car. It wasn't until he had started work on a successor to the Model A, however, that Ford really determined to put an eight into production.

During the winter of 1930–31 twenty experimental eight-cylinder cars were secretly built in the old Edison laboratory, which has been re-erected in Ford's Greenfield Village museum, but the project was temporarily shelved because of the Depression.

Then, after the improved Model A' (better known as Model B) had

**Ford Model Y**

**Ford V8**

### 1932 FORD V8

**Engine:** V8 side-valve
**Bore × stroke:** 77.8 mm × 95.25 mm
**Capacity:** 3622 cc
**Maximum power:** 65 bhp
**Transmission:** three-speed manual
**Chassis:** pressed steel channel
**Suspension:** non-independent with transverse leaf springs front and rear
**Brakes:** four wheel mechanical drum
**Bodywork:** roadster, coupé, phaeton, victoria, sedan
**Maximum speed (approx):** 75 mph (120 kph)

gone into production at the end of 1931, it was noticed that Henry Ford was 'getting madder and madder', despite the busy production lines.

Henry rationalised his feelings thus: 'The public has its part in these matters. Sometimes it knows when the time is ripe for something new …we developed a corking good four, and were all ready to let it go, but we found it was not the new effort which the public was expecting. That's why we're bringing out the eight now….'

Ford's engineers had analysed every V8 engine sold on the US market within recent years, and had achieved a production miracle in adapting the complex V8 unit for mass production.

Of course, there were teething troubles, and many of the car's mechanical components were redesigned during those first months on sale. The chassis of the original V8 was not really up to its power unit's

sportscar performance, particularly where braking was concerned and in 1933 was redesigned in body and chassis.

The V8 engine lasted in production for over 21 years substantially unchanged, thus outliving even the Model T.

The last private car with the 30 hp V8 engine was the British Ford Pilot, of which over 22,000 examples were built between 1947–52; the estate car derivative was King George VI's last and favourite car.

## Ford Thunderbird

At the 1953 Paris Salon, top Ford design executives George Walker and Lewis Crusoe saw the first Chevrolet Corvette, with the result that a phone call went back to Dearborn instructing designer Bill Boyer to build a fullsize clay model of a sports car design he had been working on.

The prototype was shown at the February 1954 Detroit Auto Show, and, in a competition to choose a name for the new car, a Ford car stylist won a suit of clothes for suggesting Thunderbird.

The first production T-Bird was built at Dearborn on 9 September, 1954; the first cars were fitted with a power-operated canvas hood for fine weather, and a detachable hardtop for bad weather.

In 1956, the hardtop gained the distinctive oval portholes that were a distinctive feature of the T-Bird.

Though the Thunderbird line has remained in production for over 30 years, it was the original 1955–57 T-Bird line, of which 54,000 examples were built, which has become a modern classic. Its purely intuitive aerodynamic styling was derived from Boyer's background in naval aviation. Unfortunately those good looks were progressively devalued.

### 1954 FORD THUNDERBIRD

**Engine:** V8, overhead-valve
**Bore × stroke:** 96.52 mm × 87.37 mm
**Capacity:** 5113 cc
**Maximum power:** 225 bhp
**Transmission:** three-speed plus overdrive (Ford-O-Matic automatic optional)
**Chassis:** pressed steel
**Suspension:** independent front with coil springs. Live rear axle with semi-elliptic leaf springs
**Brakes:** four-wheel drum
**Bodywork:** two-seater sports
**Maximum speed (approx):** 116 mph (187 kph)
**Brakes:** front disc, rear drum
**Bodywork:** two-door saloon
**Maximum speed (approx):** 100 mph (160 kph)

**Ford Thunderbird**

# A-Z OF THE CAR

## Ford Cortina

Designed by Roy Brown, the ex-dance-band crooner who had been banished to England for having designed the Edsel, the original Cortina was Dagenham's reply to the BMC Mini.

Thoroughly conventional, the Cortina nevertheless pioneered aeroflow ventilation (devised by a Tasmanian-born Ford engineer named Ken Teesdale), a feature which was adapted and adopted by virtually every other maker.

The Cortina theme was developed over 20 years, in which time well over 4 million cars were built at Dagenham bearing the Cortina

### 1962 FORD CORTINA

**Engine:** in-line four-cylinder, overhead-valve
**Bore × stroke:** 80.8 mm × 58.2 mm
**Capacity:** 1198 cc
**Maximum power:** 53.5 bhp
**Transmission:** four-speed manual
**Chassis:** integral
**Suspension:** independent front with coil springs. Live rear axle with semi-elliptic leaf springs
**Brakes:** four-wheel drum
**Bodywork:** saloon
**Maximum speed (approx):** 77 mph (124 kph)

## Ford Mustang

Introduced in May 1964, the Mustang was one of the most remarkable post-war automobile success stories. Yet it was mechanically unremarkable, consisting of a melange of componentry taken from a fairly mediocre set of Ford's range of popular cars – Falcon, Fairlane and Mercury Comet.

Designed to sell, the Mustang had instantly attractive 2+2 styling which epitomised the American concept of the sporty 'personal car', and within a year of its introduction, over 400,000 had been sold.

**Ford Mustang**

name – including overseas production and the similar German-built Taunus models, production of this line reached some 10 million before it was replaced by the Sierra.

An exciting development along the way was the launch in 1963 of the Lotus Cortina, powered by a twin-cam 1.5-litre Lotus engine developing 105 bhp and initially equipped with Lotus A-frame rear suspension. Top speed of this limited production Cortina was 108 mph (174 kph). A MkII Lotus Cortina came with the MkII Cortina in 1966 but by then the troublesome Lotus suspension was long gone.

Only early MkI Lotus Cortinas had light alloy bootlid, doors and bonnet, steel was later used.

There was a choice of power units, either a 2786 cc straight six or a V8 engine. There were initially two V8s, a 4260 cc unit and a 4736 cc engine available in various states of tune. It was hardly surprising that the rorty 289 (4736 cc) should ultimately become the car's standard V8.

With a wide range of options, the Mustang could be tailored to fit any specification, from a mild town runabout to a 130 mph (210 kph) plus performance car. There was even a Shelby racing version, the 350GT: the 350 came from the power unit's output, attained by using Cobra components.

### 1966 FORD MUSTANG

**Engine:** V8, overhead-valve
**Bore × stroke:** 101.6 mm × 72.9 mm
**Capacity:** 4736 cc
**Maximum power:** 210 bhp
**Transmission:** three-or four-speed or automatic
**Chassis:** steel platform frame
**Suspension:** independent front with unequal length arms and coil springs. Live rear axle with semi elliptic leaf springs
**Brakes:** four-wheel drums (front discs optional)
**Bodywork:** convertible, coupé
**Maximum speed (approx):** 110 mph (177 kph)

## Ford Escort Mexico

It was in 1968 that the Ford 105E Anglia was supplanted by a new small car, the Escort, which was the first new model to be launched during the tenure of the newly-organised Ford of Europe.

A lively little car, the Escort was capable of handling far more performance than its standard overhead-valve power unit provided, and consequently a potent twin-cam power unit was installed in a limited number of Escorts.

But when Ford entered for the longest car rally of all, the London-Mexico event, in 1970, the company placed its trust in a normal Cortina power unit which could be relied upon to hold its tune even under the most adverse conditions.

It was a wise choice: some 25,000 km (15,000 miles) later, the Escort of Hannu Mikkola and Gunnar Palm crossed the finishing line convincingly in the lead, and in honour of the win, a production version of the victorious car was offered. Naturally, the Mexico name tag was applied.

Ford Advanced Vehicle Operations announced the Escort Mexico in November 1970, at a price of £1150. It was not a precise duplicate of the rally-winning car – its engine was the 1600GT unit from the Capri. Ideal for club rallying, the Mexico was distinguishable from ordinary Escorts by its front bumpers, flared wheel arches and fat tyres.

**Ford Cortina**

**Ford Escort Mexico**

## 1971 FORD ESCORT MEXICO

**Engine:** in-line four-cylinder, overhead-valve
**Bore × stroke:** 80.98 mm × 77.62 mm
**Capacity:** 1598 cc
**Maximum power:** 99 bhp
**Transmission:** four-speed
**Chassis:** integral
**Suspension:** independent front with MacPherson strut. Live rear axle with semi-elliptics
**Brakes:** front disc, rear drum
**Bodywork:** two-door saloon
**Maximum speed (approx):** 100 mph (160 kph)

# FRANCO
### Sesto San Giovanni, Italy
### 1908-1912

Attilio Franco's sole claim to fame was victory in the toughest road race of the era, the Targa Florio. He first exhibited a prototype, built in his workshop in Milan's Via a Aleardi, at the 1908 Salone Dell' Automobile di Torino, and produced a few more cars before going into full production in a larger factory in Sesto San Giovanni at the beginning of 1910.

**Franco**

# Ford Escort RS Cosworth

Following the unrivalled success of the earlier Escort in rallying during the 1960s and 1970s, Ford were determined to build another and win the 1993 World Rally Championship.

The new four-wheel-drive car was designed over a Sapphire floorpan shortened by 4 in, and thus still an inch longer than the standard Escort Mk 4, allowing a longitudinal mounting for the well proven Cosworth four-cylinder twin-cam engine, carried over from the Sapphire and tuned to give up to 227 bhp and 221 lb ft of torque and for homologation reasons a larger-

## FORD ESCORT RS COSWORTH

**Engine:** in-line, twin-cam, four-cylinder turbocharged
**Bore x stroke:** 90.8 mm x 77.0 mm
**Capacity:** 1993 cc
**Maximum power:** 227 bhp
**Transmission:** five-speed manual, four-wheel drive
**Chassis:** monocoque
**Suspension:** independent
**Brakes:** ventilated discs all round
**Bodywork:** two-door four-seater
**Maximum speed (approx):** 137 mph (220 kph)

than-ideal Garrett turbocharger was fitted to the first road cars, with resultant turbo-lag problems, to be replaced when the 2500 homologation cars had been sold.

Visually, the new Escort was highly distinctive, having no panels in common with other Escort models. At the rear, the pillar-supported wing produced considerable high-speed downforce and the body's drag factor (Cd) or 0.38 indicated that stability had been more important than sheer slipperiness.

The result was a car with outstanding traction, able to reach 60 mph (96 kph) in 6.2 seconds and 100 mph (160 kph) in 17.4 secs and go on to 137 mph (220 kph).

## 1907 FRANCO

**Engine:** in-line four-cylinder, side-valve
**Bore × stroke:** 110 mm × 130 mm
**Capacity:** 4942 cc
**Maximum power:** 50 bhp
**Transmission:** four-speed chain drive
**Chassis:** pressed-steel channel
**Suspension:** non-independent with semi-elliptic leaf springs front and rear
**Brakes:** rear wheel
**Bodywork:** two or four-seat sport tourer
**Maximum speed (approx):** 65 mph (105 kph)

Business was on a small scale, though the Franco was a handsome car of sporting appearance. Only one model, the chain-driven 35/50 hp, was built.

A 6.8-litre Franco racer, driven by Cariolato, entered the 1909 Targa Florio, but failed to finish. However, the same car and driver won the 184.8-mile (277 km) race in 1910, at an average speed of 29.1 mph (46.8 kph).

The Franco was one of only two official finishers, the second place being taken by the Sigma driven by de Prosperis. Perhaps significantly, the Franco finished in much the same time as the Fiat that had won in 1907, and was slower than the Peugeot that won the concurrent voiturette race.

**Ford Escort Cosworth**

Franklin Airman

# FRANKLIN
Syracuse, USA
1902–1934

In a nation of conformist cars, the Franklin stood out as a glorious monument to eccentricity. Every Franklin built had an air-cooled engine, until 1927 every Franklin had a wooden chassis and, until 1932, they all rode on full elliptic leaf springs.

H.H. Franklin was already established as a manufacturer of die castings when, in 1901, he met John Wilkinson, who had designed an air-cooled power unit, and decided to build cars incorporating Wilkinson's engine.

The first Franklin cars had transverse four-cylinder engines with overhead valves; in 1905 the range was widened with cars powered by in-line four and six-cylinder engines under a circular bonnet. With seven main bearings – a feature of all subsequent Franklin sixes – the six-cylinder model was of advanced design.

Automatic ignition advance and retard was introduced on 1907 models, while a new design of crocodile bonnet and full pressure lubrication were featured on 1912 Franklins.

In 1915, Franklins became America's first production cars fitted with aluminium pistons; the same year, the two upper speeds were removed from the gearbox of

a Franklin, which was driven in bottom gear the 860 miles (1385 km) from Walla Walla, Washington, to San Francisco without overheating.

In 1922, a sloping dummy radiator replaced the Renault-style bonnet, but was itself supplanted three years later by the handsome Series LL designed by J. Frank De Causse; an advanced feature was an electric primer for the carburettor.

Steel chassis frames first appeared on long-chassis 1927 models, while, in an effort to stem falling sales, a range of custom bodies designed by Ray Dietrich was offered alongside 26 standard body styles on the 1931 Series 15 chassis. Nevertheless, sales were only 2851, a quarter of the 1926 level.

By 1932, Franklin had built its last wooden chassis: that year the company unveiled a 95 mph (153 kph) V12 styled by Ray Dietrich, but at $4400 it was the wrong car for the Depression. Even a forty per cent price cut failed to sell the V12; the last Franklin, the 1934 Olympic, was built for cheapness and everything bar the power unit was built by Reo.

## Franklin Airman

*The first Franklin equipped with four-wheel brakes was the 1927 26 hp Airman model. When the news of Charles Lindbergh's Atlantic flight broke, Franklin advertising manager Hugh H. Goodhart suggested that the company's export representative, Eddie Williams, based in Paris, should offer Lindbergh, for publicity, a free car.*

*The 'Lone Eagle' had his car changed for the latest model every year under this scheme; one of the four Franklins he owned is today exhibited in the Henry Ford Museum in Dearborn, Michigan.*

*Amelia Earhart and Orville Wright were other famous flyers to own Franklins.*

### 1927 FRANKLIN AIRMAN
**Engine:** in-line six-cylinder, overhead-valve
**Bore × stroke:** 82.6 mm × 101.6 mm
**Capacity:** 3262 cc
**Maximum power:** 26 hp
**Transmission:** three-speed
**Chassis:** laminated ash
**Suspension:** non-independent with full elliptic leaf springs
**Brakes:** four-wheel drum
**Bodywork:** runabout, coupé, tourer, sedan
**Maximum speed (approx):** 70 mph (113 kph)

# FRAZER NASH
Kingston/Isleworth, England
1924–1960

Like its direct ancestor, the GN, Archie Frazer-Nash's idiosyncratic sports car had a transmission in which the ratios were provided by chain-and-sprocket gearing and selected by dog-clutches. There was a solid rear axle devoid of differential and suspension was by quarter-elliptic leaf springs.

After GN collapsed in 1923, the Frazer Nash company was founded as a partnership between Archie Frazer-Nash and F.N. Pickett. The latter had made his fortune by salvaging unexploded shells from the ammunition dumps around Boulogne.

Production was always limited, and was preceded by a short run of cyclecars assembled from GN components, and re-radiatored Deemster light cars, both sold as 'Frazer Nash' vehicles.

The first true Frazer Nashes were equipped with Plus-Power 1.5-litre engines, and offered the degree of performance normally provided by a £1000 sports car for a mere £350. Plus-Power subsequently went out of business

and the British Anzani engine was adopted: then British Anzani went into receivership twice in a year, and after being bailed out by Eric Burt of the Mowlem building company was moved into the same factory complex as Frazer Nash.

When control of Frazer Nash passed out of the hands of Archie Frazer-Nash in 1928, via Richard Plunkett-Greene to H.J. Aldington, the decision was taken to replace the Anzani engine with the overhead-valve Meadows power unit (British Anzani then turned to the manufacture of cement mixers and pneumatic drills).

Every 'chain-gang' Frazer Nash was built to bespoke order; the mainstay of production during the early 1930s was the TT Replica, derived from the Frazer Nash Boulogne II model. Most TTs were fitted with the Meadows engine, and the bodywork had a radiator stone-guard, louvred bonnet, 'bathtub' tail and no driver's door.

A six-cylinder double-overhead-cam Blackburne engine of 1667 cc was introduced in 1933, then from 1934 an overhead-cam 1.5-litre four-cylinder power unit assembled at the Frazer Nash factory was also fitted. This engine, designed by Albert Gough, was fitted in both the Shelsley and TT Replica models.

In 1934 H.J. Aldington began to import BMW cars from Germany, as the traditional chain-driven Frazer Nash cars were becoming increasingly outdated. However, they were built in diminishing numbers until 1939.

After the war, Frazer Nash adopted the 2-litre BMW 328 power unit, developed jointly by the Aldington brothers and the Bristol Aeroplane Company. In addition to the conventional transmission, other signs of modernity were the tubular chassis with independent transverse leaf front suspension and torsion bar rear suspension. Derived from the 1948 High Speed Model was the Le Mans Replica, named after the marque's third placing in the 1949 24-hour race.

Developed from the MkII competition model, the Sebring Frazer Nash appeared in mid-1954. It had the engine mounted lower and further back in the frame, had full-width bodywork and was capable of 140 mph (225 kph).

From 1956, Frazer Nashes were available with BMW V8 engines of 2.6 litres and then 3.2 litres. The marque last appeared at the 1959 Motor Show; production ended in 1960 and thereafter Frazer Nash concentrated on its Porsche agency.

## Frazer Nash TT Replica

Based on the team cars built for the 1931 Tourist Trophy, the TT Replica was one of the most significant of all the 'chain gang' Frazer Nash models. Originally known as the Boulogne II, it soon became known as the 'TT Replica', and had steel-panelled bodywork instead of the fabric used on the Boulogne II, which had proved even less durable than aluminium panelling.

'Being essentially a car which is built to order', commented the catalogue, 'the general specification may always be modified to meet an owner's individual requirements'. Therefore, while the TT Replica normally had the overhead-cam 1496 cc engine, it could also be specified with double overhead-cam or pushrod overhead valve power units.

Altogether some 90 TT Replicas (including such variants as the almost identical Byfleet model, the Ulster 100 and the rare supercharged Shelsley) were built before the model went out of production in 1938.

**Frazer Nash Le Mans Replica**

### 1932 FRAZER NASH TT REPLICA

**Engine:** in-line four-cylinder, overhead-cam
**Bore × stroke:** 69 mm × 100 mm
**Capacity:** 1496 cc
**Maximum power:** 11.9 hp (rated)
**Transmission:** four-speed chain-and-dog transmission
**Chassis:** pressed steel channel
**Suspension:** non-independent, with inverted semi-elliptic cantilever leaf springs with tubular radius arms front, and quarter-elliptic leaf springs rear
**Brakes:** cable-operated drums all round
**Bodywork:** TT two-seater
**Maximum speed (approx):** 90 mph (145 kph)

## Frazer Nash Le Mans Replica

Developed from the 1948 High Speed Model, the Le Mans Replica was named after the car which came third at Le Mans in 1949, driven by H.J. Aldington and Norman Culpan.

A similar car, driven by Franco Cortese, won the 1951 Targo Florio, the only British car ever to have taken first place in the gruelling Sicilian race. The Le Mans was light and its road-holding excellent.

Stirling Moss won the British Empire Trophy in the Isle of Man the same year, and another Frazer Nash was second.

However, the glassfibre-bodied Le Mans MkII Replica, driven in 1952 by Ken Wharton, failed to share the success of its progenitor, although it led to the development of the handsome and potent Sebring of 1954.

### 1950 FRAZER NASH LE MANS REPLICA

**Engine:** in-line six-cylinder, cross-pushrod-operated overhead valves
**Bore × stroke:** 66 mm × 96 mm
**Capacity:** 1971 cc
**Maximum power:** 140 bhp
**Transmission:** four-speed manual
**Chassis:** tubular steel
**Suspension:** independent front, with wishbones and transverse leaf spring; rear, torsion bars and A-bracket or de Dion layout
**Brakes:** hydraulic drums all round
**Bodywork:** open-top sports two-seater
**Maximum speed (approx):** 130 mph (209 kph)

# GAGGENAU

**Gaggenau, Germany
1905–1911**

Theodor Bergmann's factory began production in 1895 with the Orient Express, one of the worst cars ever marketed. After the Orient Express marque died in 1903, Bergmann built the 567 cc single-cylinder Liliput, (designed by Willy Seck) at that time the cheapest car on the German market.

The automobile division of Bergmann became independent in 1905, although production of the Liliput continued until 1907. Its products were variously known as Gaggenau or SAF (for Suddeutsche Automobil Fabrik) and chief engineer was Josef Vollmer, one of Germany's leading designers.

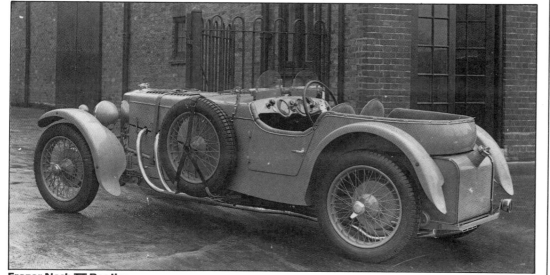

**Frazer Nash TT Replica**

After 1906 Gaggenau built high-efficiency pair-cast four-cylinder cars of 35 hp (4991 cc) and 60 hp (8830 cc) with shaft-driven overhead camshafts.

The 1908–09 6.3-litre Prinz Heinrich model had a crankshaft running in two ball- and one plain bearing, with full pressure lubrication. It was also the first German car with light-alloy cylinders and screwed-in liners: one of these advanced cars was still winning races, driven by Karl Kappler, in the early 1920s.

Gaggenau cars took part in many sporting events, such as the Kaiserpreis and Prinz Heinrich Trials, while in 1907-09 a Gaggenau was the first car to cross Africa from east to west, taking 630 days for the arduous journey.

The factory also built racing cars and aero engines. Otto Hieronymus was one of Gaggenau's leading designer-drivers.

Then Gaggenau was bought by Georg Wyss, and production

**Galloway**

thereafter was concentrated on commercial vehicles, though some manufacture of cars continued.

The Gaggenau factory worked in close co-operation with Benz at Mannheim from 1907, and in 1910 Benz took over the company, which ceased car production in 1911 to devote itself to the manufacture of Benz commercials.

# GALLOWAY
## Tongland/Heathall, Scotland
## 1921–1928

The Galloway was a light car built by an offshoot of Arrol-Johnston, and was mainly remarkable for the fact that the company's first works,

at Tongland in Kirkcudbright, was mostly staffed by women, under the leadership of Miss Dorothee Pullinger, daughter of the car's designer T.C. Pullinger.

The 10/20 hp Galloway had a 1528 cc four-cylinder engine and was produced until 1925. 'The seats are set higher than on many cars in this class', noted a 1923 report, 'so that hedges are less likely to obscure the view'. The 10/20 was then replaced by a 12 hp model with a pushrod overhead-valve engine. Unusually, the rear quarter-elliptic springs were splayed outwards; this was claimed to improve the car's roadholding.

Production was transferred from Tongland to Heathall, Dumfries, in 1923.

---

## 1908 GAGGENAU PRINZ HEINRICH

**Engine:** in-line four-cylinder, overhead-cam
**Bore × stroke:** 110 mm × 165 mm
**Capacity:** 6272 cc
**Maximum power:** 95 bhp
**Transmission:** four-speed chain-drive
**Chassis:** pressed steel channel
**Suspension:** non-independent, with semi-elliptic leaf springs front and rear
**Brakes:** rear/wheel drums
**Bodywork:** sports two or four seater
**Maximum speed (approx):** not known

---

## 1921 GALLOWAY 10/20HP

**Engine:** in-line four-cylinder, side-valve
**Bore × stroke:** 66.5 mm × 110 mm
**Capacity:** 1528 cc
**Maximum power:** 20 bhp
**Transmission:** four-speed
**Chassis:** pressed steel channel
**Suspension:** non-independent, with semi-elliptic leaf springs front, quarter-elliptic leaf springs rear
**Brakes:** rear-wheel drums
**Bodywork:** two and four seater, coupé
**Maximum speed (approx):** 50 mph (80 kph)

---

**Gaggenau Prinz Heinrich**

# A-Z OF THE CAR

Georges Irat was partly taken over by Ruby in 1934, and production was transferred to the Ruby works in Levallois. Here they made perhaps the best-remembered Georges Irat, a popular front-wheel-drive roadster with a Ruby engine. It was followed by a similarly-propelled Citroën-engined roadster.

During World War II the company produced electric cars.

Georges Irat exhibited a prototype after the war with a body of magnesium alloy and 1100 cc flat-twin, but it failed to go into production.

## GEORGES-RICHARD; RICHARD-BRASIER

**Ivry-Port, France
1897–1905**

Georges Richard's first cars were crude copies of the Benz; the steering, by horizontal chain-and-sprocket gearing, looked suicidal. Final drive was by twin belts. By 1900 the Georges Richard factory was offering licence-built Belgian

## GENERAL

**London & Mitcham, England
1902–1903, 1903–1905**

The only really notable thing about the General Motor Car Company was the bizarre and frankly dangerous looking 40 hp racer built in 1902. Unfortunately it did not appear to have made the mark in the racing world its aggressive styling threatened.

In the few years before its demise General built more conventional cars with Aster or Buchet engines of 6½ or 12 hp. By 1905 engine size had escalated to 30 or 40 hp, again from Buchet engines.

*Georges Irat 1100 cc Roadster*

### 1902 GENERAL

**Engine:** in-line four-cylinder, side-valve
**Bore × stroke:** 110 mm × 120 mm
**Capacity:** 4562 cc
**Maximum power:** 40 bhp
**Transmission:** four-speed manual and chain drive
**Chassis:** pressed steel channel
**Suspension:** non-independent, with semi-elliptic leaf springs front and rear
**Brakes:** rear-wheel contracting-band
**Bodywork:** two-seat racing car
**Maximum speed (approx):** 70 mph (113 kph)

## GEORGES IRAT

**Chatou/Neuilly/Levallois, France
1921–1946**

Georges Irat started by making cars fitted with his own overhead-valve 1990 cc four-cylinder engine, which was replaced by a 2985 cc six-cylinder in 1926.

In 1923 and 1925 Georges Irat cars won the arduous Circuit des Routes Pavees, and came third in 1926.

When the company moved from Chatou to Neuilly in 1929, they began to install six- and eight-cylinder American-built Lycoming engines in their cars.

### 1935 GEORGES IRAT SPORTS

**Engine:** in-line four-cylinder
**Bore × stroke:** 60 mm × 70 mm
**Capacity:** 1100 cc
**Maximum power:** 50 bhp
**Transmission:** four-speed manual
**Chassis:** pressed steel channel
**Suspension:** independent front. Beam rear axle with semi-elliptic leaf springs
**Brakes:** four-wheel servo-assisted
**Bodywork:** sports
**Maximum speed (approx):** not known

Vivinus cars, and then, in 1901, introduced a shaft-driven voiturette.

In 1902 the company was joined by designer Brasier and began to produce larger cars on conventional lines – mostly chain-driven – under the name 'Richard-Brasier'. This line of development culminated in the refined racing cars – based on the company's touring models, with an engine tested in a racing motorboat – which achieved worldwide fame by winning the Gordon Bennett Trophy in 1904 and 1905.

Georges Richard resigned in 1905 to found a new marque, the Unic. The company then became plain Brasier.

**General 40 HP**

### 1904 RICHARD-BRASIER GORDON BENNET

**Engine:** in-line four-cylinder
**Bore × stroke:** 150 mm × 140 mm
**Capacity:** 9896 cc
**Maximum power:** 85 bhp
**Transmission:** four-speed chain-drive
**Chassis:** pressed steel channel
**Suspension:** non-independent, with semi-elliptic leaf springs
**Brakes:** rear-wheel drums
**Bodywork:** two-seater racer
**Maximum speed (approx):** 80 mph (130 kph)

**Richard-Brasier Gordon Bennett**

# GERMAIN

**Monceau-sur-Sambre, Belgium**
**1897–1914**

Established as railway and
tramway engineers in 1873,
Germain began car production by
building the twin-cylinder 6CV
Daimler-Belge under licence from
Panhard-Levassor; a four-cylinder
12CV was added in 1900.

In 1902 Germain started
making Renaults under licence; the
axles had to be specially
strengthened to cope with Belgian
roads. Cars of 'improved Panhard'
pattern were also offered.

The first of Germain's own cars
appeared at the 1903 Paris Salon;
these were the 16/22CV (3685 cc),
24/32CV (5401 cc) and 35/45CV
(9852 cc). Well made, these L-head
cars had dual ignition, four-speed
gearboxes and good performance.

In 1905 came the 14/20CV
shaft-driven 'Chainless' Germain
with its distinctive oval radiator and
2929 cc engine.

A team of three 3.7-litre cars ran
in the 1907 French Grand Prix. The
following year three powerful 70/
80 hp racers took part in the same
race; one of them was
subsequently bought by Prince
Albert of Belgium and fitted with
touring coachwork.

In January 1907, Germain
announced their first six-cylinder
model, the 60 CV of 8822 cc; it was
replaced at the end of 1908 by a
3834 cc six with a ball-bearing
crankshaft, although the six-
cylinder line was abandoned soon
after.

**Germain 14 HP**

The 1909 range was complex,
ranging from the 14/20CV of
2925 cc to the monstrous 70/80CV
four of 12,454 cc.

The 1912 range had full
pressure lubrication and included
an overhead-cam 15CV and two
cars with Knight sleeve-valve
engines, the 20CV GCK and 26CV
SDK.

Germain did not resume car
production after the war, although
a few cars were assembled from
existing parts. The factory returned
to the manufacture of railway
material, although a 5-ton diesel
truck was shown in 1937 and
experiments with steam vehicles
were made after World War II.

---

**1905 GERMAINE
CHAINLESS 14/20**

**Engine:** in-line four-cylinder
side-valve
**Bore × stroke:** 92 mm ×
110 mm
**Capacity:** 2925 cc
**Maximum power:** 20 bhp
**Transmission:** three-speed
**Chassis:** pressed steel channel
**Suspension:** non-independent,
with semi-elliptic leaf springs
front and rear
**Brakes:** rear wheel drums
**Bodywork:** to order
**Maximum speed (approx):**
60 mph (97 kph)

---

# GILBERN

**Llantwit, Wales**
**1958–1977**

The name Gilbern was an amalgam
of the names of the company's
founders, German ex-prisoner of
war Bernard Frieze, who worked
for a glassfibre manufacturer, and
Giles Smith, who was a butcher.
The two men built the first Gilbern
car in a shed behind the butcher's
shop, then went into production in
a small factory in Llantwit in 1959.

Production started with a 2+2
coupé using many BMC
components, and 11 were made in

**Gilbern Invader**

the first year. By 1962 production had risen to one a week, and the cars were usually fitted with the 1622 cc MGA engine. Many of Gilbern's sales were in kit form, thus avoiding purchase tax.

A new model, the Ford V6-engined Genie, appeared in 1966: a major fault with this car was the steering, which would go over-centre with hard cornering. This was overcome with changes to the suspension geometry, and with a top speed of 120 mph (193 kph) and a 0-60 mph time of 9 seconds the Genie was fast for its day, albeit rather expensive.

Sales were not good, and in April 1968 the company was taken over by Ace Holdings of Cardiff, themselves absorbed by the Mecca group soon after.

The last Gilbern car was the Ford-powered Mk III Invader, a well-equipped GT car, but the subsequent introduction of VAT on car kits like the Gilbern, and new safety regulations that called for cars to be crash-tested, proved too much for Gilbern: the drop in car sales during the petrol crisis after the Arab-Israeli War proved the final blow for Gilbern, and shortly after another change of ownership, all production ceased.

### 1969 GILBERN INVADER
**Engine:** overhead-valve V6
**Bore × stroke:** 97.3 mm × 72.4 mm
**Capacity:** 2995 cc
**Maximum power:** 144 bhp
**Transmission:** four-speed manual
**Chassis:** square-tube space frame
**Suspension:** independent front with coil and double wishbone; live rear axle located by radius rods and Panhard rod
**Brakes:** discs front, drums rear
**Bodywork:** two-door glassfibre coupé
**Maximum speed (approx):** 120 mph (193 kph)

## GINETTA
**Woodbridge/Witham, England 1957–**

The Ginetta company was formed by the four Walklett brothers, following the construction of a Wolseley Hornet-based special called the Ginetta G1. Their first production car was the G2, a Lotus-like sports car with a space frame, powered by an 1172 cc Ford engine.

Next came the glassfibre-bodied G3 coupé, again Ford powered, which was sold in kit form. Its successor was the G4, launched at the 1961 Racing Car Show, powered in standard form by the 997 cc Ford Anglia engine, with the 1340 cc Ford Classic unit available as an option.

Ginetta moved to Witham, Essex, in 1962, and the following year brought out a G5 variant of the G4, with a 1498 cc Cortina engine. A G4R sports racer with disc brakes and independent rear suspension proved successful in racing and helped boost sales of the standard G4, of which over 500 were sold before production ended in 1967. The G4 was unsuccessfully revived in the '80s.

Since then Ginetta have produced a variety of competition and road cars, including the three-cylinder DKW-powered G6, 4.7-litre V8 Ford-powered G10, the similar MGB-powered G11 and the mid-engined G12 competition coupé, the latter with 1-litre Cosworth or Lotus-Cortina power.

The most successful Ginetta of the period was the rear-engined, Imp-powered G15, over 800 of which were made by the time production ended in 1974. It was

succeeded by the 1974-introduced G21, with a choice of Ford V6 or Chrysler Rapier power.

At the end of the 1970s Ginetta moved back to their original factory in Witham, after a brief excursion to Suffolk, where they refurbished G15s and developed a new G23 open-topped glassfibre sports car powered by the Ford 2.8-litre fuel injection engine.

Ginetta's current offering is the mid-engined G25, with a 1.6-litre Ford Escort engine, and the G26 front-engined, Cortina-based sports saloon.

## Ginetta G4

Designed by Ivor Walklett, the G4 kit car first appeared at the 1961 Racing Car Show, and like its predecessors featured a tubular steel space frame, on this model cut away at the sides to allow for doors. The front suspension was from the Triumph Herald and the live rear axle from the Ford Anglia. With the standard Ford Anglia 105E engine and all components the car retailed for only £499, and for another £16 it was supplied with the 1350 cc Ford Classic unit.

With its low weight and low centre of gravity the G4 had good performance and roadholding. The factory raced a disc-braked G4 very successfully, and in club races driver Chris Meek frequently beat larger GT cars like E-Type Jaguars and AC Cobras. This racing G4 had a 1600 cc engine and independent rear suspension, and the latter modification was made available as an option for road cars.

Ginetta G4

**1965 GINETTA G4**
**Engine:** in-line, four-cylinder, overhead valve
**Bore × stroke:** 80.97 mm × 72.75 mm
**Capacity:** 1498 cc
**Maximum power:** 90 bhp
**Transmission:** four-speed manual
**Chassis:** tubular steel space frame
**Suspension:** independent front with coil springs and wishbones. Live rear axle with 'A' brackets and trailing arms
**Brakes:** discs front and drums rear
**Bodywork:** glassfibre two-seater sports
**Maximum speed (approx):** 120 mph (193 kph)

Ginetta G15

## Ginetta G15

Originally priced at £849 in kit form, the small, two-seat rear-engined coupé was fitted with the Hillman Imp Sport engine and transaxle at the rear, complete with the trailing arm rear suspension. The motor was slung between the upswept side members of the steel chassis, and the front suspension came from the Triumph Spitfire.

The Imp engine produced 55 bhp, and as the G15 only weighed 1120 lb (509 kg) it could propel the car to 100 mph (161 kph) and deliver 45 mpg.

Towards the end of the production period a G15S model was offered. This had a much fuller trim and equipment package and was fitted with the larger 1000 cc Imp engine, tuned by the Chrysler Competition department.

During the '70s the price of the G15 (like everything else) rose dramatically, and in 1974, for a com-

plete, car inclusive of VAT, it had reached £1395. Other increases were imminent, and the company decided to cease production. A total of 800 had been built.

**1969 GINETTA G15**
**Engine:** in-line, four-cylinder, overhead-cam
**Bore × stroke:** 68 mm × 60 mm
**Capacity:** 875 cc
**Maximum power:** 55 bhp
**Transmission:** four-speed manual
**Chassis:** square section tubular steel perimeter chassis
**Suspension:** independent with wishbones coil springs front and semi trailing arms rear
**Brakes:** discs front, drums rear
**Bodywork:** glassfibre two seater sports coupé
**Maximum speed (approx):** 100 mph (160 kph)

## GLADIATOR

**Pré-St Gervais, Puteaux, France**
**1896–1920**

The first Gladiator was a simple 4 hp voiturette with a single-cylinder engine, cycle wheels and handlebar steering, but by the turn of the century the company was making larger and more conventional 2½ and 3½ hp Aster-engined cars with two-speed gearboxes and chain-drive. These models were imported into Britain.

In 1901 Aster-engined 6½ and 12 hp models were offered, the latter with an armoured wood chassis. An 18 hp four-cylinder racer entered the Paris-Berlin race that year but was not placed.

In 1903 cars were offered with 2.1 and 2.7-litre four-cylinder engines made by Gladiator, the latter with mechanically-operated side-valves and single camshaft. A

4-litre 28 hp model appeared two years later, and at this time the company continued to offer smaller, Aster-engined cars.

In 1906 the range was wide, and many models were very similar to Cléments, though the latter used bevel drive instead of chains. One Gladiator, a 12/14 hp four-cylinder, had shaft drive and four speeds.

In 1908 the catalogue included the 18/24 hp and 40 hp fours and the 60 hp six, and there was a range of fours from 2.2 to 6.3 litres of which all but the smallest were chain-driven. In 1909 the company was bought by Vinot et Deguingand and moved to Puteaux; Gladiators subsequently looked very much like Vinots, with the same specifications and prices.

In 1914 the Gladiator range was composed of four-cylinder models of 1.7 and 4.1 litres, and the 12 hp and 15/20 hp were listed as late as 1920, but thereafter Vinot concentrated on his own range.

**Gladiator 12/14 HP**

## 1907 GLADIATOR 12/14 HP

**Engine:** in-line four cylinder, side-valve
**Bore × stroke:** 80 mm × 110 mm
**Capacity:** 2212 cc
**Maximum power:** 15.9 hp
**Transmission:** four-speed manual
**Chassis:** pressed steel channel
**Suspension:** non-independent with semi-elliptic leaf springs front and rear
**Brakes:** rear-wheel drums
**Bodywork:** to order
**Maximum speed (approx):** 40 mph (64 kph)

# GLAS
**Dingolfing, Germany**
**1955–1966**

Hans Glas GmbH had long been established as manufacturers of agricultural machinery before entering the automotive field in 1951 with the Goggo scooter; this ceased production in 1954 and was followed in 1955 by the tiny four-wheeled Goggomobil with a rear-mounted 247 cc two-cylinder two-stroke engine.

In 1958 Glas launched their first 'real' cars, the front-engined Isar T600 and T700 saloons, with overhead-valve flat-twin engines of 584 cc and 688 cc. Then, in 1961, Glas progressed still further, launching the S1004, with a four-cylinder in-line engine of 992 cc, progressively developed in 1189 cc, 1290 cc and 1682 cc forms. This range of power units was significant in being one of the very first to feature the application of a cogged rubber belt to drive an overhead camshaft.

Glas cars were also notable for their handsome Frua-designed bodywork, but the company got into financial difficulties through its failure to rationalise its range, which grew ever more complex.

The last straw was the advanced 2600 introduced in 1966. Its overhead-cam 2580 cc V8 engine was basically two 1300GT fours on a common crankcase, each overhead cam driven by a separate cogged belt. This handsome car boasted Frua sporting four-seater coupé bodywork and a de Dion rear axle, but it was too costly to produce and Glas found themselves with a financial crisis on their hands. Unable to find the millions of Deutschmarks needed for new machinery to produce these luxury cars economically, Glas were taken over by BMW in 1966. BMW immediately carried out the necessary surgery on that complex range, and kept only the 1700 GT and 2600 in production. By 1969 the name of Glas had disappeared from the BMW line-up.

## 1965 GLAS 2600 V8

**Engine:** V8 overhead-cam
**Bore × stroke:** 75 mm × 73 mm
**Capacity:** 2580 cc
**Maximum power:** 140 bhp
**Transmission:** four-speed manual
**Chassis:** integral
**Suspension:** independent front with transverse swinging arms, coil and rubber springs; non-independent rear with semi-elliptic leaf and rubber springs
**Brakes:** discs front, drums rear
**Bodywork:** 2 + 2 coupé
**Maximum speed (approx):** 124 mph (200 kph)

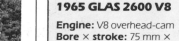

**Glas 2600 V8**

**MODEL**
Delaunay-Belleville F6 (1908)

**ENGINE**
**Location:** Front, longitudinal
**Type:** Individually cast six-cylinder, water-cooled
**Cubic capacity:** 5521 cc
**Bore × stroke:** 98 mm × 122 mm
**Valve-gear:** Side-valve
**Fuel supply:** Single up-draught Claudel-Hobson carburettor
**Ignition:** Magneto
**Maximum power:** 35 hp

**TRANSMISSION**
**Layout:** Gearbox in unit with engine driving rear wheels
**Gearbox:** Four-speed non-synchromesh manual
**Final drive:** Crown wheel and pinion

**SUSPENSION**
**Front:** Non-independent with semi-elliptic leaf springs
**Rear:** Non-independent, with live axle, semi-elliptic leaf springs and transverse leaf spring

**STEERING**
**Type:** Worm and nut

**BRAKES**
**Type:** Internal-expanding metal-to-metal drum brakes on rear wheels

**WHEELS AND TYRES**
**Type:** Rudge-Whitworth detachable wooden artillery wheels, with metal rims and 880 × 120 beaded-edge tyres

**BODY/CHASSIS**
**Type:** Steel U-section ladder-frame chassis with wooden body

**DIMENSIONS AND WEIGHT**
**Length:** 189 in (4800 mm)
**Width:** 66 in (1676 mm)
**Wheelbase:** 139 in (3530 mm)
**Track – front:** 56 in (1422 mm)
       **– rear:** 57 in (1447 mm)
**Weight:** 4480 lb (2032 kg)

**PERFORMANCE**
**Maximum speed:** 65-70 mph (105-113 kph)
**Fuel consumption:** 12 mpg

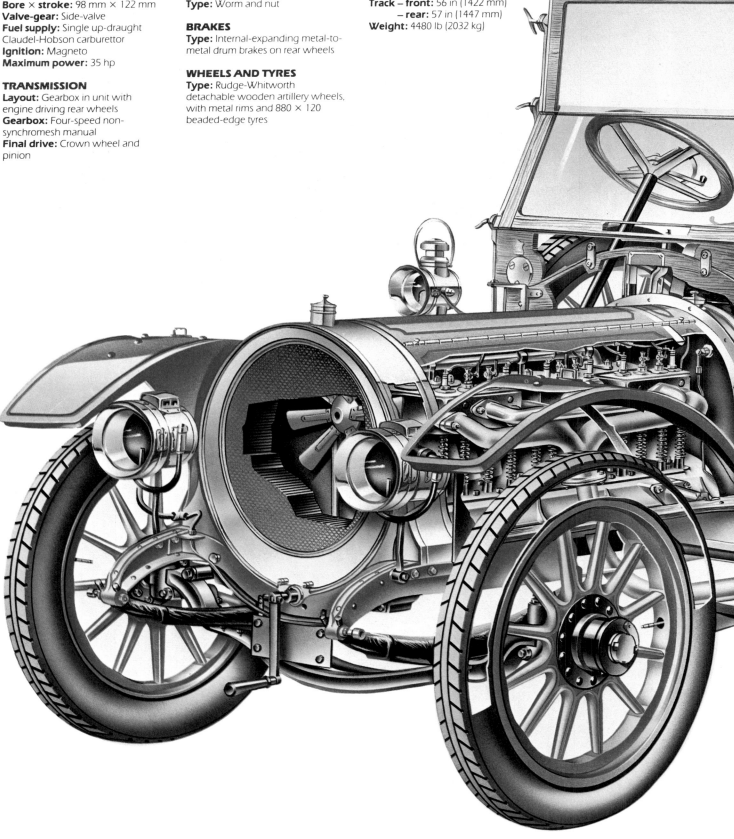

**ABOVE** The Delaunay-Belleville was built for the pillars of society, clearly intimated in the solidity and sobriety of the styling and engineering. The product of a time when aerodynamics was virtually unknown (and in the case of cars like this, virtually unnecessary), the lofty seating and dignified appearance of the car was primarily intended to reflect the owner's status. Mechanically it was not a particularly adventurous design, but the Delaunay-Belleville was renowned for the quality of its construction, for they were built in such small numbers as to be made almost entirely by hand. The six-cylinder engine consisted of three pairs of twin-cylinder blocks, and the single carburettor was mounted on the far side of the engine, the inlet manifold pipe (shown in brown) crossing the engine and entering the block next to the exhaust manifold.

# GN

**Hendon/Wandsworth, England
1910–1925**

Ron Godfrey and Archie Frazer-Nash met as young engineers in 1905, and soon collaborated in the construction of a 'creepabout' powered by a Clement motorcycle engine. Other one-off prototypes followed, then, in 1909, Frazer-Nash built a sporting cycle-car which was written up in the press and attracted three firm orders. Consequently, Frazer-Nash invited Godfrey to join him in the manufacture of similar cyclecars whose crude nature was dictated by the minimal tools at the partners' disposal.

These GN (for 'Godfrey and Nash') cyclecars had wooden chassis and cable-and-bobbin steering, and originally used 1100 cc JAP and Antoine vee-twin motorcycle engines. By 1911, however, backing from a satisfied owner enabled GN to manufacture their own engine, with Peugeot cylinder barrels mounted at 90 degrees and the automatic inlet valves converted to mechanical operation. The following year, GN also started to make their own cylinders and inlet-over-exhaust cylinder heads.

The two-speed transmission was by dog-clutches engaging chain drives of different ratios although belt final drive was subsequently incorporated.

The roadholding of these little cars was excellent, and together with light steering and a weight of little over 720 lb (327 kg) for the basic 2-seat model, the performance was lively.

Three-speed and reverse (or four-forward speed) transmissions were added later, and then, in 1916, an employee named Sheret devised a transmission in which the chains directly drove the rear axle. This was the transmission adopted as standard after World War I, when a steel chassis replaced the original ash and conventional geared steering was adopted.

The company took over the British Gregoire works at Wandsworth, where a staff of 500 was soon building up to 58 cars a week, demand being boosted by such sporting variants as the tuned Legere and the Vitesse, which boasted a 1087 cc overhead-camshaft engine based on that used in the 1913 Grand Prix GN. Later models had twin-camshaft engines and large inclined valves.

The slackening of demand after the post-war boom led to a receiver being appointed in 1920, and Godfrey and Frazer-Nash left in 1922, following disagreement with the new management. The GN had now lost its sporting appeal, for in the search for comfort four-cylinder water-cooled engines by DFP and Anzani were being offered. Only a handful was made before production ceased.

---

## 1913 GN GRAND PRIX

**Engine:** vee-twin, overhead-valve
**Bore × stroke:** 84 mm × 98 mm
**Capacity:** 1086 cc
**Maximum power:** 10 hp
**Transmission:** four-speed chain and dog, belt final drive
**Chassis:** ash, ladder frame
**Suspension:** non-independent, with quarter-elliptic leaf springs and radius rods front and rear
**Brakes:** rear-wheel drums
**Bodywork:** two-seat sports
**Maximum speed (approx):** 60 mph (97 kph)

---

**GN Grand Prix**

# GOBRON-BRILLIE

**Boulogne-sur-Seine/Levallois, France
1898–1930**

Gustave Gobron, politician and industrialist, had escaped from Paris by balloon during the seige of 1870; in 1898 he joined with engineer Eugene Brillie, who had designed an unorthodox engine which had two pistons working in the same cylinder, the explosion taking place between them.

The partners began by building rear-engined cars in Paris, and moved to Boulogne-sur-Seine in 1900. Output from the new factory was in the region of 75-150 cars annually, and a front-engined model made its debut in 1901. Until 1906 most production cars had tubular chassis frames with twin-cylinder engines of 2290 cc or four-cylinder units of 4580 cc.

As early as 1901, Gobron-Brillies were being entered in major races, but the marque's finest hour came on 17 July 1904, when a 15-litre Gobron-Brillie racer, driven by Rigolly, recorded a speed of 103.56 mph (166.6 kph) over the flying kilometre at Ostende, the first time that 100 mph (161 kph) had been exceeded.

Brillie resigned from the company at the end of 1903, but the cars continued to be called Gobron-Brillie until the war. M. Guichard, who succeeded Brillie as designer, claimed that the Gobron-Brillie engine could run on any fuel – including brandy or whisky!

The company had begun in 1904 to make more conventional engines with side valves, and also introduced pressed steel chassis at the same time.

In 1906 Gobron-Brillie listed a four-cylinder 24/35 hp, a 40/60 hp four of 7.6 litres and a 60/75 hp six of more than 11 litres. Two large cars were introduced in 1911; these had inlet-over-exhaust engines of 8165 cc and 9123 cc.

In 1907 a fleet of 40/60s was used as London Ritz-Paris Ritz taxis. A return fare was 12 guineas and the trip 12 hours.

After the war Gobron moved into a new factory at Levallois, where in 1922 they introduced the remarkable 25 hp six-cylinder of 7490 cc, which combined the opposed-piston engine with sleeve valves, camshaft braking and triple carburettors! It lasted less than a year in production, and was succeeded by a thoroughly conventional 1495 cc Chapuis Dornier-engined car. This model sold equally badly, even when disguised as a Stabilia.

The last Gobron-Brillies were powered by side-valve 1327 cc and 1500 cc engines, the latter fitted with a Cozette supercharger and sold under the name Turbo-sport.

**Gobron-Brillié**

### 1906 GOBRON-BRILLIE 40/60HP

**Engine:** in-line opposed-piston four-cylinder
**Bore × stroke:** 110 mm × 200 mm
**Capacity:** 7603 cc
**Maximum power:** 60 bhp
**Transmission:** four-speed manual
**Chassis:** pressed steel channel
**Suspension:** non-independent, with semi-elliptic leaf springs front and rear
**Brakes:** rear-wheel drums
**Bodywork:** to order
**Maximum speed (approx):** 70 mph (113 kph)

# GORDINI

Paris, France
1936–1957

Italian-born, Amédée Gordini is said to have been forced to stay in France after spending his return fare to Italy during a riotous party; he established a tuning business in 1926 and his skill at extracting surprising amounts of power from unremarkable engines earned him the nickname 'Le Sorcier' (the sorcerer).

During the 1930s he began building competition specials, both sports-racing two-seaters and monoposti, evolved from Simca-Fiat cars.

In 1951 the first proper Gordini cars appeared, using his own engines, but lack of finance was a perennial problem. Gordini built racing cars of 1500 cc, 2 litres and 3 litres, but the 2.3-litre sports car he showed at the 1952 Paris Salon never reached the public.

A 2.5-litre coupé took sixth place at Le Mans in 1953, and in the same year a straight-eight 3-litre sports racer also appeared, but

### 1955 GORDINI LE MANS SPORT

**Engine:** in-line eight-cylinder, double overhead-cam
**Bore × stroke:** 78 mm × 78 mm
**Capacity:** 2982 cc
**Maximum power:** 265 bhp
**Transmission:** five-speed manual
**Chassis:** tubular
**Suspension:** independent front and rear, with wishbones and torsion bars
**Brakes:** discs all round
**Bodywork:** two-seat sports
**Maximum speed (approx):** 125 mph (201 kph)

**Gordini Le Mans Sport**

this model was plagued by handling problems.

Unable to make the leap from motor racing to true production, Gordini decided to close his Paris workshop in 1957 to join Renault as a consultant engineer; his Dauphine Gordini was the first of a series of specially tuned versions of production Renault models, though inevitably Gordini himself had less and less to do with their development.

# GORDON-KEEBLE
**Slough/Eastleigh, England
1964–1969**

John Gordon, late of Peerless cars, and designer Jim Keeble produced the Gordon GT at Slough in 1960, but this Chevrolet-engined grand tourer proved too expensive to build. The Bertone coachwork was translated from metal into glassfibre, and production of the Gordon-Keeble began at Eastleigh in January 1964, with the original (and now obsolete) Chrysler 4.6-litre V8 supplanted by a 5.3-litre Chevrolet Corvette engine with a four-barrel Carter carburettor. Unfortunately the Gordon-Keeble

**Gräf & Stift 28/32**

---

## 1965 GORDON-KEEBLE GKI

**Engine:** V8, overhead-valve
**Bore × stroke:** 101.6 mm × 82.6 mm
**Capacity:** 5357 cc
**Maximum power:** 300 bhp
**Transmission:** four-speed manual
**Chassis:** multi-tubular
**Suspension:** independent front with coils and wishbones; rear, de Dion axle with coil springs and Watts linkage
**Brakes:** discs all round
**Bodywork:** Bertone-designed glassfibre coupé
**Maximum speed (approx):** 140 mph (225 kph)

---

was still uneconomic to build, and only some 100 examples of this fine car were built.

The company went into liquidation in 1965 and was taken over by motor agents Harold Smith (London) Ltd, who built a few Gordon-Keebles up to 1967, when the Newmarket firm of de Bruyne took over, with ambitious production plans for a new mid-engined Gordon-Keeble, but only one car was built before the venture folded.

# GRAF & STIFT
**Vienna, Austria
1907–1938**

The three brothers Gräf – Karl, Franz and Heinrich – were the technical experts behind this ambitious venture. They claimed to have built a front-wheel-drive De Dion-engined voiturette in 1897,

but the date was probably inaccurate and in any case the car was never manufactured.

Willy Stift, formerly connected with the Celeritas car factory, joined the Gräfs in 1902 to build cars for five years on behalf of Vienna's leading motor agent, Arnold Spitz.

These cars were marketed under the Spitz name until 1907, when 'Gräf & Stift' was first used.

It was Stift's ambition to build big cars of the highest quality regardless of cost, and the company's products ultimately earned the nickname 'Rolls-Royce of Austria'.

After 1908 production was concentrated on big four-cylinder models of 4240 cc, 5880 cc, 7320 cc and 7684 cc.

The 5.9-litre 28/32 hp earned its place in history in 1914 when it was the official car in which Archduke Franz Ferdinand and his morganatic wife Sophie were riding

---

## 1910 GRAF & STIFT 28/32 HP

**Engine:** in-line four-cylinder, side-valve
**Bore × stroke:** 115 mm × 140 mm
**Capacity:** 5880 cc
**Maximum power:** 28 hp
**Transmission:** four-speed manual
**Chassis:** pressed steel channel
**Suspension:** non-independent front with semi-elliptic leafsprings; de Dion rear-axle
**Brakes:** rear-wheel drums
**Bodywork:** to order
**Maximum speed (approx):** 47 mph (75 kph)

---

when they were assassinated at Sarajevo by Gavrilo Princip, thus sparking off World War I.

In 1921 Gräf & Stift introduced the spectacular Type SR4, an overhead-cam 7745 cc six-cylinder

**Gordon-Keeble GK1**

**Graham-Paige Straight Eight**

and then in 1938 the company introduced the controversial shark-nosed 3½-litre six. With an inwardly-raked snout, the styling was of surpassing ugliness. 'Vacumatic' gear-shift and overdrive were optional.

The firm's last offering was the Graham Hollywood, whose body was pressed from Cord 810/812 body dies and mounted on a Hupmobile chassis; in 1945 Graham-Paige was absorbed by Kaiser-Frazer, who wanted the factory for the production of their post-war models.

# GREGOIRE

**Poissy, France**
**1903–1923**

The first Gregoire cars were an 8 hp single, 12 hp twin and 20 hp four; the company then switched to the manufacture of quality voiturettes, the most famous of which was the 1905 8 hp twin, built until 1912.

---

capable of 90 mph (145 kph). A new 1940 cc model appeared in 1922; the SP4 was developed into the 5-litre SP5 in 1927.

The last Gräf & Stift model, the luxurious SP8, was a derivative of the SP5. Its overhead-cam 5993 cc eight-cylinder engine had a silumin block and cast-iron liners, and developed 125 bhp at 3000 rpm. Such leading coachbuilders as Armbruster, Kellner, and Jech created spectacular bespoke bodywork on this enormous chassis, which had a 148 in (376 cm) wheelbase.

The factory had built lorries during World War I, and when car manufacture ceased they devoted themselves to commercial vehicle production, building light tracked vehicles for the Wehrmacht during World War II.

In addition to their own designs, the Gräf & Stift factory also built Ford, Citroën and Aero Minor cars under licence.

# GRAHAM-PAIGE

**Detroit, USA**
**1928–1940**

The three Graham brothers, Robert, Ray and Joseph, took over Paige-Detroit in 1928, and continued manufacture of the old Lycoming-engined 8-85 Straightaway Eight alongside three new six-cylinder Continental-engined models of 3128 cc, 2666 cc and 4740 cc. The latter models were also built briefly at a Graham factory in Berlin, but this offshoot was soon swept away by the Depression.

At the time of the takeover, Graham-Paige was the 12th largest US car company, but from then on its market share declined.

---

### 1935 GRAHAM-PAIGE

**Engine:** in-line eight-cylinder, side-valve
**Bore × stroke:** 82.5 mm × 101.5 mm
**Capacity:** 4350 cc
**Maximum power:** 140 bhp (supercharged)
**Transmission:** three-speed manual
**Chassis:** pressed steel channel
**Suspension:** non-independent, with semi-elliptic leaf springs front and rear
**Brakes:** drums all round
**Bodywork:** saloon
**Maximum speed (approx):** 95 mph (153 kph)

---

The Blue Streak range of 1932, with vee-grille, pontoon wings and rear axle slotted through the chassis to lower the height, proved to be a stylistic trend-setter but sales did not benefit.

A centrifugal supercharger was fitted to the 1934 4350 cc Custom Eight, which formed the basis for the Bertelli-bodied Graham British Special sports saloon of 1935-36.

After 1936 Graham-Paige concentrated on the Crusader and Cavalier six-cylinders of 2780 cc and 3679 cc, while the outdated Special Six body dies were sold to Nissan (builders of the Datsun), who also used Graham engines.

A new supercharged six-cylinder Graham appeared in 1937,

---

### 1913 GREGOIRE 16/24 HP

**Engine:** in-line four-cylinder, side-valve
**Bore × stroke:** 80 mm × 160 mm
**Capacity:** 3217 cc
**Maximum power:** 24 bhp
**Transmission:** four-speed
**Chassis:** pressed steel channel
**Suspension:** non-independent, with semi-elliptic leaf springs front and three-quarter elliptic leaf springs rear
**Brakes:** rear-wheel drums
**Bodywork:** to order
**Maximum speed (approx):** 50 mph (80 kph)

**Grégoire**

**Grégoire Sports**

There was also a 15 hp four, while an 18/24 hp six – often described as 'very strong' – appeared in 1909. In 1912 Gregoire marketed the single-cylinder Dumont voiturette, built in Asnieres, under the name Gregoire-Dumont.

In 1911-12, Gregoire began experiments with overhead-camshaft engines with hemispherical combustion chambers, but although trials of racers with four-carburettor, hemi-head engines were carried out in 1912, the cars actually entered for the Coupe de l'Auto race had side-valve power units.

Gregoire also produced a number of aerodynamic two-seaters and saloons, mostly built on the 3217 cc 16/20 hp chassis, which also appeared with extraordinary double and triple berline bodywork, endowed with switchback roof and four-pane side windows. The passenger compartment of these cars looked like two or three little horse-drawn coaches joined end to end. The car was in fact an early type of caravan-car.

The sporting 14/20 hp of 1913 was the basis of post-war production, and it acquired overhead valves in 1921. The 1919 Gregoire-Campbell was actually a Bignan-Sport built in the Gregoire factory. M. Gregoire died in 1923, and his company only survived him by a few months.

The ultimate Gregoire was not the genuine article, anyway, for it was built by Hinstin at Maubeuge and powered by an 1100 cc CIME proprietary engine.

## GREGOIRE
**Asnieres, France**
**1945–1962**

Jean A. Grégoire had pioneered front-wheel drive in France with his Tracta of the 1920s. After the war, Grégoire began production of cars under his own name, starting in 1945 with a 600 cc flat-twin prototype for which there were ambitious, unfulfilled plans for British production as the Kendall. It ultimately evolved into the Dyna Panhard.

Grégoire's flat-four 2-litre of 1947 was built by Hotchkiss under the Hotchkiss-Grégoire name; from this Grégoire developed Chapron-bodied sports roadsters which were sold under his own name from 1956-62.

Grégoire, who had displayed a gas-turbine car with rear-wheel drive at the 1952 Paris Salon, subsequently showed a prototype electric car. Among his best post-war designs was variable-rate suspension, used by many automobile companies, including Renault.

### 1956 GREGOIRE SPORTS

**Engine:** supercharged flat-four, overhead-valve
**Bore × stroke:** 90 mm × 86 mm
**Capacity:** 2188 cc
**Maximum power:** 130 bhp
**Transmission:** five-speed manual (overdrive top)
**Chassis:** die-cast light alloy
**Suspension:** independent, with variable-rate coil springs front and rear
**Brakes:** drums all round
**Bodywork:** cast-aluminium sports three-seater
**Maximum speed (approx):** 120 mph (193 kph)

### GUY
**Wolverhampton, England**
**1919–1925**

Guy Motors had built commercial vehicles since 1914, and decided to break into the lucrative luxury car market in 1919. Their offering was a 4-litre V8 with detachable heads

and side valves; it had automatic chassis lubrication actuated every time the steering went on to full right lock, when a cam-operated plunger pump forced oil through a complex circuit of copper pipes to all moving parts of the chassis.

This 20 hp Guy was joined in 1922 by cheaper models fitted with in-line four-cylinder engines of 2.0 and 2.5 litres.

A new four-cylinder, the 13/36, appeared at Olympia in 1923, and its power unit appeared to be half of a V8. Guy's venture into car manufacture proved unsuccessful, and after 1929 the company reverted exclusively to commercial vehicle production. However, in 1929 they acquired Star, another Wolverhampton motor manufacturer, and continued to build cars alongside Star trucks and buses until 1932.

### 1919 GUY

**Engine:** V8, side-valve
**Bore × stroke:** 72 mm × 120 mm
**Capacity:** 3909 cc
**Maximum power:** 60 bhp
**Transmission:** four-speed manual
**Chassis:** pressed steel channel
**Suspension:** non-independent, with semi-elliptic leaf springs front and rear
**Brakes:** rear-wheel drums
**Bodywork:** to order
**Maximum speed (approx):** 60 mph (96 kph)

**Guy V8**

# A-Z OF THE CAR

## GWK

**Datchet/Maidenhead, England
1911–1931**

Grice, Wood and Keiller's original GWK cyclecar was friction-driven and had a two-cylinder rear-mounted Coventry-Simplex engine. Production was transferred to Maidenhead from Datchet in 1914, by which time over 1000 GWKs had been built. The top speed of these cars was 35 mph (56 kph).

The original engine reappeared briefly after World War I, but was soon replaced by a 1368 cc

### 1923 GWK 10.8 HP

**Engine:** in-line four-cylinder, side-valve
**Bore × stroke:** 66 mm × 100 mm
**Capacity:** 1368 cc
**Maximum power:** 23 bhp
**Transmission:** friction disc
**Chassis:** pressed steel channel
**Suspension:** non-independent, with quarter-elliptic leaf springs front and rear
**Brakes:** rear-wheel drums
**Bodywork:** two- and four-seat tourer, coupé
**Maximum speed (approx):** 45 mph (72 kph)

## GWYNNE

**Chiswick, England
1922–1929**

Gwynne Engineering were best-known as manufacturers of centrifugal pumps, and they had also built rotary aero engines during the Great War. In 1920 they took over production of the Albert car (for which they already built the engines) and from 1923 the cars became known as Gwynne-Alberts.

In 1922 Gwynne had begun

**Gwynne 8 HP Sports**

Coventry-Climax four-cylinder. In 1924 a 1½-litre power unit was fitted, but two years later GWK went out of business.

Grice had resigned from GWK in 1920 to make a similar design of car under the name Unit; he tried unsuccessfully to resurrect the company in 1930.

manufacture of the Gwynne Eight, based on the Spanish Victoria light car, designed by Arturo Elizalde. It had an overhead-valve 950 cc four-cylinder engine; a 1247 cc Ten subsequently became available. There was also a handsome 1021 cc Sports Eight, while at the other end of the scale a miniature fire-engine was offered on the Gwynne Eight chassis.

The Gwynne cars were noisy and uncomfortable, but provided both performance and economy at a low price. However, by the mid-1920s other cheaper and more comfortable cars had appeared.

### 1924 GWYNNE SPORTS

**Engine:** in-line four-cylinder, overhead-valve
**Bore × stroke:** 57 mm × 100 mm
**Capacity:** 1021 cc
**Maximum power:** 25 bhp
**Transmission:** three-speed manual
**Chassis:** pressed steel channel
**Suspension:** non-independent, with semi-elliptic leaf springs front and rear
**Brakes:** rear-wheel drums
**Bodywork:** sports two-seater
**Maximum speed (approx):** 65 mph (105 kph)

## HAMPTON

**King's Norton/Stroud, England
1911–1933**

Named for its birthplace of Hampton-in-Arden, Warwickshire, where the Hampton company was founded as a motor agency, Hampton moved to Lifford Mills, King's Norton, Birmingham, in 1912 and began car production with a 1726 cc four-cylinder 12/16 hp. Two years later, Hampton was a latecomer to the cyclecar craze, offering a short-lived twin-cylinder two-stroke alongside Precision and Chapuis-Dornier engines.

Following the Armistice, Hampton moved to Stroud in Gloucestershire, and brought out the 10/16 hp in 1919, powered by a 1496 cc Dorman engine; this was subsequently replaced by a 1795 cc unit.

At the beginning of 1920 output was six Hamptons a week, and sales were boosted by the cars' sporting successes: in 1922 Brian Marshall lapped Brooklands at over 89 mph (143 kph) and in 1924 J.W. Leno took a 'gold' in the Scottish 1000 miles trial.

In 1923, Hampton adopted Meadows engines, and launched the 1247 cc 9/21 hp. Finance was a constant problem; the company was reformed in 1920, 1924 and 1927. A 14 hp model appeared for 1925, and a new 12 hp model was added to the range at the end of

**GWK 10.8 HP**

**Hampton 14 HP**

In 1928 the Kommisbrot was succeeded after 15,775 had been built by a more conventional 745 cc four-cylinder model, available from 1929 in supercharged form.

Further new Hanomags appeared in the early 1930s, powered by overhead-valve four-cylinder engines of 896 cc, 1089 cc, 1299 cc and 1494 cc. The 1089 cc engine was used in the popular Garant and Kurier models.

The overhead-valve 2241 cc six-cylinder Sturm was offered from 1934 to 1939, while a 1910 cc four-cylinder diesel-engined Hanomag Rekord was available between 1937 and 1939. Streamlined bodywork was a feature of 1930s Hanomags, and a 1.3-litre saloon of 1939 managed 70 mph (113 kph) with only 32 hp.

During the war, Hanomag built cars for the German Wehrmacht; a new Hanomag, the 697 cc three-cylinder two-stroke Partner, was exhibited after the war, but failed to enter production.

## 1925 HAMPTON 14 HP

**Engine:** in-line four-cylinder, overhead-valve
**Bore × stroke:** 75 mm × 120 mm
**Capacity:** 2122 cc
**Maximum power:** 40 bhp
**Transmission:** four-speed manual
**Chassis:** pressed steel channel
**Suspension:** non-independent with semi-elliptic leaf springs front and three-quarter-elliptic leaf springs rear
**Brakes:** drums all round
**Bodywork:** two-seater, tourer, coupé
**Maximum speed (approx):** 60 mph (97 kph)

# HANOMAG
**Germany**
**1924–1939**

'The Hanomag is very quaint; it's only made of tin and paint,' ran a popular couplet of the 1920s, though the Hanomag, with its rear-mounted 10 hp single-cylinder 499 cc water-cooled engine, was Germany's first 'people's car'. It was nicknamed Kommisbrot (army loaf) because of its rounded all-enveloping body. The Kommisbrot was started by a lever mounted between the seats; it was cheap but well-made, ideally suited to rough and hilly country. It even enjoyed a brief competition career.

## 1925 HANOMAG KOMMISBROT

**Engine:** single-cylinder, overhead-valve
**Bore × stroke:** 80 mm × 100 mm
**Capacity:** 503 cc
**Maximum power:** 10 bhp
**Transmission:** three-speed chain drive
**Chassis:** integral
**Suspension:** Non-independent with coil springs front and rear
**Brakes:** rear wheel only
**Bodywork:** two-seater enclosed coupé
**Maximum speed (approx):** 40 mph (64 kph)

# HANSA
**Varel/Bielefeld, Germany**
**1905–1939**

The Hansa Automobil Gesellschaft was founded by August Sparkhorst and Dr Robert Allmers, and began production with cars strongly influenced by French designs such as the Alcyon voiturette. The company also built De Dion-engined models under the name HAG, available with single-cylinder 720 cc and 1050 cc power units, as well as a 1360 cc twin.

Hansa also used 1410 cc four-cylinder Fafnir engines, as well as a 6/14PS unit of its own manufacture.

Hansa produced a number of

that year.

In 1928, Hampton introduced both a new six-cylinder model, the 1683 cc 15/45 hp, and a revived 9 hp car.

With production running at 300 cars a year, a new 3-litre six-cylinder Hampton was launched at the 1929 Motor Show; in a desperate move to halt yet another slide into financial collapse during the Depression, in 1930 Hampton ordered 100 2262 cc straight-eight engines and sheet-steel chassis from the equally insolvent Rohr company in Germany.

The resultant model was available with the Rohr straight-eight in either its own or a Hampton chassis. There was also a 'gearless-gearbox' design and a new 1196 cc 12 hp, neither of which saved the company from yet another reorganisation.

By the end of 1931, the Rohr engine had been dropped, and only a 16 hp model was available. The company staggered on through 1932 and then closed for ever.

**Hanomag Kommisbrot**

sports cars, including overhead-valve 2.5-litre and 3.8-litre models, in the pre-World War I period; from 1910 Hansa built RAF cars under licence. Hansa bought the Westfalia car works at Bielefeld in 1913; Westfalia cars were built alongside Hansas for a year after the takeover.

During 1914, Hansa merged with Lloyd of Bremen to create Hansa-Lloyd, though Hansa cars continued to be produced, in capacities ranging from 1550 cc to 3815 cc. The cars were renowned for the high quality of their manufacture and engineering.

In 1920 Hansa, Hansa-Lloyd, NAG and Brennabor combined to form the GDA, or Gemeinschaft Deutscher Automobilfabriken; Hansa-Lloyd's speciality was large cars like the 1923 Model H, with a 4-litre power unit or the 1924 Trumpf AS (or Ace of Trumps), Germany's first straight-eight, launched with a silumin block, overhead-cam 4.5-litre engine, later increased to 5.2 litres.

Subsequently, Hansa offered side-valve 2063 cc four-cylinder 36 hp and Continental-engined six- and eight-cylinder models of 3262 cc, 3996 cc and 4324 cc, all built at the original Varel works.

In 1929, Hansa-Lloyd was taken over by the Borgward-Goliath group.

From 1930 onwards, Bremen-built Hansas had 2098 cc and 3253 cc four-cylinder and 2577 cc six-cylinder side-valve engines. There were also overhead-valve models of 1088 cc and 1640 cc with Hansa's own-make engines.

The rear-engined 498 cc twin-cylinder two-stroke built in 1934–35 was derived from an earlier version with a similar 348 cc engine, produced in small numbers only.

New models with 3485 cc and 1962 cc overhead-valve six-cylinder engines appeared in 1936 and 1937; the company's products were thereafter marketed under the Borgward name, though the Hansa and Lloyd names were revived on Borgward economy cars of the 1950s.

**Hartnett-Grégoire**

# HARTNETT
### Melbourne, Australia
### 1949–1955

Having set up General Motors-Holden after the war, Larry Hartnett resigned over policy but was then persuaded into seeking a small car that could be built for the Australian market. On a holiday in Europe, he met French engineer Jean Gregoire, whose front-wheel-driven small car was derived from the pre-war Hotchkiss Gregoire and made extensive use of aluminium. With four-wheel independent suspension, rack-and-

pinion steering and an air-cooled flat-twin engine, the Gregoire weighed only 950 lb (432 kg).

Hartnett paid £10,000 for the rights to the design and spoke of plans to build 10,000 Hartnett-Gregoires a year, but ran into problems when the body manufacturer failed to deliver the panels for the car.

Hartnett began to assemble chassis without the bodies, and some 120 rolling chassis were completed and fitted with hand-built timber station wagon bodies.

Though Hartnett won a protracted law suit, victory took him over four years, by which time the ambitious project was defunct.

# HAYNES-APPERSON/ HAYNES,
### Kokomo, USA
### 1898–1925

Elwood Haynes, a gifted metallurgist (he invented stainless steel), built his first car in 1894. For many years Haynes claimed this was America's first motor vehicle, though production did not begin until 1898, when Haynes teamed up with the Appersons.

The first production Haynes-Appersons were boxy cars with tiller steering, powered by rear-mounted flat-twin engines. Wheel steering was introduced in 1903, making the Haynes-Apperson one of the first left-hand-drive cars built in America. Though the Apperson brothers broke away in 1902, the cars were called Haynes-Apperson until 1904.

Front engines were adopted in 1904, though the 12 hp flat-twin

**Hansa Telegram**

**Haynes Light Twelve**

**HE 14/40**

was retained; the five-seater aluminium-bodied Haynes Roi-des-Belges cost $2550. The last year of the flat-twins was 1905, when Haynes introduced a vertical-four 35/40 hp.

Haynes catalogued big pair-cast fours from 1906 to 1914, in which year they introduced their first six, the Model 27. Again, this was a pair-cast engine, displacing 7763 cc. A novel feature was an electric gear-shift.

In 1916, Haynes added a 60-degree V12 to the range; each bank of cylinders was a monobloc. Swept volume of this Light Twelve was 5839 cc; it remained in production until 1921, and was offered in chassis lengths of 10 ft (305 cm) and 11 ft (335 cm). Any body type could be fitted, but most were conservative in style. In 1920 a large seven-seat limousine was catalogued at $4200, but prices were reduced, and in 1925 a five-seat sedan was priced at $2300.

The last Haynes was the 5291 cc six-cylinder Model 60, an attractive four-seater coupé.

# HE
**Reading, England
1920–1931**

The HE – the initials stood for Herbert Engineering, from the christian name of the firm's backer, Herbert Merton – was a sports car of great character designed by R.J. Sully.

The car was distinguished by its oval radiator and, on early sporting cars, by handsome 'Dutch clog' three-seater bodywork.

HE's first model was a 1795 cc side-valve four-cylinder tourer, quickly succeeded by the 1982 cc 13/30 hp of 1920; in 1922 came

the first HE sports car, the 14/40, built on a shortened tourer chassis and featuring dual coil ignition, specially tuned power unit with the bore enlarged to 75 mm (giving a swept volume of 2121 cc), full pressure lubrication and close ratio gearbox. From late 1923 both the 13/30 and 14/40 used the 72.5 mm

bore measurement.

During 1927, HE joined the craze for six-cylinder cars, introducing a 2.3-litre 15.7 hp side-valve model. Its performance was similar to that of the four. A sports model was also offered.

HE discontinued four-cylinder models in 1928. The company's last fling was a 1.5-litre six launched in 1930, and equipped with quarter-elliptic springs all round in the interests of economy. A few super-charged 1.5-litre sixes were sold.

# HEALEY
**England
1946–1953**

With an enviable reputation as a highly accomplished driver and experienced engineer, Donald Healey had been responsible for both the Gloria and Dolomite while working at Triumph in the 1930s. Then he moved to Humber, and laid plans for manufacturing a car bearing his own name.

**Healey Silverstone**

## 1949 HEALEY SILVERSTONE

**Engine:** in-line four-cylinder, overhead valve
**Bore × stroke:** 80.5 mm × 120 mm
**Capacity:** 2443 cc
**Maximum power:** 104 bhp
**Transmission:** four-speed manual
**Chassis:** 'top hat' section steel channel
**Suspension:** independent front with trailing arms and coil springs. Live rear axle with semi-elliptic leaf springs and Panhard rod
**Brakes:** drums all round
**Bodywork:** two-seater sports
**Maximum speed (approx):** 110 mph (177 kph)

After the war, he founded the Donald Healey Motor Company in Warwick, and began production of Healey Elliot saloon and Westland sports tourers, with overhead-valve Riley engines, in October 1946. The Elliot was, on its introduction, the fastest series-production saloon made in Britain, and with its 104 bhp engine and four-speed Riley gearbox was capable of 104.7 mph (168 kph) for the flying mile. Aluminium-bodied and aerodynamic, the Elliot was priced at £1598, and strong demand soon had the factory working flat out.

The marque enjoyed sporting success, and in 1949 the Silverstone sports two-seater was launched; 105 Silverstones were produced, and were particularly popular with club racers in Britain.

Built for export only, the Nash-Healey used the 3.8-litre Nash overhead-valve six-cylinder engine: it took fourth place at Le Mans in 1950, the year of its introduction. Healey built 253 of these Nash-engined cars. The marque reached a wider fame with an 2.7-litre Austin-engined two-seater, production of which was taken over by Austin as the Austin-Healey 100.

# HILLMAN

**Coventry, England**
**1907–1976**

Pioneer cycle manufacturer William Hillman entered the car industry in style, commissioning Louis Coatalen to design the first Hillman car, a 24 hp four-cylinder model, for the 1907 Tourist Trophy. It was, however, put out of the race by a crash. After creating the Hillman-Coatalen, the Breton engineer left to join Sunbeam; Hillman then produced throughly conventional models, which included a 6.4-litre four and a 9.7-litre six-cylinder. A 12/16 hp model appeared in 1909.

The company achieved its first real success with the 1913 9 hp, a 1357 cc four which survived into the 1920s. By the time it was discontinued in 1925 it had grown to 1.6 litres. An attractive pointed-radiator Sports brought a young driver named Raymond Mays his first successes.

Hillman introduced a 14 hp model in 1926; two years later the company was taken over by the Rootes brothers, who already handled export sales. In 1928 Hillman launched a 2.6-litre overhead-valve straight-eight with some sporting pretensions; a Segrave sports saloon was among the body styles offered.

The 1931 Wizard six was an unmitigated disaster, but a landmark year for Hillman was 1932, when the company introduced the 1185 cc Minx. It was thoroughly redesigned by A.G. Booth, late of Clyno and AJS in 1933, when a sporting derivative, the Aero Minx, appeared. For 1935, the Hillman Minx became the first British small car with a four-speed synchromesh gearbox.

Among the six-cylinder models of the 1930s was the Hawk but this had been discontinued by 1939 and only the four-cylinder Minx and 14 hp models were offered.

The Minx was still produced after the war; for 1949, it was equipped with full-width bodywork. The following year its power unit was enlarged to 1265 cc. Overhead valves were,

however, not adopted until 1955, along with a 1390 cc engine. The Minx name survived until 1970, by which time the car was powered by a 1725 cc engine.

At the beginning of the 1960s Hillman built a new factory at Linwood in Scotland, where they produced an advanced mini-car, the Imp, launched in 1963. It had a rear-mounted 875 cc all-aluminium overhead-camshaft engine, originally designed by Coventry-Climax, plus all-independent suspension. Its planned high level of sales never materialised, and the Hillman company found itself in what proved to be fatal financial difficulties.

Consequently, a majority interest in Rootes was acquired by the American Chrysler Corporation in 1964; one result of the take-over was the 1294 cc Avenger of 1970. But the distinct, if undistinguished, identity of Hillman was being increasingly overlaid by that of Chrysler, and there was little surprise when the Hillman name was discontinued in 1976 and replaced by that of Chrysler. Just two years after that, Chrysler's British operations were acquired by the French Peugeot-Citroën group.

## 1934 HILLMAN AERO MINX

**Engine:** in-line four-cylinder, side-valve
**Bore × stroke:** 63 mm × 95 mm
**Capacity:** 1185 cc
**Maximum power:** 37 bhp
**Transmission:** four-speed channel
**Chassis:** pressed steel channel
**Suspension:** non-independent with semi-elliptic leaf springs
**Brakes:** drums all round
**Bodywork:** sports tourer or saloon
**Maximum speed (approx):** 70 mph (113 kph)

**Hillman Aero Minx**

# A-Z OF THE CAR

## HISPANO-SUIZA
**Barcelona, Spain/Paris, France
1904–1944**

Swiss engineer Marc Birkigt was persuaded to move to Barcelona at the turn of the century, where he joined an electrical company, La Cuadra. He quickly persuaded them to let him build Spain's first production car, though output was very limited, since La Cuadra was in financial difficulties and failed in 1901 after a strike.

The chief creditor, Sr J. Castro, acquired the assets, and car production was resumed under his name, but still on a small scale.

Again, lack of finance brought the venture to a halt, but the far-sighted Damien Mateu created the Fabrica La Hispano-Suiza de

Automovils to succeed Castro. Its title recorded the marriage of Swiss brains and Spanish cash.

Initially, the Castro four was continued, becoming the first Hispano-Suiza, then, at the Paris Salon of 1906, the company launched two pair-cast fours of 3.8 and 7.4 litres; in 1907 these were followed by two big sixes.

Already, Spain's young King, Alfonso XIII, had bought the first of some 30 Hispano-Suizas he would own.

A racing Hispano built for the 1910 Coupe des Voiturettes sired the famous 3620 cc Alfonso XIII sports model which brought the marque such international acclaim that Hispano-Suiza opened an assembly plant at Levallois-Perret, Paris, in 1911 to serve its fashionable French clientele.

Hispano-Suiza moved to a larger factory in nearby Bois-Colombes in 1914; it was the French affiliate which was responsible for the immortal 32 hp

H6B of 1919, with its ohc 6597 cc light-alloy engine and the even more exciting 7983 cc Boulogne sports derivative of 1924. It was from France, too, that the famous flying stork mascot of the Hispano-Suiza came, based on the squadron insignia of France's Ace of Aces, Georges Guynemer, whose SPAD fighter was Hispano-powered. While the H6B was principally built at the Bois-Colombes plant, Barcelona did turn out a limited number as the T41 (T56 8-litre from 1928): the gutless Spanish T49 used a 3750 cc six-cylinder engine in the same chassis.

Barcelona also built the overhead-valve 4.7-litre T30 (1914–24) and 3089 cc T16 (1921–24): the 2500 cc T48 of the 1920s was built for the Spanish Government's public services. Regrettably, when Alfonso was deposed and fled Spain, he did so at the wheel of an American ReVere, and in his exile drove a Ford V8.

In 1930, Hispano-Suiza took over Ballot, and the 4580 cc Junior six-cylinder was built in the Ballot plant. At the 1931 Paris Salon Hispano-Suiza showed its contempt for the Depression by bringing out the sybaritic Type 68 V12 of 9425 cc; it was subsequently developed into the superlative 11,310 cc Type 68 bis. A six-cylinder version of the Type 68, the K6, followed in 1934.

Between 1932 and 1943, Barcelona built a series of six-cylinder Hispano-Suizas, the last being the depressing T60RL of 1934, which had servo-assisted Lockheed hydraulic brakes and central gear-change.

Hispano-Suiza struggled on in Barcelona after the Spanish Civil War and built the small six-cylinders into the 1940s, when the Pegaso truck firm took over the factory.

The French branch of Hispano-Suiza stopped car production in 1938 to concentrate on the more lucrative business of making armaments and aero engines. The French factory did build a front-wheel-drive prototype post-war, powered by a Ford V8 engine, but it failed to reach production. After a merger with Bugatti in 1963 the company became an important part of the French aerospace industry.

## Alfonso XIII

The starting point for the Type 15T Hispano-Suiza was the 1910 Coupe de l'Auto racer, which had an engine with the outrageous bore/stroke dimensions of 65 × 200 mm; Birgikt moderated this for production

### 1912 HISPANO-SUIZA ALFONSO XIII

**Engine:** in-line four-cylinder, side-valve
**Bore × stroke:** 80 mm × 180 mm
**Capacity:** 3619 cc
**Maximum power:** 64 bhp
**Transmission:** four-speed manual
**Chassis:** pressed steel channel
**Suspension:** non-independent with semi-elliptic leaf springs
**Brakes:** drums on rear only
**Bodywork:** to order
**Maximum speed (approx):** 75 mph (120 kph)

**Hispano-Suiza Alfonso XIII**

**Hispano-Suiza H6**

to 80 × 180 mm, and created one of the first great sports cars.

The model took its name from its most illustrious customer, the English-born Queen Ena of Spain gave her husband one of the first 15T Hispano-Suizas as a birthday present.

The heady performance of the Alfonso Hispano also claimed a notable victim, for aviation pioneer Charles Voisin was killed in the 15T of his mistress, the self-styled Baronne De la Roche, born plain Elise Delaroche.

Early Alfonsos had three-speed transmissions, but four speeds were later adopted; there was also a transition from a multiple-disc metal-to-metal clutch to a leather-faced cone.

## Hispano-Suiza H6

Birkigt drew on his experience of aero-engine design during the Great War to create the remarkable H6, launched in 1919. Its engine was a monobloc six-cylinder with an overhead cam, and to match its performance the H6 was endowed with an innovative installation of four-wheel servo-assisted braking.

Writing in 1923, *The Autocar* commented: 'A show-finished chassis of the Hispano-Suiza sometimes strikes one not so much as a car for everyday use as a fine example of craftsmanship staged for exhibition. In fact, the Hispano is a really practical car, as any motorist who has visited France will testify. It stands, in its way, alone, because it can satisfy the 'carriage folk' and the sportsman alike.'

Proof of the latter contention was amply given when André Dubonnet won the Coupe Boillot race at Boulogne in 1921, subsequently repeating the achievement with a prototype 8-litre derivative.

H6 chassis were clothed by the best European coachbuilders, and the car became a symbol of prestige and speed much favoured by all classes of the wealthy.

Licence production of the H6B Hispano-Suiza was undertaken by the well-known Czechoslovakian firm Skoda from 1924–27, and the model remained in production in France without significant alterations until 1934.

### 1920 HISPANO-SUIZA H6

**Engine:** in-line six-cylinder, overhead-cam
**Bore × stroke:** 100 mm × 140 mm
**Capacity:** 6597 cc
**Maximum power:** 100 bhp
**Transmission:** three-speed manual
**Chassis:** pressed steel channel
**Suspension:** non-independent with semi-elliptic leaf springs
**Brakes:** drums all round (servo assisted)
**Bodywork:** to order
**Maximum speed (approx):** 85 mph (137 kph)

## Hispano-Suiza Type 68

Launched at the 1931 Paris Salon, the remarkable Type 68 broke with Hispano-Suiza tradition in using overhead valves; the engine was a remarkably compact V12 which still leaned heavily on aviation practice. Its cylinder blocks were fixed-head aluminium castings with screwed-in nitralloy liners, sodium-cooled exhaust valves and a nine-bearing crankshaft with connecting rods with dove-tailed big-end caps secured by riveted pins.

The Type 68 was available in four chassis lengths – 134.6 in (3429 mm), 144.0 in (3658 mm), 150.0 in (3810 mm) and 162.0 in (4115 mm) – though the passenger accommodation was never outstanding.

The Type 68 was developed into the magnificent 68 *bis*, with the engine enlarged to 11,310 cc; like the power unit of its contemporary, the Bugatti Royale, the Type 68 Hispano-Suiza engine was also used to power high-speed railcars.

### 1932 HISPANO-SUIZA TYPE 68

**Engine:** V12, overhead-valve
**Bore × stroke:** 100 mm × 100 mm
**Capacity:** 9425 cc
**Maximum power:** 220 bhp
**Transmission:** three-speed manual
**Chassis:** pressed steel channel
**Suspension:** non-independent with semi-elliptic leaf springs
**Brakes:** drums all round (servo assisted)
**Bodywork:** to choice
**Maximum speed (approx):** 108 mph (174 kph)

# HONDA

**Tokyo, Japan**
**1962–**

Honda was well-established as a motorcycle maker before turning to cars with the S500 Sports, first exhibited at the 1962 Tokyo Show, with a choice of twin-overhead-camshaft 360 cc and 500 cc engines. It soon became the S600, and this tiny sports car was developed into the S800, whose engine could turn at 11,000 rpm.

Saloons of 360 cc and 500 cc were introduced in 1966, and then in 1969 came the Honda 1300, a front-wheel-drive model with a single-overhead-camshaft, four-cylinder, all-aluminium engine. Its output was 96 bhp, but 110 bhp could be had with the four-carburettor TS engine option.

The 1973 Civic was the world's first production car with a stratified-charge engine. It was followed by a larger model, the Accord, and BL later adopted and produced it as the Triumph Acclaim.

This was the beginning of closer cooperation between the Japanese and British companies: the 'XX' luxury car was a joint venture due for production in the mid-1980s.

**Hispano-Suiza Type 68**

## Honda S800

The S800 was the pinnacle of early Honda sports car production and was an intriguing blend of Honda's motor-cycle technology, in the form of the very high-revving 791 cc roller-bearing twin-cam, and traditional British-style chassis engineering in the shape of a heavy separate ladder frame.

That chassis contributed a great deal to the tiny car's surprisingly heavy weight of over 1700 lb (770 kg). The weight was all the more surprising when one remembers that engine and transmission were alloy and the S800 was generally a triumph of miniaturisation as typified by the miniscule dampers on the torsion bar front suspension.

It could outperform its Sprite, Midget and Spitfire rivals of the mid-'60s and was built to a higher standard — all for very little extra cost. Its

**Honda S800**

### 1967 HONDA S800

**Engine:** in-line four-cylinder, twin-cam
**Bore × stroke:** 60 mm × 70 mm
**Capacity:** 791 cc
**Maximum power:** 70 hp
**Transmission:** four-speed manual
**Chassis:** steel ladder frame
**Suspension:** independent front with wishbones and torsion bars. Live rear axle with trailing arms and coil springs
**Brakes:** discs front, drums rear
**Bodywork:** two-seater convertible or coupé
**Maximum speed (approx):** 94 mph (151 kph)

handling, however, was not quite in the Sprite class and the car was marred by a very firm ride.

Despite many good features neither the convertible nor the coupé really found favour in the UK: only 290 convertibles were sold along with 1258 coupés. British conservatism and the distrust of such a small high-revving engine accounted for its lack of success.

## Honda CRX Coupé

In 1984 Honda completely revised their Civic line, producing four quite different looking vehicles for different roles, the CRX Coupé being the sports variety. As Honda put it, 'If the New Generation Civic Shuttle's a space craft the new Civic CRX Coupé is a space rocket'.

On paper the new Civic

### 1984 HONDA CRX COUPÉ

**Engine:** in-line, four-cylinder, overhead-cam
**Bore × stroke:** 74 mm × 86.5 mm
**Capacity:** 1488 cc
**Maximum power:** 100 bhp
**Transmission:** five-speed
**Chassis:** integral steel
**Suspension:** independent front with struts and torsion bars. Dead beam rear axle with trailing arms and coil springs
**Brakes:** discs all round
**Bodywork:** two-door, two-seat coupé
**Maximum speed (approx):** 112 mph (180 kph)

appeared to have regressed with the switch from independent rear suspension to a dead beam axle but the system certainly worked better than its predecessor. In every other respect the cars were right up to the minute with lightweight corrosion-free plastic lower body panels and bumper sections and a fuel-injected three-valve-per-cylinder 1500 cc overhead-cam engine producing 100 bhp. The extra valve was mounted on the intake side of the crossflow cylinder head.

Despite its excellent power output the appeal of the CRX was really in its handling, its short wheelbase helping to give it very sharp, almost kart-like response.

## HORCH
**Köln/Reichenbach/Zwickau, Germany
1899–1939**

August Horch worked as an engineer with Benz from 1896–99 before setting up on his own at Köln-Ehrenfeld. His first car was a shaft-driven 5 hp twin-cylinder, followed by a 10 hp twin.

In 1902, production was moved to Reichenbach, and in 1903 a 16/20 hp four-cylinder shaft-driven car was introduced.

The following year, Horch again moved production, this time to a new factory at Zwickau in Saxony; an 18/22 hp overhead-valve four was the first car from the new factory, followed in 1905 by an inlet-over-exhaust 5800 cc 35/40 hp model. Ball bearings were used throughout the chassis, and

**Honda CRX Coupé**

exhaust pressure was used to operate the petrol-feed and lubrication systems. Horch cars were renowned for the casing-in of the underside of the chassis to protect the mechanism from dust and water.

Doctor Horch launched his first six-cylinder model, a 7800 cc 65 hp, in 1907. It was not a success, and proved a contributory factor in Horch's resignation to found Audi.

Success in sporting events included victory in the Herkomer Trophy for Dr. Stoess on an 18/22 Horch in 1906; the low, streamlined Halle bodies on the Horch cars entered for the 1908 Prinz Heinrichfahrt caused a sensation, and added several mph to the 2724 cc cars' top speed.

Sporting success fuelled production: among the wide array of cars leaving the Zwickau works during this period were inlet-over-

was produced in quantity.

During 1926 Horch produced its first straight-eight, with a 3132 cc twin-overhead-camshaft engine; it was followed in 1927 by derivatives of 3378 cc and 3950 cc, the larger engine developing 80 hp at 3200 rpm.

Daimler left Horch at the end of the 1920s and was succeeded by Fritz Fiedler, who from 1931 created new single-overhead-camshaft straight-eight models with engines from 3 to 5 litres.

An exciting new model of the early 1930s was the side-valve 6032 cc V12 Horch; its engine developed 120 hp and it had a ZF-Aphon four-speed gearbox. Horch was now firmly established in the luxury class, although its prices were lower than most of its rivals; the company's products were bodied by such leading names as Glaser, Neuss and Armbruster.

In 1933 Horch introduced a range of side-valve V8 models of 3004 cc, 3227 cc, 3517 cc and 3823 cc. The company also produced the overhead-camshaft 4946 cc straight-eight 850, which developed 100 bhp at 3400 rpm; the tuned 951A, of identical capacity, developed 120 bhp at the same engine speed.

The Horch plant in Zwickau also built the rear-engined, Porsche-designed Auto Union Grand Prix racing cars from 1933 to 1939.

Though the Horch marque was discontinued after World War II, there was an attempt in 1946 to revive the name at Zwickau, but as the plant was now in East Germany, and Auto Union, holder of the sole rights to the Horch name, was now operating from Dusseldorf in West Germany, the East Germans had to rename the new car 'Sachsenring'.

kick-starter was adopted, and proprietary power units – 1368 cc or 1498 cc Coventry-Climax engines – were introduced after the firm was reformed in 1921.

Sydney Horstmann pursued a racing programme to promote the company; tests took place at Brooklands with a supercharged side-valve Anzani power unit, and Horstman cars appeared in 200-mile races at the track between 1921 and '23.

Modified versions of the Horstman racers were marketed as the Sports and Super Sports models. Front-wheel brakes first appeared on the racers and were generally adopted in 1924.

The standard power unit became the 1.5-litre Anzani in 1923; in 1924 the option of an 1100 cc Coventry-Climax engine was offered.

The kick-starter was dropped in

**Horch V12**

exhaust fours of 1588 cc, 2080 cc, 2608 cc, 3175 cc, 4700 cc, 6395 cc and 8440 cc; subsequently cars with sleeve-valve engines made under Knight licence were offered.

Georg Paulmann was chief designer after the departure of August Horch; under his aegis the 2582 cc 'Pony' was produced.

After the war Horch continued to build a wide range of cars; at the 1921 Berlin Show the company exhibited models of 8/24 hp, 10/30 hp, 15/45 hp, 18/55 hp, 25/60 hp and 33/80 hp.

Paul Daimler joined Horch as chief engineer in 1923; the next year the company introduced an overhead-camshaft 10/50 hp four-cylinder model of 2630 cc, which

### 1931 HORCH V12

**Engine:** side-valve V12, cast iron
**Bore × stroke:** 80 mm × 100 mm
**Capacity:** 6032 cc
**Maximum power:** 120 bhp
**Transmission:** four-speed manual
**Chassis:** X-braced cross-frame
**Suspension:** non-independent, with semi-elliptic leaf springs and friction dampers front and rear
**Brakes:** drums all round
**Bodywork:** to order
**Maximum speed (approx):** 90 mph (145 kph)

# HORSTMAN

**Bath, England**
**1914–1929**

Sydney Horstman ran a garage in Bath before turning to car manufacture; his first car had an own-make 1-litre four-cylinder engine with detachable cylinder head and horizontal overhead valves. This power unit also formed the forward part of the chassis. The gearbox was in-unit with the rear axle assembly.

After the war the company was renamed Horstman, as the final 'n' was thought to sound too Germanic. An Archimedean screw

1924 when unit construction of engine and gearbox was standardised. In 1925 Horstman became one of the first British popular cars to adopt Lockheed hydraulic brakes.

However, Horstman was living beyond its means, and in 1925 the company went into liquidation for the second time, its capital wasted by projects like a supercharged front-wheel-drive sprint car.

Horstman nominally survived until 1929, offering the 11 hp Anzani and the old 9/25 hp models, but sales were negligible. Nevertheless, the name lives on, for an offshoot of the old Horstman company now makes electric hand-dryers and heating control units.

**Horstman Super Sports**

## 1923 HORSTMAN SUPER SPORTS

**Engine:** in-line side-valve four-cylinder
**Bore × stroke:** 69 mm × 100 mm
**Capacity:** 1496 cc
**Maximum power:** 40 bhp
**Transmission:** three-speed manual
**Chassis:** pressed steel channel
**Suspension:** non-independent with cantilever leaf springs front and rear
**Brakes:** rear-wheel drums
**Bodywork:** two-seater sports
**Maximum speed (approx):** 90 mph (145 kph)

# HOTCHKISS

**Paris, France**
**1903–1954**

Benjamin Hotchkiss was a Connecticut Yankee who arrived in France in 1867 and established an arms factory at St Denis, 6 km north of Paris, in the 1870s. The Hotchkiss works boosted its income in the unprofitable periods of peace by making components for the new motor industry, and took the logical step of building cars in 1903.

Designed by ex-Mors engineer Terrasse, assisted by Achille Fournier (whose racing driver brother Henri was the marque's first Parisien agent), the first Hotchkiss was a round-radiatored 17 hp four.

In 1906 it was joined by a remarkably durable 7.4-litre six —

one of the first of these cars was featured in Hotchkiss advertising in 1931, having covered over 300,000 km (186,000 miles).

Hotchkiss moved into the quality light car market in 1909 with the 2.2-litre 12/16 hp; in 1910 the company offered a range of three fours (12/16, 16/20 and 20/30 hp) and two sixes (20/30 and 40/50 hp).

After the Great War, Hotchkiss attempted to break into the super-luxury class with the 6.6-litre Type AK, with overhead valves operated by a miniature crankshaft and servo-assisted four-wheel brakes. Only one AK was built.

Hotchkiss then moved into a new, purpose-built factory, of which sole product from 1923–28 was the refined 2.2-litre Type AM. It started as a side-valve model but gained pushrod overhead valves in 1926. In 1928 Hotchkiss launched a new six-cylinder model, the AM 80, the basis for all subsequent Hotchkiss sixes until the end of production in 1954.

In 1933 the company launched the sporting AM80S 3.5-litre,

derived from the car which had won the 1932 Monte Carlo Rally (an event which Hotchkiss also won in 1933, 1934, 1939, 1949 and 1950). The Paris-Nice model of 1934 also commemorated a Hotchkiss sporting victory.

Hotchkiss merged with Amilcar in 1937: a result of this was the Grégoire-designed Amilcar-Compound, which never saw serious production.

The Hotchkiss 686 model was reintroduced after the Armistice and supplemented in 1949 by a new 13 hp four. Then, in 1952, Hotchkiss built the 2-litre front-wheel-drive flat-four Hotchkiss-Grégoire in small numbers alongside the 3.5-litre six (which had acquired independent front suspension in 1949).

A merger with Peugeot failed to last, but then Hotchkiss united with Delahaye. In 1954 the company stopped producing cars to concentrate on commercial vehicles and Jeeps.

## 1934 HOTCHKISS PARIS-NICE

**Engine:** in-line six-cylinder, overhead-valve
**Bore × stroke:** 86 mm × 100 mm
**Capacity:** 3485 cc
**Maximum power:** 115 bhp
**Transmission:** four-speed manual
**Chassis:** pressed steel channel
**Suspension:** non-independent, with semi-elliptic leaf springs front and rear
**Brakes:** drums all round
**Bodywork:** speed model tourer
**Maximum speed (approx):** 93 mph (150 kph)

**Hotchkiss AM Tourer**

## HRG

**Tolworth, England**
**1936–1956**

The HRG took its name from the initials of its founders, E.A. Halford, G.H. Robins and H.R. Godfrey (formerly the 'G' of GN). Very much in the idiom of the Frazer Nash, though with shaft drive instead of chains, the HRG was initially powered by the overhead-valve 1496 cc 4ED Meadows engine. Suspension was by quarter-elliptics at the front and semi-elliptics rear, and top speed was 90 mph (145 kph).

In 1939 HRG adopted an 1100 cc single-overhead-camshaft Singer engine, later replaced by a 1.5-litre Singer power unit when supplies of Meadows engines ceased.

After the war HRG brought out a 1496 cc 'Aerodynamic' model, with streamlined bodywork designed by Marcus Chambers and R. de Yarburgh-Bateson, but this model was withdrawn in 1950.

The traditional 1930s-style HRG continued in production, powered by the old 1.5-litre Singer engine until 1953 (though the SM1500 engine had supplanted this power unit on Singers in 1949). The last HRGs had the SM1500 unit linered down to bring it inside the 1.5-litre limit.

### 1939 HRG 1½-LITRE

**Engine:** in-line four-cylinder, overhead-valve
**Bore × stroke:** 69 mm × 100 mm
**Capacity:** 1496 cc
**Maximum power:** 58 bhp
**Transmission:** four-speed manual
**Chassis:** pressed steel channel
**Suspension:** non-independent, with quarter-elliptic leaf springs front, semi-elliptic leaf springs rear
**Brakes:** drums all round
**Bodywork:** sports two seater
**Maximum speed (approx):** 80 mph (129 kph)

HRG's last fling came in 1955 with a remarkable tubular-chassis model with all-round independent suspension and disc brakes. Its twin-overhead-camshaft engine was based on the SM1500 block, but developed 108 bhp instead of the standard 55 bhp. The takeover of Singer by Rootes put a stop to the development of this model, and HRG ceased car production in 1956. The company continued for another decade, and in 1965 produced a one-off streamlined sports car powered initially by a Ford Cortina engine and then by a Vauxhall VX 4/90 unit.

## HUDSON

**Detroit, USA**
**1909–1957**

Named after its backer, Detroit store magnate J.L. Hudson, this marque achieved instant success with its first offering, an unremarkable 2534 cc four-cylinder known as 'Model 20', designed by Howard Coffin. By the end of 1910, Hudson had climbed to 17th place in the US sales chart.

Hudson produced its first six-cylinder model, the 6-litre Model 6-54, in 1912, the year of J.L. Hudson's death, and by the end of 1914 the Hudson company

claimed to be the biggest manufacturer of sixes in the world.

The four-cylinder model, with its capacity increased to 4324 cc by a longer stroke, was discontinued in 1916 when Hudson adopted a one-model policy with the 4730 cc Super-Six, available in a wide range of body styles. A Super Six landaulette was ordered by the White House.

From 1927–30 the Super-Six engine had inlet-over-exhaust valves, but thereafter every Hudson car was fitted with a side-valve power unit.

The Hudson-Essex group reached third place in the USA sales league in 1929, but fell back after that.

A new straight-eight engine appeared in 1930, and was to remain in production until 1954. The six was phased out in 1931.

An unusual export order came in 1932, when six eight-wheeled tourers were built for the Japanese Government.

Between 1934, when Essex was discontinued, and 1938, Hudson and Terraplane design was very similar.

In 1935 the 'Electric Hand' gear shift was offered, while 1936 saw the 'safety engineered chassis', whose hydraulic brakes were rendered 'fail-safe' by an emergency mechanical system.

Hudson continued its 1942 models after the war, but took the bold step of introducing the unit-construction 'Step-Down' design in 1948, so named because the floor of the car was well below the level of the sills which formed the side members. Independent coil-spring suspension was introduced and the line-up consisted of five series, ranging from the low-priced Pacemaker to the high-priced Commodore Eight, with 4293 cc six-cylinder (which revived the old 'Super-Six' nomenclature) and the 4162 cc eight.

The Hornet, with the old 5045 cc L-head six-cylinder engine, was virtually invincible in stock car racing between 1951 and 1954, but failed to revitalise sales, which had been falling since 1950.

Hudson lacked the resources to re-tool, and the 1953 compact Jet range represented an unsuccessful attempt to generate the necessary capital. Hudson merged with Nash to form American Motors in 1954, and production was shifted to the Nash plant in Kenosha, Wisconsin. For a while Hudson shared the same body shell as the Nash; top of the post-merger line was the Hornet Custom Hollywood, with a V8 Packard engine. This unit was replaced in 1956 by the new 180 bhp AMC V8, while the smaller Wasp used Hudson's old 3310 cc six.

The Hudson name was discontinued by American Motors at the end of 1957.

**HRG 1½-Litre**

**Hudson Hornet**

## 1954 HUDSON HORNET

**Engine:** in-line six-cylinder, side-valve
**Bore × stroke:** 96.8 mm × 114.3 mm
**Capacity:** 5048 cc
**Maximum power:** 160 bhp
**Transmission:** three-speed
**Chassis:** separate frame
**Suspension:** front independent with coil springs, rear non-independent with semi-elliptics and live axle
**Brakes:** drums all round
**Bodywork:** sedan
**Maximum speed (approx):** 100 mph (160 kph)

# HUMBER

**Coventry/Beeston, England 1898–1976**

Thomas Humber founded his cycle company in 1868. It was involved in the grandiose schemes of H.J. Lawson, and built the improbable Pennington Torpedo tricars. The first vehicles built under the Humber name were tricycles and quadricycles, including a

curious front-wheel driven, rear-wheel-steered machine called the 'MD'.

The first Humber car worthy of the name was a 1901 voiturette, and this led the way to the little Humberette of 1903, which had a tubular frame and a single-cylinder 5 hp engine.

A four-cylinder 12 hp appeared in 1902, followed by a three-cylinder 9 hp and a 20 hp four in 1903.

After 1905 the two-cylinder cars were dropped and the range reduced to 10/12 hp and 16/20 hp models, a 15 hp appearing in 1907.

Up to 1908, Humber was producing cars in two factories, at Coventry and Beeston, the Beeston cars having a superior finish and more luxurious bodies, but financial difficulties led to the closure of the factory in 1908, in which year Humber revived twin-cylinder power units.

In 1913 a new Humberette appeared, powered by an air-cooled 8 hp vee-twin (later

examples were water-cooled).

An uncharacteristic move was the expenditure of £15,000 on a three-car team for the 1914 Tourist Trophy race. These cars, designed by F.T. Burgess, were powered by twin-overhead-camshaft 3.3-litre four-cylinder engines, but failed to live up to their promise in the race.

During the 1920s Humber established a reputation for producing solid, reliable cars of conservative design, with side-valve engines until 1922, when overhead inlet/side exhaust engines were introduced. The 8/18 of 1923 was a refined light car, with a 985 cc engine to propel its 1344 lb (610 kg) four-seat open-tourer body. It was called the 9/20 when its engine was slightly enlarged, but this model's much bigger body imposed too much work on the motor, even with a low top gear ratio of 5.5:1.

Four-wheel brakes (external contracting at first) appeared in 1925; sales were over 4000 in 1927, thanks to the 9/20 hp and 14/40 hp fours and the 20/55 hp six-cylinder model.

In 1930 control of the company passed into the hands of the Rootes brothers; two more sixes appeared, the 2.1-litre 16/50 and the solid

3.5-litre Snipe.

The overhead inlet/side exhaust engine layout was discontinued in 1932, and the following year Humber brought out a 1.7-litre four-cylinder 12 hp.

When World War II started, Humber were only producing six-cylinder models; the 4.1-litre Super Snipe and its variants were built as staff cars during the conflict, and the best-known was Field-Marshal Montgomery's 'Old Faithful'.

After the war, production of these big side-valve sixes continued, supplemented by a 2-litre four-cylinder engine of Hillman origins installed in the Hawk. In 1950 a Super Snipe driven by Maurice Gatsonides and the Baron van Zuylen de Nyvelt took a remarkable second place in the Monte Carlo Rally; 'Gatso' had deliberately chosen the most unsporting car to go rallying . . .

Overhead valves only appeared on the Super Snipe and Pullman for 1953, while the Hawk retained side valves for another year. The Super Snipe was briefly discontinued, then relaunched in 1959 with a 2.7-litre engine (later increased to 3 litres).

Following the acquisition of the ailing Rootes Group by Chrysler in 1964, the sole representative of the Humber marque was the boring Sceptre, a de luxe variant of the Hillman Minx with a 1.7-litre four-cylinder engine. After re-styling the Sceptre was phased out in 1976.

## 1933 HUMBER SNIPE

**Engine:** in-line six-cylinder, side-valve
**Bore × stroke:** 80 mm × 116 mm
**Capacity:** 3498 cc
**Maximum power:** 75 bhp
**Transmission:** four-speed manual
**Chassis:** pressed steel channel
**Suspension:** non-independent, with semi-elliptic leaf springs front and rear
**Brakes:** drums all round
**Bodywork:** saloon, sports saloon, limousine
**Maximum speed (approx):** 80 mph (129 kph)

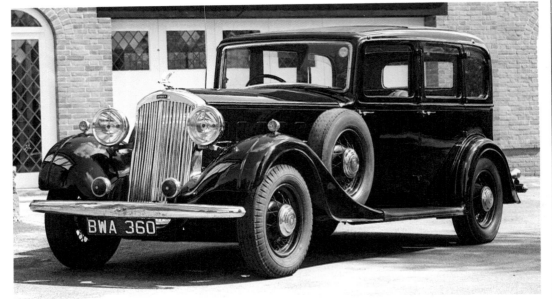

**Humber Snipe**

**Hupmobile Eight**

# HUPMOBILE

**Detroit/Cleveland, USA**
**1908–1940**

The original Hupmobile was designed by Bobby Hupp and E.A. Nelson; it was a 2.8-litre runabout with two-speed sliding gear transmission and was sold as a competitor to the Model T Ford. Priced at $750, it was an instant success, and by 1913 the company had 7.5 per cent of its market sector, with annual sales in the region of 12,000 cars. Bobby Hupp left the company in 1911 to found the RCH company.

Three-speed transmissions were available from 1911, and a refined version of the original Hupmobile was in production until the end of 1925, when it was replaced by a 3.2-litre six.

That year, Hupmobile introduced America's first low-priced straight-eight, with contracting Lockheed hydraulic brakes.

In 1929, Hupmobile acquired Chandler and transferred production of its lower-priced range to its Cleveland factory.

Sales plunged from over 50,000

---

## 1933 HUPMOBILE EIGHT

**Engine:** in-line eight-cylinder, side-valve
**Bore × stroke:** 77.8 mm × 129 mm
**Capacity:** 4470 cc
**Maximum power:** 30.1 hp
**Transmission:** three-speed
**Chassis:** pressed steel channel
**Suspension:** non-independent, with semi-elliptic leaf springs front and rear
**Brakes:** drums all round
**Bodywork:** coupé, saloon
**Maximum speed (approx):** 80 mph (129 kph)

---

to under 18,000 during the Depression; nevertheless, the Hupmobiles of 1932–33 were particularly well styled. They were supplanted by a range of advanced and aerodynamic cars, which had a three-panel D-shaped windscreen and a radio as standard equipment.

Hupmobile planned a front-wheel-drive model at this time but it failed to reach production.

By 1936, Hupmobile had slimmed down its range to a 4-litre six and a 5-litre eight, with cast aluminium wheels as standard.

In the summer of 1936 Hupmobile suspended production for several months; when it was resumed the revived eights had acquired automatically-engaged overdrive.

The last Hupmobiles appeared in 1939, rear-wheel-driven cars with bodies pressed on the dies of the front-wheel-drive Cord 810.

In 1941, Hupmobile called it a day and ceased car production, diversifying into car spares, kitchen equipment and electronics.

---

# IMPERIA

**Liège/Nessonvaux, Belgium,**
**1906–1948**

At the turn of the century, Adrien Piedboeuf was a partner in the Metallurgique agency in Aix-la-Chapelle (Aachen), Germany. In 1904 he resigned to build first motorcycles, then cars, in Liège. He chose as his emblem the crown of Charlemagne, in honour of Aix-la-Chapelle, and called his cars Imperia, after the Holy Roman Empire.

However, his first cars were sold under the Piedboeuf marque; Adrien Piedboeuf sold these 24/30 hp fours mostly to his family and friends.

In 1908, the company moved into the old Pieper factory at Nessonvaux, and began building a three-car range designed by the German engineer Paul Henze, who was later to create the Simson-Supra and Steiger sports cars of the 1920s. These Imperias were four-cylinder cars of 16/20 hp (3 litres), 24/30 hp (4.9 litres) and 50/60 hp (9.9 litres).

At this period Imperia was strongly represented in motorsport; two 8-litre cars ran in the 1907 Kaiserpreis, but neither finished.

A monobloc 1764 cc L-head 12 hp appeared in 1909; its engine was in unit with the three-speed gearbox, an unusual feature for the epoch. The same year, a shaft-driven 28 hp replaced the old 24/30 hp.

In 1910 Imperia merged with Springuel; the cars built in the Springuel factory were thereafter known as Springuel-Imperias. The most outstanding car built under

---

this title was the 1914 28/35 hp, an inlet-over-exhaust four with an elegant vee-radiator.

From the end of 1912, Imperia-Abadals were built at Nessonvaux; two sporting Imperias, the 15/22 and 20/26, were in fact Abadals with the same vee-radiator as the 28/35 hp, though Imperia kept their Spanish origins secret.

Imperia ceased all activity during the Great War, but after the Armistice the company changed hands and was acquired by Mathieu van Roggen, former owner of a marble quarry. Production was slow getting under way and less than 200 cars were built between the end of 1919 and mid-1923, all sold under the Imperia-Abadal name.

During 1921 Imperia launched an overhead-cam 5630 cc straight-eight built on aero-engine lines, but it was too costly at B.Fr 55,000 and only three or four were built.

For the Belgian Grand Prix at Spa in July 1922, Imperia prepared a team of sports cars in the amazingly short time of two months. The Imperia-Abadal 3-litre had a double-overhead cam, 32-valve four-cylinder engine of identical bore and stroke (80 mm × 149 mm) measurements as the 3-litre Bentley. Capable of 90 mph (145 kph), the Imperia-Abadal 3-litre was short-lived, as the company's management realised that there was little future for such expensive, small-production cars.

The successor to the ephemeral 3-litre was an economical 1-litre four sometimes known as the Imperia-Tili, designed by Arnold Couchard, formerly of FN. In 1924 the swept volume was increased to 1100 cc, when the car became known as the 11/22 hp. One of the first cars to have a sliding sunshine roof, the 11/22 hp Imperia had an extremely unorthodox slide-valve power unit which rotated counterclockwise. The car's transmission brake acted as a servo for the frontwheel brakes. Some 11/22 hp Imperias were assembled in Britain at the Cordwalles Works in Maidenhead, also the home of GWK. Although the 11/22 hp was fast for its size, the slide valves wore excessively after a short mileage.

A six of 1624 cc appeared at the end of 1927, and in 1929 an increase in bore size raised the swept volume to 1800 cc. In 1930, a triple-carburettor Super Sports six was offered; racing models had six carburettors and could reach 100 mph (161 kph).

Financial problems forced Imperia to restrict production from 1931, and, following a deal with Adler of Germany, the Imperia TA-9 of 1934 onwards had front-wheel-drive Adler Trumpf running gear with Belgian-built chassis and coachwork. Nevertheless, the

company continued experiments with slide-valve engines.

In 1935, Van Roggen acquired the remnants of Minerva, and a deal with Voisin saw a number of TA-9 Imperias assembled in the Voisin works at Issy-les-Moulineaux and sold in France as Minervas. . . .

Trade with Germany became increasingly difficult, the Adler components finally being bartered for woollens made by a Verviers textile company which took control of Imperia in 1940.

The works was occupied by the Germans during the war, and, after 1000 TA-8 cars had been built using surplus Hotchkiss-Gregoire power trains, Imperia ceased car production under their own name in 1949 and then assembled Standard Vanguards under licence, some fitted with Imperia-built cabriolet bodies.

The company was finally liquidated in 1959 after Standard-Triumph decided to assemble cars for the Belgian market in its own new factory at Malines.

# INVICTA

**Cobham/Chelsea/Virginia Water, England
1924–1938, 1946–1950**

Noel Macklin, previously involved with the Eric-Campbell and Silver Hawk marques, built the first three Invictas in the garage of his home at Cobham, Surrey, in 1924, using six-cylinder 2½-litre Coventry-

Climax engines, but these power units failed to live up to expectations and 2.6-litre Meadows engines were adopted on the production version, built in a factory on the Fairmile at Cobham.

Macklin's intention was to build a sports car with steam-car flexibility; his venture was backed by Oliver Lyle (of Tate & Lyle sugar) and Earl Fitzwilliam, previously behind Sheffield-Simplex.

The swept volume was increased to 3 litres in 1926, when two variants were available, the LC (large chassis) and SC (small chassis); that year, the reliability of the Invicta won the company the first of two Dewar Trophies, the second being awarded in 1929.

Invicta launched a 4½-litre model at the 1928 Olympia Motor Show; the Meadows engine was now developing 100 bhp. In 1929, a super-luxury NLC derivative of the 4½ litre Invicta with a redesigned chassis appeared, intended as a direct competitor for the 20/25 Rolls-Royce. Unfortunately, Invicta couldn't have chosen a worse time to launch a high-priced car, and it was succeeded in 1930 by the High Chassis Type A, a similar car without the luxury equipment and at a much reduced price.

Alongside the Type A, Invicta offered a low chassis Type S 100 mph 4½-litre, with underslung rear suspension. Though this was one of the most desirable cars of the period, the Depression was hardly the best time to launch a new sports car, and in 1932 Invicta attempted to appeal to a wider audience with the 12/45, powered by an overhead-cam Blackburne 1½-litre engine. It failed to achieve the anticipated success, and neither did a supercharged version, the 12/

90, announced the following year.

In the interim Macklin became involved with Railton and sold Invicta to Earl Fitzwilliam. Around seven cars are believed to have been built in the company's Flood Street, Chelsea, service depot after production ceased at Cobham.

The name Invicta reappeared after World War II on the Black Prince model, the work of ex-Lagonda designer Willy Watson, who had been responsible for the original 1924 Invicta. The Black Prince was a complex machine powered by a double-overhead-cam 3-litre Meadows engine based on an industrial unit, driving through a Brockhouse hydraulic torque converter (there was no gearbox).

Suspension was all-independent, by torsion bars, and the car was originally proposed at £3000. By the time production ceased in 1949 the price had soared to nearly £4000.

AFN Ltd, makers of the Frazer Nash, bought the remains of Invicta the following year.

## Invicta S Type

'Particularly striking is the latest model Invicta,' commented *The Autocar* in October 1930, 'and, in a way, quite unlike the preceding chassis principally because, being designed as a sports model, it has been built very low, the reduction in height having been obtained by curving the side members of the radiator downwards behind the radiator, then continuing them straight at a low level so that they extend below the rear axle instead of above it, as is more usual.'

That underslung chassis was of exceptional rigidity; the car, however, could exhibit treacherous corner-

---

**1924 IMPERIA 11/22 HP**

**Engine:** in-line four-cylinder, slide-valve
**Bore × stroke:** 66 mm × 80 mm
**Capacity:** 1094 cc
**Maximum power:** 27 bhp
**Transmission:** four-speed manual
**Chassis:** pressed steel channel
**Suspension:** non-independent, with semi-elliptic leaf springs front and rear
**Brakes:** drums all round, with servo by transmission brake
**Bodywork:** tourer or saloon
**Maximum speed (approx):** 50 mph (80 kph)

---

**Imperia 11/22 HP**

**Invicta S Type**

## 1930 INVICTA S TYPE

**Engine:** in-line six-cylinder, overhead valve
**Bore × stroke:** 88.5 mm × 120.6 mm
**Capacity:** 4467 cc
**Maximum power:** 140 bhp
**Transmission:** four-speed manual
**Chassis:** pressed steel channel, underslung at rear
**Suspension:** non-independent, with semi-elliptic leaf springs front and rear and hydraulic and friction dampers
**Brakes:** drums all round
**Bodywork:** two- and four-seat sports
**Maximum speed (approx):** 100 mph (161 kph)

ing characteristics, and it was in an S Type Invicta that S.C.H. Davis had his well-known crash at Brooklands in 1931, after skidding in the wet.

On the credit side, an S Type driven by Donald Healey won the 1931 Monte Carlo Rally outright, despite sliding off the road on ice in Norway and knocking over a telegraph pole, which bent the chassis so that the axles were out of parallel. In 1932, Healey's Invicta came second in the Monte. There were also victories in the Alpine Trial.

When production of the S Type ceased in 1934, a total of 77 had been produced. It was proposed to succeed the Type S with a double-overhead-cam 5-litre Type SS capable of 130 mph (209 kph); two of these chassis are believed to have been built, but never sold.

# IRIS
**Willesden, England**
**1905–1915**

The Iris car took its name from the Greek goddess Iris, the 'Speedy messenger of the gods', though most people thought the name came from the marque's advertising slogan, 'It Runs in Silence'.

The first Iris cars were crude, chain-driven machines of little distinction, but from late 1905 the car was distinguished by a handsome diamond-shaped radiator. Shaft drive was then adopted, and though unexciting cars, they were very well made.

Initially, Iris offered fours of 25/30 hp (4882 cc) and 35/40 hp (6757 cc), the range being supplemented for 1907 by a 7310 cc six.

The cars were built by Legros & Knowles, and were designed by Ivon de Havilland (brother of the aviation pioneer Geoffrey de Havilland) until his premature death.

Iris built a range of cars of 15 hp, 25 hp, 35 hp and the 40 hp six ('a noble looking piece of work') until the outbreak of war in 1914.

During the war Iris moved to Aylesbury, but no more cars were built, the firm continuing in business as the Bifurcated Tube & Rivet Company.

## 1908 IRIS 40 HP

**Engine:** in-line six-cylinder, side-valve
**Bore × stroke:** 108 mm × 133 mm
**Capacity:** 7310 cc
**Maximum power:** 43 hp
**Transmission:** three-speed manual
**Chassis:** pressed steel channel
**Suspension:** non-independent, with semi-elliptic leaf springs front and rear
**Brakes:** rear-wheel drums
**Bodywork:** to order
**Maximum speed (approx):** 50 mph (80 kph)

**Iris 40 HP**

# A-Z OF THE CAR

replace the Rivolta, again with Bertone styling, and this time it was a full four-seater.

In 1967, Iso brought out a Ghia-bodied limousine, the Fidia, though this model did not enjoy the expected success.

The death of Renzo Rivolta in the late 1960s led to the production of some unsuccessful models like the Bizzarini-designed mid-engined Varedo in an attempt to keep the company going; finally Rivolta's son sold out to a refrigerator tycoon in the early 1970s, but the planned revival of the company didn't happen.

range, then in 1903 came the first all-Isotta model, the 24 hp, designed by the brilliant, if self-effacing, Giuseppe Stefanini.

He was assisted from 1905 by the young engineer Giustino Cattaneo, who ultimately succeeded in ousting his mentor. One of their first projects together was Stefanini's Tipo D, a 100 hp racer with a monstrous overhead-cam engine of 17,203 cc which competed in the 1905 Coppa Florio.

In 1907 came a merger deal that was to give Isotta-Fraschini a wider fame, for a major

## ISO (ISETTA)

**Milan, Italy**
**1953–1976**

Renzo Rivolta's Iso company began by building scooters and two-stroke motorcycles after the war, progressing to the Isetta bubble-car in 1953. This 'boldly unconventional' machine arrived in nice time for the Suez crisis; its 236 cc two-stroke engine had a common combustion chamber for the two parallel cylinders, with the inlet port in one cylinder, exhaust in the other. The Isetta was also licence-built by BMW in Germany, Pilette in Belgium, VELAM in France and Isetta (GB) in Great Britain.

Manufacture of luxury GT cars began in 1962, when the first Iso Rivolta appeared, with Bertone bodywork. It was remarkably similar in chassis design to another Bertone-bodied car, the Gordon-Keeble.

Most Iso cars had Ghia or Bertone bodywork and were powered by big Chevrolet V8s.

The Rivolta coupé, with a 5359 cc power unit, was capable of some 140 mph (225 kph); it was followed by the Grifo, designed by Giotto Bizzarini, with a choice of Chevrolet or Ford V8 power ranging up to 7.4 litres. Top speed was a remarkable 186 mph (299 kph) with handling to match.

The Lele was launched to

**Isotta-Fraschini Tipo 8**

### 1965 ISO GRIFO

**Engine:** V8, overhead-valve
**Bore × stroke:** 101.6 mm × 82.6 mm
**Capacity:** 5359 cc
**Maximum power:** 296 bhp
**Transmission:** four-speed manual
**Chassis:** tubular steel
**Suspension:** independent front with coil springs, de Dion rear axle with coil springs and telescopic dampers
**Brakes:** discs all round
**Bodywork:** Bertone coupé
**Maximum speed (approx):** 137 mph (220 kph)

## ISOTTA-FRASCHINI

**Milan, Italy**
**1900–1949**

Founded by Cesare Isotta and the brothers Oreste, Vincenzo and Antonio Fraschini, Isotta-Fraschini began by selling, then assembling, the De Dion-engined Renault voiturette. Mors and Pieper cars were also sold.

Aster-engined voiturettes of 669 cc (single-cylinder) and 2251 cc (twin-cylinder) and a 785 cc one-lunger De Dion-engined car made up the 1902

### 1919 ISOTTA-FRASCHINI TIPO 8

**Engine:** in-line eight-cylinder, overhead valve
**Bore × stroke:** 85 mm × 130 mm
**Capacity:** 5898 cc
**Maximum power:** 95 bhp
**Transmission:** three-speed
**Chassis:** pressed steel channel
**Suspension:** non-independent, with semi-elliptic leaf springs front and rear
**Brakes:** drums all round
**Bodywork:** to order
**Maximum speed (approx):** 87 mph (140 kph)

shareholding was acquired by the French De Dietrich company; part of the deal called for 500 Isotta-Fraschini chassis at Luneville (the De Dietrich works) and at Marseille (where their associated company, Turcat-Mery was based). But the deal temporarily put a stop to Isotta-Fraschini's successful racing career, for the French marque didn't want its products overshadowed by those of its Italian subsidiary.

In 1908 Stefanini designed a light car, Tipo FE, with an advanced 1207 cc monobloc engine with an overhead camshaft; there was a 1327 cc derivative, Tipo FENC. An FE came eighth in the 1908 GP des Voiturettes at Dieppe: more

**Iso Grifo**

**Itala Grand Prix**

importantly, it inspired Ettore Bugatti to build his first overhead-cam light car.

Before The Great War, the Isotta-Fraschini line-up mostly consisted of four-cylinder cars of up to 11,305 cc in capacity. Particularly important was the Tipo KM of 1911–14, an overhead-cam 10,618 cc sporting model which had front-wheel brakes designed by Oreste Fraschini and tentatively introduced on some 1909 models. A 1912 derivative, the 70/80 hp Tipo TM, had a monobloc engine and was the last overhead-cam design introduced by Isotta-Fraschini.

After the war Isotta-Fraschini chief designer Cattaneo unveiled his Tipo 8, the world's first series production straight-eight, with an overhead-valve 5623 cc power unit. It was followed in 1924 by the 7372 cc Tipo 8A, and a sporting derivative, the 1926 Super Spinto Tipo 8ASS, had a power unit developing 130–150 bhp, against the standard model's 110–120 bhp. These big Isottas were spoiled by heavy steering, and although the last version, the Tipo 8B, was an improvement in this respect, only 30 were built from 1931–39.

After 1945 Isotta-Fraschini attempted to return to car manufacture with Aurelio Lampredi's 1948-49 rear-engined Monterosa, which had a 120 bhp V8 engine, initially of 2.5 litres and then of 3.4 litres. This advanced design never went into production and only some 20 of the odd-looking vehicles were built.

## ITALA

Turin, Italy
1904–1933

Itala was one of the many marques created by the Ceirano family, in this case Matteo, who founded the company in conjunction with

Guido Bigio, Angelo Moriondo, Leone Fubini and Giovanni Carenza in spring 1904. With the intervention of a Genoese financial group, the company was reformed in September 1904, with Bigio as Director General. Ceirano left the following year to found the company which ultimately became SPA, and Itala thereafter began to concentrate on building racing cars, with great success.

Alberto Balloco became chief engineer in 1905, and the company became famous for big, superbly engineered luxury and racing cars – their early four-cylinder racing cars had capacities up to 16,666 cc. The marque was also favoured by the Queen of Italy, who had a series of Itala limousines.

The company earned world fame in 1907 with victory in the Pekin-Paris race. A distinguishing feature of the marque's performance cars was the use of shaft drive at a period when most sporting models still used side chains.

At the 1911 Turin Salon, Balocco introduced an 8336 cc model with a rotary-valve engine, the concept of his subordinate Giacomo Rietti; it did not prove a success.

During the war Itala became involved in a grandiose technical-financial combination with a number of Italian companies headed by SCAT, producing V8 Hispano-Suiza engines under licence. The end of hostilities left Itala with a plant expensively re-equipped for aero-engine production and no orders....

The 'valveless' Itala engine

reappeared in 1919, followed in 1920 by new models, a 2612 cc (later 2811 cc) four-cylinder and a 4423 cc six.

In 1925, Itala's precarious financial position became untenable, and the Government Liquidator's Office assumed control; the following year Giulio Cesare Cappa was appointed technical consultant of the company, creating the Tipo 61, an overhead-valve 1991 cc six-cylinder model.

Under Cappa's direction, Itala built racing cars with front-wheel drive, overhead-cam 1094 cc and 1450 cc V12 engines and Roots-type superchargers, but the machines never reached a circuit to demonstrate their obviously enormous potential.

## Itala 35/45 hp

In February 1907 the Parisian newspaper *Le Matin* proposed an endurance trial from Pekin to Paris; Prince Scipio Borghese entered a 35/45 hp Itala touring car fitted with long-range petrol tanks, which started from Pekin on 10 June accompanied by two De Dions, a Spyker and a Contal tricar.

Once the army of 150 coolies had manhandled the 'fuel-chariots' out of Pekin, across the mountains, through the Great Wall and up to the Mongolian Plain, the Itala, driven by Prince Scipio Borghese, maintained a convincing lead across the trackless continent of Asia, despite hazards like a bridge which collapsed under it. After a shattered wooden wheel had been rebuilt by a Russian sledge-builder, the Itala arrived first in Paris, three weeks ahead of the other cars. The car had at times been dragged by camels and driven on railway lines during the 10,000-mile (16,093 km) journey.

The victorious car is today preserved in the Biscaretti Museum in Turin, along with a sister car which was the official limousine of Queen Margherita of Italy.

### 1907 ITALA GRAND PRIX

**Engine:** in-line four-cylinder, T-head
**Bore × stroke:** 175 mm × 150 mm
**Capacity:** 14,431 cc
**Maximum power:** 120 bhp
**Transmission:** four-speed manual
**Chassis:** pressed steel channel
**Suspension:** non-independent with semi-elliptic leaf springs and friction dampers front and rear
**Brakes:** rear-wheel drums
**Bodywork:** long-distance tourer
**Maximum speed (approx):** 102 mph (164 kph)

## JAGUAR

Coventry, England
1945–

When the initials SS became unusable post-war because they had been associated with the Nazi Schutzstaffel during the hostilities, the SS Car Company (based in Coventry, which of all English cities had least reason to revive wartime memories) changed its name to Jaguar.

This had first appeared in 1935 as the name of a model line, and the post-war Jaguars were so little

different from the pre-war SS Jaguars that it was virtually impossible to distinguish them from their SS counterparts; three versions, with Standard-based engines of 1½, 2½ and 3½ litres were available. The first giant step away from the mid-1930s origins of the range came with the launch at the 1948 Motor Show of the XK120, with a remarkable 3.4-litre double overhead-cam six-cylinder power unit developed by William Heynes, aided by Wally Hassan and Claude Baily, while fire-watching during the war. A four-cylinder 2-litre XK100 failed to reach production.

In 1949 Jaguar moved, in visual terms at least, into the Bentley class, with a new saloon, the MkV, which had independent front suspension and hydraulic brakes. With headlamps faired into the wings, it looked as though it cost at least twice its basic price of £975, which brought it into the most advantageous purchase tax bracket (cars costing over £1000 carried double taxation).

The XK power unit didn't find

new beginning for the Jaguar saloon range, and was soon offered with the 3.4-litre engine, too.

The D Type won Le Mans in that dreadful year of 1955 as a works entry, and in 1956-57 in the colours of the private Ecurie Ecosse team. A derivative of the D Type, the road-going XKSS, aimed squarely at the US market, could have achieved great things had production not been halted by a disastrous factory fire in February 1957, which also put an end to the works racing programme.

Before that, however, 1956 had seen the final flowering of the Jaguar tradition of racing development preceding road-going utilisation in the form of the larger-bore 3.8-litre engine. By 1960 this power unit was available in the Mk 2 saloon, which also offered the option of 2.4 and 3.4-litre engines.

Jaguar remained a remarkably autocratic company, despite acquiring Daimler in 1960, Guy Motors in 1961, Coventry Climax Motors in 1963 and merging with the British Motor Corporation in the mid-1960s; always at the helm

by a new V12 engine displacing 5343 cc.

Meanwhile, Jaguar had launched an excellent new saloon car range, the XJ Series, a four-door luxury limousine with 2.8 and 4.2-litre versions of the old twin-cam six; it was voted Car of the Year in 1969. In 1972 the XJ12 appeared, powered by the new 5.3-litre V12 engine, and again took the Car of the Year title for Jaguar. The 2.8-litre model was withdrawn from the home market and long-wheelbase and coupé variants became available.

The E Type was replaced by the XJS, which continued with the 5.3-litre V12 power unit, BL's attempt to submerge Jaguar within its corporate shroud proved happily unavailing. The marque made a dramatic step forward in 1979 with the standardisation of petrol injection for the 4.2-litre six, restoring its performance to 1969 levels despite the throttling effect of the emission control equipment subsequently added.

For the mid-1980s Jaguar began to introduce a new six-

overhead-cam six-cylinder engine, but floods of orders soon persuaded William Lyons to put the model into full-scale production.

That initial batch of just over 200 cars had aluminium coachwork over a wooden frame; the production versions had pressed-steel bodywork, still with the gloriously flowing lines that showed Lyons's flair for styling.

While the model was being readied for mass-production, public interest was fanned by a spectacular record-breaking session on the Jabbeke autoroute in Belgium, where a speed of nearly 133 mph (214 kph) was achieved, and a successful racing programme began with a first-time-out victory in the Silverstone International 1 Hour production race.

Rally success was equally noteworthy, particularly in the hands of Ian Appleyard, while the achievements of the XK120 were crowned in 1953 when a stripped and modified roadster fitted with a 'bubble' cockpit-cover achieved over 172 mph (277 kph) at Jabbeke, driven by Jaguar's chief test driver,

**Jaguar XK120**

its way into the Jaguar saloon range until 1951, when the overblown Mk VII made its debut, followed by the Mks VIII and IX.

Another new Jaguar of 1951 was the C Type, with the XK120 power unit in a special drilled channel section chassis with a triangulated tubular superstructure. This limited production competition car developed some 210 bhp (against the standard 160 bhp) and won Le Mans in 1951 and 1953, and it was also the first Jaguar to use disc brakes. These were standardised on the D Type competition car, first seen in 1954. It also saw the first use of a new 2.4-litre derivative of the XK power unit, which entered road-going production in 1956 in the 2.4 saloon. This model represented a

was the patriarchal Sir William Lyons, who remained the *eminence gris* of Jaguar after his retirement in the early 1970s right up to his death in early 1985.

The 3.4 and 3.8-litre S models of 1964 were distinguished by an excellent independent rear suspension layout first seen on the Mk X of 1962.

Jaguar entered new realms in 1961 with the launch of the sporting E Type, recognisably derived from the D Type. In 1965 this car (and the Mk X) received the new 4.2-litre version of the old XK engine, but this was really stretching things too far, for the engine was incapable of revving as high and as hard as its predecessor; it was joined in 1971 (and supplanted in the E Type in 1974)

cylinder power unit, the AJ6, first seen in the XJS Convertible.

The company made a spectacular return to private ownership in 1984; this was to be succeeded by the overdue launch of the new XJ40, an all-new (bar the AJ6 engine) luxury saloon to replace the XJ6 and XJ12. It was due to be followed by a reskinned XJS and Project 41, an AJ6-powered 'new E Type'-planned to be launched for 1987.

## Jaguar XK120

The XK120 first appeared, to tremendous public acclaim, at the 1948 Earls Court Show. It was intended as a 200-off 'teaser' for the forthcoming Mk VII saloon, to be powered by the new double-

**Jaguar E Type**

Norman Dewis.

Over 12,000 XK120s had been built by the time the model was succeeded by the XK140 in the autumn of 1954. By that time the car could be had with a special equipment power unit with a C Type cylinder head; this engine developed 210 bhp against the standard 190 bhp.

## Jaguar E Type

Announced in 1961 to succeed the XK150, the E Type, with its spectacular monocoque bodywork, was an obvious descendent of the Le Mans D Type cars of the mid-1950s; its performance (some 150 mph/ 241 kph was possible) was unmatched at the price – £2100 before tax.

The original 3.8-litre engine was replaced with a 4.2-litre version in 1965, which gave greater torque for a similar power output, with greater constraints on the revs that could be safely attained – and held....

A second series E Type range was widened to include a high-roofed 2+2 version, and optional automatic transmission was another admission that the E Type was approaching middle age.

### 1961 JAGUAR E TYPE

**Engine:** in-line six-cylinder, twin-cam
**Bore × stroke:** 87 mm × 106 mm
**Capacity:** 3781 cc
**Maximum power:** 265 bhp
**Transmission:** four-speed
**Chassis:** integral with auxiliary tubular subframes
**Suspension:** independent with wishbones and torsion bars front with wishbones and coil springs rear
**Brakes:** discs all round, inboard at rear
**Bodywork:** roadster or coupé
**Maximum speed (approx):** 149 mph (240 kph)

The third series of 1971 regained some of its lost youth with the introduction alongside the increasingly emission-bound six-cylinder power unit of the 5.3-litre V12, which was the only engine available by 1974. The coupé and 2+2 versions of this ultimate E Type were phased out so that when the model was replaced in 1975 only the roadster was available.

## Jaguar XJS

The XJS of late 1975 was not really a direct replacement for the E Type, for it was a high-speed sports coupé rather than an out and out performance car. It was also, at its launch, the most expensive Jaguar ever.

While its styling was somewhat controversial, it was the last car to come from the drawing boards of Sir William Lyons and Malcolm

### 1984 JAGUAR XJSC

**Engine:** in-line six-cylinder, twin-cam
**Bore × stroke:** 91 mm × 92 mm
**Capacity:** 3590 cc
**Maximum power:** 225 bhp
**Transmission:** five-speed manual
**Chassis:** integral with auxiliary subframes front and rear
**Suspension:** independent with wishbones and coils all round
**Brakes:** discs all round
**Bodywork:** convertible or coupé
**Maximum speed (approx):** 145 mph (233 kph)

Sayer, the skilled aerodynamicist who had created the very effective D Type in the 1950s.

The XJS was relaunched in 1981 in HE (high efficiency) form with the engine redesigned to take the May Fireball combustion chamber design. The resultant high compression ratio was said to improve fuel consumption by at least 20 per cent without impairing performance.

Then for 1984 came the XJSC convertible with the new AJ6 power unit, the first new Jaguar six for nearly 40 years (though the original Jaguar engine still soldiered on in other models).

## JENSEN
**West Bromwich, England
1936–1976**

The brothers Richard and Alan Jensen first practised car design in modifying a second-hand Austin Seven during the 1920s. It attracted the attention of a director of Standard, and the brothers were asked to create a production sports version of the Standard Nine.

This success led the Jensens to establish their own body-builders; they specialised in modifying Ford and Morris chassis, producing a series of Model Y sports tourers under the name Mistral for Bristol Street Garages. They also built a number of Ford V8 tourers, one of which went to Hollywood, supposedly for Clark Gable.

The first car to actually bear the Jensen name on its radiator was a 3.6-litre Ford V8-powered model fitted with a two-speed Columbia

**Jaguar XJSC**

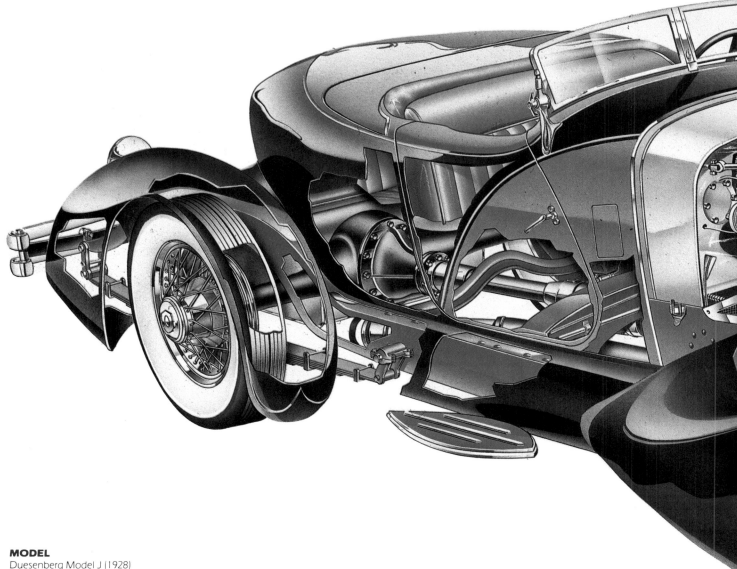

## MODEL
Duesenberg Model J (1928)

**UK price when introduced:**
$8500 (chassis only)

### ENGINE
**Location:** Front, longitudinal
**Type:** Water-cooled in-line eight-cylinder with cylinders and crankcase cast integrally. Five main bearings. Alloy sump
**Cubic capacity:** 6876 cc
**Bore × stroke:** 95.25 mm × 120.65 mm
**Compression ratio:** 5.2:1
**Valve gear:** Four valves per cylinder operated by two chain-driven overhead camshafts. Double valve springs. Intake valves 1.5 in (38 mm) diameter and exhaust valves 1.87 in (47.5 mm) in diameter
**Fuel supply:** Single 1.5 in (38 mm) duplex updraught carburettor
**Ignition:** Mechanical by coil and distributor with 6 volt system
**Maximum power:** 265 bhp at 4200 rpm

### TRANSMISSION
**Layout:** Gearbox behind engine with torque tube to rear axle
**Clutch:** Twin-plate
**Gearbox:** Three-speed manual
**Final drive:** Hypoid bevel
**Ratio:** 3.0:1 (to special order only, 3.78:1, 4.0:1, 4.3:1, 4.3:1 or 4.7:1)

### SUSPENSION
**Front:** Non-independent with semi-elliptic leaf springs, 41 in (104 cm) long
**Rear:** Live rear axle with semi-elliptic leaf springs 62 in (157 cm) long

### STEERING
**Type:** Ross cam and lever, 18:1 ratio

### BRAKES
**Type:** Duesenberg hydraulic drums, finned and of 15 in diameter. 8½ inch hand drum brake on transmission

### WHEELS AND TYRES
**Type:** Chromium plated centre lock wire wheels with 31 in × 7 inch tyres

### BODY/CHASSIS
**Type:** Alloy steel ladder frame with seven cross members. Frame depth of 8.5 in (21.6 cm). Double kickup at rear and single drop at front

### DIMENSIONS AND WEIGHT
**Wheelbase:** 142.5 in (3619 mm)
**Track – front:** 56 in (1425 mm)
     **– rear:** 56 in (1425 mm)
**Weight:** 5270 lb (2390 kg)

### PERFORMANCE
**Maximum speed:** 116 mph (186 kph)
**Fuel consumption (approx):** 11–13 mpg

**BELOW** A Model J Duesenberg Speedster by Figoni. The Model J was a massive construction, quite conventional in its chassis and suspension design but advanced in its use of the superb Lycoming-built straight-eight twin-cam and its extraordinarily comprehensive array of instrumentation which set it apart from its competition, as did such niceties as the lower driving lights which turned with the steering

rear axle; visually, it had much in common with the new SS Jaguar, and it could be said that Jensen was to Ford at this stage as SS was to Standard.

A supercharged version of this Jensen S Type was subsequently built and other engine options became available, including the V12 Lincoln-Zephyr unit, the 2.2-litre Ford V8 and the Nash straight-eight unit.

The car side of the building was bolstered by the construction of commercial vehicles, which sustained the company through the war; then there were plans to build a new model, the PW (for post-war), powered by a special 3.8-litre Meadows straight-eight. The PW was first shown in the Jubilee cavalcade of the British Motor Industry in Hyde Park in 1946. The design of the PW was copied by Austin, however, and the subsequent showdown merely led to a contract to build a sports version of the Austin A40 and a supply of 4-litre Austin engines.

This power unit appeared in the Interceptor which succeeded the PW in 1950 and the glassfibre 541 saloon of 1964. In 1957, the Jensen became one of the first British cars to be fitted with disc brakes all round. The Jensen brothers also entered into a series of negotiations at the end of the 1950s which resulted in their company becoming part of the Norcros Group in 1959; both brothers retired during the 1960s.

Jensen reverted to an American engine – a 5.9-litre Chrysler V8 – for the 1963 CV8, which was a well-specified sports saloon with a 132 mph (212 kph) top speed.

A four-wheel-drive version of the CV8, the CV8 FF appeared at the 1959 Motor Show, and won the Don Safety Award, but in 1966 the CV8 was swept aside by Kevin Beatty's spectacular new Interceptor, with Vignale-designed bodywork built in West Bromwich, and powered by a 6.3-litre Chrysler V8. An Interceptor FF appeared in 1967, using the Ferguson four-wheel-drive system in conjunction with the Dunlop Maxaret anti-lock

**Jensen 541**

### 1957 JENSEN 541

**Engine:** in-line six-cylinder, overhead-valve
**Bore × stroke:** 87 mm × 111 mm
**Capacity:** 3993 cc
**Maximum power:** 150 bhp
**Transmission:** four-speed manual plus overdrive
**Chassis:** perimeter frame
**Suspension:** independent front with coil and wishbone. Live rear axle with semi-elliptics and Panhard rod
**Brakes:** discs all round
**Bodywork:** glassfibre sports saloon
**Maximum speed (approx):** 115 mph (185 kph)

braking system.

There was a further change of ownership in 1968 when Jensen was taken over from the Norcros Group by merchant bankers William Brandt; Kjell Qvale became president and Donald Healey chairman of the rebuilt company.

A new sports car was launched in 1972 under the name Jensen-

Healey; its engine was a Lotus-built four, based on a Vauxhall cylinder block. The model didn't live up to expectations; the introduction of the GT Jensen-Healey failed to save the company from closing down the following year. Ten years later the company began to remanufacture the Interceptor.

### 1974 JENSEN INTERCEPTOR

**Engine:** V8, overhead-valve
**Bore × stroke:** 109.77 mm × 95.2 mm
**Capacity:** 7212 cc
**Maximum power:** 300 bhp
**Transmission:** three-speed automatic
**Chassis:** tubular
**Suspension:** independent front with coil and wishbone. Live rear axle with semi-elliptics and Panhard rod
**Brakes:** discs all round, servo-assisted
**Bodywork:** two-door saloon, coupé or convertible
**Maximum speed (approx):** 135 mph (217 kph)

## Jensen 541

Launched at the 1953 Motor Show, the Jensen 541 was one of the first cars with glassfibre bodywork, which Jensen were able to produce as a result of their expertise in the commercial vehicle field. The body was built in three separate sections, though the doors continued to be made of aluminium. The body was thus extremely light, easy to produce and almost corrosion-proof.

Power was provided by the 4-litre Austin Sheerline engine; it was to match the performance offered by this unit that in October 1956 Jensen made the bold step of offering the 541 with Dunlop disc brakes all round, the first production saloon so equipped.

A Rolls-Royce Hydramatic gearbox was offered on the 1961 541S; two years later the 541 series was succeeded by the similarly-styled CV8, also bodied in glassfibre.

## Jensen Interceptor/FF

Originally styled by Touring, the body design of the 1966 Interceptor was developed for production by Vignale, but then the Vignale tools and jigs were brought back to West Bromwich because chief engineer Kevin Beattie felt that the lines of communication between Staffordshire and Milan were too extended.

Flagship of the Interceptor range was the FF, which again demonstrated the pioneering flair of the Jensen company with its Ferguson four-wheel-drive system and anti-lock braking, making it probably the safest car on the roads of the mid-1960s. But the cost of this safety was an additional £1500 – the price of a reasonable up-market saloon at the time – and there were few takers, so that the FF was discontinued after only 320 had been built.

**Jensen Interceptor FF**

## JORDAN
**Cleveland, USA**
**1916–1931**

Former journalist and advertising man Edward S. Jordan was given backing to the tune of $300,000 so that he could convincingly prove that the car market had not reached saturation point. The result was one of the very best of the assembled cars built in America at that time.

Jordan always used Continental power units, starting with a 4966 cc six. The marque's best-known model was the Playboy, launched in 1921 and the subject of one of the most famous advertisements in motoring history, in which Ned Jordan extolled the virtues of the marque under the unforgettable headline, 'Somewhere West of Laramie'.

Jordan cars were fitted with hydraulic four-wheel brakes from 1924; in 1925 the marque listed its first straight-eight, of 4408 cc.

'The first truly fine American small car', as Jordan described itself, launched a 'custom' range of worm-driven 3259 cc sixes for 1927. These included models with such euphonious designations as the Blue Boy sports touring, the Tom Boy collapsible cabriolet and

### 1924 JORDAN MX SERIES

**Engine:** in-line six-cylinder, side-valve
**Bore × stroke:** 100 mm × 120.7 mm
**Capacity:** 5686 cc
**Maximum power:** 26.33 hp (rated)
**Transmission:** three-speed manual
**Chassis:** pressed steel channel
**Suspension:** non-independent with semi-elliptic leaf springs front and rear
**Brakes:** rear-wheel drums
**Bodywork:** Touring, Playboy, Blue Boy, Brougham, Sedan, Victoria
**Maximum speed (approx):** 75 mph (120 kph)

the Air Line 4380 cc eight; in remembrance of things past, the Air Line series still included a Playboy coupé.

The last new Jordan to be introduced before the Depression cut the marque down was the 5277 cc Speedway Eight of 1930; this had sporting coachwork on European lines with the typically American touch of streamlined Woodlite headlamps, but at $5000 there were few buyers.

## JOWETT
**Idle, Bradford, England**
**1905–1954**

The brothers Benjamin and William Jowett built two examples of 'the world's first light-car' in 1905; a light two-seater with tiller-steering, the Jowett didn't go into production until 1910 as the brothers were preoccupied with building motorcycles for Alfred Angus Scott.

**Jordan 25 HP**

When Scott opened his own factory, Ben and Willie decided to open a factory in Bradford to build their light car. Like all Jowetts, the 1910 model was powered by a horizontally-opposed engine, in this case an 816 cc flat-twin. Having settled on a successful formula, the Jowett brothers saw little reason to change it, though wheel steering supplanted the tiller shortly before World War I.

After the Armistice, Jowett moved to a new factory at Idle, then surrounded by fields at the end of the Bradford tram lines. The post-war cars, with the engine's capacity increased to 907 cc to make the most of the new 7 hp taxation class, began to appear in May 1920. Jowett's first four-seater, the Long Four, appeared in 1923, followed the next year by a 'Chummy' close-coupled four-seater.

Jowett built their first saloon in 1926, the year in which two Jowetts named Wait and See crossed the 'uncrossable' heart of Africa, covering 3800 miles in 60 days and rescuing a slave girl *en route*.

Although Jowett cars were renowned for their 'little engine with the big pull', they were about five years behind the rest of the motor industry – front wheel brakes finally appeared on most Jowetts for the 1929 season!

Another retrograde feature of the Jowett was fixed cylinder heads on the faithful flat-twin – detachable heads arrived in 1929, when production was running at 95 cars a week.

The company recovered quickly from a disastrous factory fire in September 1930, and in 1933 a four-speed gearbox was introduced on the streamlined Kestrel saloon (joined in mid-season by the sporting twin carburettor Weasel).

Ben Jowett began developing new power units in the mid-1930s and built three prototypes badged as La Roche, with vertical four-

cylinder engines and pre-selector transmissions before launching a far more characteristic Ten in 1936, powered by an 1166 cc flat-four.

As for the twin, it was again increased in capacity to 946 cc for 1937; it continued to be used in the Bradford van after World War II until the end of production in 1954, by which time it had been stretched to 1008 cc.

The Jowett brothers retired in 1940 and the new chief of Jowett, Calcott Reilly, began planning post-war models as early as 1942. Production restarted in 1946 with the old Bradford van, then, at the 1946 Motor Industry Jubilee parade in London, a new car, the Javelin, made its debut. Designed by Gerald Palmer, the Javelin had swept-tail bodywork inspired by the Lincoln Zephyr and suspension by torsion bars. Its roadholding was excellent, and demand was sufficient for Briggs Motor Bodies to open a special plant at Doncaster to produce Javelin bodies.

Unfortunately the Jowett-built transmission proved troublesome, and the problems contributed to a mounting financial crisis in the company.

A sports car, the Jupiter, created by ex-Auto-Union designer Eberan von Eberhorst, appeared in 1950; it had a space-frame chassis and ran at Le Mans in 1950–52, winning its class in 1950.

There were plans to produce an exciting new glassfibre-bodied sports car, the R4, but the financial problems overtook Jowett and production of all models ceased in 1954 after over 30,000 Javelins had been produced.

## Jowett Javelin

*Gerald Palmer joined Jowett in 1942 from MG, and began designing the new post-war Jowett to compete with the Citroën Traction Avant, gaining many of the space-saving advantages of front-wheel drive by using the traditional Jowett horizontally-opposed layout, though the engine, the first to use a gravity die-cast aluminium block, was all-new.*

*Designed for production by simple methods – Jowett were, after all, a small company – the Javelin was, nevertheless, technically advanced. Apart from the engine construction it had torsion-bar suspension and hydraulic tappets for its overhead valves.*

*The Javelin proved itself early on in competition, winning its class in both the 1949 Monte Carlo Rally and the Spa 24-hour race.*

*Technical advance continued with the adoption of an all-rubber-mounted front suspension, though the hydraulic tappets were dropped in the late 1940s because of supply difficulties.*

*By the early 1950s, before Jowett's ill-considered decision to*

Jowett Javelin

## 1946 JOWETT JAVELIN

**Engine:** flat four-cylinder, overhead-valve
**Bore × stroke:** 72.5 mm × 90 mm
**Capacity:** 1486 cc
**Maximum power:** 50 bhp
**Transmission:** four-speed manual
**Chassis:** integral steel body with subframe
**Suspension:** independent front with torsion bars and wishbones. Live rear axle with torsion bars
**Brakes:** four-wheel hydro-mechanical drum
**Bodywork:** fastback saloon
**Maximum speed (approx):** 82 mph (132 kph)

make its own transmissions, Javelin production was running at around 150 a week. A flat-twin inlet-over-exhaust successor, intended to be built in car, van, pickup or station wagon guise, only reached prototype stage before the factory closed down and was sold to International Harvester.

# KAISER
Willow Run, USA
1946–1955

Millionaire shipbuilder Henry J. Kaiser joined forces with Joe Frazer, president of the moribund Graham-Paige company, in a bold attempt to break the stranglehold of General Motors, Ford and Chrysler on the US motor industry. They took over the vast Willow Run plant, erected by Ford during the war to build Liberator bombers on a production line, and commissioned Howard 'Dutch' Darrin to design two cars – the Kaiser (the economy model) and

the Frazer (the luxury line).

The slab-sided prototype Kaisers built in 1946 incorporated advanced engineering ideas like all-round independent suspension by torsion bars and front-wheel drive, but by the time the car reached production, the mechanics had become entirely conventional. As sold to the public, the Kaiser had a box-section frame, coil-spring independent front suspension and live rear axle and was powered by a Continental six-cylinder L-head engine developing 100 bhp.

It was an ideal time to launch a new model, and initially the Kaiser-Frazer cars proved very popular. By 1949 the company had taken five per cent of the US market and qualified for a $44 million loan from the Reconstruction Finance Corporation.

The range included two pioneering five-door hatchbacks, the Traveler and the Vagabond, styled like normal sedans but with a two-piece tailgate and fold-down rear seats to give the flexibility of an

estate car. Top of the range was a $3000 convertible with a power-operated hood; there was also a trend-setting hardtop derivative of this model.

Unfortunately the Kaiser-Frazer organisation had already shot its bolt and discovered the hard way that the Willow Run plant, built as an aeroplane factory, was hopelessly inefficient for producing cars. In 1950, with sales of 144,000 cars, the company recorded a loss of $13 million.

In an attempt to redress the situation, the '1951' models were introduced in March 1950; the cars were attractively restyled with lower lines and more glass. There were now five Kaiser models, standard and de luxe Kaisers and a new, smaller economy range, the Henry J, with a choice of the in-line Willys Jeep engine or an in-line six. The Henry J was never a success.

The 1951 Kaisers were designed for safety, with a heart-shaped windscreen which popped out of its rubber surround if struck

with more than 35 lb (16 kg) force. That year, Kaiser reached 12th place in the USA sales league.

For 1952, the Frazer line was discontinued, leaving only its Manhattan model designation behind for the top-of-the-range Kaiser; three other models – DeLuxe, Virginian and Special – were also produced that year. The financial problems of the company were highlighted when 3000 workers were laid off in 1952.

Introduced for 1953 was the luxury Kaiser Hardtop Dragon; it had Hydramatic transmission, gold-plated exterior trim and 'interior styling in the grand manner, with rich-patterned Marie Nichols contemporary fabrics'.

The continuing fall in sales forced a merger with Willys in 1953, a union which saw the demise of the Henry J; a supercharger was offered as an option on the six-cylinder engine, and a neat two-seater glassfibre-bodied sports car with slide-away doors, the Kaiser-Darrin, made its debut.

Sales continued to fall, and it was decided to transfer production to Argentina, where the marque was known as the Carabela.

## 1953 KAISER-DARRIN

**Engine:** in-line six-cylinder
**Bore × stroke:** 84.1 mm × 111 mm
**Capacity:** 3706 cc
**Maximum power:** 118 bhp
**Transmission:** four speed manual
**Chassis:** separate chassis
**Suspension:** front independent with coil and wishbone. Live rear axle with semi-elliptic leaf springs
**Brakes:** four-wheel hydraulic drum
**Bodywork:** Aeron Armor-clad Fiberglas two-seater with Deauville top
**Maximum speed:** not known

Kaiser-Darrin

**King Touring**

---

### 1924 KING V8

**Engine:** V8, side-valve
**Bore × stroke:** 76.2 mm × 127 mm
**Capacity:** 4633 cc
**Maximum power:** 28.8 hp (rated)
**Transmission:** three-speed manual
**Chassis:** pressed steel channel
**Suspension:** non-independent with semi-elliptic leaf springs front and cantilever springs rear
**Brakes:** rear wheel only
**Bodywork:** tourer, sedan or coupé
**Maximum speed (approx):** not known

---

# KING

**Detroit/Buffalo, USA**
**1910–1924**

Charles Brady King built the first car to run on the streets of Detroit in 1896; he and Jonathan Dixon Maxwell, after working for Oldsmobile, started the Northern Manufacturing Company in 1902. The single-cylinder 'silent' Northern was the company's first product, followed in 1904 by a massive-looking flat-twin car. A four with pneumatic brakes and clutch followed in 1906.

King resigned from the Northern in 1908, and a year later the company merged with EMF.

He started manufacture under his own name in 1910 with a 'silent' 36 hp. This 5.4-litre model had unit construction of engine and gearbox; it incorporated 14 patented features, including a pressed-steel front axle.

In 1914 the first King V8 cars appeared; there were two models, of 26 and 29 hp. From 1916, eight-cylinder models were the firm's sole offering; that year the company hit a production peak of 3000 vehicles.

The inflated prices of the post-war period hit King sales badly, however, and by 1923 annual sales had slumped to just 240, and the company moved to a smaller factory in Buffalo, NY.

The King enjoyed a certain vogue in England.

# KISSEL

**Hartford, USA**
**1906–1931**

Built by a Wisconsin firm which had made its name in the manufacture of agricultural machinery, the Kissel Kar was promoted as 'Every Inch a Car'. Manufacture started with a car powered by a pair-cast four-cylinder 26 hp engine displacing 4952 cc; this was increased to 5517 cc for 1908. Virtually the whole car was made in the Kissel factory; a six of 8276 cc was launched in 1909. By 1912, the range consisted of 30 hp, 40 hp and 50 hp fours, plus the 60 hp six, with prices ranging from $1300 to $3000.

Kissel had standardised electric lighting and starting by 1913; the marque began to shed its conservative image in 1917 with the launch of the new 100 Point Six range, with a monobloc 4078 cc engine. Tourer, sedan and staggered-door all-year Sedan bodywork was available; the

---

### 1929 KISSEL WHITE EAGLE

**Engine:** in-line eight-cylinder
**Bore × stroke:** 82.5 mm × 114 mm
**Capacity:** 4881 cc
**Maximum power:** 95 bhp
**Transmission:** three-speed manual
**Chassis:** pressed steel channel
**Suspension:** non-independent with semi-elliptic leaf springs front and rear
**Brakes:** drums all round
**Bodywork:** Brougham, Sedan, Coupé Roadster convertible, Coupe Roadster solid-top, Seven-Seat Sedan, Speedster, Tourster, Touring
**Maximum speed (approx):** 90 mph (145 kph)

---

company also briefly offered a V12, powered by a proprietary Wiedely unit.

Motor agent and body designer Conover T. Silver developed a Silver Special Speedster six for 1918; this was developed into the 4660 cc Custom-built Speedster of 1919.

Feeling that the model designation of this chrome yellow speedster was somewhat prosaic, the editor of the *Milwaukee Journal*, who owned one of the first examples of this model, offered $5 for a more exciting name. The evocative winner was Gold Bug.

Alongside the Gold Bug, Kissel also offered Custom-built tourers, urban-sedans, coach-sedans and coupés.

A modified Lycoming straight-eight engine was listed in 1924, when external-contracting Lockheed hydraulic brakes became available.

In 1929 Kissel launched the splendid White Eagle speedster, with six- or eight-cylinder engine and internally expanding hydraulic brakes, but the economic climate saw to it that only 1500 White Eagles were sold.

Kissel joined Moon in the New Era Motors combine and the plant was used to build the front-wheel-drive Ruxton in 1930-31.

There were plans in 1933 to revive the Kissel marque to build a car driven by the Reverend Alvah Powell's unorthodox Lever engine, but they came to nothing.

# LAGONDA

**Staines/Feltham/Newport Pagnell, England**
**1905–1963, 1978–**

Wilbur Gunn, an American of Scots descent, served his apprenticeship in the family sheepshearing company in Ohio, then emigrated to England at the turn of the century. He built a steam launch, then turned to manufacturing

**Kissel White Eagle**

**Lagonda 4¹/₂ litre**

motorcycles in the greenhouse of his home in Staines, Middlesex. He called them Lagonda after the Indian name of the creek near the Great Lakes where he had played as a child.

At the end of 1904, aided by an engineer named A.H. Cranmer, Gunn began building twin-cylinder tricars, though by 1907 these had been superseded by four-wheeled cars powered by four-cylinder 20 hp and six-cylinder 30 hp engines. Surprisingly, most of the early production went to Russia, and the cars weren't available on the home market until 1912.

In 1913, Gunn abandoned the 20 hp and 30 hp models in favour of a single-model policy; the new 11.1 hp Lagonda light car had an 1100 cc engine built in unit with the gearbox. An advanced feature was the integral body/chassis construction; the little car had transverse front suspension.

Wilbur Gunn died in 1920, the year in which the 11.1 hp became the 11.9 hp; but this well-built light car was no match for the Morris-Cowley, so Lagonda decided to take their chance in the sports car field.

At the end of 1926 Lagonda introduced a 2-litre 14/60, subsequently developed into a Speed Model; this had twin camshafts set high up on the block operating the valves direct through

angled rockers. This, however, led to complex inlet and exhaust manifolding.

There was also a pushrod 2.6-litre six-cylinder known as the 16/65, progressively bored out to 3.2 litres – a 1931 Selector Special version of this 3 litre had a semi-automatic Maybach transmission with eight forward and four reverse ratios – and finally 3.6 litres, the latter model appearing in 1935.

In 1933 the old 2-litre was supplanted by a new 2-litre 16/80 model powered by a 1991 cc Crossley six-cylinder engine; it was only available until 1935.

Lagonda introduced a remarkable twin-cam 1100 cc sports car, the Rapier, in 1934, in which year the company began to fit a 4¹/₂ litre Meadows six-cylinder engine.

However, in 1935 Lagonda got out of its depth financially, and was purchased by solicitor Alan Good for £67,000. Good hived off Rapier and brought in W.O. Bentley as technical director. Nevertheless it was the 4¹/₂ litre Lagonda engine which powered the winning car at Le Mans in 1935; the entire three-car team still survives.

Bently refined the range and quietened the Meadows engined M45, developing it into the LG45, produced from 1935–41. Alongside this was produced the similar LG6, with torsion-bar independent front suspension and hydraulic brakes; the same chassis was used for Bentley's short-stroke 4¹/₂ litre V12 power unit of 1937.

Post-war, Lagonda was

acquired by the David Brown group for £55,000, thus allowing Brown to fit the Bentley/Watson designed twin-cam 2.6-litre six-cylinder engine to the DB2 Aston Martin of 1950. Lagondas continued to be produced by the new owners, with the engine enlarged to 2922 cc in 1954, the same year that a special 4.4-litre V12 powered Lagonda sports racer was created on an Aston Martin DB3S chassis (and crashed at Le Mans).

Production of Lagondas ceased in 1958 when Aston Martin-Lagonda moved to the old Tickford coachworks in Newport Pagnell, but the Lagonda name was briefly revived in 1961 on the DB-engined Rapide, which was produced until 1963.

In 1974 the name Lagonda was used on a four-door Aston Martin.

An angular Lagonda luxury car with elaborate electronic controls began to reach private owners in 1978; by the mid 1980s this £70,000 model was selling well to oil-rich Arabs.

## Lagonda 4¹/₂ Litre

The 4¹/₂ litre Meadows engine used in the M45 Lagonda, which made its debut at the end of 1933, had been used by Invicta since 1928; as installed in the Lagonda it gave a slightly greater output than when fitted to the Invicta.

It was raced to good effect by Kingston Bypass garage owners Fox & Nicholl, previously associated with Talbot. A Fox & Nicholl Lagon-

### 1933 LAGONDA 4¹/₂ LITRE

**Engine:** in-line six-cylinder, overhead-valve
**Bore × stroke:** 88.5 mm × 120.6 mm
**Capacity:** 4453 cc
**Maximum power:** 115 bhp
**Transmission:** four-speed manual
**Chassis:** pressed steel channel
**Suspension:** non-independent with semi-elliptic leaf springs
**Brakes:** drums all round
**Bodywork:** tourer or saloon
**Maximum speed (approx):** 95 mph (153 kph)

da came fourth in the 1934 Tourist trophy, its first race, and won the 1935 Le Mans 24 Hour Race, driven by Hindmarsh and Fontes, at an average speed of 77 mph (124 kph).

The racing M45 Lagondas used the 4¹/₂ litre engine in the shorter-wheelbase 3¹/₂ litre chassis, and formed the basis of the M45R Rapide, with a tuned power unit.

Under W.O. Bentley's supervision, the car was transformed into the LG45, and in 1937 fitted with the crossflow Sanction III engine, which developed 130 bhp; there was a 150 bhp short-chassis Rapide variant.

For 1938, the model was transformed into the LG6, lower-built and with independent front suspension outboard rear springs and hydraulic brakes. The very stylish LG6 was a fast tourer rather than a sports car, built for speed with comfort.

**Lagonda V12**

## 1939 LAGONDA V12

**Engine:** V12, four-cam
**Bore × stroke:** 78 mm ×
90 mm
**Capacity:** 4453 cc
**Maximum power:** 180 bhp
**Transmission:** four-speed
manual
**Chassis:** pressed steel channel
**Suspension:** independent front
with torsion bars. Live rear
axle with semi-elliptic leaf
springs
**Brakes:** drums all round
**Bodywork:** tourer or saloon
**Maximum speed (approx):**
105 mph (170 kph)

## Lagonda V12

The inspiration and much of the detail of Bentley's 4½ litre V12 engine came from ex-Rolls-Royce engineer Stewart Tresilian, while the chassis and body styles came from the LG6.

With a single chain-driven camshaft to each bank of cylinders, the V12 was a remarkable car whose development was curtailed by the war.

Had it not been halted by the outbreak of hostilities, Lagonda's racing programme planned for victory for the V12 in the 1940 Le Mans; as it was, V12 Rapides equipped with quadruple carburettors and increased compression to bring the power output to around 225 bhp took third and fourth places in the 1939 Le Mans race, behind a Type 57 Bugatti and a Delage D6.

# LAMBERT

**Macon/Reims/Giromagny,
France
1926–1954**

Germain Lambert was a persistent and ingenious builder of small sporting cars who never broke through into the big time. He started manufacture in Macon, Saône-et-Loire, building 1100 cc Ruby-engined cars with all-round independent suspension by leaf springs under the marque name Sans Choc, then moved to Reims, Marne, in 1931.

Here he built front-wheel-drive sports cars and, from 1933–36, a tiny front-wheel-driven cyclecar with single cylinder engines of 2 or 4½ hp known as the Baby Sans

Choc. During the war, Lambert built battery-electric runabouts; in 1948 he moved to Giromagny, near Belfort, where be built front-wheel cars with power units described as Lambert-Ruby, as the Ruby engine company had ceased trading. The post-war range was available in three models, the Grand Sport, Sport Luxe and Modèle Course, the latter with twin carburettors and racing bodywork. Germain Lambert raced his cars in the Bol d'Or between 1947–51, winning his class in 1951.

In 1952 a streamlined coupé model with full-width bodywork appeared, but production was extremely small.

In his decling years, Lambert ran a garage with a motor museum adjoining.

## 1951 LAMBERT MODEL COURSE

**Engine:** in-line four-cylinder,
overhead-valve
**Bore × stroke:** 62 mm ×
90 mm
**Capacity:** 1087 cc
**Maximum power:** 50 bhp
**Transmission:** four-speed
manual
**Chassis:** tubular steel
**Suspension:** non-independent
with beam front axle and
semi-elliptic leaf springs front
and rear
**Brakes:** drums all round
**Bodywork:** two-seater sports
or Gran Turismo coupé
**Maximum speed (approx):**
100 mph (160 kph)

**Lambert**

187

# LAMBORGHINI

Sant'Agata Bolognese, Italy
1963–

Ferruccio Lamborghini was well-established as a tractor manufacturer before turning to car production in 1963 (though as a young man just after the war he had built a few sports cars as a hobby, using modified Fiat parts).

Lamborghini realised that there was a demand for big, exclusive sports cars, and employed Giotto Bizzarrini and Gianpaolo Dallara to create such a vehicle for him. Bizzarini scaled up a V12 racing car engine he had designed and Dallara designed the tubular chassis with all-round independent suspension.

After commissioning body designs from Ghia, Scaglione, Touring and Zagato, he settled on the Touring design, which went into production in 1964.

In 1966 came the first truly classic Lamborghini, the 3929 cc V-12 Miura (charging bull) a rear transverse engine and styling attributed to Bertone's chief designer Giorgetto Giugiaro (though much of the work was done by his assistant). The flamboyant rear-engined six-cylinder Marzal of 1967, with glass gull-wing doors, never got past the prototype stage, but the less controversial aspects of its styling appeared on the front-engined 4-litre V12 Bertone-bodied Espada.

In 1970–71, Lamborghini introduced the 2463 cc mid-engined eight-cylinder Urraco P250; around the same time the company produced the less-successful Jarama 400GT with V12 power. While the Jarama was a 2 + 2, the Espada 400GT was a four-seater with Bertone bodywork. In its ultimate form, the Miura P400SV developed 385 bhp; it was replaced by the mid-engined Lamborghini Countach LP400/400S, with Bertone coupé bodywork.

In its ultimate form, the Urraco was available with V8 engines of 1994 cc, 2463 cc or 2996 cc, with 260 bhp available from the most powerful version. It was succeeded in the latter part of the 1970s by the limited-production Silhouette (killed off when Lamborghini ran into new financial problems in 1979) and in the early 1980s by the 3.5-litre Jalpa, of similar layout.

In 1974 Lamborghini was sold to a Swiss group. The new management ran into trouble in 1981, and Lamborghini was then acquired by the Mimram family, who stabilised production of both Countach and Jalpa at around three cars a week while developing the LMA off-road vehicle with a 400 bhp 7-litre V12.

A new 2 + 2 model was planned for the latter half of the 1980s.

## Lamborghini Miura

The Miura, which took its name from a fierce Spanish fighting bull – Ferruccio Lamborghini's Zodiac sign is Taurus, the Bull – was conceived by Dallara, his assistant Stanzani and chief development engineer Bob Wallace, and a rolling mock-up chassis built in time for the 1965 Turin Show. The V12 Lamborghini engine was placed transversely ahead of the rear wheels to keep the wheelbase short; Bertone built the exciting coupé body, the design of which was completed by Marcello Gandini after Giugiaro left to join Ghia.

The production Miura appeared in 1965, equipped with triple-throat Weber carburettors; because of the pioneering transverse engine installation, the carburettors (designed for inline installation) suffered from fuel starvation under heavy braking. The central chassis monocoque bore a superficial resemblance to that of the Ford GT40, and the Miura was instantly remarkable for its outstanding roadholding. As the boss said, he had made 'a dream car for a few crazy people', and orders were soon received.

Stanzini took over as chief engineer after Dallara went to De Tomaso in 1968, and produced a new version of the Miura, the S, in 1970. Capable of covering a standing kilometre in 24.4 seconds at a terminal 136 mph (219 kph) the 370 bhp Miura S had a maximum speed in the region of 175 mph (282 kph).

Even that wasn't the end of the development story, for Bob Wallace built a 'super Miura' known as the Jota with a 440 bhp engine, and the lessons learned from this chassis-development vehicle (of which nine replicas were constructed) were incorporated in the Miura SV – the V standing for veloce – launched at Geneva in 1971. This had a new sump/transaxle casting which for the first time separated the engine and transmission oil reservoirs, plus new cylinder heads which boosted the road-going horsepower to 385 bhp and the top speed to 180 mph (289 kph).

Total Miura production is estimated in the region of 800 cars.

## Lamborghini Countach

Hunched and angular, with vertically-pivoting doors, the Countach – the name is the Neapolitan equivalent of Blimey! – was engineered by Stanzani and styled by Gandini, an uncompromising statement as to what Lamborghini regarded as the true meaning of the term supercar.

After two years of testing, the Countach went into production in 1973; unlike the Miura, it had a north-south engine location: the prototype had a specially-built 5-litre power unit, although production

### 1968 LAMBORGHINI MIURA

**Engine:** V12, four-cam
**Bore × stroke:** 82 mm × 62 mm
**Capacity:** 3929 cc
**Maximum power:** 350 bhp
**Transmission:** five-speed
**Chassis:** steel semi-monocoque
**Suspension:** independent with coils and wishbones all round
**Brakes:** discs all round
**Bodywork:** aluminium and steel coupé
**Maximum speed (approx):** 170 mph (273 kph)

**Lamborghini Miura**

**Lamborghini Countach Quattrovalvole**

models reverted to the established 4-litre alloy engine developed for the front-engined Lamborghinis.

Early Countachs made extensive use of magnesium in their construction, though this was subsequently replaced with aluminium for cost reasons. Another feature of early Countachs was a periscope arrangement for the rear-view mirror, sighted down the 'valley' above the engine.

Full-scale production of the Countach started in mid-1974; as if the performance of the standard Countach was not sufficient, the Countach S was introduced in 1977, designed to make maximum use of the latest developments in tyre and suspension technology (and incorporating lessons learned from Lamborghini's unfulfilled involvement in the BMW M1 project).

An optional extra on the S was a huge rear wing, adjustable to vary the downforce, and so flamboyant that it was banned in some countries as a dangerous projection!

In 1981 the Countach's engine was developed into a 5-litre version in the interests of better bottom-end performance, though top speed remained in the region of 190 mph (306 kph).

In 1985 Lamborghini announced the new Countach Quattrovalvole; with its power output, engine size and top speed all increased, it is probably the fastest car on the road.

# LANCHESTER
Coventry, England
1895–1956

Frederick Lanchester began developing a motorcar in 1894 as a stepping-stone to his ultimate aim of developing a powered aeroplane, and, in 1895, aided by his younger brother George, built the first successful British four-wheeled car. It was fitted with the first Dunlop pneumatic car tyres ever made.

The Lanchester car first ran early in 1896, fitted with a single-cylinder air-cooled engine of unorthodox design, with twin contra-rotating crankshafts in the interests of balance and smooth running. But the unit was found to be lacking in power, so was rebuilt with two cylinders; the two contra-rotating crankshafts then carried six connecting rods....

That first Lanchester also saw the introduction of Frederick Lanchester's famous wick carburettor, which was capable of coping with fuels of different density, and which was used on all Lanchesters up to 1914. In its single-cylinder form that first Lanchester was advanced enough, with a mechanical, rather than automatic, inlet valve; the twin-cylinder version set the pattern for subsequent production vehicles by using one valve per cylinder to serve as both inlet and exhaust, thanks to a 'crossover' disc valve which alternately opened the inlet and exhaust tracts.

Final drive was by Lanchester worm gearing, said to be 97.6 per cent efficient; side-tiller steering was another feature.

The brothers' efforts to raise capital finally succeeded at the end of 1899, and production Lanchesters began to leave the Birmingham factory in 1900.

But in the interval between prototype and production, the

public concept of what was normal in car design had become hardened, and by those standards the advanced design of the Lanchester looked decidedly odd: there was no bonnet, and the driver sat well forward behind a hinged leather dashboard, steering with a right-hand tiller.

The first Lanchesters had 4034 cc twin-cylinder air-cooled engines; a water-cooled version appeared in 1902, a larger 18 hp model in 1904. 'Reserve' disc brakes were offered in 1903, but though they worked well, wore too quickly, and were replaced by conventional drum brakes.

Among the most enthusiastic of early Lanchester owners was the author Rudyard Kipling.

In 1904, Lanchester introduced its first four-cylinder, the over-square 2471 cc 20 hp. But the company's finances reached crisis point, and when the firm was duly reformed, Frederick Lanchester lost his control over the company.

In 1907 wheel steering became available as an option; tiller steering was dropped altogether in 1911.

Lanchester's first six-cylinder, the 28 hp, appeared in 1906. Four years later it was joined by the 3295 cc 38 hp six-cylinder; it was to solve problems of six-cylinder vibration that Lanchester devised his famous crankshaft damper.

By now, Frederick Lanchester was becoming increasingly engrossed in his aeronautical work, so his youngest brother George took over as chief engineer. In 1914 the board ordered George to design a thoroughly conventional long-bonnetted 'Sporting Forty'.

War intervened before many Forties were built, but a similar chassis was used on the 6178 cc overhead-valve Forty of 1919.

Though it was very different from the pre-war Lanchesters, George's new Forty proved a worthy rival to the Rolls-Royce 40/50 hp, though it never enjoyed its commercial success.

The company launched a 4440 cc straight-eight, again with overhead cam, at the 1928 Southport Rally; this proved to be the last true Lanchester, for in 1931 the company was taken over by

Daimler, and Lanchesters became merely re-radiatored Daimlers. The 1932 Lanchester Ten was still in production in the late 1940s, updated with independent front suspension and a Briggs body similar to that of the Ford Pilot.

A special 32 hp model based on the straight-eight Daimler was built in 1936 for British and foreign royalty; among the enthusiastic owners of a 32 hp was the future King George VI.

In 1952 Lanchester introduced a Fourteen, whose chassis was used on the six-cylinder Daimler-engined, Hooper-bodied Lanchester Dauphin; the company's last model appeared in 1956 in the short-lived shape of the Sprite 1.6 litre, endowed with Hobbs automatic transmission.

## Lanchester Twin-Cylinder

The first production Lanchester, the 10 hp air-cooled twin-cylinder, incorporated the lessons learned on the experimental cars, although, instead of the tubular chassis, sidemembers of plate aluminium were employed, reinforced at the top with an angle steel girder and at the base with a U-section girder which supported the engine and suspension mountings. This rapid structure was a major step towards the development of integral body/chassis construction.

The cantilever springs of those early Lanchesters were designed to match the rhythm of a walking man, as was the driver's eye level. The pre-selector transmission incorporated compound epicyclic gearing to give three forward speeds, while final drive was by Lanchester worm gearing.

An optional extra from 1903 on was reserve braking to supplement the transmission brake drum. Initially, the reserve brakes were caliper-operated discs, with steel discs and copper pads, but the pads wore badly on dusty roads, and later models had drum reserve brakes.

An outstanding feature of Lanchesters right from the start was the rigorous insistence on absolute interchangeability of parts, both mechanical and body panels.

**Lanchester Twin-Cylinder**

## 1904 LANCHESTER TWIN-CYLINDER

**Engine:** flat-twin, air or water-cooled
**Bore × stroke:** 133.4 mm × 144.5 mm
**Capacity:** 4034 cc
**Maximum power:** 22 bhp
**Transmission:** two-speed epicyclic
**Chassis:** aluminium plate and steel girder
**Suspension:** cantilever with parallel motion lever
**Brakes:** transmission brake on clutch cone and reverse gear drum. Emergency disc brakes
**Bodywork:** tonneau
**Maximum speed (approx):** 40 mph (64 kph)

A water-cooled 12 hp version was available from 1902, and more powerful versions of 16 hp (air-cooled) and 18 hp (water-cooled) were produced from 1903–04. The 18 hp was, however, not a success; an early example was lent to Rudyard Kipling for his comments. He immediately named it Jane Cakebread after an old Cockney with an unmatched record of convictions for drunkenness. And after a week Kipling sent the following enigmatic telegram to Lanchester: 'Jane disembowelled on village green, Ditchling. Pray remove your disorderly experiment'.

## Lanchester 40 HP

While the chassis of the post-war 40 hp Lanchester was a development of the unsatisfactory 1914 Sporting Forty, the engine was entirely new, and greatly influenced by contemporary aero-engine design, with inclined valves operated by a single overhead camshaft driven by skew gearing from the forward end of the crankshaft. The vertical shaft also drove a short cross-shaft operating the magneto and water pump, and the engine was remarkably efficient.

A short layshaft at the back of the engine drove two short vertical shafts, one carrying the dynamo, the other the starter, through skew gearing; this unusual arrangement was chosen as it saved space and made the commutators and brushes of the electrical equipment easily accessible for servicing.

Bodywork was novel, too, being constructed of oxy-acetylene-welded aluminium panelling over a cast aluminium framework.

The 40 hp Lanchester was one of the finest cars of the early 1920s, though the interior finish on the saloon shown at the 1919 London Motor Show, with marquetry panelling on doors and roof, was so ornate that King George V was heard to remark: 'Very fine, Mr Lanchester, but more suited to a prostitute than a prince, don't you think?'

Nevertheless, the future King George VI bought a Lanchester 40 hp in 1925, and the present Queen made her first public appearance in this car.

## 1925 LANCHESTER 40 HP

**Engine:** in-line six-cylinder, overhead-cam
**Bore × stroke:** 101.6 mm × 127 mm
**Capacity:** 6178 cc
**Maximum power:** 95 bhp
**Transmission:** three-speed epicyclic
**Chassis:** pressed steel channel
**Suspension:** non-independent with semi-elliptic leaf springs front and cantilever springs rear
**Brakes:** drums, on transmission and rear wheels
**Bodywork:** to order
**Maximum speed (approx):** 78 mph (125 kph)

**Lanchester 40 HP**

# A-Z OF THE CAR

## Lanchester Straight Eight

The last all-Lanchester design was the Straight Eight, which made its debut at the Southport International Motor Rally in July 1928, where it won the Concours d'Elegance. Derived from the 23 hp six-cylinder Lanchester, with which it shared components, conrods and valves, the Straight Eight was designed to supplant the old 40 hp, which was gradually phased out.

Careful design of the inlet manifolding made the Straight-Eight exceptionally sweet-running; its performance was good for its day.

### 1928 LANCHESTER STRAIGHT-EIGHT

**Engine:** in-line, eight-cylinder, overhead-cam
**Bore × stroke:** 78.7 mm × 114 mm
**Capacity:** 4436 cc
**Maximum power:** 90 bhp
**Transmission:** four-speed
**Chassis:** pressed steel channel
**Suspension:** non-independent with semi-elliptic leaf springs front and cantilevers rear
**Brakes:** drums all round
**Bodywork:** to order
**Maximum speed (approx):** 89 mph (143 kph)

## LANCIA
**Turin, Italy**
**1906 –**

Vincenzo Lancia was the son of a wealthy soup manufacturer who became an apprentice with Ceirano in 1898, and was taken over with the company when it was acquired by Fiat two years later. A fine driver, Lancia raced Fiats until 1908, even though he had founded his own factory in Turin in 1906. Production was halted by a fire at the Lancia works in February 1907, but later that year the 2543 cc Alpha appeared, followed in 1908 by the 3815 cc DiAlpha, of which only 23 examples were produced, against 108 Alphas.

Lancia then progressed through the Greek alphabet; in 1909 they announced the 3117 cc Beta, followed in 1910 by the 3460 cc Gamma. In 1911, Lancia offered the 4082 cc Delta plus a competition version, the DiDelta, replaced the following season by the similar Epsilon and Zeta models. The 1913 Eta, also of 4082 cc, was the first Lancia with optional electric lighting.

The 4939 cc Theta of 1914 was said to be the first European car with electric lighting and starting as standard. Lancia's first post-war model, the Kappa, was a development of the Theta, but now fitted with a detachable head.

A narrow-angle monobloc overhead-cam V12 of 6032 cc shown at the 1919 Paris Salon failed to reach production; it had curious rear suspension which attempted to combine cantilever and semi-elliptic springs, with cables linking the axle to the cantilever.

The Kappa was succeeded by the overhead-valve DiKappa; then an overhead-cam V8 engine of 4595 cc was installed in the same chassis to create the TriKappa.

In appearance, this presaged the classic Lambda, first revealed in 1922, which had a narrow-angle V4 engine of 2124 cc, sliding-pillar independent front suspension and integral body/chassis construction. Never intended as a sports car, nevertheless the outstanding handling of the Lambda ensured that it was regarded as such; in 1926, the Seventh Series Lambda acquired a 2370 cc power unit, which became 2570 cc on the Eighth Series of 1928–29.

At the end of 1929, Lancia introduced the luxury DiLambda, of more conventional construction and powered by a 3960 cc V8 engine. Some 1700 were built.

In 1931, the Lambda (of which around 13,000 were built in nine series) was replaced by the 1925 cc overhead-cam V4 Artena and the 2605 cc V8 Astura; later Asturas had 2972 cc power units.

Lancia readopted unit construction in 1932 with the 1196 cc Augusta, renowned for its outstanding roadholding; it was the inspiration for Vincenzo Lancia's last design, the pillarless Aprilia, announced just before his death in 1937. A smaller derivative, the 903 cc Ardea, appeared in 1939; it was built until 1953, outliving the Aprilia by three years.

The Aprilia's successor was the 1950 Aurelia, designed by Vittorio Jano, with a 1754 cc V6 engine which was latterly produced in 1991 cc, 2261 cc and 2451 cc form; additionally, the Aurelia GT formed the basis of the sports-racing D23 and D24, which had 2693 cc and 2983 cc twin-cam power units, some with superchargers.

In 1953 Vincenzo Lancia's son Gianni – who had already collaborated with Vittorio Jano to create the 1950 Aurelia GT – designed the 1091 cc Appia V4. However, the company ran into financial difficulties and a couple of years later Gianni Lancia was forced to sell his company to Fiat.

In 1956, the Aurelia was succeeded by the Flaminia, powered by a developed version of the 2458 cc Aurelia GT engine.

A complete break with Lancia tradition took place in 1961 with the launch of the front-wheel-drive Flavia, designed by Professor Fessia, best known as the creator of the Fiat Topolino; it was driven by a 1498 cc flat-four engine, increased to 1798 cc in 1964.

Another front-wheel-drive model, the 1100 cc Fulvia, succeeded the Appia as the smallest car in the Lancia range in 1964; by the end of the decade 1216 cc and 1298 cc engines were also available.

First announced in 1972, the Beta was available with overhead-cam four-cylinder engines of 1298 cc, 1585 cc and 1995 cc; it was contemporary with the Gamma, which had 1999 cc and 2484 cc overhead-cam flat fours.

**Lanchester Straight Eight**

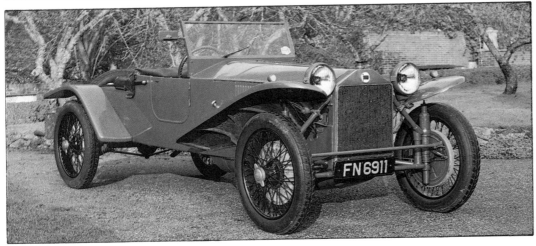

**Lancia Lambda**

The Stratos, a limited-production sporting model, began leaving the production line in 1973. It had a mid-mounted Fiat Dino 246 twin-cam V6 unit of 190 bhp.

After the Stratos had faded from sight in the late 1970s, Lancia seemed to lose its aura as Italy's leading maker of mass-market sporty saloons; the hatchback Delta of the 1980s and its three-box derivative, the Prisma, had powertrains in common with the Fiat Ritmo, though there was a rapid 1600 Turbo version.

The Volumex versions of the Beta and the larger Trevi and HP Executive were unusual in having positively-driven superchargers; also included in the complex Lancia line-up of the mid-1980s, which began with the Y10 minicar, were the sporting rear-engined Montecarlo and Rally coupés. Though both had 1995 cc engines, the twin-cam Rally, with a top speed of 137 mph (220 kph) was some 16 mph (26 kph) faster than the Montecarlo, and, at over 47 million lire, nearly two and a half times the price!

## Lancia Lambda

One of the great landmarks in the history of the motor car, the Lancia Lambda combined stressed-hull construction, sliding-pillar independent front suspension and a narrow-angle V4 engine.

The basic concept was patented by Lancia in 1919, and the prototype Lambda was running in 1921. The design went into production in 1922, and was the sensation of the Paris Salon that year.

A total of 13,000 Lambdas in nine series was built between 1922–32, the initial models being fitted with a 2120 cc engine and three-speed transmission. Towards the end of the Third Series, Lambdas became available with a four-speed transmission, while the engine was enlarged to 2370 cc for the Seventh Series and to 2570 cc for the Eighth and Ninth Series. On the latter model, coil ignition replaced magneto. The design was altered on the Seventh Series so that the body sides and bulkhead no longer formed part of the chassis, thus making it easier to fit specialist bodywork.

## Lancia DiLambda

Despite its name, the DiLambda was not a derivative of the Lambda, but was, instead, powered by a development of the old TriKappa engine. It also had a more conventional chassis structure so that bespoke bodywork could be more easily fitted by coachbuilders.

### 1930 LANCIA DILAMBDA

**Engine:** V8, overhead-valve
**Bore × stroke:** 79.4 mm × 100 mm
**Capacity:** 3960 cc
**Maximum power:** 100 bhp
**Transmission:** four-speed manual
**Chassis:** pressed steel sections
**Suspension:** independent front with sliding pillars. Live rear axle with semi-elliptic leaf springs
**Brakes:** drums all round
**Bodywork:** to order
**Maximum speed (approx):** 80 mph (129 kph)

### 1922 LANCIA LAMBDA

**Engine:** V4, overhead-cam
**Bore × stroke:** 75 mm × 120 mm
**Capacity:** 2120 cc
**Maximum power:** 49 bhp
**Transmission:** three-speed manual
**Chassis:** stressed hull with sheet steel side-members and integral bulkheads
**Suspension:** independent front with sliding pillars. Live rear axle with semi-elliptic leaf springs
**Brakes:** drums all round
**Bodywork:** tourer
**Maximum speed (approx):** 72 mph (116 kph)

Low speed torque of the narrow V8 engine was remarkable; the two-ton DiLambda could pull away from a standstill in top gear. Unfortunately that massive construction also meant that the 3960 cc DiLambda was no faster than the Lambda of little over half the capacity.

The DiLambda was withdrawn from normal production in 1933 but available to special order until 1937. A total of some 1700 was built.

## Lancia Aprilia

Vincenzo Lancia's last design – he died shortly before it was launched in 1937 – the Aprilia broke new ground with an unusual chassis with Z-section side-members welded to a flat floor.

Among the unusual features of the light-alloy engine were permanently fitted plug spanners and a water pump located in the bottom of the radiator.

The Aprilia was notable for its outstanding performance and roadholding, and survived with remarkably little modification until 1950, except for the enlargement of the engine to 1486 cc in 1939.

Post-war, many Aprilias were fitted with specialist coachwork by *carrozzerie* such as Ghia.

### 1937 LANCIA APRILIA

**Engine:** V4, overhead-cam
**Bore × stroke:** 72 mm × 83 mm
**Capacity:** 1352 cc
**Maximum power:** 47.8 bhp
**Transmission:** four-speed manual
**Chassis:** Z-section side-members with welded-on steel floor
**Susupension:** independent front with sliding pillars. Live rear axle with transverse semi-elliptic leaf spring, radius arms and torsion bars
**Brakes:** drums all round
**Bodywork:** saloon or drophead coupé
**Maximum speed (approx):** 80 mph (129 kph)

Lancia Lambda

**Lancia DiLambda**

**Lancia Aprilia**

# Lancia Flavia

Launched late in 1960, the Flavia was Lancia's first front-wheel-drive car. Designed by Fessia, who had designed the Fiat 500 pre-war, the Flavia was developed from the unsuccessful Cemsa-Caproni of 1948.

Square and low-built, the quadruple-headlamp Flavia had a top speed of over 90 mph (145 kph) an excellent performance for a 1.5-litre car; at the 1963 Frankfurt Show a new 1.8-litre version appeared, capable of over 100 mph (161 kph).

A number of specialist coachbuilders produced special bodywork for the Flavia; there were Pininfarina coupés and Vignale convertibles, plus a competition model with lightweight Zagato coachwork.

# Lancia Stratos

Designed to replace the Fulvia as Lancia's rallycar, the Stratos was originally built with a 2.0-litre Lancia/Fiat engine which had insufficient power, and production versions had the Ferrari 246 Dino engine; much of the development work was carried out by Gianpaolo Dallara, best-known for the Lamborghini Miura and the De Tomaso Pantera.

It was necessary to build 500 cars to homologate the Stratos, although it's uncertain whether that many were actually completed; in any case, many of the cars and the spares were destroyed when the roof of the Turin warehouse where they were stored collapsed.

Eventually killed off by the energy crisis of the late 1970s, the Stratos succeeded brilliantly, bringing Lancia the World Rally Championship three years in succession – 1974, '5 and '6 – and also won many sports car road and endurance events be-

---

### 1960 LANCIA FLAVIA

**Engine:** flat-four, overhead-cam
**Bore × stroke:** 82 mm × 71 mm
**Capacity:** 1500 cc
**Maximum power:** 90 bhp
**Transmission:** four-speed
**Chassis:** fabricated steel
**Suspension:** independent front with wishbones and transverse leaf spring. Beam rear axle with semi-elliptic leaf springs
**Brakes:** discs all round
**Bodywork:** saloon, coupé or convertible
**Maximum speed (approx):** 90 mph (145 kph)

---

fore the works withdrew from racing at the end of 1978.

Exceptionally fast, the Stratos was described by one enthusiastic owner as 'one of the world's worst-made but most marvellous cars'.

---

### 1975 LANCIA STRATOS

**Engine:** V6, four-cam
**Bore × stroke:** 92.5 mm × 60 mm
**Capacity:** 2418 cc
**Maximum power:** 190 bhp
**Transmission:** five-speed manual
**Chassis:** semi-monocoque
**Suspension:** independent with coil springs and wishbones front and MacPherson struts rear
**Brakes:** discs all round
**Bodywork:** Bertone glassfibre coupé
**Maximum speed (aprox):** 143 mph (230 kph)

---

**Lancia Flavia**

**Lancia Stratos**

# A-Z OF THE CAR

## LASALLE

**Detroit, USA**
**1927–1940**

That larger-than-life Californian stylist Harley Earl had his first great success for General Motors with the 1927 LaSalle, launched as a lower-priced running mate for Cadillac. Created in the image of the Hispano-Suiza, the LaSalle had a 5-litre V8. In common with the other GM marques, LaSalle acquired safety glass, chrome plate and synchromesh in 1929.

By 1930, the LaSalle was powered by a 5.8-litre engine, having passed through 5.4 and 5.6-litre versions in the interim.

In 1934, LaSalle reiterated its role as the GM style leader by pioneering the controversial turret-top styling; it also acquired a straight-eight engine, though a V8 reappeared in 1937.

By this time the LaSalle was sharing bodyshells with Buick and Oldsmobile and no longer had anything special to offer; production ended in 1940.

## LAURIN & KLEMENT

**Mlada Boleslav, Czechoslovakia**
**1906–1928**

Laurin & Klement pioneered motorcycle construction in the independent state of Bohemia in 1899, moving into cars in 1906. The first Laurin & Klement cars were powered by vee-twin 7 hp and 9 hp engines, while subsequent models used four-, six- and even eight-cylinder engines.

Laurin & Klement's 3 hp, Vee twin four-stroke voiturette of 1905 had the distinction of being the first car to be designed and produced in the Austro-Hungarian Empire (which included Czechoslovakia).

In 1907 a 4877 cc eight-cylinder appeared, designed by L & K's chief engineer, Resler, who drove it to the Paris salon, where it was declared a 'jewel of engineering'; the factory also built buses and lorries.

Laurin & Klement had agencies

### 1930 LASALLE

**Engine:** V8, side-valve
**Bore × stroke:** 86 mm × 110 mm
**Capacity:** 5840 cc
**Maximum power:** 95 bhp
**Transmission:** three-speed manual
**Chassis:** pressed steel channel
**Suspension:** non-independent with semi-elliptic leaf springs
**Brakes:** drums all round
**Bodywork:** roadster, tourer or sedan
**Maximum speed (approx):** 75 mph (120 kph)

### 1907 LAURIN & KLEMENT EIGHT

**Engine:** V8, side-valve
**Bore × stroke:** 84 mm × 110 mm
**Capacity:** 4877 cc
**Maximum power:** 45 bhp
**Transmission:** four-speed
**Chassis:** pressed steel channel
**Suspension:** non-independent with semi-elliptic leaf springs
**Brakes:** drums on rear
**Bodywork:** double phaeton
**Maximum speed (approx):** 60 mph (97 kph)

**Laurin & Klement Eight**

all over the world, and the marque achieved many competition successes. In 1913, Laurin & Klement acquired the RAF car factory and its Knight sleeve-valve-engine licence; sleeve-valve models of 3.3 and 4.7 litres were built after the merger, though Laurin & Klement also offered a wide variety of cars with side-valve engines up to 3.8 litres in capacity. At the same time the company also became increasingly preoccupied with aero engines.

Karl Loevenstein's Skodovy Zavody armaments firm took over Laurin & Klement in 1925, and from 1929 L & K cars bore the group's shortened and far more manageable Skoda name.

**La Salle Coupé**

## 1928 LEA-FRANCIS S-TYPE HYPER

**Engine:** in-line supercharged four-cylinder, overhead-valve
**Bore × stroke:** 69 × 100 mm
**Capacity:** 1496 cc
**Maximum power:** 61 bhp
**Transmission:** four-speed
**Chassis:** pressed steel channel
**Suspension:** non-independent, with semi-elliptic leaf springs
**Brakes:** servo-assisted drums
**Bodywork:** tourer
**Maximum speed (approx):** 90 mph (145 kph)

**Lea-Francis Hyper TT**

# LEA-FRANCIS

**Coventry, England**
**1904–1906, 1920–1935, 1937–1953, 1960**

R.H. Lea, formerly with the Singer cycle company, joined G.J. Francis in 1895 to manufacture bicycles. The first Lea-Francis car, designed by Alex Craig, appeared in 1904.

Although Lea and Francis reverted to the manufacture of bicycles in 1906, they began making motorcycles in 1911, and recommenced car production in 1920. Their first cars were heavy 11.9 hp and 13.9 hp models which sold badly. However, their London agent, C.B. Wardman, was also agent for Vulcan cars, and felt that cooperation between the two companies could be beneficial; thus in the early 1920s Lea-Francis amalgamated with Vulcan.

The link with Vulcan gave Lea-Francis access to the Meadows

engine, which became a characteristic feature of the marque for many years. The first Meadows-engined Lea-Francis was a new version of the C-Type, the D-Type, with a 1247 cc Meadows overhead-valve power unit. This did extremely well in reliability trials, winning 16 events in 1924.

By late 1924 the D-Type had grown into the E-Type, with a four-speed transmission instead of the three-speed unit previously used.

In mid-1925 Lea-Francis adopted the 1496 cc Meadows engine: this power unit was employed in the 12/40 sports car, which was announced in 1925 and remained in production until 1935. This engine in its 4ED version was robust enough to stand supercharging, and appeared thus, equipped with a Cozette blower, in the Lea-Francis S-Type Hyper Sports of 1928, the first series-production supercharged model from any British manufacturer.

Driving a competition version of the S-Type, with a special needle-roller crankshaft, Kaye Don won the 1928 Ulster TT.

At this period the Lea-Francis range, which included an admixture of Lea-Francis -badged Vulcans, was particularly complex, and this ultimately led to financial problems for the company.

A new 2-litre overhead-cam six-cylinder model, the Ace of Spades — so called because of the shape of its timing chest — appeared at the 1930 Motor Show, but only a few

weeks later Lea-Francis went into receivership. The Receiver, Charles Turner, managed to keep Lea-Francis running until 1935.

In 1937 the firm was re-constituted as Lea-Francis Engineering (1937) Ltd. Two models were offered, of 1.5 and 1.6 litres capacity, the engines designed by one of the partners in the new company, Hugh Rose; he had previously designed the Riley 12/4, and the new Lea-Francis engines bore a striking resemblance to that unit, with twin low-set camshafts and pushrods to eliminate the complexities of double-overhead-cam valve-gear.

Production of the new Lea-Francis models continued after the war, though sales were badly affected by the new Purchase Tax; this tax was doubled on cars costing over £1000, and Lea-Francis soon exceeded that price. The 14 hp 1.6-litre car was the mainstay of post-war production, joined by a tuned sports model in 1948. In 1950 Lea-Francis introduced a new 18 hp 2.5-litre model with the torsion-bar front suspension seen earlier on the 14 hp model, but this was not enough to ensure the survival of Lea-Francis and the company ceased production in 1953.

In 1960 new management attempted a revival of Lea-Francis with the controversially styled Ford Zephyr-engined Leaf Lynx. It was displayed at the 1960 Motor Show but no orders resulted.

# LEON LAISNE

**Lille/Nantes, France**
**1920–1937**

The Leon Laisne was intended as a demonstration of the merits of a new suspension system, and production was therefore on a very limited scale until an Englishman, Harris, joined the company in 1927, when the marque name became Harris Leon Laisne.

The unique feature of the Harris-Leon Laisne was that it had no axles in the conventional sense; its tubular chassis side-members housed the suspension units, each wheel being mounted on a radius arm which acted against discs working in rubber-filled cylinders.

The first Harris-Leon Laisnes were powered by a 12 hp CIME engine, and then a straight-eight SCAP engine was used. The company finally adopted the six-cylinder Hotchkiss power unit, and some 150 cars were reported to have been built up to 1932.

In that year a front-wheel-drive Harris-Leon Laisne was launched, with a 1231 cc four-cylinder engine, and in 1933 a British-built 12 hp Standard six-cylinder power unit was adopted.

The company also converted cars of other makes to incorporate the rubber-block suspension; it was reported that a Model A Ford so converted rode eight inches (20 cm) lower than standard.

## 1930 LEON LAISNE

**Engine:** in-line six-cylinder, overhead-valve
**Bore × stroke:** 80 mm × 100 mm
**Capacity:** 3015 cc
**Maximum power:** 70 bhp
**Transmission:** four-speed manual
**Chassis:** tubular steel
**Suspension:** all-independent, with discs working in rubber-filled cylinders
**Brakes:** drums all round
**Bodywork:** tourer or saloon
**Maximum speed (approx):** 70 mph (113 kph)

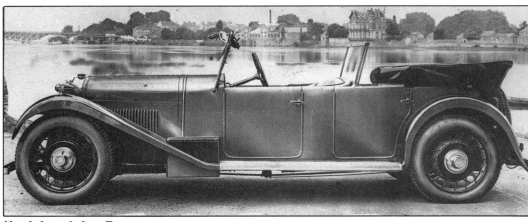

**Harris-Leon Laisne Tourer**

**Leyland Eight**

# LEYAT

**Meursault/Paris, France
1913–1927**

Marcel Leyat, who qualified as a pilot in 1911, built a propellor-driven Helicocycle in 1923: it was followed a year later by a remarkable car called the Helica, propelled by an airscrew driven by a vee-twin motorcycle engine and steered by the single rear wheel.

The advantages claimed for Leyat's invention were: 'no clutch, no gearchanging, no back axle, no tyre wear'.

Production Leyat Helicas appeared after the war, and were initially powered by flat-twin ABC motorcycle engines, later by Anzani vee-twin and three-cylinder engines.

In 1921, Leyat drove from Paris to Bordeaux in 12 hours in an Hélica that he was delivering.

Leyat's output was, like so many of those French inventor-constructors, never large, but he built both open and closed cars.

In the early 1920s, Leyat sold the Licence to produce Hélicas for France and its colonies to an engineer named Archer, then sued to get the licence back again. As a result of the court case, 600 orders were said to have been left unfilled.

Some experimental Leyats were built in the latter part of the 1920s, and then, in 1933, Leyat (whose ultimate aim was an 'aeroplane for everyman') fitted an Hélica with wings and flew it....

## 1920 LEYLAND EIGHT

**Engine:** in-line eight-cylinder, overhead-cam
**Bore × stroke:** 89 mm × 146 mm
**Capacity:** 7266 cc
**Maximum power:** 110 bhp
**Transmission:** four-speed manual
**Chassis:** pressed steel channel
**Suspension:** non-independent, with semi-elliptic leaf springs front and torsion-bar-assisted cantilever leaf springs rear
**Brakes:** rear-wheel drums, vacuum-servo-assisted
**Bodywork:** tourer, coupé, saloon
**Maximum speed (approx):** 90 mph (145 kph)

## 1921 LEYAT HELICA

**Engine:** Anzani vee-twin, side-valve
**Bore × stroke:** 85 mm × 87 mm
**Capacity:** 984 cc
**Maximum power:** 30 bhp
**Transmission:** direct drive by air-screw
**Chassis:** integral, of wood and fabric
**Suspension:** front wheels by cantilever leaf springs; none at the rear
**Brakes:** front-wheel drums
**Bodywork:** open tandem-two-seater or aerodynamic saloon
**Maximum speed (approx):** 50 mph (80 kph)

# LEYLAND

**Leyland, England
1920–1923**

Leyland Motors were one of Britain's oldest-established commercial vehicle builders, having built their first steam wagon as early as 1897. In common with others in the same field – like Guy – Leyland decided to enter the luxury car market in the euphoria following World War I.

The Leyland Eight of 1920, designed by John Godfrey Parry Thomas, assisted by Reid Railton, was the first British production straight-eight; it was also the most expensive British-built car of the times priced at £2500 in chassis form when it was launched at the 1920 Olympia Show.

When introduced, the engine was of 6967 cc, but an increase in

**Leyat Helica**

stroke brought the swept volume of later engines up to 7266 cc.

'The only car which we consider worth while having as a sparring partner to the Leyland Eight is the Rolls-Royce,' wrote Parry Thomas in 1920, but in terms of engineering innovation the Leyland Eight was actually far ahead of the 1906-designed Rolls-Royce 40/50 hp, for it featured servo-assisted brakes, torsion-bar-assisted suspension and leaf-valve springs acting on inclined tulip valves in hemispherical chambers.

The problem was that the price was too high, although the few customers included such people as the Maharajah of Patiala. Only 14 Eights were built.

Parry Thomas then built a couple of racing versions of the Leyland Eight: the 'Leyland-Thomas No. 1' was said to have been the most successful racing car ever seen at Brooklands.

**Lincoln KB**

# LINCOLN

**Detroit, USA**
**1920–**

Henry Leland's next venture into car manufacture after leaving Cadillac came with the launch of the Lincoln car – named after his boyhood hero – at the end of 1920, aided by his son Wilfred. But the uncompromising excellence of the Lincoln's engineering was offset by dull coachwork styled by Leland's son-in-law, ex-milliner Angus Woodbridge.

Although the Lincoln was powered by proprietary 5.8-litre V8 engines, many of the chassis assemblies were bought in.

After only a couple of years, Lincoln was plunged into a financial crisis by a bill for alleged wartime tax arrears; the Lelands appealed to Henry Ford for help and the company was bought by Ford. However, the two Henrys were unable to work together and the Lelands resigned soon after.

Lincoln was then put under the control of Edsel Ford, and the car quickly acquired the elegance it needed to match its engineering. The rapid acceleration of the Lincoln V8 made it a favourite with police and gangsters alike, and, to improve the score on the side of the law, a special police model with four-wheel brakes was offered in 1924 (brakes on the front wheels only became generally available in 1927).

In 1924, Calvin Coolidge became the first of many US Presidents to own a Lincoln. The engine size was increased to 6.3

litres in 1928, while further engineering innovation came with the introduction in 1932 of the V12 KB model.

Sales of the KB were disappointingly low, and in 1936 Lincoln moved into a lower-priced sector of the market with the ultra-streamlined Lincoln-Zephyr, styled by John Tjaarda.

The value of the move was shown when it was seen that out of 18,994 Lincolns sold in 1936, no less than 17,715 were Lincoln-Zephyrs.

The Lincoln-Zephyr was also the basis on which Edsel Ford's classic Lincoln Continental was constructed, a low-slung coupé first seen in March 1939. However, when America entered the war at the end of 1941, the Lincoln-Zephyr line was discontinued – permanently.

After the war the Lincoln Continental and the Lincoln were reintroduced, still powered by the pre-war 4998 cc flathead V12; the Continental was dropped in 1948 but reappeared as a separate marque in 1956.

The 1949 Lincoln Cosmopolitans had new slab-sided styling plus a new power unit, a side-valve V8 displacing 5555 cc; when completely new designs appeared for 1952, powered by an overhead-valve 5203 cc V8, the Cosmopolitan was the only model listed, available in five series, including the Capri coupé and convertible.

Yet another all-new Lincoln range was launched in 1956, with a long, low look and a 6030 cc V8; top of the range was the Lincoln Premier. The Lincoln was facelifted for 1957 with vertical dual headlamps and sharply pointed tailfins, while after 1957 the Continental became the top model of the Lincoln line, rather than existing as a separate marque.

The year 1958 saw Lincoln endowed with a 'longer, lower, wider' look: they were over 19 feet (579 cm) long, weighed nearly 2.2 tons (2235 kg) and were powered by a 7047 cc V8.

Three years later an about-turn brought more compact designs, inspired by the 1956–57 Continental Mk II, and available only in four-door form as sedans or convertibles; the Lincoln was the only four-door convertible offered by an American manufacturer. The same bodyshell was now retained until 1969 with detail improvements, though the convertible was dropped in 1967 and 1968 saw the introduction of a separate Mk III line. The 1970 Lincoln was a new car using many Ford/Mercury chassis components, though its styling was evolutionary rather than a dramatic change, with a coffin-shapped bonnet and a smaller radiator grille flanked by retractable headlights. The range, powered by 7538 cc V8 engines, consisted of a two-door coupé, four-door sedan and a Town Car, soon joined by a Town Coupé.

This range was the mainstay of production through the 1970s, though in 1979 a concession to 'down-sizing' was made when a 6555 cc engine was adopted. In mid 1977 the Mercury Monarch-based Lincoln Versailles was added to the range; its 1979 version had a 4949 cc V8.

The Continental, at that time in Mk V form, moved into Mk VI guise the following year; by 1984 Lincoln was offering three series, the Continental/Designer range (Continental, Valentino and Givenchy), the square-cut Town Car/Signature/Designer range, with options like 'Cartier equipment', and the aerodynamic Mk VII, with computer control of engine and suspension. It was also available in Sport Coupé form.

### 1932 LINCOLN KB

**Engine:** V12, side-valve
**Bore × stroke:** 82 × 114 mm
**Capacity:** 7238 cc
**Maximum power:** 150 bhp
**Transmission:** three-speed manual
**Chassis:** pressed steel channel
**Suspension:** non-independent, with semi-elliptic leaf springs front and rear
**Brakes:** drums all round
**Bodywork:** to choice
**Maximum speed (approx):** 80 mph (129 kph)

## Lincoln KB

With Ford having moved into the V8 field in 1932, Lincoln brought out its own new power unit the same year; this was the KB V12, one of only seven twelve-cylinder cars on the US market that year (the others being made by Auburn, Cadillac, Franklin, Packard and Pierce-Arrow).

Described by *The Autocar* as 'one of those exceptional cars which in both construction and performance rise much above the general practice of contemporaries,' the KB was capable of accelerating from a standstill to 60 mph (97 kph) in just 26 seconds in top gear alone. *The Autocar* also considered the Lincoln to be 'reminiscent of the best European practice'.

Sales of the KB and its slightly smaller stablemate, the KA, proved disappointing, and for 1934 a new 6.8-litre Model K was launched, its engine almost exactly midway in size between the KB and the KA; 21 different models were available, and sales, at 2170, were just 58 more than the 1933 KA/KB aggregate.

Model K was finally dropped in 1940 after only 120 cars had been sold in two seasons, including Franklin Delano Roosevelt's famous Presidential car, the Sunshine Special.

**Lincoln Continental**

# Lincoln Continental

The Lincoln Continental was the direct outcome of Edsel Ford's establishment of a styling studio at Ford in the early 1930s under former yacht designer Eugene Gregorie, who in 1930 designed the first of a series of European-inspired sporting cars for Edsel, who called them Continentals.

Despite Gregorie's pleadings, none of these custom designs was adapted for production. Until, that was, the Lincoln-Zephyr appeared and Gregorie suggested that a distinctive custom car could be created from the standard Convertible Coupé body panels. By cutting a four-inch strip from the doors and body sides an elegant coupé was created for Edsel Ford's personal delight: but when he took the car on holiday with him to Florida, he was overwhelmed by the interest aroused. He returned home with over 200 'money no object' orders

for replicas of the car, and in October 1939 the first production Lincoln Continental came off the line, its hallmark the vertically-mounted spare wheel housing behind the boot (which survives in symbolic form on modern Lincolns).

Architect Frank Lloyd Wright

---

**1939 LINCOLN CONTINENTAL**

**Engine:** V12, side-valve
**Bore × stroke:** 70 mm × 95 mm
**Capacity:** 4378 cc
**Maximum power:** 110 bhp
**Transmission:** three-speed manual
**Chassis:** pressed steel channel
**Suspension:** non-independent, with transverse leaf springs
**Brakes:** hydraulic drums all round
**Bodywork:** coupé, cabriolet
**Maximum speed (approx):** 90 mph (145 kph)

---

praised the Continental as 'the most beautiful car ever made', and three years after production ceased in 1948, the Continental was one of only eight cars selected by New York's Metropolitan Museum of Art for their 'excellence as works of art'.

## Lincoln Mk VII

The most fundamental change in American luxury cars for many years, the Mark VII was an aerodynamic sedan with the remarkable feature of electronically controlled air suspension, developed in conjunction with Goodyear.

The system consists of four air springs, a compressor, three height sensors and a microprocessor, all working to maintain a constant ride height. The idea behind this revolutionary concept was to give ride quality equal to that of the bigger Lincolns of yesterday, but with far superior handling.

The Mark VII was also the first American car with flush-glazed

headlamps, made legal just before the model went into production.

A straight-six BMW turbo-diesel option is also available.

---

**1984 LINCOLN MK VII LSC**

**Engine:** V8, overhead-valve
**Bore × stroke:** 101.6 mm × 76.2 mm
**Capacity:** 4950 cc
**Maximum power:** 140 bhp
**Transmission:** three-speed automatic
**Chassis:** integral box-type ladder frame
**Suspension:** front independent with MacPherson struts, non-independent live rear axle with coil springs and trailing arms; electronic control of ride height
**Brakes:** discs all round
**Bodywork:** five-seat saloon
**Maximum speed (approx):** 100 mph (160 kph)

---

**Lincoln Mk VIII LSC**

# A-Z OF THE CAR

## LOCOMOBILE

**Bridgeport, USA
1899–1929**

The Locomobile company was founded by magazine magnate Amzi Lorenzo Barber to exploit the light steam car designed by the Stanley brothers, and was soon – while briefly America's biggest manufacturer – turning out 4000 cars by 1902. Their steam buggy was widely plagiarised, but was really too frail for lasting success.

In 1902, therefore, Locomobile built their first petrol car, a four-cylinder model designed by A.L. Riker, which proved so successful that the manufacture of steam cars was abandoned in 1903.

Locomobile soon established an equal fame as makers of big, expensive petrol cars, among them the 1903 two-cylinder Type C 9/12 hp and the Type D 18/20 hp, the latter a chain-drive four on Mercedes lines.

These were succeeded by the Type E 15/20 hp, the 40/45 hp Type F and the 30/35 hp Type H of 1905–06. The company also catalogued a replica of their 17.7-litre four-cylinder Gordon Bennett racer.

In 1911 Locomobile introduced their longest-running model, the six-cylinder Model 48; this survived until the end of production in 1929.

Locomobile was briefly linked with Mercer and Crane-Simplex as part of the Hare's Motors group in 1920; three years later it became part of Billy Durant's final empire, and new models, the 1925–27 Junior Eight and the luxury Model 90, were introduced. During this period, the Locomobile factory also built the low-priced Flint Six.

The last new Locomobile, Model 88, was powered by a 4.9-litre Lycoming straight-eight engine and priced at $2850.

## Locomobile Steamer

The Locomobile runabout could – if properly handled – provide far more pleasurable motoring than most of its petrol-engined rivals.

It was, perhaps, too lightly built for the road conditions of the day, though one was used by its British officer owner for mine-laying in the Boer War. However, owner Rudyard Kipling condemned it as 'a wicker willow lunch basket on wheels'.

If the steam reserve in the boiler was properly husbanded, the car could be 'sprinted' to double its normal maximum speed of just over 20 mph (32 kph) for brief periods; it also provided effortless hill-climbing in an era when cheap cars were not normally noted for this attribute.

### 1902 LOCOMOBILE STEAMER

**Engine:** twin-cylinder double-acting steam unit
**Bore × stroke:** 63.5 mm × 88.9 mm
**Maximum power:** 6.5 hp
**Transmission:** direct chain drive to rear axle
**Chassis:** fully-sprung body, with tubular links between front and rear axles
**Suspension:** non-independent, with full-elliptic leaf springs front and rear
**Brakes:** band-brake on differential
**Bodywork:** two or four-seater
**Maximum speed (approx):** 48 mph (77 kph)

### 1918 LOCOMOBILE 48

**Engine:** in-line six-cylinder, side-valve
**Bore × stroke:** 114.3 mm × 139.7 mm
**Capacity:** 8599 cc
**Maximum power:** 90 bhp
**Transmission:** four-speed manual
**Chassis:** pressed steel channel
**Suspension:** non-independent, with semi-elliptic leaf springs front, three-quarter-elliptics rear
**Brakes:** rear-wheel drums
**Bodywork:** Sportif, Touring, Limousine, Brougham, Sedan Cabriolet
**Maximum speed (approx):** 70 mph (113 kph)

## Locomobile 48

'The Exclusive Car for Exclusive People' was launched in 1911 with an engine of 6982 cc, though this was subsequently enlarged to 8.6 litres.

Offered with a range of attractive body styles – the Sportif and Gunboat Roadsters offered during the Great War period were particularly distinctive – the 48 was in many ways the American equivalent to the Renault 45, a survival of the Edwardian dinosaurs produced in small numbers during the 1920s for an ultra-conservative – but rich – clientele.

## LORRAINE-DIETRICH

**Lunéville/Niederbronn/Argenteuil, France/Germany
1897–1935**

La Société Lorraine des Anciens Etablissements de Dietrich & Cie was part of one of France's oldest industrial groups, founded at Niederbronn, near Strasbourg, in the 17th century, and which had come to specialise in railway rolling-stock by the mid-19th century. With the annexation of Alsace-Lorraine by Germany after the 1870 Franco-Prussian war, Niederbronn became German, and De Dietrich & Cie founded a new branch company at Lunéville in French Lorraine, 24 km (15 miles) from the new border. This plant started to build motor cars under licence from Amédée Bollée in 1897, progressing to designs by Turcat-Méry of Marseille in 1902.

At the Niederbronn plant the Bollée design was supplanted by a voiturette designed by the Belgian Vivinus company. From 1902 the young Milanese engineer Ettore Bugatti worked at Niederbronn, where he designed a 5304 cc four-cylinder car and a 50 hp racer; in its original form the latter had the seat behind the rear axle. Production of cars at Niederbronn ended in 1904.

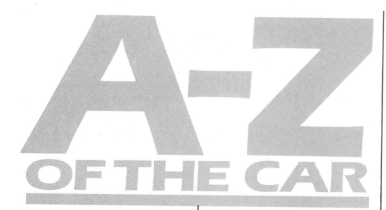
**Locomobile Steamer**

**Locomobile 48**

After that, the Alsatian market got Turcat-Mérys imported by E.E.C. Mathis and fitted with 'De Dietrich' badges. A family quarrel between Adrien de Turckheim, who headed Lunéville, and Eugene de Dietrich, who ran Niederbronn, culminated in enough finance being raised to separate the two companies.

De Dietrich cars were well-engineered but slightly old-fashioned; they did, for instance, retain the old pattern of gilled-tube radiator until 1905. However, the company's reputation was firmly based on competition successes.

During the period 1905-8, the company built a number of extremely costly and luxurious six-wheeled cars. In order to obtain more space at Lunéville for the reviving railway carriage business, a modern factory planned by Leon Turcat was built at Argenteuil, in the suburbs of Paris.

In 1908 the marque name was changed to Lorraine-Dietrich. During this period an expansionist policy saw the acquisition of a majority holding in Isotta-Fraschini and the acquisition from Ariel of a British factory in Birmingham. Both ultimately proved too expensive,

and were written off in 1909.

That year the complex Lorraine-Dietrich range consisted of an 11,460 cc six-cylinder car, four-cylinder models from a small 12 hp of 2120 cc to a huge 12,053 cc 60 hp, and a diminutive 10 hp twin-cylinder of 1060 cc.

After the war – when Alsace was restored to France – Lorraine-Dietrich was joined by a new technical director, Marius Barbarou (formerly with Delaunay Belleville). He designed an overhead-valve 15 hp six of 3446 cc, a model which sold well for many years; the 15 hp Sport was the great rival of the 3-litre Bentley at Le Mans, coming second and third in 1924, when Duff's Bentley won; first and third in 1925 and finishing first, second and third in the 1926 24-hour race. Alongside the 15 hp, Lorraine-Dietrich also offered an overhead-valve 12 hp of 2297 cc and a 30 hp six of 6107 cc.

In 1932 Lorraine introduced a side-valve 20 hp six of 4086 cc to replace the 15 hp, which had missed victory in the 1931 Monte Carlo Rally by 0.1 of a point; it was a complete failure, and car manufacture ceased in 1935.

# LOTUS
**Hornsey/Cheshunt/Hethel, England**
**1952–**

Anthony Colin Bruce Chapman, a talented young engineer, began his car manufacturing career in 1947 by building Austin Seven-based 750 specials. The growing demand for replicas led to the foundation of Lotus Engineering in 1952, and the first successful production car was the Lotus 6, sold as a kit car. Around 100 examples were built by 1955, and the model achieved numerous successes in racing and

hillclimbing.

In contrast to the square-cut Mk 6, the Lotus 8 was an aerodynamic sports car with bodywork designed by Frank Costin. This was progressively developed into the Mks 9 and 10, and paved the way for the Lotus 11, a car which ultimately won its class at Le Mans.

In 1957 the company built its first pure racing car, the Mk 12, the beginning of a competition career which grew to be of vital importance and which led to Lotus becoming many times Formula One World Champion Constructors.

That same year, the company launched the finely-styled Elite, whose aerodynamic bodywork concealed real technical originality in the shape of stressed-skin construction in bonded glassfibre. After production of the Elite ended in 1961, the Elan was launched, an open two-seater with a X-shaped backbone frame. Its Ford-based twin-cam engine was also used in the Lotus-Cortina, initially built for Ford in the factory at Cheshunt, Hertfordshire, to which Lotus had moved at the end of the 1950s.

In 1966 another new Lotus was launched, the rear-engined Europa, powered by a Renault 16 engine. Originally for export only, the Europa was built at the company's new factory in Hethel, Norfolk; from 1968 it was sold in the UK.

Lotus finally broke away from its kit-car image with the Elan Plus 2 of 1967, a 2+2 coupé derived from the original Elan, and only available in built-up form. A further move up-market came with the launch of the Elite in the early 1970s, powered by a Vauxhall-based twin-cam 16-valve 2-litre engine. At the time of Chapman's death in 1982, the Lotus line-up consisted of the Elite, Eclat and Esprit, all powered by the same 2174 cc twin-cam engine; two years later the range had been reduced to the new Excel and the Series 3 Esprit.

## 1924 LORRAINE-DIETRICH 15 CV

**Engine:** in-line six-cylinder, overhead-valve
**Bore × stroke:** 75 mm × 130 mm
**Capacity:** 3446 cc
**Maximum power:** 80 bhp
**Transmission:** three-speed manual
**Chassis:** pressed steel channel
**Suspension:** non-independent, with semi-elliptic leaf springs front, cantilever leaf springs rear
**Brakes:** Perrot-type drums all round
**Bodywork:** open tourer or saloon
**Maximum speed (approx):** 87 mph (140 kph)

**Lorraine-Dietrich 15 CV**

## 1961 LOTUS SUPER SEVEN

**Engine:** in-line four-cylinder, overhead-valve
**Bore × stroke:** 80.96 mm × 72.75 mm
**Capacity:** 1498 cc
**Maximum power:** 65 bhp
**Transmission:** four-speed manual
**Chassis:** tubular steel
**Suspension:** independent front with wishbones and coil springs. Live rear axle with coil springs
**Brakes:** discs all round
**Bodywork:** sports two seater
**Maximum speed (approx):** 105 mph (169 kph)

**Lotus Super Seven**

# Lotus Super Seven

Developed from the Lotus Six, the Seven first appeared in 1957, powered by the faithful 10 hp Ford Ten engine, a side-valve 1172 cc unit: there was also a 1498 cc Super Seven with Coventry-Climax power. Available in kit form, this stark open two-seater was the mainstay of clubman racing. When the fourth series was reached, glassfibre bodywork replaced light alloy.

Though the Seven has long ceased to be produced by Lotus, it is still built under licence by Caterham Cars, while the number of imitators is legion....

# Lotus XI

With a delightful aerodynamic body designed by Frank Costin, the Lotus XI went into production at Hornsey in 1955. There were three versions – the Le Mans with 1.1 or 1.5-litre Coventry-Climax engine, de Dion rear end, disc brakes and a choice of final drives, the Club model, with live rear axle, drum brakes and a smaller Coventry-Climax engine and the cheaper, lighter Sports model powered by a side-valve Ford Ten engine.

Costin's aerodynamic skills were shown when an XI with a perspex canopy over the driver, but otherwise standard, turned in a 143 mph

**Lotus XI**

(230 kph) lap and a 137.5 mph (221 kph) average for an hour at Monza. Another indicator was the fact that a road-going XI would record 32.5 mpg at a constant 100 mph (161 kph).

During 1957, wishbone independent front suspension replaced the divided axle layout used on the earlier Lotus cars, with a consequent improvement in stability for the Lotus XI.

The enduring appeal of this engineering tour-de-force is shown by the fact that in 1985 there were ready sales for a lookalike with glassfibre bodywork, known as the Westfield which retained the appeal of the original XI.

## 1958 LOTUS XI

**Engine:** in-line four cylinder, overhead-cam
**Bore × stroke:** 72.4 mm × 66.6 mm
**Capacity:** 1098 cc
**Maximum power:** 84 bhp
**Transmission:** four-speed
**Chassis:** tubular steel
**Suspension:** independent front with wishbones and coil springs. De Dion rear axle
**Brakes:** discs all round
**Bodywork:** aerodynamic two-seater
**Maximum speed (approx):** 125 mph (201 kph)

# Lotus Elite

When Colin Chapman decided to build a closed car, it became apparent that it would be prohibitively expensive to make dies for the production of a pressed steel body, while hand-beaten light alloy would again be too costly. So Chapman adopted the new medium of glassfibre, designing a self-supporting hull for the new model, the Elite, with attachment points for suspension and engine mounting moulded in; it was the first monocoque glassfibre car to be built.

The Elite, whose pretty body was designed by Chapman's friend Peter Kirwan-Taylor, prompted Lotus's move to Cheshunt; at the time of its launch at the 1957 London Motor Show, it was the only overhead-cam British sports car in production, using the light-alloy Coventry-Climax power unit originally designed for a portable fire-pump. Just 988 Elites were built, and though the car was originally designed for road use, there were inevitably racing derivatives; Elites were, for instance, first and second in their class at Le Mans in 1961, '62 and '63.

The cost of building the Elite continued to escalate, and when it was decided to build an open car for export markets, Lotus reverted to separate chassis construction for the new Elan model of 1962.

## 1962 LOTUS ELITE

**Engine:** in-line four cylinder, overhead-cam
**Bore × stroke:** 76.2 mm × 66.6 mm
**Capacity:** 1216
**Maximum power:** 80 bhp
**Transmission:** four-speed
**Chassis:** integral glassfibre
**Suspension:** independent with wishbones and coil springs front and Chapman struts rear
**Brakes:** discs all round, inboard at rear
**Bodywork:** glassfibre coupé
**Maximum speed (approx):** 120 mph (193 kph)

**Lotus Elite**

**1967 LOTUS EUROPA**

**Engine:** in-line four-cylinder, overhead-valve
**Bore × stroke:** 76 mm × 81 mm
**Capacity:** 1470 cc
**Maximum power:** 82 bhp
**Transmission:** four-speed manual
**Chassis:** steel backbone
**Suspension:** independent with wishbones and coil springs front and Chapman struts rear
**Brakes:** discs front, drums rear
**Bodywork:** glassfibre coupé
**Maximum speed (approx):** 111 mph (179 kph)

Lotus Europa

## Lotus Europa

Intended as an export-only model, the mid-engined Europa was launched in December 1966; its power unit was the drivetrain from the front-wheel-drive Renault 16 turned through 180 degrees and fitted at the rear of the car. This gave racing-car standards of handling and roadholding, though it was apparent that the chassis could handle more power than the 1470 cc Renault engine could produce.

A Series 2 Europa appeared in 1969, in which year the car at last became available on the British market. No longer were chassis and body permanently bonded together, while cars intended for the American market got a 1565 cc power unit.

Then, in 1971 came the Europa Twin-Cam, powered by the famous Mundy-designed 1558 cc twin-cam, which boosted power output to 105 bhp; the following year the alloy-head Big Valve power unit from the Elan Sprint was adopted, with a new Renault five-speed transmission.

In this guise, the car was known as the Europa Special: the Europa line was phased out in late 1974, after a total of 9320 had been built.

## Lotus Esprit

The Esprit originated as a design study by Giorgietto Giugiaro based on a stretched Europa chassis, first shown in Turin in 1972; by the time it reached production in 1975, the design had been refined, with a new triangulated rear suspension mounting, modified body panels and the light-alloy Lotus 907 twin-cam engine that had first appeared three years earlier in the ill-fated Jensen-Healey. Transmission was by Citroën, the same five-speed unit as fitted to the Maserati Merak.

The Esprit was not as initially successful as hoped, so an S2 version appeared in 1978, the same year in which Surrey dealers Bell & Colvill offered a Turbo conversion of the car.

A production Turbo Esprit appeared at the 1980 Geneva Show; it used the 2.2-litre version of the 16-valve 907 engine developed for the Sunbeam Lotus, was fitted with a Garrett AiResearch turbocharger installation developed by Martin Cliffe, and produced a massive 210 bhp.

Also in 1980, Lotus unveiled a normally-aspirated version of this new Esprit, the Esprit S 2.2. It would achieve 0-60 mph in 6.7 seconds, against the 5.6 seconds of the Turbo version.

**1980 LOTUS ESPRIT S**

**Engine:** in-line four-cylinder, twin-cam
**Bore × stroke:** 95.3 mm × 76.2 mm
**Capacity:** 2174 cc
**Maximum power:** 160 bhp
**Transmission:** five-speed
**Chassis:** steel box-type
**Suspension:** independent with wishbones and coil springs front, trailing arms rear
**Brakes:** discs all round
**Bodywork:** glassfibre coupé
**Maximum speed (approx):** 138 mph (222 kph)

Lotus Esprit Turbo

**Marcos 1800**

# LOZIER

**Plattsburgh/Detroit, USA**
**1905–17**

Lozier began as bicycle makers; their first hesitant venture into car manufacture came in 1900 when George A. Burrell, superintendent of their Toledo branch factory, built a three wheeled motor carriage.

When H.A. Lozier Sr retired from the company in 1900, his son E.R. Lozier and Burrell established the Lozier Motor Company in Toledo, though production didn't actually get under way until 1905, when Lozier, now based in Plattsburg, NY, introduced a chain-driven 40 hp model with a pair-cast power unit; selling price varied from $5500–6500 according to bodywork.

The marque soon acquired a sporting image; thus, when shaft-driven Loziers first appeared in 1907, they retained dummy chain-cases.

Best-known of the early Loziers was the Briarcliff tonneau, named after the 1908 Briarcliff Trophy Race (though the marque's

showing in the event was not particularly distinguished); it was available with a 7450 cc four or 9083 cc six-cylinder power unit.

Lozier shifted production to Detroit in 1910 but though new models were introduced – the 77 pair-cast 6378 cc six and the 84 monobloc 6044 cc four– and prices cut dramatically, sales of 'the quality car for quality people' declined, finally ceasing in 1917.

# MARCOS

**Luton/Bradford-on-Avon/**
**Westbury, England**
**1958–1971, 1981–**

Named for its progenitors, Jem MARsh and Frank COStin, the Marcos was inspired by aircraft techniques, with a light but torsionally-rigid plywood body/chassis structure clad in glassfibre panelling.

The cycle-winged prototype, with an 1172 cc side-valve Ford Ten engine, was capable of 120 mph (193 kph), could accelerate from 0–60 in around seven seconds and dominated the

1-litre sports-car racing class.

Marcos Cars began its formal existence in 1952, and the following year moved to Bradford-on-Avon in Wiltshire, where in 1964 the attractive Marcos Volvo made its debut – the same bodyshell was subsequently fitted with the Ford 1.6-litre pushrod power unit and the V4 2-litre and V6 3-litre engines.

A 3-litre Volvo unit was also fitted, the larger radiator required by this unit forming a very effective air dam which cured the aerodynamic problems experienced by earlier versions of this car.

The 3-litre Volvo unit coincided with the abandonment of the wooden chassis in favour of a cheaper steel square-tube chassis.

From 1965, Marcos also marketed the Jem Marsh-designed Mini-Marcos, which proved to be ugly but successful; in 1970, Marcos moved to a larger factory at Westbury in Wiltshire to produce the Dennis Adams-styled Mantis with the aim of developing a substantial export business with America. Unfortunately new American regulations trapped the cars – unsold – in the USA, and

## 1909 LOZIER BRIARCLIFF SIX

**Engine:** in-line six-cylinder, side-valve
**Bore × stroke:** 101.6 mm × 139.7 mm
**Capacity:** 9083 cc
**Maximum power:** 50 bhp
**Transmission:** four-speed manual
**Chassis:** pressed steel channel
**Suspension:** non-independent with semi-elliptic leaf springs
**Brakes:** drums on rear only
**Bodywork:** four-seater sports tourer
**Maximum speed (approx):** 85 mph (137 kph)

## 1965 MARCOS 1800

**Engine:** in-line four-cylinder, overhead-valve
**Bore × stroke:** 84.1 mm × 80 mm
**Capacity:** 1778 cc
**Maximum power:** 114 bhp
**Transmission:** four-speed manual with overdrive
**Chassis:** plywood monocoque
**Suspension:** independent front with wishbones and coil springs. Live rear axle with coil springs
**Brakes:** discs front, drums rear
**Bodywork:** glassfibre coupé body
**Maximum speed (approx):** 116 mph (187 kph)

Marcos were forced to close.

The Mini-Marcos survived the closure, and manufacture was eventually taken over by D & H Fibreglass Techniques.

In 1981, Jem Marsh resumed production of the Ford-powered 3-litre Marcos, building 51 cars in his first year. It was later joined by the Mantula, powered by a 3.5-litre Rover V8 engine.

**Lozier**

## MODEL

Ferrari 365 GTB 4 Berlinetta
(Daytona) (1970)

**UK price when introduced:**
£6700

## ENGINE

**Location:** Front, longitudinal
**Type:** Water-cooled 60 degree V12
with light alloy cylinder heads and
block. Seven main bearings
**Cubic capacity:** 4390 cc
**Bore × stroke:** 81 mm × 71 mm
**Compression ratio:** 8.8:1
**Valve gear:** Two valves per
cylinder inclined at 46 degrees
operating in hemispherical
combustion chambers via bucket
tappets by two chain-driven
overhead camshafts per bank of
cylinders
**Fuel supply:** Six Weber 40 DCN-20
downdraught twin-barrel
carburettors
**Ignition:** Mechanical with twin
coils and distributors
**Maximum power:** 353 bhp (DIN)
at 7500 rpm
**Maximum torque:** 319 lb ft (DIN)
at 5000 rpm

## TRANSMISSION

**Layout:** Gearbox in-unit with final
drive in rear of chassis
**Clutch:** Borg and Beck single dry
plate
**Gearbox:** Five speed manual

| | |
|---|---|
| 1st 3.075:1 | 4th 1.250:1 |
| 2nd 2.120:1 | 5th 0.964:1 |
| 3rd 1.572:1 | |

**Final drive:** Spiral bevel
**Ratio:** 3.300:1

## SUSPENSION

**Front:** Independent with double
wishbones, coil springs, telescopic
dampers and anti-roll bar
**Rear:** Independent with double
wishbones, coil springs and
telescopic dampers and anti-roll bar

## STEERING

**Type:** ZF worm and roller. 3.5 turns
lock to lock

## BRAKES

**Type:** Discs front and rear.
28.8 sq in (126 sq cm) rear

## WHEELS AND TYRES

**Type:** Alloy wheels 7.5 in with 215/
70 × 15 radial tyres

## BODY/CHASSIS

**Type:** Tubular chassis with two-
door coupé body

## DIMENSIONS AND WEIGHT

**Length:** 174.21 in (442 cm)
**Width:** 69.29 in (176 cm)
**Wheelbase:** 94.49 in (240 cm)
**Track – front:** 56.69 in (144 cm)
**– rear:** 56.1 in (142 cm)
**Weight:** 2641 lb (1200 kg)

## PERFORMANCE

**Maximum speed:** 174 mph
(280 kph)
**Acceleration 0–60 mph:**
5.4 seconds
**Fuel consumption:** 13 mpg

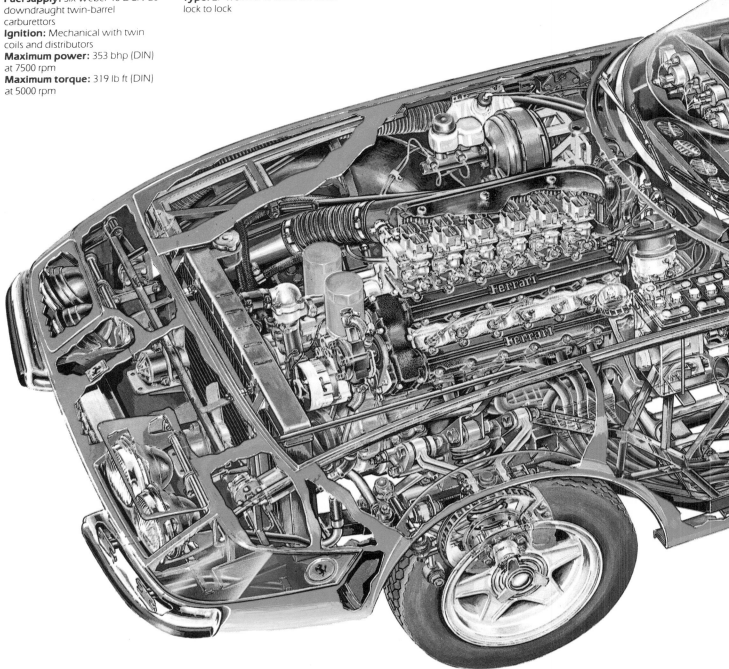

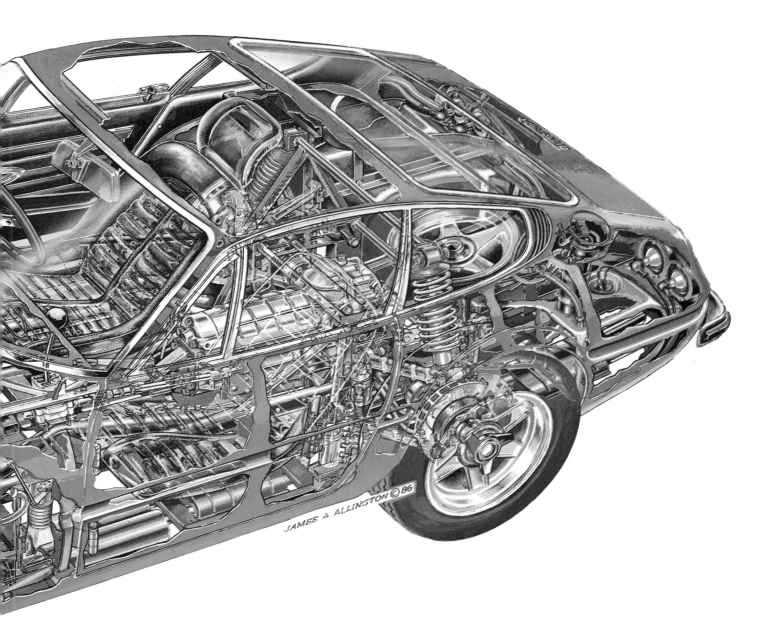

JAMES A. ALLINGTON © 86

The fact that the 365GTB/4 Daytona had its engine located at the front rather than behind the driver originally daunted certain people. The chosen layout proved its worth though and the rear mounted gearbox/final drive assembly helped to balance the overall weight distribution. The distance between these two essential masses, however, while endowing the Daytona with predictable handling, also gave each end of the car greater inertia than in a mid-mounted arrangement. As a result, oversteer, for instance, could be difficult to contain. The Daytona was renowned for its throttle sensitivity and this was one good reason.

## MARENDAZ

**London/Maidenhead, England
1926–36**

Captain D.M.K. Marendaz, formerly a partner in the company making Marseal light cars, progressed to the manufacture of this attractive small sports car with a Bentley-like radiator and flexible external exhaust pipes in the late '20s. The first Marendaz Special cars were powered by side-valve 1.5-litre Anzani engines, and known as the 11/55 hp; sometimes a supercharger was fitted, when the car was known as the 11/120. There was also an 1100 cc version.

Production of these handsome sports cars was transferred from south-west London to the infamous Cordwalles Works in Maidenhead (erstwhile home of GWK, Burney Streamline and other lost causes) in 1932, when Marendaz offered a small six of 1900 cc, the 13/70, followed in 1933 by the 2.5-litre 17/97 Marendaz Special.

For 1935 a new 2-litre six by Coventry-Climax was offered, though in recent years D.M.K. Marendaz has resolutely refused to admit that his cars used proprietary power units!

Known as the 15/90, this model could be fitted with a supercharger; among its more notable drivers was Mrs Alfred Moss, (mother of Stirling), who competed in an attractive white two-seater, subsequently sold to Joby Bowles of Epping, in whose garage the first Lotus was created.

**Marendaz 15/90**

### 1935 MARENDAZ 15/90

**Engine:** in-line, six-cylinder, side-valve
**Bore × stroke:** 65 mm × 100 mm
**Capacity:** 1991 cc
**Maximum power:** 90 bhp
**Transmission:** four-speed manual
**Chassis:** pressed steel channel
**Suspension:** non-independent with semi-elliptic leaf springs front and cantilever springs rear
**Brakes:** drums all round
**Bodywork:** two or four-seater sports
**Maximum speed (approx):** 84 mph (135 kph)

## MARLBOROUGH

**Aubervilliers, France/London & Weybridge, England
1906–1926**

Although the chassis and engine of the Marlborough were originally made in France by Malicet & Blin, the car was assembled for sale in Britain; it was first exhibited at Olympia in 1906 in single-cylinder 8 hp, twin-cylinder 10/12 hp and four-cylinder 14 hp variants.

In 1909 the agency was acquired by T.B. Andre (later famous as the maker of Hartford friction shock absorbers), and the Marlborough became steadily more British in content.

Early Marlboroughs had round radiators and bonnets; in 1912 Marlborough launched the vee-radiatored 8/10 hp light car of 1094 cc. Post-war, Marlborough introduced a 1087 cc CIME-engined model; there were also some sporting versions with British Anzani and Coventry-Climax engines.

The latter, a 2-litre six with four-wheel brakes, was announced in 1925, but never went into production. When manufacture ceased, some 2000 Marlboroughs had been built.

But the most exciting car to bear the Marlborough name was the 1923–24 Marlborough-Thomas, built as a private venture by T.B. Andre and Parry Thomas in a shed at Brooklands.

The engine of the Marlborough-Thomas was built to Parry Thomas's designs by Peter Hooker & Co; it was a twin-overhead-camshaft 1.5-litre unit with the distinctive Thomas feature of leaf-valve springs.

At a chassis price of £575 (the standard Marlborough was only £160), few Marlborough-Thomas cars were sold, though the streamlined '200-miles' bodywork with flared wings was particularly handsome.

### 1923 MARLBOROUGH-THOMAS

**Engine:** in-line four-cylinder, twin-cam
**Bore × stroke:** 70 mm × 97 mm
**Capacity:** 1493 cc
**Maximum power:**
**Transmission:** four-speed manual
**Chassis:** inverted U-section channel steel
**Suspension:** non-independent with torsion bars all round and friction dampers
**Brakes:** drums all round
**Bodywork:** streamlined sports two seater
**Maximum speed (approx):** 80 mph (123 kph)

## MARMON

**Indianapolis, USA
1902–1933**

The Nordyke & Marmon Company had been founded in 1851, and entered the automotive field in 1902 with pressure-lubricated air-cooled V4s designed by Howard Marmon. These were joined in 1908 by a 60 hp V8.

A new range – big fours of 40/45 and 50/60 hp – appeared for 1909; by 1911 only the 5.2-litre Model 32, with gearbox in the rear axle, was available. That year, the specially-built six-cylinder Marmon Wasp won the first Indianapolis 500.

In 1914 Marmon listed two models – the four-cylinder 5213 cc 32 and the six-cylinder 9383 cc 48. The advanced 34, powered by an overhead-valve six of 5565 cc first appeared in 1916: a development of this car was still in production eleven years later, alongside the unsuccessful 3115 cc Little Marmon

**Marlborough-Thomas**

straight-eight.

Marmon – who offered an eight at under £1000, under the Roosevelt marque name – only built eight-cylinder cars from 1928 to 1931, when the superlative 8046 cc alloy-engined V16, styled by Walter Dorwin Teague (later responsible for the cabin of the Boeing 707) appeared. Capacities ranged from 8.0 to 9.1 litres in the model's two-year life. Though an eight-cylinder derivative was offered in 1932, the V16 was the sole model offered for 1933; a backbone-chassis V12 designed by George A. Freers only reached prototype stage before car production ceased; the Marmon name survived on trucks.

### 1932 MARMON V16

**Engine:** V16, overhead-valve
**Bore × stroke:** 82.5 mm × 101.59 mm
**Capacity:** 8699 cc
**Maximum power:** 200 bhp
**Transmission:** three-speed manual
**Chassis:** pressed steel channel
**Suspension:** non-independent with semi-elliptic leaf springs
**Brakes:** Bendix Duo-Servo drums
**Bodywork:** sedan or convertible
**Maximum speed (approx):** 100 mph (161 kph)

# MARTINI

**Frauenfeld/St-Blaise, Switzerland
1897–1934**

This famous armaments factory founded by Friedrich de Martini in 1860 built its first stationary engines in the 1870s; at the initiative of Friedrich's son Adolf, in 1897 the company built a rear-engined twin-cylinder car with tube ignition.

Further prototypes appeared in 1898 and 1899, the latter being the first front-engined Martinicar. After yet more prototypes, a production

### 1926 MARTINI 3-LITRE

**Engine:** in-line six-cylinder, side-valve
**Bore × stroke:** 74 mm × 120 mm
**Capacity:** 3096 cc
**Maximum power:** 70 bhp
**Transmission:** four-speed manual
**Chassis:** pressed steel channel
**Suspension:** non-independent with semi-elliptic leaf springs
**Brakes:** drums all round
**Bodywork:** sports tourer
**Maximum speed (approx):** 75 mph (120 kph)

**Marmon V16 Convertible**

series of thirty V4 cars was built in 1902.

In 1903, Martini began to build Rochet-Schneider cars under licence in a new factory at St-Blaise; a hundred were built in 1903 and 130 in 1904. Martini sold the St-Blaise factory to an English combine in 1906, and two new models – the 20/24 and 30/40 – were launched; two 80 hp racers ran in the 1907 Kaiserpreis race,

finishing 13th and 15th. Martini was re-acquired by Swiss capital in 1908.

Big pair-cast four cylinder cars were the company's principal products, although overhead-valve 1087 cc voiturettes appeared in 1908, when a team of these Martini light cars ran in the Coupe des Voiturettes at Dieppe.

Martini listed a sleeve-valve 25 hp in 1913, while in 1914 the

company announced an advanced the 2614 cc 12 hp Sport, whose overhead-camshaft engine boasted four valves per cylinder in hemispherical combustion chambers. The models on offer ranged from a 1357 cc four to the 3563 cc 18 hp.

In 1921, the first new post-war Martini, the 1845 cc type FN, appeared; in 1923, the Swiss Army began taking delivery of 1800 cc

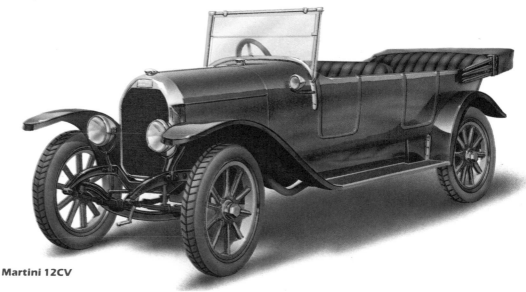

**Martini 12CV**

**Maserati Khamsin**

Martinelli voiturettes, which it used until World War II.

In 1924 the firm was acquired by the Swiss engineer Steiger, who reduced production in recognition of the fact that export sales, which pre-war had represented 50 per cent of output, had fallen dramatically.

Martini brought out a 3.1-litre six in 1926; a total of 150 cars was sold in the first six months of 1928. Two sixes of 15 hp and 20 hp were listed in 1929, but in order to escape the immense costs of developing another new model, in 1930 Martini began licence production of the German 2.5-litre Wanderer six.

This didn't find favour with the Swiss, so Martini introduced the Type NF 4.4-litre monobloc six early in 1931. When it was decided to liquidate the company in 1934, total Martini production had reached an estimated 2000 cars.

# MASERATI

**Bologna/Modena, Italy
1926–**

There were originally six Maserati brothers – Alfieri, Bindo, Carlo, Ettore, Ernesto and Marco. Marco became an artist and Carlo, who had raced cars and motorcylces in the early days of this century, died in 1910. Alfieri and Bindo Maserati went to work for Isotta Fraschini, and then in 1914 Alfieri opened a small garage near Bologna, where he was soon joined by Ettore, Bindo and Ernesto.

During the Great War the brothers made spark plugs, and then in the early 1920s Ernesto

began to race a car powered by one bank of a V8 Isotta aero engine. The company's next step was the tuning and racing of Diatto cars; the Maseratis built two 2-litre Grand Prix cars for Diatto in 1925 and then in 1925 took them over when Diatto withdrew from racing.

The engines of these former Diatto racers were linered down to 1.5 litres and the cars became the first Maseratis, bearing the trident badge of Bologna on their radiators. One of them, driven by Alfieri Maserati, won its first race, the 1926 Targa Florio.

Maserati established their reputation with racing cars with four, six and eight – and even 16 – cylinders, with swept volumes from 1088 cc to 4995 cc, although road-going cars with detuned racing engines appeared during the '30s.

One of the fearsome 'Sedici Cilindri' was converted into a road car, its 16-cylinder power unit confected from two straight-eights mounted in parallel, with their crankshafts geared together.

The death of Alfierei in 1932 was a bitter blow which led in 1937 to a take-over by Adolfo and Omer Orsi, and the company moved to their home town of Modena in 1941. However, the three Maserati brothers stayed on until their contract expired in 1947, when they left to found OSCA. Before they left, the Maseratis created the overhead-cam A6G sports car, derived from the 6CM racing voiturette and available in 1.5 or 2-litre forms.

Racing cars were again the mainstay of the company after the war. Most famous of all was the 250F, designed by Giaocchino Colombo in 1953 and raced by drivers such as Moss, Hawthorn and Fangio in various forms until 1958.

Omer Orsi then decided to withdraw from Grand Prix racing, and from 1958 Maserati concentrated on expensive sports cars, powered by the six-cylinder 3485 cc 300S engine.

Nevertheless, the 1994 cc and 2890 cc 'Birdcage' Maserati sports-racers enjoyed some competition success in private hands in the early 1960s.

Sports car production continued with the 170 mph (274 kph) 5000GT in 1959 and then the 1963 Quattroporte. In 1967 the 4-litre six-cylinder Mistrale and Sebring were announced.

Shortly afterwards, the Mistrale was replaced by the 195 mph (313 kph) Ghibli, and then in 1969 Citroën took control of Maserati for some 1000 million lire; production at Modena was then running at about 2.5 cars per day, including the new Citroën Maserati SM grand touring model.

**1972 MASERATI KHAMSIN**

**Engine:** V8, four-cam
**Bore × stroke:** 93.9 mm × 89 mm
**Capacity:** 4930 cc
**Maximum power:** 280 bhp
**Transmission:** five-speed manual
**Chassis:** tubular steel frame
**Suspension:** independent with wishbones and anti-roll bars front and rear
**Brakes:** discs all round
**Bodywork:** 2+2 coupé
**Maximum speed (approx):** 160 mph (258 kph)

Unfortunately, Citroën had its own problems, and the liaison proved to afford only temporary relief. In 1975 Maserati announced that it was going out of business, and it was only saved at the last minute by Alejandro De Tomaso.

At the end of the 1970s, Maserati's product line-up included the mid-engined 2965 cc V6 Merak and the smaller Merak 2000, the mid-engined 4719 cc V8 Bora, the 4930 cc Khamsin V8 and the twin-overhead-camshaft 4236 cc V8 Quattroporte, available with coupé or limousine coachwork.

This had all changed by 1984, when Maserati offered only the Biturbo turbocharged V6 saloon and the V8 Quattroporte, now displacing 4930 cc.

In the spring of 1985 came the news that Alejandro de Tomaso had signed a deal with his old friend Lee Iacocca of Chrysler whereby Maserati would build an open two-seater to be sold through the Chrysler network in the US.

**Maserati Biturbo**

# Maserati Khamsin

Designed as a replacement for the Giugiaro-styled, Ghia-bodied Ghibli, the Khamsin appeared just in time for the energy crisis. Nevertheless, it survived, and earned much praise for its well-balanced handling.

Evidence of Maserati's involvement with Citroën could be seen in the use of a powered hydraulic system which even raised and lowered the headlamps and adjusted the seat, in addition to providing the suspension and powering the brakes.

Since the Ford takeover had closed Ghia to Maserati, the Khamsin had Bertone bodywork, a neat 2+2 of sleek appearance with a glazed panel across the tail.

Despite its somewhat ponderous chassis construction, the Khamsin was a 160 mph (257 kph) car, though its optimistic makers claimed over 10 mph (16 kph) more, in typical Italian fashion.

# Maserati Bora

The Bora, introduced in 1971, broke new ground for Maserati in being the company's first mid-engined road-going sports car. Like many Italian exotics, it owed its powerful stylish lines to Giorgetto Giugiaro.

Power was supplied by Maserati's venerable four-cam V8 mounted longitudinally ahead of the transmission. The rear suspension was by double wishbones, the spring/damper units having been moved above the top wishbones to make room for the drive shafts.

The Bora was a true supercar, capable of spectacular acceleration in the order of 6.9 seconds to 60 mph (97 kph), but it was an expensive and thirsty beast and a logical development of the Bora theme saw the introduction of the smaller V6-engined mid-engined Merak in 1972. The Bora continued in production until 1980, survived by the Merak.

# Maserati Biturbo

When Alejandro de Tomaso took over the ailing Maserati concern in 1975 he was concerned to broaden the company's appeal. One result was the Biturbo, introduced in 1982.

### 1974 MASERATI BORA

**Engine:** V8, four-cam
**Bore × stroke:** 93.9 mm × 85 mm
**Capacity:** 4719 cc
**Maximum power:** 310 bhp
**Transmission:** five-speed manual
**Chassis:** tubular steel frame
**Suspension:** independent with wishbones and anti-roll bars front and rear
**Brakes:** discs all round
**Bodywork:** two-seater sports coupé
**Maximum speed (approx):** 165 mph (266 kph)

### 1984 MASERATI BITURBO

**Engine:** V6, overhead-cam, twin-turbo
**Bore × stroke:** 82 mm × 63.5 mm
**Capacity:** 1996 cc
**Maximum power:** 180 bhp
**Transmission:** five-speed manual
**Chassis:** integral
**Suspension:** independent by MacPherson struts
**Brakes:** discs all round
**Bodywork:** coupé
**Maximum speed (approx):** 130 mph (209 kph)

It was deliberately styled to resemble the far larger Quattroporte saloon to give it something of the large car's undoubted charisma.

The Biturbo got his name from its use of twin turbochargers, one for each bank of the overhead-cam

**Maserati Bora**

V6. That powerplant was also notable for having three valves per cylinder; the net result was 180 bhp from the 2-litre engine.

The Biturbo's appeal was enhanced when the Biturbo 425 was introduced with its V6 bored out to give a displacement of 2491 cc and a further 10 bhp and, more importantly, another 35 lb ft of torque.

# MATHIS
**Strasbourg, Germany/France**
**1905–1950**

In the early years of this century, Emile E.C. Mathis was a prominent motor agent in Strasbourg, Alsace; he imported Fiat, De Dietrich and Panhard-Levassor cars, and first became a manufacturer with the Hermes (or Hermes-Simplex) car, designed for him by the young Ettore Bugatti.

The next Mathis cars, designed by racing-driver Esser, were 2025 cc and 2253 cc models built under licence from Stoewer.

The first true Mathis appeared in 1913, in the guise of the 951 cc Babylette, a neat voiturette on similar lines to the Type 13 Bugatti.

Other pre-1914 Mathis cars included the Baby, with unit construction of engine and gearbox, available with 1327 cc or 1406 cc power units, two side-valve models of 1850 cc and 3453 cc, and the 4.4-litre sleeve-valve Mathis-Knight.

After the war, Alsace was returned to France, and production of the small Mathis cars increased to the extent that the marque soon became the fourth biggest in its new homeland.

In 1921 Mathis launched the vee-radiatored SB overhead-valve 1.5-litre, developed from an

overhead-camshaft racer. Mathis challenged the new 5 hp Citroën with a basic 760 cc car without instruments or differential.

On top of a bewildering variety of small cars, Mathis switched to a single-model policy in 1927 with the 1.2-litre four-cylinder side-valve MY, later joined by the Emysix.

These unexciting cars established the pattern for the early 1930s (though in 1930 there were bigger sixes of 2.4 and 4.1 litres, while 1931 saw two short-lived straight-eights).

The more modern Emyquatre, with independent front suspension and synchromesh, appeared in 1933, but its Emyhuit sister had only just been launched when Emile Mathis signed a contract with Henry Ford under which the Ford V8 was produced at Strasbourg under the name Matford.

The relationship between Ford and Mathis was a stormy one, and it resulted in Mathis regaining his factory just before the war.

His post-war projects, an Andreau-styled streamlined three-wheeler and a front-wheel-driven 2.8-litre flat-six, failed to go into production.

**Mathis Emysix**

# MATRA
**Romorantin, France**
**1965–1979**

Matra (Mecanique-Aviation-Traction) grew out of a small aeronautical contracting firm named CAPRA founded before the war; the company, then based in the Free French Zone, changed its

name to Matra in 1942, and after the war became France's leading manufacturer of guided missiles.

In 1965 Matra (by now a major force in French aerospace research), took over the manufacturer of René Bonnet's Renault-powered sports cars; they also plunged into an ambitious race and rally programme.

Matra's first own-design road-going car, the V4 Ford-engined Matra 530, could not be sold in sufficiently large numbers to be a viable proposition, so Matra linked with Chrysler at the beginning of the 1970s to develop the Simca-powered Bagheera sports coupé with three-abreast seating.

The Bagheera was joined at the end of the 1970s by the Rancho, a 1442 cc plastic-bodied station wagon which looked like an off-road vehicle.

Matra ceased to be an independent company when Chrysler sold its European operations to the expanding Peugeot group in 1979.

**Matra Simca Bagheera**

## MAYBACH

**Friedrichshafen, Germany**
**1921–1940**

Wilhelm Maybach, the brilliant designer who created the original Mercedes, resigned from the Daimler Motoren Gesellschaft in 1907 and joined his old friend Graf Ferdinand von Zeppelin to design airship engines. By 1912 a factory was in operation at Friedrichshafen to build aero engines designed by Maybach's son Karl. This works also made marine engines and motorcycle power units before introducing a side-valve 5738 cc six-cylinder car engine after the Great War, when the manufacture of aero engines was proscribed. The engine was sold to Spyker in Holland, but no other buyers could be found, so Maybach entered manufacture with the W3 car, first

shown in 1921.

Karl Maybach was obsessed with the idea of making driving as foolproof as possible, so the original Maybachs had two-speed pedal-controlled gearboxes. They were also the first production German cars with four-wheel braking. Among the coachbuilders who clothed this high-quality chassis with exclusive bodywork were Spohn, Glaser, Armbruster, Erdmann & Rossi and Voll-Ruhrbeck.

The W5 of 1926 had an overhead-valve 6995 cc engine, and was available with a *schnellgang* auxiliary two-speed gearbox. This gave a top speed of 75 mph (121 kph), but the six-cylinder engine was felt to be lacking in prestige, so a 6922 cc V12 made its debut in 1929. This 'small' DS7 model (built on a 147 in/373 cm wheelbase, it needed an omnibus licence) was

developed into the Zeppelin model of 1930, which had a tiny model Zeppelin airship on its badge bar.

In 1931 Maybach launched the 7977 cc V12 DS8, which soon replaced the DS7: the six-cylinder DSH of 5.2 litres was introduced at the bottom of the range. At first, the DS8 had a five-speed transmission, but from 1938 this model was fitted with a seven-speed gearbox.

Some of these cars were fitted with Spohn aerodynamic bodywork built to the designs of Paul Jaray; this streamlined coachwork was also available on the overhead-camshaft SW series current from 1934 to 1940; this included the 3435 cc SW35 (1935–36), the 3790 cc SW38 (1936-39) and the 4199 cc SW42 (1939–41) models. Total production was around 2000 units.

### 1930 MAYBACH ZEPPELIN

**Engine:** V12, overhead-valve
**Bore × stroke:** 92 mm × 100 mm
**Capacity:** 7977 cc
**Maximum power:** 200 bhp
**Transmission:** seven-speed vacuum assisted manual
**Chassis:** steel channel
**Suspension:** non-independent with semi-elliptic leaf springs all round
**Brakes:** drums all round
**Bodywork:** to order
**Maximum speed (approx):** 100 mph (161 kph)

## MAZDA

**Hiroshima, Japan**
**1960–**

The Toyo Kogyo company, founded in 1920, was originally concerned with cork products. Then it built motorcycles in the mid-1920s, and introduced the Mazda three-wheel truck in 1930. It went into full production in October 1931.

Prototype cars were built in the late 1930s before the war intervened, and the company did not actually enter the passenger-car market until 1960, when the R-360 Coupé appeared.

In 1962 Mazda launched the Carol range, the styling of which was inspired by the contemporary Ford Anglia; the Carol 360 was a two-door saloon, while the Carol 600 was a four-door model. For 1964, Mazda, who had just produced their millionth vehicle, launched the Familia pickup, which soon became the Familia Sedan.

The Mazda 1000 was introduced in 1965, the 1500 in 1966, but the most significant new model of the decade was the 1967 Wankel-engined R-100.

A new Wankel-engined model, the RX-2, appeared for 1970, and by 1977 a developed version of this engine theme, with Mazda's REAPS emission-control system by thermal reactor and air injection, was available alongside conventionally engined cars of up to 1800 cc.

The most powerful 1978 Mazda was the 135 bhp Cosmo AP Limited

*Maybach Zeppelin*

**Mazda RX7**

Coupé, which gave a maximum speed of 118 mph (190 kph).

In 1979 came a new rotary-engined sports car, the Mazda RX-7; the company was now capable of building a million cars a year.

The 323 small car launched for 1980 was a front-wheel-drive hatchback with a lightweight low-friction overhead-cam power unit: following the company's accord with Ford, the 323 was assembled in Australia as the Ford Laser.

The company updated its Cosmo/Luce range for 1981, adopting the company's first independent rear suspension set-up on rear-drive cars.

That same year, an improved rotary engine was launched, the six-port induction VIPS unit, which gave an optimum compromise between bottom-end torque and high speed power. In 1982 Mazda introduced a turbocharged rotary engine in the 125 mph (201 kph) Cosmo, and launched the 626 range, an all-new front-wheel-drive model assembled in a purpose-built automated plant, and fitted with electronically-adjustable dampers.

In 1983 Mazda showed an interesting concept car, the MX-02, which had four-wheel steering.

Although Mazda was expected to retain the Wankel engine in its successor to the RX-7, due to be launched for 1986, it was anticipated that the company would switch to a reciprocating V6 of around 3 litres capacity for its forthcoming large car range.

---

**1983 MAZDA RX-7**

**Engine:** Wankel type rotary, twin-rotor
**Capacity:** 2 × 573 cc
**Maximum power:** 130 bhp
**Transmission:** five-speed manual
**Chassis:** integral
**Suspension:** independent front with MacPherson struts and anti-roll bar front. Live rear axle with trailing arms and Watt's linkage
**Brakes:** discs all round
**Bodywork:** 2+2 coupé
**Maximum speed (approx):** 112 mph (180 kph)

---

# McFARLAN
**Connersville, USA**
**1910–1928**

John B. McFarlan founded his carriage works in 1856, and created one of the world's first 'industrial parks' around it. Late in 1909, his grandson Harry decided to go in for motor-car manufacture. The McFarlan was always large, expensive and prestigious, and several makes of engine were used in those first models, starting with a Brownell six of 4058 cc. This was continued for 1911 as the Little Six, joined by an overhead-valve Big Six

---

**1920 McFARLAN TV**

**Engine:** in-line six-cylinder, bi-block 24-valve
**Bore × stroke:** 114.3 mm × 152.4 mm
**Capacity:** 9382 cc
**Maximum power:** 120 bhp
**Transmission:** three-speed
**Chassis:** pressed steel channel
**Suspension:** non-independent with semi-elliptic leaf springs front and McFarlan cradle type rear
**Brakes:** rear only
**Bodywork:** to order
**Maximum speed (approx):** 76 mph (122 kph)

**McFarlan TV Roadster**

with a capacity of 6177 cc.

For 1912 a new 6177 cc 40/45 hp model appeared, alongside an overhead-valve, 6973 cc 55/60 hp; compressed air starters were standard equipment. The following year McFarlan announced that they were abandoning the annual model change, and that three series were to be produced instead – the Series S (6177 cc), T (7412 cc) and M (7817 cc). That year, 23 different body styles were proposed, but actual McFarlan production was just 55 cars....

The Series S and M were discontinued for 1914, when – unusually for a maker of high-class cars – McFarlan decided to adopt left-hand steering. The power unit of Series T was made by Teetor-Hartley; a second Teetor engine, this time of 9382 cc, was used in the same chassis to create the Series X. The compressed-air starter was soon replaced by electric starting equipment.

The Ninety McFarlan, introduced for 1916, used a similar power unit to the Series X; unusual accessories available at this period were a tilting, electrically-heated steering wheel and push-button-controlled electric gearshift.

Although many proprietary components were used in the manufacture of the McFarlan, it never acquired the stigma of being regarded as an assembled car.

In the autumn of 1920, McFarlan at last began to manufacture its own power units, and the TV or Twin-Valve series was introduced; the enormous 9382 cc six-cylinder engines, of McFarlan design and manufacture, had 24 valves and 18 spark plugs, with double magneto and single coil ignition. Eleven different models were offered, at prices ranging from $69000 to $9000, the latter price for the Knickerbocker Cabriolet, an extraordinarily ornate town car for the traveller who had everything and liked to take it with him (or her). But few were sold.

Some fire engines and ambulances were also built on the TV chassis (the power unit was similar to that used on Maxim fire engines, built in Middleboro, Mass.; Maxim were New England distributors for the McFarlan).

In 1924, the company introduced the cheaper SV or Single-Valve Six with a 4397 cc Wisconsin engine; it was not a success and was withdrawn in 1926.

In 1926, however, the Eight-in-Line series, which used a 4893 cc Lycoming eight-cylinder engine, was introduced; like the TV, it was built to the end of production.

The 1926 models were lower-built than their predecessors, but few were made. Some 235 cars were built in McFarlan's best year, 1922; the total production was some 2090 chassis.

**McLaughlin**

# McLAUGHLIN
Oshawa, Canada
1908–1922

The McLaughlin Carriage Company dated back to 1867 but by 1908 Robert McLaughlin and his sons had decided to build an all-Canadian car, a plan that foundered when their chief engineer fell ill. At that time, however, General Motors were looking for a foothold in Canada and McLaughlin came to a very advantageous agreement to use Buick engines and other parts.

Based on the contemporary Buick four-cylinder, 200 cars were produced in 1908 and output rose steadily thereafter, peaking at around 15,000 in 1922, McLaughlin's last year. McLaughlin's versions of the Buick were renowned for being far better built and finished than the American model. The company also built Chevrolet-based cars as well as examples based on the Buick four and six-cylinder engines and the Oakland six-cylinder.

By 1918 McLaughlin had become a wholly owned subsidiary of General Motors, and GM Canada is today based in Oshawa where McLaughlin started. From 1923, when the original agreement ran out, their cars were known as McLaughlin-Buicks to make the GM link more obvious.

## 1920 McLAUGHLIN

**Engine:** in-line six-cylinder, overhead valve
**Bore × stroke:** 86 mm × 116 mm
**Capacity:** 4043 cc
**Maximum power:** 18 bhp
**Transmission:** three-speed manual
**Chassis:** pressed steel channel
**Suspension:** non-independent with semi-elliptic leaf springs front and rear
**Brakes:** drums on rear only
**Bodywork:** convertible or sedan
**Maximum speed (approx):** 50 mph (80 kph)

# MERCEDES
Germany
1901–1926

During the 1890s the Austro-Hungarian Consul in Nice, Emile Jellinek, was also the local agent for Daimler cars. He commissioned batches of cars which he sold to his wealthy acquaintances, and was therefore able to persuade Daimler engineer Wilhelm Maybach to design for him ever more powerful cars, culminating in the 1899 24 hp four-cylinder Phönix-Daimler.

The serious dynamic deficiencies of this model led Jellinek to order a new model, 'the

car of the day after tomorrow', which first appeared in 1901 and combined the most modern design features in a manner which finally broke with horse-carriage traditions. Jellinek named this sensational new model after his eldest daughter, Mercedes, to boost its sales prospects in France.

The first Mercedes, the 35 hp, had a 5913 cc four-cylinder engine; it set the pattern for quality car design in Europe and America. The Daimler company soon adopted the Mercedes name for all their private cars, and developments of the 35 hp were built under the name 'Mercedes-Simplex'; most famous were the 18/22 hp, the 6780 cc 40/45 hp and the mighty 9240 cc 60 hp, with overhead inlet valves and 80 mph (129 kph) performance. When the official team of 90 mph cars for the 1903 Gordon Bennett Cup Race in Ireland were destroyed in a fire, a standard 60 hp, stripped of its touring body, won the race, driven by 'Red Devil' Camille Jenatzy.

However, Maybach didn't get on with the Daimler management, and resigned in 1907 to join his old friend Graf Zeppelin. He was succeeded as chief engineer by Paul Daimler, son of Gottlieb.

The Mercedes marque dominated the international motor-racing scene before the outbreak of the Great War; it was also the chosen marque of the Kaiser, and touring models of the period included cars from 1570 cc to a 9575 cc four. Knight sleeve-valve-engined models were also built, and the 4055 cc Mercedes-Knight survived until 1923.

The post-war range also included the 7250 cc overhead-camshaft six, which was used by Paul Daimler as the basis for his supercharging experiments. The first production supercharged cars appeared in 1921–22, in the shape of two small overhead-camshaft fours of 1568 cc (the 6/25/40PS) and 2600 cc (the 10/40/65PS).

Ferdinand Porsche became chief engineer in 1923; shortly before the 1926 amalgamation between Mercedes and Benz he introduced a blown overhead-camshaft six-cylinder of 6240 cc, known as the 24/100/140PS. This was developed by Porsche into the Type K (for 'Kompressor'), which produced 110 bhp in unblown form, and 160 bhp when blown.

**Mercedes 60HP**

## Mercedes 60HP

The 60 hp Mercedes made its debut at the 1903 Nice Week, winning a number of events, but also causing the death of the popular Count Eliot Zborowski when he lost control of his 60 hp and crashed into a rock.

The 60 hp was favoured by wealthy sportsmen, not least when the standard tourer belonging to the American Clarence Gray Dinsmore was stripped of its coachwork after the 1903 fire which had destroyed the works team, and won the event against purpose-built racers.

Priced at £1800, the 60 hp Mercedes was intended only for the fortunate and discriminating few: its specification even included variable-opening inlet valves.

---

**MERCEDES 60HP**

**Engine:** in-line four-cylinder, inlet-over-exhaust
**Bore × stroke:** 140 mm × 150 mm
**Capacity:** 9236 cc
**Maximum power:** 60 hp (rated)
**Transmission:** four-speed manual
**Chassis:** pressed steel channel
**Suspension:** non-independent, with semi-elliptic leaf springs front and rear
**Brakes:** rear-wheel drums and transmission
**Bodywork:** to order
**Maximum speed (approx):** 85 mph (137 kph)

---

**1924 MERCEDES 24/100/140**

**Engine:** in-line six-cylinder, overhead-camshaft
**Bore × stroke:** 94 mm × 150 mm
**Capacity:** 6246 cc
**Maximum power:** 100 bhp (140 bhp supercharged)
**Transmission:** four-speed
**Chassis:** pressed steel channel
**Suspension:** non-independent with semi-elliptic leaf springs front and cantilever springs rear
**Brakes:** drums all round
**Bodywork:** tourer or saloon
**Maximum speed (approx):** 85 mph (137 kph)

---

## Mercedes 24/100/140

Ferdinand Porsche's first super-charged sports cars for Mercedes were the Type 400 4 litre and the Type 630 6 litre, better known as the 24/100/140, the figures representing the taxable, unblown and blown horsepowers of the car, since the supercharger was only clutched in when required for ultimate perform-ance.

The 24/100/140 went on sale in 1924, and it quickly became clear that Porsche was far more skilful at designing engines than he was at chassis, for the handling of the car was a long way behind its perform-ance; some improvement was made by replacing the cantilever rear springs with semi-elliptics.

With a light-alloy dual-ignition overhead-camshaft power unit built in unit with the four-speed gearbox, the 24/100/140 obviously had great potential; this began to be realised when Porsche redesigned the car to create the Model K, first of the great supercharged Mercedes-Benz sports cars of the 1920s.

## MERCEDES-BENZ

Stuttgart-Untertuerkheim, Germany
1926–

**Mercedes 24/100/140**

Following the amalgamation between Mercedes and Benz, the newly-formed group could draw on the technical expertise of a team of engineers headed by Ferdinand Porsche, and including Hans Nibel and Fritz Nallinger, who were all three appointed to the board of the Daimler-Benz company.

Nevertheless, the first new cars to be produced following the merger were pedestrian side-valve sixes of a very dull nature.

Far more exciting, although built in limited numbers, were Porsche's overhead-camshaft supercharged six-cylinder sports cars, starting with the 1926 6250 cc 24/100/160 K Type, nicknamed the Death Trap because of its unforgiving handling; it was followed by the 6789 cc 26/120/180 S Type, and the 7067 cc 27/140/200 SS, 27/170/225 SSK and 27/170/300 SSKL Types.

Nibel took over as chief engineer after Porsche's departure in 1928, and under his regime were built the 4.9-litre Nürberg eight-cylinder (a development of Porsche's 4.6-litre Nürburg of 1928), the 3.7-litre Mannheim six (again, developed from a Porsche design, the 3.5-litre model of 1928) and the ostentatious straight-eight Grosser Mercedes, with a 7655 cc overhead-valve engine available with or without a supercharger, which in its initial form was built from 1930 to 1937.

Mercedes entered the economy class in 1931 with the popular Type 170; this had a 1692 cc six-cylinder engine and Mercedes' first application of independent front suspension, and was followed in 1933 by the 1962 cc Type 200; however, the rear-engined 1308 cc four-cylinder Heckmotor 130H of 1934–35 and its successors, the 150H and 170H, all enjoyed little success.

The 3796 cc 15/90/140 Type 380 of 1932 was the first Mercedes supercharged sports car with independent front suspension; it was developed into the 5018 cc 500K the following year.

Ex-racing driver Max Sailer became chief engineer in 1935; under his leadership Mercedes introduced the 260D of 1935, the first series-production diesel-engined car, a new Grosser Mercedes with a more modern oval tubular chassis and swing axles (launched in 1938) and the 540K of 1937, which developed 115 bhp normally aspirated and 180 bhp with the blower engaged. A one-off 580K was built for *Korpsfuhrer* Huhnlein, head of the Nazi state motorsport body, the NSKK, with whose backing the Mercedes and Auto Union racing cars dominated the major races of the 1934–39 era.

Rebuilding the factory after the war took some time; the first post-war model, the 1697 cc 170V side-valve four-cylinder of pre-war

origin, only appeared in 1947. In 1949, Mercedes brought out a diesel-engined version of this car.

The first departure from pre-war design came with the unitary-construction 180 series of 1953–54, though without doubt the classic Mercedes of that decade were the 2996 cc overhead-camshaft six-cylinder 300S and 300SL sports models of 1952 onwards, most famous in its original gull-wing coupé form. Over 3250 were built, and the straight-eight sports-racing derivative, the 300SLR, won many competition victories and gave Juan-Manuel Fangio world championships in 1954 and '55.

A new Grosser Mercedes, the long-wheelbase luxury Type 600, powered by an overhead-camshaft V8 of 6330 cc appeared in 1964.

In 1971, Mercedes launched the

produced a top speed of 143 mph (230kph). In 1985, the new W124 range of mid-sized executive saloons was launched, with engines of 2 to 5 litres.

In 1969, the SL range, which had been launched in 1971, was finally discontinued and the long-awaited new two-seater SL range was launched, offering an almost flawless blend of comfort, handling and performance.

## Mercedes-Benz S/SS/SSK/SSKL

Derived from the K Type, which was claimed to be the world's first genuine 100 mph (161 kph) touring car, the 36/220S was launched in 1927. Its lowered chassis improved the handling; production in 1927 totalled 80, while in 1928 75 S Type Mercedes were built.

Caracciola's 1929 Ulster TT car had aircraft-type wire bracing to avoid this unwelcome effect.

Though all the SS Mercedes were built in 1928–29, most were sold in 1930–31, and the model was catalogued until 1934.

Also, a short-chassis variant with a slightly larger blower, the SSK, designed for success in hillclimbing competition, was produced at the same time; 11 were manufactured in 1928, 25 in 1929 and 1 in 1931; a liberally-drilled derivative with 'elephant' blower, the SSKL (L for *Leicht* – Light) was built as a works competition car, though a few were said to have been sold to 'very special order' from 1930 on. With a top speed in the region of 150 mph (241 kph), the SSKL took the world 200 kilometre (124 mile) record in 1932 at the Berlin AVUS track, averaging 121.6 mph (196 kph)

**Mercedes-Benz SSK**

six- and eight-cylinder fuel injected S-class cars, the marque's flagships during that decade, the most powerful being the 6834 cc V8 450 SEL 6.9, capable of 140 mph (225 kph)

At the end of the decade came the new S-class range with alloy engines of 3.8 and 5 litres with four-speed automatic gearboxes and so efficient that the new 380 matched the performance of the old 450, the new 500 was better than the old 6.9 and all were more fuel-efficient.

In 1982, the 190 saloon range appeared, with engines of between 1.9 and 2.5 litres; the fastest was the 190E 2.3-16, with a Cosworth-developed 16-valve head for its four-cylinder engine. This was the first four-valve-per-cylinder Mercedes-Benz engine and it

Late in 1928, Mercedes began production of a new model, the SS (for Super Sports), of which 102 were built in 1928–29; the potential of the model was shown by 'Scrap' Thistlethwayte, who made the fastest lap (74.39 mph/119.7 kph) in the 1928 Ulster Tourist Trophy; he also made fastest lap (83.8 mph/1344.9 kph) in the 1929 Irish Grand Prix before retiring with a blown gasket. But in the 1929 Tourist Trophy race, Rudy Caracciola came in first, beating a team of three 4½ 'Blower' Bentleys; his car was subsequently acquired by Earl Howe, who made fastest lap in the 1930 Ulster TT with it.

Though the handling of the SS Mercedes was said to be good, some cars had a tendency to chassis whip, to the extent that the fan blades could hit the radiator core.

### 1929 MERCEDES-BENZ SS

**Engine:** in-line six-cylinder, overhead-cam
**Bore × stroke:** 100 mm × 150 mm
**Capacity:** 7069 cc
**Maximum power:** 170 bhp
**Transmission:** three-speed manual
**Chassis:** pressed steel channel, ladder frame
**Suspension:** non-independent with semi-elliptic leaf springs and friction dampers all round
**Brakes:** drums all round
**Bodywork:** competition two-seater or cabriolet
**Maximum speed (approx):** 110 mph (177 kph)

# A-Z OF THE CAR

## Mercedes-Benz 540K

Though their flowing lines and external exhaust systems were the very embodiment of *Sturm und Drang*, the 500/540 Mercedes range which began with the 5-litre 500K (for *Kompressor* – supercharger) of 1933 never made any impression on national or international competition, apart from entry in German reliability runs – a surprising fact in view of Mercedes's dominant record in Grand Prix racing over the same epoch of the mid '30s.

But as the symbol of the Party member who had arrived in the Nazi heirarchy, the 500/540K cabriolet was unsurpassed.

Since the supercharger was still the intermittently-engaged type pioneered by Mercedes at the beginning of the 1920s (and ignored by everyone else), the blower was more for dramatic effect than out-and-out performance, its Wagnerian scream being totally distinctive.

The 540K of 1937 had both bore and stroke enlarged, while the gear-

box. was fitted with a direct-drive top rather than the overdrive fourth of the 500K. At the beginning of 1939 a five-speed transmission with overdrive top was adopted; it was optimistically stated that 'even at full speed the running of the engine is now practically inaudible...'.

A prototype 580K was shown at the 1939 Berlin Show, with a claimed top speed of 140 mph (225 kph), which would have made it the fastest production car of the 1930s, but it got no further than the prototype stage.

## Mercedes-Benz 300SL

The 300SL Mercedes first appeared in 1952 as a tubular-framed sports coupé derived from the new 300 model: its distinctive gull-wing doors were adopted by chief designer Dr Nallinger and head of the research department Rudi Uhlenhaut to solve the problem of driver access across the high, wide sill of the space frame. When a team of three alloy-bodied 300SLs made

their competition debut at the 1952 Mille Miglia, the Italians protested the legality of the revolutionary new door design of the Mercedes, but were over-ruled.

Starting well down the pack, Karl Kling was leading as far as Florence, maintaining a 90 mph-plus average on wet roads, but eventually Bracco's Ferrari won by five minutes, with Kling second and Caracciola fourth in another 300SL.

The production version of the 300SL, which appeared a couple of years after the competition version, had its 3-litre power unit tilted to give a low bonnet line, and initial cars had triple Solex carburettors, though fuel injection was soon standardised.

The road-going capabilities of the 300SL – a roadster was added later in the model's life, but lacked the charisma of the Gullwing – were only restricted by the roads and traffic of the 1950s; *The Autocar* summed up its performance as 'electrifying'.

## Mercedes-Benz 500SL

There has been an SL in the marque's range since 1954 and in styling the new model Bruno Sacco and his team followed aerodynamic principles and yet managed to evoke the SL heritage, with a subtly timeless look. The new cars, with engines of 3, 5 and 6 litres, bristled with high technology; there was a roll-over bar, which usually lay flat and which sprang up instantly if an accident was sensed, ride-height control for the suspension, and adjustable anti-skid control.

The SL offered the choice of open or closed motoring at the touch of a button, with an automatic, hydraulically controlled soft top, and there was an option of a sophisticated hard top, detached by the use of a few simple controls. The leather seats had multi-way adjustment, thanks to

**Mercedes-Benz 540K Cabriolet**

### 1937 MERCEDES-BENZ 540K

**Engine:** in-line eight-cylinder, overhead-valve
**Bore × stroke:** 88 mm × 111 mm
**Capacity:** 5401 cc
**Maximum power:** 115 bhp normally aspirated, 180 bhp with supercharger engaged
**Transmission:** four-speed manual
**Chassis:** pressed steel channel
**Suspension:** independent with wishbones and coil springs front and swing axles and coil springs rear
**Brakes:** drums all round, servo-assisted
**Bodywork:** roadster, cabriolet or coupé
**Maximum speed (approx):** 106 mph (170 kph)

### 1952 MERCEDES-BENZ 300SL

**Engine:** in-line six-cylinder, overhead-cam
**Bore × stroke:** 85 mm × 88 mm
**Capacity:** 2996 cc
**Maximum power:** 240 bhp
**Transmission:** four-speed manual
**Chassis:** tubular steel space frame
**Suspension:** independent with wishbones and coils front and swinging axles and coil springs rear
**Brakes:** drums all round
**Bodywork:** gullwing coupé or roadster
**Maximum speed (approx):** 135 mph (217 kph)

**Mercedes-Benz 300SL**

five motors, and the seat belt system could be set to fit comfortably.

The monocoque was designed with computers to provide maximum safety and the all-independent suspension included anti-dive, anti-squat and anti-lift geometry.

The 500 SL weighed a hefty 4167 lb (1890 kg) and yet the alloy V8 could take it to 100 mph (160 kph) in just 14 seconds.

## 1991 MERCEDES-BENZ 500 SL

**Engine:** V8, quad-cam, 32-valve
**Bore x stroke:** 96.5 mm x 85 mm
**Capacity:** 4973 cc
**Maximum power:** 326 bhp
**Transmission:** automatic
**Chassis:** unitary body/chassis
**Suspension:** independent with multi-links, coil springs front, MacPherson struts, anti-roll bar rear
**Brakes:** discs all round
**Bodywork:** two-door hardtop/convertible
**Maximum speed (approx):** 157 mph (253 kph)

# MERCER
**Trenton, USA**
**1910–1925**

Before the Mercer, there was the Roebling-Planche, built from 1906–09, which took its name from the Roebling family (builders of Brooklyn Bridge) and designer Etienne Planche; the Mercer was launched in 1910, and took its name from Mercer County, New Jersey, in which its factory was located.

The first Mercers were powered by T-head Beaver engines, the fastest 1910 model being a Speedster. During 1911, chief engineer Finlay Robertson Porter produced a roadgoing adaptation

## 1913 MERCER 35J RACEABOUT

**Engine:** in-line four-cylinder, side-valve
**Bore × stroke:** 111 mm × 127 mm
**Capacity:** 4926 cc
**Maximum power:** 50 bhp
**Transmission:** three-speed manual
**Chassis:** pressed steel channel
**Suspension:** non-independent with semi-elliptic leaf springs front and rear
**Brakes:** rear wheels and transmission
**Bodywork:** two-seater raceabout
**Maximum speed (approx):** 70 mph (113 kph)

**Mercedes-Benz 500SL**

of Mercer's Type 30-M racer, and called it the Type 35-R Raceabout. This stark two-seater was intended to be 'safely and consistently' driven at over 70 mph (113 kph). The 4926 cc 35-J was produced alongside less exciting Mercers, like the M and O, which had 5211 cc engines and – initially – four speeds against the Raceabout's three. By 1914, the M and O had gained electric lighting and starting, too, whereas the 35-J still had Prestolite acetylene lamps and a crank-start; but it had gained a fourth speed.

That year, Finlay Robertson

Porter resigned to build the FRP, but only a few examples of this vee-radiatored 170 bhp luxury car were ever produced.

Porter was succeeded as designer by Erik H. Delling, who produced the 80 bhp F-head 22/70 to succeed the 35-J; it boasted such effete adornments as a body with sides and a windscreen, left-hand drive, central gearshift and an optional hood.

In 1918, Mercer became part of the Hare's Motors Group, along with Locomobile and Crane-Simplex, and Delling was replaced

by A.C. Schultz; he designed the Series 4 and 5 Sportsters which even had electric starters (though they maintained magneto ignition instead of coil, along with a fixed-head engine).

A development of these powered by a 5.5-litre Rochester overhead-valve engine was the 'Car of Calibre's' sole product in the two years before production ended in 1925.

An attempt to revive the marque name in 1931 resulted only in two prototypes, powered by Continental straight-eights.

**Mercer Raceabout**

# MERCURY

**Detroit, USA**
**1938 –**

Ford originally planned to use the name Mercury for the 1932 19-Y 8 hp car, but finally announced the Ford-Mercury in 1938 as a 3.9-litre V8 model intended to plug the gap between Ford and Lincoln.

A four-door convertible was introduced for 1940 but did not prove particularly popular. The 1942 models were restyled, with a wide grille.

Post-war, the Mercury began to

move upmarket with the 'new-look' 1949 models, which had a new 4179 cc engine and coil-spring independent front suspension; automatic transmission was offered in 1951, power-assisted steering in 1953.

From 1952, the Mercury Monterey name first used on a vinyl-roofed hardtop of 1950 was applied to a new de luxe line.

In 1954, Mercury adopted Lincoln-style ball-joint independent front suspension. The company also launched the Sun Valley, a transparent-roofed hardtop. In 1954 came Mercury's first overhead-valve V8, a 4785 cc unit which would later appear in the Ford Thunderbird.

Mercurys of the 1956–59 era,

like the 1957 Turnpike Cruiser, were notably overstyled; the company's first car with other than a V8 power unit was the 1960 Comet compact, an enlarged Ford Falcon with the Ford 2360 cc short-stroke six, also available in the bigger Monterey.

Mercury acquired a 'muscle car' image with the 1965 320 bhp Comet Cyclone, while in 1967 came the Cougar coupé, with a 'waterfall' grille.

The 1969 Marquis Brougham had the same bodyshell as the Lincoln Continental, though with a 7030 cc engine instead of the Lincoln's 7538 cc power unit. By 1972, the Comet had become little more than an upmarket Ford Maverick; Mercury was also importing German-built Ford Capris, the 7538 cc Grand Marquis retained Lincoln styling, the four-cylinder Bobcat paralleled Ford's 1540 cc Pinto, and the Monarch became a de luxe version of the Ford Granada. Four-wheel disc brakes were fitted to the 1977 Marquis; the 1978 Zephyr, a 'brand new European-size compact', was just a rebadged Ford Fairmont.

The 1979 Mercury line-up consisted of the Detroit-built and engineered Mercury Capri which had replaced the European model, the Zephyr, Monarch, Cougar and

## 1957 MERCURY TURNPIKE CRUISER

**Engine:** V8, overhead-valve
**Bore × stroke:** 101.6 mm × 92.9 mm
**Capacity:** 6030 cc
**Maximum power:** 290 bhp
**Transmission:** three-speed manual or automatic
**Chassis:** separate X frame with box-section side members
**Suspension:** independent front with wishbones and coil springs. Live rear axle with semi-elliptic leaf springs
**Brakes:** drums all round
**Bodywork:** saloon
**Maximum speed (approx):** 115 mph (185 kph)

Marquis; the Grand Marquis had tinted glass and coach lamps.

A turbocharger was offered on the 1980 Mercury Zephyr, while a small 2+2 sports coupé, the Mercury LM7, was based on the Ford Escort. For 1981, the Mercury Capri was available with a 160 hp 5-litre V8; that year's Mercury Cougar was (with the Ford Granada) the first propane-fuelled car to be offered for sale by a major American manufacturer. The 1984 season saw a new aerodynamic compact model, the front-wheel-drive Mercury Topaz, while for 1985, the Lincoln-Mercury Division began bringing German-built Sierra XR4s into America under the Merkur brand name at the rate of 20,000 a year.

# METALLURGIQUE

**Marchienne-au-Pont, Belgium**
**1898–1927**

Long-established manufacturers of locomotives, rolling-stock and trams, La Société Anonyme La Métallurgique built prototypes of a car and a voiturette at their La Sambre works in 1898, and decided to proceed with the voiturette. But since none of their three works had the right machinery for car manufacture, a purpose-built car factory was opened at Marchienne-au-Pont in 1900.

The first production Metallurgiques appeared at the 1901 Paris Salon, in the shape of a rear-engined twin-cylinder voiturette with vis-à-vis coachwork and a front-engined light car with a twin-cylinder 726 cc power unit. Shortly afterwards, a 1452 cc four-cylinder model appeared.

In 1903 ex-Mercedes engineer Ernst Lehmann became chief designer of Métallurgique, producing a range of advanced Mercédès-like cars in 1905; they had pressed-steel chassis, high-tension ignition and the option of an electric lighting dynamo.

A 10-litre 60/80 hp sports model was added to the range in

1906; in 1907 a handsome vee-radiator became a distinctive feature of the marque – it first appeared on the large cars and was adopted for smaller models in 1908 – and the company took the name L'Auto-Métallurgique to differentiate it from the railway side of the business.

The last two-cylinder Métallurgique appeared in 1908 (in which year the first overhead-inlet-valve Métallurgique engines appeared); it was replaced in 1909 by a 12/14 hp four built under Métallurgique licence in Germany by the Bergmann electrical company, which had formerly built the dreadful Orient Express.

In 1910, Métallurgique entered the Prince Henry Tour with a 5.7-litre car which had one inlet and *four* exhaust valves and developed a remarkable 110 bhp, which propelled it at 95 mph (153 kph)….

Big four-cylinder luxury cars, like the 26/60, and sporting models like the 38/90 which echoed the company's successful involvement in motorsport were the hallmark of Métallurgique in Edwardian days; there was even a 7363 cc 40 hp sporting model which developed 95 bhp.

Thanks to Métallurgique's skill in concealing their jigs and spares from the occupying German forces during the Great War, the 5027 cc 26/60 continued from 1919 with the addition of Adex four-wheel-brakes; the 15/20 and 20/40 were also re-introduced, though the 15 hp was finally dropped in 1922, to be succeeded by a new 1970 cc 12 hp with pushrod overhead valves, designed by Paul Bastien (who had originally created the design in 1921 for the now-defunct SOMEA company); sales of this 75 mph (121 kph) sports model were disappointing. Impéria-Excelsior took over in 1927, stripped the factory of its machinery and sold the empty shell to Minerva.

When Métallurgique was closed down, Paul Bastien emigrated to America and joined the Stutz company.

**Mercury Turnpike Cruiser**

## 1913 METALLURGIQUE 38/90

**Engine:** in-line four-cylinder, side-valve
**Bore × stroke:** 125 mm × 150 mm
**Capacity:** 7363 cc
**Maximum power:** 90 bhp
**Transmission:** four-speed manual
**Chassis:** four-speed manual
**Suspension:** non-independent with semi-elliptic leaf springs
**Brakes:** rear wheels only
**Bodywork:** to order
**Maximum speed (approx):** 70 mph (113 kph)

**Metallurgique 30/90**

# MG

Oxford/Abingdon/Longbridge, England
1923 –

Nobody knows precisely when the first MG was built, though it's certain that it wasn't FC-7900, the Hotchkiss-engined car known as MG Number One, which was Cecil Kimber's first attempt at building a car solely for competition, and which didn't appear until 1924.

Two years earlier, Kimber, who was General Manager of the Morris Garages – hence MG – in Oxford, commissioned six Raworth-bodied, two-seater sports cars on Morris-Cowley chassis, the first of which was sold to a young man named J.O.A. Arkell in June that year for £300. However, the first MG to be

built in any numbers (about 400) was the 14/28 Super Sport, derived from the Morris-Oxford, which came with two or four seats and open or closed 'Salonette' bodywork.

This developed into the 14/40, then in late 1928 Kimber launched the 18/80, a new car built round the 2468 cc overhead-camshaft engine from an unsuccessful six-cylinder Morris which never reached full production.

But the car which really made the name of MG famous was the Midget, based on the 847 cc Morris Minor, which appeared in 1929, the year in which MG took over the former Pavlova leather works in Abingdon in order to expand production to meet the ever-growing demand for this cheap and reliable small sports car.

From this M-Type Midget, the racing 746 cc C-Type Midget was derived, capable of 90 mph (145 kph) in supercharged form; in 1932, the M-Type was developed into the J-Type with a twin-carburettor crossflow cylinder head.

In 1933, Kimber launched the K3 Magnette, with an 1100 cc supercharged six-cylinder power unit; in its first year, the Magnette won the team prize in the Mille Miglia and, driven by Tazio Nuvolari, won the Ulster Tourist Trophy at a speed that would not be beaten until 1951.

The competition aspect of MG peaked in the blown Q-Type and R-Type, the latter a 750 cc with Y-shaped backbone chassis and all-round independent suspension. Then, after 1935, the works ceased racing, and concentrated on the road-going MGs, like the TA Midget of 1935, the 2-litre SA and its derivative the 2.6-litre WA, and the 1½ litre VA.

It was a pre-war carryover, the TC (differing from the TA and TB of the 1930s mainly in the marginally greater width of the cockpit), which gave the MG international fame in the 1940s.

The 1250 cc Y-Type, available as saloon or tourer – there was also an export-only drophead coupé – appeared in 1947; its chassis with independent front suspension was adapted for the next Midget, the 1949 TD, which enhanced its image in America by winning the team prize in the Sebring 12-hour race in 1952. That same year, the Nuffield Group – of which MG was a component – amalgamated with the Austin Motor Company to form the British Motor Corporation.

TC was followed by TF for 1954, and the Y-Type gave way to the Wolseley-based ZA Magnette; both models gave the impression that the company was suffering from middle-age spread.

A new image came with the introduction of the sleek MGA in late 1955, though the twin-cam version of 1958 proved to be too temperamental for the average MG owner.

Following the formation of BMC, Austin-Healey production was shifted to join MG in Abingdon, and a new MG Midget was an offspring of the move; it was an Austin-Healey Sprite with a new and characterless front end.

In 1962 came the MGB sports car, which was still popular at the end of the 1970s; then, just after Abingdon had celebrated its Golden Jubilee, BL closed it down, and it seemed as though the MG marque had gone for good.

But in recent years, the MG name has appeared on hot-shoe versions of the Metro, Maestro and Montego, although rumours that MG were to reintroduce a two-seat sports car in the Midget tradition have been vehemently denied.

## MG Midget

It was the Wolseley heritage which made the MG Midget possible, for the overhead-cam engine had its origins in the Hispano-Suiza-derived Wolseley Viper aero engine of World War I.

Wolseley, however, had never fully realised the performance potential of the overhead-cam layout, but when Kimber acquired a prototype of the 847 cc power unit intended for the new Morris Minor, he realised its capabilities, and produced a neat lowered version of the Minor with a lightweight pointed-tail fabric body.

It was the first British small sports car to rival foreign marques like Salmson and Amilcar at a popular price; the huge sales increase it unleashed was the foundation for the lasting fame of MG.

## 1929 MG MIDGET

**Engine:** in-line four-cylinder, overhead-cam
**Bore × stroke:** 57 mm × 83 mm
**Capacity:** 847 cc
**Maximum power:** 20 bhp
**Transmission:** three-speed manual
**Chassis:** pressed steel channel
**Suspension:** non-independent with semi-elliptic leaf springs
**Brakes:** drums all round
**Bodywork:** two-seater sports
**Maximum speed (approx):** 60 mph (97 kph)

**MG Midget**

**MG TD**

# MG TD

The TD was introduced in 1949, a more comfortable car than its predecessor and featuring a more rounded body design. It was based in part on the MG Y-type four-seat tourer, with its chassis shortened and the rear side-members curved over the axle. This stiffer chassis was necessary because the TD had independent front suspension and rack and pinion steering.

The TD was powered by the same Morris-based 1250 cc engine that had been introduced on the pre-war TB, but because the TD was heavier than the TC its gear ratios were lower, maintaining its acceleration but giving it heavier fuel consumption.

A tuned TD Mk II was also offered, mainly for homologation purposes, and its modifications included a re-worked cylinder head, larger carburettors and valves, stronger valve springs, twin fuel pumps and a higher compression ratio. Three works Mk IIs won their class

in the 1950 TT race at Dundrod.

In all, 29,664 TDs were produced before the advent of more modern designs from other companies made the MG's already dated styling look positively antiquated. Thus the 1953 TF was only a short-term face-lift of the TD.

---

**1949 MG TD**

**Engine:** in-line four-cylinder, overhead-valve
**Bore × stroke:** 66.5 mm × 90 mm
**Capacity:** 1250 cc
**Maximum power:** 54 bhp
**Transmission:** four-speed manual
**Chassis:** pressed steel channel
**Suspension:** independent front with coil and wishbones, non-independent rear with semi-elliptic leaf springs
**Brakes:** drums all round
**Bodywork:** two-seater sports
**Maximum speed (approx):** 78 mph (126 kph)

---

# MGA

The MGA's life really began in 1951, when the company produced a one-off for photographer George Phillips to race at Le Mans, and although it didn't last for many of those 24 hours, it played a substantial part in inspiring the much-needed replacement for the T-series cars.

When the car was launched in 1955 it was again at Le Mans, and of the three cars entered the best result was 12th.

Based on a robust box-section chassis, the MGA had coil and wishbones at the front and a live rear axle, very similar to the TD and TF layout, and the first production cars were powered by the 1489 cc BMC B-series engine, fitted with twin carburettors.

In 1958 the short-lived twin-cam version appeared, with much-improved performance. In 1959 engine capacity of the pushrod engines was increased to 1588 cc to form the MGA 1600.

In 1961 engine capacity was further increased to 1622 cc, but the 1600 Mk II was the last of the line, and in 1962 production ceased after a total of 101,081 had been built.

---

**1961 MGA 1600**

**Engine:** in-line four-cylinder, overhead-valve
**Bore × stroke:** 74.4 mm × 88.9 mm
**Capacity:** 1588 cc
**Maximum power:** 80 bhp
**Transmission:** four-speed manual
**Chassis:** box-section steel
**Suspension:** independent front with wishbones and coil springs. Live rear axle with semi-elliptic leaf springs and lever-arm dampers
**Brakes:** discs front and drums rear
**Bodywork:** two-seater sports coupé or convertible
**Maximum speed (approx):** 100 mph (161 kph)

---

**MGA**

# A-Z OF THE CAR

**Miesse Type J**

## MGB

By 1962 100,000 MGAs had been produced and it was time for a change. The MGB appeared at the 1962 Motor Show and although it looked heavier and bulkier than the sleek MGA it was actually shorter. Mechanically it broke no new ground, with the same live axle on semi-elliptic leaf springs. The original B was powered by a 1798 cc four-cylinder producing 95 bhp at 5400 rpm. That gave it a top speed of 105 mph (169 kph) with the ability to reach 60 mph (96 kph) in a respectable 12.2 seconds.

In 1965 the MGB GT appeared;

### 1973 MGB GT V8

**Engine:** V8, overhead-valve
**Bore × stroke:** 88.9 mm × 71 mm
**Capacity:** 3528 cc
**Maximum power:** 137 bhp
**Chassis:** integral
**Suspension:** independent front with wishbones and coil springs. Live rear axle with semi-elliptic leaf springs. Lever-arm dampers all round
**Brakes:** discs front and drums rear
**Bodywork:** two-door 2+2 coupé
**Maximum speed (approx):** 124 mph (199 kph)

its greater weight was compensated for by better aerodynamics. Both the roadster and coupé proved enduringly successful but the car suffered a lack of development over the years which led to Ken Costello's V8 conversions proving popular. That in turn led to MG's own V8 with a 137 bhp version of Rover's V8, which unfortunately never sold in the volumes the company wished. By the mid-'70s increasingly strict Federal regulations in the USA led to all MGBs (including those for the home market) being raised and equipped with large and unattractive black bumpers. Corporate neglect of the MGB continued until its demise in 1980 when it was essentially the same car as it had been 18 years before.

## MIESSE

**Brussels, Belgium
1896–1926**

Jules Miesse built his first experimental steam car in 1896, a design strongly influenced by the work of Leon Serpollet. His prototype, 'La Torpille', had a flash boiler feeding a three-cylinder engine mounted transversely in an armoured wood chassis, and to prepare for production (which didn't begin until 1900), Jules Miesse entered this prototype in

competition, with some success.

By 1902 the Miesse range consisted of three-cylinder steamers of 6 hp and 10 hp, still with flash boilers, transverse engines and armoured wood chassis. In that same year a subsidiary company was established in England to promote the sales of the Miesse steamers, and by the beginning of 1903, licence production had started in Wolverhampton, where the Miesse steamers were built as the Turner-Miesse in both 6 hp and 10 hp forms. Turner-Miesse steamers continued to be built until 1913, long after the Belgian company had abandoned steam altogether in favour of petrol.

In fact the last Belgian Miesse steamers were four-cylinder 20 hp trucks built during 1906 for the Congo Free State – where Miesse engines also powered river steamers – to the designs of Robert Goldschmidt.

Miesse had begun experiments with petrol cars in 1900, and began production of internal-combustion-engined vehicles around 1903. At the January 1904 Brussels Salon, Miesse exhibited a monstrous 40/50 hp car, designed by Goldschmidt, which dispensed with a gearbox, control being purely by the throttle and by slipping the clutch. When Miesse abandoned this ludicrous design it

### 1920 MIESSE TYPE J

**Engine:** in-line overhead-cam straight-eight
**Bore × stroke:** 69 mm × 130 mm
**Capacity:** 3889 cc
**Maximum power:** 80 bhp
**Transmission:** three-speed manual
**Chassis:** pressed steel channel
**Suspension:** non-independent, with semi-elliptic leaf springs front and rear
**Brakes:** rear-wheel drums
**Bodywork:** to order
**Maximum speed (approx):** 75 mph (121 kph)

was taken up by the Baudouin company, who attempted to market it under the name Direct during 1904–5.

The 1907 Miesse range consisted of a 3670 cc, four-cylinder, 24 hp model and a 5505 cc, 35 hp monobloc six, both with side valves and three-speed transmissions.

In 1908, Jules Miesse built an unorthodox 100 hp aero engine for the unsuccessful flapping-wing ornithopter of Adhemar de la Hault; it had two rows of star-formation four-cylinder engines with a total swept volume of 13,804 cc weighing a total of only 240 lb (109 kg).

A 2213 cc four-cylinder 14/16 hp machine, the Type D, was added to the range in 1908, followed in 1911 by the 2816 cc, L-head, 15 hp model and a valveless 20 hp variant, combining piston and slide-valves in a system invented by Jules Miesse.

In 1913 Miesse adopted an elegant vee-radiator and a badge incorporating the coat of arms of Brussels.

After the Great War an overhead-camshaft, 1944 cc four was the mainstay of Miesse production, which recommenced in 1920; the company was also one of the first in the world to offer a production straight-eight, the overhead-camshaft, 3889 cc, straight-eight Type J.

In 1923, Miesse added a 2917 cc six to the range, with the

**MGB GT V8**

**Miller 122 Racer**

same cylinder dimensions as those of the eight, as well as the 1357 cc Type K light six. Two years later, front wheel brakes were available, and the swept volume of the straight-eight was increased to 4600 cc.

Private car construction ceased in 1927, but Miesse continued to build commercial vehicles until 1972; the company finally ceased activity in 1974.

## MILLER

**Los Angeles, USA
1915–1932**

Harry Armenius Miller of Los Angeles was best known for his racing cars – particularly the advanced front-wheel-drive cars he built from 1924 to 1930 – and the overhead-camshaft racing engines which he built from 1915 (his overhead-cam straight-eight introduced in 1923 founded a dynasty which dominated the Indianapolis 500 until the mid-1960s). However, Miller also produced extremely advanced road cars, starting with the V8 Chancellor-Miller of 1928, built as 'the most advanced and perfect touring car that the world has ever known'.

Commissioned by Philip Chanceller, the Chancellor-Miller had an aluminium body designed by Gerald Kirchoff, and its chassis and engine were designed by Leo Goossen, aided by C.W. Van Ranst (who had recently designed the front-wheel-driven L-29 Cord).

When racing regulations

### 1928 MILLER 91
**Engine:** Straight-eight, twin-overhead-cam, supercharged
**Bore × stroke:** 55.54 mm × 76.2 mm
**Capacity:** 1478 cc
**Maximum power:** 154 bhp
**Transmission:** hypoid-bevel front-wheel drive, four-speed
**Chassis:** pressed steel channel
**Suspension:** non-independent, with de Dion axle front, with superimposed quarter-elliptic leaf springs, dead axle rear with semi-elliptic leaf springs
**Brakes:** drums all round
**Bodywork:** speedster
**Maximum speed (approx):** 134 mph (216 kph)

changed in 1930, Miller turned to aviation.

Two further Miller road cars followed in 1930–32, the second a four-wheel-driven 400 bhp speedster, powered by a twin-overhead-camshaft, 5096 cc, V16, built at a reputed cost of $35,000.

## MINERVA

**Antwerp, Belgium
1904–1939**

Dutch-born cycle maker Sylvain de Jong showed his first experimental car at the Antwerp Cycle & Automobile Show in 1899, but this Panhard-like prototype doesn't appear ever to have been offered for sale.

Between 1899 and 1907, Minerva was Belgium's leading

maker of motorcycles and power units to convert pedal cycles into light motorcycles; over 25,000 of the Minerva power units were built.

The first production Minerva cars appeared in 1902, designed by the engineer Museur; however, demand for the company's two-wheelers prevented them from being put into full-scale production until 1904, when a new factory was erected. The range consisted of two-, three- and four-cylinder cars of 1463 cc, 2195 cc and 2926 cc. The range was completed at the end of 1904 by a basic single-cylinder model, the 6336 cc Minervette, which sold for only £106 in England, where a subsidiary company headed by David Citroën, a cousin of André

Citroën, had been formed in 1900.

Minerva made its name with big four-cylinder cars, including models of 3.8, 5.9 and 6.2 litres; then at the London Motor Show of 1908 the company exhibited a new model with a four-cylinder Knight sleeve-valve engine, the first marque in mainland Europe to adopt the

'Silent' Knight power unit.

The 1909 range still included poppet-valve fours of 15, 18 and 25 hp, plus a 40 hp six alongside the new sleeve-valve 38 hp, but for 1912 only sleeve-valve cars were listed. By this time Minerva had become Belgium's biggest car manufacturer, employing some 1600 workers and producing nearly 3000 cars a year.

The sleeve-valve Minervas even went racing, and three 3.3-litre Minervas came second, third and fifth in the 1914 Isle of Man TT.

The 38 hp, dual-ignition, 6.3-litre four, favoured by King Albert of the Belgians, was followed by 2.3 and 4.25-litre models. By 1914, and the outbreak of war, the 38 hp Minerva had grown to 7.4 litres, and there was also a 2.1-litre 14 hp.

The first new post-war Minerva was the NN 20 hp four of 1919, joined in 1921 by a 30 hp, 5.3-litre six, which acquired four-wheel brakes in 1923. The 15 hp Minerva of 1923 had a four-cylinder, sleeve-valve engine of 2 litres and central gear-change; Minerva was then producing 2500 cars a year, mostly luxury models of which some 50 per cent were exported to England. In 1925 a new 16 hp model of 2251 cc was added to the range, while the 5344 cc, 30 hp six was succeeded by the 32/34 hp Type AK and its short-chassis sporting derivative, Type AKS, in 1928.

About this time, Minerva experimented with engines with Bournonville rotary valves, but the 2433 cc four and 1991 cc six never reached the production stage.

In 1930 Minerva launched the Type AL straight-eight of 6616 cc,

**Minerva 30 HP**

### 1928 MINERVA TYPE AKS

**Engine:** in-line six-cylinder, sleeve-valve
**Bore × stroke:** 95 mm × 140 mm
**Capacity:** 5954 cc
**Maximum power:** 150 bhp
**Transmission:** four-speed manual
**Chassis:** pressed steel channel
**Suspension:** non-independent, with semi-elliptic leaf springs front and cantilever leaf springs rear
**Brakes:** drums all round, servo-assisted
**Bodywork:** to order
**Maximum speed (approx):** 93 mph (150 kph)

but the Depression was already making savage inroads into the luxury car market and an attempt to counter imports of American luxury cars with the 3958 cc straight-eight Type AP (or M-8), launched in December 1929 and using mass-produced American transmission and steering, failed to halt Minerva's gradual decline.

Minerva was acquired by Mathieu van Roggen's Imperia group in 1936, and thereafter Minerva cars were only built in limited numbers from the stock of spare parts. An attempt to revive the marque in 1937 with the TAM 18, a front-wheel-drive model with automatic transmission and modified Ford V8 engine, failed to pass the prototype stage, and the company known as the 'Goddess of Automobiles', built its last cars in 1938. However, the company survived into the mid-1950s with the construction of Land-Rovers under licence. An attempt to revive car production in 1953 with the Cemsa-Caproni, designed by Fessia, came to nothing, though the Antwerp company did build some Rovers and Armstrong-Siddeleys.

# MITSUBISHI

**Kobe, Tokyo, Japan**
**1917—**

The first Mitsubishi, the Model A, was a Fiat copy, and as it was produced at a time when the Japanese populace was quite unused to cars, only about 20 were sold. Development continued until 1921, and thereafter the factory concentrated on trucks and buses. During World War II the factory turned to tank manufacture.

It took the company until 1959 to recover from the devastation of the war, and its first model was the air-cooled twin-cylinder 500, a small four-seat saloon.

By the mid-1960s the range included the 356 cc Minica saloon, with two-stroke engine, and the Colt saloons, the smallest using a 41 bhp two-stroke.

In the '70s Mitsubishi introduced larger pushrod 1088 cc and 1189 cc engines into the range, as well as a new range of Colt Galants. These latter had Dodge badges for the American market after Chrysler bought into

Mitsubishi. Other models included a top-of-the-range 1.6-litre 126 bhp twin-cam, and there were overhead-cam engines for the Debonair and Minica.

In 1974 the Lancer was announced, in 1.2, 1.4 and 1.6-litre forms. In '77 the Debonair was only available with automatic transmission, and the Colt range was extended from the smaller Colt Lancer and Celeste to the Sigma

### 1984 MITSUBISHI STARION TURBO

**Engine:** in-line four-cylinder, overhead-cam
**Bore × stroke:** 85 mm × 88 mm
**Capacity:** 1997 cc
**Maximum power:** 170 bhp
**Transmission:** five-speed manual
**Chassis:** integral
**Suspension:** independent with MacPherson struts and anti-roll bar
**Brakes:** discs all round
**Bodywork:** two-door coupé
**Maximum speed (approx):** 135 mph (217 kph)

and Lambda, all with overhead-cam engines of up to 2 litres.

In '78 the Sapporo was announced, with coil suspension all round, and in the same year the front-wheel-drive Mirage was announced, with transverse engine, MacPherson-strut front suspension and a dual-range eight-speed gearbox.

In 1980 the Sigmas and Sapporos were offered with 1.8, 2 and 2.6-litre engines, and the option of a 2.3-litre diesel, the latter available with a turbocharger.

The following year saw the range further extended. The 1.6-litre Minica and Mirages were made available with automatic transmission, more power was given to the Lancer and Celeste, and these variations on the Galant, Sapporo and Eterna models — top of the range was the 2.6-litre coupé with petrol injection, power steering and automatic transmission.

By the mid 1980s Mitsubishi's cars had improved dramatically in all respects and cars like the Starion Turbo and the Galant Turbo offered realistic opposition to the best of their European opposition.

**Mitsubishi Starion 2000 Turbo**

## 1969 MONICA

**Engine:** V8, overhead-valve
**Bore × stroke:** 102.5 mm × 84 mm
**Capacity:** 5572 cc
**Maximum power:** 290 bhp
**Transmission:** five-speed manual, three-speed automatic
**Chassis:** square-tube space-frame with sheet steel reinforcements
**Suspension:** all-independent, with coils and wishbones, front, de Dion axle rear
**Brakes:** discs all round
**Bodywork:** four-door coupé
**Maximum speed (approx):** 150 mph (240 kph)

Monica

# MONICA

**Balbigny, France**
**1969–76**

This desirable sporting car, backed by railway-rolling-stock manufacturer Jean Tastevin and designed by Englishman Chris Lawrence, never made full-scale production. Originally conceived as a Triumph-powered two-seat sports car, the Monica evolved into a prestigious four/five-seater whose elegant steel body was mounted on a very strong semi-space-frame chassis. The original plan was to use the double-overhead-cam 3-litre Martin V8 engine, whose origins lay in motor racing, but reliability problems meant that the Monica was eventually powered by a 5.6-litre Chrysler V8, which gave a top speed of over 140 mph (225 kph) and a 0-60 mph (97 kph) time of 7.7 seconds.

Some 30-35 Monicas were ultimately made (though 25 of them were prototypes) before the pilot production run ceased.

# MONTEVERDI

**Basle, Switzerland**
**1967–**

Garage owner Peter Monteverdi had already built his own racing cars under the MBM name before beginning production of the Chrysler V8-engined 375S luxury model and its sporting 400SS derivative in 1967. In 1968 the range was increased by the introduction of the long-wheelbase 375L, a model which was mechanically similar to the two-seaters, but with two rear seats.

By 1971 sales were good enough to inspire Monteverdi to launch the mid-engined Hai ('Shark') 450SS, but the following year he brought out a short-lived luxury GT called the 375/4 and the Hai 450 GTS. The former, 17 feet (204 cm) long and weighing two tons, was nevertheless capable of 140 mph (225 kph). The Hai had a top speed of 160 mph (257 kph).

Monteverdi managed to survive the oil crisis, launching the Palm

Beach convertible (derived from the 375 coupé) in 1975 and the Sierra saloon and cabriolet in 1977. There was also a Range-Rover-like four-wheel-drive vehicle called the Sahara.

Latest model of this limited-production marque is the Tiara luxury limousine, built around Mercedes-Benz running gear.

## 1967 MONTEVERDI 375L

**Engine:** V8, overhead-valve
**Bore × stroke:** 109.7 mm × 95.2 mm
**Capacity:** 7211 cc
**Maximum power:** 375 bhp
**Transmission:** four-speed manual
**Chassis:** tubular
**Suspension:** all-independent, with coils and wishbones front, de Dion axle and coil springs rear
**Brakes:** discs all round
**Bodywork:** two-door coupé
**Maximum speed (approx):** 140 mph (225 kph)

# MOON

**St Louis, USA**
**1905-1931**

Former Peerless designer Louis P. Mooers created the first cars offered by Scots-born Joseph W. Moon's St Louis-based buggy factory. Since Mooers had designed some formidable racing cars while with Peerless, the Model A Moon bore no signs of its horse-buggy inheritance: instead, it was a large, well-made car powered by a proprietary 30/35 hp Rutenber four-cylinder engine. By 1912, Moon listed two four-cylinder models, the 30 and 40, of 5211 cc and 5806 cc, joined the following year by a 5700 cc six. The 1914 Moons were distinguished by a streamlined coachwork of smart appearance.

Continental-built sixes of 3.6 and 5 litres were offered in 1916, and the marque was fitted with an imitation Rolls-Royce radiator by 1920.

The 1922 Moons had side-

Monteverdi 375L

valves instead of overhead valves, and the odd combination of quarter-elliptic front springs and three-quarter elliptics at the rear. For 1924, Moon offered four-wheel Lockheed hydraulic band brakes plus detachable disc wheels with detachable rims.

The 1928 Moon was powered by a 4.4-litre straight-eight, previously used in the marque's defunct alter ego, Diana. In 1929 the eight acquired a double-dropped chassis and four-speed transmission to become the Windsor. There was a handsome coupé model known as the 'Windsor White Prince' in honour of Britain's popular Prince of Wales.

In the same year Moon became part of the New Era Motors group, and built the production run of the bizarre front-wheel-drive Ruxtons – estimates vary between 52 and 500 cars – before being dragged down by the collapse of New Era Motors in 1931.

# MORGAN

**Malvern Link, England
1910–**

Malvern motor agent H.F.S. Morgan built his prototype Morgan three-wheeler in the workshops of Malvern College in 1908–09, while recovering from a motorcycle accident. Assisted by Mr Stephenson-Peach, the engineering master, Morgan produced a design the general layout of which remained in production until 1950, the little cyclecar having a tubular chassis frame and sliding-pillar independent front suspension (which is basically the same design as that used on today's Morgans).

Production of Morgan three-wheelers began in 1910; power was provided by an air-cooled, vee-twin motorcycle engine, mounted

out in the open at the front of the car, while the chain drive transmission used sprockets of different sizes engaged by dog clutches for the two forward ratios (reverse was considered an unnecessary luxury until 1930).

Boosted by sporting successes like victory in the 1913 Cyclecar Grand Prix – which gave rise to the popular Grand Prix sports model – the Morgan was soon established as the most successful of all the cyclecars, and the design continued with minimal change after World War I, though a lowered chassis was adopted on the Super Sports Morgan of 1928. The air- or water-cooled vee-twin power units used by Morgan were mainly provided

**Moon 20HP**

---

### 1921 MOON 6-48

**Engine:** in-line six cylinder, side-valve
**Bore × stroke:** 82.6 mm × 108 mm
**Capacity:** 3669 cc
**Maximum power:** 48 bhp
**Transmission:** three-speed manual
**Chassis:** pressed steel channel
**Suspension:** non-independent, with semi-elliptic leaf springs front and rear
**Brakes:** rear-wheel drums
**Bodywork:** roadster, tourer, coupé, sedan
**Maximum speed (approx):** 60 mph (97 kph)

---

by JAP or Blackburne, though more obscure marques such as British Vulpine, Blumfield and Precision were also seen, and normal wear during the 1930s, when a three-speed and reverse transmission and detachable wheels at last made their appearance, was the Matchless vee-twin engine.

A refinement of the Morgan theme finally came in 1933 with the option of a 933 cc four-cylinder Ford 8 engine.

A four-wheeled Morgan, the 4/ 4 appeared in 1935, powered by an 1122 cc overhead inlet/side exhaust Coventry-Climax four-cylinder engine. When supplies of this engine dried up in 1938, Morgan adopted the 1.3-litre overhead-valve Standard engine, which remained the standard fitting until 1950, when they replaced it with the 2088 cc wet-liner Standard Vanguard engine; however, the Plus Four of 1955 used the livelier TR engine.

A year later the Series 2 4/4 appeared, powered by the well-proven side-valve 1172 cc Ford engine which had been used in the three-wheelers until their demise in 1952. The sidevalve Ford unit was followed by Dagenham's new overhead-valve 105E engine introduced in 1959; the later Series V 4/4 used the 1498 cc Ford power unit and current 4/4s offer the alternative of the 1600 cc Ford XR3 or the Fiat Mirafiori twin-cam.

The Plus-Four-Plus of 1964 broke away from Morgan's traditional styling, but did not appeal to Morgan's traditional clientele. Only 50 examples of this glassfibre coupé were built.

Since 1968, Morgan have offered the Plus Eight, fitted with a 3.5-litre V8 Rover power unit.

## Morgan Aero

Successor to the Grand Prix Morgan, the Aero Morgan first appeared in 1919, deriving its name from the twin aeroscreens fitted instead of a full windscreen; an improved model with a vee-deflector behind the radiator and a streamline tail appeared in 1920.

With a weight in the region of 448 lb (985 kg), and an engine producing more than 40 bhp, the Aero was capable of quite dramatic performance, and in terms of acceleration was a match for any car.

The Olympia Show Aero Morgan of 1922 had a nickel-plated brass body and boa-constrictor horn; Aero Morgans acquired front wheel brakes as an optional extra (at a cost of £4) a year later.

Though the M-type dropped chassis appeared in 1927, and was adopted on the new Super Sports the following year, the Aero continued in production, the last significant change in its specification being the adoption of a new, detachable, rear chassis and bevel box with underslung springs and internal-expanding rear brake.

---

### 1920 MORGAN AERO

**Engine:** Vee-twin, overhead-valve
**Bore × stroke:** 85.7 mm × 95 mm
**Capacity:** 1096 cc
**Maximum power:** 45 bhp
**Transmission:** two-speed chain and dog clutch
**Chassis:** tubular steel
**Suspension:** independent front with sliding pillar. Quarter-elliptic rear fork with single wheel
**Brakes:** drums
**Bodywork:** two-seater sports
**Maximum speed (approx):** 75 mph (120 kph)

---

**Morgan Aero**

# Morgan Plus 8

Launched at the end of 1968, the Morgan Plus 8 continued the 1930s styling that Morgan had successfully retained, with only minor concessions to modernity, like the adoption of faired-in headlamps when the supply of free-standing headlamp shells dried up.

But under the bonnet, instead of the traditional four-in-line power unit, the Plus 8 had the 3.5-litre engine from the new Rover 3500, which provided tremendous performance, only limited by the car's quaint aerodynamics.

Fitted with alloy wheels, the Plus 8 has continued in production ever since; the options currently available include light alloy bodywork and leather upholstery.

An even faster version, the Vitesse appeared in 1985 with a fuel-injected version of the V8. It was capable of reaching 60 mph in 6.3 seconds.

Production of all Morgans remains modest, though the waiting list of several years per car proves that the appeal of this time-warped sports car built in the old style remains undiminished.

---

## 1985 MORGAN PLUS 8 VITESSE

**Engine:** V8, overhead-valve
**Bore × stroke:** 89 mm × 71 mm
**Capacity:** 3528 cc
**Maximum power:** 190 bhp
**Transmission:** five-speed manual
**Chassis:** Z-section ladder frame
**Suspension:** independent front with sliding pillars. Live rear axle with semi-elliptic leaf springs
**Brakes:** discs front and drums rear
**Bodywork:** two-seater sports
**Maximum speed (approx):** 130 mph (209 kph)

---

# MORRIS

**Oxford, England**
**1913–**

Oxford cycle and motor agent William Morris went into car production with the two-seater Morris Oxford in 1913. The little car cost £180, and was powered by a 1017 cc White & Poppe engine in unit with the gearbox. With front and rear axles by Wrigley, wheels by Sankey and bodywork by Raworth of Oxford, the Morris-Oxford was one of the better-assembled cars of the period.

The Oxford was supplemented in 1915 by the Morris-Cowley, with a 1496 cc engine and gearbox supplied by the Continental Motors Company of Detroit, thus avoiding the supply problems experienced by other British manufacturers, who had ceased car production to concentrate on war work; in 1916, however, the import of American cars and parts was banned, save for components used to make commercial vehicles. Naturally, Morris introduced a van version of the Cowley.

Production began again in earnest after the Armistice; Continental had stopped production of the Red Seal engine, so copies of the American engine were manufactured by Hotchkiss of Coventry. The addition of a cork clutch running in oil in the Coventry-built model was one of the few alterations that Morris made to the engine design.

The affectionate Bullnose nickname was inspired by the handsome rounded radiator of the Morris cars. After the war, the Oxford became a de luxe version of the Cowley, but Morris was threatened by the slump in sales that followed the post-war boom in 1920. With impeccable timing, Morris emulated Ford in 1921 with a sensational series of price cuts that dramatically boosted the flagging sales and set the Oxford and Cowley en route to becoming the best-selling British cars of the decade.

In 1923, an 1802 cc engine was offered as an option in the Oxford, and was standardised from 1924. The Oxford and Cowley Bullnoses remained in production until 1926,

**Morgan Plus 8 Vitesse**

though their peak production year was 1925; then 54,151 cars had been built, representing 41 per cent of new car production in Britain. For 1927, the Bullnose radiator was supplanted by the less inspiring – though undoubtedly more efficient – Flatnose cooler. An attempt to move into the export market with the 2513 cc four-cylinder Empire Oxford failed, despite ingenious features like a wide-track axle which could be fitted with flanged wheels to run on standard-gauge railways.

Morris also attempted to establish a foothold in the French

market with a takeover of the Leon Bollée factory at Le Mans, but the Morris Leon Bollée (which was entirely different from the home product) did not sell well, and the MLB factory was sold in 1931.

Morris, who had made an unsuccessful attempt to introduce a six-cylinder in 1921–22, finally adopted this engine configuration in 1928 with a 2.5-litre car, whose overhead camshaft was a reminder that Wolseley, who had adopted this engine layout after wartime experience with building Hispano-Suiza aero engines, had been bought by Morris the previous year. Morris entered the small-car market in 1929 with the 847 cc Minor, which had an overhead-camshaft engine, though this unit, successfully used in the MG Midget, was dropped from the Minor in 1931 and replaced by a

simple side-valve unit. The two-seater side-valve Minor was priced at £100, though sales proved disappointing.

Lockheed hydraulic brakes were first used on Morris cars in 1930 with the six-cylinder range; during the next four years the whole range acquired them.

Morris did not do too well during the early 1930s, despite the launch in 1933 of the 1.3-litre 10/4, but the company's fortunes were revived in 1935 – a season in which Morris offered no fewer than 32 different models – when Morris launched his 918 cc Series I Eight, whose styling was unashamedly cribbed from that of the successful Ford Model Y. The Series I Eight remained in production until 1938, by which time 250,000 had been built, making it the best-selling British car of the 1930s.

For the 1939 season, the Series I Eight was succeeded by the Series E Eight, which boasted entirely new bodywork and faired-in headlamps. Alongside the side-valve Eight, Morris offered four other Series II models, ranging from the Ten to the 3.5-litre 25, and all fitted with overhead-valve engines. The year 1939 also saw Morris's first venture into integral construction with the series M 1141 cc Ten, which continued to be built in India after the war.

Immediately after the war, Morris resumed production of the Eight and Ten; the first new model appeared in late 1948, in the significant form of the Issigonis-designed Minor. Initially powered by the 919 cc engine of the Series E Eight, the Minor had torsion bar independent front suspension, rack-and-pinion steering and 14-inch road wheels. The overhead-valve 803 cc engine from the Austin A30 replaced the Morris unit in 1953 and the engine capacity was progressively increased thereafter to 1098 cc. The Morris Minor remained in production until

1971 and was the first British car to sell over a million. The side-valve 1476 cc Morris Oxford and overhead-camshaft 2.2-litre Series MS Six appeared at the same time as the Minor, and had similarly styled bodywork.

The inevitable result of the creation of the British Motor Corporation in 1952 by the merging of Austin and Morris was rationalisation, and thus the Cowley and Oxford were fitted with overhead-valve Austin-built engines in 1954. The differences between the Cowley and Longbridge products were further blurred by the appearance of the Farina-bodied 1.5-litre saloon in 1959, for now the only difference between Austin and Morris was the badge and the body colours.

Though the sensational Issigonis-designed front-wheel-drive 848 cc Mini of the same year was originally sold as the Morris Mini-Minor, and its big sister, the best-selling 1100 of 1963, first appeared as a Morris, both models were later also sold under the Austin banner. But Austin was ahead in the badge-engineering stakes, the larger Austin 1800 appearing in 1965, some eighteen months earlier than the Morris equivalent, which appeared in 1966.

In 1968, BMC was taken over by Leyland Motors to form British Leyland. The new corporation announced the boringly conventional Marina in 1971 – front-engined and rear-wheel driven, it was available in 1.3 and 1.8-litre form. A year later came the front-wheel-drive 2200 model, and by 1979 the Morris range simply consisted of 14 variations on the Marina theme.

Two years later, the Marina was supplanted by the restyled Ital range, but this characterless car offered few attractions to the customer, and the Morris name was discontinued in 1983.

## Morris Cowley

Though the Morris-Oxford had proved popular, it was very definitely only a two-seater, so William Morris decided to produce a low-cost four-seater. The modest prices asked by American component makers led him to adopt the Detroit-built Continental Red Seal engine which its makers were delighted to supply since, at 1496 cc, it had proved too small for the US market. It cost just £18, against £50 for the White & Poppe unit of the Morris Oxford.

Axles and steering gear for a production run of 3000 cars were also ordered from Detroit suppliers, and, despite the outbreak of war in August 1914, the first of the new Morris-Cowleys was shown to the British press in April 1915, and production began in September of that year. Orthodox in appearance, its most notable features were the permanently engaged Dynamotor, which made starting a silent operation, and the three-speed gearbox, renowned for its shrieks and moans.

However, German submarine action sent half the 3000 engines ordered for the Morris-Cowley to the bottom of the Atlantic and this, coupled with the fact that the 1915 War Budget of Reginald McKenna added 33.3 per cent tax to imported non-essentials like private motorcars and their components, restricted production of the Continental Cowley to 1450 cars. And in 1919, Continental announced that, due to low demand, they were stopping production of the Red Seal engine. So the Coventry branch of the Hotchkiss armament works, which needed work, began to build an Anglicised version of the Red Seal.

In the post-war Morris strategy, the Cowley comprised the low-priced model range, with the Oxford a de luxe range on the same chassis. Sales of the Hotchkiss Cowley were good at first, but the post-war slump hit Morris hard, and by February 1921 the factory was full of unsold motorcars. So Morris emulated Henry Ford, and cut prices

**Morris Cowley**

<table>
<tr><td colspan="2">

**1923 MORRIS COWLEY**

**Engine:** in-line four-cylinder, side-valve
**Bore × stroke:** 69.5 mm × 102 mm
**Capacity:** 1548 cc
**Maximum power:** 26 bhp
**Transmission:** three-speed manual
**Chassis:** pressed steel channel
**Suspension:** non-independent with semi-elliptic leaf springs front and three-quarter elliptics rear
**Brakes:** drums on rear only
**Bodywork:** two-seater, four-seater, coupé, sports, saloon
**Maximum speed (approx):** 50 mph (80 kph)
</td></tr>
</table>

dramatically; their sales soared, from 1932 cars in 1920 to 3077 in 1921 and 6937 in 1922, boosted by the fact that at a rated horsepower of 11.9, the Cowley attracted half the road tax of its rival, the 22 hp Model T Ford.

In 1923 sales of 20,024 saw Morris overtake Ford to become the biggest car manufacturer in Britain.

## Morris Eight

The Morris Eight, launched in September 1934, was unashamedly inspired by the styling of the Model Y Ford, though the Morris had the advantage over the Dagenham product of semi-elliptic suspension and hydraulic brakes. Other distinctive features were two-tone paintwork and the option of a tourer version, which was only available on the Model Y chassis from specialist coachbuilders.

As a result, it sold well, even though its price was higher than that of the Ford, and 10,000 Morris Eights were sold in the first four months, 100,000 by July 1936, and some 250,000 by late 1938.

The first redesign of the Eight came in July 1935 with the Series II model; Series III was adopted for 1938, with overhead-valve engines, painted radiator shells and single-colour bodywork.

Then, in October 1938 the Series E was unveiled, mechanically similar, apart from a four-speed transmission, but completely restyled, with such advanced features as headlamps in the wings and an alligator bonnet. It survived until late 1948 when it was swept away by the Issigonis-designed Morris Minor.

**Morris Eight**

## Morris Minor

It was in late 1944 that Alex Issigonis began design studies for a post-war small car. Initially he planned to power it with a new side-valve flat-four power unit driving the front wheels, but the inevitable lack of finance meant that the old 919 cc engine of the series E and rear wheel drive had to be used. Torsion bar independent front suspension gave an excellent ride, while the full-width styling was inspired by contemporary American practice: 'It may be said to be something of a triumph in good looks on a small

chassis,' commented The Autocar.

There were changes: rumours that Europe was to follow America's minimum-height requirement for headlights meant that the lamps were moved from the grille to the leading edge of the wings, the split windscreen was replaced by curved glass, and in mid-1952, following the Morris-Austin merger, the side-valve engine was replaced by the smaller but more efficient overhead-valve Austin A30 unit of 803 cc. In 1957 a 948 cc overhead-valve engine was installed to create the Minor 1000, and the ultimate engine size when production ended in

1971, after well over 1.5 million Minors had been built, was 1098 cc.

The popularity of the Minor has proved to be so enduring that in the 1980s a number of garages came into being solely to minister to Minors, to repairing, restoring and rebuilding this individual, long-lived and extremely reliable light car.

### 1934 MORRIS EIGHT

**Engine:** in-line four-cylinder, side-valve
**Bore × stroke:** 57 mm × 90 mm
**Capacity:** 919 cc
**Maximum power:** 23.5 bhp
**Transmission:** three-speed manual
**Chassis:** double box section steel
**Suspension:** non-independent with semi-elliptic leaf springs
**Brakes:** drums all round
**Bodywork:** two-seater, four-seater, saloon
**Maximum speed (approx):** 60 mph (97 kph)

### 1948 MORRIS MINOR

**Engine:** in-line four-cylinder, side-valve
**Bore × stroke:** 57 mm × 90 mm
**Capacity:** 919 cc
**Maximum power:** 29.5 bhp
**Transmission:** four-speed manual
**Chassis:** integral
**Suspension:** independent front with wishbones and torsion bars. Live rear axle with semi-elliptic leaf springs
**Brakes:** drums all round
**Bodywork:** saloon or tourer
**Maximum speed (approx):** 62 mph (100 kph)

**Morris Minor**

*Mors Paris-Vienna Racer*

# MORS

**Paris, France
1889, 1895–1956**

Emile Mors was one of France's leading electrical engineers who dabbled in steam car construction in the late 1880s, building the first steamer with an oil-fired boiler. After seven or eight Mors steamers had been built, Mors devoted himself to the construction of light petrol-powered railway trolleys before turning in 1895 to the manufacture of air-cooled V4 cars with water-cooled cylinder heads and flexible engine mountings. By 1898, production was running at the level of 200 cars a year, flat-twin power units were used on the Petit Duc Mors that year, and the company gained tremendous publicity from its involvement in motor sport.

By 1902, most Mors engines were water-cooled, with capacities ranging from 2.3 to 8 litres and chain drive had become the norm. But the great days of Mors in competition drew to an end in the years following the marque's famous victory in the 1903 Paris–Madrid race.

In 1908, Mors introduced a monstrous four-cylinder 100 hp of 12,831 cc, but the company was in deep financial crisis, and André Citroën was called in to save the day. Citroën became a director,

introducing his 'double chevron' final drive gearing to the marque.

In 1912, Mors adopted Knight sleeve-valve engines supplied by Minerva of Antwerp, whose London agent was Citroen's cousin. The Silent Knight featured on the 2120 cc 10/12 HP, 3308 cc 14/20 HP, 4398 cc 20/30 HP and 7245 cc 28/35 HP. However, the marque also continued to offer side-valve cars like the four-cylinder 2120 cc 10/12 HP and 3404 cc 14/20 HP, and the 5107 cc 20/30 HP six. All these models remained in

production until the outbreak of war, though post-war Mors cars only used sleeve-valve power units. Indeed, the Mors factory was being used for the production of the Type A Citroën, so output of Mors cars was spasmodic, though the cars were extremely handsome, and carried on their Bentley-like radiators the legend SSS – *Sans Soupapes Silencieuse* (silent,

without valves). The cars offered included a 14/20 HP Sport of 3562 cc and a 12/16 HP of 1824 cc.

After 1925, Mors made only components, although during World War II they did build a range of cheap electric cars. In the 1950s, the Mors name appeared finally on powered road vehicles, but these were only scooters sold under the name Mors-Speed.

# MOTOBLOC

**Bordeaux, France
1902–1930**

Gunmaker Schaudel, whose first car was built in 1897, was the first man in the world to mount engine, clutch and transmission in one rigid casing – he called it *le bloc-moteur*. It was the sensation of the 1901 Paris Salon, and the Motobloc company was established to exploit this ingenious design. Shortly afterwards, Schaudel resigned to take over as chief engineer of the Manufacture Francaise d'Armes et Cycles at St-Etienne, where the Svelte car was built. He was succeeded by Emile Dombret, who had previously set up a small firm making petrol engines in St-Etienne.

The first Motoblocs were close replicas of the Schaudel – they were sold in England as the British Ideal – with a transverse *bloc-moteur* beneath the floor.

---

**1902 MORS PARIS-VIENNA RACER**

**Engine:** in-line, four-cylinder, side-valve
**Bore × stroke:** 140 mm × 150 mm
**Capacity:** 9236 cc
**Maximum power:** 60 bhp
**Transmission:** four-speed manual
**Chassis:** wood and flitchplate
**Suspension:** non-independent with semi-elliptic leaf springs
**Brakes:** rear wheel and transmission
**Bodywork:** open racer
**Maximum speed (approx):** 80 mph (129 kph)

---

However, by 1905, in-line fours, still with the gearbox in unit, were catalogued. In 1907 Emile Dombret devised a new engine, with the flywheel mounted between the middle pair of cylinders for smooth running and in that year, seven different chassis were listed, ranging from a 9 hp single to a four-cylinder 50 hp, with the option of shaft or chain drive.

Motobloc became known for the production of strongly-constructed and powerful touring cars, which enjoyed wide export sales, the six-cylinder model being particularly successful. In 1914, the range had risen to eight models, plus commercial vehicles, but production was interrupted by

**Motobloc 12 HP**

**Nacional Pescara**

### 1929 NACIONAL PESCARA

**Engine:** in-line straight-eight, twin-cam
**Bore × stroke:** 72.2 mm × 90 mm
**Capacity:** 2948 cc
**Maximum power:** 125 bhp
**Transmission:** two-speed manual
**Chassis:** box section steel
**Suspension:** non-independent with semi-elliptic leaf springs
**Brakes:** drums all round
**Bodywork:** sports, roadster, saloon
**Maximum speed (approx):** 115 mph (185 kph)

### 1912 MOTOBLOC 12HP

**Engine:** in-line, four-cylinder, side-valve
**Bore × stroke:** 80 mm × 148 mm
**Capacity:** 2976 cc
**Maximum power:** 12 hp
**Transmission:** four-speed
**Chassis:** pressed steel channel
**Suspension:** non-independent with semi-elliptic leaf springs front and three-quarter elliptics rear
**Brakes:** drums on rear wheels and transmission
**Bodywork:** to order
**Maximum speed (approx):** 50 mph (80 kph)

## NACIONAL PESCARA

Barcelona, Spain
1929–1932

Raùl Pateras Pescara, Marquis de Pescara, aided by his brother Henrique, founded this car factory in Barcelona under Royal patronage; he had already flown an experimental helicopter in 1922. The company built a number of sporting 2948 cc straight-eights making extensive use of Elektron alloy, including the wheels; standard models had a single overhead camshaft, competition cars had twin cams. Though production was limited – it is believed to have totalled only 14 cars – the Nacional Pescara was successful in international hillclimbing events. In one of the model's last competition appearances in 1935, the marque's ace driver Zanelli came second to Hans Stuck's 16-cylinder Auto Union Grand Prix car at the Kesselburg hill climb.

The company also proposed a 3993 cc luxury car with the unique engine configuration of ten cylinders in line in 1931; two were said to have been built, but it's unlikely that either found its way into private hands.

During the political unrest in Spain after the exile of King Alfonso XIII, Raùl Pateras Pescara moved to Switzerland, where he had three prototype engines built by the SLM locomotive company of Winterthur. These supercharged V16 power units developed 150 bhp, but only one was installed in a car, in Paris in 1935; it was subsequently taken to Spain. During the Civil War the car was said to have been destroyed.

World War I, during which Motobloc went into munitions manufacture, and made 2000 Salmson nine-cylinder rotary aero engines.

Though the plant was considerably larger at the end of the war, only three chassis (one a light commercial) and two types of engine, 12 hp and 15 hp, were offered; the sports version of the 15 HP was a pioneer of four-wheel braking. But Motobloc suffered from competition from the new breed of popular cars, and while at the beginning of the 1920s there were 300 workers producing a chassis a day, by 1927 the workforce was down to 90, and the company was reformed in 1929.

A new 15 hp Super-Confort six with independent front suspension was shown at that year's Bordeaux Fair, with a two-ton truck which was ordered by the Government, but Motobloc quickly became a victim of the Depression.

# NAG

**Berlin, Germany**
**1902–1934**

The Allgemeine Automobil-Gesellschaft had been in operation since 1900, building 5 hp single-cylinder voiturettes designed by Professor Klingenberg. The AAG was acquired by the major electrical concern, AEG, who initially continued the Klingenberg designs under the name NAG (Neue Automobil-Gesellschaft), but then acquired the Kuhlstein Wagenbau, which were building electric cars and second-rate petrol vehicles designed by Joseph Vollmer, creator of one of the worst cars ever, the 1895 Orient Express.

For NAG, Vollmer designed thoroughly conventional two- and four-cylinder 10 hp and 20 hp cars, as well as commercial vehicles. A variety of models followed, including an 1866 cc twin-cylinder car and four-cylinders of 5185 cc and 7956 cc; one of the latter models was delivered in 1907 to the Kaiserin Auguste Victoria, who became a regular customer of the Berlin marque.

The company achieved popular acclaim with the 1570 cc four-cylinder model, known as the Puck (a later version was known as the Darling, and won the Gothenburg Cup in the Swedish Winter Trials of 1912–13–14).

In the years before the Great War, NAG produced a wide range of cars; in 1912–14 the company offered the 10/12 hp Type K2 (1502 cc), the 14/20 hp Type K3 (2085 cc), the 18/22 hp Type K4 (2597 cc), the 20/25 hp Type K5 (3308 cc) and the 20/25 hp (5193 cc); there was also a massive 50/60 hp of 8495 cc.

Designer/racing driver Christian Riecken, who had been working with Minerva in Belgium, returned to NAG in 1914 and subsequently designed their 1921–26 sports cars.

During the war NAG manufactured 200 hp Benz aero engines under licence; in 1919, NAG became a member of the GDA car production group together with Brennabor, Hansa and Hansa-Lloyd, and in 1920 resumed car production with a side-valve 2536 cc four-cylinder car. This was quickly joined by a sports version, which won a number of races.

In 1923 an overhead-valve 2640 cc four-cylinder went into production and was joined three years later by overhead-valve sixes of 3075 cc and 3594 cc.

These were the direct result of the NAG takeover of Protos, which NAG took over that year, and were marketed as NAG-Protos; in 1927, NAG acquired the Presto and Dux car companies, too, and also created profitable links with Bussing trucks.

Designer Paul Henze, formerly with Imperia in Belgium, joined NAG in 1929, and created the 1931 overhead-valve V8 of 4540 cc – it was the first German V8 – and the 1930–32 overhead-valve 3963 cc six-cylinder. Aided by Richard Bussien, who had joined NAG as a result of their takeover of Voran in 1928, Henze also created a front-wheel-drive version of the V8, the Type 212, in 1932. It boasted a forked tubular backbone frame and independent suspension all round, with transverse springs and radius rods at the front, and swinging arms at the back.

The last new design to be produced by NAG was the front-wheel-drive Type 220 developed by Bussien and built from 1933 on. Only a few had been built before NAG decided that commercial vehicles were more profitable than cars, and merged with Bussing.

## 1931 NAG V8

**Engine:** V8, overhead-valve
**Bore × stroke:** 85 mm × 100 mm
**Capacity:** 4540 cc
**Maximum power:** 100 bhp
**Transmission:** four-speed synchromesh
**Chassis:** X-braced channel steel
**Suspension:** non-independent with semi-elliptic leaf springs
**Brakes:** drums all round
**Bodywork:** cabriolet
**Maximum speed (approx):** 80 mph (129 kph)

**NAG V8**

## MODEL
Hispano-Suiza 15T Alfonso XIII

**Spanish price when announced:**
Ptas. 14,000 (chassis only)

### ENGINE
**Location:** Front longitudinal
**Type:** Water-cooled in-line four-cylinder monobloc in cast iron with alloy crankcase. Three main bearings
**Cubic capacity:** 3619 cc
**Bore × stroke:** 80 mm × 180 mm
**Valve gear:** 2 per cylinder, either side of cylinder in T-head side-valve formation
**Fuel supply:** Hispano-Suiza three-jet automatic carburettor pressure-fed from rear-mounted fuel tank
**Ignition:** Bosch HT magneto
**Maximum power:** 63 bhp at 2300 rpm

### TRANSMISSION
**Layout:** In unit with engine
**Clutch:** 42-plate dry metallic disc
**Gearbox:** Three-speed manual
**Final drive:** Straight-cut bevels, live axle
**Ratio:** 3.0:1 or 3.25:1

### WHEELS AND TYRES
**Type:** Rudge-Whitworth detachable 885 × 105 beaded edge wire wheels

### BODY/CHASSIS
**Type:** Pressed steel perimeter chassis with cross members. Bodywork to order

### DIMENSIONS AND WEIGHT
**Wheelbase:** 104 in (2650 mm) or 118 in (3000 mm)
**Track – front:** 48 in (1220 mm)
 **– rear:** 51 in (1295 mm)
**Chassis weight:** 1450 lb (660 kg) or 1570 lb (710 kg)

### SUSPENSION
**Front:** Non independent with semi-elliptic leaf springs
**Rear:** Non independent, live axle with semi-elliptic leaf springs

### STEERING
**Type:** Worm and sector. 1.25 turns lock-to-lock

### BRAKES
**Type:** Drums on rear wheels (hand) and transmission (foot)

### PERFORMANCE
**Maximum speed:** 78 mph (125 kph)
**Fuel consumption:** 17 mpg

**BELOW** The Hispano-Suiza Alfonso mirrored the American raceabouts in being basically a chassis with very skimpy bodywork, giving excellent performance for a relatively low power output. The Alfonso was in fact based on a successful racing voiturette. Despite the apparent crudity of a simple leaf-sprung front axle ride and steering feel were both good thanks to the low unsprung weight – helped by the absence of front brakes

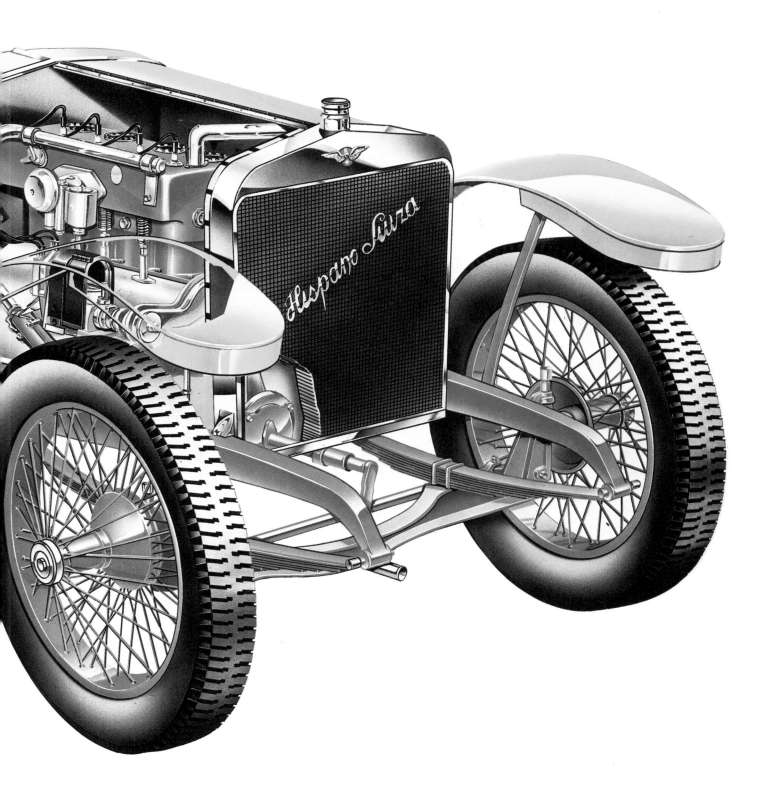

Nagant

# NAGANT

**Liège, Belgium**
**1899–1927**

Liègeois arms manufacturer Leon Nagant was renowned for the quality of his guns; the Russian army was equipped with Nagant repeating rifles and revolvers. In 1896 the Nagant works built a twin-cylinder voiturette for a local inventor, Raoul de Meuse, but did not put it into production despite encouraging results. Instead, they built a number of prototypes before starting licence production of opposed-piston Gobron-Brillies in 1899.

In 1900 the company changed its name to Fabrique d'Armes et d'Automobiles Nagant Frères, headed by Leon's brother Maurice. Licence-built Gobrons were constructed until 1904 at the rate of some 150 chassis a year; Prince Albert of Belgium owned two of them, and Gobron-Nagants appeared in competition with some success.

When the Gobron design became obsolete, Nagant began licence-production of the French Rochet-Schneider under the name La Locomotrice, building some 200 in the years 1904 and 1905. Their contract having expired, Nagant decided to build cars of their own design, and engaged the German engineer Ernst Valentin to design a new model; in the interim, they supplied components for other firms, including a batch of engines for Berliet.

In 1906, Nagant moved into a new factory, still in Liège, and the following year launched a 6872 cc chain-driven 35/40 hp four and a 4589 cc 20/30 hp. The 1908 season saw the introduction of a three-speed shaft-driven 14/16 hp 'for the man of moderate means'; by now, Nagants were being sold in France under the name 'Busson-Dedyn' and built under licence in Germany as the 'Hexe'.

The entire range acquired shaft-drive in 1911, and in 1912 a new 10/12 hp appeared. The 1913 range, designed by the new chief engineer Dufresne, consisted of the Type 8000 10/12 hp (1816 cc), the Type 7000-I 14/16 hp (3054 cc), the Type 7000-II 18/24 hp (3308 cc), the Type 9000 20/28 hp (3817 cc), the Type 6000-I 24/30 hp (4589 cc) and the Type 6000-II 30/40 hp (5297 cc). An entirely new 20/25 hp of 4563 cc was launched in 1914; its monobloc cylinder casting was also used in the company's twin-cam 4433 cc Grand Prix cars, which had a remarkable five-speed transmission on which the two upper ratios were overdrives. During the war, Nagant refused to work for the occupying Germans, so when the firm took repossession of its factory in 1919, they found that it had been stripped of machinery. Post-war production began in 1920 with models derived from the 1914 range, the Type 2000 of 3016 cc with side valves

**1921 NAGANT 2000 SPORT**

**Engine:** in-line four-cylinder, overhead valve
**Bore × stroke:** 80 mm × 150 mm
**Capacity:** 3016 cc
**Maximum power:** 50 bhp
**Transmission:** four-speed manual
**Chassis:** pressed steel channel
**Suspension:** non-independent with semi-elliptic leaf springs
**Brakes:** rear wheel and transmission
**Bodywork:** to order
**Maximum speed (approx):** 65 mph (105 kph)

and the choice of flat or vee radiator; in 1921 it gained overhead valves in a detachable head, and was produced in this form until the end of 1922.

New models were launched at the end of 1921, a 10 hp of 1954 cc and a 15 hp of 2120 cc; the 10 hp was quickly replaced by a 2001 cc 11 hp, but it was the 15 hp which became Nagant's sole offering in 1923. This overhead-valve sporting four boasted Adex four-wheel brakes. It won Nagant's last sporting victory with first and second places in the 3-litre class at the Spa Belgian Grand Prix in 1925.

At the December 1925 Brussels Salon, Nagant introduced an overhead-valve 20 hp six of 2931 cc, followed in 1926 by a light side-valve six of 1983 cc.

Nagant's last fling was a supercharged 1500 cc engine shown at the 1927 Paris Salon; designed by Hanocq and Dewandre, it developed the excellent power of 42 bhp/litre. However, due to a lack of funds, it was never fitted in a chassis, and soon after, Imperia swallowed Nagant. The factory was sold to FN, who used it as a repair workshop, then, in 1933, sold the building to the army, who were still there in the 1980s.

# NAPIER

**London, England**
**1900–1924**

The Napier engineering works in Lambeth was famed for precision manufacture for some 90 years before it became involved with motor cars, though its founder, David Napier, had patented 'Certain Improvements in Machinery for Propelling Locomotive Carriages' in 1831. It was the third generation of Napiers at Lambeth, Montague, who was first involved with cars, through his old cycling friend S.F. Edge, who had left the Dunlop Tyre Company in 1899 and bought an 1896 racing Panhard-Levassor from H.J. Lawson. Edge wanted the car modernised – the tiller steering replaced with wheel steering, electric ignition and pneumatic tyres – but as Napier worked on the car, he decided to fit a new engine as well, and built a vertical-twin power unit of 8 hp which proved so successful that a first series of six Napier cars was undertaken for Edge's newly-formed Motor Power Company, and fitted with aluminium bodies by Mulliner of Northampton.

The very first Napier car, a 2471 cc vertical-twin, was ready in time to compete in the Automobile Club's 1000 Miles' Trial in the spring of 1900; it won its class and a bronze medal. A 4942 cc four-cylinder 16 hp model appeared later that year; it had a one-piece aluminium cylinder block with pressed-in iron liners and three atmospheric inlet valves per cylinder. Eight orders were immediately forthcoming, for the 16 hp Napier was the fastest car in England in 1900. But when Edge and the Hon. C.S. Rolls entered it for the Paris-Toulouse race in July 1900, they found the car outclassed by the Continental racers (it failed to finish because of cooling and ignition problems).

Under Edge's influence, Napier pursued an active racing policy, which won the Gordon Bennet Trophy for Great Britain in 1902; consequently, Napier Green became the official British racing colour. In 1903, the year in which the company moved its works across London to Acton, Napier launched the world's first series-production six-cylinder car, the 4942 cc 18/30 HP, and set a fashion

that was quickly followed by other leading luxury car makers; the Napier six was initially plagued by periodic crankshaft vibration which caused whip and even breakage. Edge sought to minimise the problem, describing it as 'power rattle'; nevertheless, the overall smoothness and flexibility of the six proved strong selling points, particularly to a generation of motorists who disliked changing gear. In 1905 Edge's cousin Cecil proved it was possible to travel from Brighton to Edinburgh on top gear alone in a Napier six.

By 1906 Napier offered two sixes of 40 hp (5001 cc) and 60 hp (7753 cc), plus two four cylinder models of 18 hp (3160 cc) and 45 hp (5309 cc).

### 1907 NAPIER 60 HP

**Engine:** in-line six-cylinder, side-valve, L-head
**Bore × stroke:** 127 mm × 101.6 mm
**Capacity:** 7725 cc
**Maximum power:** 60 hp
**Transmission:** three-speed
**Chassis:** pressed steel channel
**Suspension:** non-independent, with semi-elliptic leaf springs front and rear
**Brakes:** transmission and rear-wheel drums
**Bodywork:** to order
**Maximum speed (approx):** 65 mph (105 kph)

The marque entered the record books in 1907 with a spectacular one-man 24-hour drive by Edge, who averaged 65.9 mph (106.1 kph) on a 9653 cc 60 hp six on the recently-completed Brooklands race track; this record stood for 18 years.

The year 1907 also saw the launch of the biggest production Napier, the 90 HP, which had a swept volume of 14,565 cc.

Napier's 1911 range was particularly complex, consisting of two-, four- and six-cylinder models, but was simplified to just half a dozen models for 1912 – a 15 hp four and sixes of 30, 40, 45, 65 and 90 hp.

During World War I, Napier built aero engines, but the famous

24-litre broad-arrow Lion twelve-cylinder designed by A.J. Rowledge, who also created the post-war Napier car, arrived just too late to play a part in the hostilities. In contrast with its pre-war profligacy, Napier now concentrated on just one model, the light-alloy 6227 cc overhead-camshaft 40/50 HP six. But production was halted after only 187 had been built; at that point,

Napier had built a total of 4258 private cars.

Napier attempted to re-enter car production in 1931 with a bid to acquire Bentley, but was thwarted at the eleventh hour by Rolls-Royce.

## Napier 40/50 HP

Designed to compete with the Rolls-Royce Silver Ghost, the Napier 40/50 was the work of A.J. Rowledge, who had just created the remarkable twelve-cylinder Napier Lion aero engine which would, over a quarter of a century later, power John Cobb's Railton Mobil Special when it broke the land speed record, achieving over 400 mph (644 kph) in one direction.

Production of the 40/50 began in late 1919, at a chassis price of £1750; the car, in the best Napier tradition, earned admiration for its 'almost amazing top-gear performance'.

It seems, however, as though the new Napier had a magnificent engine in an old-fashioned chassis, though early examples suffered from low-speed roughness which was cured by reducing the compression ratio in the rear cylinder.

Certainly the 40/50 was both robust and reliable, but only 187 of the planned production run of 500 cars had been built when Napier decided to withdraw from car production; Rowledge then joined Rolls-Royce, where he worked until he retired in 1945.

**Napier 60 HP**

**Napier 40/50**

### 1920 NAPIER 40/50

**Engine:** in-line six-cylinder, overhead-cam
**Bore × stroke:** 102 mm × 127 mm
**Capacity:** 6177 cc
**Maximum power:** 82 bhp
**Transmission:** four-speed manual
**Chassis:** pressed steel channel
**Suspension:** non-independent with semi-elliptic leaf springs front and cantilever rear with anti-roll device in torque tube anchorage
**Brakes:** rear wheel and transmission
**Bodywork:** to order
**Maximum speed (approx):** 60 mph (97 kph)

## NASH

Kenosha, USA
1917–1957

Though former farm labourer Charles W. Nash rose through sheer merit to become President of General Motors at the age of 48 in 1912, his burning ambition remained the building of a car bearing his own name. So when Billy Durant bought his way back into GM in 1916, Nash resigned and bought the Jeffery company; 'We shall build up to a standard, not down to a price,' he told the company's dealers and employees.

During 1917 the Jeffrey name was phased out in favour of Nash; the first Nash car, an overhead-valve 4-litre six, appeared in the autumn of 1917. It was immediately successful, and even though Nash was one of the first

victims of the post-war recession, closing down in November 1920 'for inventory and adjustment of plans', the company had recovered sufficiently for the launch of a 2.5-litre overhead-valve four late in 1921. Further evidence of recovery was given by the takeover of LaFayette and Mitchell in 1922 and 1924 respectively; however, the Mitchell's successor, the Ajax, was a flop, and was only built in 1925–26.

Nash's Model 328 of 1928 was claimed to be 'America's cheapest seven-bearing six', and helped to boost the company's sales to a record of 138,137 that year; the figure would not be surpassed until 1949. The 1930 Nash range included no fewer than 32 variants, including the all-new Twin-Ignition Eight of 3920 cc, which featured a starter operated by the clutch pedal, as well as the Single Six and Twin-Ignition Sixes, both of 3378 cc.

As sales slumped during the Depression, Nash attempted to arrest the slide by boosting their model range to 25 First Series body styles plus 28 Second Series in 1932, and additionally launched a Big Six. This gave them two sixes and two eights; apart from General Motors, Nash were the only US manufacturers to record a profit in that dismal year.

The 1934 range introduced revised styling, with spatted wings, raked tails and rear-mounted spare wheels; and a low-priced model line was added to the range, reviving the defunct LaFayette name. In 1934, too, Nash built its millionth car; a drastic rationalisation was carried out the following year, when the range was reduced to only two six-

cylinder body styles and four eight-cylinder styles, which featured swept-tail 'Aeroform design'.

An unconventional option was offered in 1936; customers could choose conventionally-styled models which incorporated a boot which, in conjunction with a fold-down rear seat, could be converted into a double bed. Power options that year included the low-priced side-valve 400 six, or 3037 cc or 3779 cc, and the overhead-valve Ambassador Six and Eight models.

A direct result of a 1937 merger with Kelvinator refrigerators was the 1938 announcement of Weather Eye conditioned air heating and ventilation; vacuum-operated gearboxes were another new feature for 1938.

The 1940 Nash models had a tall, narrow grille, which curved inwards at the base, while there was also a limited edition of some 50 Nash Special convertibles, with styling by Count Alexis de Sakhnoffsky.

Nash cars for 1941 models featured an integral body/chassis, which was claimed to be the first application of this method of construction in America; the company advertised their new 2.8-litre 600 six as being capable of covering 600 miles (965 km) on one 20 gallon (US) tankful of petrol, equivalent to 36 miles (58 km) per Imperial gallon.

After the war, in which the group's plants produced aero engines, propellors, helicopters, bomb fuses, flying-boat sub-assemblies, cargo trailers and binocular cases, Nash quickly returned to car production, at first with 1942 models.

A novel model for 1946 was the Ambassador Suburban Sedan,

which had wooden side panels.

The 1949 models were distinguished by overblown AirFlyte styling, in which enclosed wheels front and rear made tyre changing next to impossible. Seat belts were optional, a very early use of this now universal safety feature; a recurrent Nash theme was evident in the interior, for the front seatback dropped down to convert the seating into a double bed, with mattress and curtains available as options....

The best year of all for Nash was 1950, when they launched the first successful post-war compact, the Rambler, powered by the old side-valve six; Nash sales that season reached 191,865, and the post-war frugality of the old 600 was replaced by the Super-Power of the Statesman.

A meeting aboard the liner *Queen Elizabeth* between Donald Healey and Nash president George Mason (successor to Charles Nash, who had died in 1948) led to the Nash-Healey, built in Warwick, England, and powered by a tuned Ambassador six-cylinder engine. Offered between 1951 and 1954, the Nash-Healey distinguished itself by taking fourth place at Le Mans in 1951.

In 1954, Nash acquired Hudson, creating American Motors; Mason died unexpectedly after a few months, and his executive vice-president, George Romney, took control. He was only interested in building compact cars, and concentrated AMC's efforts on the Rambler; another small car marketed by the group in 1954 was the Metropolitan, an ugly little two-seater car with scaled-down AirFlyte styling built for Nash by Austin of England, and powered by

**Nash Metropolitan**

the A40 engine. Initially produced only for export to the States, the Nash Metropolitan was described in the catalogue as 'a practical car for small families, a sensible second car for any family'; Europe, it was felt, wasn't quite ready for the concept of two cars per family. Flamboyant two-tone colour schemes included pink/cream, red/cream, Croton green/cream, spruce green/cream and blue/cream; reading between the lines in contemporary road tests, one gets the impression that British testers were quite glad that the Metropolitan was intended for

# American Motors

export only, with 'riding and handling characteristics which are not by any means easy to describe'. The Metropolitan survived until 1961, several years after Nash had been phased out.

Restyling in 1955 brought the option of the 5244 cc Packard V8 in the Ambassador, though in 1956 the Ambassador gained AMC's new 4097 cc V8.

Though 1957 group sales were 118,990, Nash, despite flamboyant styling with dual vertical headlamps, only represented 9474 of that total – and the new Rambler marque accounted for 114,084.

It came as little surprise when AMC announced that Nash was being phased out at the end of the 1957 model year, and that all AMC products would be known as Ramblers from then on.

---

## 1954 NASH METROPOLITAN

**Engine:** in-line four-cylinder, overhead-valve
**Bore × stroke:** 65.48 mm × 89 mm
**Capacity:** 1199 cc
**Maximum power:** 42 bhp
**Transmission:** three-speed manual
**Chassis:** integral
**Suspension:** independent front with coils and wishbones. Live rear axle with semi-elliptic leaf springs
**Brakes:** drums all round
**Bodywork:** two-seater coupé or convertible
**Maximum speed (approx):** 75 mph (120 kph)

---

# NISSAN

**Tokyo/Osaka/Yokohama, Japan 1912–**

The Nissan story goes back to 1912 when the three partners in the Kwaishinsha Motor Car Works of Tokyo – Den, Aoyama and Takeuchi – built an experimental car. Two years later a second, more successful car was completed, and named DAT from the initials of the partners. The Model 31 went on sale in 1915, followed a year later by the Model 41, and production in Tokyo continued until 1926, when the company merged with the manufacturers of Lila cars, based in Osaka. Production of private motor vehicles was suspended in favour of trucks until 1931, when car manufacture was resumed with the Datson (or 'Son of Dat'). But Son signifies 'loss' in Japanese, so the model name was changed to Datsun in order to capitalise on the national symbol of the rising sun, which featured on the car badge.

The company, now known as the Jidosha Seizo Kabushiki Kaisha,

moved to Yokohama in 1933 and a year later it was renamed Nissan Jikosha Kaisha and began producing a light car on Austin Seven lines. A deal to build Model C Fords for the Japanese market came to nothing, and while big cars based on the American Graham appeared in 1937, by 1938 Nissan was mainly occupied in building trucks for the forthcoming war, in which its factory was badly damaged. Later Nissan built trucks for the occupying forces.

Nevertheless, by 1947 Nissan was back in car production with vehicles based on the contemporary Austin range, and when the occupying forces finally released all Nissan's factories in 1955, the Datsun 110 and its Datsun 120 pickup derivative began to appear in quantity. Three years later, Nissan landed the spearhead force for its invasion of America, concentrating on California with the new Bluebird, the basis of future production and exports. By 1961, Nissan was Japan's top car exporter, though the figures were as yet not sufficient to give the complacent European industry much cause for concern, since Nissan exports didn't pass 100,000 until 1962.

However, by 1964 the Bluebird was leaving the lines at the rate of 10,000 a month, and Nissan was engaged in a major programme of factory expansion, opening new plants at Oppama and Zama and merging with Prince Motors to acquire Murayama in 1966, which made Nissan the biggest car producer in Japan though it would soon be overtaken again by Toyota. By now, Nissan was establishing a firm foothold in Europe, and in 1968, the year in which the new 1800 Laurel made its debut, the first Datsun cars appeared on the British market.

An important move for Nissan was the launch of the Datsun 240Z, a six-cylinder sports coupé which

established Nissan as the world's biggest maker of sports cars, and twice won the East African Safari Rally. This successful sports coupé looked remarkably out of place in the Nissan range of the 1970s, which was as notable for its complexity as for the ineptness of its styling. The 240Z (known in some markets as the Fairlady) was succeeded by the 260Z (and 280Z in North America) and, in 1978, by the 280ZX.

In 1979, Nissan introduced Japan's first turbocharged cars and although the names Cedric and Gloria scarcely had much macho appeal, the Cedric/Gloria Turbo was voted Car of the Year.

In the 1980s came the new Leopard range, with a choice of three power units plus turbo. A joint venture with Hitachi gained Nissan a substantial slice of Japan's electronic engine-management industry and it continued to expand the turbo range through the decade with the Silvia/Gazelle range. In 1983, when the Datsun name was dropped, came the Nissan 300ZX sports car, with a 230bhp V six and a top speed of 112 mph (180 kph). Even in 1988, this was the marque's only sports model, but by the early 1990s new smaller-engined fast coupés had been launched, along with a superb 300ZX capable of 155 mph (249 kph).

By 1993, the range included the Micra, voted Car of the Year, four other Sunny models, the Primera saloons (built in Britain), the 140 mph (225 kph) 200ZX and the 300ZX.

# A-Z OF THE CAR

*Datsun Nissanocar*

## Datsun Nissanocar

The little Datsun Nissanocar of 1934 was, claimed its makers, 'the world's finest baby car', and represented the culmination of 'fifteen years of experiment and making of light cars'. 'Graceful in appearance, reliable in operation and extremely economical in use, Datsun is a value for every yen invested; no examination for driver's licence nor garage required makes the car doubly more pleasing to prospective buyers in Japan,' boasted the catalogue.

But beneath its Ford-inspired styling, the diminutive Nissanocar revealed its true origins for, apart from the semi-elliptic rear springs, it owed much to the British Austin

Seven – the power plant especially was a close copy, though the crank ran in ball-bearings. Nevertheless, in its home country, its price of 1975 yen (£127) undercut the imported Model Y Ford by £100, supporting its slogan, 'Car that appeals – prices that make sales'.

## Nissan 300ZX

The third-generation 300ZX showed how well the company had learned from previous models and was a true supercar, easily capable of challenging the best German and Italian rivals. Aimed primarily at the North American market, this two-seater had a sleek bodyshell with a drag coefficient (Cd) of 0.31 over a

sophisticated chassis with all-independent suspension, ABS braking, a viscous-coupled differential and up-to-the minute electronics. For instance, the models exported to Europe featured Nissan's HICAS system (High Capacity Actively Controlled Suspension), which had computer-controlled rear-wheel alignment and four-wheel steering, thanks to chassis sensors reading the car's cornering behaviour.

The engine, the twin-turbo quad-cam 3-litre V6, delivered 280 bhp.

With the turbo power really coming in from 2700 rpm, the 3219 lb (1450 kg) car could accelerate to 100 mph (162 kph) in 14.5 seconds. Autocar & Motor reported that the 300 ZX had 'stunning power, stupendous presence and tremendous dynamic ability'. Inside, air-conditioning was standard.

### 1934 DATSUN NISSANOCAR

**Engine:** in-line four-cylinder, side-valve
**Bore × stroke:** 56 mm × 76 mm
**Capacity:** 748 cc
**Maximum power:** 12 bhp
**Transmission:** three-speed
**Chassis:** pressed steel channel
**Suspension:** non-independent, with transverse leaf-spring front, semi-elliptics rear
**Brakes:** drums all round
**Bodywork:** roadster, phaeton, sedan, light van
**Maximum speed (approx):** 45 mph (73 kph)

### 1989 NISSAN 300ZX

**Engine:** V6, twin-turbo, quad-cam
**Bore x stroke:** 87 mm x 83 mm
**Capacity:** 2960 cc
**Maximum power:** 280 bhp
**Transmission:** manual or automatic, rear-wheel drive
**Chassis:** integral
**Suspension:** independent with multi-links, lower wishbones front, multi-links rear, anti-roll bars
**Brakes:** discs all round
**Bodywork:** steel two-seater, 2 + 2 coupé, Targa coupé or convertible
**Maximum speed (approx):** 156 mph (249 kph)

## NSU

**Neckarsulm, Germany**
**1905–1929, 1958–1977**

Founded in 1886, the Necharsulmer Radwerke built first bicycles and then, from 1900, motorcycles, adopting the more euphonic brand name of NSU in 1892. In 1905, NSU started building Belgian Pipe cars under licence, and, in 1906 began production of the 1420 cc 6/10PS

*Nissan 300ZX*

## 1967 NSU Ro80

**Engine:** twin-rotor Wankel rotary, front mounted
**Capacity:** 1990 cc
**Maximum power:** 115 bhp
**Transmission:** three-speed hydraulic torque-converter
**Chassis:** integral
**Suspension:** all independent, with MacPherson struts front, semi-trailing arms and coil springs rear
**Brakes:** discs all round, servo-assisted
**Bodywork:** four-door saloon
**Maximum speed (approx):** 112 mph (180 kph)

**NSU RO80**

four-cylinder light car designed by Otto Pfaender, who had recently joined Pipe as technical director. The 6/10PS was followed by models of up to 2608 cc, although the vertical-twin 1105 cc voiturette which appeared in 1909 was not a great success. In 1911 the popular 1131 cc four-cylinder arrived, produced until 1913, and also available in a 1555 cc version; the biggest pre-war NSU was a 3399 cc four. The 1200 cc 5/15PS was introduced in 1913 and was still in production in 1926.

An outstanding post-war model, the 5/25/40 was a supercharged development of the 1307 cc 5/30PS, and there was a 1476 cc version, with a Roots-type supercharger driven from the gearbox, capable of more than 80 mph (129 kph). Racing cars of this type won the 1925 Taunus race, the 1925–26 AVUS races and the 1926 Solitude race as a curtain-raiser to the announcement of the touring side-valve six of 1568 cc. Other models of the mid-1920s had four-cylinder engines of 2100 cc and 36610 cc, and a six of 1781 cc.

NSU shifted car production to a new factory at Heilbronn in 1927,

but this only lasted until 1929, when financial problems compelled an end to car manufacture and the sale of the Heilbronn works to Fiat. However, in 1934–35 the Neckarsulm factory produced three flat-four VW-like prototypes, designed by Ferdinand Porsche with assistance from NSU's English designer Walter Moore; these 1.4-litre cars had a backbone frame and torsion-bar suspension, but car production was not resumed until 1958, with the 583 cc overhead-cam vertical-twin Prinz. At the same time NSU sold its entire motorcycle production set-up to Pretis of Sarajevo, Yugoslavia.

An improved 598 cc version of the vertical-twin car was capable of developing 30 bhp in the Sport Prinz coupé, styled by Bertone, while racing versions were considerably more powerful.

In 1963, NSU created a sensation by introducing the first quantity-production car with a Wankel rotary engine, whose

epitrochoidal layout had first been used in a supercharger on record-breaking NSU motorcycles. The Wankel-engined Spider was an open version of the Sport Prinz, which was said to be capable of developing 50 bhp from the equivalent of 500 cc, and it was manufactured until 1967.

Alongside this unorthodox machine, NSU continued to build reciprocating-engine cars – the 1964 four-cylinder overhead-cam 996 cc Prinz was followed by derivatives of 1085 cc and 1177 cc

The Spider was succeeded in 1967 by the elegant and truly advanced Ro80 saloon, which was produced for nearly a decade, despite early durability problems with its rotary power unit. However, in 1969 NSU were taken over in a complex merger which linked them with Audi under Volkswagen. VW produced the K70 as a piston-engined alternative to the Ro80, and in 1977 NSU was phased out.

# OAKLAND

**Pontiac, USA**
**1907–1932**

The first car to leave Oakland's factory was a twin-cylinder 20 hp runabout designed by Alanson P. Brush. Its power unit possessed his typical hallmark, for it cranked anti-clockwise, and the epicyclic gear-change was incorporated in the rear axle.

Oakland became part of the new General Motors combine in 1909, the same year in which the company introduced its first four-cylinder model, which had a conventional sliding gear transmission.

By 1912, Oakland was producing fours of 3 and 4 litres, followed in 1913 by a vee-radiatored 5999 cc 40 hp six. In 1916 Oakland launched a 5.5-litre V8, but this proved shortlived, for the 2955 cc overhead-valve 15/20 hp Sensible Six, launched that year, proved so popular that it soon became Oakland's sole model. The Sensible Six was succeeded in late

## 1929 OAKLAND ALL AMERICAN SIX

**Engine:** in-line six-cylinder, side-valve
**Bore × stroke:** 85.5 mm x 107.9 mm
**Capacity:** 3038 cc
**Maximum power:** 68 bhp
**Transmission:** three-speed manual
**Chassis:** pressed steel channel
**Suspension:** non-independent, with semi-elliptic leaf springs front and rear
**Brakes:** rear-wheel drums
**Bodywork:** roadster, coupé, sedan
**Maximum speed (approx):** 65 mph (105 kph)

**Oakland All-American Six**

1923 by a 3038 cc side-valve six, which boasted centralised chassis lubrication, driven by the engine pump, and external-contracting four-wheel brakes.

The 1924 Oakland was the first car finished in Duco cellulose, and it was not long before the car industry had universally adopted this new quick-drying, high-gloss finish.

Oakland sales reached 58,000 in 1926, but the introduction in the same year by GM of the Pontiac, a lower-priced running-mate for the Oakland, had a disastrous effect on sales. The side-valve six was phased out after the 1929 season, and a 1930 V8, based on the unsuccessful Olds Viking, was the last Oakland. Pontiac had proved to be a cuckoo in the GM nest.

# OLDSMOBILE

**Lansing/Detroit, USA**
**1896 –**

Ransom Eli didn't like the smell of horses, so he decided to invent an automobile. He was one of the first Americans to produce gasoline engines, and subsequently claimed to have built a car in 1886. His first substantiable motor vehicle was a three-wheeled steamer built in the early 1890s and reviewed by *Scientific American*. However, Olds produced few cars until 1899, when copper and lumber magnate S.L. Smith bought the Olds Gasoline Engine Works to provide his two sons with a lucrative hobby, and shifted operations from Lansing, the state capital of Michigan, to the growing city of Detroit.

Originally, the Smiths planned to build a $1250 luxury car with pneumatic clutch and electric starter, but it failed to sell and involved the company in a $80,000 loss during 1900. To save the day, Ransom Olds designed the immortal single-cylinder tiller-steered Curved-Dash Oldsmobile, which, after a disastrous fire had destroyed the factory and the blueprints, made its debut in 1901, an event only made possible by a quick-witted timekeeper who had saved the prototype Oldsmobile from the holocaust. The little car proved such a success that during 1904, production exceeded 5000 units. In the same year Ransom Olds retired from the company, although he was soon persuaded, by a group of friends who had raised $500,000, to found the Reo company at Lansing.

By 1905, Oldsmobile had moved to Lansing, too, attracted by the offer of a 52-acre factory site. That year, flat-twin and wheel-steered variants of the Oldsmobile were introduced, and the 1906 season saw the launch of a vertical-twin two-stroke, the 20/24 hp Double-Action Model L, and the

first four-cylinder Oldsmobile, the 26/28 hp Model S. These models didn't sell well, however, and though the 'Merry Olds' was still selling well, it couldn't compensate for the profligacy of the management. Thus, the ailing company became part of the new General Motors combine in 1908.

Although it had been the large luxury cars that had got Oldsmobile into financial trouble, in 1910 the company launched the colossal 11,581 cc Limited six, which stood so far off the ground that it needed two-tier running boards! By 1912, however, the biggest Olds in the range was a mere 6998 cc, and the company added a low-cost four to the range in 1915, joined a year later by an efficient 4-litre V8 with aluminium pistons, which was built until 1923. From 1921–23,

Oldsmobile offered an overhead-valve four-cylinder whose 2.8-litre power unit was shared with another GM company, Chevrolet.

Along with the V8, the 2.8-litre four was replaced for 1924 by a 2774 cc six with Buick-like radiator. This one-model policy lasted until 1929, with four-wheel brakes and chromium plating available from 1927. The 4244 cc Viking, a low-priced V8 based on the LaSalle, was offered from 1929, but was a flop.

Oldsmobile was now establishing a reputation as the technical leader of GM, and in 1932 a new 3933 cc straight-eight appeared, while 1935 saw the controversial 'turret-top' styling launched on the Oldsmobile range. Their growing reputation for technical innovation was maintained with the introduction of GM's first production automatic transmission as an optional extra in 1938, although American historians reported that the new transmission 'didn't become reliable' until 1940. As an indication of the eagerness with which American motorists abandoned manual transmissions, it's worth noting that, as early as 1948, three-quarters of the Oldsmobiles sold were equipped with the Hydramatic transmission.

Although, in 1948, the top of the range Olds 98 was given GM's first new post-war body with 'Futuramic' styling (whose noteworthy features were a split

curved windscreen and wraparound rear window), a new power unit did not materialise until the following year, in the shape of the short-stroke overhead-valve 4977 cc Rocket V8 designed by Gilbert Burrell. In its initial form, the Rocket developed 135 bhp, and by 1965 this had been virtually doubled, to 240 bhp.

The questionable advantage of 'Autronic Eye' automatic headlamp-dipping came in 1953, while 1958 – the year in which Oldsmobile unveiled the dubious delights of the Dynamic 88 Starfire Coupé – saw the introduction of quadruple headlamps, exaggerated tail fins and air springing.

Oldsmobile became involved in the manufacture of smaller cars in 1961 with the F85 compact, powered by a light-alloy 3523 cc V8. Sporting derivatives included the 185 bhp Cutlass range and the 1963 Jetfire, which was available with turbocharger.

Bigger Oldsmobiles were powered by a 6457 cc V8 developing between 280 and 345 bhp depending on its state of tune, although the F85's V8 had been replaced by the more economical Buick V6 in 1964. There was also a range of full-size Jetstar eights of 5407 cc, intended as 'economy' models.

Introduced in 1966, the Toronado sports coupé was the first successful front-wheel-drive automatic. In its original form with drum brakes, it proved too fast for its chassis, its 6965 cc V8 power unit – 7456 cc from 1968 – driving the front wheels via silent inverted-tooth chains. As late as 1971, Oldsmobile still catalogued three different convertibles, based on the Cutlass Supreme, 442 and Delta 88, and all but the cheapest models were fitted with front disc brakes.

In 1973 the Omega compact was a sister model to the Pontiac Ventura, with which it shared the option of a 4097 cc six or a 5736 cc V8. In 1975, Oldsmobile brought out its last convertible, the Delta Royale, while the new Starfire had equivalent models in the Chevrolet, Pontiac and Buick ranges. Five-speed transmissions were introduced on the 1976 Starfires

and Omegas, and that year Oldsmobile claimed the Cutlass to be America's most popular model, with sales of 515,000. In reaction to the oil crisis, Oldsmobile offered the option of a 5.7-litre diesel unit.

For 1981, Oldsmobile introduced its version of the new GM J-car, the Firenza, plus the X-car Cutlass Ciera, powered by a transverse 2.5-litre four-cylinder engine driving the front wheels; it was said to have a low bonnet and a high boot to improve aerodynamics, though it looked uncompromisingly square-cut to European eyes in fact it looked rather like the Volvo 760.

The 1984 launch of a new C-car, the Ninety-Eight, was delayed, along with its Cadillac and Buick counterparts, because of problems with the automatic transmission, and it was announced that Oldsmobile, Cadillac and Buick would be consolidated in a new large-car group within GM.

## Curved-Dash Olds

The tiller-steered Curved-Dash Olds-mobile was little more than a single-cylinder gas engine given mobility by a two-speed epicyclic transmission, but its cheapness and simplicity, backed by the motor industry's first real attempt at production-line assembly, made this America's first truly popular car. A total of 425 was built in the latter part of 1901, 2100 in 1902, 3750 in 1903, 5000 in 1904

| 1901 CURVED DASH OLDS | |
|---|---|
| **Engine:** | horizontal single-cylinder |
| **Bore × stroke:** | 114.3 mm × 152.4 mm |
| **Capacity:** | 1564 cc |
| **Maximum power:** | 5 bhp |
| **Transmission:** | two-speed epicyclic |
| **Chassis:** | angle-iron frame |
| **Suspension:** | full-length springs linking front and rear axles |
| **Brakes:** | on final drive only |
| **Bodywork:** | curved-dash runabout |
| **Maximum speed (approx):** | 20 mph (32 kph) |

**Curved Dash Olds**

**Oldsmobile Limited**

and 6500 in 1905.

Supplying engines for the Curved-Dash Olds was Henry Leland's entrée to automobile manufacture, and thus the genesis of Cadillac and Lincoln. Leland's precision methods enabled him to get 7 hp out of the standard Olds engine, but when he started to get 10, Ransom Olds wouldn't use it because he thought it too powerful.

Despite its utter simplicity, the Curved-Dash Olds was capable of quite remarkable endurance; in 1904 two drivers with the curious names of T.R. McGargle and Dwight Huss, raced two Oldsmobiles – 'Old Steady' and 'Old Scout' across America. The little Curved-Dash also starred in one of the big song hits of 1905, which invoked the heroine to 'come away with me Lucille, in my Merry Oldsmobile'.

## Oldsmobile Limited

The biggest car ever to bear the Oldsmobile name, the 60 hp Limited took its name from the fact that an early example of this model raced the 20th Century Limited express train from Albany to New York – and beat it! The exploit was commemorated in a dramatic painting by William Hornden Foster.

Everything about the Limited was gigantic: it rode on wheels that were 43 in (109 cm) in overall diameter, had a 140 in (356 cm) wheelbase and stood so high that two-tier running boards were necessary to climb aboard. The price was big too; the Limited cost £5000!

### 1910 OLDSMOBILE LIMITED

**Engine:** in-line pair-cast six-cylinder, side-valve
**Bore × stroke:** 127 mm × 152 mm
**Capacity:** 11,581 cc
**Maximum power:** 60 hp (rated)
**Transmission:** four-speed manual
**Chassis:** pressed steel channel
**Suspension:** non-independent, with semi-elliptic leaf springs front and rear
**Brakes:** rear-wheel drums
**Bodywork:** roadster, tourer, limousine
**Maximum speed (approx):** 70 mph (113 kph)

## Oldsmobile Rocket 88

Oldsmobile emerged from World War II as GM's technical trend-setter. The corporation used Oldsmobile's official golden jubilee in 1948 as the opportunity to launch the new Futuramic styling that would be used on other GM marques for 1949.

The following year, Oldsmobile gained the first new post-war power unit from GM, the short-stroke overhead-valve 4977 cc Rocket V8 designed by Gilbert Burrell, which took its name, apparently, from the fact that the old six-cylinder engine plant had been converted for the manufacture of bazooka rockets. In its initial form, the Rocket developed

### 1958 OLDSMOBILE ROCKET 88

**Engine:** V8, overhead-valve
**Bore × stroke:** 98.4 mm × 87.3 mm
**Capacity:** 5138 cc
**Maximum power:** 130 bhp
**Transmission:** four-speed Hydramatic
**Chassis:** separate frame
**Suspension:** front independent with coil springs, rear non-independent with semi-elliptic leaf springs and hydraulic dampers
**Brakes:** hydraulic drums all round
**Bodywork:** convertible, saloon
**Maximum speed (approx):** 100 mph (161 kph)

**Oldsmobile Rocket 88**

135 bhp, but this had been virtually doubled by 1965 to 240 bhp, while swept volume had been raised to 5318 cc in the early 1950s.

The first Oldsmobile Rocket 88s had coil rear suspension, but with the launch of the Super 88 in 1951, this was replaced by conventional leaf springing.

## Oldsmobile Toronado

The Toronado was unusual in that its 7-litre V8 engine drove the front wheels through an automatic transmission and chain drive, and it received much technical acclaim when it was launched in 1966.

At that time it was the most powerful (and least economical) car that the British magazine *Motor* had ever road-tested, and 'proved that front-wheel drive will work extremely well with 7 litres', though there was inevitably wheelspin when stepping smartly off the mark. The Toronado won many plaudits for its ride and handling, though it was seriously deficient in the braking department.

Swept volume was raised to 7456 cc in 1968 when a one-off special-bodied Toronado was built by Ghia in Turin to the design of a young stylist Giorgetto Giugiaro.

## OM

**Brescia, Italy
1918–1934**

The SA Officine Meccaniche of Milan, a machine tool factory founded in 1899, succeeded Zust after the Great War, initially taking over the pre-war 4712 cc Zust 25/35 design as the Tipo S305. It was followed in 1919 by an original light car designed by the Austrian

---

### 1966 OLDSMOBILE TORONADO

**Engine:** V8, overhead-valve
**Bore × stroke:** 104.8 mm × 101 mm
**Capacity:** 6965 cc
**Maximum power:** 385 bhp
**Transmission:** three-speed Hydramatic driving front wheels via wide, inverted-tooth chains
**Chassis:** perimeter frame
**Suspension:** front independent, with torsion bars and wishbones, rear non-independent with dead beam axle and single-leaf springs
**Brakes:** drums all round, servo-assisted
**Bodywork:** six-seat two-door fastback saloon
**Maximum speed (approx):** 130 mph (209 kph)

---

Barratouche, the 1327 cc 12/15 hp Tipo 465, whose model designation, like all succeeding OM cars, referred to the number of cylinders and the cylinder bore. (Almost all succeeding OMs had strokes of 100 mm, save some six-cylinder models of 1930–32 which had 105 mm strokes.) A 1410 cc sporting derivative, Tipo 467 Sport, appeared in 1921, while the 1496 cc Tipo 469S of 1922–23 was the first OM with front wheel brakes.

The company's first six, the Tipo 665 Superba, appeared in 1923, founding a line that would run through until 1932; three 665 Superbas competed in the first-ever Mille Miglia in 1927, and took the first three places.

At the Milan Show in 1928, OM showed a 3-litre eight-cylinder touring car, but this remained at the prototype stage. In the same year OM decided to separate their car and railway rolling stock activities, so a new company – OM Fabbrica Bresciana di Automobili – was established.

Despite the simplicity of their power units, most of which had side-valves, OM enjoyed an excellent sporting reputation and achieved many successes. The British agent, L.C. Rawlence, produced a succession of tuned

sports OMs which had much better performance than the home-grown variety, and which led the works to produce in 1929 some special low-chassis OMs with Roots-type superchargers.

After 1925 OM built commercial vehicles, a side of the business which proved far more profitable than car-building, and in 1930 the factory's entire stock of cars was sold to a company called

---

**Oldsmobile Toronado**

---

Esperia, run by two former OM managers.

OM became part of the Fiat group in 1933, at which time it was only making commercial vehicles. There was, however, a prototype six called the OMV Alcyone which was shown at the 1934 Milan Show. It had a swept volume of 2130 cc and side-inlet/overhead-exhaust valves, but the car never reached production.

---

### 1923 OM 665S SUPERBA

**Engine:** in-line six-cylinder, side-valve
**Bore × stroke:** 65 mm × 100 mm
**Capacity:** 1991 cc
**Maximum power:** 55 bhp
**Transmission:** four-speed manual
**Chassis:** pressed steel channel
**Suspension:** non-independent, with semi-elliptic leaf springs front and rear
**Brakes:** rear-wheel drums
**Bodywork:** tourer, saloon
**Maximum speed (approx):** 75 mph (120 kph)

---

**OM Superba**

# A-Z OF THE CAR

## OMEGA-SIX

**Boulogne-sur-Seine, France**
**1922–1930**

Engineer Gadoux, late of Hispano-Suiza, designed the advanced Oméga-Six, which was intended to be a smaller equivalent to the Hispano. It made its debut at the 1922 Paris Salon, and production began with an overhead-cam 1991 cc six-cylinder car with a three-speed transmission and front-wheel brakes.

The 1928 Oméga-Six had an overhead-cam six of 2915 cc, whose cylinder head was integral with the cast-iron block; the four-speed transmission was in unit with the engine. Some Oméga-Sixes also had a two-speed rear axle designed for high-speed cruising, and all models were extremely well made.

Unfortunately, the venture was always undercapitalised, and few cars were delivered. The company planned to run at Le Mans in 1924 with a Henry-designed double-overhead-cam Oméga-Six, but failed to complete it in time.

### 1928 OMEGA-SIX

**Engine:** in-line six-cylinder, overhead cam
**Bore × stroke:** 75 mm × 110 mm
**Capacity:** 2915 cc
**Maximum power:** 122 bhp
**Transmission:** four-speed plus two-speed rear axle
**Chassis:** pressed steel channel
**Suspension:** non-independent, with semi-elliptic leaf springs front and rear
**Brakes:** drums all round
**Bodywork:** sports tourer
**Maximum speed (approx):** 105 mph (170 kph)

## OPEL

**Russelsheim, Germany**
**1898–**

Adam Opel founded his sewing machine works in 1863, having built his prototype in a disused cowshed at Russelsheim: in 1887 the company followed the example of the Coventry sewing machine industry and diversified into bicycles. Adam Opel, who had dismissed the new-fangled motorcar as 'a stink carriage for the rich', died in 1895, but his five sons thought that the car offered the possibility of compensating for a slump in the cycle market which occurred in 1897, and consequently bought the Anhaltische Motorwagenfabrik of Friedrich Lutzmann, who had been building massive Benz-like cars since 1894. Encouraged by the Grand Duke of Hesse, the brothers announced the first Opel car ('System Lutzmann') in 1898; a total of 11 cars was built in 1899, the first year of production.

A difference of opinion with Lutzmann led to the closure of the Motorcar Department in 1900, after 24 cars had been built; the Opel company took up the slack by importing Renaults and Darracqs from France, and soon acquired the production licence for Darracqs. In 1902, the Opels revealed their own twin-cylinder 10/12PS 1884 cc models, initially offered alongside the Opel-Darracqs. Soon afterwards, an enlarged 2365 cc Opel 12/14PS was added to the range.

In 1903, the first four-cylinder Opel appeared, the L-head 20/24PS, which had the option of three- or four-speed transmissions. A 6880 cc 35/40PS appeared in 1905, but the small single- and twin-cylinder Opel 'Volksautomobils' remained the company's mainstay, and were particularly popular in two-seater 'Doktorwagen' guise.

However, the one- and two-cylinder cars were replaced in 1909 by a range of three small four-cylinder models. By 1914 the Opel range had become particularly complicated, consisting of four-cylinder cars ranging from 1392 cc to 10,200 cc; the latter model had a 100 hp three-valve inlet-over-exhaust engine and four-speed gearbox.

The company's first six-cylinder prototype was completed in 1916, and formed the basis of two post-war models, the 21/60PS and 30/75PS, though these did not prove particularly popular in the depressed conditions of the 1920s.

The most popular Opel of the early 1920s was the 1984 cc 8/25PS, a vee-radiatored derivative of a pre-war model; it was subsequently developed into the 10/35PS. There was also a 14/38PS four of 3430 cc, and a few sports cars were built which used the 14/38PS engine in the 8/25PS chassis.

However, Opel decided that there would be a more profitable future in mass-producing a truly popular car that would respond to

**Oméga-Six**

the changed automobile market in Germany, so, after installing a moving assembly line in 1924, Opel copied the Citroën 5CV 'Trèfle' and began turning out the 951 cc four-cylinder Laubfrosch or 'Tree-frog' (so-called because it was painted green) in large numbers.

Priced initially at 4500 marks, then at 4000 marks, the Laubfrosch was an instant success, and its engine was soon enlarged to 1016 cc. Within three years, Russelsheim was turning out over 100 cars a day.

Alongside the Laubfrosch, Opel introduced the Type 80 10/40PS in 1925; this was a 2594 cc four, still on Citroën lines, while in 1927 Opel launched a new range of American-inspired sixes of 1735 cc (enlarged the following year to 1924 cc), 3540 cc and 4170 cc.

A notable series of experiments was carried out in the late 1920s by young Fritz von Opel, grandson of

the company's founder, who, already an accomplished racer of Opel motorcycles and cars, became interested in the rocket-propulsion projects of Max Valier. In 1928, trials were made with the Rak I rocket car, which proved promising enough for a public demonstration of the more refined Rak II, which, complete with variable-incidence wings, reached speeds up to 145 mph (233 kph) on the Avus race track.

General Motors of Detroit took control of Opel in 1928, and the same year Opel offered the eight-cylinder 5972 cc Regent built on American lines, though it was apparently Packard rather than any of the GM lines that it copied.

Following the GM takeover, Opel introduced a popular range of small cars, including a 995 cc four and 1790 cc six. De luxe versions of these cars were sold under the Regent name, while in 1934 their engines were enlarged to 1279 cc and 1932 cc respectively.

The 1279 cc engine was used in the 1935 Olympia, named after the Berlin Olympic games: it was Germany's first mass-production car with integral body/chassis construction. A year later came the 1074 cc Kadett, which rapidly became a best-seller. In December 1937 a new overhead-valve 1488 cc four-cylinder engine became standard in the Olympia,

and was so successful that the basic design was used until 1960.

Six-cylinder Opels of the late 1930s included the 2473 cc Super-Six of 1937, succeeded in 1938 by the unit-construction Kapitan. The top model in the range was the 3626 cc Admiral, launched in 1937. In that year Opel had captured over 40 per cent of the German market, and were exporting some 25 per cent of all its production. This success was based on its popular small cars, and between 1927 and 1941, Opel built 107,000 Kadetts.

One of the oddest fighting machines produced during World War II, the NSU Kettenkrad half-track motorcycle, was powered by the 1488 cc Olympia engine.

After the war, Opel could not resume production until 1947, for all the production machinery and jigs had been taken by the Soviets as reparations (the Kadett design was used as the basis of the Moskvitch 400 model). Production was resumed with trucks in 1946, and the first post-war Opel car was the Olympia, which entered production in 1947. The 2473 cc six-cylinder Kapitan, again changed only in detail from the pre-war model, reappeared in 1948.

A face-lifted Olympia was launched in 1950, with the oddly retrograde replacement of the four-speed transmission by a three-speed column change. It was

shape of a major redesign of the Kapitan. For 1959, the Kapitan was again redesigned, following the general styling trend of GM's contemporary American models.

It was the Kadett's turn in 1962, which saw the introduction of a new, modern Kadett with a 993 cc four-cylinder engine, produced in a new, purpose-built factory at Bochum in the Ruhr valley. In 1963 a new Rekord appeared, with a choice of 1488 cc and 1680 cc overhead-valve four-cylinder motors, and a 2605 cc six from the Kapitan was available the following year. New overhead-cam engines, a 1897 cc four-cylinder and a 2605 cc six-cylinder, were fitted to the Rekord in 1965.

The big Opels were spectacularly restyled in 1964, and gained hydraulic tappets: the line-up now consisted of the six-cylinder Kapitan, a de luxe version reviving the pre-war 'Admiral' designation, and the Diplomat, which was the same basic car powered by a 4638 cc Chevrolet V8. A Karmann-built Diplomat coupé appeared at the end of 1964, powered by a 5358 cc V8 which gave it a top speed of 127 mph (204 kph). The 4638 cc V8 became an option in the Kapitan and Admiral in the spring of 1965.

At that year's Frankfurt Show, Opel showed an experimental GT coupé, and three years later it went

into low-volume production.

The year 1966 brought a new Rekord range, with a 2239 cc six-cylinder option available for the first time. In March 1967, Opel launched the new Commodore range, basically the Rekord powered by a 2490 cc six; a high-performance GS version appeared in 1968.

Electronic fuel injection was offered on a new range of Kapitan, Admiral and Diplomat models announced in 1969. The following year a new medium car range, the Ascona, was launched, although its performance coupé derivative, the Manta, designed to compete with the newly-launched Ford Capri, was introduced two months ahead of the rest of the line-up. Power was by a 1584 cc overhead-cam engine, with a Rallye Manta available with 1.9-litre engine.

By 1979 the Opel range consisted of Kadett, Ascona, Manta, Rekord, Commodore and Senator/Monza models, powered by engines ranging from 1196 cc to 2969 cc.

A new front-wheel-drive Kadett appeared for 1980, while the 1981 Ascona also acquired front-wheel drive and became a great success in an increasingly competitive sector of the market. A year later came the Corsa minicar, which marked a determined expansion into Spain, and in 1984 a new, aerodynamic Kadett came onto the market.

**Opel Laubfrosch**

succeeded in April 1953 by the new Rekord, which boasted pontoon front wings and a curved windscreen, though the basic mechanics stayed much the same. It remained in production until 1957, when over half a million had been built; the new 1958 Rekord which succeeded it was the first Opel to be exported to the United States. A four-door version appeared in July 1959, while a low-priced derivative, the Opel 1200, appeared the following month, with an 1196 cc power unit in the Rekord bodyshell. It remained in production until 1962, even though a new-look Rekord had been launched in 1960.

Another new-look Opel had appeared in November 1953, in the

### 1924 OPEL 4/12PS LAUBFROSCH

**Engine:** in-line four-cylinder, side-valve
**Bore × stroke:** 58 mm × 90 mm
**Capacity:** 951 cc
**Maximum power:** 12 bhp
**Transmission:** three-speed manual
**Chassis:** pressed steel channel
**Suspension:** non-independent, with quarter-elliptic leaf springs front and rear
**Brakes:** rear-wheel drums
**Bodywork:** roadster, tourer, saloon
**Maximum speed (approx):** 45 mph (72 kph)

## Opel Laubfrosch

This was the car that transformed Opel into a mass-producer, but the 4/12PS was such an unashamed copy of the 5CV Citroën that the French company took legal action against Opel. The reason for the copying was that, having decided to make a modern production facility out of the Russelsheim works, Opel had dropped their entire product range in favour of a (short-lived) one-model policy. But the time needed to develop that entirely new model from scratch was a luxury they could not afford.

Nevertheless, there were significant differences between it and the French prototype: the German car had a magneto instead of coil ignition, 12 volt electrics instead of six and engine dimensions of 58 mm × 90 mm instead of 55 mm × 90 mm. It was, too, painted green instead of yellow (and that earned the car its 'Treefrog' nickname), and bore a distinctive radiator.

Not long after the launch, the engine was bored out to 60 mm, increasing the swept volume to 1016 cc, and the wheelbase was extended to enable four-seater bodies to be fitted. Such detail differences rendered Citroën's suit invalid, although it went before three courts.

Despite its plagiaristic origins,

**Opel GT 1900**

the Laubfrosch fulfilled its makers aims by selling in large numbers. When it was launched, Opel planned to produce 25 cars a day, twice Russelsheim's previous best, but within three years the plant was producing over 100 cars daily, and by 1928 Opel had a 37.5 per cent share of German car output.

## Opel GT

The first experimental Opel GT was built for the September 1965 Frankfurt Show. With its smooth lines and retractable headlamps it was quite unlike anything that the company had made before, and when the new Kadett line appeared, in late 1967, the time was ripe to put the GT into production, using the running gear of the new model. The prototype design was slightly modified, mostly in the interests of practicality, and, because the planned production volume of 20,000 units annually was too low for Russelsheim, a deal was struck with French coachbuilders Brissoneau & Lotz to produce the GT.

Homologated as a Grand Touring car, the GT proved an effective competition machine and Italian tuner Virgilio Conrero managed to achieve quite surprising speeds.

A less expensive version of the GT, the GT/J, appeared at the 1971 Geneva Show; production of both GT and GT/J continued until August 1973, when over 100,000 GTs had been built.

---

### 1967 OPEL GT 1900

**Engine:** in-line four-cylinder, overhead-valve
**Bore × stroke:** 93 mm × 69.8 mm
**Capacity:** 1897 cc
**Maximum power:** 90 bhp
**Transmission:** four-speed manual
**Chassis:** integral
**Suspension:** front independent with transverse leaf spring, rear non-independent with rigid axle and coil springs
**Brakes:** discs front, drums rear
**Bodywork:** two-seat coupé
**Maximum speed (approx):** 106 mph (170 kph)

---

## Opel Manta Berlinetta 1.8

The Opel Manta's venerable origins were veiled by a comprehensive face-lift in 1982, which also brought it GM's new 1.8-litre Family Two power unit. These factors boosted 1983 sales to nine times the 1982

---

### 1982 OPEL MANTA BERLINETTA 1.8

**Engine:** in-line four-cylinder, overhead-cam
**Bore × stroke:** 84.8 mm × 79.5 mm
**Capacity:** 1796 cc
**Maximum power:** 90 bhp
**Transmission:** five-speed manual
**Chassis:** integral
**Suspension:** front independent with coils and wishbones, rear non-independent with live axle and coil springs
**Brakes:** discs front, drums rear
**Bodywork:** four-seat coupé
**Maximum speed (approx):** 109 mph (175 kph)

---

level, a most remarkable increase.

Fitted with a large rubber rear wing, chin spoiler and alloy wheels, the Manta Berlinetta hatchback was very obviously aimed at the same clientele as Ford's equally venerable Capri. And like the Capri, it maintained a hardcore enthusiastic clientele who valued sporting looks and performance allied to four-seat family-car practicality.

## OSCA

**Bologna/San Lazzaro di Savena, Italy**
**1947–1967**

---

The three Maserati brothers, Bindo, Ettore and Ernesto, hit a financial crisis in 1937 and sold their company to the wealthy Orsi family of Modena. However, they also signed a 10-year contract, which meant that they stayed on until 1947, when they left to establish a new company, OSCA (Officine Speciallizate Costruzione Automobili Fratelli Maserati), in part of their old factory at Bologna.

Their first design was an 1100 cc sports car which appeared in 1948, and was raced with success in Formula Two events by such drivers as 'Gigi' Villoresi.

Anxious to return to Grand Prix racing, the brothers designed a 4472 cc V12 racing engine which could be fitted to existing 1.5-litre 4CLT Maseratis and this was raced by Prince Bira with moderate success.

OSCA built further racing cars, but the company's chief success came in sports car racing. From the original 1089 cc model, OSCA developed 1342 cc and 1453 cc derivatives, and a victory in the 1954 Sebring 12-hour race by Moss and Lloyd caused a flood of inquiries from the United States. This led to expansion into a new factory at San Lazzaro di Savena, just outside Bologna. By the late 1950s, a workforce of 40 was building 20–30 cars a year. At that

**Opel Manta Berlinetta 1.8**

## 1963 OSCA 1600 GT

**Engine:** in-line four-cylinder, double-overhead-cam
**Bore × stroke:** 80 mm × 78 mm
**Capacity:** 1568 cc
**Maximum power:** 140 bhp
**Transmission:** four-speed manual
**Chassis:** tubular steel
**Suspension:** front independent with double wishbones and coil springs, rear non-independent with rigid axle (Fissore) or independent with double wishbones (Zagato) and coil springs
**Brakes:** discs all round
**Bodywork:** sports coupé
**Maximum speed (approx):** 145 mph (233 kph)

Osca 1600

period, OSCA introduced a fast double-overhead-cam 749 cc four-cylinder based on the original 1100 cc engine.

In 1959 an agreement was reached whereby Fiat built the 1500 cc OSCA engine (with the capacity increased to 1568 cc) for their Farina-bodied 1200 model, while the Maseratis fitted the unit in specially-bodied sports coupés of their own design.

In 1963, OSCA became part of the MV Agusta group. OSCA 1600GT cars were built for a while after the merger, and the brothers worked on various projects – including a desmodromic valve engine – for Count Domenico Agusta until they retired in 1966.

# PACKARD

**Detroit, USA
1899–1958**

Disappointed with the new Winton horseless carriage which he had just bought, and convinced that he could build a better car, electrical equipment manufacturer James Ward Packard of Warren, Ohio, began production of single-cylinder cars with automatic ignition advance in November 1899. His automotive company was taken over in 1901 by Detroit businessman Henry Bourne Joy; two years later the factory moved to Detroit and the first four-cylinder Packard, designed by French engineer Charles Schmidt (formerly with Mors), appeared. The 1904 Model L four-cylinder was the first Packard to be fitted with the distinctive shouldered radiator shell that became the make's hallmark.

Packard introduced its first six-cylinder model in 1912, by which time the company was firmly established as a maker of high-priced luxury cars.

In 1915, Packard's chief engineer Jesse G. Vincent, taking inspiration from the pioneering V12

aero engines produced by Sunbeam in Britain (one of which had found its way to America in a Sunbeam racing car), launched the world's first series-production V12 car, the Packard Twin-Six. This 6950 cc model represented virtually half that year's sales, and remained in production until 1923, by which time 35,046 had been built, and Warren Gamaliel Harding had become the first US President to ride to his inauguration by car… in a Twin-Six.

Packard launched a 4395 cc Single-Six in 1921, and in June 1923 the Twin-Six was replaced by the 5681 cc Single Eight, with four-wheel brakes and four-speed transmission. The smooth-running Single Eight gave Packard pre-eminence in the luxury car field; instead of annual model changes, the Single Eight was produced in Series, and was well-established enough by 1928 for Packard to embark on a policy of eight-cylinder cars.

In 1928 Packard also began limited production of a Speedster Eight based on the new Sixth Series Eight. Although the Speedster line lasted into the Seventh Series, only 220 examples of this performance model were built.

Even though 5744 examples of a new Vincent-designed 7298 cc V12, initially bearing the famous Twin-Six name, were built between

1931–1939, eight-cylinder cars remained Packard's mainstay during the 1930s. The company moved into a more moderate price bracket in 1935 with the eight-cylinder Packard 120, which had the marque's first independent front suspension system, and sold for a basic price of only $ 990. It was followed two years later by a six, which helped boost production to a record 109,518 in 1937.

The Senior Series 160 and 180 luxury eights were produced until America entered the war; then, as a gesture of American goodwill, their body dies were sold to Russia, who introduced their version of the Packard as the 1945 ZIS–110 series.

As a result, immediately after the war Packard had no luxury car line to compete with Lincoln and Cadillac, and had to rely on a relaunch of its 1941 Clipper series, which ranged from the 4015 cc Clipper Six to the DeLuxe Clipper and Super and Custom range, powered by 4621 cc and 5834 cc eights.

A slab-sided restyling of the old body earned the 1948 Packards the 'Pregnant Elephant' nickname, though the cars initially proved popular; Packard sales reached a post-war high of 104,593 in 1948, and then began to fall.

The 1948 models were available in three series – Eight, Super Eight and Custom Eight – with a choice of 4720 cc or 5359 cc engines. Six-cylinder engines were available in taxis and export models.

Packard's own automatic transmission, the 'Ultramatic Drive', was launched in the spring of 1949, though the arrival of the first completely new post-war Packards, in the shape of the Twenty-Fourth Series 200, 200 DeLuxe, 250, 300 and 400 models, was delayed until 1951.

The 4720 cc eight was standard on the Clipper 200, 250 and 300, while the 5359 cc eight was optional on these models and standard on the 400 Patrician.

Packard's new president, James J. Nance, who joined the company

from Hotpoint in 1952, was convinced that a return to luxury cars was the way to revive the ailing company, so the low-priced Clipper line was designated a separate marque. Nance also tried to destroy all links with the past in the shape of spares stocks for obsolete models and historic archives.

In 1953 Packard returned to the custom-body market with a short run of Derham-bodied Patricians and 750 Caribbean convertibles (based on the 1952 Pan American show cars).

Nance had initiated an over-ambitious plan of expansion and diversification, and in June 1954 made the fatal mistake of buying Studebaker, which was in dire financial straits, in an attempt to widen the company's market.

Three months later, Packard introduced the new 1955 Packards, known as the First Series. Although the body was a clever re-skin of the old model, beneath it were some revolutionary features, chief of which were electrically-actuated Torsion-Level suspension, automatically compensating for different loads, on all four wheels, and electric pushbutton Twin-Ultramatic transmission as standard. There was a brand-new 5801 cc V8, too. Unfortunately, insufficient development time had been allowed, and the new models suffered from annoying teething troubles which alienated customers.

Sales for 1955 rose to almost 70,000, and then tumbled to just over 13,000 the following year, when, dragged down by the millstone of Studebaker, the group was taken over by the Curtis-Wright Corporation as a tax loss. Nance, having brought the once-proud Packard name to its knees inside four years, had already quit.

The last true Packards appeared in 1956, in which year the company attempted to forecast its future styling trends with an unspeakable concept car called the Predictor, designed by their chief stylist Dick Teague and built by

Ghia in Turin. In the 1956 range a new Executive model was introduced to bridge the gap between Clipper and Packard, but by 1957 the Packard had become nothing more than a Studebaker decorated with left-over Packard trim items. The ugly Hawk (of which only 588 were built) had a wide-mouthed, glassfibre snout and huge tailfins. When Packard sales collapsed to 1745 cars in 1958, the marginally more successful Studebaker company (whose directors had assumed control after the departure of Nance) killed off the marque.

## Packard Twin-Six

Launched in May 1915 for the 1916 model year, the Twin-Six was the world's first series-production V12. It was the creation of the brilliant chief engineer of Packard, Jesse G. Vincent, who had taken his inspiration from the V12 aero engines built in England by Sunbeam.

So instantly popular was this

**Packard Twin-Six**

### 1915 PACKARD TWIN-SIX

**Engine:** V12, L-head
**Bore × stroke:** 76.2 mm × 127 mm
**Capacity:** 6950 cc
**Maximum power:** 85 bhp
**Transmission:** three-speed manual
**Chassis:** pressed steel channel
**Suspension:** non-independent, with semi-elliptic leaf springs front and rear
**Brakes:** rear-wheel drums
**Bodywork:** runabout, tourer, landaulet, coupé, brougham, limousine
**Maximum speed (approx):** 60 mph (97 kph)

7-litre luxury car that nearly 50 per cent of Packard's 1916 output of 18,572 cars consisted of Twin-Sixes.

The side-valve power unit of the Twin-Six had only three main bearings, but nevertheless it could accelerate smoothly up to a maximum of 3000 rpm.

Moreover, the Twin-Six left an important legacy: a young Italian named Enzo Ferrari was inspired by photographs of a racing Packard V12 and the sight of US Army officers in Twin-Six staff cars during the Great War to formulate plans for the manufacture of his own V12 cars.

## Packard Sixth Series Eight

Introduced on 1 August, 1928, the Sixth Series Eight was available in five different models and 10 different body types. The most distinctive of these was the limited production Speedster – of which only 70 were built – equipped with a high-compression Big Eight power unit with a high-lift camshaft and elarged manifold. These engines produced 145 bhp, and the Speedsters were capable of 100 mph.

At the same time Packard laun-

### 1928 PACKARD SIXTH SERIES EIGHT

**Engine:** in-line eight-cylinder, side-valve
**Bore × stroke:** 88.9 mm × 127 mm
**Capacity:** 6305 cc
**Maximum power:** 106 bhp
**Transmission:** four-speed manual
**Chassis:** pressed steel channel
**Suspension:** non-independent, with semi-elliptic leaf springs front and rear
**Brakes:** drums all round
**Bodywork:** Roadster, Phaeton, Sedan, Coupé, Speedster
**Maximum speed (approx):** 80 mph (129 kph)

ched the 640 Custom Eight, which had a new wheelbase length of 140 in (356 cm) as opposed to the Standard Eight's 126.5 in (321 cm) and 133.5 in (339 cm), and offered a range of bodywork broadly similar to that of the earlier Fourth Series.

There was, however, a range of new semi-custom bodies by Dietrich on the De Luxe chassis and this was augmented a month later by the arrival of the De Luxe Eight line, which offered a choice of eight factory-built bodies and 13 semi-custom styles.

The Sixth Series is also notable for having been the first Packard car to carry the 'pelican in her piety' emblem of the Packard family.

By the time the Sixth Series was supplanted by the Seventh Series in late 1929, Packard was selling 50 per cent of the world's prestige cars.

**Packard Sixth Series Eight**

# A-Z OF THE CAR

## PAIGE, PAIGE-DETROIT

**Detroit, USA**
**1908–1927**

The original 1908 25 hp Paige-Detroit was powered by a 2172 cc three-cylinder two-stroke engine, built in unit with a two-speed gearbox. The company built 302 of these cars in 1908–09, before adopting four-stroke fours.

The first of these was the 2896 cc 25, which remained in production until 1914, when it was succeeded by the 4118 cc 36.

In 1915, Paige-Detroit adopted a policy of only building six-cylinder cars, powered by 3771 cc Rutenber and 4967 cc Continental engines. The company was only three years behind Ford when, in 1916, it installed a moving assembly line.

Paige became known as 'the Most Beautiful Car in America' from 1921, when it gained a handsome plated radiator which looked like a Bentley cooler with shoulders and which was particularly effective on the handsome Daytona roadster of 1922–26. From 1923–26, the Paige company also built the Jewett car.

The 1927 Paige range was made up of three sixes and an eight; the following year, the three Graham brothers took control of the company, and the marque became known as the Graham-Paige.

### 1921 PAIGE

**Engine:** in-line six-cylinder, side-valve
**Bore × stroke:** 95.25 mm × 127 mm
**Capacity:** 5429 cc
**Maximum power:** 66 bhp
**Transmission:** three-speed manual
**Chassis:** pressed steel channel
**Suspension:** non-independent, with semi-elliptic leaf springs front and rear
**Brakes:** rear-wheel drums
**Bodywork:** sport, tourer, coupé, sedan
**Maximum speed (approx):** 65 mph (105 kph)

## PANHARD ET LEVASSOR

**Paris, France**
**1889–1967**

The origins of Panhard & Levassor go back to 1847, when Perin & Pauwels founded a firm to make woodworking machinery. When Perin died in 1886, control of the company passed to two young engineers, René Panhard and Emile Levassor.

Levassor's friend, Edouard Sarazin, acquired the French rights to the Daimler engine patents, but died young, in 1887. His widow subsequently married Levassor, and brought the patent rights as her dowry.

At first, Panhard & Levassor were content merely to sell engines to other constructors, like Peugeot, but in 1891 they built their first car. Although it was rear-engined, like all the early designs, Levassor soon developed the layout of a front engine under a bonnet driving the rear wheels through a sliding gear change. This was adopted by most subsequent constructors, though it became – unjustly – known as the 'Système Panhard'.

For Panhard & Levassor, racing really did improve the breed; the marque's fame was established by joint first place in the 1894 Paris-Rouen trial, and by arriving first in the 1895 Paris–Bordeaux–Paris race (though, as a two-seater, Levassor's car wasn't eligible for first prize!). Other racing successes included victories in the 1896 Paris–Marseille–Paris, the 1898 Paris–Amsterdam and the 1899 Tour de France.

Out of the company's involvement in racing came wheel steering, as a replacement for 'the cow's tail' tiller (an accident in a tiller-steered racer contributed to Levassor's premature death in 1897), and their first four-cylinder engine, fitted to a racer in 1896 and available to customers in 1898.

The original Daimler vee-twin power unit was succeeded in 1895 by the 2.4-litre vertical-twin Phenix engine, which became the company's mainstay for the next few years.

But the early supremacy of the Panhard & Levassor company was rapidly eroded when Daimler's new 'Mercedes' appeared in 1901, for thereafter it was the Mercedes and not the Panhard which 'set the pattern to the world'. Without Levassor, it seems, the company couldn't keep abreast of technical developments. It continued to expand its range of cars in the early 1900s, however, and a 1.8-litre three-cylinder 8/11 hp was a popular model.

In 1906 Panhard & Levassor introduced two monsters, a 10.5-litre 50CV four-cylinder and an 11-litre six-cylinder.

The company's products had become more modest by 1909, when a four-model range included a 1206 cc Phenix twin-cylinder, a 10 hp (2412 cc), a four-cylinder 15 hp (3380 cc) and a 25 hp six of 4962 cc.

The Phenix was at last discontinued in 1910; new models introduced that year included a 5231 cc four-cylinder 25 hp and a 6597 cc six-cylinder 28 hp, and more significantly, Panhard & Levassor's first production model with a Knight sleeve-valve engine, the 4398 cc 20 hp.

The company's next sleeve-valve model, with a 2613 cc engine, was launched in 1912 and from then on, the Knight sleeve-valve engine held sway at Panhard & Levassor; a 7363 cc 35 hp was soon added to the range, while in 1914 the company launched its first sleeve-valve six, the 6597 cc 30 hp.

Poppet-valves reappeared briefly after the war on the 2280 cc

10 hp, but Knight-engined cars soon reappeared, Panhard & Levassor even producing an 1187 cc 10 hp sleeve-valve in 1922, and by 1925 all Panhards had sleeve-valve engines. They also had an idiosyncratic X-gate gearchange and push-on handbrakes.

The range then consisted of four-cylinder 10, 16 and 20 hp models plus the 6355 cc eight-cylinder 35 hp. In 1925, the 10 hp was enlarged in swept volume to 1480 cc, and in 1927 a new six-cylinder, the 2344 cc 20/60CV was launched.

Panhard & Levassor returned to the sleeve-valve eight-cylinder layout in 1931, but this 5-litre car proved a failure, not least on account of its cost – 95,000 F, as compared with 80,000 F for the

**Paige Daytona Speedster**

most expensive Renault. The best-selling Panhard & Levassors at that time were the 1.8-litre 16/45HP and the 2.3-litre 18/50HP.

A bizarre, futuristic design was introduced in 1937. The Dynamic had three seats at the front with the steering wheel in the centre, streamlined styling with faired-in headlamps and wheels and a backbone chassis, and was available with 2.5, 2.7 and 3.8-litre engines.

After the war, Panhard & Levassor completely reversed its production policy and launched a high-performance economy car, the 610 cc front-wheel-drive air-cooled flat-twin Dyna, which was enlarged to 750 cc in 1950 and 800 cc in 1952, while a sports car based on the Dyna, the Junior, appeared in 1952. Panhard's last new model was the 24CT coupé, launched in 1964.

After the Citroën takeover of Panhard & Levassor in 1967, the company was compelled to stop manufacturing cars as Citroën wanted the factory space; the only Panhard's produced thereafter were armoured cars.

## Panhard 3HP

Though the front-engined, rear-wheel-drive layout had been used in the 1880s on Bollée's Mancelle steamers, the 1891 Panhard & Levassor was the first petrol car to adopt this configuration, which became accepted as normal by virtually every other constructor, and is still dominant today.

Power was supplied to the 1891 3 hp Panhard & Levassor by a licence-built vee-twin Daimler engine, which drove through the cu-

### 1894 PANHARD & LEVASSOR

**Engine:** vee-twin, automatic inlet valves
**Bore × stroke:** 70 mm × 110 mm
**Capacity:** 847 cc
**Maximum power:** 3 bhp
**Transmission:** three speeds forward, three reverse
**Chassis:** armoured wood
**Suspension:** non-independent, with full-elliptic leaf springs front, semi-elliptics rear
**Brakes:** shoes on rear tyres
**Bodywork:** two-seater, dog cart, wagonette
**Maximum speed (approx):** 12 mph (19 kph)

**Panhard et Levassor 3HP**

rious medium of a brush clutch to a 'gearbox' in which the gears were totally exposed; a bevel-geared countershaft carried sprockets at each end for the side chains which drove the rear wheels.

Despite the crudities of the design, one of the very first Panhard & Levassors was acquired by a French priest, Abbé Gavois, who used it every day for well over two decades; it was still in running order in the late 1920s – a tribute either to its reliability or to the Abbe's persistence.

'The wheels are in wood with steel tyres,' said the company's 1892 catalogue, 'but can equally be supplied with solid rubber tyres, which give good results, but are fairly expensive.'

Hot tube ignition and a surface carburettor were also part of the specification. In 1895 the swept volume of the engine was increased from 847 to 1325 cc, and a Maybach

spray carburettor replaced the temperamental surface device. In the same year the parallel-twin Phenix engine made its bow, but the old vee-twin continued to be offered alongside it for a while.

## Panhard Dynamic

One of the most advanced designs to be put into production by the French motor industry during the 1930s, the Dynamic first appeared at the 1936 Paris Salon.

Naturally, it was powered by a sleeve-valve engine – there was a choice of 2.5, 2.7 and 3.8-litre capacities – but the backbone chassis integral with the body, all-round independent suspension by torsion bars and worm final drive were all unorthodox.

It was, however, the styling which really attracted interest in the Dynamic, for the car was super-streamlined in the Art Deco mode, with flowing lines and deep spats on all four mudguards; moreover, the driver sat centrally, and there were curved bay windows at either

end of the windscreen (which had triple wipers) to give him panoramic vision. The headlamps were recessed in the wings and concealed behind grilles which matched the radiator, thus subordinating practicality to styling.

The 1939 models saw a rever-

### 1936 PANHARD DYNAMIC

**Engine:** in-line six-cylinder, sleeve-valve
**Bore × stroke:** 85 mm × 112 mm
**Capacity:** 3813 cc
**Maximum power:** 70 bhp
**Transmission:** silent four-speed with free-wheel
**Chassis:** steel backbone integral with body
**Suspension:** independent, with torsion-bar springs front and rear
**Brakes:** drums all round
**Bodywork:** streamlined coupé
**Maximum speed (approx):** 75 mph (120 kph)

**Panhard Dynamic Coupé**

**Panhard 24CT Coupé**

# Panhard Dyna

During World War II, the Panhard factory was supposed to be working for the German occupiers, but managed to slow things up by bombarding the Germans with so much paperwork that no significant production took place. Instead, a design team led by Jean Panhard worked clandestinely on a post-war economy car, based on designs by Jean Grégoire.

Fifty pre-production prototypes were built in 1947, and the new Panhard Dyna went into production in 1948. It was powered by a 610 cc air-cooled flat-twin engine with torsion-bar springs for the valve gear.

With its aluminium-alloy frame and bulkhead, plus alloy bodywork, the Dyna was capable of a surprisingly good performance on a modest 15 bhp power output and, weighing some 42 lb (19 kg) per hp, it was capable of over 60 mph.

Novel features included seats which folded down into a bed, and the Dyna design was progressively developed, first into a 32 bhp 750 cc version, and then into an 850 cc version for 1952.

A major step forward came with the Dyna 54, the first model to be fitted with front-wheel-drive, and capable of averaging 31.5 mpg at a constant 70 mph (113 kph).

The alloy bodywork was replaced by steel in 1958: the sporting derivatives of the 1960s, like the Tigre and the 24CT, were handsomely streamlined coupés whose styling was, in many respects, well ahead of its time.

# PANTHER

**Weybridge, England
1972–**

Robert Jankel started building cars as a hobby, but the demand for replicas of his work led him to establish the Panther Westwinds company in 1971, and the first production model, the J72, appeared in June 1972. Bearing a strong resemblance to the pre-war Jaguar SS100, the Panther J72 was originally powered by the 3.8-litre Jaguar engine, though the 4.2-litre six or 5.3-litre V12 Jaguar units later became available as options. Remarkably, it retained a solid front axle throughout the 1970s.

The success of the J72 set the scene for the production of a wide variety of Panthers, mostly replicas that tended toward exaggerated caricature rather than exact reproduction. Among these were Panther's interpretations of the Ferrari FF, the Bugatti Royale and the Lancia D24.

The Panther De Ville, a luxury limousine loosely inspired by the Bugatti Royale and powered by a Jaguar V12 engine, was launched at the 1974 London Motor Show.

Other Panther creations of the 1970s included a one-off, three-seater 'beach-buggy' called the Lazer, Jaguar-powered and capable of 150 mph (241 kph), an extremely expensive special-bodied Triumph Dolomite Sprint known as the Rio, and an astonishing 8.2-litre turbocharged Cadillac-engined six-wheeler, of which two examples were built.

In 1975, Panther acquired the rights to build the Monica, which had just gone out of production in France, but little came of this.

The great success for Panther came with the launch, in the mid-1970s, of the low-cost Lima, a slightly overblown glassfibre-bodied two-seater sports car with a Vauxhall engine. However, by the early '80s the company had over-reached itself and run into financial trouble, and in January 1981 it was taken over by the Korean Jindo Industries conglomerate and reformed under the dynamic Young C. Kim.

Production was concentrated on the Lima, now renamed the Kallista and equipped with Korean-built aluminium coachwork. The Kallista used the 2.8-litre Ford V6 which gave the car far better performance than the old Lima as it was capable of reaching over 120 mph (193 kph). In 1984 the company unveiled an exciting modern mid-engined sports car, the Solo.

## 1964 PANHARD DYNA 24CT

**Engine:** horizontally-opposed twin-cylinder with overhead valves (torsion-bar valve springs)
**Bore × stroke:** 85 mm × 75 mm
**Capacity:** 851 cc
**Maximum power:** 42 bhp
**Transmission:** four-speed manual, front-wheel drive
**Chassis:** reinforced sheet-aluminium platform with tubular extensions
**Suspension:** front independent with double transverse leaf springs, rear non-independent with rigid dead axle and coil springs
**Brakes:** drums all round
**Bodywork:** sports coupé
**Maximum speed (approx):** 100 mph (161 kph)

## 1984 PANTHER KALLISTA

**Engine:** V6, overhead-valve
**Bore × stroke:** 93 mm × 68.5 mm
**Capacity:** 2792 cc
**Maximum power:** 150 bhp
**Transmission:** five-speed manual
**Chassis:** box-section ladder-frame
**Suspension:** front independent with coils and wishbones, rear non-independent with rigid axle, radius arms and coil springs
**Brakes:** discs front, drums rear
**Bodywork:** two-seat sports
**Maximum speed (approx):** 123 mph (198 kph)

**Panther Kallista**

## PARAMOUNT

Swadlincote/Linslade, England
1950–1956

The first Paramount sports car, 'of very modern lines', made its appearance in the mid-1950s. Power was by the ubiquitous 1172 cc Ford Ten engine, mounted in a simple ladder chassis of welded steel tube with independent front suspension.

The four-seater coachwork was of neat streamlined appearance, with spatted rear wings, and was panelled in aluminium over an ash framework. Twin SU carburettors were fitted as standard, although early cars were offered with the option of a Shorrock supercharger.

Although the Paramount seemed an attractive proposition, only six were built in the first three years or so. The company then moved south to Linslade, near Leighton Buzzard, where production really got under way.

Most of the Paramounts built were attractive four-seater tourers, although a few closed cars were also constructed. Late in 1955, the 1508 cc Ford Consul engine was adopted, but manufacture ceased in the following year and the remaining cars were sold off.

### 1950 PARAMOUNT

**Engine:** in-line four-cylinder, side-valve
**Bore × stroke:** 63.5 mm × 92.5 mm
**Capacity:** 1172 cc
**Maximum power:** 40 hp
**Transmission:** three-speed manual
**Chassis:** cold-drawn steel tube
**Suspension:** front independent with transverse leaf spring and wishbones, rear non-independent with underslung rigid axle and semi-elliptic leaf springs
**Brakes:** drums all round
**Bodywork:** coupé or roadster
**Maximum speed (approx):** 70 mph (113 kph)

**Peerless V8**

## PEERLESS

Cleveland, USA
1900–1931

Peerless had established themselves as manufacturers of cycles and clothes-wringers before turning to motor cars in 1900 with the 3.5 hp single-cylinder Motorette, which retailed for $1300; a cheaper version, the Type B, appeared during 1901.

The 1902 Peerless range was designed by Louis P. Mooers, who was to have a decisive effect on company policy. He introduced more advanced models, with twin-cylinder engines, shaft drive and side-entrance bodies, and created a massive 80 hp racer with a wire-gauze bonnet which he drove in the 1903 Gordon Bennett race.

In the same year, Peerless introduced their first production four-cylinder models, T-head cars of 24 hp and 34 hp. They also introduced what is believed to be America's first catalogued closed car.

Peerless obtained much useful publicity from the 11,118 cc 'Green Dragon' racer – derived from the Gordon Bennett car of 1904 – which was spectacularly driven by the barnstorming speed-ace Barney Oldfield.

The marque had been accepted as a prestige marque by 1907, when Peerless launched their first six-cylinder model.

Peerless standardised self-starters in 1913, while in 1915 'The Equipoised Eight' V8 model supplanted the six-cylinder models, of which there were no more until 1924.

In 1925, for the first time, Peerless adopted a proprietory engine – a Continental six – and this was followed by a Continental V8 in 1929.

The Depression proved fatal to Peerless, and sales continued to plummet despite restyling by Count Alexis de Sakhnoffsky.

An advanced 1931 7.6-litre V16 which made extensive use of light alloys – the frame weighed a mere 42 lb – never made production. The factory lay idle for two years, until the repeal of Prohibition, when the Peerless Motor Car Company re-emerged, phoenix-like, as the brewers of Carlings Ale . . . .

### 1918 PEERLESS V8

**Engine:** V8, side-valve
**Bore × stroke:** 82.6 mm × 127 mm
**Capacity:** 5437 cc
**Maximum power:** 65 bhp
**Transmission:** three-speed manual
**Chassis:** pressed steel channel
**Suspension:** non-independent, with semi-elliptic leaf springs front and rear
**Brakes:** rear-wheel drums
**Bodywork:** roadster, tourer, coupé, sedan, limousine
**Maximum speed (approx):** 64 mph (103 kph)

## PEERLESS

Slough, England
1958–1962

Designed by Bernie Rodgers, this glassfibre GT coupé was produced by Peerless Motors, whose name came from the fact that they had sold reconditioned ex-US Army Peerless trucks from the Slough vehicle park after the Great War. The four-seater Grand Touring Peerless was powered by a Triumph TR3 engine, had a multi-tubular chassis and was quite a brisk performer.

In 1958 a Peerless took 16th place at Le Mans, which brought the company some 250 orders in the next 12 months. The car was somewhat lacking in refinement, however, and production soon came to an end. In 1963 Chris Lawrence produced his own one-off interpretation of how the Peerless could have developed. The car had Lawrence's own design of chassis and used components from two recently defunct TR-engined Rodgers designs, the Peerless and the Warwick, hence its unlovely name – Peewick.

**Paramount Ten**

**Peerless**

# PEGASO

### Barcelona, Spain
### 1951–1957

After Enasa (the Spanish state truck company) took over the old Hispano-Suiza factory to produce Pegaso commercials, it was decided to undertake the limited production of a luxury sports car as an exercise in apprentice training. Designed by Don Wifredo Ricart, the Pegaso car was powered by a 2474 cc V8 engine with twin camshafts.

Introduced at the 1951 Paris Salon, the Z-102 Pegaso was claimed by its makers to be 'the fastest car in the world', in proof of which a Pegaso achieved a speed of 156 mph (251 kph) and set up flying kilometre and mile records of 151.05 mph (243 kph) and 151.99 mph (245 kph) respectively on the Jabbeke autoroute in Belgium in September 1953.

Although Pegaso offered stylish standardised bodywork, many of the leading carrossiers of the day constructed breathtaking coachwork on the Pegaso, such as the 1953 Touring 'Berlinetta Thrill'.

During the production span of the Pegaso, variants with engines of 2.8 litres (Z102B), 3.2 litres (Z102SS) and 4.0, 4.5 and 4.7 litres (Z103) were produced, and the option of a Roots supercharger was also available. The high-compression engines and particularly the 'blown' variety were extremely powerful devices.

In total, 125 Pegaso Z102s were produced, and three Z103s.

### 1958 PEERLESS

**Engine:** in-line four-cylinder, overhead-valve
**Bore × stroke:** 83 mm × 92 mm
**Capacity:** 1991 cc
**Maximum power:** 100 bhp
**Transmission:** four-speed plus overdrive
**Chassis:** square-section steel tube
**Suspension:** all-independent, with coils and wishbones front, de Dion axle and semi-elliptic leaf springs rear
**Brakes:** discs front, drums rear
**Bodywork:** glassfibre coupé
**Maximum speed (approx):** 110 mph (177 kph)

### 1951 PEGASO Z102

**Engine:** V8, four-cam
**Bore × stroke:** 75 mm × 70 mm
**Capacity:** 2474 cc
**Maximum power:** 170 bhp
**Transmission:** five-speed
**Chassis:** fabricated multi-square tube
**Suspension:** all-independent, with paired wishbones and torsion bars front, reversed de Dion axle and torsion bars rear
**Brakes:** discs all round
**Bodywork:** sports coupé
**Maximum speed (approx):** 155 mph (250 kph)

**Pegaso Z102**

# PEUGEOT

**Beaulieu/Audincourt/Sochaux, France
1889–**

The Peugeot family had become established as the leading dynasty in France's ironmongery business many decades before young Armand Peugeot, foreseeing the potential of the horseless carriage, built a three-wheeled steam car in conjunction with Leon Serpollet in 1889. Steam proved to be a fairly troublesome motive source, so Peugeot sought another form of engine. He showed the steamer at the 1889 Paris Exposition, where it attracted the attention of Emile Levassor, who went with Gottleib Daimler to the Peugeot factory at Valentigny in Eastern France to convince Peugeot of the potential of Daimler's internal combustion engine, for which Panhard & Levassor held the French agency.

Peugeot was convinced, and from 1890 began to produce rear-engined cars inspired by Daimler's 1889 'Stahlrad' car; these had Panhard-built Daimler engines in tubular chassis which reflected Peugeot's dominant position in the French cycle industry.

Sales multiplied steadily, from four cars in 1891 to 29 in 1892; in 1896, when 78 cars were sold in 10 months, Armand Peugeot decided to establish a separate automobile manufacturing company, and moved out of the family works at Beaulieu to establish a new factory at nearby Audincourt. Later that year, Peugeot started to make their own engines, vertical twin-cylinders designed by Gratien Michaux. Despite early teething troubles with this power unit, by 1899 Peugeot had attained annual sales of 323 cars, all still recognisably descended from the first rear-engined design.

In 1901 Peugeot revealed its first front-engined production cars, which included an 8 hp twin and a 15 hp four; most popular of these new models was the 652 cc single-cylinder 'Bébé'. By 1904, the Peugeot range included cars from 1.7 litres to 7.1 litres. The first six-cylinder Peugeot, with a 10.4-litre engine, appeared in 1908, followed the next year by a smaller six of 3317 cc. The biggest of all the pre-Great War Peugeot sixes had a swept volume of 11,150 cc, and was current in 1908-09.

Between 1906-10 a separate company run by Armand Peugeot's cousin Robert manufactured cars in the old Beaulieu-Valentigny factory (where Robert was already building motor-cycles) under the name 'Lion-Peugeot'; these light cars had single, vee-twin or V4 power units of up to 1.9 litres (plus some ferocious ultra-long-stroke racers, typical of which was a 100 mm × 250 mm single-cylinder of 1952 cc, with two plugs and *six* valves).

The two Peugeot companies were merged in 1910 by the creation of the 'SA des Cycles & Automobiles Peugeot', and a new works at Sochaux – which would later become the principal Peugeot car factory – was opened.

In 1912, Peugeot introduced a new Bugatti-designed 855 cc four-cylinder Bébé, with an unusual two-speed transmission consisting of two concentric propellor shafts and crown wheels and pinions of different diameters.

Although in the years 1912–14 the twin-overhead-camshaft Peugeot racers designed by Ernest Henry in conjunction with a trio of racing drivers named Boillot, Goux and Zuccarelli achieved tremendous racing success, including victories in the French Grand Prix and the Indianapolis 500, this camshaft layout didn't find its way into production vehicles, and at the outbreak of war, Peugeot's most popular products were the model 153

2613 cc 12CV and the 1452 cc 7CV, both with side-valve power units.

Peugeot resumed production of these two models after the war, with the addition of a 1525 cc 10CV and a 5954 cc 25CV cuff-valve six.

A new small car in the same idiom as the pre-war Bébé, the 667 cc Quadrilette was introduced in late 1920; it was replaced in 1923 by the 5CV, based on the same platform chassis, though the engine of this new model was enlarged in 1925 to 719 cc.

Peugeot continued to expand during the 1920s, buying factories from the moribund Bellanger and De Dion Bouton companies in 1927, and new models began to appear, starting in 1928 with the 1991 cc Type 183.

The mainstay of the Peugeot range for a decade, the 1122 cc Type 201 was launched in 1929; a year later came the exciting Type 201X, powered by a supercharged overhead-cam 995 cc engine designed by Ettore Bugatti, and, in effect, half a Bugatti Type 35. Few 201X cars were built; the model was discontinued in 1932 after racing driver André Boillot was killed during a testing session.

In 1931, the 'Lion-Peugeot' name was revived for a new version of the 201 with independent front suspension, while in March 1932 the company introduced the 1465 cc 301, a development of the 201.

The last of Peugeot's pre-war six-cylinders, the 601, appeared in 1936; a year later came the streamlined Peugeot 402 which lasted until the war, alongside the similarly-styled 302 and 202; it was the 302 chassis plus the powertrain and axles of the 402 which was used as the basis for the Darl'Mat sports car.

Peugeot, a pioneer of the diesel lorry, built a few diesel-engined 402s before the war. Another field of experiment was aerodynamics, and several 402s were fitted with streamlined bodywork designed by Jean Andreau; some were equipped with 802 V8 power units.

During the Occupation, Peugeot built a limited number of VLV crab-tracked electric-powered cyclecars. After the war, production of the 202 was resumed, and in 1947 Peugeot launched a new 1.3-litre model, the 203, with independent front suspension, rack and pinion steering and hydraulic brakes. It was produced until 1960.

Peugeot took over Chenard-Walcker in 1950; the company already owned a considerable share in Hotchkiss.

Another best-seller arrived in 1955 in the shape of the 1500 cc 403, followed in 1960 by the 1600 cc 404; these cars were also available in diesel form.

Peugeot launched an advanced small car – the transverse-engined 1100 cc 204 – in 1965; it had an all-aluminium power unit with the gearbox housed in the sump. The 204 was replaced in 1969 by the 1300 cc 304.

The 504, with a 1796 cc power unit developed from the 404 engine, was launched as the top-of-the-range model in 1968.

In the 1970s, Peugeot swallowed first Citroën, then Chrysler Europe, but found the Chrysler operations – which were rechristened Talbot – somewhat indigestible.

The V6-engined 604 was prematurely launched in 1974 because of press leaks, and went into production the following year. A further model launched in the early 1970s was the 104 small car, which was also sold with a Citroën power unit as the Citroën LN.

In 1978 came the new 305, followed the next year by the 505. The 305 saloon and estate models were available with a choice of five four-cylinder engines, ranging between 1290 cc and 1905 cc, four and five-speed manual gearboxes and four-speed automatic transmission. These medium-size front-wheel-drive cars sold extremely well.

In 1983 an excellent small car, the 205, was launched, available with power units of 954 cc, 1124 cc, 1360 cc and 1580 cc, plus a 1768 cc diesel.

## Peugeot Bébé

In his early days, Ettore Bugatti designed a number of cars for licence-production by other manufacturers. Such a vehicle was the Bébé Peugeot, a diminutive four-cylinder car of which the original prototype (which still survives) was built at Molsheim in 1911. Fitted with a Bugatti radiator, the prototype Bébé was shown – fruitlessly – to the German Wanderer company before Peugeot decided to take up the production licence, signing the agreement in November 1911. Manufacture of the Bébé Peugeot began in 1913.

By comparison with the contemporary Bugatti, the Bébé Peugeot was a touch *vieux style*, for it had side valves in a T-head and a cone clutch instead of the overhead valves and multiple-plate clutch seen on the Type 13 Bugatti. It also had Bugatti's ingenious two-speed transmission, consisting of twin concentric propellor shafts, each carrying at its extremity a pinion which meshed with one of two rows of teeth on the crown wheel (this was subsequently replaced by a conventional three-speed manual gearbox).

Between 1913 and 1916, Peugeot built over 3000 Bébés at its Beaulieu factory. The tiny car even took part in races, despite its slightly unpredictable roadholding.

**Peugeot Bébé**

# Peugeot Quadrilette

The Bébé formula had proved so successful that Peugeot re-used it after the war, with another diminutive economy car, the Quadrilette, designed to fit neatly into the low-taxation 'cyclecar' class (engine under 6 hp, weight under 350 kg/722 lb). Most cyclecars, inevitably, were the product of tiny workshops operating on the proverbial shoestring, and were extremely crude. The Quadrilette was a clever design with a new L-head four-cylinder power unit mounted in a pressed steel punt chassis with Z-shaped side-members. It was extremely economical and easy to maintain.

Capable of over 56 mpg, the Quadrilette was also claimed to be the most economical French car. Because space on its tiny chassis was so limited, the Quadrilette was frequently fitted with tandem-seat bodywork, though there was a side-by-side two-seater with staggered seating for thin people.

The basic powertrain was employed throughout the 1920s, though by 1922 the design had evolved into a proper small car, the 5CV. The engine size was enlarged, first to 720 cc, then to 746 cc, and the final-drive ratio progressively lowered to cope with the increasing weight of the bodywork, for some of these long-suffering baby cars were sold as four-seat saloons.

Nevertheless, the Quadrilette name survived into the 5CV era, and was used on the 172 BC, a low-cost 1925 version of the 5CV which retained the punt chassis.

**1912 PEUGEOT BEBE**

**Engine:** in-line four-cylinder, side-valve
**Bore × stroke:** 55 mm × 90 mm
**Capacity:** 855 cc
**Maximum power:** 10 bhp
**Transmission:** two-speed manual
**Chassis:** pressed steel channel
**Suspension:** non-independent, with semi-elliptic leaf springs front, reversed quarter-elliptics rear
**Brakes:** rear-wheel drums
**Bodywork:** two-seater
**Maximum speed (approx):** 37 mph (60 kph)

**1920 PEUGEOT QUADRILETTE**

**Engine:** in-line four-cylinder, side-valve
**Bore × stroke:** 50 mm × 85 mm
**Capacity:** 667 cc
**Maximum power:** 9.5 bhp
**Transmission:** three-speed
**Chassis:** pressed steel 'punt'
**Suspension:** non-independent, with transverse leaf spring front, quarter-elliptic leaf springs rear
**Brakes:** hand-brake on one rear wheel, foot-brake on the other
**Bodywork:** tandem or staggered two-seater
**Maximum speed (approx):** 37 mph (60 kph)

**Peugeot Quadrilette**

## Peugeot 402

The 'Sochaux Rocket', as it was nicknamed, was an attempt by Peugeot to give an impression of modernity equal to that of the Citroën Traction Avant, but without the troublesome technical features that had brought the Quai de Javel to its knees.

Beneath the bold aerodynamic styling with the headlamps con-

---

**1937 PEUGEOT 402**

**Engine:** in-line four-cylinder, overhead-valve
**Bore × stroke:** 83 mm × 92 mm
**Capacity:** 1991 cc
**Maximum power:** 55 bhp
**Transmission:** three-speed manual
**Chassis:** Bloctube 'top-hat' section boxed steel frame
**Suspension:** front independent with transverse leaf spring and radius arms, rear non-independent with cantilever leaf springs
**Brakes:** hydraulic drums all round
**Bodywork:** roadster, cabriolet, saloon
**Maximum speed (approx):** 65 mph (105 kph)

---

Peugeot 402

cealed behind the radiator grille, the Peugeot 402 conserved the 'Bloctube' chassis construction of its predecessor and rear-wheel drive, although cantilever rear springs were fitted to control the tendency of the rear axle to twist under torque from the engine.

The 402 was perhaps the first mass-produced car to be fitted with aesthetically-successful aerodynamic bodywork, and its lines have weathered well. Among the range of bodies available was a remarkable 'transformable coupé', whose hard-top could be electrically (or manually on the cheaper models) retracted into the boot. There were also 'commercial saloons' with hatchback bodywork capable of taking large loads.

The 1938 models were fitted with dry-liner power units, and the de luxe versions had aluminium cylinder heads which boosted the power output to 58 bhp.

## Peugeot 205 GTI

Every now and again a manufacturer gets a model almost completely right, and the Peugeot 205 GTI certainly fitted into that category.

Introduced as a rival to the ubiquitous Renault 5 in 1983, it soon swept the floor with the standard-setting 5 and Peugeot quickly realised that the chassis could cope easily with considerable power. The GTI version was equipped with a 105 bhp 1580 cc engine, and the large-engine/small car approach worked extremely well in that the small Peugeot could manage a very competitive top speed of 116 mph (187 kph) and reach 60 mph in 8.6 seconds while still being very fuel efficient – average consumption was well over 30 mpg.

Just as impressive as the performance were the handling and road-holding, both nothing short of delightful, while there was only a slight penalty in ride terms, thanks to the compliant strut-front and

---

**1984 PEUGEOT 205 GTI**

**Engine:** in-line four-cylinder, overhead-cam
**Bore × stroke:** 83 mm × 73 mm
**Capacity:** 1580 cc
**Maximum power:** 105 bhp
**Transmission:** five-speed
**Chassis:** integral
**Suspension:** independent front with MacPherson struts; non-independent rear with beam axle and torsion bars
**Brakes:** discs front, drums rear
**Bodywork:** two-door four-seater
**Maximum speed (approx):** 116 mph (187 kph)

---

torsion-bar rear suspension.

With Peugeot trying hard to improve its rather staid old-fashioned image, the 205 GTI came at just the right time and was soon being bought by the type of person who might otherwise have bought the more powerful and trend-setting VW Golf GTi.

Peugeot 205 GTI

**Pic-Pic Cabriolet**

# PIC-PIC

**Geneva, Switzerland**
**1905–1924**

In December 1904, four Swiss businessmen representing the Société d'Automobiles à Genève (SAG) approached hydraulic engineers Piccard-Pictet of Geneva and proposed that they should build cars designed by the expatriate Swiss engineer Marc Birkigt, who was working in Spain and had just created the Hispano-Suiza.

Piccard-Pictet began production of cars for SAG in 1906 with shaft-driven 20/24 hp and 35/40 hp models powered by pair-cast four-cylinder engines. At the 1907 Paris Salon a 5655 cc six-cylinder appeared.

Confusingly, while the marque was known as SAG in Switzerland until 1910, when the Société d'Automobiles à Genève failed and was taken over by Picard-Pictet, in export markets the cars always seem to have been sold under the Pic-Pic name.

In 1910 the first 'non-Birkigt' Pic-Pic appeared, a 14/18 hp monobloc four of 2413 cc, followed by an 18/22 hp four.

Pic-Pic adopted the Burt-McCollum single-sleeve-valve engine, which appeared in 1912; by 1913, the range – curiously – consisted of two 16/20 hp models, one of 2815 cc with poppet valves and one of 2951 cc, with sleeve valves, plus two poppet-valve 20/30 hp fours, differing only in the length of the stroke, with capacities of 3817 cc and 4236 cc respectively, and a sleeve-valve 30/40 hp of 4712 cc.

Front-wheel brakes and hydraulic shock-absorbers were

---

### 1913 PIC-PIC 16/20 HP

**Engine:** in-line four-cylinder, side-valve
**Bore × stroke:** 80 mm × 140 mm
**Capacity:** 2815 cc
**Maximum power:** 20 bhp
**Transmission:** four-speed manual
**Chassis:** pressed steel channel
**Suspension:** non-independent, with semi-elliptic leaf springs front and rear
**Brakes:** rear-wheel drums and transmission
**Bodywork:** to choice
**Maximum speed (approx):** 50 mph (80 kph)

---

used on the firm's unsuccessful 1914 Grand Prix cars, which introduced the handsome shouldered vee-radiator used on the post-war Pic-Pics. One of the GP cars was subsequently used on the road, rebodied as a coupé for Claude Wallis of *The Autocar* by the London Improved Coachbuilders.

Piccard-Pictet expanded rapidly during the Great War, producing army vehicles for the neutral Swiss Army: the workforce grew to a remarkable 7500. Inevitably, peace brought financial problems, and the company failed in 1920. It was reformed in 1921 by the Ateliers de Charmilles, who were mostly interested in the company's hydraulic engineering capabilities, although they continued to build Pic-Pic tourers at the rate of two a day.

In 1922 the car-building activities were sold off to a group of financiers with plans for mass-production, but the 3-litre sleeve-valve shown at the 1924 Geneva Salon proved to be the last Pic-Pic.

# PIERCE-ARROW

**Buffalo, USA**
**1901–1938**

George N. Pierce started in business making cages for birds and squirrels in 1865; he then utilised his wire-forming skills in the manufacture of cycle spokes and thus progressed to building complete shaft-drive cycles.

His cycle company built an unsuccessful steam car designed by Overman in 1900, and followed this with a De Dion-engined quadricycle, which was better received. This led to the first production Pierce, the De Dion-engined Motorette, designed by Yorkshireman David Fergusson, who had arrived in America as part of the entourage of the 'motor charlatan', E.J. Pennington, in 1899.

Later in 1902, Pierce launched a 15 hp twin, the Arrow, while in 1904 Fergusson introduced the Great Arrow, a 3770 cc Mercedes-inspired 24/28 hp four. This was joined the next year by 28/32 hp and 40/45 hp Great Arrows, and Pierce won the 1000-mile (1609 km) Glidden Tour reliability trial for the first of four wins in succession when a standard 28/

---

32 hp Great Arrow, driven by George N. Pierce's son Percy, scored 996 points out of a possible 1000.

From 1905, Pierce cars used cast aluminium body panels, while the first Pierce six-cylinder made its debut in the 1906 Glidden Tour; four years later, the company offered nothing but sixes.

The marque name Pierce-Arrow was adopted in 1909, and the range that year consisted of sixes of 36 hp (5686 cc), 48 hp (7423 cc) and 66 hp (10,619 cc).

The marque's distinctive trademark of headlamps set into the wings appeared with the 1913 Second Series, which also saw the end of annual model changes.

There was a major revision of the model range in 1918, when the Fifth Series was launched. The 66 hp and 38 hp were discontinued and a new pair-cast 47 hp with four valves per cylinder was introduced. This lasted just over a year before it was replaced by a revised monobloc version. In 1920, Pierce-Arrow finally dropped right-hand steering, and steel-panelled bodywork became predominant.

For 1925, a 'cheap' model, the Series 80, was introduced: this was the first four-wheel-braked Pierce-Arrow, and was replaced by the Series 81 in 1928. This had unfortunate Art Deco styling by James R. Way, which had an adverse effect on sales, and the Model 81 was soon discontinued.

Frightened by the sales slump, the Pierce-Arrow shareholders voted for an ill-starred merger with Studebaker in 1929, during which period Pierce-Arrow brought out an excellent new 5998 cc straight-eight.

During the eight's first season, sales totalled 8000, and even in the Depression year of 1930, 7000 were sold, but by 1932 Pierce-Arrow's total sales had crumbled to 2692, despite the introduction of an exciting new V12, the capabilities of which were proven when a prototype, driven by 'Mormon Meteor' Ab Jenkins, set up an unofficial American 24-hour record of 112.9 mph (182 kph) at Bonneville Salt Flats, Utah. The following year, Jenkins broke 14 international and 65 other records with a production V12, averaging 117 mph (188 kph) for 24 hours. With a modified Pierce-Arrow, Jenkins eventually averaged 127.2 mph (205 kph) for 24 hours.

A consortium of Buffalo businessmen bought Pierce-Arrow back from Studebaker in 1933, and shortly afterwards an ultra-streamlined Silver Arrow was built for the Chicago World's Fair.

An outstanding 1936 range – Model 1601 eight and Models 1602 and 1603 12s – was promoted as 'the safest cars in the world', but sales continued to slide. Although the Pierce-Arrow company tried to bolster its sagging finances with the production of trailer caravans, it was declared insolvent in 1938 and sold off. Its assets, valued at nearly $1 million, were auctioned for a mere $40,000.

## Pierce-Arrow 66

The mighty Pierce-Arrow 66 first appeared in 1909 with the relatively modest swept volume of 10,619 cc from its six separately-cast T-head cylinders. Despite this somewhat outmoded specification, the 66 proved popular, and for 1910 its engine was enlarged to 11,700 cc.

Sales – they varied between 66 and 206 units a year – were encouraging enough for the 66 to be

**Pierce-Arrow 66**

once again uprated, to 13,514 cc in 1912, making it the biggest-ever American production car.

The 66 remained in production for 10 years, during which time 1638 chassis were constructed, and when they went out of fashion many of them ended their days as fire-engines – Fire Chief Walter Ringer of Minneapolis devised a conversion whereby the chassis was lengthened, and the live rear axle of the 66 bolted to the extended frame and fitted with sprockets to drive a dead axle by chain. Some of these fire-engines served for 20 years.

## Pierce-Arrow Silver Arrow

The Pierce-Arrow 'Silver Arrow' was described as 'the car built in the 1930s for the 1940s'; it grew out of a meeting in October 1932 between Pierce-Arrow Vice President Roy Faulkner and his designer friend Philip Wright, who had conceived an automobile with a totally new appearance, based on wind-tunnel

experiments and developments.

The prototype Silver Arrow took just three months to build, and was one of the automotive stars of the 1933–34 Chicago Century of Progress Exposition. Its styling was a pretty good forecast of the shape that luxury cars would take in the

### 1933 PIERCE-ARROW SILVER ARROW

**Engine:** V12, L-head
**Bore × stroke:** 85.7 mm × 101.6 mm
**Capacity:** 7030 cc
**Maximum power:** 175 bhp
**Transmission:** three-speed manual
**Chassis:** box-girder frame
**Suspension:** non-independent, with semi-elliptic leaf springs front and rear
**Brakes:** drums all round, servo-assisted
**Bodywork:** streamlined saloon
**Maximum speed (approx):** 115 mph (185 kph)

### 1909 PIERCE-ARROW 66

**Engine:** in-line six-cylinder, T-head
**Bore × stroke:** 127 mm × 177.8 mm
**Capacity:** 13,514 cc
**Maximum power:** 85 bhp
**Transmission:** four-speed manual
**Chassis:** pressed steel channel
**Suspension:** non-independent, with semi-elliptic leaf springs front, three-quarter elliptics rear
**Brakes:** rear-wheel drums
**Bodywork:** runabout, touring, suburban, landau, brougham, landaulet
**Maximum speed (approx):** 60 mph (97 kph)

1940s: its headlamps, set either side of a raked radiator shell, were faired into the front wings in the best Pierce-Arrow tradition, but those wings were then continued back into the rising belt line of a full-width passenger compartment.

Twin spare wheels were concealed in the front wings, while the rear wheels were hidden behind skirts; the only jarring note of the ensemble was the tiny 'eyebrow' window breaking the smooth curve of the tail.

The car's styling can be seen retrospectively as an incongruous blend, though its stylist managed to maintain the company's feature of faired-in headlamps.

Five prototypes and five production Silver Arrows were built; the production cars were priced at $10,000 each, and their rear compartments were fitted with a duplicate set of instruments.

**Pierce-Arrow Silver Arrow**

## MODEL

Lamborghini Miura, 1967.
UK price when announced: £7455
(£9165 inc. tax).

## ENGINE

**Location:** Mid, transverse
**Type:** Water-cooled 60 degree V12 with aluminium alloy cylinder heads and block
**Cubic capacity:** 3929cc
**Bore x stroke:** 82mm x 62mm
**Compression ratio:** 9.8:1
**Valve gear:** 2 inclined valves per cylinder operated in hemispherical chambers by twin chain-driven overhead camshafts per bank of cylinders
**Fuel supply:** 4 Weber 40 IDL3Cs downdraught triple choke carburettors
**Ignition:** Twin coil and distributor, mechanical
**Maximum power:** 350bhp (net DIN) at 7000rpm
**Maximum torque:** 271lb ft (net DIN) at 5100rpm

## TRANSMISSION

**Layout:** Clutch and gearbox transversely mounted behind and in unit with the engine with direct gear drive
**Clutch:** Single plate, diaphragm spring, hydraulically operated
**Gearbox:** Five-speed manual synchromesh on all forward and reverse gear

| | |
|---|---|
| 1st 2.520:1 | 4th 1.00:1 |
| 2nd 1.735:1 | 5th 0.815:1 |
| 3rd 1.225:1 | |

**Final drive:** Helical spur with limited slip differential
**Ratio:** 4.08:1

## SUSPENSION

**Front:** Independent by double wishbones, coil springs and concentric telescopic dampers and anti-roll bar
**Rear:** Independent by double unequal wishbones, coil springs and concentric telescopic dampers and top-mounted anti-roll bar

## STEERING

**Type:** Rack and pinion, manual

## BRAKES

**Type:** Girling discs front and rear

## WHEELS AND TYRES

**Type:** 7 x 15in Atesia alloy with radial-ply Pirelli Cinturato 210HS 15

## BODY/CHASSIS

**Type:** Steel spaceframe chassis with alloy body. Coupé body, 2 doors, 2 seats

## DIMENSIONS AND WEIGHT

**Length:** 171.6in (4360mm)
**Width:** 69.3in (1760mm)
**Wheelbase:** 98.4in (2500mm)
**Track – front:** 55.6in (1412mm)
– **rear:** 55.6in (1412mm)
**Weight:** (kerb) 2850lb (1292kg)

## PERFORMANCE

**Maximum speed:** 172mph (277kph)
**Acceleration 0-60mph:** 6.7 seconds
**Fuel consumption:** 14mpg

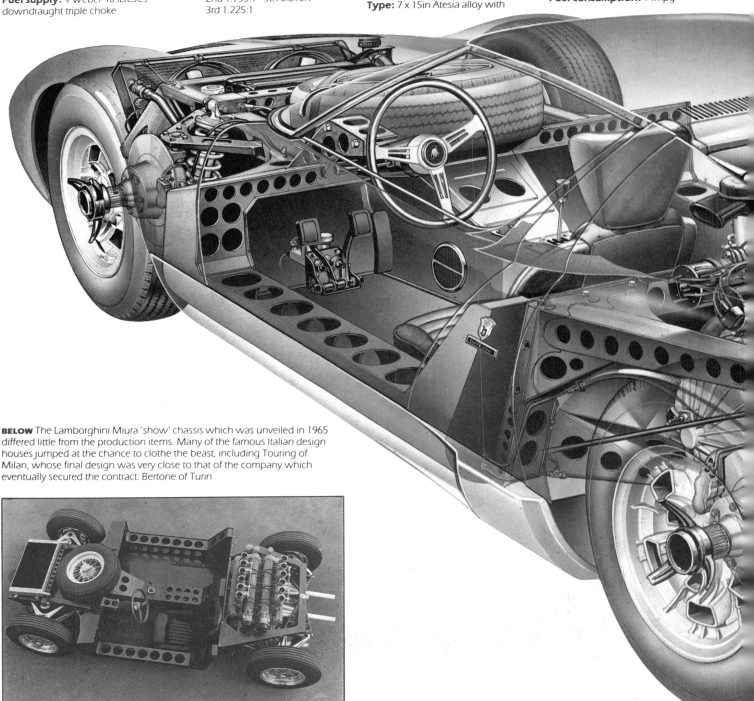

**BELOW** The Lamborghini Miura 'show' chassis which was unveiled in 1965 differed little from the production items. Many of the famous Italian design houses jumped at the chance to clothe the beast, including Touring of Milan, whose final design was very close to that of the company which eventually secured the contract: Bertone of Turin

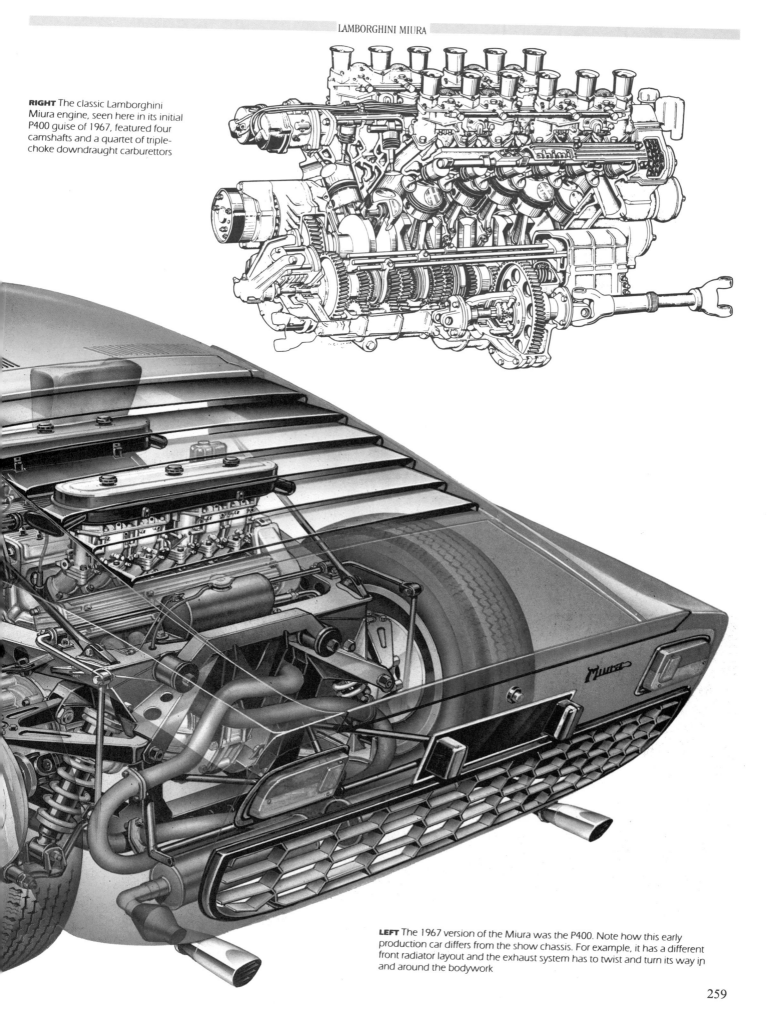

**RIGHT** The classic Lamborghini Miura engine, seen here in its initial P400 guise of 1967, featured four camshafts and a quartet of triple-choke downdraught carburettors

**LEFT** The 1967 version of the Miura was the P400. Note how this early production car differs from the show chassis. For example, it has a different front radiator layout and the exhaust system has to twist and turn its way in and around the bodywork

# A-Z OF THE CAR

## PILAIN (SLIM-PILAIN)

**Lyon, France**
**1894–98, 1902–1920**

François Pilain, the son of a miller, was one of the pioneers of motoring in France; trained as a mechanic in Chalons-sur-Saône, Pilain was hired by Léon Serpollet from 1887–9 to work on his steam cars.

In 1890 Pilain joined the Chantiers de la Buire as a designer, then left in May 1894 to run his own machine shop, where he built a number of twin-cylinder cars.

Four years later he joined Vermorel in Villefranche-sur-Saône, and established a short-lived automobile department; Vermorel dropped out of car manufacture around 1902, and didn't resume until 1908.

By 1901, François Pilain was back in Lyon repairing cars, and in the following year began production of cars with two and four-cylinder engines, though the twin-cylinder was dropped in 1903.

Pilain's original four-cylinder model was the Type 4A 5702 cc 20HP, followed in 1905 by the Type 4B, an 8621 cc 40HP with separately-cast cylinders. Working with him was his nephew Emile, who left in 1905 to found the Rolland-Pilain company in Tours.

The Pilain cars were distinguished by their transmission, which was on similar lines to the De Dion, with the gearbox incorporated in the final drive and the weight of the car supported on a dead rear axle. The 1905 20/30 HP was unusual in having direct drive on both third and fourth speeds. Apart from the very first cars, the Pilain marque was distinguished by an elegant round radiator.

Though François Pilain was a brilliant engineer, he was incapable of standardising his products, and thought nothing of modifying cars in the course of manufacture. Consequently the financial backers of the Société des Automobiles Pilain grew impatient for results; the company ran into financial difficulties and was placed in receivership in 1907, after five years of continual losses.

François Pilain resigned from his company in 1909 and established a research workshop in Lyon, where he designed and built a revolutionary prototype with a two-stroke engine, front-wheel drive and four-wheel brakes, which was completed in 1913. After thorough testing, in July 1914 he formed a company – la Société des Automobiles François Pilain – to market his design, only to have his plans brought to nothing by the outbreak of war. He died in 1924.

In the meantime the original Pilain company had been reorganised and in 1909 launched a number of new models, including the Type 40 1944 cc 12/15 HP, and the 3054 cc Types 4L and 4P.

The year 1912 saw the launch of a new 1593 cc 10/12 HP monobloc four, Type 4R, and a 15/18 HP six with the same cylinder dimensions, giving a swept volume of 2389 cc.

In 1913, Pilain announced a long-stroke (85 mm × 185 mm) 18/24 hp four of 4199 cc, plus the smallest car ever produced by Pilain, the 1045 cc Type 4U.

The factory was occupied by Hotchkiss at the start of the war for the production of lorries, and sold to them in 1917 for 2 million francs. In accordance with the agreement, the production machinery was handed back to Pilain after the Armistice.

In 1920 Pilain took over the factory of the Sté. Lyonnaise d'Industrie Mécanique et Automobile, where a neat 16-valve 15 HP of 2484 cc was built under the name of 'SLIM-Pilain'; the first SLIM-Pilains used compressed air to actuate the starter, horn, built-in jacking system and brakes.

---

### 1912 PILAIN 16/20CV

**Engine:** in-line four-cylinder, T-head
**Bore × stroke:** 90 mm × 120 mm
**Capacity:** 3053 cc
**Maximum power:** 30 bhp
**Transmission:** four-speed manual gearbox in unit with final drive
**Chassis:** pressed steel channel
**Suspension:** non-independent, with semi-elliptic leaf springs front and three-quarter elliptics rear
**Brakes:** rear-wheel drums and transmission brake
**Bodywork:** tourer
**Maximum speed (approx):** 65 mph (105 kph)

---

## PLYMOUTH

**Detroit, USA 1928–**

Chrysler – which within two years of its foundation had climbed to fourth position in the sales charts – 'went into the low-priced field with the throttle wide open' in June 1928 with the Plymouth Four, the replacement for the old Maxwell-based Chrysler 52. The model name, it was claimed, 'symbolised the endurance and strength, the rugged honesty, enterprise and determination…of the Pilgrim band who were the first American colonists'.

The new Plymouth was up-to-the-minute in style and specification, and demand exceeded supply so dramatically that a second factory with a daily capacity of 1800 cars was opened in May 1929.

The 1930 Plymouth U sedan cost the same as comparable Ford and Chevrolet models, but was ahead of both in offering a radio as an option – the first commercially-produced car radio had appeared only three years before.

The pace of change was maintained with an all-new 1931 Plymouth PA range, available in eight different body styles; this was succeeded in 1932 by the PB (which boasted a rigid X-braced chassis).

Plymouth's first six, the 70 bhp PD, appeared for 1933, the fruit of a $9 million research programme, and it cost a mere $495. These 1933 models had the curious feature of an automatic clutch which disengaged every time the throttle was released.

Plymouth production reached its first million on 10 August 1934,

**Pilain Torpedo**

by which time the marque had adopted independent front suspension. Unlike its sister marques, Chrysler and DeSoto, Plymouth never produced an Airflow model; their styling was more restrained, with emphasis on such safety features as padded seatbacks and recessed controls.

The safety message seemed, however, to be over-emphasised by an eccentric 1936 model, convertible from sedan to ambulance to hearse 'in a matter of seconds', and by the 1939 'safety-signal' speedometer which flashed a green light at speeds up to

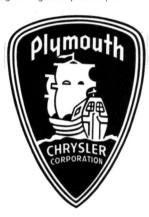

30 mph (48 kph), an amber one between 30–50 mph (48–80 kph) and a red one at speeds over 50....

A design award for safety was presented to Plymouth in 1940, when sealed-beam headlamps were standardised; the 1942 Plymouth 14C had full-width styling and interior lights which

came on when the door was opened.

The 14C was developed post-war into the 15S, which formed the basis of production up to 1949; in that year three series with all-new styling were introduced – the P17 DeLuxe, P18 and P18 Special DeLuxe, powered by the same 3569 cc side-valve six. Just as Plymouths had been sold in Britain as 'Chryslers', so the Special DeLuxe was sold in some export markets as the 'DeSoto Diplomat' or 'Dodge Kingsway'.

Despite its record of innovative engineering, the Chrysler Corporation was losing sales to its competitors in the early 1950s because of its conservative styling. For this reason Plymouth forfeited their third place in sales to Buick. One antidote was the production of a number of exciting 'dream cars' by Ghia of Turin, based on Chrysler, Plymouth and DeSoto chassis, to the designs of the corporation's new chief stylist, Virgil Exner.

Styling changes followed. The 1955 cars were longer and lower, and powered by a new 4621 cc 'Hy-Fire' V8, unique to Plymouth, though the antique side-valve six was not finally replaced until 1960.

Plymouth sales rose to a record 742,991 in 1955, although the marque did not regain its third place in sales until 1957, when Virgil Exner's new FlightSweep styling appeared. Based on a concept car built at Ghia in 1955, the Flightsweep cars offered more glass, less chrome and taller tail-fins than the opposition. The marque introduced its first Fury

performance model, powered by a potent 5211 cc V8 which was optional on other models; Plymouth also adopted the Chrysler Corporation's torsion-bar front suspension.

The good work performed by Exner's restyling of the range was undone by poor quality control, and production fell to half the 1957 level in 1958, when a new 5736 cc V8 appeared.

Unitary construction made its debut in the restyled 1960 models, which had engines up to 6276 cc. The tail-fins became bigger than ever and then vanished entirely a year later, when a brand new compact, the Valiant – powered by Chrysler's new 3687 cc slant six engine – was launched. It did not prevent Plymouth once again losing its third place in the sales league, this time to Rambler.

Exner's last designs for Plymouth were seen on the 1962 models, which included Belvedere and Fury I, II and III; the Belvedere Satellite 'muscle car' was powered by a 425 bhp, 6981 cc V8.

In 1964, Plymouth launched the Barracuda fastback, which was totally redesigned in 1967, with the slant six power unit as standard; in that year, 38 models with an amazing variety of engine options were available.

The Belvedere was used as the basis for the performance GTX as well as for the 1968 Road Runner which was claimed to be the world's fastest coupé with a top speed of up to 160 mph (257 kph).

The Belvedere line was discontinued in 1970, however, as

was the 1966-launched VIP, and heading the 1971 range was the Sport Fury with 'Brougham luxury interior'; the Belvedere was replaced by the Satellite.

By 1975 the big, powerful Plymouth cars like the Road Runner, Satellite and Barracuda had disappeared, victims of the 1973 oil crisis, although the Fury was still available, and in three sizes – 'intermediate, large and full-size'. The Valiant and Duster were still available, too.

A new compact line, the Volare, appeared in 1976, and had completely supplanted the Fury by 1978, though the Gran Fury derivative continued. For 1979 the Volare became the biggest Plymouth, with engines up to a 5211 cc V8 and models including a reborn Road Runner; there was also, ominously, a Police Package, powered by a 5899 cc V8 and with a top speed of 120 mph (193 kph).

The front-wheel-drive, 1716 cc Horizon with all-round independent suspension was entirely new, whilst the Sapporo and Arrow were Plymouth-badged Mitsubishi imports from Japan.

The Gran Fury, swept away in Chrysler's corporate crisis, re-emerged in the early 1980s as an up-market model powered by a 5211 cc V8. New for 1984 was the Voyager 'mini-van', while the mid-range car of the revitalised Plymouth marque was the Reliant, with transverse overhead-cam power units of 2.2 or 2.5 litres driving the front wheels.

## Plymouth Fury

American cars, said *The Motor*, were 'undoubtedly backed by more man-hours of experimental work but incorporated far fewer man-hours of skilled work in their construction, using steel and nylon where polished wood and leather would appear on the British model'. They also relied far more on styling for sales, and the products of the Chrysler Corporation were notably deficient on the style front in the early 1950s.

**Plymouth Fury**

### 1957 PLYMOUTH FURY

**Engine:** V8, overhead-valve
**Bore × stroke:** 90.5 mm × 82.55 mm
**Capacity:** 4260 cc
**Maximum power:** 167 bhp
**Transmission:** three-speed with semi-automatic overdrive
**Chassis:** box-section frame
**Suspension:** independent front with coils and wishbones. Live rear axle with semi-elliptic leaf springs
**Brakes:** drums all round
**Bodywork:** sedan
**Maximum speed (approx):** 100 mph (161 kph)

**Plymouth Road Runner**

The appointment of Virgil Exner as chief stylist, however, put an end to all that. He began by creating, in conjunction with the old-established Italian coachbuilder Ghia of Turin, a series of eyecatching show cars designed to improve the corporate image of Chrysler.

In 1955 he created an exaggerated style which he called Flight-Sweep, with huge tailfins and a dummy spare wheel housing formed in the boot lid; it went into production in 1957, producing spectacular looking cars like the Fury which, in its powerful 5211 cc V8 form, was as fast as it looked. A two-door Fury took the flying-mile Stock car record at Daytona at 124.01 mph (199.65 kph).

Distinctive huge fins adorned the Fury line until 1959. Later Fury models had the fins turned outwards and lacked the confident style of Exner's original.

## Plymouth Road Runner

Claimed to be the world's fastest coupé, the 1968 Road Runner, derived from the GTX intermediate, had a top speed of nearly 160 mph (258 kph). Power came from a tuned version of the standard 383 cu in block fitted with cylinder heads and manifolding from the 440 cu in unit. The Road Runner was equipped with a horn which made the same 'Beep, Beep!' sound as the zany

---

### 1968 PLYMOUTH ROAD RUNNER

**Engine:** V8, overhead-valve
**Bore × stroke:** 108 mm × 95.25 mm
**Capacity:** 6974 cc
**Maximum power:** 431 bhp
**Transmission:** automatic or four-speed manual
**Chassis:** perimeter box-section frame
**Suspension:** independent front with wishbones and torsion bars. Live rear axle with semi-elliptic leaf springs
**Brakes:** drums all round
**Bodywork:** coupé
**Maximum speed (approx):** 165 mph (265 kph)

---

cartoon character from which the car took its name!

Even faster was the limited edition – 1200 were built – 'Super Bird' Road Runner, which was a carbon copy of the 1969 Dodge Daytona 'street stocker', with high-mounted rear spoiler and 19 in (48 cm) long droop snoot front end. The 1970 Duster, with power by either a 3244 cc slant six or 5572 cc V8, was known as the 'pocket Road Runner'. But there was no comparison with the real thing, which from 1969 could be specified with the mighty 426 cu in hemi-head engine for even greater performance and with only drum brakes to stop it!

The 1971 Road Runners, upgraded to fall into Chrysler's new 'sports personal' classification, were wider, yet shorter, thanks to new, more curvaceous sheet metal and curved side windows. By 1975, however, Plymouth's big, powerful cars like the Road Runner had disappeared, victims of the 1973 oil crisis. The name Road Runner reappeared in 1979, although the days of out-and-out gas-guzzling performance were obviously long gone, since the fastest Volare Road Runner was good for 'only' 112 mph (180 kph)!

## PONTIAC

**Pontiac, USA, 1926–**

The Pontiac Buggy Company was founded in 1893 by Edward M. Murphy, though when he entered the motor industry in 1907, he named his cars Oakland. It was as a low-priced running mate for Oakland that the Pontiac marque – promoted as 'The chief of the sixes' – was launched at the January 1926 New York Automobile Salon. However, this new 3064 cc side-valve six designed by Ben H. Anibal, former chief engineer of Cadillac, proved so successful that by 1931 it had entirely ousted the older marque. The Pontiac remains the only marque created (rather than acquired) by General Motors to have lasted longer than a couple of seasons in production.

The original side-valve six survived until 1930, when it was replaced by a Marquette-based 3277 cc overhead-valve six. The final Oakland, a 4104 cc V8 based on the Olds Viking, became a Pontiac for 1932, but was quickly succeeded by America's first straight-eight priced at under $600; this 3654 cc unit even briefly supplanted the six, and helped sales to climb to 89,000 cars, giving Pontiac fifth place on the US market.

Under a new general manager, Harry J. Klinger, the six was reinstated in 1933; Dubonnet 'knee-action' independent front suspension, 'turret-top' bodies and 'No-Draft' ventilation were introduced in 1934.

For 1935, the Pontiac was promoted as 'the most beautiful thing on wheels', thanks to 'Silver Streak' styling, and the British importer, racing driver Kaye Don, offered English-bodied coupé versions of the Pontiac.

The Silver Streak proved so popular that few changes were made until 1941, when the new Torpedo range was launched; the Streamliner and Streamliner Chieftain were more expensive versions of this design, which was reintroduced after the War.

The first post-war restyling

came in 1949, when fastback (Streamline) and notchback (Chieftain) bodies were launched, although the 1949 Canadian-built 'Pontiacs' were actually Chevrolets fitted with Pontiac grilles.

Pontiac launched its new Catalina hardtop in 1950, followed by dual-range Hydramatic transmission in 1952, and wraparound rear windows and power steering in 1953. The antique side-valve eight was replaced in 1955 by a 4703 cc overhead-valve 'Strato-Streak' V8.

A new 43-year-old general manager, Bunkie Knudsen, brought

in a 'youth image' orientation for Pontiac, which included the production of 3700 Safari sporting station wagons and a brief flirtation with fuel injection in 1958. A new, wide-track Pontiac range was launched for 1959, with exaggerated tailfins and a rear grille that matched the front-end styling.

The unit-construction Tempest, built on more compact lines, and powered by an oversquare 3179 cc four-cylinder engine, was launched in 1961; with manual or automatic transaxle, its swing-axle independent rear suspension made it, according to Road Test magazine, the 'worst riding, worst all-around handling car available to the American public' apart from the notorious Chevrolet Corvair.

But although by 1964 a more conventional Tempest had replaced this controversial model, its Le Mans version led to the legendary 125 mph (201 kph) GTO muscle

car, with a choice of 6555 cc or 7456 cc V8 engines. Almost as fast, but not so sporting, was the 1963 Grand Prix; by 1968 Pontiac was offering a family of small sporting coupés, the Firebirds, powered by a small overhead-cam six, which contributed to the marque's record sales of 943,523 units for the season. This unit was replaced in 1970 by an engine with pushrod overhead valves which was also used in the 1971 Ventura compact.

It was styling – low, wide lines – rather than high performance which characterised Pontiac's new 1973 intermediates, the Grand Am two- and four-door hardtops; an odd feature was a full width grille composed of ten vertical slots divided by a pointed 'beak'.

The fastest Pontiac was now the Trans Am coupé version of the Firebird, with a 185 bhp, 6555 cc V8 power unit; disc front brakes were standard on all Pontiacs except for the Ventura.

In 1975 in the wake of the energy crisis, Pontiac introduced the inevitable sub-compact – the Astre; a year later it evolved into the sunbird, which had a five-speed manual gearbox as an option.

Pontiac's immensely complex 1979 product range consisted of the Sunbird (offering a choice of two four-cylinder Pontiac engines, Buick's V6 or Chevrolet's 5162 cc V8), Firebird sport coupés up to 6604 cc, the Phoenix intermediate, the Le Mans range, and full-size Pontiacs, which were only available with automatic transmission.

The 1980 Pontiac Phoenix, with transverse 2475 cc four or 2835 cc V6 power units driving the front wheels, shared the 'X-body' with other GM marques, while for 1981 came Pontiac's J2000 'J-car', followed for '82 by the T1000 'mini' hatchback which was Pontiac's version of the Chevette.

The latest Pontiac, the 1984 Fiero, was selected as 'American Car of the Year' by the Detroit Auto Writers Group; it is a mid-engined sports coupé with plastic panels hung on a skeleton frame.

## Pontiac Silver Streak

'The Most Beautiful Thing on Wheels' was launched for the 1935 season; the Silver Streak styling had a 'fencer's mask' radiator grill, the vertical bars of which were continued along the bonnet top. It introduced independent front suspension to the Pontiac range: 'The softness of the springing is adequately demonstrated by the way in which the car can be rocked when stationary, yet on the road it stiffens up in a surprising manner to give quite a pronounced sense of security,' commented The Motor.

The Silver Streak was available with six- and eight-cylinder engines, which were rubber mounted to reduce vibration; in England, the Pontiac concession was handled by racing driver Kaye Don, who marketed a range of coachbuilt English bodywork alongside the standard American product. They included drophead coupés and sedanca coupés, both on the six-cylinder chassis.

The appeal of the Pontiac Silver Streak was such that sales doubled in the 1935–36 period, necessitating an enlargement of the factory to meet demand.

## Pontiac GTO

The GTO name, up till then associated with the Ferrari Gran Tourismo Omologato, was annexed in 1965 for the performance derivative of the Pontiac Tempest Le Mans. The GTO became a separate model line in 1966, offering 125 mph (200 kph) performance for $3000; over 95,000 Pontiac GTOs were sold that year.

Car & Driver, normally a more level-headed publication, claimed 'Ferrari never built enough GTOs to earn the name anyway – just to be on the safe side, though, Pontiac built a faster one!'

In fact, straight-line speed seemed to be the GTO's only claim to the sports car title, for its rear axle was prone to hop when the brakes were applied hard... .

Launched with Pontiac's then-biggest engine, the 389 cu in (6374 cc) V8, by 1967 the GTO had acquired a 400 cu in (6555 cc) power unit, which gave it what its makers termed Hi-performance.

Despite its handling deficiencies, the GTO won Motor Trend's Golden Calipers trophy in 1968 for its success in 'confirming the correlations between safety, styling and performance'.

**Pontiac GTO**

| 1935 PONTIAC SILVER STREAK |
|---|
| **Engine:** in-line eight-cylinder, side-valve |
| **Bore × stroke:** 82.6 mm × 88.9 mm |
| **Capacity:** 3801 cc |
| **Maximum power:** 85 bhp |
| **Transmission:** three-speed manual |
| **Chassis:** pressed steel channel |
| **Suspension:** independent front with 'knee action'. Live rear axle with semi-elliptic leaf springs |
| **Brakes:** drums all round |
| **Bodywork:** coupé, saloon |
| **Maximum speed (approx):** 80 mph (129 kph) |

| 1967 PONTIAC GTO |
|---|
| **Engine:** V8, overhead-valve |
| **Bore × stroke:** 103 mm × 95.25 mm |
| **Capacity:** 6555 cc |
| **Maximum power:** 335 bhp |
| **Transmission:** three speed manual |
| **Chassis:** pressed steel perimeter frame |
| **Suspension:** independent front with coil springs. Live rear axle with coil springs and telescopic dampers |
| **Brakes:** drums all round |
| **Bodywork:** convertible and coupé |
| **Maximum speed (approx):** 125 mph (200 kph) |

**Pontiac Silver Streak**

**Pontiac Firebird Trans Am**

### 1973 PONTIAC FIREBIRD TRANS AM

**Engine:** V8, overhead-valve
**Bore × stroke:** 104.6 mm × 95.2 mm
**Capacity:** 6555 cc
**Maximum power:** 330 bhp
**Transmission:** three-speed
**Chassis:** body-on-frame
**Suspension:** independent front with wishbones, coil springs and anti-roll bar. Live rear axle with semi-elliptic leaf springs and anti-roll bar
**Brakes:** discs front and drums rear
**Bodywork:** two-door, four-seater sports coupé
**Maximum speed:** 122 mph (196 kph)

## Pontiac Firebird

Pontiac's version of the GM F-car was introduced in 1967, preceded by Chevrolet's Camaro but it soon caught up lost ground.

It was one of the prettiest of all American designs and was built with a range of engines to make its appeal as wide as possible. The six-cylinder cars were not particularly quick but the top of the line Trans Ams were as fast as they were striking; with a 6.6-litre V8 they were capable of a top speed of 122 mph (196 kph) while acceleration was everything you would expect from well over 300 bhp. With the stiffer suspension settings handling was by no means bad.

Like all US muscle cars the Trans Am was emasculated after the various fuel crises of the '70s, so much so that the smaller third generation cars introduced in 1982 had to make do with only a 155 bhp 5-litre V8 as the top engine option. Since then, however, the use of fuel injection and more sophisticated electronic engine management systems have started to bring back the missing performance.

By 1985 the Firebird Trans Am was powered by a 4999 cc V8 the output of which had risen to a more respectable 205 bhp at 4400 rpm, enough to produce a top speed of just under 130 mph (209 kph). Despite the sleek looks of the third generation cars the suspension was still rather simple, retaining a live rear axle.

## Pontiac Fiero

Late in 1978, the GM fuel economy conference gave its approval to a two-seater 'personal sports car' project: this P-Car was given the final go-ahead for production in the spring of 1980. Chief project engineer Hulki Aldikacti had started with a conventional front-engined layout, but progressed to a mid-engine design using the volume-production transaxle unit from the

**Pontiac Fiero**

front-engined GM X-cars, with the steering fixed by tie-rods.

Its cast-iron power unit, producing only 92 bhp from 2.5 litres, seemed somewhat out of keeping with the advanced design of the rest of the car, for the Fiero, which went on sale in 1983, was the first large-scale production American car to use space-frame construction with separate moulded plastic body panels. These were fitted by a unique 'mill-and-drill' technique which ensured perfect fit of the plastic body panels by machining the mounting points to tolerances similar to those used in engine manufacture. The concept, chosen for the flexibility it gave to the GM design team by enabling them to transform the car completely by simply chang-

### 1984 PONTIAC FIERO

**Engine:** in-line four-cylinder, overhead-valve
**Bore × stroke:** 101.6 mm × 76.2 mm
**Capacity:** 2475 cc
**Maximum power:** 92 bhp
**Transmission:** four-speed manual
**Chassis:** steel space frame clad in Endurolux panels
**Suspension:** independent with coil springs and wishbones front and MacPherson struts rear
**Brakes:** discs all round
**Bodywork:** two-seat coupé
**Maximum speed (approx):** 97 mph (156 kph)

ing the design of the moulded body panels, seemed neither to reduce weight nor complexity, for the car weighed 2480 lb (1125 kg) – the same as a conventionally-constructed two-seater sports car – and needed some 300 stampings to make up its steel space-frame, which was assembled using some 4300 spot-welds, only 10 per cent of which were robot-applied.

Nevertheless, the concept was bold enough for the Fiero to be voted American Car of the Year 1984 by US motoring journalists, even if European writers found its performance somewhat lacking in excitement. A promised European version has so far failed to materialise, although a V6 version appeared in the US in 1985.

# PORSCHE

Gmünd, Austria/Stuttgart-
Zuffenhausen, Germany
1948–

Ferdinand Porsche, born in 1875, was one of the great geniuses of the automobile, though he was in his seventies before he built a car under his own name. But in the previous half-century, Dr Porsche had designed such immortal machines as the Prince Henry Austro-Daimler, the Mercedes-Benz 38/250, the 16-cylinder Auto-Union Grand Prix car and the Volkswagen; the Tiger tank, the Cisitalia Grand Prix car and the Austro-Daimler Sascha were also

among the multitude of designs.

After the war, Ferdinand Porsche was interned in France because of his work in designing military vehicles for the Nazis, and during this two-year period was consulted by Renault over the design of the rear-engined 4CV; following his release from internment, Porsche settled in Gmünd, Austria, where he, his son Ferry and Karl Rabe created the first Porsche sports cars, powered by 1086 cc VW-derived flat-four engines. A series of 50 Type 356 roadsters was built at Gmünd and fitted with light alloy sports roadster bodywork. Since Porsche cars were relatively cheap, demand for them was encouragingly high.

However, Porsche found working conditions in Austria too difficult, for there were chronic shortages of materials, components

and skilled labour, and moved to Stuttgart-Zuffenhausen in Germany, where he died in 1952.

Here, the rear-engined Type 356 was built in many guises – coupés, cabriolets, speedsters and convertibles – with engines from 1096 cc to 1966 cc. It was succeeded in 1965 by the Porsche 912, built until 1969 and powered by a light-alloy 1582 cc flat-four.

The first 'all-Porsche' engine, the Type 547, designed by Ernst Fuhrmann, appeared in 1953, and was installed in a new space-frame chassis clothed in glorious alloy spyder bodywork developed in the Stuttgart University wind tunnel. This Type 550 Spyder was shown in prototype form at the 1953 Paris Salon and 15 competition cars were subsequently built, followed at the end of 1954 by a production series of 75 cars which went on sale at a price of DM24,600 – twice the cost of a Speedster. Most Spyders were exported to America, where the model achieved notoriety when the young film star James Dean was killed in one.

The famous overhead-cam flat-six 1991 cc Porsche 911 made its debut in 1964; larger power units were available from 1969, culminating in a 2993 cc unit. The 911 was available in Carrera form from 1972–75, powered by a

2687 cc flat-six of 260 bhp.

Between 1969 and 1975, Porsche offered the mid-engined Porsche 914, with four-cylinder VW engines of 1795 cc or 1971 cc, or the Porsche 1991 cc six.

By 1979 Porsche's range had expanded to include the front-engined 924, with an in-line water-cooled four-cylinder Audi engine of 1984 cc (originally designed for a van), the faithful old rear-engined 911, available in SC form, with a 180 bhp 2993 cc flat-six, or as the 911 Turbo, whose 3299 cc flat-six power unit boasted Bosch K-Jetronic fuel-injection, and the 928 – voted 1978 Car of the Year – with a front-mounted 4474 cc V8.

After running three 924 Turbos at Le Mans in 1980, Porsche built a homologation special series of 400 turbocharged 924 Carrera GTS coupés, whose 2-litre engines developed 245 bhp, giving a 147 mph (237 kph) capability. These cars were only available on the European market, costing over £19,000 in Britain.

In 1981, Porsche at last introduced an engine of their own manufacture for a derivative of the 924, the 944, powered by a 2.5-litre four that was effectively half a 928 engine.

That year, too, a 4X4 Turbo convertible version of the 911 was shown at Frankfurt, though without firm production plans.

In the mid-1980s, Porsche continues its four-model range while carrying out development projects for the motor industry in its research laboratories at Weissach.

## Porsche 356

The original Porsche 356 was basically a hotted-up Volkswagen with light-alloy roadster bodywork: this first Porsche had its engine mounted ahead of the rear axle for optimum weight distribution, though this feature was abandoned on the production version in the interests of better

passenger and luggage capacity.

The first series of production Porsche 356 coupés had alloy bodywork, too, and was built in Gmünd; these cars were raced by selected drivers to establish the marque name. Since the cars were relatively cheap, demand was strong, and production was transferred to Stuttgart where there were fewer restrictions and shortages than in Austria. Steel bodies replaced alloy when production restarted in Germany.

Originally, 1131 cc VW flat-four engines were used, but these were soon reduced in capacity to 1086 cc and fitted with twin downdraught carburettors, improved manifolding and a redesigned camshaft to raise the power output from 25 bhp at 3000 rpm to 40 bhp at 4000 rpm, sufficient for an 80 mph (129 kph) top speed. Subsequently, engines of 1300 cc, 1500 cc and 1600 cc were fitted in the 356.

And when the 356 coupé was launched at the 1949 Geneva Salon, it was an instant success; sporting success was quickly achieved, too, with a class victory at Le Mans in 1951 typical of the Porsche's winning ways.

Body styles ranged from the original coupé through the convertible,

---

### 1962 PORSCHE 356 CABRIOLET

**Engine:** flat four-cylinder, overhead-valve
**Bore × stroke:** 82.5 mm × 74 mm
**Capacity:** 1582 cc
**Maximum power:** 74 bhp
**Transmission:** four-speed manual
**Chassis:** integral
**Suspension:** independent with torsion bars front and rear
**Brakes:** drums all round
**Bodywork:** convertible
**Maximum speed (approx):** 109 mph (175 kph)

---

**Porsche 356 Cabriolet**

**Porsche 914**

a hardtop and the stark open Speedster, possibly the most desirable production 356 of all. Porsche built just 4922 Speedsters between 1954–56, when the model was succeeded by the similar 356 Convertible. There was also an alloy-bodied Carrera variant with a 124 mph (200 kph) maximum from a twin-cam 1600 cc engine.

## Porsche 914

In the late '60s Porsche went back to the origins and collaborated with Volkswagen in producing a new 'cheap' sports car. The mid-engined 914 appeared at the 1969 Frankfurt Show and customers could have either the VW flat-four or the Porsche flat-six from the 911 range.

The plan was to sell the cheaper versions as VWs and, logically enough, the more expensive as Porsches. Unfortunately the car's lowly origins meant that it was never accepted as a 'true' Porsche, while the lower-priced VW wasn't particularly cheap. Its lines did not meet with universal approval either (Gugelot's original design had been altered for production reasons), and the 914 was not a commercial success. By 1975 only the VW powered version was available, with either the 1756 cc 85 bhp engine or the larger 1971 cc unit.

Porsche didn't easily lose faith in the mid-engined approach, and, in trying to revive the 914s, produced 11 916 prototypes with fuel-injected 190 bhp versions of the 2.3-litre flat-six and top speed of 145 mph (233 kph). Sadly the 916 would have been too expensive to be a commercial success and the 911 soldiered on.

---

### 1975 PORSCHE 914

**Engine:** Mid-mounted flat six, overhead-cam, air-cooled
**Bore × stroke:** 80 mm × 66 mm
**Capacity:** 1991 cc
**Maximum power:** 110 bhp
**Transmission:** five-speed manual
**Chassis:** integral
**Suspension:** independent with wishbones and coil springs front and trailing arms and coil springs rear
**Brakes:** discs all round
**Bodywork:** two-door, two-seater sports with Targa top
**Maximum speed (approx):** 128 mph (206 kph)

---

## Porsche 911

Launched to replace the four-cylinder Carrera 2, the 911 was designed by Professor Porsche's grandson, and powered by a 1991 cc flat-six power unit developing 130 bhp in its original form. Four wheel disc brakes were standard.

Even in its original form, the 911 was good for around 130 mph (209 kph); then the engine was progressively enlarged, to 2.2, 2.4 and then to 2.7 litres for the 'duck-tail' Carrera RS (there was even a 3-litre Carrera RS, but that was restricted to the Porsche's native Germany!).

In fact, the 3-litre Turbo of 1974 was claimed by Porsche to be the world's fastest-accelerating car.

Since then, the 911 has been

---

### 1984 PORSCHE 911 TURBO

**Engine:** flat six-cylinder, overhead-cam, turbocharged
**Bore × stroke:** 97 mm × 74.4 mm
**Capacity:** 3299 cc
**Maximum power:** 300 bhp
**Transmission:** four-speed manual
**Chassis:** integral
**Suspension:** independent with MacPherson struts and torsion bars front with semi-trailing arms and transverse torsion bars rear
**Brakes:** discs all round
**Bodywork:** sports coupé
**Maximum speed (approx):** 162 mph (260 kph)

---

**Porsche 911 Turbo**

progressively developed; a 3.2-litre version was standardised in 1984, the Turbo has gained a 3.3-litre engine, and it is possible to convert existing engines to 3.5 litres.

But what is most remarkable is that after over 21 years in production, the vitality and attraction of the 911 seem undiminished. Dr Ferry Porsche has said that he intends that the 911 will remain in production throughout the 1980s. The model's early reputation for rusting has been overcome, and while the ultimate 911 in terms of performance is the 162 mph (261 kph) Turbo, with its huge 'whale-tail' spoiler, many people still prefer the pure lines of the original 911.

## Porsche 928

The largest car so far to bear the Porsche name, the 928 was launched in 1976, powered by a front-mounted water-cooled V8 engine of 4474 cc developing 240 bhp. Transmission was by five-speed transaxle, and top speed was around 150 mph (241 kph). Since then, the 928 has progressed through various engine changes to the point where it is now powered by a 310 bhp 4.7-litre unit with Bosch LH-Jetronic fuel injection and computerised ignition.

Its slightly portly body has been criticised for its poor aerodynamics, though this seems to have little effect on the car's rapid performance. Roadholding is aided by the ingenious Weissach axle, with coil-sprung top links and wide-angled lower A-frames with tiny swinging links at the forward end of each bottom arm which, operating within closely-planned tolerances, counteract the car's natural tendency to oversteer during sharp braking or acceleration. It is a system that works extremely well.

**Porsche 928S**

## Porsche 944

Perhaps unfairly the 924 was never accepted as a real Porsche despite its quite acceptable performance, and it soon became clear that there was room for another model.

That model became the 944, introduced in 1981, based on the more flamboyant body style of the 924 Carrera with its aggressively flared wheel arches. Power was supplied by an in-line four-cylinder which was essentially one bank of the V8 from the 928. As it was on the large side for a four, at 2479 cc, it featured twin balance-shafts to smooth the power delivery.

In search of equal weight distribution and high polar moments of inertia for increased stability and road-holding, the 944 had its transmission at the rear to complement the front-mounted engine.

### 1984 PORSCHE 928S

**Engine:** V8, overhead-cam
**Bore × stroke:** 97 mm × 78.9 mm
**Capacity:** 4664 cc
**Maximum power:** 310 bhp
**Transmission:** five-speed manual or four-speed automatic
**Chassis:** integral
**Suspension:** independent with MacPherson struts front and Weissach axle, wishbones and semi-trailing arms rear
**Brakes:** discs all round
**Bodywork:** 2+2 coupé
**Maximum speed (approx):** 158 mph (255 kph)

### 1985 PORSCHE 944

**Engine:** in-line four-cylinder, overhead-cam
**Bore × stroke:** 100 mm × 78.9 mm
**Capacity:** 2479 cc
**Maximum power:** 163 bhp
**Transmission:** five-speed
**Chassis:** integral
**Suspension:** independent with MacPherson struts front and semi-trailing arms and torsion-bars rear
**Brakes:** discs all round
**Bodywork:** two-door sports coupé
**Maximum speed (approx):** 136 mph (218 kph)

**Porsche 944**

# A-Z
## OF THE CAR

**1919 PRAGA GRAND**

**Engine:** in-line four-cylinder, side-valve
**Bore × stroke:** 90 mm × 150 mm
**Capacity:** 3824 cc
**Maximum power:** 45 bhp
**Transmission:** four-speed
**Chassis:** pressed steel channel
**Suspension:** non-independent, with semi-elliptic leaf springs
**Bodywork:** cabriolet, saloon
**Maximum speed:** (approx): 55 mph (88 kph)

## PRAGA

**Prague, Austria/Czechoslovakia
1907–1947**

Renowned for their durability – they became known as the 'hundred-thousand-mile cars' – Pragas were built by one of Bohemia's leading engineering works, which first proposed car manufacture as early as 1904, but didn't get around to it for another three years. Praga's first products, built until 1911, were based on French Renault and Charron designs, with two- and four-cylinder engines; the first genuine Praga was the 1850 cc Mignon, designed by a young engineer named Frantisek Kec, who was the firm's first director, and designed most Praga cars and trucks up to 1933.

The 3.8-litre Grand appeared in 1912, and took team prizes in the Vienna–Trieste–Vienna alpine rally in 1912–13–14.

A 1130 cc light car, the Alfa, appeared in 1913; these three models formed the basis of post-war production. Since Prague was now capital of the newly-formed state of Czechoslovakia, Praga became the new country's leading producer.

The Grand dominated motor sport in the early days of the Czech Republic – six Praga Grands were among the nine cars to complete a 1500-mile six-day trial around Czechoslovakia without penalty points, while the model was victorious in the Great Russian Rally and the Polish Rally in 1923.

Production of these side-valve fours was on a small scale: in 1923, Praga built a hundred Grands and a similar number of Mignons, now with a new 2.3-litre Rapid engine, plus 320 trucks.

A new small model, the Piccolo, with a 707 cc engine appeared next: its engine was subsequently increased in size to 856 cc, in which form a Piccolo won the 6000-mile Grand Prix of Algiers rally.

There was a doorless wooden-bodied sporting Piccolo Special; by the end of the decade, the Alfa and Mignon had grown into sixes of 1790 cc and 2636 cc respectively,

**Praga Grand Cabriolet**

and the Grand had acquired a straight-eight 3585 cc power unit. In the early 1930s, Praga produced such new models as the 995 cc backbone-chassis Baby with all-round independent suspension, the 1450 cc Lady and the 60 mph (100 kph) 1660 cc Super-Piccolo, still mostly designed by Kec.

A proposed merger between Praga, Skoda and Tatra came to nothing when Tatra dropped out at the last minute.

At the outbreak of war, the range consisted of two light fours – a new 1128 cc Piccolo with all-round independent suspension and the 1660 cc Lady – and two sixes, the 2492 cc Alfa 23 and the six-speed 3485 cc Golden Praga. Cotal electrically-operated preselector gearboxes were optional.

Though the post-war Communist government restricted Praga to truck manufacture, nevertheless a few light cars were built up to 1947.

## PRESTO

**Chemnitz, Germany
1907–1927**

Presto were well-established cycle and motorcycle manufacturers who built a few cars from 1901, but did not enter full-scale production until 1907, when they began building French four-cylinder Delahaye cars under licence.

Their first own-design models

**1922 PRESTO 9/30**

**Engine:** in-line four-cylinder, side-valve
**Bore × stroke:** 86 mm × 101 mm
**Capacity:** 2350 cc
**Maximum power:** 30 bhp
**Transmission:** four-speed manual
**Chassis:** pressed steel channel
**Suspension:** non-independent, with semi-elliptic leaf springs front and rear
**Brakes:** rear-wheel drums
**Bodywork:** sports tourer
**Maximum speed (approx):** 63 mph (101 kph)

included a long-stroke (100 mm x 200 mm) 6238 cc four-cylinder and another of 4920 cc. As production increased, smaller four-cylinder cars of 2078 cc and 2340 cc were introduced.

After the war, Presto joined the GDA group and increased production. The largest model was now a 2350 cc four-cylinder developing 30 bhp, succeeded in 1925 by an improved 40 bhp model.

Presto's last cars were overhead-valve 2613 cc and 3141 cc sixes; in 1926 Presto took over Dux, but were then absorbed into the NAG group in 1927, and the two cars became known as NAG-Prestos. In 1934, NAG sold the Chemnitz works to Auto-Union.

## PROTOS

**Berlin, Germany
1899–1926**

Dr. Alfred Sternberg, whose wife Lilli was a well-known pioneer motorist, founded the Protos factory, and he began production with a 749 cc single-cylinder voiturette. This was followed by the curious three-cylinder 'Kompensengin', which was, in effect, a twin-cylinder unit with a third, opposed, cylinder whose piston merely acted as a balance weight to ensure smooth running. By 1904, Protos taxicabs were already running on the streets of Berlin, and in that year the company was also offering four-cylinder cars with engines of up to 45 hp.

In 1905, Protos built a 100 hp six-cylinder racer which, though it did not enter production, paved the way for a 45 hp six-cylinder car, apparently the first shaft-driven German six to enter production, which it did in early 1906.

Dr. Sternberg sold Protos to the Siemens-Schuckert electrical group in 1908, in which year a 17/35 hp

**Presto Type D**

„PRESTO"-Personenwagen
Luxus-Ausführung.

RAILTON

### 1914 PROTOS 27/62 HP TYPE E II

**Engine:** in-line six-cylinder, side-valve
**Bore × stroke:** 110 mm × 120 mm
**Capacity:** 6838 cc
**Maximum power:** 62 bhp
**Transmission:** four-speed manual
**Chassis:** pressed steel channel
**Suspension:** non-independent, with semi-elliptic leaf springs front and rear
**Brakes:** rear-wheel drums
**Bodywork:** open tourer
**Maximum speed (approx):** 75 mph (120 kph)

**Protos Type C1**

four-cylinder Protos came second (to the American Thomas Flyer) in the New York–Paris Race, bringing international renown to the marque.

The marque's most notable customer was 'Little Willy' – Crown Prinz Wilhelm – who bought a 27/62 hp six-cylinder Protos limousine.

Protos deservedly earned the reputation of being one of Germany's leading marques, offering a wide variety of cars from a 1501 cc four to the 6838 cc five-bearing, six-cylinder E II in the years preceding the outbreak of war.

The company returned to production after the Armistice with an overhead-valve four of 2612 cc and the 16/46, powered by a 4137 cc four-cylinder side-valve unit.

Then Protos adopted a one-model policy with the 30 bhp side-valve, 2596 cc four-cylinder Type C, which was succeeded by the 45 bhp Type C1 of broadly similar design. In 1926, NAG took control of Protos after Siemens-Schuckert decided to move out of car production. That was not entirely the end of the marque, however, for after the take-over some NAG models carried the badge NAG-Protos.

# PUCH

### Graz, Austria
### 1906–1923

Johann Puch was a well-known manufacturer of bicycles who began building motorcycles as early as 1898, but did not turn to four-wheelers until eight years later, when he hired the well-known German designer Karl Slevogt to create a prototype, which failed to go into production. Puch also tested a number of French cars before introducing the first Puch car in 1906, a neat, shaft-driven voiturette powered by an 8/9 hp vee-twin engine.

In 1907, Puch brought out his first four-cylinder model, the 12/18 hp, shown alongside the 8/9 hp

### 1907 PUCH 8/9 HP

**Engine:** vee-twin, side-valve
**Bore × stroke:** 78 mm × 94.6 mm
**Capacity:** 904 cc
**Maximum power:** 9 bhp
**Transmission:** three-speed manual, shaft drive
**Chassis:** pressed steel channel
**Suspension:** non-independent, with semi-elliptic leaf springs front and rear
**Brakes:** rear-wheel drums
**Bodywork:** two-seater racer
**Maximum speed (approx):** 35 mph (56 kph)

**Puch 8/9 HP Racer**

at the Vienna Automobile Show that March. At the end of 1908, Slevogt joined Puch as designer from Laurin & Klement, and the following year designed an overhead-camshaft 3996 cc four which performed well in the Prince Henry Trial.

Other Puch models available at this period had side-valve four-cylinder engines of 1580 cc and 4400 cc; the most famous model produced at this period was another side-valve four, the sporting 14/40 hp Alpenwagen, with a 40 bhp, 3560 cc power unit. This model was also produced after the war.

The last cars built by Puch had

1588 cc four-cylinder engines and four-speed transmissions. Works racers derived from this model were produced in 1921–22, and won many events in the hands of works drivers Kirchner, Weiss and Zsolnay.

Car manufacture ceased in 1923 when the first of the famous double-piston Puch motorcycles, designed by the Italian-born engineer Giovanni Marcinello, made its debut.

# RAILTON

### Cobham/London, England
### 1933–1949

Produced in the factory which had formerly built the Invicta (Captain Noel Macklin was involved with both projects) the Railton took its name from the gifted designer Reid Railton, although his main contribution to the design was to improve the handling of the 4-litre Hudson-Essex Terraplane 8 chassis on which the car was based. On this foundation, British-built coachwork and an Invicta-like radiator and riveted bonnet were fitted, to create a fast, cheap and handsome sporting car, the archetypal 'Anglo-American sports bastard'. The Terraplane straight-eight engine had such crude features as splash-lubricated big-ends, but gave the Railton a top speed of up to 88 mph (142 kph) depending on bodywork.

For 1935, Hudson announced that Terraplanes would only be available with six-cylinder power

269

**Railton**

### 1934 RAILTON

**Engine:** in-line straight-eight, side-valve
**Bore × stroke:** 76 mm × 114 mm
**Capacity:** 4137 cc
**Maximum power:** 113 bhp
**Transmission:** three-speed manual
**Chassis:** pressed-steel channel, X-braced
**Suspension:** front independent, with Axle-Flex with semi-elliptic leaf springs; rear non-independent, with rigid axle and semi-elliptic leaf springs
**Brakes:** Bendix mechanical drums all round
**Bodywork:** to order
**Maximum speed (approx):** 85 mph (137 kph)

units, so Railton adopted the 4.1-litre Hudson straight-eight power unit instead. Also used was the Terraplane's 'Axle-Flex' independent front suspension, an invention of somewhat dubious merit which was quickly abandoned by Hudson since its advantages over the cheaper and simpler beam axle were purely nominal.

A short-lived Railton model was the 1935 Light Sports Tourer, of which perhaps six examples were built; this exciting device had a top speed little short of 100 mph (161 kph).

In 1938, increased costs resulted in the production of two smaller six-cylinder models powered by Hudson engines of 2.7 and 3.5 litres, though these never

proved particularly popular. That same year, a baby Railton also appeared, based on a Standard Flying Nine chassis and endowed with a Flying Standard Ten engine; only 50 examples of this uncharacteristic Railton and only 81 six-cylinder models were built, out of the total Railton output of 1460 cars. Despite post-war austerity and supply shortages, Railton built a handful of cars after World War II, but a list price which had rocketed to over £4000 quickly put paid to the model's chances of survival.

# RAMBLER

**Kenosha, USA,
1900–1913, 1950–1971**

British-born Thomas B. Jeffrey had been building bicycles under the trade name Rambler in North America since 1878, and

constructed a prototype motor carriage as early as 1897. In 1900 he exhibited two twin-cylinder runabouts, designed by his son Charles, at shows in Chicago and New York, sold his interest in the cycle company, and bought a factory at Kenosha, Wisconsin, to manufacture Rambler cars.

The first two years were occupied in experiment, but in 1902 the Rambler Model C was placed on the market.

As time progressed the Rambler gradually changed from a spidery motor runabout to a substantial motor car, although twin-cylinder engines were only fitted until 1907, when the 40 hp Model 25 was launched. Among the novelties incorporated in Rambler design were America's first detachable spare wheel (1909), a locking petrol tap and a steering column adjustable for rake (both 1911).

The Rambler name was dropped in 1913 in a successful

attempt to boost sales; the company's products were then known as Jeffrey until after a 1916 takeover, and the marque became Nash from mid-1917.

In 1950, Nash revived the Rambler name, initially as a model name and then, because the Rambler 'compact' car sold so well, as the name of a separate marque. Since in 1956 Ramblers represented three-quarters of the American Motor Corporation's sales, AMC (formed in 1954 to control Nash, Hudson and Rambler) dropped both the Nash and Hudson names.

However, Rambler was putting on size and weight, so in 1958 the discontinued 1956 two-door sedan was revived under the name Rambler American and sold well enough to establish Rambler as the best-selling independent American company since the foundation of the industry, and by the following year Rambler moved into fourth place in the US sales league.

All things are cyclic, and once again the popularity of the Rambler marque name went into decline, despite the incorporation of some advanced technical features like dual-circuit brakes and disc brakes. New cars were launched by American Motors under their individual model names, and the Rambler name was discontinued in North America in 1970.

### 1963 RAMBLER CLASSIC 660

**Engine:** in-line six-cylinder, overhead-valve
**Bore × stroke:** 79.4 mm × 107.9 mm
**Capacity:** 3205 cc
**Maximum power:** 138 bhp
**Transmission:** three-speed automatic
**Chassis:** monocoque
**Suspension:** front independent, with coils and wishbones, rear non-independent, with rigid axle and coil springs
**Brakes:** hydraulic drums all round
**Bodywork:** four-door sedan
**Maximum speed (approx):** 93 mph (150 kph)

**Rambler 660**

# A-Z OF THE CAR

## RAPID

**Turin, Italy**
**1904–1921**

Also known as the STAR – Societa Torinese Automobili Rapid – this car was designed by Giovanni Battista Ceirano, though poor health compelled him to retire from the company in 1905 to Bordighera, where he died in 1912. He was replaced by Giovanni Battista Maggi as administrative head, and Rodolfo Chio as chief

engineer (though Chio was killed while testing a chassis in 1906).

The first Rapid cars were the 16/24 and 24/40 hp, with engines of 4562 cc and 7432 cc respectively; a round radiator was characteristic of the marque.

Surviving a world-wide depression in the motor industry during 1907, Rapid offered a range of cars with four-cylinder engines of between 1570 cc and 10,560 cc.

After the Great War, Rapid opened a repair garage for cars of all makes, but went into liquidation in 1921, when the factory was taken over by SPA.

---

### 1910 RAPID 15 HP

**Engine:** in-line four-cylinder, T-head
**Bore × stroke:** 80 mm × 130 mm
**Capacity:** 2614 cc
**Maximum power:** 15 hp (rated)
**Transmission:** four-speed manual
**Chassis:** pressed steel channel
**Suspension:** non-independent, with semi-elliptic leaf springs front and rear
**Brakes:** rear-wheel drums
**Bodywork:** to order
**Maximum speed (approx):** 50 mph (80 kph)

---

## RAPIER

**Staines/Hammersmith, England**
**1935–1940**

Lagonda began development of a small sports-racing car late in 1932, and although the Lagonda Rapier was originally announced in September 1933, it did not go into production until the following year. The 1104 cc Rapier, designed by Timothy Ashcroft, was powered by a twin-overhead-camshaft engine, a remarkably advanced layout for a car sold at a chassis price of only £270. Its hemispherical combustion chambers were fed by twin SUs

and the engine had the reputation of being unburstable.

It had originally been intended to manufacture the engine from aluminium alloy, but a cast iron cylinder block was eventually adopted on grounds of cost. With a crossflow cylinder head and hemispherical combustion chambers, the Rapier was a remarkable performer, whose speed was matched by the fitting of powerful Girling brakes.

The Rapier was sold by Lagonda until the Staines company was reformed under Alan Good in

**Rapier**

---

### 1936 RAPIER

**Engine:** in-line four-cylinder, double-overhead-cam
**Bore × stroke:** 62.5 mm × 90 mm
**Capacity:** 1104 cc
**Maximum power:** 45 bhp
**Transmission:** four-speed preselector
**Chassis:** pressed steel channel
**Suspension:** non-independent, with semi-elliptic leaf springs front and rear
**Brakes:** drums all round
**Bodywork:** sports tourer
**Maximum speed (approx):** 85 mph (137 kph)

---

1935. When it was realised that the reputation of the Rapier far outstripped the model's sales, the new management discontinued production.

A new company, Rapier Cars Ltd, was formed to rescue the Rapier by its designer Tim Ashcroft, Major W.H. Oates and N. Brocklebank; they bought the design and production machinery from Lagonda and continued manufacture under the marque name Rapier.

A supercharged Rapier was offered in 1936, and by the time production ended in 1940, some 300 Rapiers had been built.

## RELIANT

**Tamworth, England**
**1935–**

When Raleigh discontinued their three-wheeled Safety Seven its designer, T.L. Williams, took over the production of this one-wheel – forward three-wheeler, building the first Reliant van in a workshop in the garden of his home in Tamworth, Staffordshire.

Before long the company had expanded sufficiently to transfer

manufacture to a new factory at nearby Two Gates. From 1939, Reliant adopted the Austin Seven engine for their three-wheeled commercial vehicles, but it wasn't until 1952 that a private version of the design was launched, despite the lower road tax paid by three-wheeled cars weighing under

8 cwt (406 kg).

While Reliant is still well-known as a manufacturer of three-wheelers – the Rialto is the latest in a long string of such designs, which have had glassfibre bodywork since 1956 – the company moved onto four wheels in 1961 with the Les Bellamy-designed Sabre, one of

**Rapid 15 HP**

**Reliant Scimitar GTE**

three 'package deal' models created by Reliant for assembly in Israel (where the model was known as the Sabra). Powered by the four-cylinder 1704 cc Ford Consul engine, the Sabre was prone to severe scuttle shake on bad surfaces and was consequently redesigned in 1963, acquiring the 2556 cc Ford Zephyr Six power unit at the same time.

In 1962 the old Austin Seven-derived power unit fitted to the three-wheelers was finally laid to rest, and replaced by a purpose-designed 600 cc light-alloy overhead-valve engine, subsequently increased in capacity to 701 cc. This unit was used in Reliant's first economy four-wheeler, the 1964 Rebel 600 (which became the Rebel 700 in 1967).

In 1964, Reliant achieved its hoped-for breakthrough into the sports–saloon market with the David Ogle-designed Scimitar. Its hatchback derivative, the GTE of 1968, was a successful combination of sports car and station wagon.

Reliant acquired Bond Cars in 1969, and in 1970 launched the Bond Bug three-wheeled 'fun-car' whose curious handling displayed all the drawbacks of the one-wheel-forward three-wheeler configuration. In 1975, Reliant launched a four-wheeled derivative of the Robin called the Kitten. Alongside the new Rialto three-

wheeler in 1982, Reliant launched a four-wheeled utility car, the Fox.

In 1984 Reliant unveiled their replacement for the Scimitars, the Scimitar SS1 1600, a smaller, Michelotti-styled two-seater available with a choice of Ford's 1300 cc Escort engine or the 96 bhp, 1600 cc XR2 unit. Sales of this neat, glassfibre bodied car were sufficiently good for the company to announce that production of the older Scimitars – available latterly in GTC convertible or GTE estate form – would end in October 1985.

In that year Reliant's Shenstone factory began assembly of 200 Ford RS200 rally/sports two-seaters under contract.

## Reliant Scimitar GTE

Announced in 1968, the GTE was the first attempt by a company to build a sports car with an estate car's carrying capacity. The Ogle design worked brilliantly, and the rising reputation of this fast car – which was light years away from the humble three-wheelers – was further enhanced when Princess Anne bought a GTE.

The car spawned a number of similar designs, notably the Lancia Beta HPE, Volvo P1800ES, Gilbern Invader Estate and BMW Touring. In 1976 the GTE was given an extensive facelift, further adding to its

popularity.

It was initially available with Ford's V6 engines of either 2.5 or 3 litres. The latter, which produced 135 bhp and 172 lb ft of torque, enabled the GTE to reach 125 mph (201 kph) and 60 mph (97 kph) in 8.5 seconds; in 1980 (the year in which the convertible GTC was introduced) Ford ceased production of the large V6 and Reliant switched to that company's 2.8-litre V6, which had the same power output

---

### 1968 RELIANT SCIMITAR GTE

**Engine:** V6, overhead-valve
**Bore × stroke:** 93.7 mm × 72.4 mm
**Capacity:** 2994 cc
**Maximum power:** 135 bhp
**Transmission:** four-speed manual (overdrive optional) or three-speed automatic
**Chassis:** box-section ladder frame, with tubular cross-members
**Suspension:** front independent, with coils and wishbones and anti-rollbar; rear non-independent, with rigid axle, trailing arms, Watt linkage and coil springs
**Brakes:** discs front, drums rear
**Bodywork:** three-door, four-seat glassfibre sports estate
**Maximum speed (approx):** 125 mph (201 kph)

---

but a torque figure of 152 lb ft, reducing the GTE's maximum speed to 116 mph (187 kph) and the 0–60 mph time to 11 seconds.

When production ended late in 1985, nearly 16,000 Scimitars had been built.

## Reliant Scimitar SS1

The Italian designer Michelotti had a long tradition of shaping British sports cars, models like the later TRs, the Spitfire and the Stag so it seemed logical to have him design the new Scimitar. Unfortunately when the car appeared at the 1984 Motor Show in Birmingham its looks were universally regarded as rather odd.

Its slightly toy-like appearance masked the fact that under its glass-fibre and deformable plastic body-shell (designed for ease of repair) was a very good chassis easily capable of handling the power of the two engines offered, the 1300 and 1600 Ford CVH engines, the latter in 96 bhp XR2 tune giving a top speed of 111 mph (179 kph). The bigger engine in its Scimitar installation seemed rather rough and anaemic, so much so that the press quickly cried out for the fuel-injected version of the CVH from the XR3i. Despite the SS1's great agility it really needed the more powerful engine to help it compete against modern rivals.

**Reliant Scimitar SS1 1600**

**1985 RELIANT
SCIMITAR SS1 1600**

**Engine:** in-line four-cylinder, overhead-cam
**Bore × stroke:** 79.96 mm × 79.52 mm
**Capacity:** 1596 cc
**Maximum power:** 96 bhp
**Transmission:** five-speed manual
**Chassis:** steel space-frame on centre tunnel
**Suspension:** independent, with wishbones, coils and anti-roll bar front, semi-trailing arms, coil springs and anti-roll bar rear
**Brakes:** discs front, drums rear
**Bodywork:** open two-seat glassfibre sports
**Maximum speed (approx):** 111 mph (179 kph)

# RENAULT

**Billancourt, France
1898–**

Button-maker's son Louis Renault, regarded as a dunce at school, was fascinated by machinery. At the age of 13 he befriended steam-car pioneer Leon Serpollet, who gave Renault his first drive, but it ended abruptly when a wheel fell off the car!

In 1898, aged 21, Louis Renault built his first voiturette, powered by a 273 cc De Dion engine, in a shed in the garden of his parents' house at Billancourt, Seine. It featured direct drive by shaft to a live rear axle, a feature of sufficient novelty for Renault to patent it. He had no plans for quantity production of his voiturette, but having demonstrated the little car to a number of friends on Christmas Eve, 1898, Renault received a dozen orders from potential customers.

In order to begin manufacture, Louis founded Renault Frères with financial backing from his two elder brothers, Fernand and Marcel.

By 1900, Renault Frères was established as one of the largest companies in its field, and began to fit 500 cc De Dion engines to its cars. An active racing policy boosted orders, for when the Renault team won the voiturette class in the 1900 Paris-Toulouse race, the company received 350 orders.

In 1901 Renault began fitting twin-cylinder 8 hp engines of 1060 cc and the following year a Renault-built 4398 cc four-cylinder 20CV unit designed by Viet made its debut in the company's racing cars. The company temporarily withdrew from racing after the death of Marcel Renault in the 1903 Paris-Madrid event. Louis Renault himself gave up driving the company's products in races and concentrated on his inventions, some of which, like a hydraulic damper, found their way into production.

By 1904 the Renault range was based on five models: twins of 8 hp and 10 hp and four-cylinder cars of 14, 20 and 35 hp. On early models the radiator tubes formed the side of the bonnet, but Renaults appeared at the 1904 Paris Salon with the radiator at the rear of the engine, a position which was to remain characteristic of the marque until the late 1920s.

In 1905 the Paris Hackney Cab Company ordered 1500 twin-

cylinder Renaults, the first of many such orders for Renault taxis, which served for many years in Paris and London.

Renault's first six-cylinder model, a 50 hp 9.5-litre, appeared in 1908, the year in which Louis Renault, by acquiring the shares of his surviving brother Fernand (who was in poor health), gained complete control of the company, which he was to run in an increasingly autocratic manner for the next three and a half decades.

Although the company's range was large and confusing – in 1912 a choice of 15 different models was offered, from the twin to the 7539 cc six-cylinder 40CV – by the outbreak of war, Renault had expanded into one of Europe's leading manufacturers of motor vehicles.

After the Armistice the pre-war range was resumed, consisting of the twin-cylinder 9 hp, four-cylinder 10/12 hp and 18 hp and six-cylinder 22 and 40 hp, but the twin-cylinder Renault survived for only a few months and was then replaced by a new four-cylinder 10 hp designed for quantity production.

In 1923 Renault launched a new model, the three-seat 951 cc 6CV KJ, designed to compete with the new 5CV Citroën Cloverleaf. This was the first Renault to have a detachable cylinder head, and was developed into the four-seat NN of 1924. The new model was promoted by an apparently driverless car circulating in Paris.

Renault also launched the JY in 1923, a six-cylinder model of 4222 cc which was later enlarged to 4766 cc. The massive 40CV still continued in production, though since the war its swept volume had been increased to 9123 cc. A side-valve 1.5-litre Monasix was also offered in the late 1920s, though its poor acceleration earned it few friends.

By this time the products of

273

Renault, once the great innovator, had become staid and conservative, although there was an attempt to reverse this trend in 1929 when the firm launched its first straight-eight, the 7100 cc Reinastella, a replacement for the antiquated 40CV six. The Reinastella was the first Renault with a frontal radiator, and also the company's first luxury car with left-hand steering. It was joined in 1930 by the Nervastella, a 4.24-litre eight of similar design. A sporting version, the 4.8-litre Nervasport, appeared in 1932. In April 1934 a Nervasport fitted with streamlined bodywork covered 5000 miles (8046 km) at an average of 102 mph (164 kph), breaking 10 world and international records in the process. That same year, the Reinastella was replaced by the 5.4-litre Nervastella Grand Sport.

Nevertheless, none of the popular Renaults of the 1930s could be regarded as progressive in design, although the company's aviation interests were represented in the streamlined design of the standard bodywork. In 1937, however, Renault broke new ground with the Juvaquatre, the company's first monocoque car with independent front suspension; over 18,000 were sold in 1939.

During the war the Renault factory was badly damaged by bombing. Louis Renault, accused of collaborating with the Germans during the Occupation, was arrested and died in jail under mysterious circumstances. The Renault factories were taken under government control to become the Regie Nationale des Usines Renault, resuming production with the Juvaquatre.

Shortly afterwards the rear-engined 760 cc 4CV was introduced, a model which had been developed in secret during the Occupation. The factory was tooled-up for the production of this economy car at the rate of 400 a day, and manufacture continued until 1961.

The Fregate, launched in 1951, was the last front-engined, rear-wheel-drive car produced by Renault. It had all-round independent suspension, and production reached the 100,000 mark in 1955. While driving his Fregate back from Strasbourg, Pierre Lefaucheux, who had overseen Renault's post-war recovery, hit a patch of ice, crashed and was killed. He was succeeded by Pierre Dreyfus.

Renault introduced a new rear-engined model, the Dauphine, in 1956; a tuned performance model, the Dauphine Gordini, appeared in 1957. In 1960, the Dauphine became the first French car with over 2 million sales.

The Floride was new for 1959, while three years later the old 4CV was succeeded by the front-wheel-drive 747 cc R4.

After an attempt to build the American Rambler under licence had failed, Renault launched the 956 cc R8 in 1962; it pioneered all-round disc braking, and was subsequently followed by the R8 S, the R8 Major and the R8 Gordini.

In 1965 Renault introduced the R16, with a die-cast aluminium 1470 cc power unit. Renault claimed that this was the first mass-produced European car to replace the dynamo with an alternator. Three years later the Dauphine was discontinued. The R12 appeared in 1969, followed in 1970 by the R6 and in 1971 by the R15 and R17. The R12 Gordini was, however, an unsuccessful venture of the early 1970s, which also saw the launch of the Rodeo (a plastic-bodied, Jeep-like vehicle), the R5 minicar and its sporting R5-Alpine derivative (known as the R5-Gordini in Britain). In 1976 the R14 was launched, designed to fall between the R12 and R16, and in 1978 the R18 arrived (a replacement for the R12), along with the R20 and R30.

In the summer of 1978 an accord was signed between Renault and American Motors, which gave the French company a ready-made dealer network for an onslaught into the US market.

In 1980 Renault launched the Fuego coupé, a sporting derivative of the R18, available in seven versions, with a choice of 1400, 1600 and 200 cc power units. A 'hot-shoe' Turbo version of the R5 was also unveiled.

A new small car, the R9, launched in 1981, was voted Car of the Year. It was a somewhat bland design intended for production in America as well as in Europe. Renault placed great hopes on the R9 and its hatchback derivative, the R11, but by 1984 it was apparent that sales were slipping. A technically-advanced new model, the R25, replaced the R20 and R30, while in 1985 Renault unveiled the Supercinq, a modern redefinition of the old R5, which seemed to be slow at establishing itself in those mass-market sectors in which Renault was becoming dangerously uncompetitive.

## Renault AX

The little twin-cylinder Renault AX made its public debut at the 1908 London Motor Show, and was welcomed by the French magazine *Omnia* in the following terms: 'It is very much to the taste of the public, who see it as a move towards the voiturette…that car for poor people that can render so many services. I hope that they won't weigh down this nice little chassis, built to carry neat two-seater bodywork, with huge coachwork capable of carrying five people!'

But of course they did, for the twin-cylinder Renault chassis was quickly adapted as a taxicab, in which guise the model was well-known in Paris and London, its finest hour being the rushing of reinforcements to the front in 1914 when the German Army threatened Paris. This achievement earned the Renault taxi the proud title 'Taxi de la Marne', its immortality guaranteed by the preservation of a Renault taxi in the Invalides in Paris.

In 1908 a short-chassis AX cost a substantial £250.

The general model name AX actually applied to quite a variety of twin-cylinder Renaults; it was originally given to the 8CV model of 1908/09, then applied to the larger (1206 cc) 9CV which succeeded it. There was also a long wheelbase AXD, while the AG long was the 8CV taxi chassis. There were two further taxi chassis; ANB for a Parisian taxi and ALB for a short-stroke 884 cc taxi used in London. Indeed, the last twin-cylinder Renault, the 1206 cc FD which appeared in 1919, was largely destined to replace the stock of Parisian taxis after the war.

---

### 1908 RENAULT AX

**Engine:** in-line, twin-cylinder, side-valve
**Bore × stroke:** 75 mm × 120 mm
**Capacity:** 1060 cc
**Maximum power:** 8 bhp
**Transmission:** three-speed manual
**Chassis:** pressed steel channel
**Suspension:** non-independent with semi-elliptic leaf springs all round
**Brakes:** drums on rear only
**Bodywork:** two or four-seater
**Maximum speed (approx):** 35 mph (56 kph)

---

**Renault AX**

## Renault 40CV

The origins of the mighty 40CV Renault (known as the 45 hp in England) were in the 7.5-litre 50CV of 1910, which was renamed the 40CV the following year despite retaining the same engine dimensions.

A post-war development of this, the Type HD, appeared in May 1919, but seems to have remained at the prototype stage, for it was quickly followed by the Type HF, in which a 10 mm increase in bore size brought the swept volume to 9123 cc.

In 1920–23, a dozen different 40CV models were submitted for official examination by the Ministry of Mines, but only three went into limited production, varying only in detail, such as three or four speed transmissions, two or four wheel brakes.

The 40CV finally went into full production at the end of 1923; its power unit of 9.1 litres was the largest catalogued during the 1920s, and the chassis was a favourite with Parisian high society.

A Renault 40CV won the 1925 Monte Carlo Rally, and the type also set up a number of endurance records at Montlhéry, culminating in an impressive session during 1926 when a standard chassis fitted with a specially-built streamlined single-seat saloon body covered 4167.6 km (2589.7 miles) in 24 hours, at an average speed of 173.65 kph (107.9 mph); a replica of this car can be seen today in Jackie Pichon's motor museum at Clères.

**1924 RENAULT 40CV**

**Engine:** in-line six-cylinder, side-valve
**Bore × stroke:** 110 mm × 160 mm
**Capacity:** 9123 cc
**Maximum power:** 140 bhp
**Transmission:** four-speed manual
**Chassis:** pressed steel channel
**Suspension:** non-independent with semi-elliptic leaf springs front and cantilever springs rear
**Brakes:** drums all round, servo assisted
**Bodywork:** to order
**Maximum speed (approx):** 90 mph (145 kph)

**Renault 4CV**

## Renault 4CV

In the autumn of 1940, Louis Renault planned a small car for construction after the war: his design department began development without telling him, and in May 1941 Renault was astounded to walk into the design office unannounced and discover a wooden mock-up of the 4CV engine. Instead of scolding the engineers – such development work was forbidden by the occupying Germans – he ordered the manufacture of three actual power units.

A prototype car was constructed in secret by the end of 1942; Louis Renault assisted at its final trials in September 1943, though he seemed little impressed with it. A more refined second prototype was also built and secret tests of this car began in March 1944.

Launched at the 1946 Paris Salon, the 4CV earned the nickname 'little pat of butter', as at first it was painted sand yellow, using stocks of desert camouflage paint originally intended for the Afrika Korps. Demand for the 4CV was so high that Renault had to introduce their first automated transfer lines to speed production.

From 1948, the 4CV was built for the British market at Acton: early models had a 760 cc engine, but this was reduced to 748 cc to bring the car under the 750 cc limit for competition work.

By the end of its production run in 1961 over one million had been sold worldwide.

**1949 RENAULT 4CV**

**Engine:** in-line four-cylinder, overhead-valve
**Bore × stroke:** 54.5 mm × 80 mm
**Capacity:** 748 cc
**Maximum power:** 21 bhp
**Transmission:** three-speed manual
**Chassis:** integral
**Suspension:** independent with wishbones and coil springs front and swing axles rear
**Brakes:** drums all round
**Bodywork:** four-door saloon
**Maximum speed (approx):** 60 mph (96 kph)

**Renault 40CV**

# A-Z OF THE CAR

miles of development testing. One car was sent to the North Cape for trials north of the Arctic Circle, another was tried in the Swiss mountains, a third was tested in the United States while a fourth underwent endurance testing in Africa.

The first Dauphine left the production line in a new factory at Flins, near Mantes, in December 1955, with output intended to reach 550 cars a day within twelve months. The car was officially launched in March 1956.

A one-piece casting was used for the cylinder block and crankcase, which contained the wet cylinder liners. An identical crankcase to the 4CV was employed, rear swing-axle suspension was identical to the 4CV and, also like the 4CV, a Ferlec automatic electromagnetic clutch was available as an optional extra, giving two-pedal control.

The potential of the Dauphine was shown in April 1956 when four led their class in the Mille Miglia.

In the 1960s, the Dauphine became the first French car to sell over two million. Renault attempted a major assault on the North American market with the Dauphine but the car's fragility gave Renault a disastrous reputation in the USA.

## Renault Dauphine

It was in 1951 that Renault decided that there would be room, in about five more years, for a new medium-sized car to slot between the 4CV and the 2-litre Frégate. The first prototype was completed in July 1952 and, after preliminary tests, a small pre-production series was constructed, and covered over 2 million

### 1959 RENAULT DAUPHINE

**Engine:** in-line four-cylinder, overhead-valve
**Bore × stroke:** 58 mm × 80 mm
**Capacity:** 845 cc
**Maximum power:** 30 bhp
**Transmission:** three-speed manual
**Chassis:** integral
**Suspension:** independent with wishbones and coil springs front and swing axles rear
**Brakes:** drums all round
**Bodywork:** four-door saloon
**Maximum speed (approx):** 68 mph (109 kph)

**Renault Dauphine**

## Renault 25

Designed by a team led by Jacques Cheinisse, the R25 was launched for 1984 at the height of the motor industry's obsession with drag factors as 'the world's most aerodynamic production car'. This claim was based on the basic, slim-tyred R25TS, with a claimed drag factor of 0.28: the plusher versions of the R25 had CDs of anything up to 0.33.

### 1985 RENAULT 25

**Engine:** V6, overhead-cam
**Bore × stroke:** 88 mm × 73 mm
**Capacity:** 2664 cc
**Maximum power:** 144 bhp
**Transmission:** five-speed manual
**Chassis:** integral
**Suspension:** independent with MacPherson struts front and coil springs and wishbones rear
**Brakes:** discs all round
**Bodywork:** saloon
**Maximum speed (approx):** 125 mph (201 kph)

**Renault 25**

**Renault 5 Turbo**

What was remarkable about the claim was that the R25 lacked any of the voguish appurtenances of other aerodynamic models such as the Audi 100, like flush glazing; instead, this well-equipped Renault large car relied on careful fairing-in of much of the underbody, along with a sealed nose section on 2.0 and 2.2-litre versions, aerodynamic wheel trims and a carefully sealed rear hatch. Aerodynamic efficiency was not the 25's sole strong point as it was a superbly comfortable fast executive saloon – Renault's first good big car for many years.

## Renault 5

Launched at the beginning of 1972, the Renault 5 minicar was described as 'sympathetic and amusing' by the motoring press. It was intended for the growing 'supermini' class, and was intended to slot in above the basic Renault 4. The suspension was soft and with a long travel, ideal for use on the rough roads and farm tracks of rural France, but this small, economical three-door hatchback soon became an international best-seller.

Announced with an 875 cc power unit (956 cc was soon listed), the R5 was also available in eco-

---

### 1985 RENAULT 5 TURBO

**Engine:** in-line four-cylinder, overhead-valve, turbocharged
**Bore × stroke:** 76 mm × 77 mm
**Capacity:** 1397 cc
**Maximum power:** 160 bhp
**Transmission:** five-speed manual
**Chassis:** integral
**Suspension:** independent with wishbones torsion bars and anti-roll bars
**Brakes:** discs all round
**Bodywork:** two-door, two-seater
**Maximum speed (approx):** 130 mph (210 kph)

---

nomy form with a 750 cc power unit; then came a 1289 cc version for added performance. Most powerful of all the production R5 variants was the Alpine (known as the Gordini in Britain), with a 1397 cc power unit and alloy road wheels.

There was, however, also a two-seat rear-engined Turbo version, which had little in common with the ordinary R5 apart from a vague similarity in overall shape: it was an

homologation special for the firm's successful rally cars, and boasted a 160 bhp 1397 cc power unit.

In 1984, the R5 was joined by an all-new Supercinq which, though it looked similar in styling to the old R5, was completely different, being mechanically derived from the R9/R11 range and having a subtly redesigned bodyshell.

## REO

**Lansing, USA**
**1904-1936**

---

Having successfully brought quantity production to America's small car industry, Ransom Eli Olds decided to retire from Oldsmobile at the age of 40, in 1904, but a deputation of businessmen persuaded him to head a new company which they had organised. The carrot was a $260,000 share in the $500,000 company; Olds accepted at once, and within seven months the factory had been built and cars were being built. Before the end of the season, 300 railway wagonloads of single-cylinder gas buggies, worth almost $1.4 million, had been shipped. Reo quickly

added a twin-cylinder model to the range, while an unsuccessful four-cylinder Reo appeared in 1906.

But Reo's next four, launched in 1911, was, claimed Ransom Olds modestly, 'pretty close to finality'. He called his Reo the Fifth, which sold for $1055, 'The car that marks my limit…my farewell car'. But in fact Olds scarcely paused, and went on to produce a range of four- and six-cylinder models, which were fitted with distinctive vee-radiators during the war.

In 1920, Reo concentrated production on the six-cylinder Model T; with no handbrake (but *two* footbrakes), the Model T Reo had magneto ignition and underslung rear suspension. It was replaced by a new 25 hp Flying Cloud six, also available as the Wolverine, in 1927. That led to Reo's best-ever year the following season, when 29,000 cars were built.

For 1931, Reo launched the Flying Cloud Eight, as well as the Custom Royale Eight, styled by Count Alexis de Sakhnoffsky; in 1933 Reo, who had already pioneered the synchromesh gearbox, offered a two-speed automatic transmission, one of the first to be fitted to a production car.

**Reo Flying Cloud**

## 1933 REO FLYING CLOUD

**Engine:** in-line six-cylinder side-valve
**Bore × stroke:** 85.7 mm × 125 mm
**Capacity:** 4396 cc
**Maximum power:** 85 bhp
**Transmission:** three-speed manual
**Chassis:** pressed steel channel
**Suspension:** non-independent with semi-elliptic leaf springs
**Brakes:** drums all round
**Bodywork:** saloon
**Maximum speed (approx):** 60 mph (97 kph)

An auxiliary 'underdrive' was controlled by a pullout handle on the dash, which also engaged reverse. For 1936, the automatic became a four-speed, but in the middle of that year it was decided to discontinue car production in favour of trucks, for the Reo Speed Wagon commercial had gained an excellent name. It was a wise move which ensured the survival of the Reo name; as for Ransom Olds, who died at the age of 86 in 1950, history records that he also invented America's first successful motor mower... .

## RHODE

**Birmingham, England**
**1921–1933**

F.W. Mead and T.W. Deakin had collaborated before the Great War in building the Media, available with a 9 hp vee-twin or four-cylinder power units of 8/10 and 10/12 hp, but these were manufactured on a very small scale.

Serious manufacture started in 1921 with the Rhode light car, which, unusually, used a specially-manufactured 1087 cc four-cylinder overhead camshaft engine. For 1924, Rhode offered a larger 1232 cc engine; this was felt to be

rather noisy, so in 1926 quietness was sought by the introduction of pushrod overhead valves.

Two years later, Rhode launched a completely new car, the Hawk; initially, the power unit was an overhead-camshaft version of the 11/30 hp engine, but this was replaced by a 1.5-litre Meadows. The company, which came under new ownership in 1931, listed the Meadows-engined-Hawk saloon until 1933.

## 1928 RHODE HAWK

**Engine:** in-line four-cylinder, overhead-valve
**Bore × stroke:** 69 mm × 100 mm
**Capacity:** 1496 cc
**Maximum power:** 40 bhp
**Transmission:** four-speed manual
**Chassis:** pressed steel channel
**Suspension:** non-independent with semi-elliptic leaf springs front and cantilever springs rear
**Brakes:** drums all round
**Bodywork:** fabric saloon
**Maximum speed (approx):** 70 mph (113 kph)

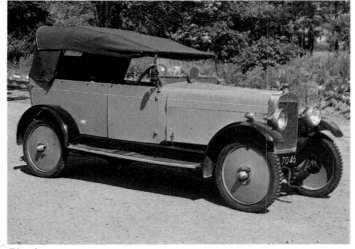

**Rhode**

## RICKENBACKER

**Detroit, USA**
**1922–1927**

Captain Eddie Rickenbacker, was the top-scoring American air ace of World War One, with a tally of 26 German planes shot down in combat, which had earned him the Legion d'Honneur, the Croix de Guerre and the American Distinguished Service Cross. So when he decided to manufacture an automobile, it was promoted as 'the car worthy of its name', and carried the Hat-in-the-Ring squadron insignia that had formerly been painted on the SPAD biplane of its promoter.

The Rickenbacker automobile was the culmination of three years of development by Harry Cunningham, Barney Everett and Walter Flanders; a handsome, well-engineered car which made pioneering use of two-tone paint schemes, the Rickenbacker's six-cylinder engine possessed double flywheels for smooth running. More crucially, in 1923 Rickenbacker introduced internal expanding four-wheel brakes, the

first time this feature had been used on a medium-priced American car.

Alarmed by the thought that they, too, would have to face the cost of fitting front-wheel brakes, Rickenbacker's rival manufacturers instigated a 'whisper campaign' which alleged that too-powerful brakes were a threat to safety. Despite its famous name, and the fact that it had even been praised in a popular song of the day – 'she won't jar your vacation for there's no vibration in my cracker-jacker Rickenbacker' – the Rickenbacker car suffered from the innuendi. Captain Eddie felt that this campaign was a contributory factor in the decline of his company. Another setback came when Walter Flanders was killed in 1922.

Rickenbacker introduced the Vertical Eight Super-Fine in 1924; the company's energetic publicity manager, LeRoy Pelletier (also responsible for that memorable catch-phrase 'Watch the Fords go by!') claimed: 'A Prince of the Purple might drive this car himself without losing caste!'.

A proposed merger with Peerless fell through later that year; in 1925, Rickenbacker launched the striking Vertical 8 Super-Sport, with aerofoil bumpers, bullet-shaped headlamps, laminated mahogany cycle wings and all-round safety glass.

But things were not well at Rickenbacker; stock sales were suspended in January 1926, and Captain Eddie resigned from the board that September. The company was reformed, and new models – 6-70, 8-80 and 8-90 – introduced. However, in the Spring of 1927, the company's assets were auctioned, and the engine, tools, dies and patterns were sold to Jørge Skafte Rasmussen, who shipped them to Europe, where Rickenbacker six- and eight-cylinder engines were fitted in the Zwickau and Dresden models produced by the Audi works, which Rasmussen had recently acquired.

# A-Z OF THE CAR

**Rickenbacker Vertical Eight**

# RILEY

**England
1898–1969**

William Riley diversified out of the weaving trade in 1890 and bought up an established cycle company, Bonnick & Co, to provide a secure future for his four sons. In 1896 the company changed its name to the Riley Cycle Company Limited and later that year young Percy Riley designed a neat four-wheeled voiturette with a single-cylinder engine, which first ran in 1898. Young Percy even cut the gearwheels by hand; an advanced feature of the design was the use, well before it became commonplace, of a mechanically-operated inlet valve.

Once that prototype had been completed, however, the Riley company failed to follow up this early lead with any kind of production motor vehicle. Indeed, it wasn't until 1900 that Riley made its first tentative venture in this field with the Royal Riley motor tricycle, powered by a De Dion Bouton engine. This basic machine quickly evolved into a tricar, with two wheels in front and a single driven wheel behind. The power unit on these three-wheelers was a 1034 cc vee-twin engine designed by Percy Riley and built by the Riley Engine Company, founded by the Riley brothers in 1904, and they were produced until 1907.

In 1905 Riley built their first four-wheeler – a development of the tricar, which retained its best features, such as the Percy Riley-designed engine and constant-mesh transmission. An important development pioneered on this car was the centre-lock detachable wire wheel, which was soon standardised on Riley cars, and the manufacture of which for sale to other car companies proved to be a profitable sideline.

In 1907 Riley brought out a new, front-engined 12/18 hp model with an improved, 2076 cc vee-twin power unit, capable of taking four or five-seat bodywork. A smaller, 10 hp derivative of the 12/18 hp appeared in 1909, with a 1390 cc engine designed by Stanley Riley.

The 9 hp Riley was phased out during 1910, and in 1912 William Riley decided that the future of the company lay with the manufacture of wheels. The Riley Cycle Company had stopped making cycles in 1911, when it was renamed Riley (Coventry) Ltd, and now William Riley announced that it would cease building cars as well.

So the four Riley brothers set up a new firm, the Riley Motor Manufacturing Company, to take over the car-building side of the business; its first new car was the 2951 cc 17 hp, launched at the 1913 Olympia Show. To confuse matters still further, Victor and Stanley Riley also set up the Nero Engine Company, which proposed to build a 1097 cc 10 hp car, although only three prototypes had been completed by the outbreak of World War I.

A factory at Foleshill, Coventry, acquired for munitions manufacture by the Nero Engine Company, formed the basis of post-war Riley expansion, becoming the principal Riley factory in 1919, when Riley (Coventry) Ltd, which had stopped making detachable wheels, amalgamated with Nero. Meanwhile, the Riley Motor Manufacturing Company had ceased making chassis and become the Midland Motor Body Company, while the Riley Engine Company was assembling 17/30 hp Rileys from its stock of pre-war parts.

Riley (Coventry) launched the first all-new post-war model in 1919; designed by Harry Rush, the 11 hp Riley had a side-valve 1498 cc engine developing 35 bhp. In 1923 a handsome sports derivative of the 11 hp, the Redwinger, was launched. With an engine tuned to give 42 bhp, the Redwinger was capable of 70 mph, and was built in both two- and four-seater versions.

The Riley Engine Company, which had turned to the manufacture of stationary and marine power units designed by Percy Riley, now re-entered the car field with the sensational 1100 cc Riley Nine, introduced for 1927. The fabric-bodied Monaco saloon was particularly successful, and the incorporation of a luggage boot into the body was an unusual feature for the period.

Harry Rush attempted to counter this new model by fitting a Ricardo head to the side-valve engine of the old 11 hp Riley (he had previously dabbled with supercharging and overhead valves), but this car was discontinued during 1928.

In that year Riley introduced both a touring version of the Nine, and the 'Brooklands' Nine, conceived by 'Welsh Wizard' Parry Thomas, whilst at Olympia they launched a six-cylinder variant of the Nine, the 1631 cc Fourteen.

The messy corporate structure of the various Riley companies was tidied up in 1931 when Riley (Coventry) Ltd took over the Riley Engine Company and the Midland Motor Body Company. During the 1930s Riley launched numerous variants of their four- and six-cylinder models, among them the fastback Kestrel and the more conventional Falcon of 1933, the sporting 9 hp Gamecock and Imp and the six-cylinder MPH. A 1.5-litre 12/4 four-cylinder engine designed by Hugh Rose was launched in 1934; it was produced alongside the faithful Nine for the next few years.

The Riley engine boasted many sporting successes, like consecutive wins in the BRDC 500 Mile race at Brooklands in 1934–35–36, victory in the 1932 JCC 1000 Mile race at Brooklands and the manifold victories of Freddie Dixon's single-seat 'Red Mongrel'.

1937 saw the launch of a 2.5-litre long-stroke four and of the V8 Autovia, built by an associated company, but Riley was heading into financial problems, and in 1938 the company was taken over by the Nuffield Organisation. Only the 1.5-litre and 2.5-litre fours survived the take-over, and these remained in production even after the war,

**Riley Nine**

powering a handsome range of post-war cars with independent torsion-bar front suspension and fabric-topped saloon bodies. Indeed, though the Pathfinder launched in 1954 shared its bodywork with the Wolseley 6/90, it retained the classic 2.5-litre Riley engine until 1957, when a 2.6-litre BMC engine was adopted.

From then on, the Riley marque degenerated into a badge-engineered variant of the BMC theme, fading away as an up-market derivative of the BMC Mini and 1100 front-wheel-drive models.

## Riley Nine

Initially built by the Riley Engine Company, the Riley created a sensation when it appeared in mid-1926. Quite apart from its handsome Monaco saloon bodywork, the Nine possessed an outstanding engine created by Percy Riley in the shape of an 1100 cc four-cylinder unit whose twin camshafts were mounted high in the block, with short pushrods actuating inclined valves in a hemispherical head, giving the advantages of twin overhead camshafts without the complication. A rigid crankshaft ran in only two main bearings, creating a compact, highly tunable power unit, whose basic valve layout remained a feature of Riley engines until 1957.

The Brooklands Nine, initiated

by Parry Thomas before his death in 1927, and brought to fruition by his assistant, Reid Railton, appeared at the end of 1927, winning its first race at Brooklands by a clear mile.

The appearance of the MK IV Riley Nine chassis in mid-1929 was a major step forward; it brought strengthened side members, more supple springing, larger brakes and stronger wheels.

By August 1929 over 6000 Riley Nines had been produced, and demand was still rising: ownership of a Riley Nine inspired Raymond Mays to use the 12/6 Riley as the genesis of the ERA.

A new dropped chassis

appeared at Olympia in 1931 for the improved Plus Ultra Nine, while in 1933 Riley launched a handsome sports car based on the Nine, the Imp. In 1935 a streamlined saloon, the Merlin, replaced the Monaco on the Nine chassis; the Riley Nine was finally discontinued after the Nuffield takeover at the end of 1938.

## Riley MPH

Based on the six-cylinder cars built for the 1933 Tourist Trophy, the Riley MPH, launched at the beginning of 1934, obviously drew styling inspiration from Italy, with its wedge-shaped profile and finned spare wheel cover. Two engine options were initially available, a 1458 cc

---

### 1930 RILEY NINE

**Engine:** in-line four-cylinder, overhead-valve
**Bore × stroke:** 60.3 mm × 95.2 mm
**Capacity:** 1087 cc
**Maximum power:** 25 bhp
**Transmission:** four-speed manual
**Chassis:** pressed steel channel
**Suspension:** non-independent with semi-elliptic leaf springs front and rear
**Brakes:** drums all round
**Bodywork:** Monaco fabric saloon, two or four-seat tourer
**Maximum speed (approx):** 65 mph (105 kph)

---

### 1934 RILEY MPH

**Engine:** in-line six-cylinder, overhead-valve
**Bore × stroke:** 60.3 mm × 95.2 mm
**Capacity:** 1633 cc
**Maximum power:** 60 bhp
**Transmission:** four-speed preselector or close-ratio manual
**Chassis:** pressed steel channel
**Suspension:** non-independent with semi-elliptic leaf springs front and rear
**Brakes:** drums all round
**Bodywork:** two-seater sports
**Maximum speed (approx):** 90 mph (145 kph)

---

**Riley MPH**

unit eligible for 1.5-litre competitions, or a 1633 cc engine; a 1726 cc engine was available in 1935.

The potency of the MPH was shown in the 1934 24 Heures du Mans, when the MPH of the Frenchmen Sebilleau and de la Roche won its class and finished second overall.

But the MPH, arguably the prettiest British sports car of its day, was a victim of the complexity of the Riley range of the mid-1930s, and was discontinued in 1935 in favour of the 12/4-engined Sprite, which had a similar body but compromised its good looks in favour of modernity with a 'waterfall' grille and skirted·wings. In all, it is believed that 18 MPHs were built.

# Riley RM

The Riley RM was one of the first new cars to be announced after the war, though it was styled very much on pre-war lines; the standard saloon had an attractive fabric top stretched over metal mesh on a timber frame.

The first cars all had the 1.5-litre four; the 2.5-litre unit was not introduced until the end of 1946.

A handsome three-abreast open Roadster was launched in 1948 for export markets, and there was also a drophead coupé. Apart from a few 1.5-litre dropheads, these cars were built on the 2.5-litre chassis. The power and reliability of the 2.5-litre unit led to its use in the Healey cars, too.

The 1.5-litre RM was updated in October 1952, and remained in production in modified, RME form until 1955; for 1954, a new look was given by the removal of the running boards, the 'helmet' section front wings and the spatted rear wings. The original 2.5 litre was revised in 1952 and replaced in 1953 by the Gerald Palmer-designed Pathfinder RMH, which retained the old 2.5-litre engine in a new, full-width bodyshell. This model lasted until 1957, when it was replaced by the Wolseley-like 2.6 in 1957.

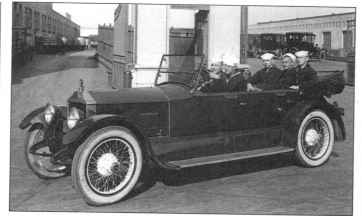
**Roamer**

# ROAMER
### Kalamazoo, USA
### 1916–1930

Built by Albert C. Barley, former manufacturer of the Halladay car, and designed by Karl H. Martin, the Roamer car was externally styled to resemble the Rolls-Royce, but was, in fact, no more than a quality assembled car, initially powered by six-cylinder Continental engines, and subsequently by Rutenber fours. In 1921 Rochester-Duesenberg horizontal-valve four-cylinder engines were introduced, remaining as the Roamer power unit until 1925. Apart from some Continental sixes which were fitted to a few 1926 Roamers, the marque transferred exclusively to Lycoming eights.

But sales fell away after 1926, and the Roamers sold as 1930 models were, in fact, unsold 1929 cars. Apart from his work for Roamer, Karl Martin also designed the Deering Magnetic and America's first straight-eight, the Kenworthy Line-O-Eight; in 1919–25 he also manufactured the limited production Wasp luxury car, of which only 18 were built. In 1930 the Depression took its toll.

---

## 1921 ROAMER D4 75

**Engine:** in-line four-cylinder, horizontal valve
**Bore × stroke:** 101.6 mm × 152.4 mm
**Capacity:** 4941 cc
**Maximum power:** 75 bhp
**Transmission:** three-speed manual
**Chassis:** pressed steel channel
**Suspension:** non-independent with semi-elliptic leaf springs
**Brakes:** drums on rear only
**Bodywork:** roadster, tourer, cabriolet, coupé, saloon
**Maximum speed (approx):** 80 mph (130 kph)

---

## 1950 RILEY RM

**Engine:** in-line four-cylinder, overhead-valve with twin camshafts
**Bore × stroke:** 80.5 mm × 120 mm
**Capacity:** 2443 cc
**Maximum power:** 90 bhp
**Transmission:** four-speed manual
**Chassis:** X-braced channel steel
**Suspension:** independent front with torsion bars. Live rear axle with semi-elliptic leaf springs
**Brakes:** drums all round
**Bodywork:** saloon, roadster, drophead coupé
**Maximum speed (approx):** 78 mph (125 kph)

**Riley RM Roadster**

## MODEL
E-type Series One, 1961

### UK price when announced:
£1480 (2098 inc. tax) Roadster,
£1550 (£2197 inc. tax) coupé

## ENGINE
**Location:** Front, longitudinal
**Type:** Water-cooled in-line six with cast-iron block and aluminium alloy head.
**Cubic capacity:** 3781 cc
**Bore × stroke:** 87 × 106 mm
**Compression ratio:** 9.0:1
**Valve gear:** 2 inclined valves per cylinder, operated in hemispherical combustion chambers by twin chain-driven overhead camshafts.
**Fuel supply:** 3 SU HD8 carburettors
**Ignition:** Coil and distributor, mechanical
**Maximum power:** 265 bhp (gross) at 5500 rpm
**Maximum torque:** 260 lb ft (gross) at 4000 rpm

## TRANSMISSION
**Layout:** Clutch and gearbox in unit with engine driving rear wheels
**Clutch:** Single plate, diaphragm spring
**Gearbox:** Four-speed manual with synchromesh on top three ratios
   1st 3.377:1   3rd 1.283:1
   2nd 1.86:1   4th 1.00:1
**Final drive:** Hypoid bevel with limited slip differential
**Ratio:** 3.31:1 or 3.07:1

## SUSPENSION
**Front:** Independent by double wishbones, longitudinal torsion bars, telescopic dampers and anti-roll bar
**Rear:** Independent with one lower lateral link and one lower radius arm per side with the drive shaft acting as the upper lateral link. 2 telescopic spring/damper units per side.

## STEERING
**Type:** Rack and pinion, manual

## BRAKES
**Type:** Discs front and rear, in-board at rear. Hydraulic with servo assistance

## WHEELS AND TYRES
**Type:** 5½J × 15in wire spoked with Dunlop 6.40 × 15in RS5 cross-ply tyres

## BODY/CHASSIS
**Type:** Steel monocoque centre section with square-tube front sub frame and pressed steel rear sub frame. Convertible or coupé bodywork, 2 doors 2 seats

## DIMENSIONS AND WEIGHT
**Length:** 175.5 in (4457 mm)
**Width:** 65.3 in (1658 mm)
**Wheelbase:** 96 in (2438 mm)
**Track – front:** 50 in (1270 mm)
     – rear: 50 in (1270 mm)
**Weight:** (dry) 2464 lb (1117 kg) roadster, 2520 lb (1143 kg) coupé

## PERFORMANCE
**Maximum speed:** 149 mph (240 kph)
**Acceleration 0-60 mph:** 7.1 seconds
**Fuel consumption:** 21 mpg

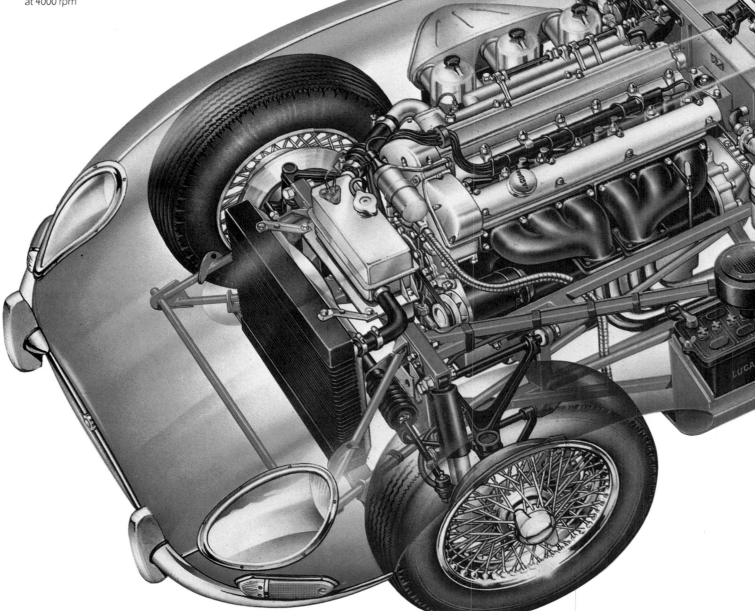

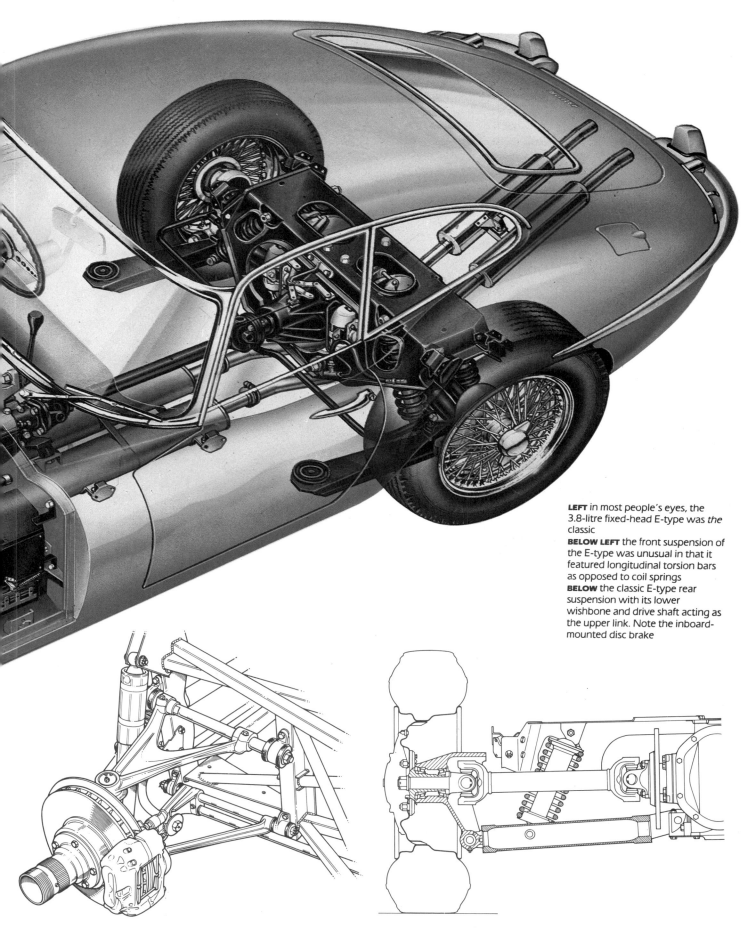

**LEFT** in most people's eyes, the 3.8-litre fixed-head E-type was *the* classic

**BELOW LEFT** the front suspension of the E-type was unusual in that it featured longitudinal torsion bars as opposed to coil springs

**BELOW** the classic E-type rear suspension with its lower wishbone and drive shaft acting as the upper link. Note the inboard-mounted disc brake

# A-Z OF THE CAR

## ROCHET-SCHNEIDER
**Lyon, France**
**1894–1932**

Edouard Rochet and his friend Theophile Schneider started building bicycles in 1889, and by 1894 had become one of the first companies in the Lyon area to begin car manufacture, initially building cars modelled on the German Benz. With backing from a wealthy motorist named Demetrius Zafiripulo, a member of a Franco-

twin- and 12 hp four-cylinder form in 1901. At the 1902 Paris Salon, these were replaced by a 6½ hp single cylinder model, a 10 hp twin and a 16 hp four, which apart from its armoured wood chassis, followed Mercedes practice closely.

Like many French firms, Rochet-Schneider was reformed as an English company for tax reasons in 1904, and by 1906 the Rochet-Schneider range had grown to include 16, 18/-22, 30, 30/35, 40/50 and 70 hp models, all four-cylinder cars. Three years later the firm was offering nine different cars, including two massive chain-driven

Rochdale Olympic

## ROCHDALE
**Rochdale, England**
**1952–1968**

Starting life as just another kit car, the Rochdale was initially available with such bodies as the Riviera drophead coupé and the Olympic 2/4 seat saloon, but developed into the stylish glass-fibre monocoque fixed-head Olympic sports coupé.

The Rochdale originally used BMC mechanicals, particularly the 1.5-litre Riley engine, but in its Phase 2 form, from 1963, the Ford Cortina engine was favoured.

In total Rochdale built approximately 400 Phase 1 and two Olympics.

### 1964 ROCHDALE OLYMPIC

**Engine:** in-line four-cylinder, overhead-valve
**Bore × stroke:** 81 mm × 72.75 mm
**Capacity:** 1498 cc
**Maximum power:** 78 bhp
**Transmission:** four-speed
**Chassis:** glassfibre monocoque
**Suspension:** independent front with wishbones and coil springs. Live rear axle with coil springs
**Brakes:** discs front drums rear
**Bodywork:** glassfibre sports coupe
**Maximum speed (approx):** 118 mph (190 kph)

Greek banking family from Marseille, Rochet-Schneider abandoned cycle manufacture in 1898 and built a new factory on the Chemin Feuillat. Here the partners began building cars on Panhard lines, announced in 7 hp

six-cylinder models, a 7135 cc 30CV and a 10,857 cc 45CV.

Rochet-Schneider's 1914 range consisted of six different models, with the largest a 7238 cc 50CV four; it also included two side-valve six cylinders, of 18CV (3619 cc) and 28CV (5228 cc).

During the war Rochet-Schneider made lorries for the French Army, resuming production in 1918 with pre-war models. The company's first new post-war car was a sidevalve 6126 cc six cylinder introduced in 1920. This model subsequently acquired overhead valves, and was replaced in 1926 by another six, this time with a 3769 cc engine. In 1930 this power unit was enlarged to 4561 cc, with pushrod overhead valves, dual

**Rochet-Schneider Cabriolet de Ville**

**1909 ROCHET-SCHNEIDER 12/16 HP**

**Engine:** in-line four-cylinder, side-valve
**Bore × stroke:** 80 mm × 120 mm
**Capacity:** 2413 cc
**Maximum power:** 20 bhp
**Transmission:** four-speed manual
**Chassis:** pressed steel channel
**Suspension:** non-independent with semi-elliptic leaf springs front, three-quarter semi-elliptic leaf springs rear.
**Brakes:** rear wheel and transmission
**Bodywork:** two-seat cabriolet de ville
**Maximum speed (approx):** 40 mph (65 kph)

ignition and a twin-choke Zenith carburettor.

But the old-fashioned four-cylinder models were becoming increasingly difficult to sell, and by 1932 Rochet-Schneider had abandoned car manufacture in favour of building lorries and buses, in which form the marque survived until 1953, two years after it had been acquired by Berliet.

# ROLLAND-PILAIN

**Tours, France
1905–1931**

Emile Pilain entered the automobile industry in 1898, assisting his uncle François, later one of Lyon's leading makers in his own right, at Vermorel, at Villefranche-sur-Saône. Emile stayed on for a year or so after François had resigned to establish his own company in 1901, and then turned up in Tours, where, with financial backing from one Rolland, he began manufacturing cars and bicycles.

The first Rolland-Pilain car was a 20/28CV monobloc four-cylinder model of 2211 cc. This was followed by a 12/16CV and a 35/45CV 'Grande Tourisme'.

In 1910 Rolland-Pilain began experimenting with sleeve-valve engines, including a 3921 cc sleeve-valve six in their complex range for that year, which also included conventionally-engineered models of 1460 cc, 2413 cc, 2724 cc, 5195 cc, 5702 cc, 6872 cc, 8760 and 14,335 cc, the five latter models available with either shaft or chain drive.

For 1913 Rolland-Pilain added a 20CV of 3969 cc and a big 60CV of 6902 cc to this range, and then, having obviously over-reached themselves, reduced it dramatically;

**1909 ROLLAND-PILAIN 16 HP**

**Engine:** in-line four-cylinder, side-valve
**Bore × stroke:** 80 mm × 110 mm
**Capacity:** 2212 cc
**Maximum power:** 42 bhp
**Transmission:** four-speed
**Chassis:** pressed steel channel
**Suspension:** non-independent with semi-elliptic leaf springs
**Brakes:** rear-wheel drums
**Bodywork:** two-seat sports racer
**Maximum speed (approx):** 70 mph (115 kph)

ROLLAND-PILAIN

by the outbreak of the Great War, Rolland-Pilain were only building the 20CV and the 1924 cc 10CV.

Rolland-Pilain reintroduced these two old models after the war, but in 1921 launched an exciting new overhead-valve 12CV of 2297 cc, with brakes on all four wheels. In 1922 Rolland-Pilain built a remarkable racer with a 1980 cc straight-eight engine originally intended for desmodromic valve operation (but as this could not be made to function satisfactorily, the team of three cars competing in the 1922 French Grand Prix had conventional valve gear). They also had the odd Rolland-Pilain four-wheel brake system, with hydraulic front and mechanical rear braking. This model was catalogued at a price of Fr 90,000.

The following year, Rolland-Pilain again competed in the French Grand Prix; this time, their team included a car with the Schmid cuff-valve engine – but it failed to reach the starting line.

In 1924 Rolland-Pilain introduced an outstanding 2008 cc 11CV overhead-valve four, followed in 1925 by a 1924 cc 10CV.

At the 1925 Motor Show, Rolland-Pilain exhibited a somewhat cheaper version of the 1924 cc sports model, the B25, and a sporting 2008 cc 11 HP, and for 1927 they produced a 1.5-litre machine. After that, however, like so many Continental marques, Rolland-Pilain began to succumb to up-market American influence.

Right at the very end, Rolland-Pilain produced a handful of luxury cars powered by American side-valve Continental engines, a 3-litre six and a 4-litre eight, which appeared in 1929. The following year, Rolland-Pilain was reduced to sharing a stand at the Paris Salon with another failing firm, Bollack, Netter et Cie, and during 1931 it vanished altogether.

**Rolland-Pilain two-seater runabout**

# ROLLS-ROYCE

**Manchester/Derby/Crewe, England 1904–**

Henry Royce was born in 1863, the same year as Henry Ford; like Ford, he found his first successful job in the new-fangled technology of electrical engineering. The third point of similarity between these two otherwise markedly different men who so dramatically made their mark on the history of motoring was that their best-known cars – the Model T Ford and Rolls Royce Silver Ghost – were built for a period of 19 years, during almost the same 19 years.

In 1884, together with his friend Ernest Claremont, Royce established an electrical engineering company in Cooke Street, Manchester, and made his name as a manufacturer of reliable dynamos and electric cranes. By the turn of the century, established as a successful businessman, Royce took to a new hobby: motoring. In 1903 he brought a Decauville, one of the better light cars of the day, and it was with the Decauville as inspiration that he built three 10 hp twin-cylinder cars under the Royce name in 1904. These were of sufficiently high quality to attract the attention of Lord Llangattock's younger son, the Hon C.S. Rolls, a pioneer motorist who had a successful West London motor agency and was looking for a refined light car to sell alongside high-class Continental imports like Mors, Panhard and Minerva.

Rolls agreed to take every car that Royce could manufacture, provided they were marketed under the name Rolls-Royce. He also persuaded Royce to prepare as wide a range of exhibits as possible for the December 1904 Paris Salon. By dint of all-out working, Royce managed to complete a 10 hp two-cylinder car which gave demonstration runs outside the Salon, a 10 hp show chassis, a three-cylinder model of 15 hp, a 20 hp four-cylinder car (though the show model's engine was a dummy) and a 30 hp six-cylinder engine. The old, Decauville-like cooler of the Royce was replaced by a new radiator of Palladian elegance, whose squared-off shape was to become the Rolls-Royce hallmark.

In order to publicise the new marque, Rolls-Royce entered two 20 hp cars – which combined strength with lightness by the pioneering use of nickel steel in frame and front axle, plus an aluminium rear-axle casing – in the 1905 Isle of Man Tourist Trophy, where one of them crossed the finishing line first, but was narrowly squeezed into second place on elapsed time. This success

persuaded Rolls and his partner Claude Johnson to drop their other agencies, and a new company, Rolls-Royce Limited, was founded in 1906 to take over the car side of Royce Ltd (which continued in the electrical business until after Henry Royce's death in 1933). In 1906 the company, having expanded quickly enough to outgrow the Manchester plant, bought a site at Derby where a new factory designed by Royce was erected. The finance for the expansion was provided by increasing the capital and going public, though the relatively new company was regarded with some suspicion by the press and public, since there had been a number of catch-penny company flotations just prior to that time, so that it was only by appealing to a wealthy owner that the minimum limit for subscriptions was passed.

An aberration was the V8 Legalimit, which Johnson asked Royce to design in 1905; it was intended to have all the advantages of the electric car with none of its drawbacks, and to run 'noiselessly, odourlessly, vibrationlessly and smokelessly' from 3 to 20 mph (5–32 kph) in top gear. Its V8 engine was so shallow that it was capable of being mounted beneath the floor. None of the planned 'bonnetless' Legalimits was built, the only car to be delivered having a low, conventional bonnet and radiator.

Though the 30 hp six had not been a conspicuous success, in 1906 Rolls-Royce launched a new six-cylinder model, the 40/50 HP, known from 1907 as the Silver Ghost. Its design was hardly innovative, but it was built with Royce's customary devotion to the highest engineering standards, and achieved immortality as 'The Best Car in the World'; production was transferred to Derby in 1908, but the Silver Ghost survived until 1925. By the time it was discontinued, Rolls was dead, killed when his Wright Flyer biplane had crashed at Bournemouth in 1910, and Henry Royce was in semi-retirement following a major breakdown in health caused by overwork. From 1911 up to his death, Royce directed the design of Rolls-Royce cars from his homes in France and Sussex, to prevent his being exposed to the daily routine of the business.

Between 1919–1931, Rolls-Royce cars for America were built in a branch factory at Springfield, Massachusetts; total production at this factory was just under 3000 cars.

In 1922, Rolls-Royce launched a new, smaller model rated at 20 hp, with a 3150 cc six-cylinder engine, the first Rolls-Royce with a detachable cylinder head. Initially, it had a three-speed transmission with central gearchange, though

popular demand compelled the adoption of a right-hand-change, four-speed gearbox in 1925.

In 1925 the Silver Ghost was supplanted by the New Phantom; this was a transitional design with a new, overhead-valve 7.7-litre engine in a broadly similar chassis to the older model. It was replaced in 1929 by the more comprehensively revised Phantom II.

In that year the 20 HP grew up into the 20/25, whose power unit was also used in the original 'Rolls-Bentley' cars introduced after Rolls-Royce's controversial take-over of Bentley Motors. The 20/25 was succeeded in 1936 by the 25/30 (whose power unit was equally fitted to the 4¼-litre Bentley launched at that period), and the 25/30 evolved into the Wraith in 1938.

Between 1936–39 Rolls-Royce built the Phantom III, a beautifully-engineered V12 of 7341 cc, often clothed in ponderous coachwork; its engine, fitted with hydraulic tappets, gained the reputation of being prohibitively costly to overhaul.

After the war, Rolls-Royce moved from Derby to Crewe, where production restarted in 1947 with the Silver Wraith; this was followed in 1949 by the Silver Dawn, which broke new ground in being the first Rolls-Royce to be available with a standardised Rolls-Royce design of coachwork made from pressed steel, rather than built by traditional coachbuilding methods.

Rolls-Royces continued to be powered by developments of the pre-war six-cylinder engine until 1959, when a 6231 cc V8 appeared in both the Silver Cloud and the Phantom V models (the Phantom IV had been a 5675 cc straight-eight of which only 16 were built).

A total break with Rolls-Royce traditions came in 1965 when the

Silver Shadow adopted integral construction and all-round independent suspension.

The year 1971 brought crisis to Rolls-Royce: aviation had killed C.S. Rolls 61 years before, and now it threatened to kill the company which he had helped to found.

Since the Great War, Rolls-Royce had created some of the world's finest aero engines, such as the Merlin used in the Hurricanes and Spitfires that had won the Battle of Britain, but in the early 1970s the advanced-technology RB211 turbofan jet ran into development problems. Rolls-Royce was hurled into serious financial difficulties.

In February 1971 a receiver was appointed and Rolls-Royce declared bankrupt. The Government was urged to help, with the result that two separate companies were formed. The car division, Rolls-Royce Motors, was hived off as a separate (and profitable) concern and sold in 1980 to the Vickers group, a giant with strong roots in the defence and engineering sectors. During the remainder of the 1970s, Rolls-Royce prospered, with a strong demand for the Silver Shadow; annual output reached 3350 in 1978 and 1979.

The Silver Shadow was joined in the late 1970s by the Corniche and Camargue models, then by the (relatively) lower-priced Silver Spur and Silver Spirit, with the Phantom VI catering to the top-bracket carriage trade with a choice of limousine or landaulette coachwork.

Rolls-Royce was hit by the second oil-shock in mid-1982, when orders fell drastically; from under 2500 units in 1982, production plummeted to 1600 in 1983, and the Rolls-royce workers staged their first strike for 23 years that autumn. A cost-cutting programme was instituted with great success, and by 1984 production had recovered to 2500 vehicles annually. Rolls-Royce, whose state had sent jitters through the Vickers shareholders in 1983, earned £14 million on sales of £149 million during 1984.

The Silver Shadow was phased out in the early 1980s; by the middle of the decade the 'cheapest' Rolls-Royce available, the Silver Spirit, cost over £55,000.

On 2 August, 1985, Rolls-Royce passed a remarkable milestone by building its 100,000th car, 81 years from the start of production. The car, a royal blue Silver Spur Centenary commemorative, went on display alongside the original Silver Ghost and a 1904 10 hp Rolls-Royce; a further 25 identical cars were produced and delivered round the world; 12 went to the United States, five to the Middle East and eight to the United Kingdom.

# A-Z OF THE CAR

## Rolls-Royce 40/50

Rolls had rushed into the six-cylinder market with the 30 hp of 1905–06, but it was hardly a success. For a start, its engine was based on components developed for the smaller, lighter 10 hp twin and 20 hp four, and, like so many early sixes, it suffered from periodic vibration.

Henry Royce realised that building a six from a combination of three two-cylinder units was inferior to combining two three-cylinder units, and that, in essence, is what he did for his next car, the 40/50 HP six, which appeared during 1906.

Apart from this, the new power unit was far more robust: the crankshaft was almost twice the diameter of its predecessor, and full pressure lubrication was adopted.

The chassis was stronger, too, although the basic design was similar to that of the 30 hp, with a four-speed gearbox (third was direct, fourth an overdrive 'sprinting gear'), leather-faced cone clutch and platform rear suspension. Royce's passion for perfection was shown in the way that the brakes were compensated by a miniature differential gearing in an aluminium housing, instead of by the customary pivoted whiffle-tree linkage, while the rear axle casing was, in Royce's words, 'sewn together with a ring of tiny bolts'.

The public launch of the 40/50 HP six took place at the 1906 Olympia Motor Show, where a Pullman limousine and a polished chassis were shown. It was Claude Johnson who really put the new model on the map when he took the 13th car of the type, christened The Silver Ghost, on a 2000-mile (3219 km) RAC-observed run (which included the course of the forthcoming Scottish Reliability Trial), and

then launched the car on a 15,000-mile (24,140 km) observed trial which it completed triumphantly with only one involuntary stop, when the petrol tap shook closed after 629 miles (1012 km) and needed only £2 2s 7d–worth of parts renewed to bring it to as-new condition after the equivalent of three years' motoring.

An increase in engine stroke to 120.7 mm late in 1909 raised the swept volume to 7426 cc and the power output to 60 bhp. Around the same time the overdrive four-speed 'box was replaced by a three-speed unit with direct drive on top gear in the interests of top gear flexibility, a much-prized virtue in those pre-

synchromesh days.

That the Silver Ghost possessed that flexibility in good measure was shown in 1911 when a new pattern car with a tapered bonnet, cantilever rear springs and an increased compression ratio, ran from London to Edinburgh on its 2.9:1 top-gear ratio with fuel consumption of 24.32 mpg, and then reached 78.26 mph (126 kph) at Brooklands. This model went into production as the 'London–Edinburgh', and is now probably the most desirable of all Silver Ghosts. In 1913–14 a four-speed transmission with direct-drive top was introduced.

During the Great War, Rolls-Royces served with great honour as armoured cars, carrying a couple of tons of armour-plating with ease.

The refined post-war version of the Ghost had electric lighting and starting as standard, aluminium pistons and dual ignition, but it didn't have four-wheel brakes, nor was this feature standardised until 1924, a year before the end of production.

From 1921 a newly-formed American Rolls-Royce company built the Silver Ghost in Springfield, Massachusetts; by the time it ceased manufacturing operations in 1931, the factory had built 1703 Silver Ghosts and 1241 Phantom Is.

In contrast a total of 6173 Rolls-Royce Silver Ghosts was built in Manchester and Derby, and by the time the Ghost was discontinued, the once pre-eminent position of the Rolls-Royce was being actively challenged by companies like Hispano-Suiza.

---

### 1907 ROLLS-ROYCE 40/50

**Engine:** in-line six-cylinder, side-valve
**Bore × stroke:** 114.3 mm × 114.3 mm
**Capacity:** 7036 cc
**Maximum power:** 48 bhp
**Transmission:** four-speed manual (overdrive top)
**Chassis:** pressed steel channel
**Suspension:** non-independent, with semi-elliptic leaf springs front, semi-elliptics and transverse platform spring rear
**Brakes:** rear-wheel drums and transmission
**Bodywork:** to order
**Maximum speed (approx):** 53 mph (85 kph)

---

**Rolls-Royce Silver Ghost**

# Rolls-Royce 20 HP

Rumours of an experimental small Rolls-Royce were confirmed in 1921 when the magazine *The Motor* published one of the first-ever 'sneak' photos showing the new model. The car was announced in 1922, and its engine differed from that of the Ghost in having pushrod-operated overhead valves and a detachable cylinder head. It also had centrally-mounted gear and brake levers at a time when the hallmark

## 1922 ROLLS-ROYCE 20 HP

**Engine:** in-line six-cylinder, overhead-valve
**Bore × stroke:** 76 mm × 114 mm
**Capacity:** 3127 cc
**Maximum power:** 53 bhp
**Transmission:** three-speed manual
**Chassis:** pressed steel channel
**Suspension:** non-independent, with semi-elliptic leaf springs front and rear
**Brakes:** rear-wheel drums
**Bodywork:** to order
**Maximum speed (approx):** 75 mph (120 kph)

**Rolls-Royce 20 HP**

of the quality car was right-hand mounting of the levers. Another point of criticism was the fitting of a three-speed gearbox, although it wasn't until the end of 1925 that a four-speed transmission was fitted.

Remarkably, the prototype engine had been fitted with twin overhead camshafts, though lack of development work forced the abandonment of this advanced feature.

The 20 HP Rolls-Royce was a particularly significant model since it

was the foundation on which the company's power units were based for the next 37 years, with the crucial dimension being the distance between bore centres (4.150 in/10.5 cm), chosen because it gave adequate water-jacketing round the cylinders. But, like its big sister, the Twenty didn't get four-wheel braking until 1925.

The Twenty was built up to 1929, when it was supplanted by the bigger-engined 20/25 HP.

# Rolls-Royce Phantom I

In many ways, the Rolls-Royce New Phantom, which appeared alongside the Silver Ghost in the first half of 1925, was an enlarged version of the 20HP, with a similar layout of combustion chambers and valve gear to the smaller car. Like the Ghost, however, it had its cylinders cast in two blocks of three (though the detachable cylinder head was

made in one piece), while the chassis was of very similar design, with separate engine and gearbox, torque tube transmission and cantilever rear springs. And like the Ghost, where the car was designed to proceed with a minimum of gearchanging, the gearchange was fitted with Henry Royce's archaic locking gate, in which the lever had to be moved round three sides of a square to disengage it; snappy gearchanges were hardly the order of

## 1925 ROLLS-ROYCE PHANTOM I

**Engine:** in-line six-cylinder, overhead-valve
**Bore × stroke:** 108 mm × 139.7 mm
**Capacity:** 7668 cc
**Maximum power:** 100 bhp
**Transmission:** four-speed manual
**Chassis:** pressed steel channel
**Suspension:** non-independent with semi-elliptic leaf springs front and cantilever rear
**Brakes:** drums all round, servo assisted
**Bodywork:** to order
**Maximum speed (approx):** 75 mph (120 kph)

**Rolls-Royce Phantom I Brewster**

the day, though the car could be started from rest in third gear.

A slightly retrograde step was that the thermostat fitted to the cooling system of the latter Ghosts (from 1923) was not retained; instead vertical hand-controlled shutters were used to promote fast warm-up of the engine.

Moreover, the steering was criticised for its heaviness, though this was probably the result of the change from high-pressure narrow-section tyres to fatter low-pressure 'balloon' tyres, and the ride of early examples tended to be a little on the 'soft' side.

Over the short life-span of the Phantom I (1925–29), the output of the engine was gradually improved, most particularly by the fitting of an aluminium cylinder head on later models. There were significant differences between the cars built in Derby and the cars built in Springfield; the first 66 American cars did not have the servo-assisted four-wheel brakes of the British product, though they were equipped with a central chassis lubricating system, a feature that wasn't picked up by Derby until the end of the decade. And the Springfield Ghost was built until 1933, because of the cost of changing over to the more comprehensively redesigned Phantom II. Springfield's best year was 1928, when just under 400 cars were produced; after that, the Depression began to bite, with 200 cars built in 1929 and 100 in 1930. Production actually stopped in 1931, though cars were assembled from spares on hand until 1933; Springfield built 1241 Phantoms against the Derby total of 2212. The American factory was in receivership in 1934, though some repair and maintenance work continued, and some of those strange Brewster-bodied Ford V8s

were sold; by 1935 it was all over and the factory had been closed down for good.

One 1926 Phantom I was fitted with a novel Amherst Villiers supercharger installation commissioned by Captain Kruse of Sunningdale, Berkshire. Its blower was driven by a separate four-cylinder 10 hp engine mounted in a streamlined housing fitted to the nearside running board. This boosted the car's top speed from the normal 75 mph to 94 mph (120 to 151 kph) and gave a corresponding increase in the normal cruising speed (55 to 75 mph, 88 to 120 kph), though fuel consumption dropped from 12 to 9 mpg with the blower engaged... .

## Rolls-Royce Phantom III

During the mid-1920s, when Rolls-Royce was searching for a replacement for the Silver Ghost, an experimental V12 engine had been built, a not unnatural format when Rolls-Royce's aero-engine expertise is considered. But it wasn't until the time came to replace the Phantom II in the mid-1930s that Rolls-Royce actually put a V12 car into production.

The Phantom III announced in late 1935 had an overhead-valve V12 with its valves operated by a single camshaft in the angle of the vee, and hydraulic tappets, an advanced engineering touch (though pioneered in 1907 on the Leon Bollée car) which eventually proved a

source of irritation when, 1930s lubrication technology being what it was, the oilways became blocked with sludge and the tappets ceased to function properly, overloading the valve gear. Consequently, many Phantom IIIs were modified to take conventional solid tappets. The other break with Rolls-Royce tradition was the adoption of independent front suspension by 'short and long' radius arms controlled by a coil spring and damper in an oil-filled housing. This was, in fact, a modified General Motors design, a hardly surprising move since Rolls-Royce of America's chief engineer, Maurice Olley, had joined General Motors in 1930 specifically to improve the ride and handling of the Cadillac and developed this very suspension for them. The Cadillac suspension was, therefore, no more than a Rolls-Royce design with an American accent (though whether it would have been specifically developed for the Rolls-Royce had Springfield continued in operation is a moot point).

Slightly smaller in swept volume than the Phantom II (7340 cc against 7668 cc), the Phantom III power unit was notably more compact – it proved possible to use a wheelbase 8 in (20 cm) shorter on the Phantom III yet provide more space for bodywork. It used wet liners and paired conrods, while the dual coil ignition showed that Rolls-Royce knew more about combustion than many of their contemporaries. There were, as on earlier Rolls-Royces, two plugs

per cylinder, and one coil fired one plug in each cylinder. Rolls-Royce so arranged things that there was a microsecond's delay between the two systems, thus promoting good flame spread. On early Phantom IIIs, a heat exchanger was fitted for quick warm-up of the oil. Fuel consumption averaged 10 mpg.

In good order, a Phantom III was a magnificent conveyance, quick, silent and well-mannered, with a top speed of over 90 mph (145 kph) and the ability to reach 70 mph (113 kph) from a standstill in under 25 seconds; in the short life of the Phantom III – output was curtailed by the war – only 704 were produced.

### 1938 ROLLS-ROYCE PHANTOM III

**Engine:** V12, overhead-valve
**Bore × stroke:** 82.6 mm × 114.3 mm
**Capacity:** 7340 cc
**Maximum power:** 165 bhp
**Transmission:** four-speed
**Chassis:** X-braced pressed steel channel
**Suspension:** independent front with wishbones and oil-damped helical springs. Live rear axle with semi-elliptic leaf springs
**Brakes:** drums all round, servo assisted
**Bodywork:** to order
**Maximum speed (approx):** 92 mph (148 kph)

**Rolls-Royce Phantom III**

# A-Z OF THE CAR

in 1938, though not introduced until after the war.

The Silver Dawn was shorter, lighter and cheaper than the coach-built Rolls-Royces; for the most part, its bodywork was built to Rolls-Royce specification by the Pressed Steel Company and finished in the company's specially-installed work-shops, which were equipped to handle trim, upholstery and paint-work. Some Silver Dawn chassis were, however, fitted with one-off bodywork, like the fastback saloon by Pinin Farina shown in 1951. Production ran from 1949–55, and a total of 760 Silver Dawns was built.

not divert from a straight line if the driver sneezed (but equally gave him little opportunity for high-speed evasive action in emergency).

In 1971, therefore, the company – at that time operating in receivership, because of the problems of its aero-engine division – launched the new Corniche, which had higher-geared steering, improved suspension and radial tyres, plus an engine enlarged to 6750 cc, which gave a top speed of 123 mph. Its performance was good and the car could reach 100 mph (161 kph) from standstill in just half a minute.

For 1975 came the Carmargue, a

## Rolls-Royce Silver Dawn

Though Bentley had bitten the austerity bullet as early as 1946 and produced a 'standard steel' body, it took another three years before a Rolls-Royce with a standardised body made its debut. It was during 1949 that the Silver Dawn appeared, initially for export only.

### 1950 ROLLS-ROYCE SILVER DAWN

**Engine:** in-line six-cylinder, side-valve (F head)
**Bore × stroke:** 88.9 mm × 114.3 mm
**Capacity:** 4257 cc
**Maximum power:** 135 bhp
**Transmission:** four-speed manual
**Chassis:** X-braced pressed steel channel
**Suspension:** independent front with coil springs and wishbones. Live rear axle with semi-elliptic leaf springs
**Brakes:** drums all round (hydraulic front, mechanical rear)
**Bodywork:** standard steel saloon or to order
**Maximum speed (approx):** 90 mph (145 kph)

**Rolls-Royce Corniche**

'Hitherto,' commented *The Motor*, 'the Rolls-Royce has been the car for those who prefer to be chauffeur-driven; today, however, there are many owners who require the traditional refinement of the fine car and who prefer to drive themselves. To meet their need the Silver Dawn was produced.'

Like its contemporary, the Silver Wraith, the Silver Dawn had the new post-war F-head inlet-over-exhaust engine originally designed

## Rolls-Royce Corniche

The 1975 Silver Shadow was the first unit-construction Rolls-Royce, which also boasted self-levelling rear suspension built under Citroën licence and the first disc brakes to be adopted by Crewe. Its steering was somewhat slow-geared to incorporate the cautious Rolls-Royce Company's celebrated 'sneeze factor', which ensured that the car would

### 1980 ROLLS-ROYCE CORNICHE

**Engine:** V8, overhead-valve
**Bore × stroke:** 104.1 mm × 99.1 mm
**Capacity:** 6750 cc
**Maximum power:** not quoted
**Transmission:** three-speed automatic
**Chassis:** integral with front and rear auxiliary frames
**Suspension:** independent with coil springs and wishbones front and semi-trailing arms rear
**Brakes:** discs all round
**Bodywork:** convertible
**Maximum speed (approx):** 118 mph (190 kph)

two-door coupé derivative of the Corniche with rather bland Pininfarina styling; it was, however, comprehensively equipped, as befitted the world's most expensive production car (though its launch price of £29,250 seems quite modest by the standards of a decade later!), and came only with automatic transmission. In 1985, the Camargue lost its position as the world's most costly car, though by now the price tag had risen to over £83,000! The conservative Corniche convertible had overtaken it by just over £400.

**Rolls-Royce Silver Dawn**

**Rosengart Supertrahuit**

# ROSENGART
**Neuilly, France**
**1928–1955**

Lucien Rosengart started his rise to fame with Citroën, where in 1921–22 he created SADIF (*Société Auxiliare pour le Developpement de l'Industrie Française*) to solve Citroën's cash-flow crisis. SADIF was a finance company which advanced cash against vehicles in stock, enabling Citroën to continue producing cars at full speed during the slack season in the last quarter of the year. His company restored to an even keel by the activities of SADIF, Citroën decided that Rosengart was dispensable; Rosengart then joined Peugeot as chief executive, though his magic touch was hardly in evidence; the parting of the ways came by mutual consent, and Rosengart set up as a manufacturer in his own right, revealing his first car at the 1928 Paris Salon. However, that first Rosengart turned out to be no more than the familiar Austin Seven built under licence, differing only from the British prototype in that the bodywork was adapted to the French taste with features like a ribbon radiator. In 1932 the chassis was lengthened to accommodate a small 1100 cc six-cylinder version of the Austin engine, which was offered alongside the original four.

That same year, Rosengart decided to make a bold technical statement by launching a new and revolutionary model, though once again he played safe by actually taking out the French production licence for a car designed abroad, in this case the Adler Trumpf.

The new Rosengart Supertraction was first shown to

## 1933 ROSENGART SUPERTRAHUIT

**Engine:** in-line four-cylinder, side-valve
**Bore × stroke:** 74 mm × 95 mm
**Capacity:** 1649 cc
**Maximum power:** 40 bhp
**Transmission:** four-speed manual
**Chassis:** pressed steel channel
**Suspension:** independent with twin transverse leaf springs front and three-quarter cantilever springs rear
**Brakes:** drums all round
**Bodywork:** cabriolet, streamlined saloon
**Maximum speed (approx):** 65 mph (105 kph)

the press on 21 December, 1932; differing only from its German counterpart in its badging, the Supertraction gave Rosengart a year's start on his old employer, Citroën, in producing the first front-wheel-driven French family car. Proof of the new model's reliability was given a little while after the launch when marathon man Francois Lecot drove 100,000 km (62,000 miles) in 98 days at an average speed of 65 kph (40 mph).

After 1933, the Supertraction began to differ increasingly from the Adler Trumpf and, at the 1934 Paris Salon, appeared in a streamlined style; the original, squarecut bodywork was offered alongside this new-look Supertraction until 1936, when the Trumpf was withdrawn from the German market. The streamlined Supertraction, however, was offered until 1938, when it was succeeded by a Citroën-based front-wheel-drive model. There

was also a rear-wheel-drive version with similar bodywork, the 8/40 Superdix.

After the war, Rosengart introduced the Supertrahuit which, powered by a 3.9-litre Mercury engine, was totally out of tune with the post-war need for economy. When it turned out to be a complete flop, Rosengart returned to his pre-war Austin Seven theme, launching two models, the Artisane and the Ariette, powered by the old 750 cc side-valve in 1952. Two years later came the Sagaie, with an overhead-valve air-cooled 750 cc flat-twin said to be capable of 75 mph (121 kph); it was not enough to compete with Renault and Panhard, and failed to save the company, which closed down the following year.

# ROVER
**Coventry, England**
**1904–**

John Kemp Starley, born in Walthamstow in 1855, was apprenticed in Coventry and became a maker of cycles in 1877 in partnership with William Sutton. The partnership was dissolved in the mid-1880s and Starley began selling cycles under the name Rover. In 1888 Rover built the first true safety bicycle, while in the same year Starley constructed what was claimed to be Coventry's first motor vehicle, an electric tricycle driven by an Edwell Parker motor. Finding the 4 mph speed limit too irksome, he took the machine over to France for testing at Deauville, and it proved capable of some 8 mph. Rover bicycles gained an international reputation, but it wasn't until 1899 that the

company made its first tentative steps into motor vehicle production with the construction of a De Dion-engined bathchair, which appeared at the Automobile Club's famous demonstration of automobiles in the Old Deer Park at Richmond, Surrey. But it was not until two years after Starley's death at the early age of 46 in 1901 that Rover began to manufacture motor tricycles.

This led to the production of a neat 8 hp single-cylinder car, designed by Edmund Lewis, which appeared in 1904 and used much cast aluminium in its construction, particularly in its backbone chassis frame.

In 1905 Rover introduced another, more conventional, single-cylinder model, this time of 6 hp, and it sold for a mere 100 guineas (£105). The new 6 hp and the 8 hp sold so well that Rover decided to broaden out into the manufacture of four-cylinder cars that same year. Designed by Lewis, the new fours were a neat, but short-lived small monobloc four, the 10/12, and the 16/20, with separately-cast cylinders displacing 3199 cc, which won the 1907 Tourist Trophy Race.

A twin-cylinder 12 hp appeared in 1908, as did a 2497 cc 15 hp four designed by Bernard Wright; its lubrication system was somewhat deficient, incorporating a vane-type pump, and the replacement of crankshafts was, apparently, by no means unknown.

Wright, however, managed to persuade the Rover directorate to adopt the Knight sleeve-valve engine, and sleeve-valve Rovers of 8 hp (single-cylinder 1041 cc) and 12 hp (twin-cylinder 1882 cc) were introduced for 1911. The cylinder dimensions indicate the use of some Daimler components in their construction.

Rover production took a new turn in the autumn of 1911 with

the introduction of an excellent 2297 cc 12 HP designed by the Yorkshireman Owen Clegg. Clegg was also a skilled production organiser, and under his guidance Rover abandoned the old haphazard system of producing small numbers of several models – in 1912 Rover boasted that it 'offered a bigger selection of vehicles than any other company in the world, ranging from cycles at £6 10s to £15 2s 6d, motor cycles from £49 to £79 and cars from 100 guineas to £600' – and by 1913 had taken up a one-model policy with the Twelve. (An 18 HP had been launched in 1911, but it had proved uncompetitive).

Clegg's Twelve formed the basis of post-war production (though Rover had built Sunbeams for the War Office during the hostilities), with some updating in 1924 by Clegg's successor, Mark Wild, when it reappeared as the Fourteen, with a four-speed gearbox. In 1920 Rover re-entered the small car class with the Rover Eight, a 998 cc flat-twin designed by J.Y. Sangster, later to become one of the most noted designers of motorcycles. This near-cyclecar proved popular, and some 17,000 were built before it was replaced in 1924 by the four-cylinder Nine. In 1923 Wild unveiled a 3.4-litre six based on the Fourteen, which proved unsatisfactory, and was quietly dropped after only three units had been completed.

Peter August Poppe designed the Fourteen's successor, the 14/45, with an overhead-cam power unit of 2132 cc. The 14/45 did not sell well, despite subsequently being uprated to 2413 cc as the 16/50 hp, and it was replaced in 1928 by a 2-litre pushrod overhead-valve 'Light Six', the basic design of

which, built in capacities up to 2565 cc, became the backbone of 1930s production.

Rover attempted to counter the Depression with a rear-engined 839 cc V4 sub-utility car, the Scarab, priced at £85, and intended to fill the gap between motor cycle and small car. Unveiled in September 1931, the Scarab failed to reach production, though its combination of sliding-pillar front suspension and rear swing-axles apparently drew praise from such authorities as Doctor Porsche.

Through the 1930s, Rover maintained a solid middle-class image with a complex range which started at the Family Ten and went up to a seven-seated six-cylinder Meteor Coachbuilt Limousine. The sporting Speed Meteor tourer was an uncharacteristic venture, of which only a handful was assembled in Rover's London Service Depot at Seagrave Road, Kensington.

From 1932 Rover underwent considerable rejuvenation under the energetic managership of S.B. Wilks and Frank Ward, which underlined the middle-class values that the customer had come to expect from the Rover with a range of cars of conservative styling and sound engineering.

The 1937 line persisted until

1948, when Rover launched new inlet-over-exhaust four- and six-cylinder models, the P3 60 and 75, which featured independent front suspension for the first time on a production Rover. A bold post-war design venture, the Mi 700 cc luxury car, failed to pass the prototype stage.

Rover took a major step into a new market sector in April 1948 with the 4WD Land-Rover which was launched at the Amsterdam Show and became the natural successor to the wartime Jeep as a go-anywhere vehicle; it was in production in the mid-1980s.

Another landmark was the launch in October 1949 of the P4 75, with full-width styling and distinctive 'Cyclops' centre headlight.

Descendants remained in production until 1964. The company was at this time doing pioneering work on prototype gas-turbine cars, and JET 1 of 1950, with a 230bhp single-stage turbine running on aviation-type kerosene, set a speed of 152 mph (245 kph) on a highway in Belgium.

The last turbine car, the T4 of 1961, looked very like the radically styled Rover 2000 of 1964, first a 2-litre and from 1968 with the former Buick 3.5-litre V8. This lightweight, all-alloy engine would

power Rovers well into the 1990s.

In 1966, Rover merged with Leyland to become the spearhead of BL's luxury car effort and in 1970 the company launched the first Range Rover, a highly successful blend of comfort and four-wheel-drive off-road ability.

In 1976 came the new Rover SD1, with Ferrari Daytona-like styling and available with 2.3 and 2.6-litre sixes and the 3.5-litre V8. In the 1980s came the Rover 213 range, an anglicised Honda model. After much rationalisation within British Leyland, only the Rover name survived, gracing the entire range of Mini, Metro, Maestro and Montego models, the Honda-inspired 200 series, the four-door 400 variants, the 600 range, based mechanically on the Honda Accord, and, at the top of the list, the 800 models, the fastest being the 138 mph (222 kph) Vitesse Fastback.

## Rover 8 HP

The new 8 hp Rover made its debut at the Bexhill Speed Trials on August Bank Holiday Monday, 1904, driven by its designer, Edmund W. Lewis, formerly with Daimler. The little car proved 'fast, remarkably free of vibration, and gave a very good account of itself,' coming second in

### 1904 ROVER 8 HP

**Engine:** single-cylinder side-valve
**Bore × stroke:** 114 mm × 130 mm
**Capacity:** 1327 cc
**Maximum power:** 8 bhp
**Transmission:** three-speed manual
**Chassis:** aluminium backbone
**Suspension:** non-independent with transverse leaf spring front with live rear axle and semi-elliptic leaf springs
**Brakes:** drums on rear only
**Bodywork:** two-seater
**Maximum speed (approx):** 28 mph (45 kph)

its class. The Rover was remarkable for its neat chassisless construction, in which engine and transmission were carried in an aluminium casting, which incorporated brackets to support the rear suspension. Steering was originally by cable and bobbin, although this basic system was soon supplanted by rack and pinion; the gear change was on the steering column.

Though the 8 hp Rover sold for only £200, it was nevertheless a robust and reliable little car, capable of achieving over 40 mpg; in 1905 R.L. Jefferson drove a specially-bodied 8 HP across Europe to Constantinople, where no motor vehicle had ever penetrated. Rover soon offered an even smaller car, the 6 HP, for just 100 guineas.

**Rover 8 HP**

# A-Z OF THE CAR

**Rover Twelve**

## Rover 16/20 HP

The 16/20 HP Rover achieved fame in the 1907 Isle of Man Tourist Trophy, the only motor-race run on the public highway in the British Isles. Driven by former champion cyclist E.L. 'Long' Courtis, one of the two-car team led all the other competitors home, having averaged 28.8 mph (46 kph) over the 241-mile (388 km) race. Replicas of the winning car were offered for sale, and one survives today in the possession of the British Motor Industry Heritage Trust.

The 16/20 HP Rover achieved other sporting successes, taking

**Rover 16/20 HP**

### 1907 ROVER 16/20 HP

**Engine:** in-line four-cylinder, side-valve
**Bore × stroke:** 95 mm × 110 mm
**Capacity:** 3119 cc
**Maximum power:** 20 bhp
**Transmission:** three-speed manual
**Chassis:** pressed steel channel
**Suspension:** non-independent with transverse semi-elliptic leaf springs front and live rear axle with semi-elliptic leaf springs
**Brakes:** rear wheels, transmission and engine
**Bodywork:** Roi des Belges
**Maximum speed (approx):** 45 mph (73 kph)

Gold Medals in the London-Edinburgh Trials and the Saltburn Speed Trials.

A notable feature of the design was the engine brake, a Rover speciality of the period, in which the cams could be slid backwards on a keyed shaft to bring different cam profiles into use. This gave no lift at all to the inlet valve, but raised the exhaust valve twice for every revolution of the shaft, so that air was drawn in from the exhaust pipe, compressed and released, forming a powerful air brake.

## Rover Twelve

Rover's infatuation with the sleeve-valve engine was brought to its conclusion when Yorkshireman Owen Clegg arrived from Wolseley and created the immensely popular Twelve, with a conventional side-valve engine. The company soon concentrated all its production on this one model, and applied Clegg's 'batch-production' theories so that Twelves were soon being mass-produced in batches of up to 500 cars. Unusually for the period, Rover built their own bodywork. Despite the fact that the Twelve was a very good car, Rover failed to secure any War Office contracts during the Great War, and had to build Sunbeams under licence; several of these Rover-Sunbeams survive.

Clegg left Rover to join Darracq in Suresnes, France, where he produced a Darracq on similar lines to the Rover Twelve.

The Twelve reappeared after the war, redesigned in many respects, including the adoption of a detach-able cylinder head; 'the new model represents a very distinct advance upon the 12 hp Rover cars hitherto turned out...and does great credit to its designers and manufacturers' claimed *The Motor*. Added *The Autocar*: 'The name of Rover has become a household word synonymous with the virtues of sound British workmanship and material, and the quality of reliable service which follows in their train.'

## Rover 8 HP

Described as 'very warm, fairly comfortable but frankly inelegant in design', the 8 HP launched in 1919 marked Rover's return to its origins. It was cheap, basic and popular, despite a somewhat compromised reputation for reliability, for early examples had the distressing tendency at high speed to shed the flat-twin engines' cylinder heads.

Until the introduction of the Austin Seven, however, the 8 HP Rover had few rivals, since it was more substantial than the average cyclecar and more comfortable than a motorcycle and sidecar. Its specification was nonetheless basic: on early

### 1911 ROVER TWELVE

**Engine:** in-line four-cylinder side-valve
**Bore × stroke:** 75 mm × 130 mm
**Capacity:** 2297 cc
**Maximum power:** 28 bhp
**Transmission:** three-speed manual
**Chassis:** pressed steel channel
**Suspension:** non-independent with semi-elliptic leaf springs
**Brakes:** rear-wheel and transmission
**Bodywork:** tourer
**Maximum speed (approx):** 50 mph (80 kph)

Rover 8 HP

**1919 ROVER 8 HP**

**Engine:** air-cooled flat-twin, side-valve
**Bore × stroke:** 85 mm × 88 mm
**Capacity:** 998 cc
**Maximum power:** 14 bhp
**Transmission:** three-speed manual
**Chassis:** pressed steel channel
**Suspension:** non-independent with quarter-elliptic leaf springs front and rear
**Brakes:** rear-wheel drums
**Bodywork:** two seater, tourer, coupé
**Maximum speed (approx):** 45 mph (72 kph)

examples, even the ignition switch was an extra and, as an indication of relative costs, the complete car cost £220. To have the car painted any colour other than the standard brown was £5 extra, side curtains for the hood were £3 extra, and a speedometer was a further £7!

Remarkably, the little Rover Eight did quite well in the Light Car Trials of the day. It was succeeded by a 1074 cc four-cylinder water-cooled 9 HP of little distinction.

## Rover 16/50

Peter August Poppe was well-known as the builder of White & Poppe proprietory engines before the Great War, though his company was ultimately absorbed by the De-

nnis commercial vehicle company in 1919. Poppe was called in by Rover to design a successor to the old Clegg Twelve, and he created the 14/45 which appeared in 1924. Its hemi-head engine layout was ingenious: the overhead camshaft operated the inclined inlet valves directly, while short horizontal pushrods actuated the exhaust valves; it was a layout similar to that used on the BMW 328 engine of a decade later.

However, the 14/45 proved underpowered for the heavy limousine bodies that were then in favour, so was joined by the six-cylinder 16/50 HP, with a similar design of engine; handsome pointed-tail sports tourers with specially-tuned engines were available on both chassis.

**1925 ROVER 16/50 HP**

**Engine:** in-line six-cylinder, overhead-valve
**Bore × stroke:** 80 mm × 120 mm
**Capacity:** 2413 cc
**Maximum power:** 50 bhp
**Transmission:** three-speed manual
**Chassis:** pressed steel channel
**Suspension:** non-independent with semi-elliptic leaf springs front and rear
**Brakes:** drums all round
**Bodywork:** tourer, saloon, sports
**Maximum speed (approx):** 85 mph (137 kph)

Poppe's ingenious engine layout proved both costly to build and prone to oil leaks, so in 1927 he designed a more conventional overhead-valve six of 2023 cc, which, initially, was produced alongside the 16/50, a muddled marketing policy which took Rover close to the brink during the Depression (it was reformed in 1932 under the able directorship of S.B. Wilks and Frank Ward). The new six, which formed the basis of all Rover engines up to 1947, powered the stylish sportsman's saloon that achieved fame in 1930 as the car that beat the 'Blue Train' from the French Riviera to Calais. This was a fabric-bodied saloon with cycle wings (available thereafter to special order as the 'Blue Train' Rover), driven by a motoring journalist.

## Rover 75

After the war, all Rover production was concentrated at the Solihull plant, and for 1948, Rover introduced the P3 range which, while it retained the pre-war styling of its predecessor, had a new power unit with an ingenious inlet-over-exhaust layout. The camshaft was set low down on the side of the engine, directly operating the side exhaust valve, while a pushrod actuated the inlet valve. These cars also featured independent front suspension, its first appearance in a production Rover. Both the car and its engine were solidly built and well-engineered.

This power unit was used in the 1950 P4 range, which adopted full-width styling; a distinctive feature of

Rover 16/50 HP

Rover 75

## 1950 ROVER 75

**Engine:** in-line six-cylinder, inlet-over-exhaust
**Bore × stroke:** 65.2 mm × 105 mm
**Capacity:** 2103 cc
**Maximum power:** 75 bhp
**Transmission:** four-speed manual
**Chassis:** pressed steel channel
**Suspension:** front independent with coils and wishbones, rear non-independent with semi-elliptic leaf springs
**Brakes:** drums all round
**Bodywork:** saloon
**Maximum speed (approx):** 78 mph (125 kph)

this model was the spotlight mounted centrally in the radiator grille, from which the P4 '75' took its nickname of 'Cyclops'. Although the central spotlight was soon deleted, the 75 formed the basis of all Rover design for the next decade and a half. In 1955 a new short-stroke engine of 2230 cc was introduced, which proved almost 10 mph (16 kph) faster than its predecessor. The depths to which general car design had sunk in the mid-1950s is indicated by the fact that *The Motor* praised the Rover's sober shape as 'free from disturbing ornament'. The timelessness of the Rover styling was proved by its not being replaced until 1958, and then only by the evolutionary 3-litre.

the design was the de Dion rear suspension, which intruded into the boot space to an unwarrantable degree, so much so that a popular option was a bracket for mounting the spare wheel on the boot lid.

The integral chassis was of ingenious design, for the exterior body panels were bolted on, making accident repair simplicity itself.

In 1968 Rover's new all-alloy ex-Buick 3½-litre power unit was installed in the 2000 bodyshell: five years later the four-cylinder 2000 also received a new power unit, the 2200 in-line four.

## 1963 ROVER 2000

**Engine:** in-line four-cylinder, overhead-cam
**Bore × stroke:** 857. mm × 85.7 mm
**Capacity:** 1980 cc
**Maximum power:** 91 bhp
**Transmission:** four-speed manual, three-speed automatic
**Chassis:** integral
**Suspension:** front independent with transverse wishbones and upper longitudinal radius arms and coil springs, rear semi-independent with de Dion axle, Watt linkages and coil springs
**Brakes:** discs all round (rear inboard)
**Bodywork:** four-door saloon
**Maximum speed (approx):** 105 mph (169 kph)

# Rover 2000

The Rover 2000 broke dramatically with company tradition, for its sleek saloon styling was meant to bring Rover quality before an expanding new market, that of young executives. Its inspiration lay in the last of Rover's jet saloons, a legacy of which could be seen in the front suspension in which coil-sprung longitudinal radius arms fed their loads into the scuttle, a neat layout which didn't intrude into the engine bay. While this was necessary to leave maximum room for a portly automotive gas turbine engine, it wasn't quite so necessary for the in-line four-cylinder piston-engine of the 2000. A major shortcoming of

Rover 2200 SC

## Range Rover

Although the Land Rover, launched after the war, had become established as the leading British off-road vehicle, even its staunchest protagonists could hardly claim that it was luxurious. With the launch of the Range Rover in 1970, however, all that changed, for this elegant and timeless design was just as at home as an elegant town carriage for the Barbour-and-green-welly Chelsea set as it was in demanding off-road use (like the expedition which crossed the Dairen Peninsula in Central America), where its level of comfort was much appreciated.

Powered by the 3½-litre V8, the Range Rover had a well-designed four-wheel drive system with a centre differential to reduce tyre wear:

### 1970 RANGE ROVER

**Engine:** V8 overhead-valve
**Bore × stroke:** 88.9 mm × 71.1 mm
**Capacity:** 3528 cc
**Maximum power:** 130 bhp
**Transmission:** four-speed dual-range
**Chassis:** ladder type
**Suspension:** non-independent, with front rigid axle and longitudinal radius arms, transverse linkage bars and coil springs, rear non-independent with rigid axle, longitudinal radius arms, upper A-racket, coil springs and Boge Hydomat self-levelling
**Brakes:** discs all round
**Bodywork:** two-door five-seat estate
**Maximum speed (approx):** 98 mph (158 kph)

**Range Rover**

Boge Hydromat self-levelling suspension was standard.

In more than a decade and a half, the only significant change in the appearance of the Range Rover has been the addition of a five-door variant; and so far the Range Rover has remained unrivalled, although its success has spawned several four-wheel-driven family saloons from competing companies.

## Rover 220i Turbo coupé

The 200 series of two-door saloons was the one that bolstered the Rover revival and in 1992 the six-model range was joined by the 220i Turbo coupé, then, at £19,316, the cheapest 150 mph (240 kph) car on sale in the UK.

### 1992 ROVER 220i TURBO COUPÉ

**Engine:** 16-valve, in-line four, turbocharged
**Bore x stroke:** 84 mm x 89 mm
**Capacity:** 1994 cc
**Maximum power:** 197 bhp
**Transmission:** five-speed manual, front-wheel drive
**Chassis:** integral
**Suspension:** all independent, with MacPherson struts
**Brakes:** discs all round
**Bodywork:** two-door coupé
**Maximum speed (approx):** 150 mph (240 kph)

It shared the wheelbase and floorpan of the saloon models, but was reshaped to be 1.5 in (30 mm) lower, with T-bar style removable glass roof panels.

Weighing 2645 lb (1199 kg), the car was powered by the turbocharged 2-litre, four-cylinder engine of the larger 800 series Vitesse models, which gave 197 bhp and 174 lb ft of torque. The coupé's performance was phenomenal, with acceleration to 60 mph (96 kph) in 6.3 seconds and 100 mph (162 kph) in 15.6 seconds.

The coupé was a real rival to the Vauxhall Calibra and VW Corrado, and was let down only by a rather vague gearchange and power-assisted steering.

**Rover 220i Turbo**

**Rumpler**

# RUMPLER

**Berlin, Germany**
**1921–1926**

Born in Bohemia, Dr. Edmund Rumpler designed his first car for Nesselsdorfer in 1897, and then joined Daimler and later Adler, where he created Germany's first unit- constructed engine/gearbox. He then became a pioneer aeroplane designer, and during the Great War, the bird-like outline of his Taube monoplane became a symbol of menace from the air. After the Armistice, forbidden to build aeroplanes, Rumpler turned to the manufacture of aerodynamic cars; his rear-engined Type 0A 104 cars caused a sensation at the 1921 Berlin Show with their aerofoil-section bodywork, although these advanced Tropfenwagen (Teardrop) cars did not sell well.

Nothing about Rumpler's cars was orthodox; even the power unit was unlike anything else on the road, although it had some aviation antecedents. Compact, though expensive to build, this double-row 'broad-arrow' engine was manufactured to Rumpler's design by Siemens of Berlin. Its overhead valves were closed by leaf springs, and a single Pallas carburettor fed all six cylinders. Mounted in the rear of the deep chassis frame, this radical power unit developed 36 bhp at 2000 rpm and drove the short three-speed transmission via a multiplate clutch. Open tourers and lofty saloons were built; the driver occupied a solitary seat in the nose of the machine.

In an effort to improve sales, Rumpler brought out an improved design in 1924, which had a conventional overhead-valve, in-line four-cylinder 50 hp engine of

2595 cc. A longer wheelbase increased passenger accommodation from 4–5 to 6–7, though at the expense of handling. In 1925 the appearance of the cars was modified to make it less radical, but sales remained minimal.

In 1926, Rumpler turned the powertrain of his Tropfenwagen back-to-front to create a front-wheel-drive car, which had a Z-section light-alloy chassis, all-round swing-axle independent suspension, four-wheel brakes and light-alloy disc wheels. The power output of the 2595 cc engine remained the same, but the poorer aerodynamics meant that top speed was now down to around 70 mph (113 kph). Despite the front-wheel-drive Rumpler's more conventional appearance and advanced specification, the project never passed the prototype stage.

Benz took out a Rumpler licence, but only used it to create their famous rear-engined 2-litre Teardrop sports and racing cars.

---

**1921 RUMPLER 0A 104**

**Engine:** double-row broad-arrow six-cylinder, overhead-valve
**Bore × stroke:** 74 mm × 100 mm
**Capacity:** 2581 cc
**Maximum power:** 36 bhp
**Transmission:** three-speed manual
**Chassis:** semi-integral, deep-sided frame
**Suspension:** non-independent with cantilever leaf springs front, swing axles rear
**Brakes:** rear-wheel drums
**Bodywork:** streamline saloon, tourer
**Maximum speed (approx):** 70 mph (113 kph)

---

# RUSTON-HORNSBY

**Lincoln, England**
**1919–1924**

Ruston and Hornsby were a long-established firm of agricultural engineers who had made their first venture into internal combustion as early as 1897, with a paraffin tractor. They also experimented with caterpillar-tracked vehicles before the Great War, experience which proved extremely valuable when it came to developing the first tanks.

During the war, Ruston-Hornsby proved their mechanical skills by building Clerget and BR2 rotary aero-engines.

They foresaw a huge market for cars following the end of hostilities, and their first car, the A1, duly appeared in 1919. Intended to

compete with low-priced American imports, the A1 was entirely conventional, powered by a 40 bhp side-valve 2613 cc four-cylinder engine rated at 15.9 hp and driving through a three-speed gearbox. The engine was bored out to create the A3 of 1920, which displaced 3308 cc and had a power output of 50 bhp. For 1923, Ruston-Hornsby launched revised versions of the existing cars, the 16 hp B1 and the 20 hp B2. They had, claimed the company, 'been under test for the past 18 months, and the experimental models during this period have covered mileage aggregating to many tens of thousands of miles, over roads as far as possible of the most hilly description and the worst condition. Scotland to a great extent supplied this test'.

Both cars were also speed-tested at the Brooklands circuit where the 20 hp climbed the 1:4 Test Hill 40 times, 'as it is an exceedingly good engine lubrication test.' They were not cheap cars, but despite the neat appearance and sound performance of the 1923 Ruston-Hornsbys, car production ceased the following year.

---

**1923 RUSTON-HORNSBY B2**

**Engine:** in-line four-cylinder, side-valve
**Bore × stroke:** 90 mm × 130 mm
**Capacity:** 3308 cc
**Maximum power:** 50 bhp
**Transmission:** three-speed manual
**Chassis:** pressed steel channel
**Suspension:** non-independent with semi-elliptic leaf springs front and rear
**Brakes:** rear-wheel drums
**Bodywork:** tourer
**Maximum speed (approx):** 59 mph (95 kph)

**Ruston-Hornsby**

**MODEL**
Mercedes-Benz 540K (1937)

**UK price when introduced:**
£1890

**ENGINE**
**Location:** Front, longitudinal
**Type:** Water-cooled in-line straight-eight. Nine main bearings
**Cubic capacity:** 5401 cc
**Bore × stroke:** 88 mm × 111 mm
**Compression ratio:** 6.13:1
**Valve gear:** 2 valves per cylinder operated by single block-mounted camshaft, pushrods and rockers
**Fuel supply:** Single Mercedes-Benz updraught carburettor with Roots type supercharger
**Ignition:** Mechanical with coil and magneto
**Maximum power:** 115 bhp nomally aspirated, 180 bhp with supercharger engaged

**TRANSMISSION**
**Layout:** Gearbox behind engine
**Clutch:** Multi-plate
**Gearbox:** Four-speed manual with preselector change on third and fourth
| | |
|---|---|
| 1st 3.89:1 | 3rd 1.419:1 |
| 2nd 2.27:1 | 4th 1.00:1 |
**Final drive:** Spiral bevel
**Ratio:** 3.03:1

**SUSPENSION**
**Front:** Independent with double wishbones and coil springs
**Rear:** Independent with swinging axles and two coil springs per side either side of drive shaft

**STEERING**
**Type:** Screw and nut

**BRAKES**
**Type:** Lockheed hydraulic, drums front and rear. Servo assisted

**WHEELS AND TYRES**
**Type:** Wire spoke wheels with Dunlop Fort 7 × 17 in tyres

**BODY/CHASSIS**
**Type:** Pressed steel chassis with two side rails and five cross members. Two-door, two-seater convertible body

**DIMENSIONS AND WEIGHT**
**Length:** 207 in (5258 mm)
**Width:** 75 in (1905 mm)
**Wheelbase:** 129.5 in (3289 mm)
**Track – front:** 59.5 in (1511 mm)
**– rear:** 58.75 in (1492 mm)
**Weight:** 5516 lb (2502 kg)

**PERFORMANCE**
**Maximum speed:** 106 mph (171 kph)
**Acceleration 0–60 mph:** 13.8 seconds
**Fuel consumption:** 10–12 mpg

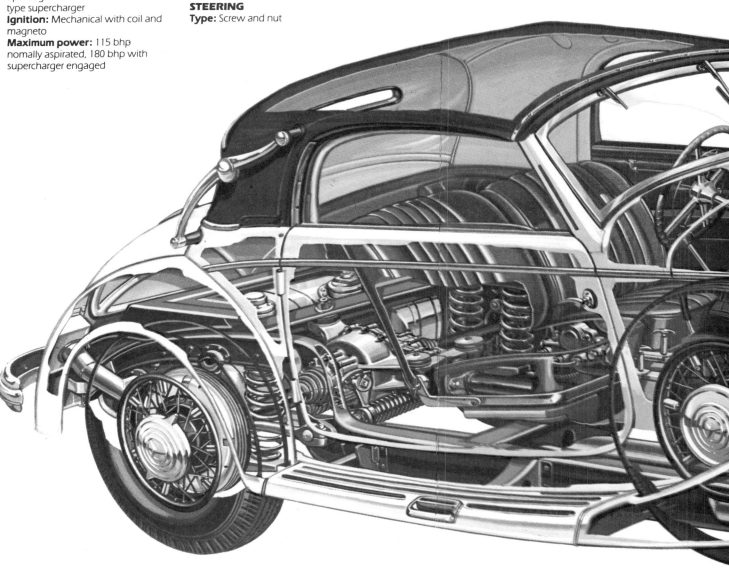

**BELOW** This cutaway of a two-seater cabriolet reveals the innovative coil spring and double-wishbone front suspension first seen on the 380 models and subsequently widely imitated. Note the use of twin coil springs at each side of the rear swinging axle shafts to support the 540K's imposing mass. The total weight of nearly 2.5 tons handicapped fuel economy but endowed the speedster with an exemplary ride quality.

# A-Z OF THE CAR

Rytecraft Scootacar

## RUXTON

New York/St Louis/Wisconsin, USA
1929–1931

Conceived by company promotor and financier Archie M. Andrews, who was also a Hupmobile director, the Ruxton was a low-slung front-wheel-drive car powered by a 5.5-litre Continental straight-eight engine. It took its name from William V.C. Ruxton, an acquaintance of Andrews, who had displayed interest in the project. Production began in 1930 in the factories of both Moon and Kissel, who were members of the New Era Motors group. Ruxton's tourer bodies were supplied by former electric-car manufacturers Raulang, while sedan bodies were built by Budd from panels pressed from dies originally used by the British Wolseley company. The garish

interior trim was created by stage designer Joseph Urban, who also produced a striking colour scheme of horizontal stripes for one of the company's demonstration vehicles. Ruxton built between 300 and 500 cars before their collapse.

### 1930 RUXTON

**Engine:** in-line straight-eight, side-valve
**Bore × stroke:** 90 mm × 108 mm
**Capacity:** 5500 cc
**Maximum power:** 94 bhp
**Transmission:** three-speed manual, front-wheel drive
**Chassis:** pressed steel channel
**Suspension:** non-independent with semi-elliptic leaf springs front and rear
**Brakes:** rear-wheel drums
**Bodywork:** tourer
**Maximum speed (approx):** 59 mph (95 kph)

## RYTECRAFT

London, England
1934–1940, 1946–48

Jack Shillan made his name selling outboard-engines for boats, and in the 1930s began to diversify into fairground attractions, including construction of electric dodgem cars. These soon acquired petrol power in the shape of 98 cc Villiers engines (also used in motor mowers) and Shillan then began building similar vehicles under the name 'Scootacar' for urban use. The first road-going Scootacars only had one speed and a centrifugal clutch, although three-speed gearing and 250 cc Villiers engines were featured on models built from 1936.

Scootacars were mostly used for publicity purposes, and several hundred were built as midget

### 1936 RYTECRAFT SCOOTACAR

**Engine:** single-cylinder, two-stroke
**Bore × stroke:** 63 mm × 80 mm
**Capacity:** 249 cc
**Maximum power:** 12 bhp
**Transmission:** three-speed manual
**Chassis:** parallel tubes
**Suspension:** none
**Brakes:** rear-wheel drums
**Bodywork:** open two-seater
**Maximum speed (approx):** 45 mph (72 kph)

replicas of the contemporary Vauxhall; there was also a miniature version of the ill-fated Chrysler Airflow cars. Sabu the elephant Boy used a Scootacar to drive round the Denham film studios during the filming of Zoltan

**Ruxton Sedan**

Korda's Technicolor epic 'The Drum'; Lord Louis Mountbatten and Prince Peter of Yugoslavia were other distinguished users of Scootacars.

Production ceased when the Scootacar factory went over to war work, producing outboard engines for life-rafts; a few cars were assembled after the war, almost certainly from existing stocks of spare parts.

During the 1960s, a Scootacar was restored and driven round the world by Surrey draughtsman Jim Parkinson (now a well-known dealer in motor books).

# SAAB

**Trollhatten, Sweden
1949–**

The Svenska Aeroplan Aktiebolaget, as an aside from the wartime production of SAAB-17 attack bombers, SAAB-18 reconnaissance bombers and J21 fighters for the Swedish Air Force, the Flygvapnet, began development of a prototype car. They showed this prototype to the Press in 1947, the year in which they also unveiled Sweden's first jet fighter, the 21R, but Saab did not start car production until late 1949.

Styled by industrial designer Sixten Skasten, the Saab 92 (it took its series nomenclature from its project number) employed unitary construction, and, inevitably, had an aerodynamic body; the car was front-wheel driven and had all-independent suspension. Its power unit was a transversely mounted two-stroke twin of 764 cc derived from the pre-war DKW unit.

The model name was changed to 92B in 1952 when small changes were made to the body design, and more powerful model, the Saab 93, arrived in 1955, powered by a three-cylinder 748 cc engine; coil-spring suspension replaced the torsion-bars of the original model.

A tuned sports model, the Granturismo 750, mainly went for export; it was capable of virtually

100 mph (161 kph). The 1959 Saab 95 had an 841 cc engine; this same power unit was also used in the 1960 Saab 96 which featured a restyled rear end. The 96 was available in various sports versions, which helped Saab to its many rally victories, including wins in the Monte Carlo Rally in 1962–1963 and the RAC Rally in 1960–1961–1962. This rallying success boosted Saab's export sales: in 1955 total sales had been 5500 cars, of which 226 were exported, while a decade later, production had risen to 48,300, with 17,000 exports.

Saab had been experimenting with sports cars for some time, starting with the Sonett Super Sport of the mid-1950s. As a result of this programme, the Sonnett II, a small glassfibre GT coupé, was introduced in 1966; it didn't prove particularly successful, nor did the Sonnett III, which used the German Ford V4, introduced with the 1967 Saab 96 (though the two-stroke engine was still available).

Ford supplied Saab with 50,000 V4 engines and the 96 was still being produced in Finland at the end of the 1970s, though the all-new Saab 99 started production in 1969, powered by an overhead-cam Triumph-designed 1700 cc four, later enlarged to 1850 cc.

Saab had merged with the old Scania-Vabis truck company in 1968, and four years later, in 1972, the car division was integrated into a new, five-division Saab-Scania group. That same year, a 1985 cc Saab-designed four-cylinder power unit went into production in Saab's Sodertalje plant; subsequent versions were the 1975 110 bhp EMS with Bosch fuel injection and the 140 bhp Turbo of 1977. The 900 – a long-nosed version of the 99, with some mechanical refinements – was launched in 1978, with a 900 Sedan following in 1981 and the 900 CD in 1982.

The 1984 Saab 9000 was supposed to be the fruit of shared design and development with Lancia, but it was difficult to find many similarities between the two cars, apart from the basic configuration of the powertrain. Powered by a four-cylinder 16-valve engine, the Saab featured electronic control of ignition and turbocharger boost, giving it exceptional protection against the effects of low-grade fuel.

# Saab 96

With a shape similar to that of the original Saab 92, the 96 was originally launched in 1960, derived from the 95 'Combiwagen' estate car model, and powered by Saab's traditional two-stroke engine. The 1967 version of the 96 broke new ground for the company in introducing its first four-stroke power unit, the German-built Ford V4 Taunus unit. This gave 0-50 mph (80 kph) in 12.5 seconds, and fuel consumption of 30 mpg.

An unusual feature of the 96 was the incorporation of a free-wheel in the transmission; like its predecessors, the V4 Saab 96 enjoyed considerable rallying success, with wins in the RAC Rally (1968 and 1971). Swedish Rally (1971–72), Scottish Rally (1969) and Thousand Lakes event (1972).

---

**1960 SAAB 96**

**Engine:** V4, overhead-valve
**Bore × stroke:** 90 mm × 58.9 mm
**Capacity:** 1498 cc
**Maximum power:** 65 bhp
**Transmission:** four-speed manual
**Chassis:** integral
**Suspension:** front independent with coils and wishbones, rear non-independent with rigid axle, trailing arms and coil springs
**Brakes:** front-wheel discs, rear-wheel drums
**Bodywork:** five-seat saloon
**Maximum speed (approx):** 90 mph (145 kph)

---

Saab 96

**Saab 99 Turbo**

## Saab 99

The 99 first appeared a surprisingly long time ago, in 1968. Naturally it was front-wheel drive with a longitudinally-mounted 1.7-litre overhead-cam engine developed from a Triumph design. Strangely, it was mounted back to front and excellent access was provided to it via a huge, ingeniously hinged bonnet which was an indication of the thoughtful design, as was the heated driver's seat.

By 1971 engine displacement had risen to 1854 cc and that old Saab feature, the freewheel, discarded. The next year displacement rose again, to 1985 cc which, with fuel injection, resulted in an output of 118 bhp. The strong chassis with

wishbone front and dead beam-axle rear suspension was easily capable of handling more power and in 1978 Saab started the current trend to turbocharged production cars with the 99 Turbo. The combination of Bosch mechanical fuel injection and a Garrett AiResearch turbo resulted in a power output of 145 bhp and an even more impressive torque figure of 174 lb foot at 3000 rpm giving impressive performance.

## Saab 9000 T16

While Ital Design's Giorgetto Giugiaro created the basic designs for both the Saab 9000 and the Lancia Thema, the two cars seemed to have little in common when the 9000 was launched in 1984. True,

both cars had five pressings in the front ends, but the 9000 was a hatchback, while the Thema was a conventional three-box saloon. And while both cars had transverse power units, they were of different capacities.

The 16-valve turbocharged twin-carburettor power unit was mounted with the majority of its mass ahead of the front axle line, with the five-speed gearbox on its left; to overcome the problem of unequal-length drive shafts, the drive to the right-hand wheel was taken by a layshaft which entered a massive bearing from which the driveshaft – the same length as that on the left – took the drive to the wheel, thus balancing the forces.

### 1979 SAAB TURBO

**Engine:** in-line, four-cylinder, overhead-cam, turbo
**Bore × stroke:** 90 mm × 78 mm
**Capacity:** 1985 cc
**Maximum power:** 145 bhp
**Transmission:** four-speed
**Chassis:** integral
**Suspension:** independent front with wishbones and coil springs. Dead beam-axle with twin longitudinal leading arms, twin swinging trailing arms and Panhard rod
**Brakes:** discs all round
**Bodywork:** two-door saloon
**Maximum speed (approx):** 125 mph (201 kph)

### 1984 SAAB 9000 T16

**Engine:** transverse, double-overhead-cam four-cylinder 16-valve, turbocharged
**Bore × stroke:** 90 mm × 78 mm
**Capacity:** 1985 cc
**Maximum power:** 175 bhp
**Transmission:** five-speed, front-wheel drive
**Chassis:** integral
**Suspension:** front independent with MacPherson struts, rear non-independent with rigid axles and leading and trailing arms and coil springs
**Brakes:** discs all round
**Bodywork:** hatchback saloon
**Maximum speed (approx):** 137 mph (220 kph)

**Saab 9000**

# A-Z OF THE CAR

## SABRA

**Haifa, Israel**
**1960–**

Israel's first home-grown manufacturer, Sabra, took its name from the juicy cactus that is the country's national emblem. Working in conjunction with the British company Reliant, Sabra began production with a sports car identical to the Reliant Sabre, a somewhat off-looking two-seater powered by the 1.7-litre Ford Consul engine, with glassfibre bodywork and a ladder frame.

In 1962, Sabra launched a small station wagon with 997 cc Ford

### 1960 SABRA SPORT

**Engine:** in-line four-cylinder, overhead-valve
**Bore × stroke:** 82.5 mm × 79.5 mm
**Capacity:** 1703 cc
**Maximum power:** 90 bhp
**Transmission:** four-speed manual
**Chassis:** ladder type
**Suspension:** front independent with tubular leading arms and coil springs, rear non-independent with live axle and leaf springs
**Brakes:** discs front, drums rear
**Bodywork:** two-seat sports
**Maximum speed (approx):** 109 mph (175 kph)

**Sabra Sport**

## SALMSON

**Paris, France**
**1921–1957**

At the turn of the century, Emile Salmson's factory was renowned for its light industrial pumps; however, the adventurous Salmson then branched out into aviation, attempting (unsuccessfully) to build a helicopter before 1910. This enlightened him as to the need for a suitable power unit, so he took a licence to manufacture the Canton-Unne radial aero-engine,

**Salmson Grand Sport**

Anglia power and styling similar to the Austin A40; it later evolved into the Sussita pickup and estate and Carmel saloon, with 1.2-litre Cortina engines. The Gilboa 12 four-door saloon, launched in 1967, was available with either Cortina or 1147 cc Triumph power.

established the Société des Moteurs Salmson close to the Issy-les-Moulineaux flying ground and began the manufacture of seven- and nine-cylinder aero-engines.

Emile Salmson died during the war, and his sons left the firm in 1919, control passing to M. Heinrick, former head of Salmson's Lyon branch factory. Like so many companies whose profitability had depended on wartime orders, the Société des Moteurs Salmson had to cast around for new business in the difficult post-Armistice period, and settled on woodworking machinery, valves, civil aero engines and cars.

Salmson's career as a car constructor began with the building of the British GN cyclecar under licence, the manufacture of which started in the autumn of 1919. The first true Salmson appeared in 1921, and was fitted with a 1086 cc engine built by freelance designer Emile Petit, who had created a four-cylinder, air-

cooled engine by drawing on his wartime experience of designing aero-engines. Petit, who was an acquaintance of a prominent Salmson sales agent, André Lombard, was persuaded to fit one of these engines in a Salmson chassis for assessment. Petit's four-cylinder unit boasted four 'push-pull-rods', one rod controlling both the inlet and exhaust valves on each cylinder. With the air-cooling replaced by water-cooling, it was adopted for production. Petit's unorthodox *monoculbuteur* power unit was mounted in unit with a conventional three-speed gearbox,

### 1926 SALMSON GRAND SPORT ST SEBASTIEN

**Engine:** in-line four-cylinder, double-overhead-cam
**Bore × stroke:** 62.2 mm × 90 mm
**Capacity:** 1086 cc
**Maximum power:** 40 bhp
**Transmission:** four-speed manual
**Chassis:** pressed steel channel
**Suspension:** non-independent with semi-elliptic leaf springs front and quarter-elliptic leaf springs rear
**Brakes:** drums all round
**Bodywork:** two-seat sports
**Maximum speed (approx):** 105 mph (170 kph)

rather than the chain-and-dog transmission of the GN-based Salmsons.

Simultaneously, Petit was working on a racing version of this power unit, this time with twin

**Sandford**

overhead camshafts. Driven by the affable André Lombard, it won the 1921 Cyclecar Grand Prix at Le Mans. To commemorate this achievement, the cross of St Andrew (for André Lombard) was incorporated in the radiator design; it was also because of Lombard that the *monoculbuteur* Salmson, which was to form the basis of production, was named the Type AL. As the Type AL came into production, so the GN-based Salmson was phased out, the last being built at Salmson's factory at Billancourt in mid-1922 (although an agency continued to import GNs from England for some time after that).

In 1923, Salmson launched its – and possibly the world's – first production twin-cam model, the 1194 cc 8/10 hp Type D, which had a more robust chassis than the Type AL (which was built light to qualify as a cyclecar under French taxation ratings) and an unusual rear suspension layout, consisting of two pairs of quarter-elliptic springs, one facing forwards, the other backwards.

A more robust version of the AL series, the VAL3, with semi-elliptic front suspension, appeared in 1925, followed by a stronger chassis in 1926.

That same year, a couple of 1086 cc twin-cam sports cars, the three-speed GS and four-speed SS, were added to the line-up; other variants on the double-overhead-cam sports car scene included a series of 18 'Grand Prix' Salmsons with Cozette superchargers, the tuned San Sebastian version and the low-chassis GS8. Petit's last design for Salmson was a straight-eight racer with desmodromic valve gear, but only two of these cars

were built.

In the autumn of 1929, Salmson launched the S4 series, with a twin-overhead-camshaft engine, initially of 1300 cc, and styling by André Kow; the heavy coachwork normally fitted to the S4 chassis quickly promoted an increase in engine capacity to 1465 cc on the S4C of 1931–32, and then to 1600 cc on the 1936 S4D (the S4C and S4D were the basis of the British Salmson cars built in Raynes Park from 1934–39). Some S4Ds had the engine bored out still further, to 1730 cc, and this power unit was used in the longer, lower S4DA of 1937. In the same year came the final enlargement of the twin-cam Salmson engine, the S4E; a six-cylinder 20/90 HP of 2590 cc was unique to British Salmson.

After the war, in 1946, Salmson resumed production with the 1.7-litre S4-61 and the 2.3-litre S4E, both revived 1939 models; the company's first ventures into modern styling were unsuccessful.

A new model, the Randonnée, appeared in 1951, powered by a light-alloy version of the old 2.3-litre engine, but was recorded as having feeble performance. Salmson's last new model, the G72, appeared in 1953, powered by a 105 bhp version of the 2.3-litre engine and clad in handsome GT coachwork; it notched up an impressive total of rally wins in the 1954 season, but plans for a 1956 long-wheelbase, four-door version failed to pass the prototype stage. Although the G72 was a well-made car, only a small number were sold, and in 1957 Salmson abandoned car production altogether, going full circle by devoting its activities to pump production.

## SANDFORD

**Paris, France**
**1922–1939**

'The cheapest always costs much more', claimed Stuart Sandford when advertising his Morgan-inspired three-wheeler, to justify the fact that the Sandford cost more than twice as much as the apparently similar Darmont. In fact, the sliding-pillar independent front suspension and chain final drive were really all the Sandford had in common with the Morgan, for it was powered by a four-cylinder water-cooled Ruby engine instead of the Moggie's vee-twin, while the three-speed-and-reverse gearbox was far more advanced than the Morgan's two-speed, chain-and-dog transmission.

Sandford, a Briton by birth, headed the French network of 'Old England' draperies and drove a Darmont for fun before throwing caution to the winds in 1923 and going full-time into cyclecar manufacture.

The Sandford was certainly beautifully put together, and far more robust than other cyclecars; yet despite this, and the fact that it had a four-cylinder engine, it weighed a mere 640 lb (290 kg). Top speed was therefore over 85 mph (137 kph), with some 105 mph (169 kph) available from supercharged Sandfords. The marque was particularly successful in endurance racing, and in 1932 won the Bol d'Or 24-hour race, when it rained 21 hours out of the race's 24.

After 1933, Sandford uncharacteristically turned to four wheels, with a total lack of success.

## 1923 SANDFORD

**Engine:** in-line four-cylinder, overhead-valve
**Bore × stroke:** 62 mm × 90 mm
**Capacity:** 1088 cc
**Maximum power:** 50 bhp
**Transmission:** three-speed manual
**Chassis:** tubular
**Suspension:** front independent with sliding pillars, rear non-independent with quarter-elliptic leaf springs
**Brakes:** three-wheel drums
**Bodywork:** two-seat sports
**Maximum speed (approx):** 87 mph (140 kph)

## SARA

**Courbevoie/Puteaux, France**
**1923–1930**

MM Tisserand and Piazzoli, who headed the Société des Applications du Refroidissement par Air – which quickly changed its name to Société des Automobiles à Refoidissement par Air – launched their first air-cooled cars in 1923 with four-cylinder 1098 cc engines. This model remained in the catalogue throughout the company's existence. The power unit had four separate and liberally-finned cylinders encased in a jacket through which air was forced by a belt-driven turbine.

Though the marque had a not-entirely-justified reputation for fragility, and a fully-justified reputation as a lethargic performer, nevertheless SARA cars appeared in competition, and performed with regularity if not aplomb.

**SARA Cabriolet**

making sporting cars with 3 and 5.1-litre engines and dual ignition.

The SAVA factory suffered tremendous damage in World War I, and began its post-armistice activity by manufacturing signalling apparatus, later bringing out a 20 HP directly derived from the pre-war exhaust-over-inlet sports chassis, but with the option of four-wheel brakes. In December 1922, SAVA unveiled its first true post-war model (originally designed as the 1915 model, with a 2-litre overhead-valve engine based on the 3.3-litre units fitted to the unsuccessful 1914 Tourist Trophy racers); only a few examples of this handsome sports car were built before SAVA was taken over and closed down by its old rival, Minerva, who had been spreading the word that SAVA stood for 'Slechste Auto van Antwerpen' – 'Antwerp's worst car' . . . .

## 1923 SARA

**Engine:** in-line air-cooled four-cylinder, overhead-valve
**Bore × stroke:** 62 mm × 91 mm
**Capacity:** 1098 cc
**Maximum power:** 35 bhp
**Transmission:** four-speed manual
**Chassis:** pressed steel channel
**Suspension:** non-independent with transverse leaf springs front, quarter-elliptic leaf springs rear
**Brakes:** drums all round
**Bodywork:** two-seat, four-seat, cabriolet
**Maximum speed (approx):** 45 mph (72 kph)

The four-cylinder sold well, but in 1927 SARA launched the ill-fated SARA 6, an 1806 cc six-cylinder model which was also built in Scotland under the marque name 'Scotsman'.

# SAVA

**Berchem-Antwerp, Belgium
1910–1923**

The Société Anversoise pour Fabrication des Voitures Automobiles was the direct descendant of the Compagnie des Constructions Mecaniques, founded by an engineer called Dodelinger in 1902, and selling cars under the marque name 'Royal Star'. In 1907 the company employed 300 workmen and built five four-cylinder models ranging from 11/12 HP to 25/30 HP, plus a single-cylinder whose components were interchangeable with the De Dion.

The marque was reorganised as 'SAVA' in 1910, but its range remained complex, including a monobloc 18 hp, 2011 cc four whose power unit was built by Fondu and which had a worm-drive back-axle (SAVA was the first Continental constructor, it seems, to adopt this method of construction).

During 1911, SAVA introduced a sporting 1966 cc 18/24 HP with the unusual configuration of side inlet and pushrod overhead exhaust valves, plus four or eight sparking plugs. For 1913 the range consisted of a 2474 cc 14/16 HP,

the 18/24 HP (now increased in capacity to 2954 cc) and a 35/50 HP four, also with exhaust-over-inlet head, which sold for £610 in England, where the marque was represented by David Brown, the group which built the Valveless and which later took over Aston Martin and Lagonda.

A handsome rounded radiator was adopted in 1913, along with a 3405 cc exhaust-over-inlet 20/60 HP, and in 1914 the company, along with Minerva, received an order for armoured cars from the Belgian Ministry of Defence. At the same time the company was

## 1912 SAVA 18/24 HP

**Engine:** in-line four-cylinder, exhaust-over-inlet
**Bore × stroke:** 82 mm × 140 mm
**Capacity:** 2954 cc
**Maximum power:** 60 bhp
**Transmission:** four-speed manual
**Chassis:** pressed steel channel
**Suspension:** non-independent with semi-elliptic leaf springs front and rear
**Brakes:** rear wheel and transmission
**Bodywork:** two- or four-seater tourer
**Maximum speed (approx):** 55 mph (90 kph)

**SAVA Sedanca de Ville**

# A-Z
# OF THE CAR

## SAXON
**Detroit, USA**
**1913–1923**

The Saxon – 'The car that makes both ends meet' – was, at one time, one of Detroit's best-selling products. Built by a company founded by Hugh Chalmers (formerly with Chalmers–Detroit) and Harry (no relation to Henry)

Ford, the Saxon started life as a four-cylinder light car selling for only $395.

This spindly two-seater sold well, and in 1915 the company introduced a $785 Saxon Six. The following year, production was running at 27,800 units annually, and Saxon moved into 10th place in the US sales league. In 1917,

however, the company dropped the popular four-cylinder roadster, and Saxon sales began to fall away.

A four-cylinder model was reintroduced in 1920, but by 1921 the Saxon overhead-valve four (now known as the Saxon-Duplex) had become one of the most expensive cars in its class, and production inevitably came to an end two years later.

## SBARRO
**Les Tuileries de Grandson,**
**Switzerland**
**1968–**

Franco Sbarro was chief mechanic of the Scuderia Filipinetti in the 1960s when they were racing Ferraris and GT40s. In 1967 he built the Filipinetti sports coupé, based on the VW1600 chassis, and then in the following year established his own little workshop near Minister Filipinetti's mediaeval

castle on Lake Neuchatel, building exclusive cars in limited numbers. He currently builds around 100 cars per year.

These vary from out-and-out

### 1916 SAXON FOUR

**Engine:** in-line four-cylinder, side-valve
**Bore × stroke:** 70 mm × 114.3 mm
**Capacity:** 1752 cc
**Maximum power:** 30 bhp
**Transmission:** three-speed manual
**Chassis:** pressed steel channel
**Suspension:** non-independent with semi-elliptic leaf springs front, cantilever leaf springs rear
**Brakes:** rear wheel only
**Bodywork:** roadster
**Maximum speed (approx):** 45 mph (72 kph)

### 1985 SBARRO REPLICA BMW 328

**Engine:** BMW in-line four-cylinder, overhead-cam
**Bore × stroke:** 84 mm × 71 mm
**Capacity:** 1573 cc
**Maximum power:** 90 bhp
**Transmission:** four/five-speed manual
**Chassis:** integral box-type, reinforced platform
**Suspension:** all-independent, with coils and wishbones front, semi-trailing arms rear
**Brakes:** discs front, drums rear
**Bodywork:** glassfibre two-seat roadster
**Maximum speed (approx):** 112 mph (180 kph)

**Sbarro replica BMW 328**

replicars like his GT40, based on the De Tomaso Pantera chassis, and his Bugatti-inspired Royale, costing over a quarter of a million Swiss francs and powered by two 3.5-litre Rover V8 engines mounted in tandem, to sports cars like the mid-engined Stash, with BMW or Mercedes power, or the four-wheel-drive Windhound, with a choice of four, six, eight or 12-cylinder engines.

Perhaps the best-known of Sbarro's products is his replica BMW 328, with modern BMW power; he also offers a glassfibre-bodied Mercedes 540K replica which costs over 240,000 Swiss Francs and is based on the Mercedes 500 SE. In contrast, Sbarro produces a gullwing polyester-bodied sports coupé on the Mercedes 500 SEC chassis.

His latest creation is the Challenger, an ultra-aerodynamic, wedge-shaped two-seater with either Porsche or Mercedes power.

**Saxon Four**

**SCAT 16/20 HP Tonneau**

## SCAT

**Turin, Italy
1906–1932**

Having founded Junior in 1904, Giovanni Ceirano resigned two years later to organise the Societa Ceirano Automobili Torino (whose products were known by the simple acronym 'SCAT'), with some financial backing from Newton & Bennett of Manchester. The SCAT was a superb car, whose quality enabled its makers to ride out the financial crisis of 1907 with relative ease. The initial model was the 2724 cc 12/16 HP, followed in 1907 with relative ease. The initial model was the 2724 cc 12/16 HP, followed in 1907 by the 3190 cc 16/20 HP and the 22/32 HP of 3770 cc. These were all bi-block four-cylinder cars with shaft drive and four-speed gearboxes.

For 1910-11, the 22/32 HP had its stroke lengthened to give it a capacity of 4398 cc, while the 12/16 HP was redesigned to become the 15/20 HP; this, too, had its swept volume increased, in 1912–14, to 2951 cc.

Other new models of 1912 were the 25/35 HP, the result of yet another increase in stroke for the old 22/32 HP, which increased its capacity fo 4712 cc, and an overhead-cam racing 60/75 HP of 6284 cc, offered until 1915.

However, it was with smalled racing cars that SCAT achieved its racing successes; Giovanni Ceirano's son Ernesto won the

### 1912 SCAT 25/35 HP

**Engine:** in-line four-cylinder, T-head
**Bore × stroke:** 100 mm × 150 mm
**Capacity:** 4712 cc
**Maximum power:** 35 bhp
**Transmission:** four-speed manual
**Chassis:** pressed-steel channel
**Suspension:** non-independent, with semi-elliptic leaf springs front and rear
**Brakes:** rear-wheel drums
**Bodywork:** tourer
**Maximum speed (approx):** 62 mph (100 kph)

Targa Florio in 1911 and 1914, while John Newton's nephew (and SCAT's test driver) Cyril Snipe won the Targa in 1912.

Production of the SCAT 25/35 HP was suspended in 1916 after Italy had entered the Great Way and resumed again in 1918, along with the 2120 cc 12/18 HP introduced in 1914; another wartime product was the 3563 cc 18/30 HP, built in 1915–16. The company built military trucks and Hispano-Suiza aero-engines during the hostilities.

Giovanni Ceirano left in 1919 to found the Ceirano company, and control of SCAT passed to the National Savings Bank. When it became obvious that a considerable chunk of SCAT's clientele had followed Giovanni Ceirano, the SCAT company (whose offerings ranged from a

1551 cc 12/16 HP to a monstrous overhead-cam 120 hp racer with a 9236 cc four-cylinder power unit) tried to undermine Ceirano sales.

There followed a compex financial sarabande, which resulted in Giovanni Ceirano taking a majority shareholding in SCAT in August 1923; the following December, the Ceirano company was liquidated and merged with SCAT, the products of the revised company being known as 'SCAT-Ceirano'.

The most notable of these was the N150, a Lancia-like small car designed by Candido Viberti, and familiarly known as the 'Ceiranina'; production of this car ceased in 1928 when SCAT-Ceirano was

taken over by the Fiat group, though the S150 VVV, with independent front suspension, was built until 1931, when SCAT car production ceased; the company, put into liquidation in 1932, was absorbed into SPA.

## SCOTT SOCIABLE

**Bradford, England
1921–1925**

Alfred Angas Scott had been famous for his water-cooled two-stroke motorcycles since 1909 (his first engines were supplied by the Jowett brothers), and his curious Sociable, an offset three-wheeler, was a development of his wartime work in building Scott-Vickers motor machine-gun outfits. 'The machine may be termed a kind of super-sidecar,' commented *Motor Cycling*, adding 'while the driver and passenger are luxuriously accommodated in a roomy body complete with windscreen and hood – a dickey seat also being provided – the layout of the chassis, in that the single front steering wheel and offside rear driving wheel are in line (the other rear wheel running free), follows

### 1921 SCOTT SOCIABLE

**Engine:** parallel twin-cylinder two-stroke
**Bore × stroke:** 63.5 mm × 76.2 mm
**Capacity:** 578 cc
**Maximum power:** 12 bhp
**Transmission:** constant-mesh three-speed manual
**Chassis:** triangulated tubular spaceframe
**Suspension:** coil springs in tension
**Brakes:** rear-wheel only
**Bodywork:** compressed-fibre two-seater
**Maximum speed (approx):** 50 mph (80 kph)

**Scott Sociable**

sidecar practice, at any rate to some small extent.'

The triangulated space-frame chassis of the Sociable was made up of standardised lengths of tubing bolted together; the unusual rear suspension consisted of coil-springs in tension, while the offset two-seat bodywork was formed from waterproofed fibre, stiffened by an internal ash framing.

The water-cooled 578 cc twin-cylinder, two-stroke engine was mounted under a sliding cover faired into the offside mudguard, which also held the two-gallon (9-litre) fuel tank. The drive was transmitted, via a three-speed contant-mesh gearbox, by shaft to the offside rear wheel.

Though a road-tester claimed that 'The front wheel maintains its course and exhibits no sidecar tendency to skid sideways across the road', the lop-sided appearance of the Scott Sociable obviously cost it sales, which remained small throughout its four year life. Its price of £178, anyway, was virtually the same as that for conventional light cars.

# SCRIPPS-BOOTH

Detroit, USA
1912–1922

In 1908 a talented 20-year-old artist named James Scripps-Booth drew a fantastic two-wheeled car, which was supported at low speeds by retractable auxilary wheels, he completed the design while on honeymoon in Paris in 1911.

Financed by his uncle, a builder of marine engines, Scripps-Booth built this colossal 'Bi-Autogo' in 1912, at a cost of \$25,000. Predictably, the steering of the Bi-Autogo, which had a 6306 cc V8 engine and weighed 3200 lb (1451 kg), was awesomely heavy; only the prototype (which still survives) was ever built.

In 1913, inspired by the French Bedelia, Scripps-Booth built a prototype tandem-seated cyclecar; this went into production with a Spacke engine under the name 'JB Rocket' in January 1914, but the Scripps-Booth Cyclecar Company was sold to the Puritan Machine Company of Detroit at the end of 1914; they continued to produce the Rocket, powered by a 10 hp De Luxe engine, under their own name for a short while.

Scripps-Booth then introduced a luxury light car based on European practice; it was designed by William Stout, who later became a famed aeronautical engineer, creating for the famous Ford Trimotor Tin Goose aeroplane.

The Scripps-Booth Model C, with a four-cylinder Sterling engine, was said to be the first American car with its horn-button in the

Scripps-Booth Model C

## 1914 SCRIPPS-BOOTH MODEL C

**Engine:** in-line four-cylinder, side-valve
**Bore × stroke:** 73 mm × 101..6 mm
**Capacity:** 1702 cc
**Maximum power:** 20 bhp
**Transmission:** three-speed manual
**Chassis:** pressed steel channel
**Suspension:** non-independent, with semi-elliptic leaf springs front and rear
**Brakes:** rear-wheel drums
**Bodywork:** roadster or coupe
**Maximum speed (approx):** 45 mph (72 kph)

centre of the steering wheel. It also pioneered the use of electrically-operated door locks, which tended to jam on open models....

Among Scripps-Booth owners were King Alfonso XIII of Spain, the Queen of Holland, Winston Churchill and the operatic singer, Count John McCormack.

In the autumn of 1916, the Scripps-Booth Company became a public corporation, and the new directors insisted on the production of the Model D, powered by a Ferro V8 engine designed by

Alanson P. Brush, and available either as roadsters or town cars.

James Scripps-Booth complained that the Model D compromised his vision of the firm that bore his name as a manufacturer of light cars, and finally, resigned over company policy in October 1916. When sales fell as a result of production difficulties the following year, when a six-cylinder model was listed, the Scripps-Booth company was absorbed by Chevrolet, which itself became part of GM in July 1918.

From then on, Scripps-Booth cars, which prior to the GM takeover were little more than re-radiatored Chevrolets, became Oakland chassis fitted with 40 hp Northway six-cylinder engines; the line was phased out in 1922 at the express order of GM boss Alfred P. Slogan the plant being turned over to production of Buick sedans.

As for James Scripps-Booth, he tried to re-enter the motor industry in 1923 with a low-slung luxury car called the Da Vinci, and powered by an Argyll single sleeve-valve engine. Although he failed to sell his designs, he accused Stutz of having copied them for the Stutz Safety Eight. By the time he proved his case, seven years later, Stutz was virtually bankrupt.

Seabrook 12/24 HP

# SEABROOK

London, England
1917–1928

Seabrook Brothers Ltd was originally formed in 1896 to make cycle components, and imported the American Regal Underslung, which they sold as the 'Seabrook-RMC' before the Great War. In 1920, Seabrook turned to manufacture; the Seabrook was a well-designed light car with a monobloc 1796 cc four-cylinder engine, which had aluminium pistons and cylinder head – an advanced touch for the period, which proved to be prohibitively expensive to manufacture.

The original Seabrook was replaced in 1921 by the 9.8 hp Dorman-engined 9/19 model. The Meadows-engined Seabrook 10/20 appeared in 1923; by 1925 it had become known as the 12/24, with a bore and stroke of 69 mm × 100 mm (which still gave a capacity of 1496 cc) and was Seabrook's sole model. Although from late 1924 Alford and Alder front-wheel brakes were fitted, this step forward was accompanied by a retrogression in the form of the adoption of a three-speed gearbox.

## 1923 SEABROOK 10/20

**Engine:** in-line four-cylinder, overhead-valve
**Bore × stroke:** 63 mm × 120 mm
**Capacity:** 1496 cc
**Maximum power:** 21.5 bhp
**Transmission:** four-speed
**Chassis:** pressed steel channel
**Suspension:** non-independent, with semi-elliptic leaf springs front and rear
**Brakes:** rear-wheel drums
**Bodywork:** tourer
**Maximum speed (approx):** 48 mph (77 kph)

# A-Z OF THE CAR

of their offerings still have strong Fiat links, being derived from Fiat's Panda, 127 (Fura), Ritmo (Ronda) and Regata (Malaga).

SEAT now have links with Porsche for engine design, Karmann for prototype development and with Giugiaro for design; the first fruit of this international cooperation is the Ibiza which was launched late in 1984, and by the time the accords expire in 1992, SEAT plans to have launched three completely new models, code-named S003 (minicar), S03 (hatchback saloon) and SXX (notchback saloon).

proprietary engines, principally made by Ruby; his first cyclecar, the B4, had a 900 cc Ruby unit in a chassis distinguished by a transverse leaf spring and a two-speed transmission. Subsequently, Sénéchal cars adopted a three-speed transmission, and were available in 'Sport' and 'Grand Sport' form, with engines of 900 cc and 972 cc. In 1923 the 900 cc Sport was discontinued and a new 1100 cc model announced. This was called the Supersport, and its engine, which had a bore and stroke of 59 mm × 100 mm, produced 33 bhp.

Robert Sénéchal was renowned for the curious competition versions of his little cars, some with tandem seating, others with wicker bodywork covered in doped fabric. His forté was the Bol d'Or contest, which he won in 1923, 1924 and 1925. A Sénéchal, its engine linered

**SEAT Ibiza**

## SEAT

**Barcelona, Spain**
**1949–**

The origins of the Sociedad Española de Automoviles de Tourismo go back to 1919, when a Spanish subsidiary of Fiat of Turin was founded; from 1931 its products were known as 'Fiat-Hispanias'. Although the company continued to produce Fiat-designed cars, it was taken over by the Spanish state holding company INI in 1949, when the SEAT name was adopted. SEAT's principal product until 1956 was the four-cylinder 1400 saloon. The rear-engine 600 followed in 1957, while in 1959, SEAT combined the angular Pininfarina bodyshell of the Italian marque's 1800 with the less powerful four-cylinder 1400. The 1500 engine became optional in 1963, and was later adopted as standard.

In 1979, Fiat took over the majority shareholding, and Lancia models powered by 2-litre SEAT engines were introduced. The Fiat

### 1985 SEAT IBIZA

**Engine:** transverse four-cylinder, overhead-cam
**Bore × stroke:** 75 mm × 67.5 mm
**Capacity:** 1193 cc
**Maximum power:** 63 bhp
**Transmission:** four-speed manual
**Chassis:** integral
**Suspension:** all independent, with MacPherson struts front, wishbones and transverse leafspring rear
**Brakes:** discs front, drums rear
**Bodywork:** three-door saloon
**Maximum speed (approx):** 96 mph (115 kph)

control lasted only two years, and when Fiat pulled out, the Spanish Government stepped back in to save the 32,000 jobs that were at stake, and today SEAT is 99 per cent owned by INI.

In 1982, SEAT signed a seven-year cooperation deal with VW, and began producing several VW models – Polo, Passat and Santana – under licence. However, the bulk

### 1925 SENECHAL GRAND SPORT

**Engine:** in-line four-cylinder, overhead-valve
**Bore × stroke:** 57 mm × 95 mm
**Capacity:** 972 cc
**Maximum power:** 50 bhp
**Transmission:** three-speed manual
**Chassis:** pressed steel channel
**Suspension:** non-independent, with transverse leaf spring front, quarter-elliptic leaf springs rear
**Brakes:** rear-wheel drums
**Bodywork:** two-seat sports
**Maximum speed (approx):** 70 mph (112 kph)

**Sénéchal Grand Sport**

## SENECHAL

**Gennevilliers, France**
**1921–1929**

The fork-bearded pioneer aviator and racing driver Robert Sénéchal (who died in his 90s in 1985), president of the Motocycle Club de France, was a dominant figure in the small world of cyclecars. His products used various French

down to 750 cc, set up a class two-seater record of 74.5 mph (119.18 kph) at Arpajon in 1924.

The company was taken over by Chenard & Walcker in 1924, and Chenard engines of 975 cc and 1100 cc were adopted. Front-wheel brakes were fitted for 1926, and the following year a 1500 cc model appeared. When the traditional Sénéchals were phased out, Robert Sénéchal offered the streamlined 1500 cc 'Torpille'.

# SERPOLLET

**Paris, France**
**1889–1907**

Leon Serpollet, a blacksmith's son from Culoz (Ain), was born in 1858 and built his first steam engine at the age of 18, later beginning work on a three-wheeled car built entirely of wood. The power unit of this vehicle produced 'more soot than motion', so Serpollet devised a 'flash boiler' which instantaneously generated steam by pumping water into red-hot iron tubes.

Serpollet left home in 1881 and established a workshop in Montmartre, where he built a single-seat steam tricycle, the only self-propelled vehicle running in Paris when it was first tested in 1887.

**Serpollet Three-Wheeler**

Four Serpollet steam three-wheelers were built at the Peugeot factory at Beaulieu (Doubs) in 1889, and one of these was shown at the 1889 Paris Exposition. Although Peugeot soon lost interest, Serpollet undertook one of France's first long-distance motor tours in 1890, driving from Paris to Lyon with his friend Ernest Archdeacon. The 290-mile (466.7 km) trip took around two weeks, and the mass of repairs made to the car added some 350 lb (158.8 kg) to its weight of 1200 lb (544.3 kg).

Serpollet continued on his own without Peugeot's backing, building twin-cylinder 4/6 hp steam cars with coke-fired boilers and (from 1891) four wheels. His foreman, François Pilain, later became a manufacturer of petrol cars in his own right, and a leading figure in the motor industry of Lyon. A frequent visitor to the Serpollet workshop in the Rue des Cloys in Montmartre was a 15-year-old schoolboy named Louis Renault, whose first ride in a self-propelled vehicle was in a Serpollet

steamer.

During the 1890s, Serpollet was constrained by his financial backers to concentrate on steam trams and railcars until he met a wealthy American, Frank Gardner, in 1898. Gardner had already dabbled in petrol car construction, and the two men went into partnership, building Gardner-Serpollet steam cars powered by flat-twin engines with paraffin-fired boilers in a new plant in the Rue Menilmontant in Paris.

Serpollet's aim was to build a steam car which would rival the petrol vehicle for simplicity of operation, and from 1900 the Serpollet steamers increasingly resembled petrol vehicles in their styling.

In 1900 a light 5 hp model appeared, while in 1901, an 8 hp V4 and flat-four engines of 6, 9 and 12 hp were introduced.

In 1902 a streamlined racing Serpollet, the *Oeuf de Paques* (Easter Egg), was the first car to exceed 75 mph (121 kph), and there was talk of a merger with the Cannstatt-Daimler company,

manufacturers of the Mercedes, but nothing came of it. At the end of 1903 a 15 hp flat-four was added to the range, as was the Serpollet Simplex, a 6 hp voiturette of uncomplicated design with a four-cylinder engine. One of the first customers for the new 15 hp was the Shah of Persia, who now owned five Serpollets.

Late in 1904, Serpollet introduced an improved 15 HP and a big 40 HP, both boasting a clutch and almost automatic engine control, though the auxiliary donkey engine which operated the steam and water pumps independently of the speed of travel gobbled some 10–15 per cent of the steam produced by the boiler.

It was reported that an eight-cylinder Serpollet was available during 1906, but Serpollet was already very ill with consumption, and when he died in February 1907, the company quickly followed.

---

### 1891 SERPOLLET THREE-WHEELER

**Engine:** twin-cylinder steam
**Bore × stroke:** 60.3 mm × 90.4 mm
**Maximum power:** 4/6 hp
**Transmission:** two-speed
**Chassis:** armoured wood
**Suspension:** front independent with full-elliptic leaf springs, semi-elliptic leaf springs rear
**Brakes:** rear-wheel drums
**Bodywork:** phaeton
**Maximum speed (approx):** 16 mph (25 kph)

---

## Serpollet Three-Wheeler

Derived from the original Peugeot-Serpollet, but more massively constructed, the first production Serpollets appeared at the end of 1890. Powered by a twin-cylinder engine, they were fired by coke, fed auto-

matically from hoppers on either side of the rear-mounted boiler. Fuel for an 18-mile (29 km) journey was carried, plus water for double the distance. Power was sufficient to enable a 1:12 gradient to be climbed in bottom gear carrying seven passengers.

Unlike most early steam vehicles, the Serpollet could be controlled with one hand, for a twist-grip on the steering bar opened and closed a valve which controlled the amount of water fed into the steam generator.

Although the first of these cars had three wheels, a four-wheeled version appeared in 1891.

## Serpollet 15HP

Serpollet's last major new steam cars were designed to look as much like petrol cars as possible. The 15 HP (uprated to 18 HP for 1905) was powered by a flat-four engine, and a boiler, operated by forced draught plus an auxiliary donkey engine to provide an automatic supply of lubricating oil and water to the engine in direct proportion to the engine speed, gave virtually automatic control. Even at that early date, however, the petrol car had all but ousted its rivals, steam and electricity, and Serpollet was fighting a rearguard action for 'the facile and elastic medium' of steam which was lost with his premature death in 1907.

---

### 1904 SERPOLLET 15 HP

**Engine:** flat-four steam engine
**Maximum power:** 15/18 hp
**Transmission:** direct drive by cardan shaft and bevel gear
**Chassis:** pressed steel channel
**Suspension:** non-independent, with semi-elliptic leaf springs front and rear
**Brakes:** rear-wheel drums
**Bodywork:** phaeton
**Maximum speed (approx):** 40 mph (64 kph)

---

**Serpollet 15 HP Steamer**

# SHANGHAI

Shanghai, China
1958–

In 1920 a small car repair business was founded in the cosmopolitan city of Shanghai, and after the Communist takeover of China, this private business was transformed into a national company in 1949, building light-duty cross-country vehicles. In 1958 the Shanghai company title was adopted, though the three-wheeled cars it produced were sold under the Phoenix marque name. Larger, four-wheeled cars appeared in 1959; with American-influenced styling.

In 1962 the marque name, too, became Shanghai. although the works in An Ting Town still manufacture the antique-looking Shanghai 760A, which is probably the only side-valve-engined car still in production (5100 were built in 1982), during 1984 they began to assemble the Volkswagen Santana. Apart from its ability to run on low-grade petrol the Shanghai Santana is substantially the same as its European prototype and marks a very significant step forward for the Chinese industry.

### 1985 SHANGHAI SANTANA

**Engine:** in-line four-cylinder, overhead-cam
**Bore × stroke:** 79.5 mm × 80 mm
**Capacity:** 1588 cc
**Maximum power:** 85 bhp
**Transmission:** four-speed
**Chassis:** integral
**Suspension:** independent front with MacPherson struts. Rigid axle with trailing arms and coil springs
**Brakes:** discs front, drums rear.
**Bodywork:** four-door saloon
**Maximum speed (approx):** 103 mph (166 kph)

**Sheffield-Simplex Gearboxless**

# SHEFFIELD-SIMPLEX

Sheffield, England
1906–1922

It was a car with the unlikely name of Brotherhood-Crocker which sired the round-radiatored Sheffield-Simplex, one of the great Edwardian marques. Built by the engineering firm of Peter Brotherhood Ltd (famed for their high-speed steam engines), the Brotherhood-Crocker had an early form of two-pedal control, with a single pedal operating brake and clutch, while the throttle pedal pivoted sideways (to avoid ankle fatigue, claimed the car's designer, Percy Richardson). In 1906 control of Brotherhood-Crocker was assumed by one of the company's directors, Earl Fitzwilliam, and production transferred to a factory at Tinsley, near Sheffield, The 'Silent Smooth-Running Six-Cylinder' Sheffield-Simplex retained the two-pedal control of the Brotherhood-Crocker. From 1908 to 1913, the 6982 cc 45 hp Sheffield-Simplex six was available in 'gearboxless' form (with direct drive for all normal use, supplemented by an 'emergency box').

The gearboxless Sheffield-Simplex was the ultimate expression of the Edwardian craze for top-gear flexibility, and one gearboxless 45 HP even contrived to travel from Land's End to John O'Groats on its single gear ('the most meritorious and useful trial ever completed').

The 1910 14/20 hp Sheffield-

### 1908 SHEFFIELD-SIMPLEX GEARBOXLESS 45 HP

**Engine:** in-line six cylinder, side-valve
**Bore × stroke:** 114 mm × 114 mm
**Capacity:** 6982 cc
**Maximum power:** 45 hp (rated)
**Transmission:** single direct speed
**Chassis:** pressed steel channel
**Suspension:** non-independent, with semi-elliptic leaf springs front and rear
**Brakes:** rear-wheel drums and transmission
**Bodywork:** tourer
**Maximum speed (approx):** 50 mph (80 kph)

Simplex was rumoured to be based closely on the Renault 14/20. In the same year. Tinsley introduced a three-speed 20/30 hp six on similar lines to the 45 hp, except that it possessed a conventional three-speed gearbox. Before long a re-designed development of the 20/30, known as the 30 hp, was the principal Sheffield-Simplex model.

Of similar design, but available with four-wheel brakes from 1921, the post-war Sheffield-Simplex was known as the 45 hp; in an odd retrogression, the bi-bloc engine was replaced in 1921 by an anachronistic unit of 7777 cc which had individually-cast cylinders.

After car production ceased in 1922, the company built the Ner-A-Car motorcycle and Shefflex lorries, production of the latter finally finishing in 1933.

**Shanghai Santana**

# A-Z OF THE CAR

## SHELBY

**Venice/Los Angeles/Ionia, USA
1962–1970**

Texan-born Carroll Shelby was a well-established racing driver – he had won Le Mans in a DBR1 Aston Martin in 1959 with Roy Salvadori as co-driver – who had the dream of producing an American sports car. When, in 1961, he learned that the Bristol engine would no longer be manufactured for the AC Ace,

### 1968 SHELBY GT 500 KR

**Engine:** V8, overhead-valve
**Bore × stroke:** 105 mm × 96 mm
**Capacity:** 7014 cc
**Maximum power:** 400 bhp
**Transmission:** four-speed
**Chassis:** integral
**Suspension:** front independent, with wishbones, coils and anti-roll bar, rear non-independent with live axle and semi-elliptic leaf springs
**Brakes:** discs front, drums rear
**Bodywork:** fastback,
**Maximum speed (approx):** 130 mph (209 kph)

Shelby had the bright idea of shoe-horning the new 4.3-litre Ford V8 engine into the AC chassis to create the Cobra, initially built at Thames Ditton in mid-1962, though production really got under way the following year, when the 4.7-litre Ford power unit was adopted, and manufacture was shifted to the former Reventlow Scarab workshops in Venice, California. The Cobra achieved sporting success on both sides of the Atlantic during 1964, and the

following year a new Shelby model, the 350GT, a highly-tuned Mustang derivative began to leave a new factory near Los Angeles airport; Carroll Shelby was also involved in the Ford GT40 programme.

Cobra production ended in 1966 after 1140 had been built, while manufacture of the 350GT and its 500GT derivative was shifted to a Ford plant in Michigan in 1968; when it ended in 1970, some 15,000 Shelby Mustangs had been built, and had won Production Car honours in the SCCA Class B series in 1965–66–67. In recent years Carroll Shelby has worked as a consultant for Chrysler, producing cars like the fast 2.2-litre Shelby Charger.

## SIATA

**Turin, Italy
1926–1970**

The Societa Italiana Applicazioni Transformazioni Automobilistiche was a small factory founded by racing driver Giorgio Ambrosini in

1926 and renowned pre-war for the manufacture of go-faster equipment for Fiat cars. They also constructed the occasional Fiat-derived sports car, like the open two-seat Topolino-Siata which appeared in the late 1930s. That in its most developed form, had the engine enlarged to 596 cc with a

### 1950 SIATA DIANA GRAN SPORT

**Engine:** in-line four cylinder, overhead-valve
**Bore × stroke:** 77 mm × 74.9 mm
**Capacity:** 1395 cc
**Maximum power:** 44 bhp
**Transmission:** four-speed
**Chassis:** integral
**Suspension:** independent front with coil springs and wishbones. Live rear axle with semi elliptic leaf springs
**Brakes:** drums all round
**Bodywork:** two-seat sports or coupé
**Maximum speed (approx):** 87 mph (140 kph)

Siata

Shelby GT 500 KR

**Sigma Torpedo**

# SIMA-VIOLET
Courbevoie, France
1924–1929

Marcel Violet was a prolific builder of cyclecars who had been involved in the production of many leading marques, starting in 1913 with the unpromisingly titled Violet-Bogey and progressing through such makes as Major, Mourre, Juascar, Galba and Leroy. Though the Violet-Bogey had been powered by a four-stroke engine of advanced design, Marcel Violet became closely linked with two-stroke power units, and the Sima-Violet, built by his Société Industrielle de Matériel Automobile, was typical, with a 496 cc twin-cylinder two-stroke engine. With a novel backbone chassis and independent front suspension, this streamlined cyclecar was capable of remarkably good performance, and in fact enjoyed a certain amount of competition success, winning its class in events like the Bol d'Or. The best of Sima-Violet's two-stroke racing cars was powered by a supercharged flat-four engine displacing 1484 cc.

After the demise of the Sima-Violet, the company built the Sima-Standard, a light car assembled from obsolete cars like the 5CV Citroën. It was not a success....

30 bhp power output boosting the top speed of the aerodynamic two-seat coupé to around 75 mph (121 kph) In 1938 one of these coupés established a class record by averaging 70 mph (113 kph) for 24 hours.

Following the war, Siata began by creating the neat 48 cc Cucciolo clip-on bicycle motor (later adopted by Ducati) then built the Bersaglieri sports car with a rear-mounted 750 cc four-cylinder twin-cam engine in a tubular chassis with all-independent suspension. Less complex was the 1948 Amica, with a tubular chassis and Fiat suspension fore and aft, plus a Fiat 500 engine as standard, though a Siata-converted 750 cc power unit was available. In 1949, Siata began the production of the Diana, based on the Fiat 1400, with a box-section steel chassis. With its engine output raised from 44 to 65 bhp, it was capable of some 90 mph (145 kph); the 1951 Rallye was also Fiat 1400-powered, though this time the car was a blatant copy of the MG TD. In 1950, Siata's commercial director, Luigi Segre, left to join Carrozzeria Ghia, where he developed the international links of that old-established coachworks, laying the foundation for their eventual acquisition by Ford.

Siata helped Fiat to develop the 8V sports, launched at the 1952 Geneva Salon and Siata built a number of sports coupés and spyders based on the 8V chassis. Then, in contrast, in 1953–54 Siata built the Mitzi, a tiny and utilitarian minicar with an engine of only 328 cc; its minimal performance scarcely justified the fitting of all-round torsion-bar suspension.

During the 1950s, Siata began to fit American power units as diverse as the 750 cc Crosley and the Chrysler V8, but in 1959, Siata went into liquidation and ceased production. A new company, Siata Abarth, was formed by Ambrosini and Carlo Abarth in 1960. The company – renamed Siata Auto in 1961 – was mostly concerned with increasing the performance of the standard Fiat product, though in 1967 came the Siata Spring, a two-seater cabriolet which aped MG T-series styling but which had a rear-mounted Fiat 850 engine.

# SIGMA
Chênes-Bougeries, Switzerland
1909–1914

The Société Industrielle Genevoise de Mécanique et d'Automobiles was formed out of the remains of the old Lusia (Picker-Moccand) company, which had employed among its draughtsmen one Ernest Henry, who moved to Paris with Picker in 1910 and there joined Peugeot where he drew up the immortal twin-cam GP Peugeot. As for the SIGMA company, in 1909 it began production of medium-sized four-cylinder Sigma cars under the direction of John Meynet; like several quality marques of the time, the Sigma had a round radiator.

The first Sigmas had side-valve engines of 8/11 hp (1593 cc) and 15 hp (2614 cc), then, in 1911, the company acquired the licence to use the Knight sleeve-valve engine, available in two models, the 2614 cc 18CV and 4576 cc 28CV.

Sigma cars quickly established a sound reputation; in 1910 their

**1912 SIGMA SS 18CV**

**Engine:** in-line four-cylinder, sleeve-valve
**Bore × stroke:** 80 mm × 130 mm
**Capacity:** 2614 cc
**Maximum power:** 35 bhp
**Transmission:** four-speed manual
**Chassis:** pressed steel channel
**Suspension:** non-independent with semi-elliptic leaf springs
**Brakes:** rear wheel only
**Bodywork:** tourer
**Maximum speed (approx):** 68 mph (110 kph)

Sicilian agent, De Prosperis, finished second (and last) in the Targa Florio, while in 1911 Hongnacher's Sigma won the Mont Ventoux hillclimb in the South of France.

A larger poppet-valve four, the 25CV Grande Tourisme, was offered alongside the Knight-engined Sigmas.

**1914 SIMA-VIOLET**

**Engine:** flat-twin, two-stroke
**Bore × stroke:** 65 mm × 75 mm
**Capacity:** 496 cc
**Maximum power:** 10 bhp
**Transmission:** two-speed manual
**Chassis:** tubular backbone
**Suspension:** independent front with transverse leaf spring and parallel links. Live rear axle and quarter-elliptic leaf springs
**Brakes:** rear wheels only
**Bodywork:** tandem two-seater
**Maximum speed (approx):** 68 mph (110 kph)

**Sima-Violet Cyclecar**

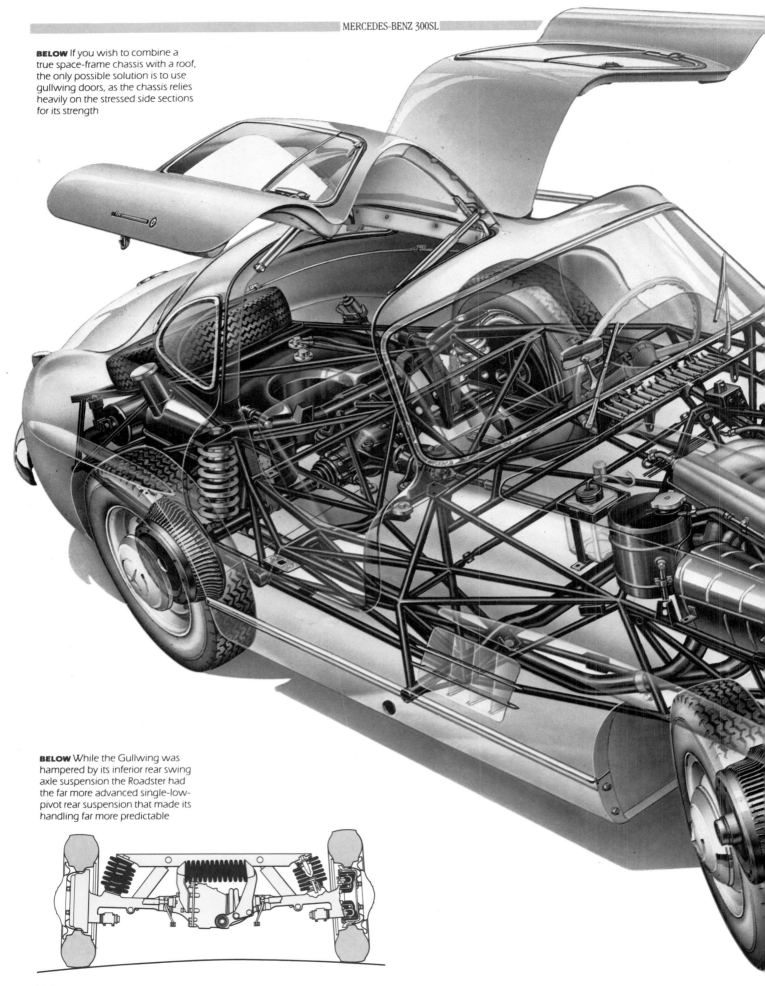

**BELOW** If you wish to combine a true space-frame chassis with a roof, the only possible solution is to use gullwing doors, as the chassis relies heavily on the stressed side sections for its strength

**BELOW** While the Gullwing was hampered by its inferior rear swing axle suspension the Roadster had the far more advanced single-low-pivot rear suspension that made its handling far more predictable

**RIGHT** The Roadster chassis varied considerably from that of the Gullwing. The use of conventional doors meant that the original high-silled space frame could not be used

## MODEL
Mercedes-Benz 300SL Coupé, 1955
UK price when announced: £4393

## ENGINE
**Location:** Front, longitudinal
**Type:** Water-cooled in-line six
**Cubic capacity:** 2996cc
**Bore x stroke:** 85mm x 88mm
**Compression ratio:** 8.55:1
**Valve gear:** 2 valves per cylinder in line operated via rocker arms by chain-driven overhead camshaft
**Fuel supply:** Bosch injection
**Ignition:** Coil and distributor
**Maximum power:** 240bhp (SAE) at 6100rpm
**Maximum torque:** 217lb ft (SAE) at 4800rpm

## TRANSMISSION
**Layout:** Clutch and gearbox in-unit
**Clutch:** Single dry plate
**Gearbox:** Four-speed manual
　1st 3.14:1　　3rd 1.305:1
　2nd 1.85:1　　4th 1.0:1
**Final drive:** Hypoid bevel with limited slip differential
**Ratio:** 3.64:1

## SUSPENSION
**Front:** Independent by double wishbones with concentric coil springs and telescopic dampers
**Rear:** Independent by swinging half axles

## STEERING
**Type:** Recirculating ball, manual

## BRAKES
**Type:** Drums front and rear, servo

## WHEELS AND TYRES
**Type:** Pressed steel 5K x 15in with 6.70 x 15 tyres

## BODY/CHASSIS
**Type:** Tubular steel spaceframe chassis with coupé bodywork

## DIMENSIONS AND WEIGHT
**Length:** 175.7in (4217mm)
**Width:** 70in (1778mm)
**Wheelbase:** 94in (2387mm)
**Track – front:** 54.5in (1384mm)
　　　　 **– rear:** 56.5in (1435mm)
**Weight:** 2850lb (1293kg)

## PERFORMANCE
**Maximum speed:** 135mph (217kph)
**Acceleration 0-60mph:** 8.8 seconds
**Fuel consumption:** 18.4mpg

# SIMCA

**Nanterre/Poissy, France**
**1934–1978**

The acronym Simca stands for the Société Industrielle de Mécanique et Carrosserie Automobile, a company established by Henri-Théodore Pigozzi in November 1934 to build Fiats for the French market under licence in the former Donnet factory at Nanterre. The first products were based on the Tipo 508 Balilla, soon followed by the Tipo 518 Ardita. The 500 Topolino became the Simca Cinq, the 1100 the Simca Huit; performance versions of these two cars were developed by Amédé Gordini, who took the Index of Performance at Le Mans with a specially-tuned Simca Huit in 1939.

Simca began to move away from the Fiat designs in April 1951 with the Aronde, designed to compete with the Peugeot 203: it was Simca's first monocoque-bodied car, and enjoyed a spectacular success. In 1951, Simca built 21,000 Arondes, a production level on a par with that of the superseded Simca Huit, while by 1959, output had soared to almost 200,000 examples annually.

It was in 1954 that Simca made another significant step in its progress as a motor manufacturer; Ford decided to sell its factory at Poissy, which was unacceptably unprofitable, and Simca bought it, along with the rights to manufacture the post-war Ford

Vedette. It became the Simca Vedette; Poissy became the main Simca plant, and Nanterre was sold to Citroën in 1961.

In 1957, Simca launched the four-cylinder Ariane, which combined the Aronde engine with the Vedette bodyshell. Two years later, Simca took over Talbot, though the marque name quickly fell into abeyance.

Meantime, Simca had sown the seeds of their own destruction: at

the time of the purchase of Poissy, 15 per cent of Simca shares had been set aside for Ford; now Simca sold these shares to Chrysler of America. The Trojan horse was within the gates....

Quickly it was announced that the Aronde would be built under licence in the Chrysler factory at Adelaide for the Australian market.

The Vedette was built overseas,

too; Simca manufactured this 22 hp side-valve V8-engined car in France until 1961, but licence-production continued in Brazil until the latter part of the 1960s.

The Simca 1000, a boxy rear-engined saloon, appeared for 1962; the following year, Chrysler increased their shareholding in Simca to 63 per cent, and the Simca 900, 1300 and 1500 were added to the range. The company's founder Pigozzi died in 1964 and in 1967, Chrysler's share in Simca was increased to 77 per cent.

In 1968, the transverse-engine front-wheel-drive 1100 appeared, followed a year later by the utilitarian 4CV. A year later, Simca took over the automobile division of Matra.

Chrysler boosted their share of Simca to 99.3 per cent in 1970, and changed the name of the company to Chrysler France, and the Simca name began gradually to be squeezed out in favour of Chrysler-badged models, though the Chrysler Simca 1610 had been introduced as late as 1977.

With the crumbling of Chrysler's European empire during the decade, what had once been Simca passed into the hands of Peugeot in 1978 and was transmuted into Talbot.

## Simca Aronde

The Aronde appeared in April 1951 as the successor to the pre-war Simca Huit, which had become unattractively obsolete alongside its rival, the Peugeot 203. Like the 203,

the Aronde had monocoque construction, though its engine was visibly derived from that of the old Simca Huit; the fact that the Peugeot power unit had detachable liners was regarded as a strong point in favour of the Sochaux marque.

The clientele was also put off to some extent by the restless programme of product development followed by Simca, who constantly modified the Aronde in tiny details. Nevertheless the new Simca model also acquired a reputation for sound performance and handling (though its suspension did not escape criticism).

By the time production ended in 1963, a total of 159,418 Arondes had been built; a new five-bearing Rush engine was fitted to Arondes from the end of 1960. Production of Arondes finally ceased in 1964.

---

### 1951 SIMCA ARONDE

**Engine:** in-line four-cylinder, overhead-valve
**Bore × stroke:** 72 mm × 75 mm
**Capacity:** 1221 cc
**Maximum power:** 45 bhp
**Transmission:** four-speed manual
**Chassis:** steel monocoque
**Suspension:** independent front with coil springs and torsion bar. Live rear axle with semi-elliptic leaf springs
**Brakes:** drums all round
**Bodywork:** saloon
**Maximum speed (approx):** 80 mph (127 kph)

---

**Simca Aronde Elisée**

# A-Z OF THE CAR

**Simson-Supra S**

## Simca 1000

The Simca 1000 was the first car to be produced under a new corporate structure assumed by Simca in 1960, in which the company was split into two divisions, Automobiles and Industries; the first 1000 appeared in 1962 with a rear-mounted 1000 cc power unit with five main bearings.

The car was instantly popular: over 154,000 were built in the first full year of production, and it took just over a decade to reach the million mark.

A Ferodo semi-automatic gearbox was launched as an option in 1966; in 1969 came the 1118 cc 1000 Special, followed in 1970 by the 1300 cc Rallye version. The 1005 and Rallye were the ultimate derivatives of the Simca 1000.

**Simca Rallye**

### 1977 SIMCA RALLYE 2

**Engine:** in-line four-cylinder, overhead-valve
**Bore × stroke:** 76.7 mm × 70 mm
**Capacity:** 1294 cc
**Maximum power:** 86 bhp
**Transmission:** four-speed manual
**Chassis:** integral
**Suspension:** independent with transverse leaf spring and wishbones front and semi-trailing arms and coil springs rear
**Brakes:** discs all round
**Bodywork:** four-door saloon
**Maximum speed (approx):** 106 mph (170 kph)

## SIMSON-SUPRA

Suhl, Germany
1911–1933

The well-known Simson & Co Thuringian armaments factory began producing cars before the Great War with 6/18 and 10/30PS models. The company began building inlet-over-exhaust valve models of 1559 cc, 2595 cc and 3538 cc after the war, then in 1924 decided to launch a no-compromises sports car designed by Paul Henze, who had previously worked for Imperia in Belgium, RAF in Austria and Cudell and Steiger in Germany. Aided by ex-Benz development driver Karl Kappler, who drove a prototype in races in 1922–23, Henze created the Type S, a sporting twin-overhead-camshaft 1960 cc four-cylinder car launched at the 1924 Berlin Automobile Show. Its dry-sump engine had a cast silumin crankcase and the chrome nickel crankshaft ran in three roller bearings; pistons were cast from Elektron alloy.

The Simson-Supra Type S was fully the equivalent of the Mercedes in terms of quality, although total production was probably only in the region of 30 cars. In parallel, Simson-Supra offered a single-overhead-camshaft derivative, the Type So, which developed 40 bhp at 3000 rpm; some 750 Type So Simson-Supras were built. There was also an overhead-valve 3108 cc six-cylinder model, while the last Simson-Supra was a side-valve 4673 cc straight-eight, the Type A, built in limited numbers in 1931 and '32.

### 1925 SIMSON-SUPRA S

**Engine:** in-line, four-cylinder, twin-cam
**Bore × stroke:** 70 mm × 128 mm
**Capacity:** 1970 cc
**Maximum power:** 66 bhp
**Transmission:** four-speed manual
**Chassis:** pressed steel channel
**Suspension:** non-independent with semi-elliptic leaf springs
**Brakes:** drums all round
**Bodywork:** two or four-seat sports
**Maximum speed (approx):** 85 mph (137 kph)

## SINGER

Coventry, England
1905–1970

Marine engineer George Singer entered the sewing machine industry in the 1860s. In 1868 he was foreman at the Coventry Sewing Machine Company when young Rowley Turner, nephew of the firm's financial backer, arrived from France on the latest novelty, the Machaux velocipede, and suggested that his uncle's firm should start manufacturing this ancestor of the bicycle.

The Singer velocipedes proved a great commercial success. In 1875, Singer left the company to set up on his own as a cycle manufacturer. The Singer company didn't enter the motor industry until 1901, when they began building the Perks & Birch Motor Wheel, a self-contained power pack for bicycles and tricycles. More substantial three-wheelers followed, but the first Singer car didn't appear until 1905. Made under licence from Lea-Francis, it had an overhead-camshaft, 15 hp three-cylinder horizontal engine with connecting rods a remarkable 39 in (99 cm) long!

In 1906 the Singer range was

entirely revised, and the Lea-Francis design replaced by cars with vertical two-, three-, or four-cylinder White and Poppe engines, rated at 8, 10 or 12 hp. There were also larger models with Aster engines of 12/14 hp and 22 hp; however, after George Singer's death in 1909, the company was reorganised, and its principal product became the White & Poppe-engined 16/20.

Singer soon developed its own power unit, launched in 1912 in the popular 10 hp model, one of the best of the first generation of four-cylinder light cars that appeared just before the Great War. This car had its three-speed gearbox mounted in the rear axle.

The Singer Ten achieved a number of sporting successes, most notably with the bullnosed Bunny and in the hands of Lionel Martin, who commemorated his hillclimbing success at Aston Clinton with his highly-tuned Singer Ten when he launched his own marque, calling it 'Aston Martin'.

The Ten was reintroduced after the war, although from 1922 its gearbox was mounted in the conventional position. The car was redesigned the following year, with its engine now an overhead-valve monoblock rather than a side-valve bi-block design.

An odd sub-species of Singer had appeared in 1921 in the shape of a vee-twin light car, a legacy of Singer's takeover of the Coventry-Premier motorcycle and cyclecar company. It acquired a four-cylinder Singer engine in 1922 but

vanished entirely the following year. A 2-litre six appeared in 1922, with semi-elliptic front and cantilever rear suspension.

The old Ten was finally replaced by the new 10/26 for 1925; in 1926, Singer took over Calcott, whose factory became the Singer spare parts depot.

Another important new model arrived at the end of 1926 in the shape of the 848 cc overhead-camshaft Junior; this and the 10/26 (now rechristened the Senior) were major factors in elevating Singer to third place in the British car production stakes after Morris and Austin.

In the autumn of 1929 the Senior was replaced by a new 1.8-litre six, while in 1931 the Junior acquired a four-speed transmission and a new 1261 cc, side-valve Ten was launched, symptomatic of the growing complication of the range, which for 1932 included the 848 cc Junior, a 972 cc Junior Special, the 1261 cc Ten, a new side-valve 12/6 of 1476 cc, the 2041 cc 18/6 and the overhead valve 2180 cc Silent-Six. The most expensive Silent-Six, the 'Kaye Don' saloon styled by stage designer-turned-car designer C.F. Beauvais, cost £480.

A new chief engineer, Leo J. Shorter, was appointed in 1932, and oversaw a rejuvenation of the range which led to the entire Singer line-up acquiring overhead-camshaft engines by 1935.

The overhead-cam power unit was particularly appropriate for the A.G. Booth-designed sports Nine, which took 13th place at Le Mans in 1933 and 7th in 1934, so that sports Nines became known as the 'Le Mans'. Singer also supplied 1100 cc and 1.5-litre engines to HRG for their sports cars.

An advanced, if doomed, venture, was the Eleven Airstream launched for 1935, which had full-width streamline bodywork even before the Chrysler Airflow was generally available in Britain.

After World War II, Singer continued to manufacture pre-war designs until the advent of the Shorter-designed SM 1500 of 1949. A 1500 Roadster appeared two years later, and during the early 1950s Shorter experimented with a steam-driven version of this car.

Another avenue of investigation was the use of plastics. The Hunter saloon of 1955 incorporated a glassfibre bonnet top and had the option of a double-overhead-cam power unit (which almost certainly never reached the public). This advanced model failed to save the company and in 1956 Singer was taken over by the Rootes Group, who replaced the Hunter with the Hillman Minx-derived Gazelle. From that point, Singers became upmarket versions of the Hillman range, and the Chamois light car of 1965 was a derivative of the rear-engined Hillman Imp.

The 1496 cc Gazelle and the 1725 cc Vogue were phased out shortly before the Singer marque finally ceased production in 1970.

## Singer Junior

Launched at the 1926 Olympia Motor Show, the Singer Junior was the progenitor of the most successful Singer models for the next three decades, for it introduced the overhead-camshaft power unit to the Singer range. A sporting version was quickly introduced, and in 1928 one of these little pointed-tail two-seaters achieved an unusual record in climbing the 1:4 Porlock Hill 100 times in 15 hours. As a consequence, the model was known as the Singer Porlock.

A Sportsman's Coupé was launched in 1929, and for 1931 the Junior acquired a four-speed transmission. For 1932 a 972 cc Junior Special was added to the range, but the days of the Junior were numbered, and the model failed to survive after 1933.

| 1926 SINGER JUNIOR |
| --- |
| **Engine:** in-line four-cylinder, overhead-cam |
| **Bore × stroke:** 56 mm × 86 mm |
| **Capacity:** 847 cc |
| **Maximum power:** 15 bhp |
| **Transmission:** three-speed manual |
| **Chassis:** pressed steel channel |
| **Suspension:** non-independent, with semi-elliptic leaf springs front and rear |
| **Brakes:** drums all round |
| **Bodywork:** two-seater, tourer, saloon |
| **Maximum speed (approx):** 45 mph (72 kph) |

**Singer Junior Torpedo**

## Singer Le Mans

The sporting version of the Singer Nine was designed by A.G. Booth, late of Clyno and AJS, and first appeared at the 1932 Olympia Show, winning a *Coupe des Glaciers* in the Alpine Trial shortly after its introduction. In 1933 a specially-built Sports Nine qualified at Le Mans – it was ninth overall and the first under-1000 cc British car to qualify for the Rudge-Whitworth Trophy – and thereafter the Sports Nine became known as the 'Le Mans' (though the true Singer Le Mans, with a fully-machined counter-balanced crankshaft, was rarely seen).

In standard form, the Le Mans was a robust little car which could achieve 6000 rpm thanks to a solid two-bearing crank, though its gearbox contained an ill-assorted set of ratios.

For 1934, Singer launched a 1.5-litre Le Mans Special Speed Model, of which only a dozen were built.

The excellent reputation built up by the sporting Singers was dashed in the 1935 Ulster Tourist Trophy when the three of the four-car team had identical accidents at the identical point on the circuit, due to the steering drop-arms fracturing . . . .

Singer never entered a works racing team again.

**Sizaire-Berwick 20 HP**

### 1932 SINGER LE MANS

**Engine:** in-line four-cylinder, overhead-cam
**Bore × stroke:** 60 mm × 86 mm
**Capacity:** 972 cc
**Maximum power:** 30 bhp
**Transmission:** four-speed manual
**Chassis:** pressed steel channel
**Suspension:** non-independent, with semi-elliptic leaf springs front and rear
**Brakes:** hydraulic drums all round
**Bodywork:** two/four-seater sports
**Maximum speed (approx):** 75 mph (120 kph)

# SIZAIRE-BERWICK

**Courbevoie, France/Park Royal, England**
**1913–1927**

Sometimes called the 'poor man's Rolls', the Sizaire-Berwick was a luxury car designed by Maurice Sizaire after he and his brother had left Sizaire-Naudin; the Berwick part of the name came from their partner, the London motor agent F.W. Berwick, who specialised in the import of French cars such as the Licorne.

Production of the Sizaire-Berwick began at Courbevoie, on the outskirts of Paris; a young apprentice seconded to the plant from London named Jack Waters later became famed as an actor under his stage name of Jack Warner.

The Sizaire-Berwick was originally powered by a 4072 cc four-cylinder engine renowned for its smooth running, and the design of its radiator was so close a copy of the Rolls-Royce cooler that Rolls sued Sizaire-Berwick (the case was, however, settled out of court when it was discovered that while Sizaire-Berwick had registered the design of their radiator, Rolls-Royce had omitted to do so).

Production was halted by the Great War, during which the Sizaire brothers served in the French Army and Berwick established a factory at Park Royal, to build aeroplanes.

Post-war, Maurice Sizaire moved to London to design a new

### 1913 SIZAIRE-BERWICK 20 HP

**Engine:** in-line four-cylinder, side-valve
**Bore × stroke:** 90 mm × 160 mm
**Capacity:** 4072 cc
**Maximum power:** 44 bhp
**Transmission:** four-speed manual
**Chassis:** pressed steel channel
**Suspension:** non-independent, with semi-elliptic leaf springs front and rear
**Brakes:** rear-wheel drums and transmission
**Bodywork:** seven-seat tourer
**Maximum speed (approx):** 65 mph (105 kph)

25/50 hp Sizaire-Berwick car, with a handsome vee-fronted radiator and the engine uprated to 4536 cc; production began at Park Royal in 1920, though the car was distinctly overweight due to modifications made by Berwick's chief engineer, a relative of the man who provided the company's financial backing.

The Austin Motor Company gained a controlling interest in the British Sizaire-Berwick operation in 1923, and thereafter, until production eventually ceased in 1925, unimpressive cars were built with 12 and 20 hp Austin engines.

As for the French Sizaire-Berwick operation, it lasted for another two years, ultimately offering cars with six-cylinder Lycoming power units.

**Singer Le Mans**

# A-Z OF THE CAR

## SIZAIRE-NAUDIN

**Paris, France
1905–1921**

Maurice Sizaire trained as an architect, but his ambition was to build cars. He even persuaded his younger brother Georges to take a job in a cycle factory so that he would have a reliable assistant in realising that ambition. Aided by a friend, Louis Naudin, the brothers began work on a three-speed belt-driven single-cylinder voiturette in 1899, but work progressed slowly, and the car wasn't completed until 1902. The transmission proved a failure, so Maurice Sizaire devised a novel gearbox in which there was direct drive on all three ratios, thanks to a triple-ratio pinion engaged with the crown-wheel by an ingenious cam device. The car was completed in this form at the end of 1904, and went on display at the Exposition des Petits Inventeurs in March 1905; there was little that was conventional about that first Sizaire-Naudin car, which had a wooden chassis, independent front suspension by a transverse spring and sliding pillars, and that system of direct drive on all three forward speeds. It was powered by a single-cylinder 6 hp engine, in which the speed was varied by altering the lift of the inlet valve.

The design was an instant success, and a company was established to produce the Sizaire-Naudin light car, which was progressively developed over the next few years and achieved a number of competition successes, such as victory in the 1906 and 1907 Coupe de l'Auto races, and in the 1906 Coupe des Voiturettes on the Targa Florio circuit in Italy. Inevitably, the Sizaire-Naudin became more conventional, and the firm's backer, the Duc D'Uzes, decided that he could do without the Sizaires and Naudin, dismissing them about the time that the company introduced its first four-cylinder model, with an overhead-valve 1593 cc 12 hp power unit.

However, the company failed to flourish without its founders and only lasted until 1921; its last new model was introduced just post-war, with a 2.3-litre engine.

Between 1923 and 1929 the Sizaires produced the Sizaire Frères, the world's first production car with all-round independent suspension.

---

**1905 SIZAIRE-NAUDIN 6 HP**

**Engine:** single-cylinder, side-valve
**Bore × stroke:** 100 mm × 120 mm
**Capacity:** 942 cc
**Maximum power:** 8 bhp
**Transmission:** three-speed (direct drive on all gears)
**Chassis:** ash frame
**Suspension:** front independent, with transverse leaf spring, rear non-independent with semi-elliptic leaf springs
**Brakes:** rear-wheel drums
**Bodywork:** two-seater
**Maximum speed (approx):** 30 mph (48 kph)

---

**Sizaire-Naudin**

**Skoda Rapid Convertible**

# SKODA

**Plzen/Mlada Boleslav,
Czechoslovakia
1924–**

The Akciova Spolecnot Skodovy
Zavody was one of the Austro-
Hungarian Empire's most important
industrial concerns, making arms,
machinery and components for
ships. After the Great War the
group – fortunately now known by
the acronym 'Skoda' – found its
Plzen base incorporated into the
new state of Czechoslovakia.
Deciding to enter the automotive
industry, Skoda acquired licences to
build Sentinel Steam Wagons and
the 37.2 hp Marc Birkigt-designed
Hispano-Suiza. In 1925, Skoda took
over the Laurin & Klement car
factory at Mlada Boleslav, and
continued to build cars derived
from L & K designs such as the
1950 cc four-cylinder Types 110
and 120, the 3495 cc sleeve-valve
six-cylinder Types 350 and 360, the

3880 cc eight-cylinder Type 860
and the 2490 cc six-cylinder Type
465. The L & K name was finally
phased out in 1929.

A major turning point for Skoda
came with the introduction of the
four-cylinder Type 430 in 1933; this
best-selling model broke away from
conventional chassis construction
and used a backbone frame with
swing axle suspension. The 995 cc
four-cylinder Popular and the
1380 cc Rapid were derived from
the 430; at the same time Skoda
offered the six-cylinder 2480 cc

**1985 SKODA RAPID
CONVERTIBLE**

**Engine:** rear-mounted in-line
four-cylinder, overhead-valve
**Bore × stroke:** 75.5 mm ×
72 mm
**Capacity:** 1174 cc
**Maximum power:** 62 bhp
**Transmission:** five-speed
**Chassis:** integral
**Suspension:** all-independent,
with coils and wishbones
front, leading arms rear
**Brakes:** discs front, drums rear
**Bodywork:** fastback
convertible
**Maximum speed (approx):**
93 mph (150 kph)

Superb.

Skoda's immediately pre-war
range included the side-valve
995 cc Popular and the overhead-
valve 1089 cc Popular; the Rapid
had been redesigned to
incorporate a modern overhead-
valve 1560 cc engine and the

Superb now featured an overhead-
valve 3140 cc six-cylinder motor.

After 1945 Skoda built mostly
overhead-valve 1089 cc and
1221 cc four-cylinder cars such as
the Octavia and Felicia. In 1959
work began on a new factory, the
largest development of its kind in
Czechoslovakia. Following the
opening of this plant in 1964,
Skoda concentrated on new rear-
engined designs, starting with the
1000MB and 1100MB cars. By
1969, a million 1000MB Skodas
had been produced. The rear-
engined Skodas acquired an evil
reputation for handling, and in fact
the Skoda Estelle was withdrawn
temporarily from the UK market
while alterations were made to its
roadholding characteristics. The
four-cylinder 120LS, which has an
1174 cc engine, was introduced in
1977.

Skoda's 1985 range consisted
of the 1046 cc 105S, the 1174 cc
120L, LS and GLS and the 1289 cc
130L and Rapid Coupé; even a
convertible was available.

**Simplex Speed Car**

# S & M SIMPLEX, SIMPLEX

**New York, USA**
**1904–1914**

Smith & Mabley, of 513–519 Seventh Avenue, was New York's fashionable agency for Mercedes, Renault and Panhard cars. Since there was a 40 per cent tax on imported models, in 1904 S & M launched an 18 hp luxury car built on European lines to sidestep this swingeing duty. A 30 hp S & M Simplex followed later that year, as did a speccial 75 hp racing car. Frank Croker, son of the corrupt local Tammany Hall politician 'Boss' Croker, raced a liberally-drilled 75 hp Simplex in the 1904 Vanderbilt Cup Eliminating Trials, but the chassis folded in half. Rebuilt, but still with a gruyère chassis, the 75 hp ran at Ormond Beach, Daytona in 1905, but wrote itself, and young Croker, off in spectacular fashion.

The S & M Simplex was a victim of the 1907 slump, but the Simplex name was bought by Herman Broesel, who financed a Mercedes-inspired model built from the finest materials available – the cylinders and pistons were of 'gun iron', the chassis of Krupp nickel steel – to the design of Edward Franquist.

Best-known of the Franquist-designed Simplex cars was the 10-litre 50 hp T-head, which established a sound reputation in competition, including a win at the October 1908 Brighton Beach 24-hour race at Coney Island, at an average speed of some 48 mph (77 kph). This feat was repeated the following year at an average of just over 45 mph (72 kph), when it finished 50 miles (80 km) ahead of the next car.

In 1911, Franquist introduced a

---

## 1909 SIMPLEX SPEED CAR

**Engine:** in-line four-cylinder, side-valve
**Bore × stroke:** 146 mm × 146 mm
**Capacity:** 9785 cc
**Maximum power:** 65 bhp
**Transmission:** four-speed manual
**Chassis:** pressed steel channel
**Suspension:** front and rear non independent with semi-elliptic leaf springs
**Brakes:** rear wheel and transmission
**Bodywork:** two-seater raceabout
**Maximum speed (approx):** 75 mph (120 kph)

---

38 hp, 7.8-litre shaft-drive Simplex, followed by the magnificent 75 hp of 1912–14; this 10-litre monster was probably America's last big chain-drive car.

The marque was taken over by Goodrich, Lockhardt and Smith, who displaced Franquist and appointed Henry M. Crane in his place; in 1914 the marque changed its name to 'Crane-Simplex'.

# SPA

**Turin, Italy**
**1906–1928**

Matteo Ceirano, having founded Itala in 1905, resigned in 1905 to join Michele Ansaldi in a joint venture which was incorporated on 12 June, 1906 as the Societa Piemontese Automobili Ansladi Ceirano (or 'SPA' for short). with a capital of a million Lire and a 12,000 sq metre factory on the Barriera Crocetta, SPA included among its directors Count Edoardo

---

Bareldi Sant'Albano and the industrialist Michele Lanza, who had built Turin's first car in 1895.

Nevertheless, the company was initially undercapitalised, a situation only remedied in 1908 when SPA absorbed the FLAG (Fabbrica Ligure Automobili Genova) company, which had been strong on backing but weak on product (it had been attempting to build the British Thornycroft under licence), and increased its share capital to 4.5 million Lire, changing its name to Societa Ligure Piemontese Automobile and moving its registered offices to the Genovese base of FLAG while keeping its factory in Turin.

The first products of SPA – the 7785 cc 40/50 hp four and the 11,677 cc 60/70 hp six – were on very similar lines to the contemporary Itala 35/45 hp four and 60 hp six, save for a 5 mm increase in stroke; like them, they were shaft-driven at a time when such large cars usually had chain final drive.

Then in 1908 SPA launched the 15/20 hp four of 3404 cc, followed a year later by the 1727 cc twin-cylinder 10/12 hp and the 2270 cc 12/15 hp four-cylinder models.

In 1908 a four-cylinder SPA completed the journey from Turin to St Petersburg and then came second in the St Petersburg-Moscow racce; in 1909 Baron Ciuppa won the Targa Florio on his 28/40 hp SPA.

In 1909/10, SPA began to diversify into the production of trucks and aero-engines, the latter being designed by ex-Fiat engineer Aristide Faccioli.

A new 15/20 hp, of 2724 cc, appeared in 1910, as did the 25/30 hp, a 4398 cc four built up to 1916, when SPA went over to the production of trucks and aero-engines for the war, and reintroduced in 1919–21. The 1847 cc 12/15 hp of 1912 also reappeared after the war. In 1911 Michele Ansaldi left SPA, followed in 1918 by Matteo Ceirano (who died in 1941).

After the war the majority

---

shareholding in SPA was acquired by Ansaldo, but the failure of the Ansaldo empire's principal bankers, the Banca Nazionale di Sconto, ended this involvement.

Most exciting of the post-war SPA cars was the sporting 30/40 hp Tipo 24S, with a twin-overhead-camshaft 24-valve 4426 cc engine; in its Super Sports form this exciting car had a handsome vee radiator on Mercedes lines. Among the model's sporting victories were first two places in the 1924 Alpine Cup and victory in the Aosta-Grand St. Bernard hillclimb, driven by Beria d'Argentina.

Fiat took over SPA in 1926 and car production rapidly ended. Thereafter, SPA concentrated on the manufacture of commercial and military vehicles.

---

## 1920 SPA TIPO 24S

**Engine:** in-line six-cylinder, double-overhead-cam
**Bore × stroke:** 85 mm × 130 mm
**Capacity:** 4426 cc
**Maximum power:** 90 bhp
**Transmission:** four-speed manual
**Chassis:** pressed steel channel
**Suspension:** non-independent, with semi-elliptic leaf springs front and rear
**Brakes:** drums all round
**Bodywork:** open two or four-seater
**Maximum speed (approx):** 78 mph (125 kph)

---

**SPA 24S**

# A-Z OF THE CAR

**Speedwell 25HP**

## SPARTAN

**Pinxton, England**
**1973–1982**

After years of repairing sports cars, Jim McIntyre's Nottinghamshire company began to manufacture traditionally-styled sports kit-cars in 1973, initially using a Triumph chassis, then progressing to a purpose-built unit. Power units ranged from Ford Mexico to Rover 3500 V8, and production by this little company exceeded 1000 cars.

### 1982 SPARTAN PLUS TWO

**Engine:** V6, overhead-valve
**Bore × stroke:** 90 mm × 60.1 mm
**Capacity:** 2993 cc
**Maximum power:** 114 bhp
**Transmission:** four-speed manual
**Chassis:** tubular space-frame
**Suspension:** front independent with MacPherson struts, rear non-independent trailing arms and coil springs
**Brakes:** discs front, drums rear
**Bodywork:** two-seat sports
**Maximum speed (approx):** 112 mph (181 kph)

## SPEEDWELL

**Reading/London, England**
**1900–1908**

Speedwell of Reading, Berkshire, were predominantly motor agents, importing the Serpollet steam car among other marques, but they also sold cars under their own name. Many of these were actually imported models of lesser-known marques badged as Speedwells, but the company also assembled cars from proprietary parts.

In 1904, three Speedwell models – 6 hp and 9 hp singles and a 10 hp twin – were available, while the company's first four-cylinder cars, with 14/16 hp and 24/30 hp engines, were launched in 1905, in which year Speedwells competed in the Isle of Man Tourist Trophy.

They raced in the 1906 TT, too. Late that year they launched a handsome 25 hp four, with a disc clutch and a double rear axle of patented design, with separate driving and load-carrying members. 'By this combination we get all the advantage, the silence and freedom from chain-troubles of the live-axle drive with the massive strength of the solid forged steel axle,' claimed the company, by now based in

### 1906 SPEEDWELL 25 HP

**Engine:** in-line four-cylinder
**Bore × stroke:** 110 mm × 130 mm
**Capacity:** 4942
**Maximum power:** 45 bhp
**Transmission:** three-speed manual
**Chassis:** pressed steel channel
**Suspension:** non-independent, with semi-elliptic leaf springs front and rear
**Brakes:** rear-wheel drums and transmission
**Bodywork:** Roi-des-Belges tonneau
**Maximum speed (approx):** 52 mph (84 kph)

Knightsbridge, London, and promoting 'the merits of Speedwell cars, the merits that particularly commend them to those who contemplate the relief or supplanting of their horses with a motor car.' A 45 hp six was offered in 1907 and uprated to 45/50 hp the following year, in which Speedwell ceased production.

## SPYKER

**Trompenburg, Holland**
**1900–1925**

The Spijker brothers, Hendrik and Jacobus, were originally carriage-builders in Hilversum, and were active as early as 1880. In 1895 they began to import Benz cars from Germany and then to modify them. By 1900 they had taken the logical step of building their own design, a horizontally-opposed two-cylinder 5 hp model; the brothers (who anglicised the name of their products to 'Spyker' in hope of export sales), equipped a new factory at Trompenburg, near Amsterdam, to cope with an anticipated demand which failed to materialise.

Undeterred, in 1902 Jacobus Spijker produced a 20 hp on more conventional lines. This had a 3770 cc four-cylinder engine whose cylinders were cast separately, and whose crankshaft ran in five bearings; an 1885 cc twin-cylinder version was also constructed.

At the end of 1903 a new Spyker appeared, powered by a 'circular engine', in which the cylinders were enclosed in a dustbin-like casing which ensured the maximum amount of water round the combustion chambers. Unfortunately, the water circulation was too sluggish and the engine boiled furiously... .

During 1903 Spyker built what is generally accepted as the world's first six-cylinder car, a one-off, four-wheel-driven, four-wheel-braked racer designed by the young Belgian engineer Joseph Laviolette. The *raison d'etre* behind this remarkable vehicle was, it seems, the elimination of skidding, however, with its dual-range, three-speed transmission, the six-cylinder Spyker also proved remarkably effective in hill-climbing contests.

It's all the more remarkable,

**Spartan**

therefore, that the company failed to exploit its technical lead to its fullest advantage; only a handful of 32/40 hp four-cylinder, four-wheel-drive tourers was subsequently built.

The advent of the four-wheel-drive six overshadowed that season's more conventional new models, a 16 hp twin and a 20/24 hp four, although their makers promoted these as 'silent as steam cars'.

During the following year, 1904, Spyker introduced their famous 'Dustless' chassis, which used a carefully-designed undershield to reduce the amount of dust raised by the car's passage over unmade roads. Another 1904 novelty was the 'magnetic carburettor', in which an electrically-operated needle valve could be used to cut off the fuel supply when the car was coasting, thus economising on petrol. On the 1905 models, Spyker adopted the round radiator that was to become associated with the marque; these were, in Edwardian times, the sign of a car of quality.

That early faith in the export business bore rich fruit when, in 1904-06, Spyker's entire output of four-cylinder cars was exported to England, where there were also many twin-cylinder Spyker taxis in service on the streets of London.

For 1906, Spyker offered a 2799 cc 12/18 hp, a 15/24 hp of 3456 cc, a 4562 cc 20/30 hp and a 7964 cc 30/40 hp.

Tragedy hit Spyker in February 1907: Hendrik Spijker, who ran the business side of the company, was drowned in the wreck of the SS Berlin in the North Sea, and, when the company books were examined, it was found that he had successfully been concealing the fact that the company was in deep financial trouble. Although Spyker survived the crisis, it never regained its former vitality.

An engaging rogue named Godard fast-talked his way halfway round the world in 1907, persuading the factory to supply him with a car to drive in the Pekin-Paris race. He scrounged his way across two continents until Jacobus Spijker finally had him evicted from the car when it reached Berlin.

1907 proved to be the last year of Spijker family involvement in the company, although at first there was little sign of the change, for the cars continued much the same for 1908, save that a vast 40/80 hp sports-racer with a 10,603 cc engine made a brief appearance.

At the end of 1909, Laviolette

**Spyker 60HP**

again revealed his penchant for unconventionality by equipping all Spyker engines with worm-driven transverse camshafts in the interests of smooth running. One transverse camshaft ran between each pair of cylinders, carrying two cams which actuated four valves. It was a system which worked well enough on four cylinders, but was prone to seize when applied to six (that being a short-lived venture of 1911).

Queen Wilhelmina of the Netherlands bought two of these transverse-camshaft cars, a 7238 cc 40 hp (which was, apparently, her first car) and a 4849 cc 25 hp. The range also contained a 1791 cc 12 hp, with the curious feature of a transmission brake fitted between the clutch and the rear transaxle so that it did not work when the car was in neutral.

After the war, Spyker re-entered car production with a side-valve four-cylinder 25/30 hp of 3.6 litres; several of these post-war chassis were fitted with curious aeroplane-styled 'Aerocoque' sports bodywork, which even incorporated vestigial tail surfaces.

The 25/30 was soon supplanted by the C4, designed by aero-engineer Frits Koolhoven, built on a French chassis and powered by a 5741 cc Maybach engine from Germany.

Over-expansion during the war proved Spyker's downfall, for the post-war models failed to sell in sufficient numbers: probably less than 500 cars were built in six years, 330 13/30s and 150 30/40s.

Attempts to break into the light car market by selling 1.2-litre Mathis cars as Spykers and to enter the commercial vehicle field by assembling American trucks failed to save Spyker from closure.

## Spyker 60 HP

The concept of Jacobus Spijker, the 60 hp six was realised by Joseph-Valentin Laviolette, the company's chief designer, and his assistant, F.W. Brand, who ran the Trompenburg development workshop.

Work began on this revolutionary car in 1902, and the idea behind the adoption of four-wheel drive was to eliminate skidding on the greasy roads of the period.

Nevertheless, the car was entered for the 1903 Paris-Madrid race, where it would have been driven by one E. Hautekeet and borne the racing number 188, but it failed to make the start. Instead, the 'double-driving six-cylinder Spyker' made its public debut at the December 1903 Paris Salon. Two months later it was displayed at the Crystal Palace Show in London, at which the new six-cylinder Napier made its first show appearance.

Among its unusual features was a dual-ratio gearbox, giving six forward and two reverse speeds, but the technical ideas incorporated in the new model were in advance of the capabilities of contemporary metallurgy, and many of its test runs ended in breakdowns. It was also a victim of Jacobus Spijker's grasshopper mind, for he was unable to concentrate on one idea for long.

It's unlikely that the planned production of six-cylinder, four-wheel-drive cars actually got underway, although a few four-cylinder, four-wheel-drive tourers were manufactured and sold.

The pioneering venture was halted after Jacobus Spijker was ousted from the company.

Nevertheless, when the contents of the works were auctioned off in 1925, it was found that the old 1903 four-wheel-drive car still survived in

### 1902 SPYKER 60 HP

**Engine:** in-line separately cast six-cylinder, T-head
**Bore × stroke:** 120 mm × 128 mm
**Capacity:** 8686 cc
**Maximum power:** 40 bhp
**Transmission:** dual-range three-speed, four-wheel drive
**Chassis:** pressed steel channel
**Suspension:** non-independent, with semi-elliptic leaf springs front and rear
**Brakes:** external-contracting rear-wheel drums plus transmission brake on front wheels
**Bodywork:** two-seater
**Maximum speed (approx):** 46 mph (75 kph)

the factory loft. It eventually came into the hands of a former director of the Spyker company named Springer, and was ultimately restored, though with little respect for its original specification. Bought by Dutch collector Max Lips to save it from being exported to America, the four-wheel-drive Spyker can still be seen in the Lips Autotron at Drunen, near s'Hertegenbosch in southern Holland.

## Spyker C4

Powered by a Maybach engine imported from Germany, the C4 Spyker was designed by aeronautical engineer Frits Koolhoven – the company had entered the aircraft industry during the Great War, in which it also adopted the Latin motto Nulla tenaci invia est via (No way is impassable to those of fixed purpose). Fitted with dual ignition, the power unit also had the unusual feature of a two-speed cooling fan. The dura-

## 1921 SPYKER C4

**Engine:** in-line six-cylinder, side-valve
**Bore × stroke:** 95 mm × 135 mm
**Capacity:** 5742
**Maximum power:** 70 bhp
**Transmission:** four-speed manual
**Chassis:** pressed steel channel
**Suspension:** non-independent, with semi-elliptic leaf springs front, cantilever leaf springs rear
**Brakes:** rear-wheel drums
**Bodywork:** tourer
**Maximum speed (approx):** 75 mph (120 kph)

**Spyker C4**

bility of the model was illustrated by its slogan 'Guaranteed for ever' and underlined by the fact that in 1921, S. F. Edge used a Maybach-engined Spyker to break his own 24-hour record at Brooklands, averaging 74.27 mph (120 kph) over two 12-hour stints.

Only minor modifications were made to the record-breaking car, such as a straight-through exhaust and Hartford friction shock-absorbers, supplemented by bungee straps, between the rear axle and chassis.

Some 150 examples of this model were built. Although Queen Wilhelmina continued her royal patronage of the marque, output was hardly viable, and in 1925 Trompenburg was closed down for good.

# SQUIRE

### Henley-on-Thames, England 1934–1936

Young Adrian Squire was obsessed by the idea of building his own sports cars; after serving as an apprentice at Bentley and as a draughtsman at MG, Squire attracted the backing of a wealthy friend from his schooldays, Jock Manby-Colegrave. A workshop was established at the top of Remenham Hill, near Henley-on-Thames, where Squire and Manby-Colegrave were joined by car salesman Reginald Slay who, aged 27, was so much older than either of the other partners that they called him 'Uncle'. The potent new supercharged double-overhead-cam 1496 cc R1 Anzani engine was chosen as the power unit for the Squire car, while transmission was by an ENV 110 preselector gear box, whose bottom gear band was forced to do duty as a clutch, coping with the 105 bhp output of the power unit. Nevertheless, the preselector box was a valuable aid to good acceleration.

The Squire car was available in two chassis lengths and fitted with bodywork by Vanden Plas or Ranalah. No compromise, either mechanical or aesthetic, was made in the construction of the Squire, and the result was probably the best-looking British sports car of the 1930s.

If the car had sold on appearance alone, the bold venture might have stood some chance of success. Unfortunately, the price of perfection was prohibitively high: basic cost of the car was £1195, while the highly-stressed Anzani engines proved unreliable unless they were regularly maintained. Furthermore the 15 in (38 cm) hydraulic brakes were so fierce that in the event of an emergency stop, the front spring shackles could fracture!

Squire attempted to boost the minimal sales with the announcement of a cheaper two-seater, with 'Skimpy' bodywork by Markham of Reading, but still failed to attract customers. A mere seven cars — two long chassis, five short — were built during the two years of production on Remenham Hill under Adrian Squire's supervision.

The original Squire company was wound up in July 1936, but a further two cars were subsequently built up by Val Zethrin, who had bought one of the two long-chassis Squires.

## 1934 SQUIRE

**Engine:** in-line four-cylinder, double-overhead-cam, supercharged
**Bore × stroke:** 69 mm × 100 mm
**Capacity:** 1496 cc
**Maximum power:** 105 bhp
**Transmission:** four-speed preselector
**Chassis:** pressed steel channel
**Suspension:** non-independent, with semi-elliptic leaf springs front and rear
**Brakes:** hydraulic drums all round
**Bodywork:** two or four-seat sports
**Maximum speed (approx):** 100 mph (160 kph)

A racing Squire single-seater driven by the 21-year-old Luis Fontes appeared at Brooklands in 1935 on a number of occasions. It only managed to finish once, in a Mountain Handicap race at the track. It expired during its biggest race, the British Empire Trophy, with a broken crankshaft, which Squire camouflaged as 'big-end failure'. In the BRDC 500 Mile Race two months later, the chassis fractured. The single-seater was subsequently rebodied with the two-seat Van den Plas coachwork from the third short-chassis car, which had been fitted with Skimpy bodywork in the interests of lightness.

Squire later rejoined his mentor W.O. Bentley at Lagonda and then moved on to join the Bristol Aeroplane Co.

Adrian Squire was killed in an air raid on Bristol during 1940; he was only 30. Six of the seven Squire cars built under his aegis remain as a testament to his unswerving perfectionism.

**Squire**

# A-Z OF THE CAR

**Standard Rhyl**

## STANDARD

**Coventry, England
1903–1963**

It was the architect of the Tower Bridge, Sir John Wolfe Barry, who started the Standard car on its sixty-year journey, by putting up £3000 to enable his young assistant Reginald Walter Maudslay, in straitened circumstances due to his father's death, to leave civil engineering and establish a motor factory in Coventry. Maudslay (whose cousin designed the Maudslay car, also made in Coventry) employed Alex Craig, formerly with Singer and Lea-Francis, as chief engineer; they called their car the Standard because it was assembled from standardised patterns and interchangeable parts, and because its design followed proven principles.

During 1905, Standard launched an 18/20 six-cylinder model, and in November exhibited at Olympia, so impressing London motor agent Charles Friswell that he offered to take the company's entire production. Standard's output was stepped up, and the company moved into a larger factory to cope with demand. In March 1906, the 18/20 was supplanted by a 24/30 hp six, while a new 50 hp luxury model appeared.

Among successful publicity activities of the period were the provision of twenty 20 hp cars for the 1909 Imperial Press Conference, plus a contract to supply all the cars for the 1911 Delhi Durbar, held to celebrate the coronation of King George V.

Standard had built their first four-cylinder light car as early as 1909, when they launched a 12 hp model which, thanks to a horrendously low-geared back axle (its 6.5:1 ratio limited top speed to around 25 mph), could carry spacious landaulette coachwork. The company's real success in the light-car field came in 1913 with the 9.5 hp Rhyl.

During the war, Standard manufactured munitions and opened a new factory at Canley to build aeroplanes, making 1300 RE-8 reconnaisance biplanes.

Post-war, Standard introduced an enlarged version of the Rhyl, the SLS, which became the 11.6 hp SLO in 1921; by 1923, Standard was building 5000 SLOs annually.

To combat a downturn in sales, Standard launched a six-cylinder model, the 2.2-litre 18/36, in 1927. It wasn't really the right car to revitalise the company, and was quickly joined by the Standard Nine, normally seen with fabric bodywork and worm-drive rear-axle.

The Nine kept financial crisis at bay for a while, but in 1929 the company had to be reorganised; Captain John Black, previously in charge of Hillman, became Standard's managing director, and a programme of revision of the company's offerings got under way.

Two years later, the Standard line-up consisted of a Big Nine plus 16 hp and 20 hp sixes, while a Little Nine was added to the range in 1932. The following year, Standard brought out two new small sixes, the Big Twelve and the Little Twelve, which gained Wilson self-changing gearboxes at the time of the Olympia Motor Show.

The Standard Ten came along in 1934; in 1936 the fastback Flying Standard range was introduced in 12 hp, 16 hp and 20 hp variants, promoted by their maker as cars 'of astonishing beauty with flowing lines simplified for practical reasons only . . . it's called the "Flying Standard" because at speed it is as silent as a bird on the wing.'

For the 1937 season, Standard offered the Flying Nine, Flying Ten, Flying Twelve, Flying Fourteen, and a short-lived 2.7-litre V8, of which only 200 examples were built; its power unit also appeared in the ephemeral Raymond Mays car.

At the 1938 Motor Show, Standard launched three new models, the 1-litre Eight, the Super Ten and the Twelve Saloon De Luxe which proved popular in 1939. All featured independent front suspension by transverse leaf spring.

After highly-varied wartime activity – the company built aircraft, armoured cars, aeroengines and military vans – in 1945 Standard bought the bankrupt Triumph company, whose factory had been destroyed in the Blitz, and Triumph cars began to be produced at Canley alongside the pre-war Standard Eight, Twelve and Fourteen.

The first truly new post-war model was the Vanguard of 1948, powered by a 2.1-litre wet-liner four-cylinder engine. It was restyled as the Phase I Vanguard in 1952, the Phase II version following a year later. A complete redesign came in 1956, when the Phase III nomenclature was adopted.

In late 1953 the company launched a new small car of basic design, the 803 cc Eight, subsequently joined by the similarly-styled Ten, whose engine and independent front suspension would eventually be transferred to the Triumph Herald in 1959.

Standard was taken over by Leyland Motors in 1961, and a sign of the changing attitude towards Standard came when the Triumph marque became the flagship of the group. The problem was that the name Standard, once a complimentary title, had become debased, and now represented merely the opposite to De Luxe. The last Standards were the 2138 cc Ensign and Vanguard Six; the engine of the latter was used in the Triumph 2000. Then, in May 1963, the marque name Standard ceased to exist. The company had scarcely passed its 60th anniversary before it was closed down.

## Standard Rhyl

Launched in March 1913, the Standard S Model Rhyl was typical of the new breed of big cars in miniature that appeared just before the Great War. It was instantly successful, and came to dominate the output of the Standard factory. In the period from 1913 to 1916, some 1300 of these little cars were built.

A remarkably modern touch was the three-year guarantee provided with every Rhyl; this was the first model to employ the classic Standard radiator with a rounded, shouldered header tank mounted on a tubular cooling element without brass side panels.

The roadholding of the Rhyl was commended, particularly because the car was one of the first in its class to be fitted with rear shock absorbers.

## Standard Nine

Faced with falling sales in the late 1920s, Standard decided to bring out a new small car, which was announced for the 1928 model year. Normally seen in Teignmouth form, with fabric saloon coachwork, the Nine proved an instant success. The 1928 Nine was the precursor of a line of extremely successful small Standard cars.

Capable of a top speed just in excess of 50 mph (80 kph) and a fuel consumption of 40 mpg, the Standard Nine offered a level of performance remarkable for the period.

The only criticisms offered by road testers were that the clutch was apt to be fierce, the steering was a little vague and the springs a little 'choppy'; The Autocar concluded that 'generally speaking, the little car would be ideal for town work, because it is very easy to handle, economical to run and not large enough to be awkward in car parks or in traffic.'

### 1916 STANDARD RHYL

**Engine:** in-line, four-cylinder, side-valve
**Bore × stroke:** 62 mm × 90 mm
**Capacity:** 1087 cc
**Maximum power:** 15 bhp
**Transmission:** three-speed manual
**Chassis:** pressed steel channel
**Suspension:** non-independent with semi-elliptic leaf springs
**Brakes:** drums on rear only
**Bodywork:** two-seater
**Maximum speed (approx):** 42 mph (68 kph)

**Standard Nine**

## STANLEY
Newton, USA
1897–1927

Identical twins Francis E. and Freelan O. Stanley made a handsome profit from the sale of their photographic dry plate business to the Eastman Kodak company; having seen an inconclusive demonstration of a horseless carriage at a fair, they were convinced that they could do better, and began building steam cars as a hobby in 1897. By that winter, they had built half-a-dozen cars, and eventually were persuaded to sell one to a Bostonian, J.F. Methot.

Then F.E. beat all-comers in a race at New England's first auto show, and the brothers were inundated with so many orders that they began building a batch of 200 steam buggies. Only one car had been completed, however, when a consortium headed by magazing publisher John Brisben Walker bought them out for $250,000 – at that point it had cost the Stanleys only $20,000 – and began building their design as the Locomobile. The Stanleys had made the sale, which debarred them from making steam cars for the year May 1899–May 1900, in the firm knowledge that their design was capable of tremendous improvement, and they spent the period until 1901 in the development of a new and better design which avoided any of the patents incorporated in the earlier car.

This new Stanley had a twin-cylinder engine geared direct to the

---

### 1930 STANDARD NINE

**Engine:** in-line four-cylinder, side-valve
**Bore × stroke:** 60 mm × 102 mm
**Capacity:** 1154 cc
**Maximum power:** 20 bhp
**Transmission:** three-speed manual
**Chassis:** pressed steel channel
**Suspension:** non-independent with semi-elliptic leaf springs
**Brakes:** drums all round
**Bodywork:** fabric covered saloon
**Maximum speed (approx):** 51 mph (82 kph)

## Standard Vanguard

In 1947, Standard concentrated its production on a single model, the rather portly unit-constructed Vanguard four-door saloon; its wet-liner four-cylinder power unit was shared with another Standard product, the Ferguson tractor. Initially shown in 1.8-litre form, the production versions of the Vanguard engine were enlarged to 2.1 litres; this power unit also found its way into the Plus 4 Morgan, Swallow Doretti, Peerless GT and the first 150,000 Triumph TR sports cars.

The transatlantic styling of the Vanguard – it looked like a 1942 Plymouth in miniature – made it easy to sell in export markets, where its dubious handling was less open to criticism, and for some time it remained a rare sight on the roads of Britain, though 185,000 were sold in the first five years of production. It sold well in Australia, and was built under licence in India, Belgium and Switzerland.

An estate car version was introduced for 1951, and the Vanguard became one of the first British cars to offer the option of Laycock de Normanville overdrive.

A mild restyling for 1952, with lower bonnet line, new grille and larger rear window was dubbed the Phase I Vanguard, followed in 1953 by a Phase II version with an extended boot replacing the rounded back of the original Vanguard. A Phase III Vanguard was launched in 1956, with entirely new bodywork, followed a year later by a two-tone Vanguard Sportsman with a high-compression twin-cylinder engine.

A Vignale Vanguard, with some cosmetic styling revisions by the Turin *carrozzeria*, appeared in 1958, with a six-cylinder Vanguard added to the range in 1962, only months before the Standard name vanished for ever; this model was chiefly notable for its 2-litre power unit.

---

### 1950 STANDARD VANGUARD

**Engine:** in-line four-cylinder, overhead-valve
**Bore × stroke:** 85 mm × 92 mm
**Capacity:** 2088 cc
**Maximum power:** 68 bhp
**Transmission:** three-speed manual
**Chassis:** integral
**Suspension:** independent front with coil springs and wishbones. Live rear axle with semi-elliptic leaf springs
**Brakes:** drums all round
**Bodywork:** four-door saloon
**Maximum speed (approx):** 75 mph (120 kph)

**Standard Vanguard**

back axle; this layout was used on all subsequent Stanleys. Originally, the twin-cylinder model carried buggy bodywork, with the fire-tube boiler beneath the seat, whence curls of flame were liable to shoot out between the driver's legs in the event of blow-back in the burners…. This was almost certainly a main factor in the relocation of the boiler, which around 1905 was shifted to the front of the car under the famous 'coffin nose' bonnet.

In 1906, a racing Stanley Steamer named *Beetle*, the first car to have its body developed in a wind tunnel, exceeded 127 mph (204 kph) at Ormond Beach, Daytona, Florida; in a subsequent record attempt the car became airborne and was destroyed.

In short bursts, Stanley Steamers were generally faster than their petrol-engined contemporaries, though care had to be taken not to let the boiler level fall too low (when it would burn out) or too high (when it would prime, sending incompressible water into the engine with dire results). Typically, the production 1907 Gentleman's Speedy Roadster could reach over 75 mph (120 kph) over short distances.

An epidemic of foot-and-mouth disease in the Stanley's New England home area in 1914 caused many roadside horse-troughs to be removed in an attempt to contain the outbreak, so Stanley Steamers, which up to then had relied on the horsetroughs to refill the boiler at regular intervals, had to be fitted with condensers from 1915 so that exhaust steam could be reconverted to water.

The cost and bother of developing the more expensive condensor models (which could cover 150–200 miles between boiler refills) cut the company's 1915 production that year to 126, compared with 743 in 1914, though it subsequently revived to rise to 500 in 1917, the last full year in which the Stanley brothers were involved in the running of the firm.

A Chicago investment group headed by Prescott Warren controlled Stanley from May 1918 but the marque never recovered from the post-war slump and was taken over in 1924 by the Steam Vehicle Corporation of America of Allentown, Pennsylvania. It is unlikely that the new owners actually built any further Stanleys before they ceased trading in 1927; an attempt to revive the marque in the mid-1930s came to naught.

## Stanley EX

In 1904, Stanley introduced a new model to supplant the old buggy-style steamer; while the twin-cylinder engine geared direct to the rear axle was retained, the boiler was moved to the front under a

**Stanley Gentleman's Speedy Roadster**

### 1908 STANLEY EX

**Engine:** horizontal single-acting twin-cylinder steam engine
**Bore × stroke:** 76.2 mm × 101.6 mm
**Maximum power:** 30 bhp
**Transmission:** direct drive to rear axle
**Chassis:** wooden frame with tubular steel underframe
**Suspension:** non-independent with full elliptic leaf springs
**Brakes:** drums on rear only
**Bodywork:** two or four-seat tourer
**Maximum speed (approx):** 60 mph (97 kph)

round-fronted bonnet. This both simplified the task of monitoring the water level in the boiler and moved the burner out from under the driver. Starting from cold was also simplified.

Front and rear axles were still linked by reach bars, but the body underframe was strengthened so that various body styles could be adopted.

Handsomest of these was the Gentleman's Speedy Roadster, launched in 1908, which had abbreviated two-seat sports bodywork and could attain 70 mph (113 kph) over short distances; it was based on the 20 hp derivative of the basic EX formula, which had a 3.5 × 4.5 in engine, and had a boiler which could operate at 650 psi. The 20 hp eventually metamorphosed into the 30 hp, with 4 × 5 in cylinders.

One drawback of the EX was a range restricted to 50 miles (80).

## Stanley 735

The only major modifications made to the Stanley Steamer during its long production life were the adoption of a condensor in 1915 and the changeover to steel boiler tubes, rendered necessary because the water returned to the boiler from the condensor contained oil, which caused leaks round the copper boil-er tubes used up to that time.

Because the condensor acted as a silencer for the exhaust steam, the latter Stanleys, such as the 735 and 740 were uncannily quiet; indeed, the only sound to be heard from a cruising Stanley was the rhythmic creak of the wooden-spoked wheels.

But such silence was bought at a price unacceptable to the average motorist; not only did the Stanley's firetube boiler take several minutes to reach working temperature, but the car needed specialist attention. Though boiler explosion was not the recurrent threat of popular misconception, nonetheless the operator of a Stanley had to bear in mind that the boiler (prevented from bursting by a wound-on strait-jacket of piano wire – three-quarters of a mile of it!) contained steam at pressures up to 550 psi which was, apparently capable of slicing through steel if a leak developed… .

### 1916 STANLEY 735

**Engine:** horizontal twin-cylinder steam engine
**Bore × stroke:** 101.6 mm × 127 mm
**Maximum power:** 60 bhp
**Transmission:** direct drive to rear axle
**Chassis:** pressed steel channel
**Suspension:** non-independent with semi-elliptic leaf springs front and full elliptics rear
**Brakes:** rear wheel drums
**Bodywork:** tourer or saloon
**Maximum speed (approx):** 60 mph (97 kph)

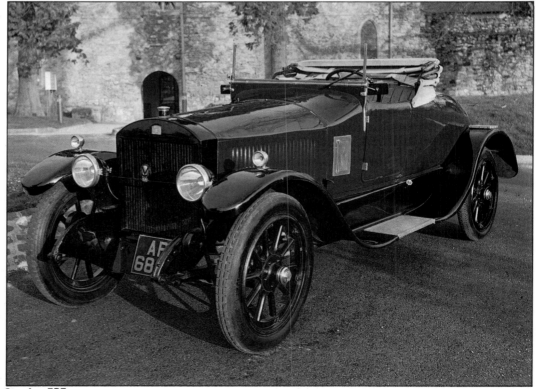

**Stanley 735**

# A-Z OF THE CAR

## STAR

**Wolverhampton, England
1897–1932**

Edward Lisle's Star Engineering Company built cycles from 1883; a pioneer motorist, Lisle built his first 3½ hp Benz-based Star car in 1897. It cost 180 guineas. A twin-cylinder version with three speeds appeared in 1900, but the Benz pattern was becoming obsolete, so Star followed this model a year later with a more modern Panhard-inspired 7 hp vertical twin. There was also a light car with a single-cylinder De Dion power unit.

Then in 1903, Star announced a 12/16 hp four built on Mercedes lines, followed in late 1905 by a 3261 cc version. The first six-cylinder Star, the 6227 cc 30 hp, was catalogued from 1906 to

1911, with an increase in bore size taking the swept volume to 6981 cc in 1909. The same year, a new 2862 cc 15 hp (actually 19.6 rated horsepower) four-cylinder model appeared, to be replaced in 1912 by the famous 15.9 four of 3016 cc.

In 1914, when Star had become one of Britain's six biggest car producers, this model and the similar 3817 cc 20.1 hp were offered with streamline torpedo coachwork and elegant bullnose radiators, apparently developed for the colonial market.

The 15.9 HP and 20.1 HP survived until 1921, when they were supplanted by a conventionally-designed side-valve 1795 cc 11.9 HP model, which was enlarged to become a 1945 cc 12/25 HP in 1924. The similar 12/40 HP Sports was fitted with front-wheel brakes to cope with the

extra performance provided by the fitment of pushrod overhead valves. There was also a six-cylinder version known as the 18/40.

In 1928, Star was acquired by Guy Motors, and the over-complicated range reduced to just two six-cylinder models, the 18/50 HP and the 20/60 HP, which were totally redesigned in 1930 as the Comet and Planet respectively; featuring four-wheel hydraulic jacks and servo-assisted brakes, these elegant cars were promoted as offering '1941 motoring luxury and economy', but the cars proved hopelessly uneconomic to build, and production of Star cars ceased in March 1932.

## Star 15.9 HP

'The right car at a moderate price, all-British and second to none', the Star 15.9 HP was launched in 1912; it proved its durability by running at Brooklands for 12 hours under RAC

observation, covering 801 miles (1289 km) at an average of 66.75 mph (107.5 kph) and establishing 24 class records.

For 1914, the 15.9 and 20.1 hp Stars gained a bullnosed radiator (available in brass or German silver) originally introduced for colonial models but so handsome that it was adopted for the home market too, plus handsome streamlined tourer bodywork. 'The bodywork of the 1914 Star cars,' commented *The Autocar*, 'has been considerably improved and the new scuttles and bonnets merge into the bodies in a most commendable and practical manner, the foot room of the front seats being ample.'

The 15.9 HP and the similar 3816 cc 20.1 hp model were reintroduced after the Great War.

---

### 1912 STAR 15.9 HP

**Engine:** in-line four-cylinder, side-valve
**Bore × stroke:** 80 mm × 150 mm
**Capacity:** 3016 cc
**Maximum power:** 40 bhp
**Transmission:** four-speed
**Chassis:** pressed-steel channel
**Suspension:** non-independent with semi-elliptic leaf springs front and three-quarter elliptics rear
**Brakes:** transmission and rear wheels
**Bodywork:** torpedo tourer
**Maximum speed (approx):** 70 mph (113 kph)

---

Star 15.9 HP

**Stearns 30/60 HP**

# STEARNS

Cleveland, USA
1898-1930

Frank B. Stearns built his first car in 1896, while he was still a student, and started production of single-cylinder gas buggies with tiller steering in 1898–9. Wheel steering arrived with the 4083 cc model – still with a single-cylinder power unit – introduced in 1900. When in 1901 Stearns announced that he planned to build ten cars a day, the press greeted the statement with scepticism.

In 1902, Stearns introduced a front-engined twin, somewhat highly priced at $3000. Stearns was now evolving confidently into a maker of expensive quality cars, and in 1904 launched a 36 hp four on Mercedes lines, which developed into the 1906 four-cylinder 40/45 HP. This model used cast aluminium body panels with a 17-coat paint finish. Each chassis had to undergo a searching test before it was released to the customer, including a 150-mile run over rough roads carrying a half-ton load of sand.

The 40/45 HP was soon joined by a 8737 cc 30/60 hp four and the 45/90 hp six of 12,913 cc, whose engine was so long that the rear cylinders were beneath the dashboard. With the euphemistically-named light tourer coachwork, the Stearns 45/90 was reckoned to be the fastest stock car of its day.

In 1909, Stearns launched a refined 4.8-litre 15/30 HP, billed as The Ultimate Car, while 1914 saw the introduction of two Knight sleeve-valve-engined models, the 5.1-litre four and 6.8-litre six. In 1917, the 5.4-litre SK-8, with a 90

degree V8 engine joined the range.

Frank Stearns retired from the company in 1919; during the early 1920s, the company pursued a one model policy with a 4072 cc four, though by 1924 Stearns had launched a 4397 cc six. The Stearns company was acquired by Willys Overland in 1925; the new owners retained the Stearns hallmark of a white line round the inside edge of the radiator shell.

Stearns was a victim of the Depression, although it retained its reputation for quality right to the end in 1930. The last new models were the Stearns-Knights of 1929–30, a lower-priced 27.3 hp six – it cost $2095 – and a nine-bearing 6.3-litre straight-eight priced at $5500.

## 1909 STEARNS 30/60 HP

**Engine:** in-line four-cylinder, side-valve
**Bore × stroke:** 136.5 mm × 149.2 mm
**Capacity:** 8737 cc
**Maximum power:** 60 bhp
**Transmission:** four-speed manual
**Chassis:** pressed-steel channel
**Suspension:** non-independent with semi-elliptic leaf springs all round
**Brakes:** rear wheel and transmission
**Bodywork:** toy tonneau
**Maximum speed (approx):** 80 mph (129 kph)

## 1923 STEARNS-KNIGHT

**Engine:** in-line four-cylinder, double sleeve valve 'Silent Knight'
**Bore × stroke:** 100 mm × 140 mm
**Capacity:** 4072 cc
**Maximum power:** 70 bhp
**Transmission:** three-speed manual
**Chassis:** pressed steel channel
**Suspension:** non-independent with semi-elliptic leaf springs front and rear
**Brakes:** drums on rear only
**Bodywork:** saloon
**Maximum speed (approx):** 75 mph (120 kph)

**Stearns Knight**

# STEPHENS
**Moline, USA**
**1916-1924**

Unusually for a quality car, the Stephens was built by a maker of agricultural machinery, the Moline Plow Company. Stephens never built anything other than a 3670 cc six-cylinder – the Salient Six – which gained overhead valves in 1918, when the company switched from buying-in Continental engines to producing their own power units, which coincidentally shared the same dimensions

In 1922, the marque adopted a high, rounded radiator, and launched a sports phaeton derivative with cycle wings and wire wheels, plus a standard paint scheme of grey with apple-green wheels.

Some 25,000 Stephens cars were built during the marque's nine-year existence.

## 1924 STEPHENS SALIENT SIX

**Engine:** in-line six-cylinder, overhead-valve
**Bore × stroke:** 82.6 mm × 114.3 mm
**Capacity:** 3670 cc
**Maximum power:** 50 bhp
**Transmission:** three-speed manual
**Chassis:** pressed steel channel
**Suspension:** non-independent with semi-elliptic leaf springs front and rear
**Brakes:** rear wheel and transmission
**Bodywork:** sport tourer, tourer and sedan
**Maximum speed (approx):** 60 mph (97 kph)

**Stephens Salient Six**

# STEVENS-DURYEA
**Chicopee Falls, USA**
**1900-1927**

When Frank and Charles Duryea, the two brothers who had built America's first commercially-produced car in 1895, quarrelled and separated, Frank joined the Stevens Arms & Tools company, of Chicopee Falls, Massachussets, as vice-president and chief engineer.

Like many other armaments manufacturers, Stevens found that their precision machining skills suited them admirably for the manufacture of motorcars; they took over the old Overman factory, where cycles and steam cars had previously been built, and in 1900 began producing a 6 hp horizontal-twin Victoria Stanhope with tiller steering and folding front seat.

This somewhat archaic-looking model was joined in 1905 by a 20 hp four-cylinder Stevens-Duryea of conventional appearance.

In 1905, Stevens-Duryea launched a 9.6-litre Big Six, incorporating three-point suspension of the engine/gearbox unit. And it was on this type of car that the Stevens-Duryea company concentrated its energy from 1907.

In 1914, for instance, Stevens-Duryea offered the Model C, with a

## 1915 STEVENS-DURYEA MODEL D

**Engine:** in-line pair-cast side-valve six-cylinder
**Bore × stroke:** 112.7 mm × 139.7 mm
**Capacity:** 8362 cc
**Maximum power:** 80 bhp
**Transmission:** three-speed manual
**Chassis:** pressed-steel channel
**Suspension:** non-independent with semi-elliptic leaf springs front and rear
**Brakes:** rear wheel only
**Bodywork:** sport, sedan and limousine
**Maximum speed (approx):** 62 mph (100 kph)

7897 cc power unit.

The last truly new model to be produced by Stevens-Duryea was the Model D of 1915.

Frank Duryea then sold his share in the company, which suspended production until 1920, when the Model D was revived – under the Model E designation. It was overpriced, however, and in 1923, the company was taken over by Ray M. Owen, who headed Owen Magnetic, and few Stevens-Duryeas were built after 1924. Indeed, it's unlikely that the factory ever built more than 100 cars a year.

Instead, the Chicopee Falls plant turned to the manufacture of Raulang electric cars and coachwork, mainly for the last of the Stanley Steamers.

Touring bodies for the ephemeral Ruxton were built in the old Stevens-Duryea plant in the late 1920s.

**Stevens-Duryea Model D Touring**

## MODEL
Porsche 911 Carrera Coupé (1984)

**UK price when announced:**
£22,537 (1984)

## ENGINE
**Location:** Rear, longitudinal
**Type:** Horizontally opposed six cylinder, air cooled
**Cubic capacity:** 3164 cc
**Bore × stroke:** 95 mm × 74.4 mm
**Compression ratio:** 10.3 : 1
**Valve gear:** 2 inclined valves per cylinder operated by single belt-driven overhead camshaft per bank of cylinders
**Fuel supply:** Bosch L-Jetronic fuel injection
**Ignition:** Electronic with DME (digital motor electronics)
**Maximum power:** 231 bhp (DIN) at 5900 rpm
**Maximum torque:** 207 lb ft (DIN) at 4800 rpm

## TRANSMISSION
**Layout:** Clutch and gearbox in unit with, and ahead of, engine
**Clutch:** Single dry plate
**Gearbox:** Five speed manual with synchromesh on all forward gears

| | |
|---|---|
| 1st 3.182 : 1 | 4th 0.966 : 1 |
| 2nd 1.833 : 1 | 5th 0.763 : 1 |
| 3rd 1.261 : 1 | |

**Final drive:** Spiral bevel
**Ratio:** 3.875 : 1

## SUSPENSION
**Front:** Independent with McPherson struts, lower wishbones, longitudinal torsion bars and anti-roll bar
**Rear:** Independent with semi-trailing arms, transverse torsion bars and anti-roll bar

## STEERING
**Type:** Rack and pinion, manual

## BRAKES
**Type:** 9.25 in diameter discs front and 9.61 in discs rear, dual circuit, servo assisted

## WHEELS AND TYRES
**Type:** Steel 6 in × 15 in front and 7 in × 15 in rear with 185/70VR15 tyres front and 215/60VR15 rear

**FAR LEFT AND LEFT** The front strut and torsion bar suspension which replaced the original double wishbones, alongside the infamous semi-trailing arm rear suspension

## BODY/CHASSIS

**Type:** Integral steel chassis with 2-door coupé body and 2+2 seating

## DIMENSIONS AND WEIGHT

**Length:** 168.9 in (4290 mm)
**Width:** 64.96 in (1649 mm)
**Wheelbase:** 89.41 in (2271 mm)
**Track – front:** 54.02 in (1372 mm)
**– rear:** 54.33 in (1379 mm)
**Weight:** 2558 lb (1160 kg)

## PERFORMANCE

**Maximum speed:** 152 mph (245 kph)
**Acceleration 0–60 mph:** 6.1 seconds
**Fuel consumption:** 21 mpg

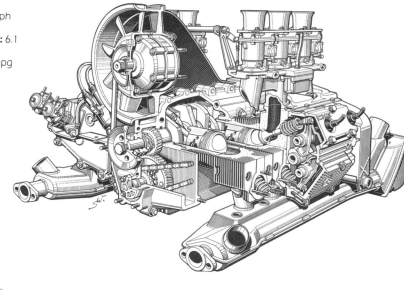

**ABOVE** Compact, light and very powerful, the Porsche flat six with Weber carburettors

# A-Z OF THE CAR

## STEYR

**Steyr, Austria
1920 to date**

The outbreak of peace posed a potential threat to the Österreiche Waffenfabriksgesellschaft at Steyr, Austria's biggest armaments works, so they recruited Hans Ledwinka, previously with Nesselsdorf, to design them a post-war car. Drawing inspiration from his pre-war Nesselsdorf Type U, Ledwinka designed the Steyr Type II Waffenauto, which appeared on the market in 1920. Powered by an overhead-camshaft 3325 cc 12/40 hp six-cylinder engine, the Type II was soon joined by the Type IV, a side-valve 1814 cc four-cylinder model. Ledwinka returned to Tatra in 1921, where he brought out his backbone chassis 1056 cc flat-twin model in 1923.

The Steyr Six underwent much development; it was bored out to produce the 4014 cc Type VI in 1922. This was one of Austria's most successful sporting models in the early 1920s, and was itself replaced by the 4890 cc Klausen Sport, named for a famous victory at the Klausen hillclimb. This limited production model developed a remarkable 145 bhp in racing trim.

In 1926, Steyr launched a smaller six-cylinder model displacing 1560 cc. The following year, Ferdinand Porsche resigned from Mercedes and returned to his native Austria, where he took over at Steyr and began by updating Ledwinka's design, which had by now reached the Type VII stage. Porsche's single overhead-camshaft Type XVI could reach speeds of 75 mph (120 kph), and found some 400 customers in the rather troubled 1928-30 period.

The Steyr range at this period also included overhead-valve 2078 cc sixes and also the overhead-valve 1990 cc Steyr 120S.

In 1929–30, Ferdinand Porsche designed a luxurious new Steyr, the 5.3-litre straight-eight Austria, the sensation of the 1929 Paris Salon. The model never went into production, however, as Steyr was holding joint venture talks with the Puch combine, of which Austro-Daimler formed part. The two factories rationalised their production at the request of the bank which was backing them both, and the Steyr Austria was dropped in favour of the Austro-Dailer ADR8. Ferdinand Porsche then resigned and set a design consultancy.

While he was with Steyr, Porsche also designed the 2-litre Type XXX, with a light-alloy overhead-valve six-cylinder engine of 2078 cc, which produced 40 bhp at 3500 rpm. The end of Austro-Daimler cars came in 1934 when the Steyr and Puch companies merged. That year, the first small Steyr appeared, in the shape of the Type 100, with a 1385 cc side-valve four-cylinder engine; in 1937, Steyr launched the 1498 cc Type 200, which was also available as Type 220 with an overhead-valve engine of 2260 cc.

The 1158 cc Steyr 55 light car of 1938 carried very streamlined bodywork; with a side-valve flat-four engine, it succeeded the 984 cc Type 50 of 1936. some 13,000 Type 50 and 55 cars were built before the war closed the factory and production ceased.

From 1949, Steyr assembled Fiat cars for Austria, and from 1957 on they built the Fiat 500 as the Steyr-Puch 500, fitted with a 493 cc flat-twin engine of their own make. The model was built mainly at the Puch factory in Graz.

Steyr also assembled Opel cars under licence in the mid-1930s.

In the 1960s, Steyr introduced the Haflinger go-anywhere vehicle, designed by Ledwinka's son Erich, followed in the early 1970s by a six-wheel-drive derivative, the Pinzgauer. During 1979 Steyr began manufacturing Explorer four-wheel-drive vehicles for Mercedes.

---

### 1934 STEYR TIPO 100

**Engine:** in-line four-cylinder, side-valve
**Bore × stroke:** 70 mm × 84 mm
**Capacity:** 1385 cc
**Maximum power:** 40 bhp
**Transmission:** four-speed manual
**Chassis:** pressed steel channel
**Suspension:** independent with semi-elliptic leaf springs front and swinging axles rear
**Brakes:** drums
**Bodywork:** two-door convertible
**Maximum speed (approx):** 80 mph (129 kph)

---

**Steyr Tipo 100**

# STOEWER

**Stettin, Germany**
**1897–1939**

The Stoewer brothers, Emil and Bernhard, owned an ironworks at Stettin, Pomerania (now Szeczin, in Poland), founded by their father, Bernhard, in 1858, and which had manufactured sewing machines, typewriters and bicycles. The latter activity led the brothers to start building Cudell De Dion-engined motor cycles, three-wheelers and quadricycles as early as 1897; they then progressed to the manufacture of more substantial rear-engined 2080 cc twin-cylinder phaeton-bodied cars.

The brothers built their first front-engined four-cylinder Stoewer in 1901; based on the French Panhard, this wooden-chassis 3052 cc machine reflected the cautious attitude of the Stoewers to motor engineering, for it was even then built on obsolescent lines. The next Stoewer was inspired by the Mercedes, with a pressed steel chassis, chain final drive and pair-cast T-head cylinders.

But by 1906 the Stoewers had gained sufficient confidence to produce a design that owed little to the work of others and that resulted in the unveiling of the new Stoewer P6, powered by an 8829 cc six-cylinder engine. It so impressed Kaiser Wilhelm of Germany that he ordered one and the model remained in production until 1910.

| **1935 STOEWER GREIF V8** |
|---|

**Engine:** V8, overhead-valve
**Bore × stroke:** 69.5 mm × 82 mm
**Capacity:** 2488 cc
**Maximum power:** 57 bhp
**Transmission:** four-speed manual, front-wheel drive
**Chassis:** pressed steel channel
**Suspension:** independent with coil springs
**Brakes:** drums all round
**Bodywork:** cabriolet
**Maximum speed (approx):** 70 mph (113 kph)

Stoewer next brought out four-cylinder models of 1501 cc (in 1908 a batch of these G4 models had been built for NAG, who fitted them with NAG radiators and coachwork) and 2544 cc; in 1910, Stoewer announced the Type B6, with a 2025 cc engine, which was also built under licence by Mathis.

Soon after World War I came a remarkable delusion of grandeur: in 1911 Stoewer had begun building aeroengines to the design of the *emigré* Russian engineer, Boris Loutsky and had produced these power units during the hostilities. After the hostilities, Loutsky suggested that his overhead-valve 11,160 cc six-cylinder aeroengine could be shoehorned into a car chassis to use up surplus parts. A racing version of the resulting Stoewer D7, known inevitably as the Grosser Stoewer, ran at the Fanoe Beach meeting in Denmark in 1922, driven by works-driver Emil Kordewan, who swept the board, reaching an average speed of 114 mph (183 kph). The Grosser Stoewer remained in production until 1923 in touring form, and in 1929, Kordewan had a special built which incorporated the D7 engine in the latest Stoewer chassis.

A smaller racing car of the early 1920s had a 2490 cc four-cylinder overhead-camshaft engine and streamlined bodywork.

More conventional production models of the early 1920s included 1570 cc, 2120 cc and 2292 cc four-cylinder models. The six-cylinder D5, with a 3107 cc side-valve engine, was enlarged to 3383 cc in 1926, when it also acquired four-wheel brakes and became known as the D12V (for *Vierradbremse*-'four wheel brakes').

The most popular model of the mid-1920s was the D10, with a 50 bhp engine of 2.6 litres. During 1928, Stoewer introduced the 1997 cc and 2462 cc straight-eight Superior models, designed by Fritz Fiedler and based closely on the American Gardner from St Louis.

Until the early 1920s, Stoewer had been a typical family business, with the founder-owners and their families taking an active part. But Bernhard Stoewer retired from the company in 1921 to breed thoroughbred horses on his Pomeranian estate, and within a

few years the factory ran into financial difficulties, and had to be baled out by the city of Stettin and the state of Prussia.

Bernhard Stoewer returned from retirement to supervise the development of two new straight-eights based on the Fiedler designs, the 3974 cc G15 Gigant (also available in a 3633 cc version, and with a supercharger as the G15K) and the 2963 cc Marschall.

The last big Stoewer was the impressive 100 hp 4905 cc straight-eight Repraesentant but the company's economic problems led to the manufacture of cheaper cars in the 1930s. The first of these, the sensation of the 1931 Berlin Show, was the V5, an 1188 cc V4 with front-wheel drive.

Bernhard Stoewer designed another front-wheel-drive car for 1934, but the new 2488 cc Greif V8 enjoyed only critical success, for sales didn't match its technical expertise. Bernhard retired for the second time once the Greif was in production (Emil had already left the firm, in 1932) and Stoewer had once again to seek technical and financial aid. The Kaiser's grandson, Prince Louis Ferdinand, proposed a union between Stoewer and Ford of Germany (which was losing sales because of its American and British links) but after Ford had loaned Stoewer half a million Reichsmarks for expansion, it became obvious that the apparently prosperous Stoewer-Werke was virtually bankrupt. Ford decided to end the deal there and then, with only 200 tourer bodies for their 10 hp Eifel to show for the RM500,000.

After the collapse of the Ford deal, Stoewer built the Greif-Junior, with an overhead-valve air-cooled 1474 cc flat-four engine, from 1936 to 1939 under Tatra licence.

Stoewer was back with its own designs in 1937, when it showed the overhead-valve 2390 cc four-

cylinder Sedina and 3585 cc six-cylinder Arcona at the Berlin Show, but these models were not rebuilt. WWII by the outbreak of World War II, during which Stoewer supplied cars to the German forces; the works, extensively damaged in an air raid during 1944 were not rebuilt, since after the Armistice, Stettin found itself behind that new Iron Curtain, transformed into the Polish port of Szeczin.

# STONELEIGH

**Coventry, England**
**1912–1914, 1922–1924**

The original Stoneleigh was a 12 hp four-cylinder model, which, apart from its radiator, was identical to its sister marque, BSA. The post-war Stoneleigh light car, sponsored by Armstrong-Siddeley, had a 1-litre vee-twin power unit with inclined overhead valves and aluminium pistons. It had reputedly been designed to use up war-surplus aeroengine cylinders, and featured unorthodox three-seat bodywork with the driver sitting in the centre with two passengers behind.

| **1922 STONELEIGH** |
|---|

**Engine:** vee-twin, overhead-valve, air-cooled
**Bore × stroke:** 85 mm × 88 mm
**Capacity:** 998 cc
**Maximum power:** 15 bhp
**Transmission:** three-speed manual
**Chassis:** pressed-steel channel
**Suspension:** non-independent with semi-elliptic leaf springs all round
**Brakes:** rear wheels only
**Bodywork:** three-seater tourer
**Maximum speed (approx):** 35 mph (56 kph)

**Stoewer Grief V8**

**Stoneleigh**

335

# STORERO

**Turin, Italy**
**1912-1919**

The Storero company developed from a Fiat sales and garage chain – the Fiat connection stemming from Luigi Storero's friendship with Fiat founding father Giovanni Agnelli. Relations became closer when

### 1913 STORERO 25/30 HP

**Engine:** in-line four-cylinder, side-valve
**Bore × stroke:** 100 mm × 140 mm
**Capacity:** 4398 cc
**Maximum power:** 25 bhp
**Transmission:** four-speed
**Chassis:** pressed steel channel
**Suspension:** non-independent with semi-elliptic leaf springs
**Brakes:** rear drums
**Bodywork:** landaulette
**Maximum speed (approx):** 45 mph (72 kph)

Fiat actually took over the chain in 1908.

Storero built his first car in 1912, the 20/30 hp powered by a four-cylinder side-valve monobloc unit of 4398 cc. A smaller 15/20 soon followed, also powered by a monobloc four, but of only 3308 cc.

A modified version of the 20/30, the 3.7-litre B20/30, was driven by Minoia in the Targa Florio but without any success although the D10/15 enjoyed more success in the Parma-Poggio event, winning its class in 1914.

The sporting theme was continued with cars like the 5-litre overhead-cam AS of 1915 but Storero's main market was in refined luxury cars before they switched to war production.

# STOREY

**Tonbridge/Clapham Park, England**
**1920–1930**

Will Storey experimented with steam cars before the Great War, but during that war his machine tool company produced munitions and, latterly, rotary aero-engines. Peace found them well capitalised and geared for expansion, but suddenly faced with a cessation of military orders.

Will Storey decided to gear up for the mass-production of motorcars to meet the postwar demand for transportation, and during 1918 experimented with a five-cylinder radial-engined prototype. This was quickly

abandoned, and during 1919 Storey built a model factory on a 40-acre (16-hectare) site at Tonbridge in Kent, while work continued on a prototype powered by an inlet-over-exhaust Coventry-Simplex engine.

This was well received and formed the basis of production, which began in a limited fashion in Storey's London workshops pending the completion of the Tonbridge factory. The choice of power unit had now been switched to the French Chaupuis-Dornier, and cars of 14.3 and 20 hp were advertised. These were fitted with rear-axle-mounted gearboxes, which, like most of the chassis components, was built in Storey's own workshops.

### 1920 STOREY 14.3 HP

**Engine:** in-line four-cylinder, side-valve
**Bore × stroke:** 76 mm × 120 mm
**Capacity:** 2178 cc
**Maximum power:** 30 bhp
**Transmission:** three speed manual
**Chassis:** pressed steel channel
**Suspension:** non-independent, with semi-elliptic leaf springs front, cantilever leaf springs rear
**Brakes:** rear-wheel drums
**Bodywork:** two-seater, coupé, tourer, salon
**Maximum speed (approx):** 50 mph (80 kph)

**Storey 14.3 HP**

**Storero Tipo A 20/30**

The Tonbridge factory went into production in the spring of 1920, but was delayed when a dock strike held up supplies of power units. Storey attempted to counter this threat by building his own power units, and by the end of 1920 engines of Storey's own manufacture were used in 10/12 hp, 15.9 hp and 20 hp forms. These cars had the gearbox in a more conventional location.

Storey's bank, alarmed by the way that the post-war car market was becoming saturated, called in Storey's overdraft and put the company into liquidation. Will Storey's brother Jack, the former works manager, acquired as many spares as possible and established an assembly operation in premises he owned at Clapham Park, London, during 1921.

At first, Storey power units were fitted, but as the supply of these ran out, Meadows power units were installed.

The company was reconstructed again during 1925, and three models – 10/25 and 14/40 hp fours and a 17/70 hp six-cylinder – were listed, although it is unlikely that more than a handful was actually built.

# A-Z OF THE CAR

**Straker-Squire 24/80 HP**

## STRAKER-SQUIRE

**Bristol/London, England
1906–1926**

Sidney Straker & Squire, of Fishponds, Bristol began building steam trucks in 1901, only turning to petrol cars five years later when they began licence-production of the French Cornilleau-St. Beuve, an obscure Parisian marque with some advanced features like monobloc construction of its 25 hp four-cylinder engine.

Described as 'a chassis of the Highest Class, possessing improvements of great merit…free from pipes, wires and encumbrances…few have so many commendable details of construction', the Straker-Squire-CSB cost £675 in four-seater tourer guise.

At the 1907 Olympia Motor Show, Straker-Squire introduced the 16/20 hp 'Car for the Connoisseur', which sold at £375; also new in 1907 was the 12/14 hp Shamrock built by a sister company.

In 1908, Straker-Squire brought out the 15 hp four-cylinder designed by A.R. (later Sir Roy) Fedden; it became the marque's most successful model. A limousine version with detachable wheels was added to

### 1921 STRAKER-SQUIRE 24/80 HP

**Engine:** in-line, separately cast six-cylinder, overhead-cam
**Bore × stroke:** 80 mm × 130 mm
**Capacity:** 3921 cc
**Maximum power:** 80 bhp
**Transmission:** four-speed manual
**Chassis:** pressed steel channel
**Suspension:** non-independent, with semi-elliptic leaf springs front, cantilever leaf springs rear
**Brakes:** rear-wheel drums
**Bodywork:** two or four-seat tourer
**Maximum speed (approx):** 90 mph (145 kph)

the range in 1911; two years later a four-speed gearbox replaced the old three-speed unit.

During the Great War, Straker-Squire built Rolls-Royce Eagle aero-engines under licence, and followed the general lines of this power unit – which was separately cast, with fixed-head cylinders and an overhead camshaft – in the power unit for the post-war sporting model, which appeared as a prototype in 1918. This car was subsequently fitted with an airship-tailed racing body and its

engine tuned to develop 115 bhp, which enabled it to lap Brooklands at 104 mph.

Manufacture had by now shifted to Edmonton, North London, but this 24/80 hp Straker-Squire 'Aeroplane of the Road' didn't actually go into production until 1921, so that the old 15 hp model had to be revived as a stop-gap, though it failed to sell. Nor, too, did the new 24/80 hp Straker-Squire find many buyers, for it was prohibitively expensive at over £1100 in chassis form, £1525 as an open two-seater.

The company then attempted to broaden into the lower-priced field with a 1460 cc Dorman-engined sports model selling at £250 in chassis form; this appeared at the 1923 Motor Show, but it was too late. In July 1924, Straker-Squire went into receivership.

## STUDEBAKER

**South Bend, USA
1902–1964**

The Studebaker family, who emigrated from Holland in 1736, founded their wagon building company in South Bend, Indiana, in 1852, and by 1875 could boast that they were the 'largest vehicle house in the world', their prosperity fuelled by settlers heading west in Studebaker-built covered wagons. By the 1890s, the Studebaker Brothers, Manufacturing Company was producing 75,000 horse-drawn vehicles a year. At the turn of the century, budding automotive tycoons placed orders for automobile chassis with Studebaker, which inspired their legal counsel, Frederick Fish (son-in-law of John Studebaker), to develop the company's automotive activities in parallel with their profitable wagon-building activities (which continued until 1921).

The first automobiles to bear the Studebaker name were 20 Studebaker electrics constructed in 1902. The company's first petrol cars, built in conjunction with the Garford firm of Elyria, Ohio, appeared in 1904, initially as flat-twin runabouts and, from 1905, in four-cylinder form.

Cheaper models built for Studebaker by the Everitt-Metzger-flanders company of Detroit, and marketed as EMF or Flanders, appeared in 1908. Studebaker merged with EMF in 1910 to create the Studebaker Corporation, and the Garford, EMF and Flanders models were all phased out by 1912.

Studebaker launched a new two-car range in 1914 with a 3146 cc four and 4736 cc six, with three-speed transmissions in unit

with the back axle; under the inspired presidency of Albert Erskine, the four was replaced by a new 3392 cc Light Six designed by the new chief engineer, Fred M. Zeder, in 1920. A Big Six of 5810 cc was also available alongside the old Special Six.

By 1925, the company was building some 108,000 cars a year, though it had fallen from third place in the industry in 1912 to eighth.

The company launched a new low-cost line, the Erskine, for 1927, and in 1928 Studebaker bought the financially troubled Pierce-Arrow company.

Studebaker's new chief engineer, 'Barney' Roos, launched an excellent straight-eight named the President in 1928, when the sixes were pretentiously renamed Dictator and Commander; the Dictator and Commander acquired eight-cylinder engines in 1929. The 1930 Studebaker eights all had nine-main-bearing power units.

In 1932, sales plunged to 36,242 units, and Studebaker declared bankruptcy. The receivers sold off Pierce-Arrow, dropped the eight-cylinder President and brought out new six-cylinder Studebakers fitted with the power units formerly used in the discontinued Rockne range. By 1935, Studebaker was back in business, with Paul Hoffmann and Harold Vance (lately with the receivers) as president.

The company hired Raymond Loewy as styling consultant in 1936, with the aim of making Studebaker's products more distinctive. With Europe visibly

moving ever nearer a state of war, the Dictator model designation was becoming increasingly embarrassing, and was dropped in 1938. A new small six, the 2687 cc Champion, was launched for the 1939 model year, firmly establishing Studebaker as a maker of – by American standards – small cars and spurring sales in both 1940 and 1941 past the 100,000 mark.

During the war, Studebaker built trucks, aeroengines and Weasel personnel carriers, and after the Armistice became one of the first companies to launch brand-new post-war models, which appeared in May 1946.

Their controversial styling, in which the front wings flowed smoothly into the bodywork, with a low-set full-width grille, earned the post-war Champion, Commander and LandCruiser sixes, powered by either 2786 cc or 3704 cc side-valve engines, the epithet 'coming or going?' Playing a key role alongside Loewy in the look of the new models was Virgil Exner, subsequently poached by Chrysler to revitalise their image.

For 1950, the Studebaker range was given a nose which resembled an aeroplane spinner, plus an automatic transmission with direct drive in the highest ratio and coil spring independent front suspension. The new model boosted Studebaker sales to their highest-ever level, 268,229 units.

Studebaker launched its first V8, a short-stroke high-compression overhead valve unit of 3802 cc, in 1951, the last year that Studebaker used the spinner nose. Two years later, Studebaker launched new coupé, two- and four-door sedan and station wagon models, with exemplary styling by Robert E. Bourke, chief designer of the Loewy studios. There were production problems, however, and Studebaker's market share plummeted, the company got into financial difficulties, and in 1954 Packard took over.

Packard's president, Jim Nance, the hot-shot ex-white-goods salesman, had the idea of creating a complete dual-dealership empire for the high-price Packard and the popular Studebaker, but Studebaker proved to be a millstone that dragged Packard down.

The classic styling of the 1953 Studebakers was impaired by chromium plate and a wraparound windscreen in 1955, then in 1956 the Loewy studios neatly re-skinned the existing body to produce the Flight Hawk (3032 cc six), Power Hawk (3671 cc V8), Sky Hawk (4244 cc V8) and Golden Hawk (5768 cc Packard V8).

But nevertheless, sales continued to plummet, and the launch of the Studebaker Scotsman, a new economy model powered by the old side-valve six, failed to halt the decline.

Studebaker-Packard signed a management agreement with the Curtiss-Wright aircraft company in 1956, who sold off Packard's plant and proving ground and concentrated production at Studebaker's South Bend factory as a prelude to the demise of Packard in 1958.

For Studebaker, there was a disastrous facelift that year, in which dual headlamps and tailfins were grafted-on. Then the advent in 1959 alongside the 4736 cc Silver Hawk V8 of the compact Studebaker Lark (readied for production by stylist Duncan McRae in a remarkable ten months) at last managed to reverse the sales trend, and sales doubled to 133,382 units. It was a false dawn; from then on it was downhill all the way.

Studebaker offered a wider Lark range styled by Brooks Stevens for 1962, then, mid-way through the year, the distinctive glassfibre-bodied Avanti sport coupé designed by Raymond Loewy was announced.

It was powered by a 4736 cc V8, with an optional supercharger (a blown Avanti took 29 stock car records) but the Avanti was slow to get into production because of difficulties in building the radical glass-fibre bodyshell. Alongside this problem, the sliding roof the the 1963 Wagonaire estate car developed an embarrassing tendency to leak.

Byers Burlingame, elected president in November 1963, decided that the time had come to diversify out of motor manufacturing. Production was transferred to Canada in 1964, where Studebaker struggled along spasmodically, building Chevrolet-engined cars until 1966, though in 1965 the Avanti managed to leave the sinking colossus and start a separate existence.

## Studebaker Commander

In terms of car equipment, the Studebaker Commander launched at the end of 1938 represented a major breakthrough, for it combined the first air-conditioning system available on a mass-produced car with a windscreen defroster and an automatically engaged overdrive. It also reintroduced the steering column gearchange, a space-saving feature not seen since the early days of motoring.

The car also dispensed with the transmission tunnel, boasting 'no humps or wells to impede you – plenty of room for three – front and rear.'

Another aid to driver comfort was a 'hill-holder' to stop the Com-

mander from rolling back on hills, while rotary catches were fitted to the doors so that they could be shut with only a light pressure. The automatic overdrive was a notable advance on similar systems tried on earlier cars, for the geared-up overdrive was automatically engaged when the throttle pedal was briefly lifted at speeds over 34 mph (55 kph) and cut out at speeds under 28 mph (45 kph), though for overtaking direct-drive top could be automatically re-engaged by flooring the throttle, which actuated a solenoid on the transmission. There was also overdrive on second gear, which gave a 70 mph (113 kph) top speed on that ratio. Overdrive could only be engaged when the free-wheel was in operation, which also permitted clutchless gear-changing.

The independent front suspension fitted to the Commander tended towards firmness, in marked contrast to earlier American independent systems, which had tended to induce excessive body roll but allow good ride comfort.

Press reports summarised the Commander as possessing 'performance allied to a highly practical make-up'.

## Studebaker Avanti

At the behest of Studebaker's new president, Sherwood Egbert, Raymond Loewy and his team of designers began work on a new model that, in Egbert's words, 'would give Studebaker renewed recognition and provide the American public with an outstanding new concept of automotive design and engineering.'

Starting from sketches made by Egbert during a flight from Chicago to Los Angeles, Loewy developed an odd-looking wedge-profiled sports coupé which combined performance and safety features in a

---

### 1939 STUDEBAKER COMMANDER

**Engine:** in-line six-cylinder, side valve
**Bore × stroke:** 84.1 mm × 111.1 mm
**Capacity:** 3703 cc
**Maximum power:** 70 bhp
**Transmission:** three-speed manual with overdrive
**Chassis:** X-braced pressed steel
**Suspension:** independent front with transverse leaf springs. Live rear axle with semi-elliptic leaf springs
**Brakes:** drums all round
**Bodywork:** saloon
**Maximum speed (approx):** 80 mph (129 kph)

---

**Studebaker Commander**

**Studebaker Avanti**

## 1982 STUDEBAKER AVANTI

**Engine:** V8, overhead-valve
**Bore × stroke:** 90.4 mm × 91.9 mm
**Capacity:** 4736 cc
**Maximum power:** 200 bhp
**Transmission:** three-speed (optional automatic overdrive)
**Chassis:** box-type ladder frame
**Suspension:** independent front with wishbones and coil springs. Live rear axle with semi-elliptic leaf springs
**Brakes:** discs front, drums rear
**Bodywork:** glassfibre coupé
**Maximum speed (approx):** 130 mph (209 kph)

manner hitherto unknown on an American automobile.

For instance, the Avanti had a padded dashboard, with recessed instruments and several of the minor controls flush-mounted above the windscreen; panel lighting was red, which was said to give the driver's eyes less problems in adjusting at night, and Avanti was claimed to be the first production American car with caliper-operated disc braking. A roll-over bar was built into the glassfibre bodyshell.

While the Avanti was being developed, Studebaker acquired the Paxton Corporation, headed by colourful motor-racing personality Andy Granatelli. Paxton supercharging was made optional on the Avanti, and Granatelli drove a blown Avanti over a measured 2.25 mile (3.6 km) course in 60.8 seconds at an average 133.334 mph (214.66 kph) and a terminal speed of 171 mph (275 .3 kph).

When the collapse of Studebaker seemed inevitable, South Bend

Studebaker dealer Nathan Altman acquired production rights to the Avanti, and began manufacture of the slightly-modified Avanti II in part of the old Studebaker plant.

Though the Avanti Motor Corporation changed hands in 1982, the Avanti is still being built in limited numbers at South Bend, still with the distinctive coke-bottle side profile (an inverse aerodynamic curve formerly seen only on supersonic aircraft) that had been Loewy's styling innovation on the original 1964 model.

## STUTZ
**Indianapolis, USA**
**1911–1935**

Harry C. Stutz had been designing cars for 14 years before the first car to bear his name appeared, starting with a crude gas buggy in 1897. Stutz was responsible for designing the American Underslung of 1907, in which the chassis was hung beneath the axles to give a low centre of gravity, then went into component manufacture, specialising in robust three-speed transaxles. To prove the quality and durability of his gearbox/rear-axle unit, Stutz built a racing car in five weeks, then entered it in the first-ever Indianapolis 500-mile race in 1911.

The Stutz racer, driven by Cal Anderson, finished 11th, earning the marque the title of 'the car that made good in a day', and production of Stutz cars, powered by 6.3-litre Wisconsin engines, began shortly after. Though there was little remarkable about those first Stutz cars, the marque did continue to compete in sporting events like the Indianapolis 500

and the Milwaukee Grand Prix. During the 1913 season, Stutz achieved the remarkable record of seven victories in seven consecutive races, a feat only equalled after World War II by Mercedes-Benz. To consolidate that sporting image, in 1914 Stutz launched its most famous model, the stark Bearcat speedster, which was little more than two seats and a cylindrical fuel tank.

It proved remarkably popular, its sporting potential enhanced by the racing successes of the Stutz

White Squadron team, whose cars were powered by totally non-standard 16-valve overhead camshaft 4851 cc Wisconsin engines; in 1915, the White Squadron drivers Earl Cooper and Gil Anderson were first and third in the National Drivers' Championship after a particularly successful season.

In 1919 Harry Stutz left the company he had founded to build a quality car named the HCS, which copied Hispano-Suiza styling but failed to made the grade.

The Stutz Motor Car Company now came under the control of steel tycoon Charles Schwab, and Stutz began to build their own four- and six-cylinder engines, while the rear-axle/gearbox unit was phased out in favour of a more conventional transmission layout.

Sales were on a downward trend, nevertheless, and in 1925 Frederic E. Moscovics took over Stutz. In an attempt to reverse the falling sales, Moscovics brought in

Belgian designer Paul Bastien, who had formerly worked with Metallurgique. Bastien created a car which exemplified 'safety, beauty and comfort', the overhead-camshaft 4.7-litre Safety Stutz Vertical Eight.

The marque's greatest sporting successes came in 1928, when Frank Lockhart's super-streamlined Stutz Blackhawk achieved 225 mph (362 kph) on only 3.1 litres on one of its record attempts (it was the smallest-ever land speed record car, but regrettably crashed and killed its driver before he could take the record) and a Black Hawk Speedster finished second at Le Mans behind the 4½ litre Bentley of Barnato and Rubin — the best American result until the GT40.

An economy model, the Black Hawk six launched in 1929, was hived off as a separate marque, then in 1931, Stutz revived the traditional Bearcat designation, though the new Bearcat was a very different proposition from its predecessor. Powered by a 32-valve twin-overhead-camshaft DV 32 power unit, it had a guaranteed 100 mph (161 kph) top speed. Car production ceased in 1935, although between 1928 and 1938, Stutz offered a rear-engined light van, the Pak-Age-Car, which also boasted all-round independent suspension. It was not a success, though the Diamond T truck company subsequently bought the production rights.

The Stutz name was revived in the 1970 with a vulgar Virgil Exner-designed Blackhawk coupé with coachwork by Carrozzeria Padana of Modena. It was in similar vein to Exner's Ghia-built Duesenberg, and sold at prices from $22,500 to $75,000; Elvis Presley owned four of them....

# A-Z OF THE CAR

## Stutz Bearcat

The 1914 Stutz Series E range was launched shortly after Gill Anderson had brilliantly won the 300-mile (483 km) Elgin National Trophy race at a record 71.4 mph (114.9 kph). Available with either bi-block four- or six-cylinder power units, the Series E Stutz was available in a choice of four body styles, including 'a racy creation known as the Bearcat' on the four-cylinder chassis.

Making liberal use of aluminium, the Bearcat retained Stutz's gearbox/rear axle unit, though a cone clutch replaced the multi-disc pattern used on earlier models. Dual ignition was standard, and bodywork was merely two bucket seats,

a bolster fuel tank and rakish wings, in a similar idiom to the Bearcat's great rival, the Mercer Raceabout, whose devotees taunted Bearcat drivers with the doggerel jibe: 'You must be nutz to drive a Stutz!' To which the Stutz aficionados retorted: 'There was never a worser car than a Mercer…'.

When one dissatisfied owner took his new Bearcat back to the works to complain that his car was no match for the smaller-engined Mercer Raceabout, the 'dud' car was handed to that indefatigable record-breaker Cannonball Smith, who used it to establish a new trans-America record, taking 11 days 7½ hours for the trip, and on one memorable day covering 592 miles (953 km) in the 24 hours. The car finished the marathon run with no more serious fault than a broken shock-absorber mounting.

The last of the original Bearcats was the 4.7-litre Speedway Six of 1924, though the name was subsequently revived on the marque's last great model, the DV-32 Super Bearcat of the mid '30s.

## Stutz Vertical Eight

Paul Bastien, formerly with Metallurgique in Belgium, designed a remarkable car for Stutz in 1926: an extremely low-built car, the new

Safety Stutz (otherwise known as the AA Vertical Eight) boasted four-wheel hydraulic brakes and wire-mesh safety glass. It had centralised chassis lubrication and a worm-drive rear axle. Originally launched in 4736 cc form, the straight-eight power unit was enlarged to 5277 cc in 1928 and the Black Hawk Speedster added to the range.

In 1928 a Stutz Black Hawk Speedster finished second to the 4½ litre Bentley of Barnato/Rubin (which lost its top gear 90 minutes from the end) in the Le Mans 24-hours race.

---

### 1914 STUTZ BEARCAT

**Engine:** in-line bi-block four-cylinder, side-valve
**Bore × stroke:** 120.1 mm × 139.7 mm
**Capacity:** 6837 cc
**Maximum power:** 60 bhp
**Transmission:** three-speed manual
**Chassis:** pressed steel channel
**Suspension:** non-independent with semi-elliptic leaf springs front. Live rear axle with semi-elliptic springs
**Brakes:** rear wheel only
**Bodywork:** raceabout
**Maximum speed (approx):** 80 mph (130 kph)

---

### 1927 STUTZ VERTICAL EIGHT

**Engine:** in-line eight-cylinder, overhead-cam
**Bore × stroke:** 85.7 mm × 114.3 mm
**Capacity:** 5277 cc
**Maximum power:** 113 bhp
**Transmission:** four-speed manual
**Chassis:** pressed steel channel
**Suspension:** non-independent with semi-elliptic leaf springs
**Brakes:** servo-assisted drums all round
**Bodywork:** tourer, sedan or coupé
**Maximum speed (approx):** 85 mph (137 kph)

---

**Stutz Roadster**

**Stutz Vertical Eight Phaeton**

It was a result which underlined the Stutz boast that 'the car which is safest has the right to be fastest', for had the race continued much longer, the Stutz could well have won, as it finished only 62 miles (100 km) behind the winner. Stutz also ran at Le Mans in 1929–30–31, but never equalled that 1928 performance.

Improvements for 1931 included a 'no-back' device in the transmission so that the car did not run back on hills, and variable servo-assistance for the brakes.

# SUBARU
## Tokyo, Japan
### 1958–

The roots of Subaru go back to 1917, when Chikuhei Nakajima founded an aircraft research laboratory in Ota City; it eventually became the Nakajima Aircraft Company, which supplied fighter aircraft – noted for their manouevrability and long range – and aeroengines to the Japanese Army air force during World War II.

The Nakajima company was reorganised in 1945 as Fuji Sangyo, manufacturing such peacetime produces as scooters, railway rolling stock, bus bodies and internal combustion engines. In 1950, by order of the occupying Allied forces, Fuji Sangyo was split up into 12 smaller companies; five of these nevertheless combined to become Fuji Heavy Industries in 1953, building scooters, railway rolling stock and aircraft power units.

Fuji Heavy Industries launched their first car, the Subaru 360, powered by a rear-mounted twin-cylinder two-stroke engine, in 1958. Early versions of this all-independently-suspended minicar had three-speed transmissions, and four speeds were not introduced until 1969. The Subaru 1000 appeared in 1966, with a sport version following a year later.

Fuji Heavy Industries joined the Nissan group in 1968, in which year they launched their first 'full-size' car, the front-engined, front-wheel-drive 997 cc Subaru FE, again with all-round independent suspension. A 1088 cc version appeared in 1970, and was followed a year later by a 1300 cc model.

Also in 1971, Subaru introduced its Leone series, originally with 1200 cc power, which by 1978 was using 1361 cc and 1595 cc engines. During the mid 1980s, the increasingly complex Leone range has grown to include several four-wheel-drive models with 1800 cc engines, some turbocharged.

The Rex minicar range, which also dates back to the 1970s, has for several years been powered by a low-emission 544 cc four-stroke engine. In its most powerful, turbocharged, form, this engine is used in the Rex Combi Turbo 4WD Sedan, and there are also four-wheel-drive derivatives of this minicar with 31 bhp engines.

Subaru also manufacture the Justy sedan range and a seven-seater 'people-mover', the Domingo; again, there are four-wheel-driven versions of these two vehicles, which are both powered by transversely-mounted three-cylinder 997 cc engines, front-mounted on the Justy, rear-mounted on the Domingo.

The fastest and most powerful show car at the 1985 Tokyo Motor Show was the Subaru F-9X, a bespoilered projectile with gull-wing doors, a vaguely Porsche-like profile and a turbocharged 16-valve 2-litre flat-four engine developing an incredible 360 bhp at 8000 rpm. Its permanent four-wheel-drive system was said to foreshadow production cars with such a transmission.

Also shown at Tokyo in 1985 was the ACX-11 coupé, powered by a brand-new 2.7-litre flat-six engine developing 150 bhp. With permanent four-wheel drive and electro-pneumatic suspension, the ACX-11 was said to be scheduled for volume production.

Further models expected to enter production soon are a 1.8GL coupé and the Justy ECVT, with an electronically-controlled continuously variable transmission.

## 1976 SUBARU 4WD 1600

**Engine:** flat-four, overhead-valve
**Bore × stroke:** 92 mm × 60 mm
**Capacity:** 1595 cc
**Maximum power:** 68 bhp
**Transmission:** four-speed
**Chassis:** integral
**Suspension:** independent with MacPherson struts front and semi-trailing arms with torsion bars rear
**Brakes:** discs front, drums rear
**Bodywork:** estate
**Maximum speed (approx):** 87 mph (140 kph)

## 1985 SUBARU LEONE TURBO

**Engine:** turbocharged flat-four cylinder, overhead-valve
**Bore × stroke:** 92 mm × 67 mm
**Capacity:** 1781 cc
**Maximum power:** 135 bhp
**Transmission:** five-speed four-wheel drive with two-speed transfer box
**Chassis:** integral
**Suspension:** independent with MacPherson struts front, and semi-trailing arms rear
**Brakes:** discs all round
**Bodywork:** four-door sedan
**Maximum speed (approx):** 112 mph (180 kph)

**Subaru 4WD 1600**

**Subaru XT Turbo**

# A-Z OF THE CAR

## SUNBEAM, SUNBEAM-TALBOT

**Wolverhampton/London/Ryton-on-Dunsmore, England
1899–1976**

Alderman John Marston of Wolverhampton started in business manufacturing japanned metal goods, then diversified into bicycle manufacture: the Sunbeam bicycles became famous for their oil-filled chain-cases. In 1899, Sunbeam decided to try their hand at motor manufacture, and built a prototype car with a 4 hp single-cylinder engine and belt drive.

A second prototype, this time with a twin-cylinder engine, was completed in 1901, the year in which the first production Sunbeam went on sale. This was a strange device called the Sunbeam-Mabley, designed by an architect named Mabberley Smith; apart from the single-cylinder 326 cc engine above the front wheel, driving the central axle by belt – the wheels were disposed in diamond formation, allegedly to reduce skidding – the Sunbeam-Mabley looked rather like a perambulating Victorian sociable sofa, and gave the impression that it had escaped from one of its designer's massive half-timbered country houses.

Fortunately, an English motor engineer named Thomas Charles Pullinger arrived in Wolverhampton from Lyon (where he had been designing cars for a local company, Teste & Moret) on a quadricycle he had built himself, and was appointed works manager. Drawing on the friendships he had made in Lyon, Pullinger secured manufacturing rights to a recently-superseded Berliet design, which went into production as a Sunbeam (with, of course, the addition of Sunbeam chain cases) in 1902. Powered by a 2.4-litre four-cylinder engine, this 12 hp Sunbeam was in production between 1902 and 1905, when Pullinger left to join Humber. Six-cylinder engines put in a brief appearance in 1904 and 1907, but the majority of Sunbeam

production at this period was composed – apart from a curious 3.2-litre twin-cylinder 'station cart' – of fours, designed, after Pullinger's departure, by his former assistant, Angus Shaw.

Sunbeam cars really took off in 1909, when the Breton-born designer Louis Coatalen joined the Wolverhampton company from Hillman. Coatalen's first design for Sunbeam was the 14/18 HP, which the Sunbeam board had apparently requested should be a three-cylinder model. Always the individualist, Coatalen ignored them, and when the surprised directors lifted the bonnet of the prototype, one of them was heard to gasp in surprise: 'Oh, Mr Coatalen, it's got *four!*'

'Why, so 'e 'ave!' said Coatalen....

A firm believer in the theory that 'racing improves the breed', Coatalen was soon building experimental racers for Brooklands – the 1910 Nautilus had both an aerodynamic single-seat body and Sunbeam's first overhead valves.

But it was with a mildly-modified version of his production 3016 cc side-valve monobloc 12/16 HP that Coatalen achieved the Sunbeam company's first major racing victory, coming in 1–2–3 in the Coupe de l'Auto race (run concurrently with the Grand Prix) of 1912. Although Coupe de l'Auto replicas were built for private sale, the Sunbeam company's first venture into twin overhead camshafts (on its Peugeot-inspired 1913 racers for the Tourist Trophy and the Grand Prix) had no road-going counterpart. The 12/16 HP model remained in production until 1921; during the Great War, it was built under licence by Rover as a staff car.

Sunbeam amalgamated with Talbot and Darracq in 1920. The old side-valve 16 hp and 24 hp Sunbeam models were redesigned, with overhead-valve engines, in 1922, and a six-cylinder car, the 16/50 HP, was added to the range in 1924.

The company continued its racing programme within the STD organisation, and, driven by H.O.D. Segrave, its double-overhead cam,

Fiat-inspired racer won an outstanding victory in the 1923 French Grand Prix, the first-ever British GP win. Seagrave repeated his success at the following year's San Sebastian event (Divo's Sunbeam had won the 1923 Spanish Grand Prix).

Sunbeam's experience in racing-car construction was reflected in the magnificent twin-overhead camshaft 3-litre six-cylinder announced for 1924; one of the great sporting cars of the decade, the 3-litre Sunbeam was built in small numbers until 1930.

Apart from this delightful car, road-going Sunbeams of the 1920s were conservatively-engineered cars of great quality, a tradition which was maintained into the 1930s with the exception of the 1934 Dawn which carried saloon coachwork too heavy for its 1.6-litre overhead-valve four-cylinder engine and preselector gearbox. More in the Coatalen tradition was the 2.9-litre Speed model of 1933, with a 'crash' gearbox although it was a direct competitor for another STD sports car, the Roesch-designed Talbot 105.

Unfortunately, Sunbeam was dragged down by the collapse of the unwieldy STD combine in 1935, and acquired by the Rootes Group, which seemed not to understand the value of what it had bought. Consequently there were no Sunbeams in 1938, and then in 1939 the name was combined with that of Talbot – which had already been thoroughly debased under Rootes ownership, to create Sunbeam-Talbot. Sunbeam-Talbots were no more than overweight luxury versions of the Hillman Minx

and Humber Snipe and Super Snipe.

Sunbeam-Talbot planned to introduce a new model based on the Hillman 14 for 1940, but it wasn't put into production until after the war, when the pre-war Minx-based Ten also reappeared. More modern derivatives with overhead valves, wraparound windscreens and column gear-change appeared in 1948 as the 80 and 90, although the 80 lasted only to the end of 1950.

The name Sunbeam re-appeared in 1953 with the announcement of the Sunbeam Alpine, a two-seater sporting variant of the Sunbeam-Talbot 90, named to commemorate the 90's success in winning the team prize in the Alpine Rallies of 1948 and 1952. Driving Sunbeam Alpines, Stirling Moss won a Gold Cup and Sheila Van Damm the Coupe des Dames in the 1954 Alpine.

In 1956, the Hillman Minx-

based Sunbeam Rapier was added to the range, initially with a 1.4-litre engine, which was later increased in capacity to 1.5 litres.

The original Alpine was discontinued in 1957, but the name was revived on a two-seater sports version of the Rapier launched for 1960.

The basic Alpine theme was developed through a number of variants, like the Italian-bodied Venezia derived from the Humber Sceptre and the 1964 Tiger, basically an Alpine with a 4.2-litre Ford V8 engine shoe-horned under the bonnet. This was really the last car worthy of the Sunbeam name: all that followed was badge engineering of the most dismal kind. The Sunbeam Stiletto of 1968, for instance, was a fastback coupé version of the Hillman Imp, and the fastback Rapier of the same year had little to offer. An Alpine version of the Rapier was introduced in 1969.

After the acquisition by Peugeot of Chrysler's European interests, the Sunbeam name was used on a hatchback Talbot series with overhead-valve aluminium engines of 928 cc, 1295 cc and 1598 cc launched in 1977. These new Sunbeams went against the fashionable front-wheel drive trend by using the front engine/rear drive layout.

A sporting derivative of this model line confused the issue still further, for it was marketed as the Talbot Sunbeam Lotus in recognition of Lotus's role in developing its 150 bhp 2172 cc overhead cam power unit. By 1982, Peugeot had discontinued the Sunbeam name, although the Alpine designation reappeared – one suspects, without any knowledge of its origins... it certainly lacked sporting pretensions.

## Sunbeam 12/16 HP

The effect of Louis Coatalen on Sunbeam was quite remarkable: from being a not-very-successful maker of cars of obsolescent design, within four years the Wolverhampton company had gained an international reputation and its profits had risen accordingly. In 1909, Sunbeam recorded a profit of just £90; four years later, the company's profits had risen a thousandfold.

That success was largely due to the 12/16, launched late in 1909; introduced with a pair-cast T-head engine, the 12/16 gained an L-head monobloc cylinder casting in 1912, when the stroke was lengthened to give a swept volume of just over 3 litres. In this form the Sunbeam was a most effective touring car, and its hidden strength was revealed in 1911, when racing cars derived from the 12/16 were entered for the Coupe de l'Auto race. These were based closely on the production

# Sunbeam 3 Litre

In 1922, Louis Coatalen, managing director of Sunbeam, decided to put the company's racing experience into a road car, and work began on the design of a twin-cam 3-litre sports model.

Sketched out in Paris by Vincent Bertarione (also responsible for the twin-cam 1923 Grand Prix Sunbeams), the design for the twin-cam six-cylinder 3-litre Sunbeam arrived at Wolverhampton for approval in late 1923. In May 1924, a prototype with integral cylinder block and timing chest plus a curious skew gear camshaft drive, appeared, but immediately vanished... .

When the 3-litre engine reappeared in March the following year, the camshaft was driven by helical spur gears.

'Capable of a road speed of over 90 mph completely equipped and with hood erected, the new three-

**Sunbeam 12/16 HP**

### 1925 SUNBEAM 3 LITRE

**Engine:** in-line six-cylinder, twin-cam
**Bore × stroke:** 75 mm × 110 mm
**Capacity:** 2916 cc
**Maximum power:** 90 bhp
**Transmission:** four-speed manual
**Chassis:** pressed steel channel
**Suspension:** non-independent with semi-elliptic leaf springs front and cantilever rear
**Brakes:** drums all round, servo assisted
**Bodywork:** tourer or fabric saloon
**Maximum speed (approx):** 95 mph (153 kph)

sports cars. The 1913 Coupe de l'Auto Sunbeams were more powerful (87 bhp) but less successful, taking third place.

During the Great War, the Sunbeam 12/16 was chosen as one of the standardised staff cars along with the D-Type Vauxhall and 25/30 Crossley, but, since Sunbeam was so busy producing aeroengines and other war material, the model was built under licence by Rover. Sunbeam reintroduced the 12/16 after the Armistice, and it was produced until 1921, little modified save for electric starting and the semi-elliptic rear suspension first seen on the Coupe de l'Auto Sunbeams. It was replaced by an overhead-valve derivative, the 16/40, for 1922; there were also a few sports versions of the 16/40, with overhead camshafts.

model, except for a 1 mm reduction in stroke to bring them within the Coupe de l'Auto capacity limits, and the replacement of the standard worm-drive rear axle by bevel drive, in anticipation of the 1912 modifications. Coatalen's further achievements included oil pump location in the sump, light 'slipper' pistons and the use of shock absorbers.

A more polished design, again closely based on the production model, and with the same cylinder dimensions as the 1911 racer, won the 1912 Coupe de l'Auto, and was also third in the French Grand Prix, which was run concurrently.

The 1912 Coupe de l'Auto Sunbeam developed 74 bhp at 2600 rpm, and its success led to the production of a limited series of replicas, marketed as Sunbeam's first

**Sunbeam 3 Litre**

**Sunbeam Alpine**

litre Sunbeam is the latest addition to the ranks of ultra-rapid sporting cars,' eulogised *Motor* magazine. 'It is at all times a touring vehicle, and can be driven through traffic on top gear at very low speeds with none of that harshness so often associated with so many so-called "sports" chassis. The engine is modelled on the lines of those used in the 1924 Grand Prix Sunbeams.'

The new model was long and lithe, with close-fitting cycle wings; a tourer body was standard, with a Weymann fabric saloon appearing later.

A 3-litre Sunbeam driven by Jean Chassagne and S.C.H. Davis finished second at Le Mans in 1925 at a creditable 55.97 mph (90.1 kph) on a course like a 'potholed pebble beach'.

Originally, the 3-litre Sunbeam was a 'homologation special' for Le Mans, which required 30 examples of competing cars to have been built, but this 'E Sanction' was followed by an 'F Sanction' 3 litre for 1926, which a strengthened chassis

frame and modified cylinder block; there were also some 25 intermediate 'FE Sanction' cars with the old engine, plus ten F Sanction chassis with E Sanction engines. Probably some 250 cars were built in 1926, though not all were sold that year. The latter sales of 3-litre Sunbeams were small – about ten a year in 1928–29–30 – and the cars were updated before they were sold and even so sales were slow.

In 1929 Sunbeam announced a supercharged version, 'a car of phenomenal performance' with a power output of some 130 bhp. Few were built.

## Sunbeam Alpine

Announced in March 1953, the Sunbeam Alpine two-seater was developed from the Sunbeam-Talbot 90. Originally intended for export only, it marked the first move away from the Sunbeam-Talbot marque name, which was finally dropped in favour of Sunbeam in October 1954.

Because the Sunbeam-Talbot 90

had been built on a separate chassis frame, the change from saloon to tourer was not as traumatic as with a unit-construction car, although an extra cross-member was fitted at the rear of the engine bay, and flitch-plates and box-sections added extra stiffness to the forward part of the chassis.

Other modifications included stiffer front suspension and a thicker anti-roll bar, a close-ratio gearbox, higher-geared steering and a redesigned high-compression cylinder head.

The Sunbeam concern re-entered the world of sports cars with the Sunbeam Alpine, a car produced as the result of the successes of the 90 sports saloon in the Alpine and Monte Carlo rallies. The Alpine was a genuine 100 mph (161 kph) car, and achieved success in the Alpine Rallies of 1953 and 1954. In the latter year, Stirling Moss came third overall and won a Gold Cup (for competing in three successive Alpine Rallies without incurring any penalty points), and Sheila Van

### 1953 SUNBEAM ALPINE

**Engine:** in-line four-cylinder, overhead-valve
**Bore × stroke:** 81 mm × 110 mm
**Capacity:** 2267 cc
**Maximum power:** 80 bhp
**Transmission:** four-speed manual (overdrive optional)
**Chassis:** X-braced separate chassis
**Suspension:** front independent with coil and wishbone, rear non-independent with semi-elliptic leaf springs
**Brakes:** four-wheel hydraulic drums
**Bodywork:** two-seater sports
**Maximum speed (approx):** 105 mph (169 kph)

Damm took the Ladies' Cup.

The original Alpine model was discontinued in October 1955, although the name was revived for 1960 on a new Sunbeam sports.

## MODEL
Rolls-Royce Silver Ghost, 1907
**UK price when announced:** £985
(chassis only)

## ENGINE
**Location:** Front, longitudinal
**Type:** Water cooled straight six, in two groups of three cylinders
**Cubic capacity:** 7046 cc
**Bore × stroke:** 114 mm × 114 mm
**Compression ratio:** 3.2:1
**Valve gear:** One two-jet Royce carburettor
**Ignition:** Coil and magneto, two sparking plugs per cylinder
**Maximum power:** 50 bhp at 1500 rpm

## TRANSMISSION
**Layout:** Clutch and gearbox in unit with engine driving rear wheels
**Clutch:** Four speed manual with reverse

| | |
|---|---|
| 1st 2.83:1 | 3rd 1:1 |
| 2nd 1.66:1 | 4th 0.8:1 |

**Final drive:** Spiral bevel drive
**Ratio:** 2.708:1

## SUSPENSION
**Front:** Forged axle on semi-elliptic leaf springs
**Rear:** Live axle supported on semi-elliptic leaf springs and transverse leaf spring

## STEERING
**Type:** Worm and nut

## BRAKES
**Type:** Rod-operated drums at rear

## WHEELS AND TYRES
**Type:** Wooden spoked, with 875 mm × 105 mm tyres at the front, 880 mm × 120 mm tyres at the rear

## BODY/CHASSIS
**Type:** Ladder type U-section steel chassis with six cross members. Special Roi-des Belges touring style body built by Barker & Co.

## DIMENSIONS AND WEIGHT
**Length:** 180 in (457 cm)
**Width:** 62.5 in (159 cm)
**Wheelbase:** 132.5 in (344 cm)
**Track – front** 56 in (142 cm)
— **rear** 56 in (142 cm)
**Weight:** 3685 lb (1671 kg)

## PERFORMANCE
**Maximum speed:** 55 mph (88.5 kph)
**Acceleration 0–60 mph:** not known
**Fuel consumption:** 20.8 mpg

The bare bones of the original Silver Ghost. The six-cylinder side-valve engine was made up of two, three-cylinder monobloc units. Note the rear suspension which featured a transverse leaf spring along with the more conventional longitudinal semi-elliptic leaf springs. The high armchair-style seats were the distinctive feature of Roi-des-Belges coachwork

# A-Z OF THE CAR

## Sunbeam Tiger

The Alpine name was revived in 1960 for a new, integral-construction two-seat Sunbeam sports car with a 1494 cc engine developing 78 bhp; this gave a top speed of over 98 mph (158 kph).

In 1964, a more potent variant of the Alpine appeared, with a 4.2-litre Ford V8 engine shoehorned in – it was a fairly tight fit! – and various modifications to enable the extra power to be used safely. Externally, only a chrome strip along each side (incorporating Tiger scripts) gave the game away.

The Tiger had the effortless performance associated with big American power units, combining the ability to accelerate from 0–60 mph (97 kph) in 9.4 seconds with the potential of accelerating from a standstill to 90 mph (145 kph) using third gear only.

Given that the rear suspension layout was as basic as could be – a leaf-sprung axle devoid of additional location – the Tiger was credited with 'outstanding' roadholding. 'On good roads the throttle can really be used to advantage in a completely controllable fashion, be the surface wet or dry, either to provoke the tail for amusement or to generate the ultimate cornering power,' commented *The Motor*. 'On bad roads, the ride gets choppy, the steering kicks and the body shakes, but it still holds the road and goes where you point it.'

The choice of the Ford engine was particularly odd considering that Chrysler had just taken their first financial interest in Rootes. The Tiger was produced until 1967, the last 600 or so being MkIIs with the more powerful 4.7-litre Ford V8 as used in the Mustang and AC Cobra.

### 1964 SUNBEAM TIGER

**Engine:** V8, overhead-valve
**Bore × stroke:** 96.5 mm × 73 mm
**Capacity:** 4261 cc
**Maximum power:** 141 bhp
**Transmission:** four-speed manual
**Chassis:** integral
**Suspension:** front independent with coil and wishbone, live rear axle with semi-elliptic leaf springs
**Brakes:** front-wheel discs, rear-wheel drums
**Bodywork:** two-seat sports with transverse occasional third seat
**Maximum speed (approx):** 118 mph (189 kph)

## SUZUKI
### Hamamatsu, Japan
### 1955–

This famous motorcycle firm, founded as a textile company with the name of Suzuki Shokkuki Seisakusho in 1909, built its first two-seater in 1936 but did not enter the car field until 1955 with the Suzulite 360 utility car. This was a front-wheel-drive model with a twin-cylinder engine.

The front-wheel-drive Fronte 360, derived from the Suzulite, appeared in 1967, followed a year later by a larger model, the Fronte 500.

The Fronte 800 was a saloon model powered by a three-cylinder two-stroke engine. By the late 1970s, Suzuki was offering the Jimny, a light (539 cc, three-cylinder) four-wheel-driven utility model as well as an updated version of the Fronte.

By the mid-1980s, the range had been swollen by the addition of the Cervo 543 cc three-cylinder, front-wheel-drive hatchback coupé, the Alto sedan (also a 543 cc front-wheel-drive model, of which there was a four-wheel-drive version) and the 993 cc three-cylinder Cultus. Of the longer-established models, the Fronte range offered four-stroke power units of 543 cc or 796 cc, while the 4WD Jimny series had a choice of a 539 cc three-cylinder two-stroke or a four-cylinder four-stroke engine of 970 cc.

For 1985, there was a 40 bhp turbocharged version of the Cultus, a 1324 cc version of the Jimny and two new variants of the Cultus, a turbocharged 993 cc three-cylinder capable of 99 mph (159 kph), and a naturally-aspirated 1324 cc four-cylinder model.

*Sunbeam Tiger Mk I*

**Suzuki SJ40**

### 1979 SUZUKI SJ40

**Engine:** in-line four-cylinder, overhead-cam
**Bore × stroke:** 65.5 mm × 72 mm
**Capacity:** 970 cc
**Maximum power:** 52 bhp
**Transmission:** four-speed manual with high/low transfer box. four-wheel drive
**Chassis:** ladder frame
**Suspension:** non-independent with rigid axles and semi-elliptic leaf springs
**Brakes:** drum
**Bodywork:** two-door jeep
**Maximum speed (approx):** 60 mph (97 kph)

### 1985 SUZUKI CULTUS TURBO

**Engine:** transverse three-cylinder, turbocharged
**Bore × stroke:** 74 mm × 77 mm
**Capacity:** 993 cc
**Maximum power:** 80 bhp
**Transmission:** five-speed, front-wheel drive
**Chassis:** integral
**Suspension:** front independent with MacPherson struts, rear rigid axle with semi-elliptic leaf springs
**Brakes:** servo-assisted discs/drums all round
**Bodywork:** two-door hatchback
**Maximum speed (approx):** 99 mph (159 kph)

At the 1985 Tokyo Show, Suzuki revealed two midget sports cars, the Targa-roofed R/P2 powered by a 100 bhp turbocharged 800 cc double-overhead-cam 12-valve three-cylinder engine and the 16-valve R/S1, which offered 130 bhp from its double-overhead-cam four-cylinder power unit. While claiming that this aerodynamic mid-engined open two-seater 'gave its rider the feeling of one-ness similar to a motorcylcle', Suzuki denied that it planned to put either the R/S1 or the R/P2 into immediate production, but they were obvious signs of things to come.

### SWALLOW DORETTI

**Walsall, England
1954–1955**

Built by the Swallow Coachbuilding Company (1935) Ltd, a descendant of Swallow Sidecars (parent of SS, and hence Jaguar, cars), this sports car used the engine and drive-train of the recently-announced Triumph TR2 in a tubular chassis strengthened by welded-on steel pressings carrying outriggers. On these were mounted two plates which – apart from the door apertures – ran the entire length of the car and to which the outer panels of the elegant two-seat body were fitted.

The Swallow Doretti was designed specifically to meet the perceived demand for two-seat sports cars that existed in America and which had been so successfully tapped by the MG T-Series cars. Unfortunately, however, the Swallow Doretti failed to find the same degree of success, and was in production for only two years. Most Swallow Dorettis were open two-seaters, although one hardtop GT coupé was built.

**Suzuki Cultus**

**Swallow Doretti**

### 1954 SWALLOW DORETTI

**Engine:** in-line four-cylinder, overhead valve
**Bore × stroke:** 83 mm × 92 mm
**Capacity:** 1991 cc
**Maximum power:** 90 bhp
**Transmission:** four-speed plus overdrive
**Chassis:** tubular with pressed steel reinforcements
**Suspension:** front independent with coil and wishbone, rear semi-elliptic leaf springs and torque rods
**Brakes:** hydraulic drums all round
**Bodywork:** two-seat sports
**Maximum speed (approx):** 101 mph (163 kph)

## SWIFT
### Coventry, England
### 1900-1931

In 1869, the European Sewing Machine Company (makers of Swiftsure sewing machines) diversified into bicycles, building Britain's first 'boneshaker' velocipedes. To cover its new activity, the company changed its name to the Coventry Machinists' Company, and in 1870 built the very first high-wheeled 'ordinary' (or penny farthing) bicycle to the design of James Starley, 'father of the cycle industry'.

But although Swift Cycles became one of the leading names in the bicycle industry, the company did not go into the car business until 1902, when it produced an unlovely device powered by an MMC-built De Dion Bouton engine. With a distinctly novel transmission – dual pinions and two sets of teeth on the crown wheel, the ratios selected by dog-clutches – this 4.5 hp voiturette was started by inserting the starting handle into a hole on the (unsprung) rear axle.

In 1904 a Swift-designed voiturette of more conventional design was announced, although it still had the 4.5 hp De Dion engine. Subsequently, three- and four-cylinder models were added to the range – some with proprietary engines by Simms and Aster – but the 1906 10 hp was significant in being the company's first model to have a Swift-designed engine. In addition, a 7 hp single was announced in 1909 and also marketed by Austin. The twin-cylinder 10 hp unit was followed by a four-cylinder 10/12 hp car, which appeared in 1912.

In 1913, Swift launched a vertical-twin cyclecar of 972 cc; at that time the range consisted of the 1327 cc 10 hp, the 1795 cc 12 hp, the 1945 cc 14 hp, the 2614 cc 15.9 hp and the 3054 cc 20 hp.

These were all swept away, save for the 12 hp, after the Great War, when the Swift company became embroiled in the ill-fated Harper Bean combine.

At the 1919 Motor Show, the 12 hp was joined by an updated version of the pre-war Ten, and a new Twelve appeared in 1920. The Ten was modernised in 1923, gaining a detachable cylinder head and unit construction of engine and gearbox. The Twelve was subsequently modified in similar fashion. A new 17.9 hp 18/50 hp arrived in 1925, while the 10 hp and the 12/35 hp acquired four-wheel brakes in 1926. The following year, the 12 hp Swift was uprated to 14/40 hp, although its mechanical specification stayed the same.

A modern version of the Ten appeared in 1930, with a four-speed gearbox and 'ribbon'

radiator, but could not be produced in large enough numbers to compete with the similar offerings from Morris and Austin. For 1931, Swift offered the cheap 8 hp Cadet, 'the Aristocrat of the Small Car World', but it was overpriced in comparison with its rivals like the Austin Seven and Morris Minor.

## Swift 7 HP Cyclecar

'The one thing that was necessary to complete Motor History' was launched by Swift at the 1912 Motor Cycle and Cyclecar Exhibition. It was to succeed the 7 hp single-cylinder model that the company had also sold to Austin, who marketed it as the 'Seven', the first time that this famous designation had appeared.

The chassis of the new Swift 7 hp reflected the company's cycle-building experience, for it was tubular, carrying the crossmembers on lugs. It was simple to make but, unfortunately, was not very strong (one surviving Swift cyclecar has been fitted with a secondary chassis to stop the car from folding in the middle); in 1914 a more substantial pressed steel chassis was fitted.

The three-speed and reverse gearbox and bevel-drive back axle were a surprise on a cheap cyclecar – the breed usually got by with some kind of dog-and-chain transmission.

Another noteworthy feature of the chassis was its rack-and-pinion steering, which was one step up from the crude wire-and-bobbin steering fitted to so many cyclecars. The 7 hp was not reintroduced after the War – and Motor History seemed to manage quite well without it… .

### 1913 SWIFT 7 HP CYCLECAR

**Engine:** vertical twin-cylinder, side-valve
**Bore × stroke:** 75 mm × 110 mm
**Capacity:** 972 cc
**Maximum power:** 7 bhp
**Transmission:** three-speed manual
**Chassis:** tubular
**Suspension:** non-independent with semi-elliptic leaf springs front and rear
**Brakes:** rear-wheel drums
**Bodywork:** two-seater sports
**Maximum speed (approx):** 35 mph (56 kph)

**Swift 7 HP**

# A-Z OF THE CAR

## Swift 10 HP

The roots of the Swift Ten went back a long way: its monobloc engine had been designed by W. Radford in 1919, although it didn't gain a detachable head until 1923. This car represented Swift's attempt to compete with the big battalions, although with Morris production running at some 60,000 a year and Swift making just 1800 or so cars annually, it was apparent that the little Coventry firm was struggling.

Nevertheless, the Ten underwent periodic updates: the 1923 redesign also brought a reduction in capacity from 1122 cc to 1097 cc, and the substitution of coil ignition for magneto. That move doesn't seem to have been popular, for in 1925 the magneto reappeared, along with a longer wheelbase better suited to four-seater bodywork.

In 1927, the P-Type Ten appeared, with the engine capacity uprated to 1190 cc. In 1928, Swift offered the novel Ten Migrant, with two sunshine roofs, one over each pair of seats.

The 'sturdy Ten' was the backbone of Swift production, and in 1929 it represented the peak of Swift's traditional approach, with fixed starting handle, nickel plating and traditional radiator, all 'quality'

### 1927 SWIFT TEN

**Engine:** in-line four-cylinder, side-valve
**Bore × stroke:** 62.5 mm × 97 mm
**Capacity:** 1190 cc
**Maximum power:** 22 bhp
**Transmission:** three-speed manual
**Chassis:** pressed steel channel
**Suspension:** non-independent with semi-elliptic leaf springs front and rear
**Brakes:** drums all round
**Bodywork:** tourer or saloon
**Maximum speed (approx):** 50 mph (80 kph)

features that were regarded by the company's rivals as being somewhat old fashioned, although the adoption of a four-speed gearbox instead of the traditional three-speed transmission was a welcome improvement.

The late 1929 redesign created the 1930 4P series with its Chrysler-like 'ribbon' radiator and chromium plating. It did not last beyond 1931.

## TALBOT
### London/Coventry, England
### 1903–1938, 1979 to date

In October 1902, a company was incorporated to build the French Clément car in London; since the company was financed by the Earl of Shrewsbury and Talbot, its products were initially known as Clément-Talbots. Indeed, until November 1904, the company merely imported cars from France and endowed them with the Earl's family crest, the Talbot (a hunting hound) and Cap of Maintenance. A magnificent new factory was erected on a five-acre site in Ladbroke Grove, North Kensington, which initially began by assembling cars from parts sent over by Clément (whose products were now known as Clément-Bayards).

However, the French connection was gradually dropped and the Talbot slowly emerged as a marque in its own right.

'The Great National Firm' offered a wide variety of models; in 1905 there were four twin-cylinder Talbots, of 7/8, 8/9, 9/11 and 10/

12 hp, and five four-cylinder models from 12/14 hp to an impressive 35/50 hp model displacing 6.3 litres.

The year 1906 saw the first truly British Talbot, a 3.8-litre 20/24 hp car designed by works manager C.R. Garrard, who had worked in France with Adolphe Clément since 1888; he had also designed the factory in Ladbroke Grove. The 20/24 was soon joined by a 2.7-litre 12/16 hp: both models were notable performers in speed trials and established a sound reputation.

A third Garrard design appeared at the end of 1906; this was a 3-litre 15 hp with dual ignition.

The marque had already earned the soubriquet of 'the Invincible Talbot'; in 1911 the company acquired a new chief designer, G.W.A. Brown, formerly with Austin, where he had designed a remarkable series of Pearley racing cars for the Brooklands driver Percy Lambert. George Brown applied his skill at extracting maximum performance from side valve power units to the 25 hp Talbot, a 4531 cc development of a power unit originally launched (in 4156 cc form) in 1908. In 1913, a streamlined 25 HP driven by Lambert became the first car in the world to cover over 100 miles in an hour.

By 1914 the range also included a six-cylinder model. In 1916 Talbot acquired a quite exceptional chief engineer named Georges Roesch, a Swiss engineer who had previously worked with Grégoire, Delaunay-Belleville and Renault in Paris and Daimler in Coventry.

Roesch was commissioned to design a light car for post-war production, and created the A12, an advanced 1750 cc car which never passed the prototype stage, for at that point Clement Talbot Ltd was taken over by Darracq, and the A12 project was dropped.

The reason for the sale of Clement Talbot to Darracq was basically that the Earl of Shrewsbury & Talbot had lost interest in the business after his only son had been killed in World War I. Hard on the heels of this takeover came a merger with Sunbeam of Wolverhampton, and

**Swift Ten Swallow**

the fortunes of Georges Roesch were embroiled in those of the complex Sunbeam-Talbot-Darracq combine. Initially, he was involved in the design of an advanced 30 cwt lorry to meet a potential War Office order which unexpectedly evaporated. He then redesigned the two-seater overhead-valve 8/18 hp Talbot imported from Talbot-Darracq in Paris into the 10/23, which appeared in 1923. This 1074 cc light car was a full four-seater, which was soon joined by the six-cylinder 12/30 hp model, also designed in Paris, but sadly deficient in power and performance.

Roesch was sent to Sunbeam in Wolverhampton for a brief period, then to Darracq in Paris. During this period, in which the fortunes of Talbot declined as part of the general malaise which pervaded the confused STD combine, Roesch formulated valuable theories on the design of efficient combustion chambers and valve gear. These theories matured on Roesch's return to Ladbroke Grove into the refined and well-engineered six-cylinder 1666 cc 14/45, with significantly light pushrod valve gear. Introduced in 1926, the 14/45 Talbot became the company's sole model for 1928–29, and was then

joined by a new, higher-performance derivative, the 70, for 1930. The 70 – so-called because that was its target speed in miles per hour – was quickly renamed the 75, since it was easily capable of greater performance than anticipated, while a sports-racing derivative was known as the 90.

In 1931, the 105 appeared, powered by a new 140 bhp 3-litre six-cylinder engine and it remained in production until 1937. The ultimate development of the Roesch six-cylinder theme came with the 110 of 1935; its cylinders had larger bores than those of the 105, increasing the swept volume to 3.5 litres.

But Talbot was dragged down in the convoluted finances of the STD combine, and when a £500,000 note fell due in September 1934, the finances to meet it were lacking. Consequently, the Rootes Group took control of Clement Talbot in 1935, and proceeded to debase the company's products, for Rootes' concern was with sales, rather than engineering, and the intelligently created cars of Georges Roesch were continued only as long as it took to use up the existing stock of components.

In 1936 Rootes launched the Talbot Ten, an 'airline' sports

saloon based on the depressing side-valve Hillman Minx, and added an equally dismal Talbot 3 litre derived from the Hillman Hawk the following year. Barely capable of reaching 80 mph (129 kph), the 3-litre Talbot was a sad swansong for the marque, for in 1938 it was renamed Sunbeam-Talbot.

In 1979 Peugeot-Citroën, which had acquired the emasculated remnants of the old STD combine from Chrysler, announced that it would use the Talbot name on all its European 'ex-Chrysler' products. By the end of 1985, though, the revived marque was being phased out in England – the company changed its name to Peugeot Talbot, since Peugeot was felt to be 'more emotive' – and the new small Peugeot 309 (replacement for the Talbot Horizon) was being built in Talbot's Coventry factory. Surviving Talbot UK models included the Solara, of which the later models were known as the Rapier and the Minx – names dredged from Rootes' past but never previously associated with the Talbot marque. The only truly new Talbot model was the Samba minicar which was being built at Poissy at the beginning of the eighties with engines of 954 cc, 1124 cc, 1219 cc and 1360 cc – the 1219 cc being the sporting model.

## Talbot 25 HP

When it was originally launched in 1908, the 25 HP was Talbot's first L-head design, though it took the skill of G.W.A. Brown to unleash the full potential of the engine, enlarged from 4156 cc to 4531 cc for 1910.

Brown succeeded in doubling the power unit of the 25 hp engine, and to demonstrate the potential of this unit Talbot built two special streamlined racing single-seaters, one for Percy Lambert, the other for Leslie Hands.

Lambert achieved the most with this remarkable design, initially establishing staggering Brooklands records for the half mile, mile and lap of 113.28, 111.73 and 109.43 mph respectively (182.4, 179.88 and 176.18 kph).

Commented the *Badminton Magazine*: 'Racing is the one and only training school for the development and perfection of the touring car. The man who can make the fastest car is the man who can make the best car, and as far as the invincible Talbot is concerned – well, there are the figures.'

In February 1913, Lambert became the first man ever to cover a hundred miles inside an hour, then, having lost the record to racing cars of greater capacity than his, he fitted a 4.75-litre engine to the car. Lapping at around 110 mph (177 kph) in October 1913, Lambert's car went out of control and crashed, killing its driver.

Five days later he was buried in Brompton Cemetery in a coffin which was streamlined to match his car. His grave was aptly marked by a headstone in the shape of a broken wheel.

The remains of his car were incorporated in a post-war racer by G.A. Vandervell (who was later to achieve fame as the head of Vandervell bearings and the builder of the racing Vanwall car), while Hands's car was bought by Malcolm Campbell.

The success of these two cars was all the more remarkable for the fact that they were basically touring chassis.

**Talbot 25/50 HP**

> ### 1910 TALBOT 50 HP
>
> **Engine:** in-line four-cylinder, overhead-valve
> **Bore × stroke:** 101.5 mm × 140 mm
> **Capacity:** 4531 cc
> **Maximum power:** 50 bhp
> **Transmission:** four-speed manual
> **Chassis:** pressed steel channel
> **Suspension:** non-independent with semi-elliptic leaf springs
> **Brakes:** rear wheel drums and transmission brake
> **Bodywork:** torpedo or landaulet
> **Maximum speed (approx):** 70 mph (112 kph)

# Talbot 14/45 HP

Although it only cost £20 more than the little 10/23 Talbot, the 14/45 Talbot launched in 1926 was a remarkably refined four-seater, which used many of the basic features of the over-priced Paris-designed 12/30 in conjunction with the brilliant ideas of Georges Roesch.

During the development of the new model, Roesch researched every available grade of steel, and had a chart drawn up which related each variety of steel to its potential use in a car. The most brilliant fruit of this research was the overhead valve gear of the 14/45, which employed ultra-thin pushrods — manufactured by a firm of knitting needle manufacturers in Redditch — acting on light rockers pivoting on an overhead knife edge. It was at once simple, light and efficient, and the clearances could be adjusted by just loosening one locking bolt. With a bore just 1 mm greater than the 12/30, the 14/45 fell in the same fiscal tax band, yet developed half as much power again, and could turn at 4500 rpm against 3000.

**Talbot 90**

### 1926 TALBOT 14/45 HP

**Engine:** in-line six-cylinder, overhead-valve
**Bore × stroke:** 61 mm × 95 mm
**Capacity:** 1666 cc
**Maximum power:** 45 bhp
**Transmission:** four-speed manual
**Chassis:** X-braced pressed steel channel
**Suspension:** non-independent with semi-elliptic leaf springs front and live rear axle with quarter-elliptics
**Brakes:** drums all round
**Bodywork:** tourer or saloon
**Maximum speed (approx):** 60 mph (96 kph)

Among the many remarkable features of the chassis was the first recorded standard fitment of direction indicators, illuminated arrow signs between the front and rear dumb irons.

Within a few months of the introduction of the new model, production had risen to 50 cars a week, putting the Barlby Road factory on a far sounder economic basis. The 14/45, one of the finest medium-sized tourers of its day, was the basis of all subsequent Roesch-designed Talbots.

# Talbot 90/105 HP

Arthur Fox, of the motor agents Fox & Nicholl, had taken on the agency for Talbot in 1927: a keen advocate of the promotional value of motorsport, Fox had just lost the contract to run the works team for Lagonda when he attended the launch of the new Talbot 70 in February 1930. He immediately saw the potential of the new power unit, and proposed to the works that they would create a special competition model by installing the new 2276 cc engine in the short wheelbase 14/45 Scout

chassis.

A racing programme was agreed upon, and a team of three cars was laid down as a prelude to the production of a new model, which was known as the 90 from its potential top speed. By raising the compression ratio to the unprecedented level of 10:1, Roesch also achieved virtually 90 bhp on the test bench — with utter reliability.

These fast, quiet cars were ready to race in less than two months from the start of the project: but their first race, the 1930 Brooklands Double Twelve, ended disastrously when two of the Talbots collided in the finishing straight, one of them killing its riding mechanic and a spectator.

Before the accident, however, the Talbots had proved themselves capable of outstanding performance, and it was decided to continue the racing programme for the rest of the 1930 season. The decision was vindicated by 3rd and 4th places in the Le Mans 24 Hours in June 1930, followed by class wins at the Irish Grand Prix, the Ulster Tourist Trophy race and the Brooklands 500 Mile event. Production of

### 1930 TALBOT 90

**Engine:** in-line six-cylinder, overhead-valve
**Bore × stroke:** 69.5 mm × 100 mm
**Capacity:** 2276 cc
**Maximum power:** 85 bhp
**Transmission:** four-speed manual
**Chassis:** X-braced pressed steel channel
**Suspension:** non-independent with semi-elliptic leaf springs front and live rear axle with quarter elliptics
**Brakes:** drums all round
**Bodywork:** tourer
**Maximum speed (approx):** 100 mph (161 kph)

the Talbot 90 ended in October 1933.

Meanwhile, in the spring of 1931, Roesch had created the 105, powered by a larger, 2969 cc engine, with an improved cylinder head, and capable of developing 100 bhp. During 1931, the Fox & Nicholl Talbot 105 team cars achieved class wins in the Brooklands Double Twelve, the Irish Grand Prix, Le Mans and the Tourist Trophy.

However, the works association with Fox and Nicholl came to an end at the end of 1932 though this did not prevent a team of 105s from attaining joint victory (with the Adler team) in the 1934 Alpine Rally, which Talbot had also won in 1932.

The versatility of the 105 was demonstrated at the 1932 Scottish Show, when, in order to secure a sale, a Talbot staffman raced an express train back to London, averaging over 53 mph (85 kph) for more than 400 miles (644 km).

Some 325 Talbot 105s were built between 1931 and 1935, then a further 97 105 chassis were assembled from existing parts in 1936–37 after the Rootes takeover, followed by a further 200 cars with modified engines with Humber preselector transmissions and streamline bodies.

**Talbot 14/14 HP**

# A-Z OF THE CAR

## TALBOT (TALBOT-LAGO)

**Suresnes/Poissy, France
1920–1959, 1979 to date**

In October 1919, the old-established Darracq company of Suresnes (which, however, was capitalised in Britain) took over Clement-Talbot of London: as a result, the firm's exhibits at that year's Paris Salon were badged as Talbot-Darracqs. The following June Talbot-Darracq merged with Sunbeam of Wolverhampton, thus creating Sunbeam-Talbot-Darracq Motors; from that point, the Parisian cars were known simply as Talbots, although the firm's racing cars sometimes ran as Talbot-Darracqs (and sometimes as Sunbeams, and occasionally as Talbot Specials).

The 4594 cc V8, launched as a Darracq in 1919, made an easy transposition to the Talbot marque; in 1921 the design was updated by the addition of a detachable cylinder head, but was eventually discontinued in 1923. Meanwhile, in 1922 the company launched the first new models to leave the Suresnes factory since the merger, the 8/18 Talbot-Darracq (a misleading name as this was only a re-radiatored London-built Talbot; Suresnes' contribution was merely a token one) and the overhead-valve 1505 cc four-cylinder 10 HP, which was increased in capacity to 1598 cc the following year. Before long there was also a 2121 cc four. Although the four-cylinder models soldiered on until 1927, they were supplanted that year by the excellent six-cylinder Talbots, available in three versions – 2687 cc and 2916 cc touring models, plus the 3034 cc sports chassis.

The last of the fours, the 1669 cc DD (a development of the old 10CV), was still catalogued in 1928, even though the last chassis had been built in 1927; it had been replaced in production by the six-cylinder M67 11 HP, which scaled 3248 lb (1470 kg), a formidable load for 1999 cc to haul around (which meant that top gear was a

dismal 5.77:1).

In 1930 Talbot catalogued the Pacific 22 hp straight-eight of 3822 cc, though very few were made before the model was discontinued in 1933. A smaller eight, the 3.4-litre Atlantic, lasted until 1935.

By that time, Talbot was running out of impetus; 1935 saw the collapse of the STD combine and the takeover of Suresnes by its former works manager, the brilliant Italian-born engineer Antonio 'Tony' Lago, who modified the existing range while creating two new six-cylinder models of 2.7-litre and 3.0-litres, with X-braced chassis, which made their debut for 1937. Lago also commissioned his chief designer, Becchia, to modify the old Talbot 3-litre six – the cylinder head had cross-over pushrods rather like the BMW six –

**Talbot-Darracq V8**

to create the Talbot-Lago Speciale engine of 4000 cc.

A proposed joint venture with the moribund Invicta company had planned the production of Talbot-based Invictas in London from 1938, but nothing came of it.

After the war, the Talbot-Lago name was upheld by the great racing 4483 cc overhead-valve six-cylinder, originally launched in 1938, but endowed with a new cylinder head, with high-set camshafts and hemispherical combustion chambers à la Riley; this unit also powered the company's Record models, which, with a 170 bhp power output,

were said to be the most powerful production cars in the world. In 1950, Talbot-Lago countered the increasing taxation on larger cars by launching the 2690 cc four-cylinder Baby, only built in right-hand drive form. Lago's swansong came in 1958, with the limited production Lago-America, powered by BMW 2.6-litre engine; the very last of the line had Simca power. In 1979 the Talbot name was resurrected by Peugeot-Citroën, which had just taken over the remains of the company, although the Simca name was also used for the French market.

In 1979 Peugeot-Citroën, which had acquired the remains of the old STD combine from Chrysler, announced that it would use the Talbot name on all its European products, and models like the Horizon small car and the Tagora large saloon range appeared. It seemed, however, that any nostalgic appeal of the old Talbot name had all but vanished. Some Matra models, like the Rancho break and the Murena sports were also badged as Talbots.

There was a crippling strike at Poissy in the early 1980s, which at one stage threatened the future of this ex-Ford plant, and by the end of 1985, Poissy was building the Samba minicar, with engines of 954 cc, 1124 cc, 1219 cc or 1360 cc – the 1219 cc version was the sporting Rallye model – and the Solara, a somewhat characterless 1600 cc saloon car.

The attrition of the marque name was shown when, for 1986,

the new small Peugeot 309 replaced the Talbot Horizon.

## Talbot-Darracq V8

'A masterpiece of up-to-date motor engineering and design', the V8 Talbot originally appeared in 1919 as a Darracq, became a Talbot-Darracq in October that year, and a Talbot in 1920 as the STD combine coalesced. The V8 was designed by Darracq's

Yorkshire-born chief engineer, Owen Clegg, drawing upon his wartime experience of aeroengine design.

Its cylinders were cast in two blocks of four, set at an angle of 90 degrees and a dual-choke Smith four-jet carburettor, made under licence by the Darracq Company, was mounted between the cylinder banks, while the side valves were actuated, through rockers, from a single camshaft. Forked connecting rods ran on a four-throw crankshaft supported in three main bearings. The engine was built in unit with the four-speed gearbox which featured a central gearchange, an unusual feature for a quality car of the period.

With a touring fuel consumption of 15 mpg, the car was reported to have a lively performance, and to

> **1919 TALBOT DARRACQ V8**
>
> **Engine:** V8, side-valve
> **Bore × stroke:** 75 mm × 130 mm
> **Capacity:** 4595 cc
> **Maximum power:** 60 bhp
> **Transmission:** four-speed manual
> **Chassis:** pressed steel channel
> **Suspension:** non independent with semi-elliptic leaf springs front and cantilever leaf springs rear
> **Brakes:** rear wheel drums
> **Bodywork:** tourer
> **Maximum speed (approx):** 70 mph (113 kph)

run without vibration, even at top speed. Production ceased in 1922.

## Talbot-Lago Speciale Sports

The transformation of the French Grand Prix into a sports car event in the mid-1930s gave Tony Lago the excuse he needed to produce a sports racing derivative of his new six-cylinder Talbots. With a 4-litre engine designed by Walter Becchia, in which inclined valves in a hemispherical head were actuated by pushrods from a single camshaft, the Talbot-Lago Speciale sports racer appeared during 1936, clad in similar bodywork to that of the contemporary Delahaye racers.

In standard form, the 4-litre engine developed some 165 bhp, and the racing engines, with a 9.0:1 compression ratio, developed rather more, yet were flexible enough to run on Discol pump fuel on the road (alcohol was added to the fuel for track use). The potential of the new engine was great, even if the cars from Suresnes failed to win in their first season (though Talbots achieved third places in both the Marne and Comminges races, and set the lap record in the first Sports Car GP at Montlhèry).

'Hoodless, screenless and bodied almost to the limit of frugality', the Talbot-Lago Special was intended primarily as a racer, though it was also a road car with few equals.

One of the works cars had a remarkable career, for in 1937 it won the ACF Sports Car GP at Montlhèry, driven by Louis Chiron, and the Donington TT, with Gianfranco Comotti at the wheel, was sold to the British driver A.C. Lace, who drove it, partnered by Ian Connell, in the 1938 TT, finishing fifth. Connell then bought the car from his erstwhile co-driver, and had a remarkably successful racing career with the Talbot-Lago, winning many Brooklands events and coming a close second to Dobson's Delahaye in the "Fastest Road Car" race, and was only once beaten in a sprint, and then only by less than a second on a wet course at Shelsley Walsh.

**Tamplin Cyclecar**

## TAMPLIN

**Staines/Cheam, England
1919–1927**

Before the Great War, Captain Carden had, for want of a better word, designed one of the most unspeakable cyclecars, the lethal rear-engined Carden (which was revived after the Armistice as the AV). Carden himself had moved on to create other atrocities, among them the Tamplin, whose chassis was an offence against any normal engineering standards, for it was made of ash panelled with waterproof fibreboard. This seemed a little inadequate, considering that

---

---

---

the Tamplin was powered by a hefty 965 cc JAP vee-twin engine which drove the rear wheels by chain and belt through the medium of a Sturmey-Archer three-speed motorbike gearbox devoid of reverse – this didn't feature in the Tamplin's specification until 1923.

Sliding-pillar independent front suspension was an advanced feature, although one suspects that it was adopted because it was cheap to make rather than from any consideration of roadholding. A particularly thoughtful piece of design was the tandem seating, which omitted to provide any accommodation for the rear passenger's legs, which had to be hung out over the side (long plank running boards prevented them from becoming entangled in the drive belts). After three years of offering this motorised mooncalf, Tamplin turned conventional in 1922 with a side-by-side two-seater; later examples used Blackburne instead of JAP engines.

**Talbot-Lago T26 SS**

# TATRA

**Koprivnice, Czechoslovakia
1923 to date**

Designer Hans Ledwinka was born in Klosterneuberg, near Vienna and was apprenticed as a mechanic in 1878. In 1897 he moved to eastern Moravia and joined the old-established Nesselsdorf company which had turned from coachbuilding to the manufacture of railway carriages. But, inspired by the German Benz, Nesselsdorf had begun to build a motor car – known as the Präsident – shortly before the teenaged Ledwinka joined them. He too, was soon working on the Präsident, but did not play a prominent role until he succeeded in designing a gearbox for the Präsident where the firm's automotive engineers had failed. By 1901, aged 23, Ledwinka was in charge of Nesselsdorf's automobile activities. He briefly left the company twice, the first time in 1902–05 to work for a Viennese steam car builder (where he experimented with front-wheel brakes), the second time between 1916–21, when he worked for Steyr.

When Ledwinka returned to his old company, it had been renamed Ringhoffer, the town of Nesselsdorf had become Koprivnice, and Moravia was part of the new republic of Czechoslovakia. In his spare time at Steyr, Ledwinka had been working on the design of a light car with a flat-twin engine and backbone chassis. This went into production as the Tatra – the name of a local mountain range – in 1923, and the Ringhoffer company changed its name to the Ringhoffer-Tatra-Werks at the same time. The final Nesselsdorf models, the 6.5-litre models T and U, enjoyed a brief existence as Tatras, though production of these models had ceased by the end of 1925.

The original Tatra 11 was succeeded by the improved T12, which was built until 1930. These sturdy little cars even proved successful in races. The two-cylinder versions were superseded by the 1.7-litre Type 30 flat-four in 1930; it, too, was air-cooled.

A water-cooled 2-litre six had appeared in 1926, and was followed by the water-cooled 2.3-litre Type 31 in 1927. The 1160 cc Type 57 of the early 1930s was a new small air-cooled four-cylinder, still with the backbone chassis and the 1690 cc Type 75 was similar in layout.

In the late 1920s, Ledwinka designed two water-cooled overhead-valve luxury models, one with a 3850 cc six-cylinder engine, the other with a 5990 cc V12. Although both followed what had become Ledwinka's standard pattern of backbone chassis with swing axles, few examples of these expensive models were built.

Designer Hans Ledwinka was never short of unorthodox ideas, and in 1929 he built a rear-engined light commercial three-wheeler, the T49, powered by a single-cylinder derivative of the T11 engine. This was followed in 1931 by Ledwinka's first rear-engined car, a twin-cylinder coupé, which was developed in 1933 to become the V570, a streamlined twin-cylinder saloon with a rounded nose. However, the more orthodox T57, with a 1260 cc four-cylinder engine, was chosen for production since its power unit ran more smoothly.

Nevertheless, Ledwinka's rear-engined prototypes did lead to some litigation against Professor Porsche for patent infringement in his Volkswagen design.

In the spring of 1934, Ledwinka unveiled another interesting car, the Tatra 77, which had an air-cooled overhead-cam V8 engine of

2969 cc mounted at the rear of an aerodynamic body with a central frame.

Indeed, only air-cooled cars were being made by Tatra when war broke out; these were the flat-four front-engined side-valve 1910 cc T52 and overhead-valve 1260 cc T57, and the rear-engined overhead-valve 1760 cc T97. The rear-engined 2969 cc V8 T87 was brought out as the successor to the Tatra 77.

After the war, Ledwinka was jailed by Czechoslovakia's new Communist masters, since Tatra had built trucks for the occupying German forces during the hostilities. Despite the evidence of 1200 witnesses as to Ledwinka's probity, he was jailed for six years. On his release in 1951, he moved first to Austria, then to Germany, where he acted as a consultant engineer.

Tatra continued production with improved versions of the rear-engined cars powered by 2472 cc V8 engines, though the company was now increasingly concentrating on heavy lorries. Between 1949 and 1951 Tatra also built successful sports cars and racing monoposti – still with rear air-cooled engines – which, driven by Vermirovsky, Soyka and Pavlicek, proved successful in competition.

From 1955 different versions of

**Tatra Type II**

the restyled rear-engined Tatra 603 appeared, followed in the 1960s by the improved Vignale-styled T613. Production was on a small scale – some 6000 T603 cars were built in the model's 20 year production span, and most of these cars were supplied only to officials of Eastern Bloc governments.

Tatra's main concern since, however, has been the manufacture of commercial vehicles and railway rolling stock; between 1964 and 1966 truck production increased by 60 percent. About a third of all Tatra products are exported and this is taken care of by the Czech foreign trade corporation.

Under its rather square-cut exterior, the current T613–2 still follows the Ledwinka line, with an overhead-cam V8 engine of 3495 cc mounted above the rear swing axle. Developing 168 bhp at 5200 rpm, this latest Tatra can attain 118 mph (190 kph).

## Tatra 11

Variously nicknamed the Tatrachek or the Tin Dachshund, Ledwinka's first design for the newly-created Tatra company revolutionised existing design principles, since it had a large-diameter backbone tube instead of a conventional chassis frame. The air-cooled 1056 cc flat-twin engine was mounted transversely above the front axle, in unit with the gearbox. The rear swing axle incorporated an ingenious final drive in which the propellor shaft carried two spiral-bevel pinions, each engaging with a separate crown wheel at the end of either half shaft. Each crown wheel and pinion was of a different diameter from its counterpart, but either set had the same aggregate number of teeth. The purpose behind this seemingly complex method of construction was that it permitted either swing axle to roll around its pinion without the need for universal joints, a very simple yet brilliant piece of design.

Although the Tatra 11 was intended as a touring car, nevertheless it did appear in sporting form in

### 1923 TATRA TYPE 11

**Engine:** flat-twin overhead-valve
**Bore × stroke:** 82 mm × 100 mm
**Capacity:** 1056 cc
**Maximum power:** 15 bhp
**Transmission:** three-speed manual
**Chassis:** backbone tube
**Suspension:** non-independent with transverse leaf spring front and independent swing axle with transverse leaf spring rear
**Brakes:** rear wheel
**Bodywork:** two-seater tourer
**Maximum speed (approx):** 50 mph (80 kph)

order to enhance the marque image, a TII winning its class in the Solitude hill climb as early as 1924. These competition Tatras were for the most part specially built, with high-compression engines with dual inlet valves, roller-bearing cranks and larger carburettors.

In 1925, two racers were built with mechanical four-wheel brakes and split-axle independent front suspension, making them some of the first all-independently sprung competition cars. With the output of their engines boosted to the remarkable figure of 35 bhp, and a top speed approaching 85 mph (135 kph), these two cars finished first and second in the 1100 cc class in the 1925 Targa Florio.

Also in 1925, a standard Tatra II won the 3300-mile (5313 km) Leningrad-Tiflis-Moscow reliability trial, defeating 78 rivals; TIIs also traversed Africa from Alexandria to Cape Town and crossed the Australian desert.

A reliability run of, in hindsight, rather more dubious merit was the achievement of a Tatra II which, in the 1920s, covered over a million kilometres carrying an up-and-coming young National Socialist politician to campaign meetings; even after he had become Fuhrer, Adolf Hitler still retained his affection for the Tatra marque... .

# A-Z OF THE CAR

## Tatra 77

'The demise of the classic design of car has its origins in modern theory,' claimed an early advertising leaflet for the new Tatra 77, introduced in March 1934. 'All that science has allowed to be conceived and achieved is put into practice in the Tatra car, without regard for tradition or preconceived ideas. Everything about this car is new; its bold conception achieves perfection.'

The rearward mounting of the big air-cooled V8 engine was initially adopted in the interests of silence, but Ledwinka was quick to realise the aerodynamic benefits it brought, and designed a streamlined body for the Tatra 77 whose drag coefficient of 0.212 is remarkable even by the standards of the 1980s; a faired-in underbelly and rear stabilising fin aided the T77's aerodynamic performance.

'The aerodynamic shape, result of patient scientific research, gives the car a remarkable appearance and an unmatched speed for a very low fuel consumption,' claimed Tatra. Indeed, the T77 was ideally suited to the autobahns that were springing up in Europe; so remarkable was its high speed performance that during the war Dr Todt, the man behind Germany's high-speed road programme, lobbied for the continuation of production of the T77's successor, the T87 (introduced in 1937) on the grounds that it was the ideal car for the autobahn.

Moreover, the basic design of the T77 set the pattern for all the Tatras that have been built since – apart from the MacPherson strut front suspension, the layout of the modern Tatra 613 is recognisably that of the T77, introduced over half a century ago.

---

### 1934 TATRA TYPE 77

**Engine:** V8, overhead-valve
**Bore × stroke:** 80 mm × 84 mm
**Capacity:** 3379 cc
**Maximum power:** 70 bhp
**Transmission:** four-speed manual
**Chassis:** backbone chassis with box-section side frames
**Suspension:** independent with transverse leaf springs and double wishbones front. Independent with transverse leaf springs and swing axles rear
**Brakes:** four wheel drums
**Bodywork:** four-seater saloon
**Maximum speed (approx):** 93 mph (150 kph)

---

## TB
### Bilston, England
### 1920–1924

Thomson Brothers were (and are) a famous maker of tankers who produced one of the more attractive three-wheeled cyclecars of the 1920s, the TB. Prototypes were on the road at the end of 1919, and by late 1920, the TB was available in three models, the two-seater, with air-cooled Blackburne vee-twin, the family two-seater (it could carry two adults plus a child) and the Sports, powered by a JAP

---

### 1920 TB

**Engine:** vee-twin side-valve
**Bore × stroke:** 85 mm × 85 mm
**Capacity:** 965 cc
**Maximum power:** 15 bhp
**Transmission:** three-speed manual
**Chassis:** steel channel
**Suspension:** quarter-elliptic leaf springs front and cantilever leaf spring rear
**Brakes:** external contracting type on rear wheel
**Bodywork:** two-seater cyclecar
**Maximum speed (approx):** 45 mph (72 kph)

---

**TB Cyclecar**

engine, which had 'more the appearance of a 'road-eater' than the other models, and was 1 cwt lighter.' All models had a Bugatti-style radiator, which, in the case of the air-cooled models, was a dummy.

An unusual feature for so light a cyclecar was a three-speed and reverse gearbox driving the rear wheel by shaft and crown wheel and pinion.

## TEMPERINO
### Turin, Italy
### 1919–1925

The Temperino brothers – Maurizio, Giacomo and Carlo – opened a garage dealing in cars and motorcycles in 1907, then built a prototype small car from 1908–10 with the aid of the young engineer Giulio Cappa Bava.

However, production did not begin until after the Great War, when the brothers took over a former precision instrument factory in the Viale Stupinigi. The rotund bodywork for the Temperino cars was provided by the Stabilimenti

**Tatra Type 87**

## 1922 TEMPERINO

**Engine:** in-line twin-cylinder, overhead valve
**Bore × stroke:** 85 mm × 90 mm
**Capacity:** 1096 cc
**Maximum power:** 20 bhp
**Transmission:** three-speed manual
**Chassis:** steel channel
**Suspension:** non-independent, semi-elliptic leaf springs front and quarter-elliptic leaf springs rear
**Brakes:** rear wheel drum
**Bodywork:** two-seater
**Maximum speed (approx):** 40 mph (65 kph)

Temperino

Farina and the first cars were powered by side-valve vee-twin engines of 1010 cc; later on, the vee-twins were supplanted by overhead-valve 1096 cc in-line twins which had the unusual feature of a three-speed gearbox integral with the axle.

Another odd feature was the fact that only the right-hand rear wheel was driven, which certainly eliminated the need for a differential. Though there were plans in 1922 for the licence-production of Temperini in Britain – indeed, a British company was formed – they came to nothing, and even in the car's native Italy, output remained on a small scale. Racing driver Guiseppe Farina's first car was a Temperino, but any chance the marque might have had of making the big time faded in 1925 when the firm's bank, the Banca Nazionale di Sconto, failed abruptly, dragging Temperino down with it.

# TEMPLAR

**Cleveland, USA
1918–1925**

'The Superfine Small Car' was one of the best high-grade American cars to appear after the Great War, and initially used a 'Top-Valve' four-cylinder overhead valve engine which gave the Templar Sportette model a top speed of some 50 mph (80 kph).

The Templar had handsome aluminium bodywork resplendent in a 27-coat paint finish, and its price of $2685 included such unlikely extras as a gradient meter, a compass and a 1-A Junior

## 1922 TEMPLAR

**Engine:** in-line four-cylinder, overhead-valve
**Bore × stroke:** 85.7 mm × 139.7 mm
**Capacity:** 3225 cc
**Maximum power:** 50 bhp
**Transmission:** three-speed manual
**Chassis:** pressed steel channel
**Suspension:** non-independent with semi-elliptic leaf springs front and rear
**Brakes:** rear wheel
**Bodywork:** roadster, tourer, sportette, coupé or sedan
**Maximum speed (approx):** 50 mph (80 kph)

Autographic Kodak camera.

Towards the end of production, Templar introduced a 4397 cc side-valve six-cylinder model, available with sport, phaeton, brougham, or sedan bodywork and two-tone paint finishes.

# TERRAPLANE

**Detroit, USA
1932–1937**

The 2.5-litre side-valve six Terraplane – offering 'Land Flying' – was Hudson's replacement for the Essex marque; it was joined in 1933 by a 4-litre straight-eight offering 85 mph performance, the

**Templar 18/23**

## 1934 TERRAPLANE BIG SIX

**Engine:** in-line six-cylinder, side-valve
**Bore × stroke:** 76.2 mm × 127 mm
**Capacity:** 3474 cc
**Maximum power:** 70 bhp
**Transmission:** three-speed manual
**Chassis:** pressed steel channel
**Suspension:** independent split axle with semi-elliptic leaf springs front and rigid axle with leaf springs rear
**Brakes:** mechanical drums front and rear
**Bodywork:** saloon
**Maximum speed (approx):** 81 mph (130 kph)

**Terraplane Six**

chassis of which was reworked by Reid Railton to create the original Railton, whose weight of only a ton guaranteed shattering performance.

The 1936 Big Six was characterised by a swept-back grille and independent front suspension, plus the 3.5-litre Hudson Big Six engine, though in some export markets, the Terraplane retained the 2.6-litre engine.

Describing the Big Six, *The Autocar* claimed: 'It is not surprising that a car such as this Terraplane should be finding supporters at the present time, for at a moderate price it gives a very fine top gear performance, with power in reserve almost all the time in ordinary running and is, in addition, a thoroughly roomy five seater car … One has come to expect from this kind of car effortless, silent and smooth running with a very minimum of necessity for gear changing, acceleration when required of sports car character, and a docility in traffic which is hardly surpassed by any other form of car.'

The addition of hydraulic brakes to the restyled 1936 models was not enough to stop the Terraplane name from being dropped the following year, when the marque was replaced by a new small Hudson six-cylinder model, the 112.

# THAMES

**London, England
1906–1911**

Builders of naval dreadnoughts, and of petrol commercials since 1902, the Thames Iron Works, Shipbuilding & Engineering Company of Greenwich came straight in at the top end of the market with a 40–50 hp six-cylinder car, first shown at Olympia in 1906. It featured a patent three-speed gearbox and was commended for the quality of its design.

A 15 hp twin and a 24 hp four were added to the range for 1908, along with a massive 60 hp six. Driven by Clifford Earp, previously associated with Napier, a 60 hp Thames took 'all world's records from 50 to 300 miles' at Brooklands.

The 1910 range included an 8 hp single-cylinder, a 12 hp twin, a 15.9 hp four and sixes of 24 and 60 hp; bodies available included the quaintly-named Cynosure, Chirugeon and Conqueror styles.

However, a year later, Thames claimed that they were too busy building commercial vehicles and the motor department was shut down.

However, Thames did leave one reminder of their existence behind, for their works football team is said to have the origin of Millwall FC ….

## 1906 THAMES

**Engine:** pair-cast, in-line six-cylinder, side-valve
**Bore × stroke:** 114.3 mm × 127 mm
**Capacity:** 7817 cc
**Maximum power:** 50 bhp
**Transmission:** three-speed manual
**Chassis:** pressed steel channel
**Suspension:** non-independent with semi-elliptic leaf springs front and rear
**Brakes:** rear wheel and transmission
**Bodywork:** available to order
**Maximum speed (approx):** 60 mph (97 kph)

**Thames 50 HP**

# THOMAS

**Buffalo, USA**
**1902–c1919**

In 1900, businessman Edwin Ross Thomas, who had previously been involved in the railway industry, took over part of the facilities of the moribund Globe Cycle Company of Buffalo, New York. For two years, Thomas built bicycles and motorcycles before adding a building nearby for the manufacture of motorcars, which began in 1902 with light single and twin-cylinder vehicles with crocodile bonnets and low-slung gilled-tube radiators. A 24 hp three-cylinder model was added to the range in 1903, and the crocodile bonnet was replaced by a conventional bonnet and radiator for the 1904 season.

The 1905 range was known by the Thomas-Flyer name for the first time; it consisted of fours of 40 hp and 50 hp and a 60 hp six, offered either with touring coachwork or as a stark racer with two seats and a bolster tank.

Then during 1906 the Thomas-Flyer range was redesigned on European lines, reputedly as a carbon copy of the contemporary Richard-Brasier, though the radiator looked more like that of the De Dion. Thomas was said to have imported Richard-Brasier parts and patterns from France and copied them exactly, though the engines certainly seemed far larger than anything Brasier was producing.

Nevertheless, the new Thomas-Flyer models proved an instant success; during 1907, the Buffalo factory produced a total of 700 cars and 400 taxicabs. A side-line venture at this period was the Thomas-Detroit, an associated company founded by E.R. Thomas as the result of a chance meeting with a 26-year-old manager from Oldsmobile, Roy D. Chapin, who had been seeking financial backing to build medium-priced quality cars designed by his colleague Howard Coffin. The Thomas-Detroit marque lasted from 1906 to 1908, and then became the Chalmers Motor Company.

The parent Thomas-Flyer marque came to world notice in 1908, when a 1907 Thomas-Flyer 60 hp four won the 22,000-mile (35,000 km) New York-Paris race, 'the most difficult endurance contest ever undertaken'. The publicity brought by the victory boosted Thomas-Flyer sales to 816 in 1908, but they reached their peak level of 1036 cars in 1909, when the company's first shaft-drive model, the Model L Flyabout, proved so unreliable that sales tumbled to 913 cars in 1910. That year, E.R. Thomas – who never learned to drive, and always had a chauffeur – sold the Thomas-Flyer company to the New York banking company of Eugene M. Meyer. Meyer brought in a team of disaffected Packard executives, who had resigned when Alvan Macauley became general manager, but despite the new expertise and the much-needed financial backing, the rescue bid was too late, and Thomas-Flyer went into receivership in August 1912. Its assets, including the New York-Paris car, were auctioned off in 1913. However, Thomas-Flyer cars assembled from the stockpile of spare parts were theoretically available to special order until 1919.

E.R. Thomas died in Buffalo in 1936 at the age of 85.

## Thomas-Flyer 60 HP

'The stupendous undertaking is a veritable romance,' wrote the *Daily Mail* when the round-the-world New York-Paris Race was announced. 'Is such a journey possible? Theoretically it is, but it must be borne in mind that the motor car, after woman, is the most fragile and capricious thing on earth.'

Indeed, when he was originally told of the race, E.R. Thomas had scoffed: 'We will not enter; none of those cars will reach Chicago!' But a few days before the race, he changed his mind, and a standard 1907 60 hp four-seat roadster was taken from stock and hurriedly prepared for the round-the-world event by strapping planks to the mud-guards and fitting a detachable prairie schooner top. A straight front axle giving extra ground clearance was a subsequent modification made during the race itself.

Just six cars started from New York's Times Square on 12 February 1908, and the Thomas was the only American entry. Conditions on the TransAmerica run were so bad that only four cars were still in the race by the time the West Coast was reached, and the Thomas, in the lead despite a detour via Alaska (on the original route but abandoned as impassable) had been plagued by transmission troubles.

In a journey which included a 72-day crossing of the Siberian wastes, 'roads of every description were encountered…the car travelled over 13,000 miles under its own power, through snow, mud and swamps, fording streams, climbing mountains and, worst of all, bumping over 450 miles of cross-ties in Siberia'.

Though the competing German Protos car reached Paris ahead of the Thomas, on elapsed time and distance the American entry was judged the winner. A brief boom in sales resulted, but then unreliable new shaft-drive models undid all the good publicity generated by the round-the-world race, and four years later the Thomas Flyer company went into receivership.

The New York-Paris car was sold along with other company effects; today it is preserved in the Harrah collection in Reno, Nevada.

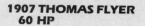

### 1907 THOMAS FLYER 60 HP

**Engine:** in-line four cylinder, side-valve
**Bore × stroke:** 146 mm × 139.7 mm
**Capacity:** 9360 cc
**Maximum power:** 60 bhp
**Transmission:** four-speed manual, chain final drive
**Chassis:** pressed steel channel
**Suspension:** non-independent with semi-elliptic leaf springs front. Live rear axle with semi-elliptic leaf springs
**Brakes:** rear wheel and countershaft
**Bodywork:** four-seater tourer
**Maximum speed (approx):** 60 mph (97 kph)

**Thomas-Flyer**

# THÉOPHILE SCHNEIDER

**Besançon/Billancourt, France
1910–1931**

Théophile Schneider, whose family was in the silk trade, had been working with Edouard Rochet since 1894 in the Rochet-Schneider company, but was ousted in a management reshuffle following the liquidation and reorganisation of Rochet-Schneider Ltd (like many leading French companies of the day, it was capitalised in London) in 1909. He moved north into Peugeot territory and formed Automobiles Théophile Schneider in Besançon, Doubs, in 1910.

Th.Schneider cars were conservative in design, with the radiator behind the engine *à la* Renault, but extremely well-

## 1913 THÉOPHILE SCHNEIDER 18CV

**Engine:** in-line four-cylinder, side-valve
**Bore × stroke:** 95 mm × 140 mm
**Capacity:** 3969 cc
**Maximum power:** 50 bhp
**Transmission:** four-speed manual
**Chassis:** pressed steel channel
**Suspension:** non-independent with semi-elliptic leaf springs front and rear
**Brakes:** rear wheel
**Bodywork:** torpedo, cabriolet, landaulet
**Maximum speed (approx):** 56 mph (90 kph)

built; the company began operations with the four-cylinder 12CV (1693 cc), followed the next year by a 1767 cc 10CV, a 2614 cc 14CV, the 3685 cc 18CV and the 5195 cc 25CV as well as the six cylinder (3181 cc) 15CV. The company promoted its products by racing them and, though the competition record wasn't particularly brilliant, nevertheless the company paid dividends from the start. In 1912, a new Th.Schneider, the 2993 cc 14/16 CV, made its debut, as did a monstrous 6082 cc 28CV. With subtle variations in bore and stroke dimensions, the same basic range continued in production until the war.

Th.Schneider was, indeed, poised for expansion in 1912, and sought to buy the Paris factory of Mors, which was heavily in debt to the bankers. But the move – which saw the acquisition of the bank's claim on Mors by Schneider – was forestalled by André Citroën, who launched a rescue operation and found a rich and eccentric Armenian diamond broker who put up the cash to buy back the bank claim.

On the rebound, Th.Schneider managed to buy the Billancourt factory that had belonged to aviation pioneer Robert Esnault-Peleterie; the Th.Schneider company was reformed in 1914 when the shareholders objected to the provision whereby Schneider and his partner Louis Ravel took fifty per cent of the profits for themselves....

After the Armistice, the factory resumed production

with the pre-war range, starting with the 5501 cc 26CV, first seen in 1913, although the radiator was moved to the front as a feeble gesture at modernity. Mainstay of post-war production was the 14/16CV, of which a six-cylinder version, the 4489 cc 20CV, was also built.

One of the best Th.Schneiders of the decade was the sports 10CV, which, fitted with open four-seater coachwork, appeared at events such as Le Mans. Overhead

# TOYOTA

**Toyota City, Japan
1935 to date**

In 1935 the Toyoda Automatic Loom Manufacturing Company, a leading Japanese textile company doubtless inspired by the forthcoming liberalisation of the national laws on automobile manufacture, built a prototype car looking like the front of a Chrysler Airflow married to the rear end of a Ford V8 tourer, which went into production as the AB in mid-1936. A saloon version, the AA, was closely modelled on the aerodynamic styling of the Airflow. The Toyoda – it became the Toyota in 1937 – was powered by an overhead-valve 3389 cc six-cylinder engine with identical dimensions to the contemporary Chevrolet Six, which developed 65 bhp.

The company aimed to undercut Japanese-assembled Ford and GM cars by 10 per cent, and recruited Shotaro Kamiya, then heading the sales division of GM Japan, to spearhead their sales

drive; developments of their first tourer and sedan models were offered up to the outbreak of war.

Toyota's first post-war model, the 27 bhp SA two-door Toyopet sedan, appeared in 1947, though production had to wait until the Allied ban on private car production was lifted in October 1949.

In 1954, with annual production approaching 10,000 units a year, Toyota announced the 1453 cc overhead-valve Crown. In 1957 they introduced the Corona 1000 cc, which was followed in 1965 by the New Corona two-door hardtop, intended to fill a gap in the US market where Toyota's previous attempt to break into the market in 1957–58 had proved unsuccessful.

Toyota's expansion was marked in 1959 by the opening of the new Motomachi plant to build the Crown and Corona models exclusively for the Japanese market. In 1960 a small batch of glassfibre-bodied sports versions of the 1.5-litre Crown, with the engine tuned to develop 72 bhp, was put into production by the Tokyo firm of Kuno Motors. In 1961 Toyota launched the Publica range, powered by 700 cc air-cooled engines.

The next year saw the production of the millionth Toyota, the launch of the conventional 1100 cc Corolla and the start of exports to Europe. It might have taken Toyota 27 years to build their first million vehicles, but the second million was reached only three years later, in 1965, and the third million came little more than a year after that.

In 1967, Toyota launched the Century model and the Corona gained 1500 cc and 1600 cc engines; the Crown was fitted with six-cylinder and V8 power units. The MkII version of the Corona was launched in 1968, while in 1969 – when the company celebrated its millionth export sale – the Corolla became the first individual Toyota model to reach a million units.

The 1158 cc Celica and 1400 cc/1600 cc Carina were launched from Toyota's new Tsutsumi plant in December 1970. In 1972, Toyota production passed the 10 million mark, three million of which had borne the Corolla name.

Two further new Toyotas, the Publica-derived Starlet, available in two-door coupé and four-door saloon models, and a redesigned Corona with engines of 1600, 1800 and 2000 cc, appeared in 1973.

The 1979 range included 993 cc and 1166 cc Starlets, 1588 cc Carina saloon and estate models, 1588 cc and 1969 cc Celicas and the 1968 cc Cressida; the biggest Toyota that year was the 2563 cc Crown luxury model. That year saw the launch of the new Tercel and Corsa models, with north-south

**Théophile Schneider 18CV**

1452 cc engines driving the front wheels.

By 1980, Toyota was outstripping Chevrolet as one of the world's best-selling nameplates, and the range was consequently more and more complex, with variants on the Tercel/Corsa, Starlet, Corolla/Sprinter, Carina, Crown, Century and 4×4 Land Cruiser available. The front-wheel drive Camry was another new entry in the early 1980s.

The 1984 worldwide sales figures saw Toyota comfortably ensconced as the third biggest manufacturer after GM and Ford, and with the aim of raising their world share from the current 8.3 per cent to 10 per cent by the turn of the century; this would mean a virtual doubling of production from the present level of 3.4 million to a staggering 6.7 million.

Toyota is currently upgrading its technical image, with striking new models like a well-designed front-wheel drive Celica coupé with a transverse double-overhead-camshaft, 16-valve 1998 cc engine, which began appearing in Europe at the beginning of 1986 (and which was shown in 4×4 form at the 1985 Tokyo Show), and the Corolla GT 'hot hatchback' powered by the same 1587 cc double overhead-camshaft engine as the mid-engined MR2 sports coupé.

## Toyota MR2

Perhaps the most outstanding Toyota design of recent years, the MR2 is a dedicated two-door sports coupé with a mid-mounted double overhead-camshaft 1600 cc power unit with sixteen valves, also seen in the Corolla GT.

In its field, it has become an instant success, receiving great praise for its overall design, its handling and roadholding. Capable of accelerating from rest to 60 mph in some 7.9 seconds the MR2 is also notable for good fuel economy, not always a feature expected of small sports cars.

Though the Toyota MR2 still has some of the stylistic shortcomings that mar many Japanese cars, like an uninspired dashboard layout and overfussy exterior ornamentation, nevertheless in many respects – not least, its outstanding dynamic characteristics – it is proving a serious challenge to Europe's manufacturers of sporting cars.

### 1985 TOYOTA MR2

**Engine:** transverse, mid-mounted four-cylinder, double-overhead camshafts and four valves per cylinder
**Bore × stroke:** 81 mm × 77 mm
**Capacity:** 1587 cc
**Maximum power:** 122 bhp
**Transmission:** five-speed manual
**Chassis:** integral
**Suspension:** independent with MacPherson struts front and rear with anti-roll bar front and trailing and transverse arms rear
**Brakes:** discs all round
**Bodywork:** two-door coupé
**Maximum speed (approx):** 122 mph (196 kph)

**Toyota MR2**

# A-Z OF THE CAR

**Toyota 2000GT**

## Toyota Corolla

Introduced in Japan in 1966, the Toyota started life as a humble two-door saloon with a four-cylinder, overhead-valve, 1077 cc engine and no claim whatsoever to fundamentally innovative design concepts.

Aimed very much at the more impecunious 'man in the street', market, the Corolla very soon took pole position as the Japanese 'people's car' and in late 1966 Toyota's newly developed Takaoka plant lifted Corolla production capacity to 30,000 a month – an impressive figure for the day and even more impressive when it is borne in mind that early production was for the home market.

The Corolla range grew in the '60s to encompass four-door models and a Coupé which offered greater performance from its tuned version of the 1166 cc engine.

Engine sizes have increased over the years from 1100 cc to 1400, 1500, 1600 and more recently, 1800 cc. Current models are now rather less austere than the original specification allowed and they also follow the generally universal trend of front wheel drive.

From as early on as 1972 the Corolla range offered five-speed manual transmission in this country, while many other manufacturers waited for the '80s before daring to make such a departure from tradition; this is one area in which the Corolla has broken convention.

The current Corolla range has four generations of forebears – each one a significant improvement on its predecessor in terms of engineering, comfort and styling, although simple suspension and an essentially conservative design brief have been adhered to throughout.

In 1983 the 10 millionth Corolla rolled off the production line at Takaoka in 'Toyota City' and in doing so it joined that select band of motor cars, like the Model T Ford and the Volkswagen Beetle, whose production numbers have reached eight figures.

The Corolla still has the highest production volume for a car sourced from a single country and almost from a single plant.

---

### 1985 TOYOTA COROLLA GT

**Engine:** in-line, four cylinder double-overhead camshaft and four valves per cylinder
**Bore × stroke:** 81 mm × 77 mm
**Capacity:** 1587 cc
**Maximum power:** 119 bhp
**Transmission:** five-speed manual
**Chassis:** integral
**Suspension:** independent MacPherson struts all round with transverse and trailing links rear
**Brakes:** discs all round
**Bodywork:** four-seater saloon
**Maximum speed (approx):** 122 mph (145 kph)

---

## Toyota 2000GT

Launched during the 1966 season, the Toyota 2000GT was a sleek coupé powered by a double overhead-camshaft six-cylinder engine. Like the 1600GT saloon, powered by a four-cylinder double overhead-camshaft engine, the 2000GT was launched on the strength of a successful racing programme.

With such 'European' features as wire wheels and a five-speed transmission, the 2000GT was evidence that Japan was firmly established as a serious contender in the world markets and could produce competent sports cars.

---

### 1966 TOYOTA 2000GT

**Engine:** in-line six cylinder, double overhead-camshaft
**Bore × stroke:** 75 mm × 75 mm
**Capacity:** 1988 cc
**Maximum power:** 150 bhp
**Transmission:** five-speed manual
**Chassis:** integral
**Suspension:** independent all round with wishbone and coil spring
**Brakes:** discs all round
**Bodywork:** two-seater coupé
**Maximum speed (approx):** 137 mph (220 kph)

---

**Toyota Corolla GT**

# TRABANT

**Germany (East)**
**1958 to date**

The ancestry of the Trabant is complex, for the marque descends from the IFA of 1948–56 (itself derived from the old DKW, one of a number of companies swallowed up by the nationalised East German car industry after World War II had divided Germany) via the Zwickau of 1956–58.

Uncompromisingly utilitarian, all Trabants have followed the layout of their Zwickau exemplar in featuring front-wheel drive and two-stroke twin-cylinder in-line engines. These are air-cooled, with a rotary inlet-valve. Initially offered with 499 cc engines, in 1963 the Trabant became available with a 594 cc power-unit.

An open version of the Trabant, the Tramp, was added to the range in 1979 which, like the closed model, had bodywork in resin-reinforced papier-mâché!

Current Trabant line-up includes the 601 Limousine and the Universal estate car, both names seeming far too grandiose for this machine.

### 1985 TRABANT 601 LIMOUSINE

**Engine:** in-line two cylinder, two-stroke
**Bore × stroke:** 72 mm × 73 mm
**Capacity:** 595 cc
**Maximum power:** 26 bhp
**Transmission:** four-speed manual
**Chassis:** integral
**Suspension:** independent with transverse leaf spring and wishbones front and transverse leaf spring and swing axles rear
**Brakes:** drums all round
**Bodywork:** saloon or estate
**Maximum speed (approx):** 62 mph (100 kph)

**Tracta**

# TRACTA

**Asnières, France**
**1926–1934**

One of the pioneering front-wheel drive cars, the Tracta was built by two young engineers, Jean Grégoire and Pierre Fenaille. They first tested their transmission in a prototype racer called the Gephi, powered by a Cozette-supercharged 1100 cc SCAP engine and built in the works of Langlois and Journaud at Courbevoie in the summer of 1926.

The secret of the Tracta was a homokinetic joint designed by Grégoire; the Gephi proved – apart from some understandable teething problems – so rapid that production was underwritten by Fenaille's father, and several hundred Tracta sports and touring cars were built at Asnières.

The low-built Tracta cars had outstanding roadholding, though the in-line layout of engine and transmission gave an exceedingly long bonnet, which was fine from the point of view of aesthetics, but poor from the accommodation standpoint; the crankshaft-

### 1929 TRACTA

**Engine:** in-line four-cylinder, overhead-valve
**Bore × stroke:** 70 mm × 104 mm
**Capacity:** 1616 cc
**Maximum power:** 40 bhp
**Transmission:** four-speed manual, front wheel drive
**Chassis:** pressed steel channel
**Suspension:** independent with sliding pillar front, non-independent with inverted quarter-elliptic leaf springs rear
**Brakes:** drums all round (inboard front)
**Bodywork:** roadster or coupé
**Maximum speed (approx):** 65 mph (105 kph)

mounted Dynastart projected through the bulkhead into the driving compartment.

The proprietary engines employed on the Tracta were the SCAP 1100 cc and 1600 cc fours (sometimes in supercharged form) and the 1700 cc sidevalve continental or 3000 cc overhead-valve Hotchkiss six-cylinder engines.

Sadly, the Tracta faded away just as the Traction Avant Citroën began to make front-wheel drive truly popular.

The Tracta design was blatantly copied by the Belgian Juwel company, whose TA-4, shown at the December 1928 Brussels Salon, was a close copy of Grégoire's design, apart from the 1131 cc overhead-camshaft Juwel engine. The design was taken over by a new company, Astra, and shown at the 1929 Brussels Salon. This time, the car was externally identical to the Tracta and even boasted a SCAP engine, though the car went one better than its French prototype in being equipped with independent rear suspension by a transverse leaf spring.

Only a handful of Astras was built before the company went out of business in 1931.

# TRACTION AERIENNE

**Neuilly, France**
**1921–c1926**

Like the Leyat (Hélica), this odd little streamlined saloon car was propeller-driven. Unlike the Leyat, the Traction Aérienne (also sold as

### 1922 TRACTION AERIENNE

**Engine:** flat twin-cylinder, air-cooled
**Bore × stroke:** 90 mm × 120 mm
**Capacity:** 1527 cc
**Maximum power:** n/a
**Transmission:** airscrew
**Chassis:** tubular
**Suspension:** non-independent with leaf springs front and rear
**Brakes:** drums all round
**Bodywork:** aerodynamic saloon
**Maximum speed (approx):** 62 mph (100 kph)

**Trabant 601 Limousine**

**Traction Aerienne**

**Trident Clipper II**

the Eolia) was steered by the front wheels, and had four-wheel brakes, doubtless to compensate for the lack of transmission braking. Its four-bladed propeller was prevented from decimating the populace by somewhat sketchy wire guards; contemporary reports speak of its good suspension and poor acceleration. All-up weight of this strange device, which looked like the result of an illicit liaison between a light aircraft and a perambulator, was said to be 300 kg (660 lb).

# TRIDENT
**Woodbridge/Ipswich, England**
**1966–1978**

When TVR of Blackpool ran into financial trouble in 1965, and was unable to proceed with production of a fixed-head coupé design by Trevor Fiore based on the Healey 3000 chassis, which had been built in prototype form by Italian coachbuilder Fissore, the design was acquired by their agent W.J. Last, of Woodbridge, Suffolk. Last established the Trident Car company, and first showed a convertible derivative of Fiore's striking design powered by a 4.7-litre Ford V8 engine.

With a new chassis, and glassfibre bodywork, the Trident went into full production in 1967 in Market Harborough, but manufacture was soon transferred to Woodbridge.

The Trident was offered with both open and closed bodywork in 1967, along with the option of the 3.0-litre Ford V6 Essex engine. A new derivative, this time with a stretched Triumph TR6 floorpan appeared in 1969, when production was transferred to

---

## 1976 TRIDENT CLIPPER

**Engine:** V6, overhead-valve
**Bore × stroke:** 102 mm × 91 mm
**Capacity:** 5899 cc
**Maximum power:** 230 bhp
**Transmission:** three-speed Torque Flite automatic
**Chassis:** X-braced box-type ladder frame ·
**Suspension:** independent coil springs and wishbones front, independent coil springs and trailing arms rear
**Brakes:** discs front and drums rear
**Bodywork:** 2+2 coupé
**Maximum speed (approx):** 140 mph (225 kph)

---

Ipswich. This model was known in its V6 version as the Venturer and with the V8 as the Clipper.

Body design was improved during 1970, and the Clipper II became available with the 5.4-litre Chrysler V8 engine. The following year, a new model with a 2.5-litre Triumph engine appeared, with the name Tycoon, but Trident was under fire frrom the hyperactive safety and pollution lobbies, and went into liquidation early in 1972. The marque reappeared sporadically, the last time being 1976, when the Venturer and Clipper were offered, the latter with an American Ford V8 engine driving through an automatic transmission.

During its chequered career

Trident notched up over 200 sales in both kit and built-up form, some 50 per cent of which went for export.

# TRIKING
**Marlingford, England**
**1980 to date**

Commercial artist Tony Divey revived the Morgan Super Sports concept with this delightful three-wheeler, powered by a vee-twin Moto Guzzi engine more normally seen in light Italian military transport vehicles, and available in 844 or 950 cc guise.

With positive stop five-speed motorcycle-type gearchange, immense flexibility allied to a three-figure top speed and outstanding roadholding, the Triking is built in limited numbers to individual order.

In 1983 one enterprising Norwegian Triking owner drove his three-wheeler from Oslo to Sicily and back.

---

## 1982 TRIKING

**Engine:** vee-twin, overhead-valve
**Bore × stroke:** 88 mm × 78 mm
**Capacity:** 949 cc
**Maximum power:** 71 bhp
**Transmission:** five-speed manual
**Chassis:** tubular
**Suspension:** independent with coil springs and parallel arms front, swinging arm and coil spring rear
**Brakes:** discs all round
**Bodywork:** two-seater sports
**Maximum speed (approx):** 110 mph (175 kph)

---

**Triking**

**MODEL**
3-litre Super Sports Sunbeam

**UK price when announced:**
£1125

**ENGINE**
**Location:** Front longitudinal
**Type:** Six fixed-head cylinders in line with dry sump lubrication
**Cubic capacity:** 2916 cc
**Bore × stroke:** 75 mm × 110 mm
**Compression ratio:** 6.4:1
**Valve gear:** Twin overhead camshafts driven by helical gear trains, two valves per cylinder inclined at 110 degrees
**Fuel supply:** Two Claudel Hobson H42A carburettors fed by Autovac from rear-mounted 18 gallon fuel tank
**Ignition:** BTH CE6 magneto
**Maximum power:** 90 bhp at 3800 rpm

**TRANSMISSION**
**Layout:** Gearbox in unit with crankcase. Rear wheel drive
**Clutch:** Single dry plate, 11.85 in (301 mm)
**Gearbox:** Four-speed manual
  1st 3.17:1    3rd 1.44:1
  2nd 2.04:1    4th 1.00:1
**Final drive:** Spiral bevel
**Ratio:** 4.5:1

**SUSPENSION**
**Front:** Non-independent with semi-elliptic leaf springs (eight leaves 2 in wide)
**Rear:** Live rear axle with cantilever springs (six leaves 2.25 in wide)

**STEERING**
**Type:** Screw and nut

**BRAKES**
**Type:** four wheel vacuum-servo assisted drums 15.75 in (400 mm) diameter

**WHEELS AND TYRES**
**Type:** Detachable wire wheels 5.25 × 21 (originally 820 × 120 mm beaded edge)

**BODY/CHASSIS**
**Type:** Pressed steel channel chassis with four-seat tourer, Weymann body

**DIMENSIONS AND WEIGHT**
**Length:** 188 in (4475 mm)
**Width:** 67 in (1702 mm)
**Wheelbase:** 130.5 in (3315 mm)
**Track – front:** 55 in (1397 mm)
    **– rear:** 55 in (1397 mm)
**Weight (chassis only):** 2954 lb (1340 kg)

**PERFORMANCE**
**Maximum speed:** 95 mph (153 kph)
**Acceleration 0–75 mph:** 35 seconds
**Fuel consumption:** 21 mpg

**BELOW** The simple lines of the 3-litre Sunbeam. Although the Sunbeam rivalled the more famous Bentley 3 Litre in some respects, performance for example, it was certainly nowhere near as robust as the car described by Bugatti as 'the fastest lorry in Europe'. Its spindly construction is obvious to the eye and in fact one of the long chassis cars for Le Mans 1925 broke a chassis side member on the drive down to the race. That weakness was soon remedied, however, and the Sunbeam earned a reputation for its light controls and precise handling

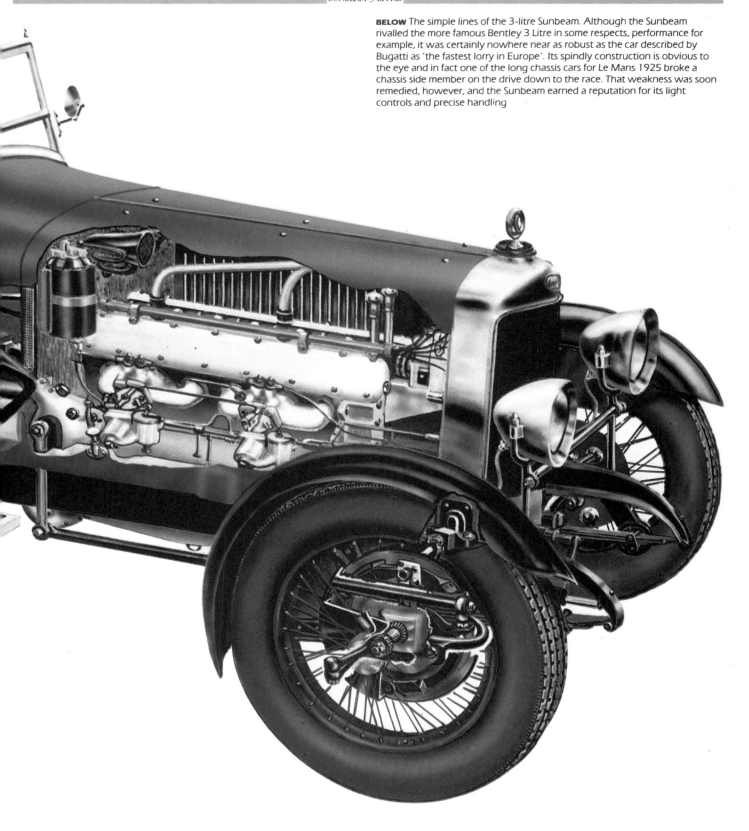

# A-Z OF THE CAR

## TRIUMPH

**Coventry, England**
**1923–1984**

German immigrant Siegfried Bettman's Triumph company had been making motorcycles since 1901, but did not enter the car industry until 1923, after taking over the Coventry factory of the recently defunct Dawson company. Triumph's first car was the 1.4-litre 10/20, replaced two years later by the 1900 cc 13/30, the first British car to be fitted with Lockheed external contracting hydraulic brakes.

In 1928, Triumph announced a well-designed light car, the 832 cc Super Seven, followed in 1931 by the Scorpion, powered by a fashionably small 1.2-litre six-cylinder engine.

The Super Nine of 1932 featured a Coventry-Climax overhead inlet-side exhaust engine, and was joined the following year by the Ten.

On the sporting front, Triumph celebrated success in the Australian market with a sports tourer, the Southern Cross, followed for 1934 by the Gloria, named after a well-known mannequin and available with either 1100 cc four-cylinder or 1500 cc six-cylinder Coventry-Climax engines.

By now, Donald Healey was chief experimental engineer, and it was under his aegis that the supercharged twin overhead-camshaft 2-litre Dolomite, an unashamed copy of contemporary Alfa Romeo design, was created; the ambitious programme proved short-lived, and few Dolomites were built.

Triumph-made overhead-valve engines were listed in addition to the Coventry-Climax units by 1937, when the range included the 1.5-litre Gloria plus four and six-cylinder Dolomites, though these flashily-styled cars were a long way from the twin-cam eight that had first borne the name.

In 1939, Triumph lost its long battle against insolvency, and the company was placed in receivership. Triumph was bought by Sir John Black's Standard Motor Company in 1944, and Triumph's first post-war models, the razor-edge 1800 saloon and the Roadster – the last series-production car with a dickey seat – were powered by an 1800 cc overhead-valve engine intended for the 1.5-litre Jaguar.

It was not long before a new engine appeared in the shape of Standard's wet-liner Vanguard four-cylinder, fitted to Triumphs from 1949. The 2.1-litre version of this engine powered the 1953 TR2 sports car, the first of a distinguished line to use this unit, which appeared in all the TR variants until the TR5 of 1967, when it was replaced by a 2.5-litre six.

After the razor-edged Renown (the former 1800 saloon) had been phased out in 1955, saloon car production did not regain its stride until the 948 cc Herald of 1959. In 1962, Triumph announced the Vitesse, a six-cylinder version of the Herald. The Spitfire sports two-seater was another Herald derivative, whose sporting theme was continued by the 2-litre GT6 of 1967.

Standard-Triumph was taken over by Leyland Motors in 1961, with a resultant rapid expansion of the range: the 2000 saloon of 1964 was followed by the 2.5 PI derivative in 1969; meanwhile, the front-wheel-drive 1300 had appeared in 1966, the sporting TR6 in 1969, and the rather disappointing wedge-shaped TR7 in 1976.

The 3-litre Stag, launched in 1970, lasted until 1977 despite a temperamental V8 power unit,

while the 1972 Dolomite and the overhead-camshaft 2-litre Dolomite Sprint offered sports car performance and handling in a comfortable family saloon bodyshell.

In 1979 a convertible version of the TR7 was launched, and a TR8 powered by the Rover 3.5-litre V8 engine was built for the US market only. In late 1981, the TR7 and TR8 were discontinued, and the Triumph name survived only on an Anglicised Honda Accord, the Acclaim, which was phased out in 1984.

## Triumph Super Seven

Introduced at the 1927 Olympia Show, the Triumph Super Seven was intended to rival the Austin Seven and Morris Eight, and went one better in having a three-bearing crankshaft; it also boasted a Ricardo turbulent head and hydraulic brakes. Another unusual feature was a worm-drive rear axle.

The fabric saloon version of the Super Seven, upholstered in diamond-patterned moquette, was described by *The Light Car & Cyclecar* as offering 'an amazing amount of comfort and, in fact, sheer luxury'; road test reports spoke of its 'almost phenomenal' ability to maintain a high cruising speed and the excellent top gear performance.

In 1930, *The Autocar* described the Super Seven as 'a very likeable little car for the way in which it tack-

### 1928 TRIUMPH SUPER SEVEN

**Engine:** in-line four cylinder, sidevalve
**Bore × stroke:** 56.5 mm × 83 mm
**Capacity:** 832 cc
**Maximum power:** 14 bhp
**Transmission:** three-speed manual
**Chassis:** pressed steel channel
**Suspension:** non-independent with semi-elliptic leaf springs front and rear
**Brakes:** drums all round, hydraulically-operated
**Bodywork:** two-seater, tourer or saloon
**Maximum speed (approx):** 45 mph (72 kph)

**Triumph Super Seven**

**Triumph Dolomite Roadster**

les hard work' and predicted that 'its popularity should increase'.

However, despite its specification, and the introduction of a lively sports version that fell within the 750 cc capacity limit, the 'Perfect Miniature' never sold in large numbers. A six-cylinder derivative, the Scorpion, was built in the early 1930s.

## Triumph Dolomite

Donald Healey was the moving spirit behind the remarkable Triumph Dolomite of 1934, which drew its inspiration from the supercharged 2.3-litre straight-eight Alfa-Romeos designed by Vittorio Jano. The power unit, largely made of Hiduminium alloy, closely followed its Milanese prototype, even down to the length of the stroke, though the bore was slightly smaller, bringing the car just under the 2-litre mark.

Initial reports on the car were enthusiastic, bolstered by early

### 1934 TRIUMPH DOLOMITE

**Engine:** in-line eight cylinder with double overhead-cam and supercharger
**Bore × stroke:** 60 mm × 80 mm
**Capacity:** 1991 cc
**Maximum power:** 140 bhp
**Transmission:** four-speed preselector
**Chassis:** pressed steel channel
**Suspension:** non-independent with semi-elliptic leaf springs front and rear
**Brakes:** drums all round, hydraulically operated
**Bodywork:** two-seater sports
**Maximum speed (approx):** 105 mph (169 kph)

rumours of secret dawn testing at speeds of 120 mph (193 kph). 'All parts of the car, frame, brakes, gearbox, engine, have been designed to play their part with one idea in view

– efficiency!' wrote Brian Twist of *The Autocar* after touching 105 mph (169 kph) with a fully road-equipped Dolomite at Brooklands.

The original intention was to market the Dolomite (guaranteed to have covered a flying mile at a speed in excess of 100 mph/161 kph) for 1000 guineas in chassis form, or £1225 complete and the company stated: 'Although we do not intend to race, we are prepared to offer the utmost cooperation to any private owner who desires to compete in any of the classic events of the year.'

Donald Healey entered a Dolomite in the 1935 Monte Carlo Rally, but the car was hit by a train in a level-crossing accident, and Healey was more than lucky to escape with his life.

The ambitious project was wound up after only six cars had been completed, and these were sold off by an outside company as HSM-Dolomites. The Dolomite name reappeared on a mildly sporting Triumph shortly afterwards.

Remarkably, two of the 'real' Triumph Dolomites still survive today.

## Triumph 1800 Roadster

The first new cars to be built by Triumph after it had been acquired by Standard appeared in the spring of 1946, in the shape of a 'razor-edged, town and country' saloon and a handsome sports tourer. 'They are similar in chassis design, but the saloon has an entirely different styling of its coachwork from that of the tourer, and also has a slightly longer wheelbase,' commented *The Autocar*. The 1800 roadster was a 'speed-looking' car with a long bonnet, one of the most handsome sporting cars of the immediate post-war period, and the last production car to incorporate a dickey seat. A novel touch was the fact that the boot lid opened forward and incorporated two glazed areas which became the windscreen for the rear dickey

**Triumph Roadster**

was marketed as the TR2; it was the cheapest 100 mph (161 kph) car on the British market at the time.

Mildly modified, mainly by fairing in the cockpit cover, a TR2 exceeded 120 mph (193 kph) on the Jabbeke autoroute in Belgium; in standard trim, the TR2 could cruise at a steady 90 mph (145 kph) in overdrive while consuming only one gallon every 27 miles (43 km) – at a constant 40 mph (64 kph) the TR2 achieved a remarkable 54 mpg.

In 1956, the TR3 appeared, with a redesigned grille, a 100 bhp power unit, and the option of a bench seat in the back so that children could be accommodated where there had previously been only luggage space. In late 1957, the TR3 became the first mass-production British car to be fitted with front disc brakes.

---

### 1954 TRIUMPH TR2

**Engine:** in-line four cylinder, overhead-valve
**Bore × stroke:** 83 mm × 92 mm
**Capacity:** 1991 cc
**Maximum power:** 90 bhp
**Transmission:** four-speed manual (overdrive optional)
**Chassis:** box-section steel
**Suspension:** independent with coil spring and wishbone front, live axle with semi-elliptic leaf springs rear
**Brakes:** drums all round
**Bodywork:** sports two-seater
**Maximum speed (approx):** 108 mph (174 kph)

---

### 1946 TRIUMPH 1800 ROADSTER

**Engine:** in-line four cylinder, overhead-valve
**Bore × stroke:** 73 mm × 106 mm
**Capacity:** 1776 cc
**Maximum power:** 65 bhp
**Transmission:** four-speed manual
**Chassis:** square-section steel tube
**Suspension:** independent with transverse leaf spring and wishbone front, live axle with semi-elliptic leaf springs rear
**Brakes:** self-adjusting drums all round, hydraulically operated
**Bodywork:** roadster or saloon
**Maximum speed (approx):** 75 mph (120 kph)

---

they perceived as the gap between the MG T series and the Jaguar XK120, and showed their new car, the TR, powered by a 2-litre version of the Triumph Renown engine, at the 1952 Olympia Motor Show.

The 'simple but distinctive lines' of the open two-seater body attracted favourable comment, though the lack of luggage accommodation provided by the bobtailed rear end, with its exposed spare wheel mounting, was a drawback.

This was rectified by the following March, when a revised TR, with an extended boot, was shown at Geneva; 'The effect of the straight, clean lines is a great improvement on the rather beetle-like shape used originally,' commented *The Autocar*.

However, at the same time Sir John Black, managing director of Standard-Triumph, was demonstrating a prototype with the original tail line to Willys-Overland in America, since that company was considering taking the American agency.

The car wasn't available to the public until August 1953, when it

passengers.

Power came from a new 1800 cc engine, and the recently-introduced self-adjusting Girling Hydrostatic brakes were fitted; but a modern feature which was not so desirable was the steering column gearchange, which, for the direct linkage of a floor change substituted a dozen pivot points, three levers and a bell-crank, in the dubious interests of enabling three passengers to sit abreast in the front seat. 'If the driver can remember that he is operating the normal four-speed gear change upside down, he has mastered it,' optimistically claimed *The Autocar*, ignoring the possibilities for wear inherent in the system.

## Triumph TR2/3

Perhaps the most renowned postwar Triumphs, the TR series established a remarkable reputation; Triumph's original intention was to produce a sports car to plug what

**Triumph TR2**

# A-Z OF THE CAR

**Triumph Acclaim**

## Triumph Stag

The Triumph Stag was introduced in 1970 as the result of Triumph's policy of 'gap-filling' in the British car market.

With no other competition in its home country and very little throughout the rest of the world, the Stag was well-received. It offered excellent performance from its relaxed 3-litre engine and combined it with the luxury and equipment levels of its saloon counterparts – the 2000 and 2.5 series, upon which it was closely based.

This heavy, notoriously unreliable, but nonetheless desirable classic sports car ceased production in 1977, as did the six-cylinder saloons, the outcome of drastic range-trimming.

### 1973 TRIUMPH STAG

**Engine:** V8 overhead-camshaft
**Bore × stroke:** 86 mm × 64.5 mm
**Capacity:** 2997 cc
**Maximum power:** 145 bhp
**Transmission:** three-speed automatic
**Chassis:** integral
**Suspension:** independent with McPherson struts front and coil springs and semi-trailing arms rear
**Brakes:** discs front and drums rear
**Bodywork:** four-seater convertible
**Maximum speed (approx):** 120 mph (193 kph)

## Triumph Acclaim

The product of a deal made in 1979 between BL Cars and the Japanese firm of Honda, the Triumph Acclaim was essentially a Honda model (known overseas as the Honda Ballade).

The Acclaim was assembled at Cowley although some of it was British sourced and constructed (the interior trim, for instance). Power units and suspension components were supplied ready-assembled direct from Japan, however.

Intended primarily as a stop-gap vehicle between the Dolomite and the new generation Maestro range, the competent little Acclaim was produced only between 1982 and 1984 and was the last BL car to bear the Triumph name.

### 1984 TRIUMPH ACCLAIM

**Engine:** transverse in-line four cylinder, overhead-camshaft
**Bore × stroke:** 72 mm × 82 mm
**Capacity:** 1335 cc
**Maximum power:** 70 bhp
**Transmission:** five speed manual
**Chassis:** integral
**Suspension:** independent with McPherson struts all round and trailing and transverse links
**Brakes:** discs front and drums rear
**Bodywork:** four-door saloon
**Maximum speed (approx):** 96 mph (155 kph)

**Triumph Stag**

# TROJAN

**Kingston/Croydon, England**
**1922–1936, 1961–1965**

'Can you afford to walk?' was the slogan adopted by the makers of the ingenious Trojan utility car – the only make of car advertised in the *Church Times* – originally designed by Leslie Hounsfield before the Great War (the 1910 prototype still survives).

At the heart of this idiosyncratic machine was a 1.5-litre horizontal two-stroke engine with a minimum of moving parts, for it had two pairs of cylinders with common combustion chambers and long V-shaped connecting rods which flexed instead of pivoting. The engine was set in motion by a long 'mechanical seat starter' lever rising through the floor; ignition switch and petrol tap were combined, and since the inlet manifold was four feet long, on the first Trojans this tap/switch also operated a gravity feed primer for the inlet ports.

In the interests of reducing vibration, the flywheel of the engine was linked to the transmission through coil springs; the two-speed epicyclic gearing, which emitted curious noises like a small animal in pain, drove the solid rear axle through double chains. The punt-type chassis carried long, extremely flexible cantilever springs, which Trojan referred to as 'Wondersprings'.

The Trojan was initially built for Hounsfield's Trojan Ltd at Kingston-upon-Thames by the Leyland commercial vehicle company but manufacture was eventually taken over by Trojan Ltd and moved to Croydon in 1928.

The move was followed by the

launch for 1930 of the new RE (Rear Engined) model, which had the same engine and transmission layout – now with three speeds – transferred to the rear of the car, where it hid in a dummy boot with the power unit mounted vertically.

Production fell away to a trickle in the 1930s, though commercial versions of the Trojan, favoured by such companies as Brooke Bond continued to sell well.

A dumpy saloon, the Cheviot, and the Exmoor tourer were available in 1934, though even at the competitive price of £185 few customers wanted them.

In a last-ditch attempt to attract private customers, Trojan announced a streamlined saloon, the Mastra, for the 1936 season; its 2.2-litre six-cylinder two-stroke engine still lived at the rear of the chassis. The Mastra did not go into

production, and though Trojan continued to build vans, the Trojan name did not feature on a private car again until 1962, when the company took over manufacture of the Heinkel bubble car.

# TUCKER

**Chicago, USA**
**1946–1948**

Preston Tucker was an inventive engineer who had worked with the great Harry Miller in the 1930s, and saw the opportunity for producing a super-safe 120 mph (193 kph) dream car to meet the new perceptions of the atomic age.

Styled by ex-Duesenberg designer Alex Tremulis, the 1946 Tucker Torpedo seemed to have

**Tucker Torpedo**

## 1923 TROJAN

**Engine:** horizontal four-cylinder, two-stroke
**Bore × stroke:** 63.5 mm × 117.5 mm
**Capacity:** 1488 cc
**Maximum power:** 11 bhp
**Transmission:** two-speed epicyclic
**Chassis:** pressed steel punt
**Suspension:** non-independent with cantilever 'wondersprings' all round
**Brakes:** rear wheel drums and transmission
**Bodywork:** chummy tourer
**Maximum speed (approx):** 35 mph (56 kph)

## 1946 TUCKER TORPEDO

**Engine:** flat six helicopter unit, overhead-valve
**Bore × stroke:** 127 mm × 127 mm
**Capacity:** 9651 cc
**Maximum power:** 150 bhp
**Transmission:** Tuckermatic torque converter
**Chassis:** perimeter frame
**Suspension:** independent, rubber in torsion and wishbone links all round
**Brakes:** discs all round
**Bodywork:** streamline saloon
**Maximum speed (approx):** 130 mph (210 kph)

met Preston Tucker's demand for a car that was truly ahead of its time. At the rear of the streamlined body

**Trojan**

– its drag coefficient was said to be only 0.30 which is impressive even by today's standards – was originally mounted a massive 9651 cc flat-six engine designed by Ben Parsons.

The intention was that this huge power unit would be low-stressed and thus long-lived, but problems in readying this engine for production prompted the adoption of a flat-six Franklin helicopter engine, which had been converted to sealed-system water-cooling to overcome customer prejudices. Tucker planned that later Torpedoes would have a specially-built Caproni turbine engine.

The Torpedo was full of safety features that would not become general practice for another 20 or 30 years, like all-round disc brakes, a pop-out windscreen and padded dashboard.

Suspension was independent all-round, and early cars were fitted with Tuckermatic transmissions which had only 30 basic parts. Problems, however, dictated that production Torpedoes used an ex-Cord four-speed manual gearbox with electric preselector shift.

Tucker had produced some 50 cars in a former Dodge aircraft plant in Chicago when he was taken to court by the Securities Exchange Commission and accused of stock fraud after he had applied for a $30 million loan from the US Reconstruction Finance Committee.

Though Tucker was exonerated, the damage had been done; the court hearing had labelled Tucker a fraud, and the public was all too ready to believe the smear campaign. Production never restarted.

Preston Tucker died of lung cancer in 1956 while negotiating to build a small car, the Carioca, in Brazil.

# TURCAT-MERY

**Marseille, France**
**1896–1928**

Léon Turcat and his cousin Simon Méry, both aged 22, built their first car in 1896; it had a horizontal four-cylinder engine and chain drive. Over the next three years, the cousins built a handful of cars, then set their business on a proper footing as a manufacturing company, the Société des Ateliers de Construction d'Automobiles Turcat, Méry & Cie, established in May 1899 with capital of Fr 350,000 (about £14,000). But business remained small until December 1901 when, on a visit to the Paris Salon (the cousins couldn't afford to exhibit their cars) Turcat met the Baron Adrien de Turckheim of De Dietrich. The upshot was that in February 1902, Turckheim visited Nice, was taken for a ride in a

**Turcat-Méry**

Turcat-Méry car, and arranged for a licence under which the Turcat-Méry cars would be built by De Dietrich and the cousins would receive royalties.

In 1905, Adrien de Turckheim quarrelled with Eugene de Dietrich, resulting in the Lunéville De Dietrich automobile company splitting away from the parent group. For the time being, Turcat-Méry introduced a big chain-drive 10,200 cc six-cylinder, and the following year their complex range included a 6333 cc 28CV, a 3053 cc 18CV and a 2412 cc 14CV.

That year, however, saw a serious financial crisis for De Dietrich, which had made some unwise expansions into Britain and Italy, and by 1912, Turcat and Méry were back in Marseille heading their own company again, building monobloc fours of 2.6, 3.3, 4.1, 4.7 and 6.3 litres. After the war, Turcat-Méry's finances were unsure, and the company was reformed in 1921 and 1924. Inbetween times, they introduced a 3015 cc 15CV in 1922, followed in 1923 by a 2978 cc 15CV.

In 1925, Turcat-Méry launched their first truly modern post-war car, the overhead camshaft 2388 cc 12CV. Finances were still unsteady,

and after 1926, Turcat-Méry was forced to fit proprietary engines – including 1500 cc and 1700 cc SCAP and CIME units – in order to survive. There was even a handful of 2.3-litre SCAP engined straight-eights, though very few of this model were made. No new cars were built after 1928.

# TURNER

**Wolverhampton, England**
**1902–1930**

Turner built the Belgian Miesse three-cylinder steam car under licence until 1913 – indeed, the flash-boilered Turner-Miesse continued some seven years after the Miesse steamer had ceased production. In 1906, Turner temporarily turned to petrol, building the Seymour-Turner, which had a 4.1-litre four-cylinder engine and shaft drive, for Seymours of London. Steam took over again, however, and it was not until 1911 that another internal-combustion car appeared, in the shape of the Turner cyclecar, powered by an 1100 cc vee-twin, and with a two-speed transmission.

A more refined small car, the Ten, appeared the following year,

as did a 2.1-litre Fifteen.

Though the Turner company built some Varley-Woods chassis from 1918 in a specially-rented plant, the Turner marque itself did not reappear until 1922, when 1.8-litre and 2.3-litre models were announced. During 1923, the 1.8-litre engine was replaced by a 1.5-litre Dorman power unit, while in 1924 a 2.1-litre Colonial model was added to the range, gradually ousting the 2.3-litre model. In the latter part of the 1920s, Turner only built the 12 hp car, which gained front-wheel brakes from 1928; production ceased in 1930.

**Turner-Miesse Steam Car**

# TURNER

**Wolverhampton, England**
**1951–66**

Though this Turner company also came from Wolverhampton, it was an entirely distinct concern from the other Wulfrunian Turner firm. Founded by John Turner to build racing cars, Turner soon began building sports cars with proprietary power units, by such makers as Ford, Vauxhall, Lea-Francis and Austin. With a simple tubular chassis incorporating Austin A35 independent front suspension, the Turner 950 was the company's best-known model.

In 1958, a Turner driven by ex-ERA racer Bob Gerard won the *Autosport* Series Production Sports Car Championship; the company introduced the option of the 1100 cc FWA Coventry-Climax power unit, though initially for export only. Indeed, exports played a considerable role in the Turner story, for though most Turners sold on the UK market were in kit form (which avoided purchase tax), it was claimed that 90 per cent of their output went to North America and South Africa. At the end of 1959, it was announced that an Alexander-tuned version of the Turner, known as the Turner-Alexander, with an alloy-head 948 cc BMC power unit capable of developing 80 bhp (against the standard 43 bhp) would be sold by a separate company in Haddenham, Bucks, but little seems to have come of this.

## 1959 TURNER CLIMAX

**Engine:** in-line four-cylinder, overhead-valve
**Bore × stroke:** 72.4 mm × 66.6 mm
**Capacity:** 1098 cc
**Maximum power:** 75 bhp
**Transmission:** four-speed manual
**Chassis:** tubular steel with welded steel sub-frame
**Suspension:** Independent with wishbones and coil springs front and trailing links, radius rods and transverse torsion bars rear
**Brakes:** discs front, drums rear
**Bodywork:** glassfibre sports
**Maximum speed (approx):** 104 mph (167 kph)

# TVR

**Blackpool, England**
**1956 to date**

Designed by Trevor (hence TVR) Wilkinson and Bernard Williams, the TVR first appeared on the export market, as it was 'race-tested' in America under the name Jomar by sports/racing car dealer Ray Saidel, from about 1956 before going into production at the end of 1957 (a 1.2-litre Austin A40-engined prototype with glass fibre bodywork by R.G. Shattock had been built in 1954).

TVRs were available in kit form from about 1957, but full production did not begin until after the first of countless financial crises which dogged the early history of TVR had been resolved by the formation of a new company at the end of 1957.

Publicly announced in January 1958, the original production TVR was available with either the 1172 cc sidevalve Ford engine or the 1098 cc Coventry-Climax engine; the Ford unit could be equipped with a Shorrock supercharger, which boosted the power output to 54 bhp, giving a top speed of 110 mph (177 kph) – though the Climax-engined version was quicker still, at 125 mph (201 kph).

The TVR coupé was known as the TVR Grantura, from Bernard Williams's Grantura Plastics company; the Mk I Grantura was succeeded by the Mk II, with revised bodywork, in 1959. The Shorrock-supercharged Ford 100E engine was replaced by the new 997 cc 105E Anglia power unit, while other engines available in TVRs included the 1216 cc FWE Coventry-Climax and the 1489 cc MGA unit. In the early 1960s the 1340 cc Ford Classic and 1612 cc MGA engines were available alongside the eternal Coventry-Climax.

At the 1962 New York Motor Show, the TVR Mk III was introduced, with redesigned, Triumph Herald-based suspension; though the new model secured £1.5 million-worth of orders for TVR, an over-ambitious competition programme quickly ran the company into trouble, and a new company, Grantura Engineering, took over production with an MGB-engined Mk III 1800 appearing soon after. In 1963 Grantura Engineering was succeeded by TVR Cars Ltd.

A new turn for TVR came when an American customer couldn't obtain delivery of an MGB engine for his TVR, and the agents, White Griffith Motors, installed a 4727 cc Ford V8 instead, creating the TVR Griffith 200 (1964) and 400 (1965). When Griffith folded, the TVR Griffith V8 was continued as a British model.

TVR Cars went into liquidation in 1965, shortly after the Fiore-styled Trident had appeared; this model was taken over by a separate company, Trident Cars, which survived until 1974.

The production of TVR cars was continued by TVR Engineering, headed by Arthur Lilley and his son Martin, who took over at the end of 1965. Halfway through the following year, the Mk IV appeared, with the engine moved forward in the frame and the overall quality improved.

A short-lived 1966 venture was the Hillman Imp-based Tina, another Fiore design, which failed to reach production.

In 1967 the Vixen 1600 succeeded the 1800 cc Mk IV, followed a year later by the long wheelbase Vixen S2 (the S3 was a 'federalised' version for the American market, launched in 1970). A new V8 model, the Tuscan, appeared in 1967, followed in 1969 by the 3-litre Ford-engined Tuscan V6.

A new design of chassis appeared in 1971; into this were fitted the Triumph 1300 cc (as used on the Spitfire) the six-cylinder 2500 cc engines, while in 1972 the availability of more modern bodywork created the 1600M, 2500M and 3000M.

The company survived a major setback in January 1975, when a fire caused £250,000-worth of damage and destroyed a year's supply of pre-formed chassis tubing. Nevertheless, within three months TVR was back in production and the 150 mph (242 kph) Ford V6 powered Turbo appeared later in 1975, followed by the Taimar hatchback at the end of 1976.

The original, rather humped look of the TVR was outdated by

**Turner Sports**

1980, when the more square-cut Tasmin coupé and convertible appeared; the same basic shape is currently in production as the 280i (with Ford V6 power) and the V8-engined 350i and 390SE Convertible.

## TVR Mk I Grantura

Named for ex-dirt track racer Bernard Williams's Grantura Plastics company, which made its glass fibre bodywork, the original TVR coupé first appeared as a kit car, and made its debut in fully built-up form in January 1958 at the Manchester garage of H & J Quick, Ltd, Ford main dealers. It was offered with a choice of either the 1172 cc Ford sidevalve of the far better double overhead-camshaft 1098 cc Coventry-Climax FWS engine.

Even with the heaviest power unit option, the 54 bhp Shorrock-supercharged Ford engine, the little TVR scaled only 1450 lb (658 kg); this excellent power/weight ratio made for a lively performance, and the car possessed the advanced feature for 1958 of all-round independent suspension.

Raced in America under the name Jomar, the original TVRs were lively little cars, though the cramped cockpit and harsh ride restricted their ownership to the more dedicated enthusiasts. The Mk I TVR Grantura was supplanted by the restyled Mk II version in 1959.

**1958 TVR Mk I GRANTURA**

**Engine:** supercharged, in-line four cylinder, sidevalve
**Bore × stroke:** 63.5 mm × 92.5 mm
**Capacity:** 1171 cc
**Maximum power:** 54 bhp
**Transmission:** three-speed manual
**Chassis:** tubular backbone
**Suspension:** full-independent with laminated torsion bars and trailing arms
**Brakes:** drums all round
**Bodywork:** glassfibre, coupé
**Maximum speed (approx):** 110 mph (117 kph)

TVR Mk I Grantura

## TVR 350i

Powered by the Rover V8 engine, the current TVR 350i has a distinctive, angular look that nevertheless possesses excellent aerodynamics. Its V8 engine underlines the fact that this powerful sports two-seater is very definitely aimed at the export market in the United States; its level of performance is indicated by the fact that the TVR 350i will cover a quarter mile from rest in less than 15 seconds and go from 0–50 mph (81 kph) in just 5.1 seconds.

Though the 350i is recognisably the spiritual successor to the old TVR Griffith, it has modern ride and handling characteristics that put it a world away from its predecessor; nevertheless the high transmission tunnel is one of the features that provide a clue to the TVR's origins.

**1984 TVR 350i**

**Engine:** V8 overhead-valve
**Bore × stroke:** 88.8 mm × 71 mm
**Capacity:** 3528 cc
**Maximum power:** 190 bhp
**Transmission:** five-speed manual
**Chassis:** tubular backbone with perimeter tubes
**Suspension:** independent with coil spring and wishbone front and lower transverse link, radius arm and coil spring rear
**Brakes:** discs all round
**Bodywork:** glassfibre coupé or convertible
**Maximum speed (approx):** 140 mph (225 kph)

## UNIC

**Puteaux, France**
**1904–1939**

When Georges Richard resigned from the Richard-Brasier concern in 1904, he founded the Georges Richard Company in Puteaux, Seine; since he intended to follow a one-model policy, his new company was also known as 'Unic'.

Production started with a handsome twin-cylinder 10/12CV of 1797 cc, and the one-model policy was quickly abandoned,

TVR 350i

## 1922 UNIC TYPE L

**Engine:** in-line four-cylinder, side-valve
**Bore × stroke:** 70 mm × 120 mm
**Capacity:** 1843 cc
**Maximum power:** 30 bhp
**Transmission:** four-speed manual
**Chassis:** pressed steel channel
**Suspension:** non-independent with semi-elliptic leaf springs front and superimposed cantilever and quarter elliptic leaf springs rear
**Brakes:** rear wheel drums
**Bodywork:** tourer or saloon
**Maximum speed (approx):** 55 mph (88 kph)

**Unic Type L**

another model, the 2615 cc 16/20CV four, appearing the following year, followed shortly after by the 1943 cc 12CV (later enlarged to 2120 cc), which was sold mainly as a taxicab chassis and survived in this form for nearly 20 years.

Unic cars were almost universally dull, but notable among them were the 4085 cc six-cylinder produced from 1909–1911 and the long-stroke 1914 23/40CV of 6242 cc.

After the war, Unic's staple product (apart from the 12CV taxi) was the 1847 cc four, which had curious rear suspension with a single cantilever spring superimposed over a short quarter-elliptic. Unic was also becoming noted for the construction of lorries of all sizes.

A 1997 cc sports model arrived in 1923, distinguished by horizontal bonnet louvres and capable of 70 mph (113 kph). Unic also essayed sleeve-valve engined cars without great success, and in 1927 joined a short-lived alliance with Chenard-Walcker and Delahaye (Rosengart also participated in 1929).

In 1929, Unic launched two overhead-valve eight-cylinder models with double cantilever rear suspension; there was then an hiatus during which only commercial vehicles were built, broken by the appearance of a new model with independent front suspension by semi-elliptic springs and articulated arms bolted to the centre of the spring and hinged to the opposite side of the frame.

The old overhead-valve 2-litre chassis continued, joined by an overhead-valve 3-litre six-cylinder, which, in its sports version, had a double-reduction rear axle. Only trucks were produced after 1939.

# UNIPOWER

### Perivale/London, England
### 1966–1970

One of the best of the Mini-based specials, the mid-engined Unipower GT was the brainchild of Ernest Unger and Val Dare-Bryan, and first appeared in prototype form in 1963 with aluminium bodywork on a spaceframe chassis, and built in racing driver Roy Pierpoint's workshop.

But the project was taken over by financiers Tim Powell and Andrew Hedges, and reappeared with a very strong two-seater glass fibre body – with coupé or targa top – bonded to the complex space-frame. Power was by either Mini Cooper or Cooper S engines.

A Mk II version appeared in 1968, and new models with Triumph Stag and BMC six-cylinder engines were proposed. About 75 Unipower GTs were built, over half of which were exported.

The stillborn BMC six-cylinder model was the genesis of the Bohanna Diablo, which became the AC ME3000.

## 1968 UNIPOWER GT

**Engine:** transverse, mid-mounted overhead-valve, four-cylinder
**Bore × stroke:** 70.64 mm × 81.33 mm
**Capacity:** 1275 cc
**Maximum power:** 76 bhp
**Transmission:** four-speed manual
**Chassis:** tubular steel
**Suspension:** independent with coil spring and wishbone
**Brakes:** discs front and drums rear
**Bodywork:** two-seater coupé
**Maximum speed (approx):** 115 mph (185 kph)

**Unipower**

# A-Z OF THE CAR

## VALE

**Maida Vale, England
1932–1936**

'The Hand-Made Car at a Mass-Production Price' took its name from the site of the works where it was built, in London's Maida Vale. Designed by 'Pow' Pellew (later the Earl of Exmouth), the Vale Special was initially powered by a side-valve 832 cc Triumph engine, which gave a top speed of some 72 mph (116 kph)

The Vale Special cars were

### 1932 VALE SPECIAL

**Engine:** in-line four-cylinder side-valve
**Bore × stroke:** 56 mm × 83 mm
**Capacity:** 832 cc
**Maximum power:** 21 bhp
**Transmission:** four-speed manual
**Chassis:** pressed steel channel
**Suspension:** non-independent with semi-elliptic leaf springs
**Brakes:** drums all round
**Bodywork:** two-seater sports
**Maximum speed (approx):** 72 mph (116 kph)

nearly all built as two-seaters, though the four-seater Tourette was offered in 1933.

In the interests of performance, in 1934 it was announced that larger engines – Coventry-Climax fours and sixes of 1098 cc and 1476 cc respectively – would be fitted, and the company offered to re-engine existing cars.

Possibly the last of the 103 Vale Specials built was the supercharged six-cylinder racing car built in 1935 for Ian Connell, and capable of some 130 mph (209 kph) when it could be persuaded to run properly.

## VANDEN PLAS

**London/Abingdon, England
1960–1980**

Founded in 1923 as the British branch of the famous Belgian coachbuilding firm, Vanden Plas became a subsidiary of Austin in June 1946, for the initial purpose of building the bodywork for the 4-litre A135 Princess. In 1960, Vanden Plas became a separate marque, building the de luxe Austin-based Princess; in 1964 the company also built the Vanden Plas 1100.

### 1960 VANDEN PLAS PRINCESS

**Engine:** in-line six-cylinder, overhead-valve
**Bore × stroke:** 83.3 mm × 89 mm
**Capacity:** 2912 cc
**Maximum power:** 108 bhp
**Transmission:** three-speed automatic
**Chassis:** integral
**Suspension:** independent coil spring and wishbone front and live axle with semi-elliptic leaf springs rear
**Brakes:** front disc, rear drum
**Bodywork:** saloon
**Maximum speed (approx):** 98 mph (158 kph)

The typical Vanden Plas treatment consisted of a superior level of trim and paint, a distinctive grille with the discreet crown badge, walnut dashboard and leather seats.

The 1965 Princess R used the 3.9-litre Rolls-Royce military engine, while in June 1967 the Vanden Plas 1300 appeared, and by 1973, had become the sole car bearing the Vanden Plas nameplate. The last Vanden Plas model, the 1500, was a de luxe version of the Austin Allegro. Vanden Plas also produced coachwork for Daimler and Jaguar cars in their Park Royal, London, factory; in 1979 the factory was closed and Vanden Plas production transferred to the Abingdon MG factory, was closed down in 1980.

**Vanden Plas Princess**

**Vale Special**

# VARLEY-WOODS

**London/Wolverhampton,
England
1918–1921**

The Varley-Woods took its name from the two partners in the project, Ernest Vernon Varley Grossmith and John Robert Woods. The former, a member of the famous acting and soap-making family who dropped his surname in 1919, had previously been involved in the manufacture of canned soups and mouth organs, while Woods was a Near East river trader.

The Varley-Woods was a handsome, if pedestrian, car with a Rolls-Royce-type radiator and polished aluminium bonnet, built in a specially-rented factory by Turner of Wolverhampton.

An aluminium block overhead-camshaft 1795 cc Dorman engine was used on the first Varley-Woods cars, but from mid-1920 the

---

## 1920 VARLEY-WOODS

**Engine:** in-line four cylinder, overhead-camshaft
**Bore × stroke:** 69 mm × 120 mm
**Capacity:** 1795 cc
**Maximum power:** 27 bhp
**Transmission:** four-speed manual
**Chassis:** pressed steel channel
**Suspension:** non-independent with semi-elliptic leaf springs front and cantilever leaf springs rear
**Brakes:** rear wheel drums
**Bodywork:** tourer
**Maximum speed (approx):** 50 mph (80 kph)

---

company fitted a more conventional 14.3 hp Tylor engine (made by a well-known manufacturer of lavatory cisterns who also built power units for London buses).

Woods returned to Africa and was eaten by a lion, and the company eventually succumbed to bankruptcy after a brief, but chequered, career.

# VAUXHALL

**London/Luton, England
1903 to date**

The Vauxhall Ironworks had been founded by one Alexander Wilson back in 1857, and had gained a sound reputation as makers of marine engines long before the company decided to venture into the manufacture of horseless carriages in 1903 (the company had in fact experimented with marine petrol engines as early as 1896). The vehicle produced was an American-inspired runabout powered by a horizontal single-cylinder 5 hp engine, with chain drive, coil-spring suspension and tiller steering. A similar design was built for the Brush company under the name Brushmobile. The following year, Vauxhall built a 6 hp version of this design, which boasted the luxury of a reverse gear!

In 1905, the company moved from its original base at London's Vauxhall to Luton, Bedfordshire, coincidentally the country estate of the Norman knight Fulk le Bréant, whose London residence, Fulk's Hall, had been the origin of the district of Vauxhall. Fulk's crest, a griffin, had been adopted as the

trademark of the Vauxhall Ironworks. This move heralded the introduction of three new models with three-cylinder vertical engines, which competed successfully in trials and hillclimbs (although an entry in the 1905 Tourist Trophy proved abortive, despite the fitment of an overdrive six-speed gearbox).

The original buggy-type design remained popular, but was phased out from 1906, when a more conventional shaft-driven car, the T-head four-cylinder 18/20 hp, was introduced, the header tank of its radiator bearing concave 'flutes'; this styling feature, which distinguished all Vauxhalls up to 1959, was apparently inspired by the ornate top of a wardrobe....

A smaller 12/16 hp four-cylinder on similar lines followed, then chief engineer Laurence Pomeroy introduced the L-head 20 hp, one of which won the 1908 2000-mile Reliability Trial. Pomeroy then designed a sporting 3-litre Vauxhall, which performed so convincingly in the 1910 German Prince Henry Trials that, with the cylinder capacity increased to 4 litres, the model went into production as the famous Prince Henry Vauxhall, which gave rise to the most famous of all Vauxhalls, the 30/98, for which Pomeroy increased the engine capacity to 4.5 litres. A few 30/98s were made before World War I, during which the Vauxhall company was one of the few firms to continue car manufacture, as the D-Type Vauxhall was produced in considerable numbers as Army staff cars.

The side-valve E-Type 30/98 reappeared in 1919, but was given a new overhead-valve 4.2-litre

engine and front-wheel brakes in 1922, and was known thereafter as the OE.

In 1922, Vauxhall introduced a new, cheaper model, the 14/40; that same year, the D-Type acquired overhead valves. Vauxhall was still a small-scale manufacturer (in 1924 the company produced just 1400 cars) but nevertheless the American General Motors giant was anxious to buy into an established British company and, after negotiations with Austin had fallen through, took over Vauxhall in December 1925.

Although it was only some three years later that the first GM-inspired Vauxhalls appeared in the shape of the 20/60, which featured overhead valves, coil ignition and central gear-change, Vauxhall continued to introduce new models like the S-Type 'Silent 80', a 3.9-litre six-cylinder sleeve-valve luxury car, priced at £1250.

The 20/60 cost only £475, far cheaper than any other Vauxhall — the R-Type 'Hurlingham' was the stylish sports version — but the 2-litre Cadet six of 1931 was even less costly, for it sold at £280 in 17 hp form and £295 in 26 hp guise. Despite that, in 1932 the Cadet became the first car on the British market to offer a synchromesh gearbox, beating Rolls-Royce by several months.

The A-Type Light Six, the first British car with 'no-draught' ventilation, was introduced in 12 and 14 hp form in 1933 and, by 1934, the model had taken some 40 per cent of all new-car registrations in the 14 hp class. At the other end of the scale, Vauxhall brought out the 20 hp BY-Type of 2.4 litres and the 3.2-litre BX-Type 'Big Six' in 1934; the 'Big Six' survived until late 1936, when it was replaced by the 25 hp G-Type, with independent front suspension of knee-action type, which had originally appeared on the 12 hp DY-Type and 14 hp DX-Type in 1935.

The unitary construction of the four-cylinder H-Type 10 hp of 1938 was another technical innovation for Vauxhall, as this was the first integrally constructed British car. The H-Type was priced at only £158; it had a three-speed gearbox, and returned a fuel consumption of 40 mpg.

**Varley-Woods**

In 1939, all Vauxhalls were fitted with hydraulic brakes; the newly introduced 14 hp J-Type, with its 1781 cc six-cylinder engine, cost a highly competitive £220, which gave an early boost to sales.

For the duration of the war, the Vauxhall factory was engaged in producing jerrycans, Bedford trucks, Churchill tanks, armour-piercing shells, rocket-launcher tubes and, towards the end of hostilities, jet engines.

The post-war era saw the reintroduction of the four-cylinder 10 hp and 12 hp and the six-cylinder 14. However, by 1948 all of these cars had been phased out, and replaced by the 1442 cc Wyvern four and the 2275 cc Velox six L-Type models, with completely new styling on markedly trans-Atlantic lines, with faired-in headlights. A steering-column gear-change was another American feature of the L-Type Vauxhalls, which were both re-styled in 1952 as the E-Type range, with short-stroke engines replacing the original power units. A luxury version of the six known as the Cresta appeared in 1955 at a price of £844. The E-type models remained in production until 1957, when the four-cylinder 1.5-litre Victor, with its distinctive wrap-around 'dog-leg' windscreen, appeared; the six was similarly restyled in 1958.

The Victor was re-styled in 1962, while the Velox and Cresta received similar treatment the next year. More powerful engines were introduced in 1964, the Victor power unit was increased in capacity to 1.6 litres, while the six went up to 3.3 litres.

A major departure from previous practice came in 1964, when Vauxhall announced a new small car, the square-cut 1057 cc Viva, which was re-styled for 1967 and again in 1970, when the Viva HC was offered in 1159 cc and 1256 cc forms.

An entirely new Victor appeared for 1968 with 1.6 or 2-litre inclined ohc engines; the camshaft was driven by a cogged neoprene belt, the first occasion that this feature had been seen on a British production car. The old 3.3-litre six was fitted into a similarly-styled bodyshell to create the Ventora.

In 1971, the Victors were restyled on more chunky lines, using many of the same body inner skin panels as the equivalent Opel models, and with engines whose capacity had been increased to 1800 cc and 2300 cc; similar body styling changes were made to the Ventora. The old 1600 cc Victor engine was now available in the Viva bodyshell, while a coupé version of this model, the Firenza, appeared in 1971, offering a choice of 1256 cc, 1600 cc or 2300 cc power units. The entire Viva/Firenza range was revised in 1973, with the Viva name being retained on the models with the smallest engines; the 1800 and 2300 now became known as Magnums.

In 1975, Vauxhall introduced a new model, the Chevette hatchback which was powered by the 1256 cc Viva engine. The following year, the Cavalier, a mid-sized saloon identical to the Opel Ascona, was imported from GM's Belgian plant, with a choice of 1300, 1600 or 1900 cc engines; by August 1977, this model was being built in Britain.

Early in 1979, Vauxhall introduced the Carlton and Royale, two new 2.8-litre Opel-based luxury models and, by the following year, a 3-litre Royale was also available. The last Viva was built in mid-1979, and replaced by an Anglicised Vauxhall Kadett marketed as the Astra.

A new front-wheel-driven Cavalier with a choice of 1.3-litre and 1.6-litre engines was launched for 1982; again, the German Opel Ascona was identical. With this model, Vauxhall managed to steal a march on their rivals, Ford, whose Sierra replacement for the Cortina was still a year away.

A new Spanish plant was opened in Zaragoza to produce a minicar launched for 1984 and known as the Corsa in Europe and Nova in Britain (in its native Spain, 'no va' means 'doesn't go'). completely restyled Astras, with more aerodynamic lines, appeared for 1985.

In early 1986, Vauxhall introduced the Belmont notchback, derived from the Astra and intended to fill the gap between that model and the Cavalier. It was due to be followed in the autumn by a new Carlton with virtually flush glazing, independent rear suspension and revised four-cylinder engines. A 16-valve version was also planned.

# Vauxhall Prince Henry

Developed from Vauxhall's first L-head car, the 20 hp car which won the 1908 2000-Mile Trial, a 3-litre sports car with a wickedly pointed pointed radiator, was designed by Laurence Pomeroy for the 1910 Prince Henry Trial. In the competition, two of the team of three made non-stop runs, and by late 1910 the first Prince Henry Vauxhalls were being supplied to private owners.

When bodied as a streamlined single-seater the Prince Henry became the first car (in its class) to reach 100 mph (161 kph) at Brooklands.

Fitted as standard with sporting torpedo bodywork, the Prince Henry cost only £580, and soon established a sound reputation for top-gear flexibility allied to excellent handling and outright performance; it was one of the first true sports cars. For 1913, Vauxhall fitted a new 3969 cc engine which produced 75 bhp against the 60 bhp of the previous power unit; when this engine began to prove inadequate in competition with rival marques, Pomeroy developed a new 4526 cc sporting car, the 30/98 with a power output of 90 bhp.

## 1914 VAUXHALL PRINCE HENRY

**Engine:** in-line four cylinder side valve
**Bore × stroke:** 95 mm × 140 mm
**Capacity:** 3969 cc
**Maximum power:** 75 bhp
**Transmission:** four-speed manual
**Chassis:** pressed steel channel
**Suspension:** non-independent with semi-elliptic leaf springs
**Brakes:** rear wheel and transmission brakes
**Bodywork:** torpedo tourer
**Maximum speed (approx):** 80 mph (129 kph)

*Vauxhall Prince Henry*

# A-Z
## OF THE CAR

**Vauxhall Cadet**

## Vauxhall 30/98

John Higginson was a Lancashire businessman who, apart from having invented the Auto-Vac fuel feed system, was also a skilled amateur competitions driver, who had achieved considerable success with such cars as the 60 hp Mercedes and La Buire. He suggested to Pomeroy that a viable new competition car could be created by fitting a bigger engine into the Prince Henry chassis. The new power unit was known, for no very definite reason, as the 30/98. It was initially very much what would nowadays be known as a homologation special, for Vauxhall were in the beginning reluctant to sell 30/98 chassis, save to the kind of rich amateur who could be trusted to enhance the company's image in competition (the chassis price of £900 also helped to restrict sales).

Higginson was by far the most successful of the few customers who bought the dozen or so 30/98 Vauxhalls built before World War I, achieving fastest times at such hill-climbs as Waddington Pike, Shelsley Walsh and Aston Clinton during 1913.

Post-war, the 30/98 entered full production as the E-Type, using a shortened version of the D-Type chassis. It soon established an excellent reputation as a fast tourer, although it never achieved the sporting *éclat* of the 3-litre Bentley. In 1922, the side-valve E-Type was supplanted by the ohv OE-Type,

---

**1922 VAUXHALL 30/98 OE**

**Engine:** in-line four cylinder overhead-valve
**Bore × stroke:** 98 mm × 140 mm
**Capacity:** 4234 cc
**Maximum power:** 115 bhp
**Transmission:** four-speed manual
**Chassis:** pressed steel channel
**Suspension:** non-independent with semi-elliptic leaf springs
**Brakes:** drums all round
**Bodywork:** sports tourer
**Maximum speed (approx):** 85 mph (137 kph)

---

which was both quieter and more powerful than the old model, developing around 115 bhp against the 90 bhp of the E-Type.

The optional aluminium 'Wensum' sports bodywork was among the most atractive styles of the 1920s, with its flared wings and vee-stern with wood decking.

Braking was never the strong point of the 30/98, although cable-operated front-wheel brakes, introduced in 1923, ameliorated the system somewhat, even if the cables needed frequent adjustment. Hydraulics made their appearance towards the end of the 30/98's life, in 1926. Surprisingly, the 30/98 survived well into the GM era, with the last few cars being built late in 1927. Total production was around 580, of which more than 50 per cent were exported to Australia.

## Vauxhall Cadet

Launched at the beginning of October 1931, the Cadet was by far the cheapest car that Vauxhall had built

---

**1932 VAUXHALL CADET**

**Engine:** in-line six cylinder overhead-valve
**Bore × stroke:** 67.5 mm × 95.25 mm
**Capacity:** 2048 cc
**Maximum power:** 40 bhp
**Transmission:** three-speed manual
**Chassis:** pressed steel channel
**Suspension:** non-independent with semi-elliptic leaf springs
**Brakes:** drums all round
**Bodywork:** tourer, coupé, saloon
**Maximum speed (approx):** 62 mph (100 kph)

---

up to that point, the standard saloon selling for £280 and the chassis for a mere £185. The car was designed on straightforward, American-influenced lines. Following on the success of the 20/60 hp, the Cadet really established Vauxhall as a mass-producer of motor cars.

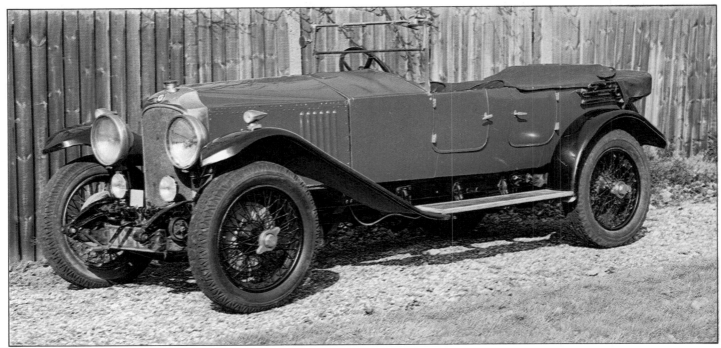
**Vauxhall 30/98**

**Vauxhall Wyvern**

For 1932, Vauxhall made a number of improvements to the Cadet, including the replacement of the 6 volt electrical system by 12 volts, Marles-Weller cam and lever steering instead of the Bishop cam system and, most importantly, the adoption of a synchromesh gearbox. This had previously been seen in America on Buick and Cadillac cars, but this was the first time that the 'easy-change' transmission had been fitted to a British car. Remarked *The Autocar*, 'The car is unusually easy to control by reason of the synchromesh gear, which does not call for double clutching in changing down from top to second or in changing up from first to second or from second to top… As regards silence of operation, second gear runs so quietly that it is hardly possible to tell whether the car is on top or second except by the increased revolutions of the engine.'

A 26 hp version of the Cadet was also built, chiefly for 'Colonial' markets.

## Vauxhall Velox & Wyvern

Launched in 1951, the 1.5-litre, four-cylinder Wyvern and 2.25-litre, six-cylinder Velox E-Type models introduced curved windscreens and novel side-opening bonnets (although the latter feature was soon replaced by a conventional rear-hinged layout). The power units were initially those used on the L-Type Velox and Wyvern produced in 1948-51, then in 1952 a new 'square engine' was introduced, with capacities of 1507 cc for the Wyvern and 2262 cc for the Velox. Furthermore, in 1953, an optional 7.6:1 high-compression cylinder head was offered for the Velox as a result of the reintroduction of branded fuels after so many years of

**1953 VAUXHALL WYVERN**

**Engine:** in-line four cylinder overhead valve
**Bore × stroke:** 79.4 mm × 76.2 mm
**Capacity:** 1507 cc
**Maximum power:** 40 bhp
**Transmission:** three-speed manual
**Chassis:** integral
**Suspension:** independent with coil spring and wishbone front and non-independent with semi-elliptic leaf springs rear
**Brakes:** drums all round
**Bodywork:** four-door saloon
**Maximum speed (approx):** 70 mph (113 kph)

wartime 'Pool' petrol

Apart from minor trim changes, like a new grille in 1956, the body shape remained unchanged throughout the production life of the Wyvern and Velox (1951-57), although in 1954 the Cresta was launched as a luxury version of the Velox.

It was in 1953 that Vauxhall not only produced its millionth vehicle, but output exceeded 100,000 vehicles a year for the first time; total production of the E-Type series was 341,626 cars.

## Vauxhall Viva

Mechanically, the original HA Viva, which appeared in 1964, was very similar to the Opel Kadett; its basic price was just £478 (plus £100

purchase tax), for which the customer got a basic, boxy saloon. Its styling showed how poverty-stricken Vauxhall had become.

'World-wide tests,' claimed its makers, 'have proved its superiority in speed, steering, handling, roominess, suspension and all-round finish', although the car suffered from a bouncy ride (and some early examples were known to drop their propellor shafts in the road).

Press reports categorised the Viva as having no vices: 'It is safe and unsporting with a limit of adhesion that is quite high, but not exceptional…the Viva commanded respect rather than great enthusiasm for its virtues from our testers,' commented *Motor*.

The HA model lasted until 1967, although the van-based Beagle estate car kept the square HA line, with its clinched-over seams, until 1973.

The Viva name survived until mid-1979; a 2-litre variant of the Viva was built in Canada under the 'Pontiac' label in the early 1970s.

**1964 VAUXHALL VIVA**

**Engine:** in-line four cylinder overhead-valve
**Bore × stroke:** 74.3 mm × 60.96 mm
**Capacity:** 1057 cc
**Maximum power:** 44 bhp
**Transmission:** four-speed manual
**Chassis:** integral
**Suspension:** independent front with double wishbones and transverse leaf spring, non-independent rear with semi-elliptic leaf springs
**Brakes:** drums all round
**Bodywork:** two-door saloon
**Maximum speed (approx):** 80 mph (129 kph)

**Vauxhall Viva**

## Vauxhall Cavalier

Launched for 1982, the Cavalier was Vauxhall's version of the General Motors J-car bodyshell, and had transversely mounted power units of either 1.3 or 1.6 litres driving the front wheels, and the choice of saloon or hatchback bodywork.

The new transverse engine was 15 per cent shorter and 18 per cent lighter than the units it replaced, and featured hydraulic tappets in the interests of reduced noise and maintenance. The engine incorporated eight counterweights on the camshaft and a torsional damper to ensure smooth running.

GM invested a total of £20 million in new assembly facilities for the Cavalier at Luton, and with a year's start over Ford's 'Project Toni' Cortina replacement (which emerged as the Sierra), GM made a concerted attack on the valuable British fleet-car sector, in which their showing had previously been less

**Velie**

### 1982 VAUXHALL CAVALIER

**Engine:** transverse four cylinder overhead camshaft
**Bore × stroke:** 80 mm × 79.5 mm
**Capacity:** 1598 cc
**Maximum power:** 90 bhp
**Transmission:** four-speed manual
**Chassis:** integral
**Suspension:** independent with MacPherson strut front and compound crank with coil springs rear
**Brakes:** disc front, drum rear
**Bodywork:** saloon or hatchback
**Maximum speed (approx):** 106 mph (170 kph)

than brilliant. The new Cavalier succeeded in establishing a firm foothold in what had formerly been very much Ford territory, and the Cavalier became a best-seller among fleet buyers.

However, that didn't disguise the fact that Luton had become very much an assembly plant, and there were Government calls for Vauxhall to increase the UK content of their cars, which it was felt had fallen unacceptably low.

## VELIE

**Moline, USA**
**1909–1928**

The W.L. Velie Company was a well known Illinois carriage-builder long before the dawn of the motor car age, and had built anything up to 25,000 carriages annually for more than 40 years before finally — and late in the day — building its

first car, the Velie 30, early in 1909. The 30 was powered by a four-cylinder, 3295 cc American & British engine, and its projected sales of 10,000 in 1910 dictated its competitive price of $1750.

Backing for Velie's automotive venture came from the John Deere Plow Company, who distributed Velie cars until 1915, when the company launched its 40 hp Biltwell Model 22 continental-engined six, priced at $1065. This was followed for 1917 by the Greater Velie Biltwell. The Velie marque was so popular in Shreveport, Louisiana, that a suburb of the town was named Velie in 1916. In 1918, Velie launched perhaps its most famous model, the four-seat Sport Car, which had a long-stroke, 4966 cc six-cylinder Continental engine.

During the 1920s, Velie cars became cheaper and their lines more angular; in 1922, the company began to build its own

### 1918 VELIE SPORT CAR

**Engine:** in-line six cylinder side-valve
**Bore × stroke:** 88.9 mm × 133.4 mm
**Capacity:** 4965 cc
**Maximum power:** 60 bhp
**Transmission:** four-speed manual
**Chassis:** pressed steel channel
**Suspension:** non-independent with semi-elliptic leaf springs front and cantilever leaf springs rear
**Brakes:** rear wheel drums
**Bodywork:** sports tourer
**Maximum speed (approx):** 65 mph (105 kph)

overhead-valve, 3335 cc six-cylinder engines, although right at the end of production, some 1927–28 models were fitted with an '8–88' in-line, eight-cylinder power unit manufactured by Lycoming.

**Vauxhall Cavalier**

# A-Z OF THE CAR

**Vermorel 12CV**

## VERITAS

**Messkirch/Rasstatt/Nürburgring, Germany
1946–1952**

Former German motor-cycle racing champion Ernst Loof founded the Veritas company in the French-occupied zone of Germany immediately after the war, in conjunction with a number of ex-BMW employees, to build sports

### 1948 VERITAS SPORTS

**Engine:** in-line six-cylinder overhead-valve
**Bore × stroke:** 66 mm × 96 mm
**Capacity:** 1971 cc
**Maximum power:** 80 bhp
**Transmission:** four-speed manual
**Chassis:** tubular steel
**Suspension:** independent with double wishbones front and non-independent with de Dion tube rear
**Brakes:** drums all round
**Bodywork:** single-seater sports
**Maximum speed (approx):** 110mph (177 kph)

and racing cars powered by the pre-war 1971 cc BMW 328 six-cylinder engines fitted with a special cylinder head, and backed by French aid. In 1947, Karl Kling won the 2-litre German sports-racing championship for Veritas, and a monoposto Veritas driven by ex-motor-cycle ace Georg Meier took the German Formula 2 title. Veritas also produced a small number of coupés and cabriolets with the BMW engine and with overhead-camshaft 1988 cc six-cylinder, BMW-based engines built for Veritas by the Heinkel aircraft company; production was small, a total of perhaps 35–40 cars being delivered. The Veritas Komet was a two-seater with a choice of 100 bhp or 140 bhp Heinkel-Veritas power units, while the Scorpion 2+2 convertible and Saturn three-seater coupé had the 100 bhp engine. Bodies were mostly built by Zipperich and Heinkel, and the company had an ample order book when it was forced to suspend production in 1950 after the Mark had been revalued.

Production was moved to the Nürburgring, where a few cars were constructed by Ernst Loof under the name Veritas-Nürburgring.

Between 1950–52, Veritas built the Dyna-Veritas in small numbers in conjunction with the French Panhard company. These had overhead-valve, 744 cc flat-twin Panhard engines and running gear and Veritas-designed coachwork built by Baur of Stuttgart.

Lack of finance led to the demise of the Veritas marque, which also produced Meteor 2-litre F2 racing cars.

## VERMOREL

**Villefranche-sur-Saône, France
1902–1930**

Vermorel, founded in 1850 to manufacture wood-working machinery, built their first experimental cars in 1902, designed by François Pilain (who left to establish his own marque in Lyon soon after); these were 2598 cc horizontal twins, but serious production did not get under way until 1908, when Vermorel brought out a pair-cast four-cylinder model of 1874 cc, which was soon uprated to 2064 cc.

A T-headed 3308 cc four was added to the range for 1912; L-headed Vermorels appeared for

### 1913 VERMOREL 12CV

**Engine:** in-line four-cylinder side-valve
**Bore × stroke:** 74 mm × 120 mm
**Capacity:** 2064 cc
**Maximum power:** 35 bhp
**Transmission:** four-speed manual
**Chassis:** pressed steel channel
**Suspension:** non-independent with semi-elliptic leaf springs front and three-quarter elliptic leaf springs rear
**Brakes:** rear wheel drums
**Bodywork:** saloon
**Maximum speed (approx):** 50 mph (81 kph)

1913 in the shape of a 1642 cc 8/10CV light car and a 16/20CV of some 2.8 litres capacity.

A 2.3-litre 15/18CV, introduced shortly before the outbreak of war, was Vermorel's staple offering in the post-Armistice period, although a more modern 1.7-litre four-cylinder 12CV with dual rear springing appeared in 1924, gaining pushrod ohv the following season. In 1926, when Vermorel at last abandoned cone clutches in favour of the more modern plate clutch, a 1131 cc light car was introduced. The last new model introduced before Vermorel abandoned car production was an ohv, 2-litre six-cylinder, the Type AH3, which made its debut in 1929.

## VINOT-DEGUINGAND

**Puteaux/Nanterre, France
1901–1925**

Vinot-Deguingand started production with belt-driven cars with 1500 cc vertical twin-cylinder engines mounted in a pressed-steel frame; their early models were sold in Britain under the name 'La Silencieuse'. In 1903, the company introduced four-cylinder models of 12CV (2211 cc) and 18CV (3685 cc), although the retrograde step of using armoured wood

**Veritas Sports**

## MODEL
Tatra 77 (1934)
**UK price when announced:** £990

## ENGINE
**Location:** Rear, longitudinal
**Type:** Air-cooled 90-degree V8 with alloy block and detachable cylinder heads
**Cubic capacity:** 2969 cc
**Bore × stroke:** 75 mm × 84 mm
**Compression ratio:** 5.6:1
**Valve gear:** 2 overhead valves per cylinder operated by single overhead camshaft per bank of cylinders
**Fuel supply:** Single downdraught Solex carburettor. 12-gallon fuel tank at front of car
**Ignition:** Coil and distributor
**Maximum power:** 75 bhp at 3500 rpm
**Maximum torque:** 98 lb ft at 2400 rpm

## TRANSMISSION
**Layout:** Gearbox and clutch in-unit with engine and rear axle
**Clutch:** Single dry plate
**Gearbox:** Four-speed manual with dog-clutch engagement of 2nd and synchromesh on 3rd and 4th
  1st 4.70:1   3rd 1.56:1
  2nd 2.95:1   4th 1.04:1
**Final drive:** Jointless drive by means of spur-wheel differential driving two concentric pinion shafts
**Ratio:** 3.15:1

## SUSPENSION
**Front:** Independent with transverse leaf spring and twin-wishbone assemblies, plus hydraulic dampers
**Rear:** Independent, with swinging half axles and transverse semi-elliptic leaf spring

## STEERING
**Type:** Rack and pinion

## WHEELS AND TYRES
**Type:** Pressed-steel 16 in wheels with 650 × 16 cross-ply tyres

## BODY/CHASSIS
**Type:** Box-section steel chassis frame with central single tube backbone, with fork at rear to support engine and gearbox. Aerodynamic four-door six-seat saloon body

## DIMENSIONS AND WEIGHT
**Length:** 212.6 in (5400 mm)
**Width:** 66 in (1670 mm)
**Wheelbase:** 124 in (3150 mm)
**Track – front:** 49 in (1250 mm)
  – rear: 49 in (1250 mm)
**Weight:** 3968 lb (1799 kg)

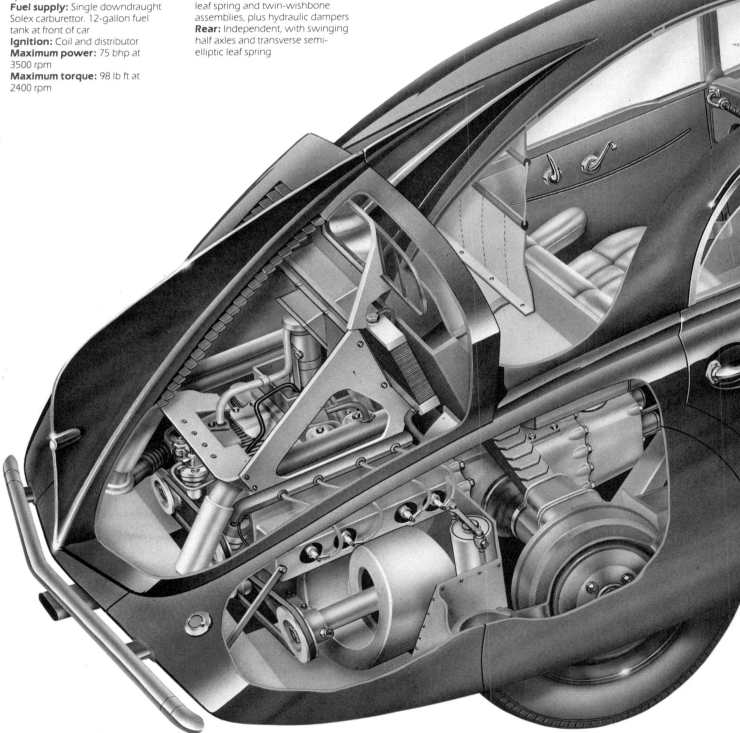

**PERFORMANCE**
**Maximum speed:** 90 mph
(145 kph)
**Acceleration 0–60 mph:** 14
seconds
**Fuel consumption:** 20 mpg

**BELOW** The truly cavernous interior of a Type 77 Tatra. Its huge wheelbase, coupled with the rear-mounted V8 meant that there was more than ample room for the passengers. Note the central spine chassis, one of the Tatra's main features, as is the swing-axle rear suspension with the upper transverse semi-elliptic leaf spring

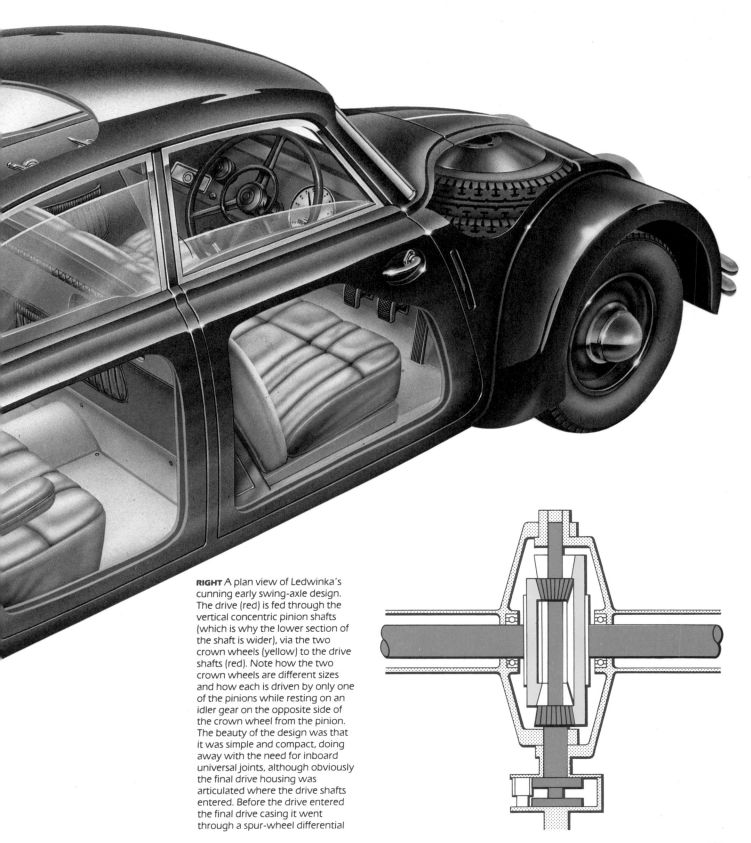

**RIGHT** A plan view of Ledwinka's cunning early swing-axle design. The drive (red) is fed through the vertical concentric pinion shafts (which is why the lower section of the shaft is wider), via the two crown wheels (yellow) to the drive shafts (red). Note how the two crown wheels are different sizes and how each is driven by only one of the pinions while resting on an idler gear on the opposite side of the crown wheel from the pinion. The beauty of the design was that it was simple and compact, doing away with the need for inboard universal joints, although obviously the final drive housing was articulated where the drive shafts entered. Before the drive entered the final drive casing it went through a spur-wheel differential

**Vinot-Deguingand 12CV**

## 1912 VINOT-DEGUINGAND 12CV

**Engine:** in-line four cylinder
  side-valve
**Bore × stroke:** 80 mm ×
  130 mm
**Capacity:** 2613 cc
**Maximum power:** 35 bhp
**Transmission:** four-speed
  manual
**Chassis:** pressed steel channel
**Suspension:** non-independent
  with semi-elliptic leaf springs
**Brakes:** rear wheel drums
**Bodywork:** tourer
**Maximum speed (approx):**
  50 mph (80 kph)

chassis was taken at the same time.

By 1906, Vinot-Deguingand had a complex line-up which ranged from a 2212 cc 12/16CV to a 35/50CV six of 6999 cc.

New for 1908 was a neat shaft-drive 16/24CV with four-speed transmission, and a similar 24/32CV model.

In 1909, Vinot-Deguingand acquired Gladiator, and the products of the two marques were virtually identical, save for the design of their radiators, for the following decade.

A new pressure-lubricated 12/16CV appeared in 1910, while the range was comprehensively revised in 1911 and new fours of 10/12CV (1693 cc), 15CV (2212 cc) and 25/30CV (4166 cc), plus a 50cv six (8101 cc) were added to their range.

The 1693 cc four was continued after the war, alongside new models like the archaic 2613 cc 12CV and the ohv 1795 cc 11/25 CV, which was uprated to 12/25CV and 1847 cc in 1923. When Vinot failed in the mid-1920s, their factory was bought by Donnet, and few more Vinot-Deguingands were built.

In 1928, the Deguingand name was resurrected on a limited-production 735 cc Duplex-engined cyclecar designed by the ubiquitous Marcel Violet (although this became a Donnet in 1932, a year before Donnet itself expired).

## VOISIN

**Issy-les-Moulineaux, France
1919–1939**

Pioneer aviator and insatiable womaniser, Gabriel Voisin was forced to convert his aviation works for car production work after the Armistice since there were no more orders forthcoming for military aircraft. Since Voisin was above all a strong individualist, his cars were anything but conventional; all of them used Knight double sleeve-valve engines, which Voisin managed to endow with quite remarkable performance.

The first Voisin car was actually a Citroën design that had not gone into production; this 3969 cc 18/23CV remained current for nearly ten years.

Voisin exhibited a 7238 cc V12 as early as 1921, a year in which he also launched the 1244 cc C4 four-cylinder model.

In 1927, Voisin introduced the first six-cylinder sleeve-valve-engined cars to be sold in France; of the three models launched that year, the best was the 13CV of 2300 cc, capable of 75 mph in standard form. The 'Charmant' sports derivative incorporated a two-speed rear axle.

Two low-chassis models with striking razor-edge coachwork, the 4800 cc Sirocco V12 and the 5800 cc Simoun six arrived in 1930 – the Sirocco was derived from the Diane, also launched in 1930.

In the 1930s, Voisin built a number of Minervas – again, sleeve-valve engined cars – under licence without much success. The year 1936 saw the construction of a strange 6-litre straight-twelve, which never passed the prototype stage. At the very end of

production, some Voisins were built with the American Graham six-cylinder 3500 cc engine, the sole exception to the sleeve-valves, although these were not the work of Gabriel Voisin, but of a syndicate which had taken control.

Voisin created many of the unorthodox bodies for his cars – he was, it was said, helped in their design by architect Le Corbusier – and, while these controversial styles may not have been to conventional taste they certainly attracted much attention. Voisin's engineering drew heavily on aircraft practice, making great use of light alloy. After World War II, Voisin made the tiny and ugly Biscuter for Spain.

## Voisin 18/23CV

During 1918, two young Panhard engineers named Artaud and Dufresne appeared in Gabriel Voisin's office with plans for an improved version of the sleeve-valve 16CV Panhard-Levassor, which had been rejected for production by their employer. Convinced that their design had potential, Artaud and Dufresne acquired the prototype from Panhard and offered the design to Citroën who, after building three cars, decided instead to go for the cheaper end of the market. So the two engineers offered the design to Voisin instead. He, seeing that the sleeve-valve offered the steam-engine silence he was seeking, snapped up the design and proceeded to exploit the performance potential of the sleeve-valve configuration as no other manufacturer ever did.

The first 18/23CV was ready for test on Gabriel Voisin's 39th birthday, 5 February 1919; but when Voisin let in the clutch, he discovered that, in their haste to get the car ready, his men had assembled the rear axle back to front, so that the car had four speeds backward and only one forward! Trying the car backwards, Voisin discovered the advantage of front-wheel braking . . . .

Although by Gabriel Voisin's exacting standards, the original 18/23CV was slow and fragile, nevertheless it was capable of reaching

## 1920 VOISIN 18/23CV

**Engine:** in-line four-cylinder,
  sleeve-valve
**Bore × stroke:** 95 mm ×
  140 mm
**Capacity:** 3970 cc
**Maximum power:** 100 bhp
**Transmission:** four-speed
  manual
**Chassis:** pressed steel channel
**Suspension:** non-independent
  with semi-elliptic leaf springs
  front and rear
**Brakes:** drums on rear wheels
  only
**Bodywork:** tourer
**Maximum speed (approx):**
  81 mph (130 kph)

**Voisin 18/23CV**

Volga M-21

### 1960 VOLGA M-21

**Engine:** in-line four-cylinder, overhead-valve
**Bore × stroke:** 92 mm × 92 mm
**Capacity:** 2445 cc
**Maximum power:** 80 bhp
**Transmission:** three-speed manual
**Chassis:** integral
**Suspension:** independent front with coil springs and wishbones. Live rear axle with semi-elliptic leaf springs
**Brakes:** drums all round
**Bodywork:** saloon
**Maximum speed (approx):** 78 mph (126 kph)

some 75 mph (121 kph) and formed the basis of Voisin production for the next decade or so; with a high-compression head and magnesium pistons, its engine could be persuaded to develop some 150 bhp and in this form powered Voisin's streamlined entries which won the French Touring Car Grand Prix in 1922.

In slightly more standard form, and driven by veteran racer Dominique Lamberjack, an 18/23CV with a 150 litre fuel tank went from Paris to Nice in just eleven and a half hours in 1920 to beat the crack Blue Train express by six hours.

## Voisin V12

Gabriel Voisin's first V12 appeared at the 1920 Paris Salon, with a 30 degree engine displacing 7260 cc, and so advanced in design that Voisin called it 'an exercise in science fiction'; it had, for instance, an hydraulic coupling instead of a conventional clutch. Its development costs were, however, horrific, and the project never passed the prototype stage.

In 1930, Voisin again turned to

the V12, launching two models powered by the same 4860 cc engine. The Diane was a conventional enough car, 'with a big carrying capacity'; the Sirocco was intended as a sports model, with a remarkable underslung chassis, with both front and rear axles above the frame members, and a deep transmission tunnel. Outriggers beyond the chassis members supported the wide bodywork, 'with the result that there is considerable room inside, and although the total height is low, head room is ample'.

Voisin's final 12-cylinder design came in the autumn of 1936. This time, the cylinders were in line, and the rearmost cylinders of the 5988cc

### 1930 VOISIN SCIROCCO

**Engine:** V12, sleeve-valve
**Bore × stroke:** 72 mm × 100 mm
**Capacity:** 4860 cc
**Transmission:** three-speed manual
**Chassis:** pressed steel channel
**Suspension:** non-independent with semi-elliptic leaf springs front and rear
**Brakes:** drums all round
**Bodywork:** sports saloon
**Maximum speed (approx):** 95 mph (153 kph)

power unit projected into the driving compartment . . . .

## VOLGA
**Gorkij, USSR**
**1955 to date**

Launched in 1955 to replace the Pobieda (Victory) – which continued to be built in Poland as the Warszawa – the Volga was designed by Andrei Lipgart, and though bold claims were made for a 'hydro-converter' transmission on the prototype, production cars had a conventional three-speed transmission.

Heavily-built, and heavy on the controls, the Volga was strongly influenced by contemporary American styling. Remarkably, its hand-brake acted on the transmission, while the rugged use to which the Volga was expected to be subjected was reflected in the front seat – which converted into a bed – and in the well-filled twin tool rolls, which even included two wooden blocks for chocking the car while changing wheels.

The original Volga M-21 continued in production until 1968 with only minor modifications; it was joined by the M-22E ambulance and M-22G estate car and supplanted by the lower-built M-24, which at last offered a four-speed transmission, though the M-21 persisted alongside this model until 1971.

The Volga M-24 gave way to the similar 3102, still with the old faithful 2445 cc engine, in 1982. A diesel-engined version using a 2112 cc unit was also available.

Voisin V12

# VOLKSWAGEN

**Wolfsburg, Germany**
**1938 –**

Ferdinand Porsche's design office in Stuttgart had produced a number of small-car prototypes during the 1930s before in 1936 refining a design concept originally created for NSU, with a flat-four engine mounted at the rear, into the first prototypes of the Volkswagen (people's car) which the Führer, Adolf Hitler, had promised the faithful of the Nazi party.

A pilot series of 30 cars was constructed in 1937 by Daimler-Benz, since the Porsche-Buro lacked the production facilities. Then, in 1938, Adolf Hitler laid the cornerstone of the Volkswagen factory at KdF-Stadt, named after the cars, officially known as KdF-Wagen (*Kraft durch Freude* – 'Strength through Joy'), and unofficially known as the Käfer (beetle).

Though the KdF-Wagen was theoretically available on subscription, and orders were secured from the Germany public for almost 170,000 of them to finance the building of the new factory, no cars were actually delivered to the public before the war broke out and production was turned over to military requirements.

Among the variants on the VW built for the German armed forces was the amphibious Schwimmwagen; because the 985 cc engine of the original VW was considered not powerful enough for military use, a larger air-cooled flat-four of 1131 cc was fitted. This power unit was adopted for the post-war models which were produced by loyal employees in the bomb-flatened ruins of the factory, whose location was now officially known as Wolfsburg instead of KdF-Stadt.

Both an Allied investigation team and Henry Ford II dismissed the VW Beetle as having no commercial future, but under the leadership of the remarkable Heinrich Nordhoff, production of the VW increased apace. The Beetle went on to become the most

successful car in motoring history, outselling even the Model T Ford (although over a longer period).

In the 1950s, VW achieved great success with an Italian-designed variant of the Beetle, the Karmann-Ghia, built in Osnabruck by the old-established coachbuilder, Karmann.

As far as mainstream production went, the first break with the Beetle tradition came with the introduction of the VW1500 in 1961; engines of up to 1795 cc were subsequently fitted in this fastback model.

Then in 1965 VW acquired Auto-Union – including NSU and Audi – from Mercedes, and since the 1675 cc VW 411 of 1969 did not enjoy great success, this typically VW air-cooled rear-engined car was phased out in favour of the new NSU K70. This broke new ground for Wolfsburg, since it was powered by a front-mounted overhead-cam water-cooled vertical four of 1594 cc or 1795 cc, and was produced as a VW from 1970 to 1974.

Between 1969–75, a joint venture between VW and Porsche, based at Ludwigsburg, produced a sports car known as the VW-Porsche or Porsche 914, powered

by a 1679 cc flat-four or 1991 cc flat-six. It was succeeded by the front-engined Porsche 924.

In 1973, VW introduced the Passat, with engines of 1297 cc to 1471 cc; this was followed a year later by the Scirocco (available with power units ranging from 1093 cc to 1457 cc) and the Giugiaro-styled Golf, which sold a million within 31 months of its launch.

In 1975, the highly successful hatchback Polo minicar, with an 895 cc engine, was added to the range; 1093 cc and 1272 cc versions were subsequently offered, while a version with a conventional boot was introduced under the name Derby.

A lightweight 4X4, the Iltis, appeared in 1979.

In 1980 VW introduced the Jetta, a booted variant of the Golf, and the Scirocco and Passat were restyled in 1981. The Santana, a notchback derivative of the Passat, followed a year later, available with four- or five-cylinder petrol engines or a four-cylinder diesel.

In the early 1980s, VW bit the corporate bullet and replaced their best-selling Golf with Golf II, which was a logical derivative of the old

model rather than a complete breakaway, and though it was felt that VW's deliberate conservatism might have militated against sales of the new model, in fact it soon became accepted.

The mid-1980s saw VW increasingly investigating four-wheel drive, with Syncro 4X4 versions of the Passat and Golf introduced.

## Volkswagen Beetle

As early as 1931, Dr Porsche's design office drew up plans for a stream-lined, rear-engined family car with a backbone frame, to be built by Zündapp, well-known motorcycle makers, who planned to break into the car market to speed their recovery from the slump. But by the time that Zündapp were ready to go into production with this car – which had a five-cylinder radial water-cooled engine – the worst of the slump was behind them, so the project was shelved after a prototype had been built.

---

**1953 VOLKSWAGEN BEETLE**

**Engine:** flat-four air-cooled, overhead-valve
**Bore × stroke:** 77 mm × 69 mm
**Capacity:** 1285 cc
**Maximum power:** 44 bhp
**Transmission:** four-speed manual
**Chassis:** integral backbone
**Suspension:** independent trailing arms with torsion bars front and independent swing axle with torsion bars rear
**Brakes:** drums all round
**Bodywork:** two-door saloon or convertible
**Maximum speed (approx):** 75 mph (120 kph)

---

*Volkswagen Beetle*

Porsche next designed a similar car for NSU, but this time with a flat-four air-cooled engine. Three prototypes were constructed before NSU decided the investment was too great to proceed.

Then Porsche submitted his plans for a 'people's car' to the newly-proclaimed Führer, Adolf Hitler, and had the project approved. Working for minimal expenses, Porsche drew on his Zündapp and NSU designs to create the original Volkwagen prototypes. The three handbuilt prototypes were subjected to thorough testing, and came through so successfully that a further 30 prototypes were built by Mercedes for extended testing by members of the SS. The Volkswagen Development Corporation was set up by the state and work began on the factory at KdF-Stadt (which became Wolfsburg after the war).

After producing 100,000 military VWs during the war, Wolfsburg – badly battered by Allied bombing – was nursed back into life by its devoted workers, who persisted with the Beetle even when Allied experts (including Henry Ford II) said it was not a commercially viable proposition.

In the early 1950s, VW began exporting an improved model, with a synchromesh gearbox, hydraulic brakes and larger-section tyres.

Between 1945 and 1974, Wolfsburg built 11,916,519 Beetles, and millions more were constructed in other VW plants round the world, particularly in Brazil, where the Beetle was known as the Fusca; the Beetle was still – just – in production in Mexico in the mid-1980s, 50 years and over 20 million cars since it was first introduced. The Mexican version was the 1200L which was powered by the 1192 cc, 34 bhp version of the flat-four which gave it the less than impressive top speed of 71 mph (115 kph).

## Volkswagen Karmann-Ghia

In 1953, the old-established Turin *carrozzeria*, Ghia, shipped a prototype 2+2 coupé to Wolfsburg. Though Ghia's head, Luigi Segre, claimed credit for the design, in fact all he had done was to scale down a design by Virgil Exner of Chrysler, the d'Elegance, which Ghia had built in limited volume.

The design was accepted by the VW management, and, because Ghia lacked the capacity for quantity production, the coupé was produced by the Osnabruck coachbuilder, Karmann.

At the peak of production Karmann was building 42,000 Karmann-Ghias annually. Between 1957–73, Karmann also produced the Karmann-Ghia Cabriolet, and from 1962–69 there was also a Karmann-Ghia coupé based on the VW1500, designed by Sergio Sartorelli.

**Volkswagen Karmann-Ghia**

### 1955 VOLKSWAGEN KARMANN-GHIA

**Engine:** flat-four air-cooled, overhead-valve
**Bore × stroke:** 77 mm × 64 mm
**Capacity:** 1192 cc
**Maximum power:** 30 bhp
**Transmission:** four-speed manual
**Chassis:** integral backbone
**Suspension:** independent trailing arms with torsion bars front and independent swing axle with torsion bars rear
**Brakes:** drums all round
**Bodywork:** two-door coupé or convertible
**Maximum speed (approx):** 71 mph (115 kph)

## Volkswagen Golf

Intended as the successor to the Beetle, the VW Golf was launched in mid-1974, at the height of the first energy crisis. The Golf represented a clean break with tradition being styled by Giorgetto Giugiaro's Ital Design studio and having a transverse in-line engine in front – capacities of 1093 cc and 1471 cc were originally available – driving the front wheels. An engine of 1588 cc was subsequently added to the range.

Sales of the Golf got off to a rapid start – nearly 190,000 were built in the first six months of production, and the 500,000 mark was passed in 1976, while a million was reached in October the same year, just 27 months after its launch.

### 1974 VOLKSWAGEN GOLF 1500S

**Engine:** four-cylinder transverse, overhead-cam
**Bore × stroke:** 76.5 mm × 80 mm
**Capacity:** 1471 cc
**Maximum power:** 70 bhp
**Transmission:** four-speed manual
**Chassis:** integral
**Suspension:** independent with MacPherson struts and wishbones front and independent with trailing arms and coil springs rear
**Brakes:** discs front, drums rear
**Bodywork:** five-door saloon
**Maximum speed (approx):** 100 mph (161 kph)

**Volkswagen Golf**

In 1978 VW began assembly of the Golf – renamed the Rabbit – in Pennsylvania. The Rabbit proved so successful that US-built VW sales outstripped American Motors in December 1978, only a few months after the factory had gone into operation. The Golf is also offered with a 1471 cc overhead-camshaft diesel engine and the diesel Rabbit was the first small economy diesel model on the American market.

A new 1.8-litre engine preceded a courageous decision by VW to redesign the Golf while it was still a best-seller – production had passed six million in ten years – and the Golf II appeared during 1983.

At the beginning of 1986, VW unveiled a four-wheel-drive version of the Golf, the Syncro.

# VOLVO

**Goteborg, Sweden/Eindhoven, Holland**
**1927 –**

The first Volvo left the factory on the morning of 14 April, 1927. Planning for the Volvo car began in 1924, when Assar Gabrielsson and Gustaf Larson considered the feasibility of assembling a car from Swedish components which would be suitable for Swedish roads. With backing from the SKF ball-bearing company, the tiny concern built 10 prototypes in 1926.

Styled by the artist Mass-Olle, the first Volvo (the name is Latin for 'I roll') was heavily American-inspired; it had a 1.9-litre side-valve four-cylinder engine. At least two of the team involved in designing the original Volvo had worked in the USA, while the car was first tested by a Swedish-born Hupmobile employee, who was later employed by Volvo to develop their six-cylinder cars.

Volvo sold some 1000 OV4 tourers and PV4 fabric saloons in two years, then, in 1929 the 3.1-litre PV651 six-cylinder Volvo, still designed very much on American lines, appeared.

The PV652 of 1930 was a similar design, but with hydraulic brakes replacing the mechanically-operated brakes of the earlier model; it was produced until 1936.

Volvo suddenly revealed their adventurous side with the PV36 Carioca of 1935, which looked like a Chrysler Airflow, and had independent front suspension and all-steel bodywork. Sad to say, it was not a success, and was quickly replaced by the more conventional PV51/52 models at the end of 1936.

Volvo production rose to nearly 2000 cars in 1937, although only 56 of these were exported, and commercial vehicles were still far more crucial to Volvo's well-being.

In 1938, Volvo introduced the streamlined PV53–56, developed

from the PV51/52, and produced in small numbers during the war; it was often sold with a wood-burning gas-producer unit.

Prototypes of a new model, the PV60, were tested in 1942, though it did not go into production until 1947. It was to be the last six-cylinder Volvo for many years.

Just before the war, Volvo experimented with a small rear-engined car, the PV40, which had an eight-cylinder radial engine and unit body construction, but almost inevitably production problems caused this brave project to be abandoned.

Volvo at once began planning the more conventional PV444, with a four-cylinder 1.4-litre pushrod engine, independent front suspension and unit body construction.

Though the car was shown as early as 1944, lack of suitable body steel prevented production from getting under way until 1947. The car was redesigned in 1958 as the PV544, while a five-bearing 1.8-litre B18-engine appeared on the 1962 model. Altogether nearly half a million examples of this model were built.

In 1956, Volvo brought out a new model, the 120 or 122 (there were many variations) which in Sweden was known as the

Amazon. Though the 120/122 had a totally new body, many mechanical components were common with the older model.

Volvo attempted to reach the speciality market with the P1900 sports car, which had glass-fibre bodywork and was built in 1956/7.

Its successor was the Ghia-styled P1800, a two-seater coupé with the B18 engine. Pressed Steel built the bodies in Scotland, while the cars were assembled at West Bromwich by Jensen. There were embarrassing production delays, and the first cars only began leaving the Jensen factory in 1961, three years after the car had first been exhibited in New York. Production remained slow, and assembly was eventually transferred to Goteborg in 1963; the Swedish-built car was known as the P1800S. In 1966, and again in 1969, the power output of the engine was increased; the 1800E had electronic fuel injection and developed 130 bhp, giving the car a 110 mph (177 kph) top speed.

In 1971 Volvo produced a 2+2 version of this model, known as the 1800ES: a total of 39,414 examples of the various models of this distinctive car were built.

In 1966, this model gained the 2-litre B20 engine, and in 1972, fuel injection was introduced.

A year later, the 144 was redesigned and acquired new overhead-camshaft engines; in 1968 it was joined by the six-cylinder 164, which had the 3-litre B30 engine, although a subsequent joint venture with Renault and Peugeot resulted in the fitting of a new V6 engine from 1975. That year saw the introduction of the new 240 series, with 2.1-litre four-cylinder overhead-cam engines.

Volvo broke new ground in 1979 by fitting a six-cylinder diesel engine, while the 244GLT of 1980 had a fuel-injected engine with a turbocharger. For 1982, the four-cylinder engine was enlarged to 2.3 litres and the V6 power unit to 2.8 litres.

A new, larger model, the 760GLE, appeared in 1982, with styling aimed at the American market. This big V6-engined car was supplemented by the in-line 2.3-litre four as the 740 series, also available for export with the turbocharged 2-litre four.

As for the Dutch-built Volvos, these now have the five-speed de Dion transaxle as standard, and the CVT automatic available as an option in the 1.4-litre-engined 340 series. The 360 series has a 2-litre engine, with manual transmission.

## Volvo PV444

Launched in 1944, the PV444 was heavily influenced by American styling of 1940, when work had started on the design. The shortage of steel prevented the car from entering production before 1947, but it quickly earned a sound reputation. The press remarked that 'although the performance of this car is by no means abnormal, it has many other excellent qualities which commend themselves to the buyer, particularly

if the car is to be driven under severe road conditions.'

However, the unexceptional performance of the original PV444 was transformed in 1957 by the fitting of the 1.6-litre power unit previously used in the heavier four-door Amazon saloon. *The Motor* summed up the PV444L as 'a Swedish family car of modest appearance and prodigious performance', and certainly the conventional-looking pushrod power unit was quite surprisingly lively. 'The bhp figure is one commonly associated with double overhead camshafts; the road speed in relation to engine capacity conjures a picture of an entirely different kind of car with a truly aerodynamic body,' *Motor* commented.

The basic PV444 design was in production for 14 years, though there were substantial revisions throughout that period; as the first Volvo to be sold in numbers outside Sweden it established the marque's international reputation for safe, strong construction.

When production ceased in 1958, a total of 196,000 had been built; the PV544 which succeeded the PV444 was very similar in appearance, with production reaching 440,000 between 1958–65.

---

**1947 VOLVO PV444L**

**Engine:** in-line four cylinder overhead valve
**Bore × stroke:** 80 mm × 80 mm
**Capacity:** 1580 cc
**Maximum power:** 85 bhp
**Transmission:** three-speed manual
**Chassis:** integral
**Suspension:** independent with coil springs and wishbones front and rigid axle with coil springs and torque arms rear
**Brakes:** self-adjusting drums all round
**Bodywork:** fastback two-door saloon
**Maximum speed (approx):** 97 mph (156 kph)

---

**Volvo PV444**

# A-Z OF THE CAR

**Volvo 760 Turbo**

## Volvo P1800

Until very recently the P1800 was the only really sporty car that Volvo had ever built. It was introduced first on the US market in 1959 and two years later appeared in the UK. From 1961 to 1964 the cars were built at Jensen's factory in West Bromwich.

With the introduction of the P1800S in 1964 production switched to Sweden. Early P1800S models retained the 1.8-litre engine but in 1968 the displacement was increased to 2 litres. Electronic fuel injection arrived in 1969 and the model designation changed to 1800E. The last variant on the theme was the 1800ES, the fast estate version inspired by the Reliant Scimitar. Although by that time it had a power output of 130 bhp and a top speed near 120 mph (193 kph) the ES was not a great success.

### 1970 VOLVO 1800S

**Engine:** in-line four-cylinder, overhead-valve
**Bore × stroke:** 88.9 mm × 80 mm
**Capacity:** 1986 cc
**Maximum power:** 110 bhp
**Transmission:** four-speed manual with overdrive
**Chassis:** integral
**Suspension:** independent front with coil springs and wishbones. Live rear axle with trailing links, torque arms, Panhard rod and coil springs
**Brakes:** discs front and drums rear
**Bodywork:** sports coupé
**Maximum speed (approx):** 115 mph (185 kph)

## Volvo 760

New for 1982, the 760 Series Volvo was described by journalist L.J.K. Setright as 'scarcely credible even as a car of the present, though some of its best qualities are redolent of a sadly lost past', and certainly its styling ran counter to every European trend of the early 1980s. With not a curve in sight, the square-cut bodywork of the 760 series epitomised the 'metallic Origami' school of design, and was very evidently aimed at the American luxury car market. Early in the model's life, the 760 GLE Turbodiesel option was offered, powered by a turbocharged six-cylinder Volkswagen diesel of 2.4 litres, followed soon after by the four-cylinder 740 Series. A turbocharged 2 litre version is available in export markets only, producing 155 bhp.

### 1983 VOLVO 760 TURBO

**Engine:** in-line four cylinder, overhead-cam with turbocharger
**Bore × stroke:** 96 mm × 80 mm
**Capacity:** 2316 cc
**Maximum power:** 182 bhp
**Transmission:** five-speed manual
**Chassis:** integral
**Suspension:** independent with MacPherson struts front and rigid axle with trailing arms and coil springs
**Brakes:** discs all round with servo assistance
**Bodywork:** four-door saloon
**Maximum speed (approx):** 124 mph (200 kph)

**Volvo 1800S**

# WALTER
### Jinonice, Czechoslovakia
### 1908–1937

In 1898 Josef Walter began the manufacture of motorcycles, adding a bathchair-like three-wheeler to the range in 1908. The three-wheeler gradually became more car-like, and eventually was even available with closed four-seat bodywork.

Walter began production of high-quality four-wheelers in 1912 with the 14 hp WI model; alongside this was offered a sporting cyclecar with the same 1250 cc vee-twin power unit as the three-wheeler.

Increases in engine capacity created the WII and WIII models, then after the war the company built the side-valve 1540 cc WZ and its overhead-valve sporting derivative, the WIZ, launched in 1921.

In 1922 Josef Walter lost control of the factory and set up a new gear manufacturing company at Kosire, near Prague; control of the Walter company passed to Vitoz Kumpera and his son Teny, who had worked with Peugeot, Hispano-Suiza and Gnome & Rhone. A 1920s development with far-reaching consequences was the start of aero-engine manufacture; Walter car production was, in any case, always on a very limited scale, with the accent on performance, and many of the company's touring models had a racing equivalent. Thus the single-overhead-camshaft 1945 cc four launched in 1924 had a racing version capable of over 100 mph (161 kph). The principal works driver was Jindrich Knapp, often aided by the two Kumperas.

An overhead-valve 2496 cc six-cylinder was added in 1928, followed by a 2860 cc racing model built for Jindrich Knapp. It developed 125 bhp, and this model was so popular that Walter was forced to put a detuned version, the 6B, into full production. A sports version with a Cozette supercharger was available, and later models had a four-speed synchromesh gearbox with Maybach overdrive. A team of 6Bs won the foreign car class in the 1931 German ADAC 10,000 km trial.

In the late 1920s and early 1930s, Walter was offering a range made up of the 980 cc Junior, the 1438 cc Bijou (both fours) and the Prince and Lord with the 2496 cc six-cylinder engine, plus the Super and Regent 3257 cc sixes.

Many of the chassis produced by Walter were bodies by such famous Czech coachbuilders as Sodomka, Jech, Brozik, Aero (who were licencees for the Weymann fabric body) and Uhlik.

The most expensive and luxurious car made by the Walter

**Walter 6B**

## 1930 WALTER 6B

**Engine:** in-line six cylinder, overhead valve
**Bore × stroke:** 80 mm × 108 mm
**Capacity:** 3257 cc
**Maximum power:** 95 bhp (115 bhp supercharged)
**Transmission:** four-speed manual plus overdrive
**Chassis:** x-braced pressed steel channel
**Suspension:** non-independent with rigid axles and semi-elliptic leaf springs
**Brakes:** drums all round, hydraulically operated and servo assisted
**Bodywork:** to order
**Maximum speed (approx):** 100 mph (160 kph)

factory was the 5879 cc V12 Royal, built in small numbers between 1931 and 1934; some sources say production of the Royal was no more than a dozen cars. Nevertheless, Walter even built a bus with a 7354 cc V12 engine in 1931.

During the early 1930s the six-cylinder Standard 3-litre and Super 3.3-litre touring cars were popular. Walter also built Fiat Balillas with overhead-valve 995 cc and 1089 cc four-cylinder engines under licence from 1933, along with the 1438 cc Fiat 514 and 2516 cc Fiat 521, the later model being marketed as the Walter Lord.

Walter works-driver Jindrich Knapp crowned his competition career with outright victory in the 1934 Czech 1000 miles race, driving a 3257 cc 6B Super six-cylinder with bodywork modelled on that of the Fiat Ballila sports.

In 1936 the Walter factory ceased car production entirely to devote itself to the manufacture of aero-engines.

In 1936 the Walter factory ceased car production entirely to devote itself to the manufacture of aero-engines.

# WANDERER
### Chemnitz/Siegmar, Germany
### 1911–1939

Wanderer were toolmakers who began building bicycles in 1887, adding motorcycles to their output in 1902; though they built a few experimental cars in the first decade of this century, it was not until 1910 that they decided to go into series production of four-wheelers.

Having apparently turned down a young designer named Ettore Bugatti, who offered them a light four-cylinder car which was subsequently built as the Peugeot Bébé, Wanderer began building a tandem-seated car called the Püppchen (doll), initially with an F-head 1145 cc four-cylinder engine. In 1914, the company introduced a more powerful overhead-valve 1220 cc version with oddly-disposed three-seat bodywork in which the driver sat alone in front, with the two passengers behind; the tandem-seated Püppchen was used as a patrol vehicle by the German Army during the Great War.

Improved versions of the 1220 cc car were built until 1925, although in 1924 Wanderer introduced an overhead-valve 1550 cc four-cylinder car, followed

in 1926 by a 1940 cc version.

The first six-cylinder Wanderer, the dreary 2540 cc W10, appeared at the November 1928 Berlin Show, followed soon after by the 2.5-litre W11, also built under licence in Switzerland by Martini. The year 1930 saw a 2995 cc sports car, the W11S, added to the Wanderer range.

Wanderer joined DKW, Horch and Audi in the newly founded Auto-Union in 1932. This brought a new shape and swing axle rear suspension to these cars, and the 1692 cc four-cylinder Wanderer of 1933–34 was very similar to the contemporary DKW.

The Wanderer works also built

a range of Porsche-designed six-cylinder models, and in 1936 announced the W25K supercharged 1963 cc Porsche-designed two-seater sports cars. Unfortunately its wet-liner light-allow engine proved to be short-lived, and over-enthusiastic owners replaced terminally-damaged W25K engines with the more reliable Cologne-built Ford V8 unit. War ended Wanderer car production; the final models were the 1767 cc W24 and the six-cylinder 2632 cc W23, both with side-valve engines and all-round independent suspension.

**Wanderer W25K**

---

### 1936 WANDERER W25K

**Engine:** in-line six cylinder, overhead valve
**Bore × stroke:** 70 mm × 85 mm
**Capacity:** 1963 cc
**Maximum power:** 85 bhp
**Transmission:** four-speed manual
**Chassis:** x-braced box channel
**Suspension:** transverse lead springs
**Brakes:** drums all round
**Bodywork:** two-seater sports
**Maximum speed (approx):** 95 mph (153 kph)

## WARTBURG

**Eisenach, Germany**
**1898–1904, 1956 –**

The Fahrzeugfabrik Eisenach was an offshoot of Heinrich Ehrhardt's arms factory at Eisenach in Thuringia (now East Germany) which began by building French Decauville cars under licence under the name Wartburg, taken from a local mountain. The cars had either air-cooled 3.5 hp or water-cooled 5 hp inlet-over-exhaust twin-cylinder engines mounted at the rear of the chassis.

In 1903, the factory became independent of the parent company, building cars with 4 hp, 5 hp, 8.5 hp and 10 hp twin-cylinder power units.

In 1903, Willi Seck, the former designer of two leading Aix-la-Chapelle companies, Scheibler and Cudell, joined Eisenach to create a new range of cars, which went into production under the Dixi name. BMW took over the Dixi works in

1928, and produced the Austin Seven under licence in 1929–31, calling it the BMW Wartburg, but the Wartburg name then lay in abeyance for a quarter of a century.

It was then revived for a new model built at Eisenach to succeed

---

### 1984 WARTBURG 353W

**Engine:** in-line three cylinder two-stroke
**Bore × stroke:** 73.5 mm × 78 mm
**Capacity:** 992 cc
**Maximum power:** 50 bhp
**Transmission:** four-speed manual
**Chassis:** box-type ladder frame
**Suspension:** independent with coil springs and wishbones front and independent with semi-trailing arms and coil springs rear
**Brakes:** disc front and drum rear
**Bodywork:** saloon or estate car
**Maximum speed (approx):** 81 mph (130 kph)

---

the old DKW-derived IFA in 1956; the three-cylinder two-stroke engine of 894 cc was retained until 1952, when swept volume was raised to 992 cc.

A new model, the Wartburg Knight, appeared in 1966 and the same basic design, now called the 353W, remains in production today. Beneath its ill-fitting bodywork, the chassis is a remarkable relic, with more in common with the 1930s than the 1980s.

## WHITE

**Cleveland, USA**
**1900–1918**

Rollin H. White of the White Sewing Machine Company designed the first 'Incomparable' White steam car in 1900; it was a typical steam buggy, distinguished only by a semi-flash boiler which ensured virtually automatic control, for the flow of water was directly

proportional to the flow of fuel.

The little runabout proved an instant success, and in the first full year of production, 1901, White sold 193 cars. Few changes were made for 1902, but in 1903 the company introduced a more robust design in the shape of a 10 hp wheel-steered tonneau, which had its double-acting compound engine mounted under a bonnet with frontal condenser, giving the appearance of a petrol car.

In late 1904, White unveiled a 15 hp model of more substantial construction and capable of 50 mph (80 kph), while in 1907 the company introduced the more powerful Model L20 hp and 30 hp Model K. All these models were equipped with a two-speed back axle and clutch mechanism, but improved design allowed these features to be omitted from the 1909 20 hp Model O and 40 hp Model M. These two models also replaced the complicated Stevenson Link motion used on the earlier cars with Joy valve gear.

Despite the ease of control of the latter White steamers, the contracting market for steam cars forced White to introduce a petrol-engined model based on the French Delahaye in 1910.

From 1912, a 60 hp petrol-engined six was available, and White became the third biggest American luxury car manufacturer, with 12 models catalogued.

Despite this, and the launch of a promising 32-valve four in 1917, White abandoned car production in favour of commercials in 1918.

From time to time, nevertheless, White were persuaded to build one-off private cars, most notably a large special sedan built in 1920, for a Philadelphia sportsman and a series of special coupés based on the White taxicab chassis, for Coca-Cola's travelling salesmen.

There were also two special sedans built for a Boston physician in 1924 and 1935, the latter with custom coachwork by Bender of Cleveland, Ohio, being mounted on a White light truck chassis.

**Wartburg Knight**

# A-Z OF THE CAR

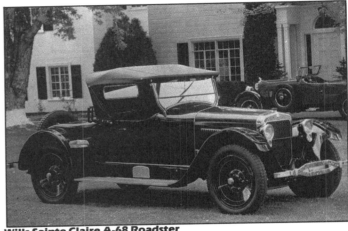

**Wills Sainte Claire A-68 Roadster**

## 1904 WHITE 15 HP

**Engine:** twin cylinder compound steam
**Bore × stroke:** 76.2 mm × 88.9 mm + 127 mm × 88.9 mm
**Capacity:** n/a
**Maximum power:** 15 hp (rated)
**Transmission:** two-speed manual
**Chassis:** armoured wood
**Suspension:** non-independent front and rear with semi-elliptic leaf springs
**Brakes:** rear wheel only
**Bodywork:** tourer, brougham or landaulette
**Maximum speed (approx):** 50 mph (80 kph)

## WILLS SAINTE CLAIRE

**Marysville, USA
1921–1927**

The unfortunately-named Childe Harold Wills, was an expert metallurgist and intuitive engineer, responsible for the success of the first Ford cars, including the Model T. Wills specified vanadium steel for it, hitherto only seen in Europe, in the quest for mechanical strength.

Finally, frustrated by Henry Ford's unwillingness to develop a car to replace the Model T, Wills resigned from the Ford Motor Company in 1919; he spent his $1,592,128 severance pay in developing a 4400-acre site at Marysville, Michigan, into a model industrial community.

After so many years with the utilitarian Model T Ford, Wills wanted to follow an entirely new course, aiming to build a luxury car which would be ten years ahead of its time in engineering terms.

His Wills Sainte Claire car appeared in 1921, taking its name from a local beauty spot, Lake Sainte Claire (on whose frozen waters Henry Ford had set a world speed record in 1904). The Wills Sainte Claire was acclaimed as a metallurgical materpiece, for it was the first car to use molybdenum steel, and its overhead-camshaft 60

## 1921 WILLS SAINTE CLAIRE

**Engine:** V8, overhead-camshaft
**Bore × stroke:** 82.6 mm × 101.6 mm
**Capacity:** 4349 cc
**Maximum power:** 65 bhp
**Transmission:** three-speed manual
**Chassis:** pressed steel channel
**Suspension:** non-independent, with semi-elliptic leaf springs front and rear
**Brakes:** hydraulic drums all round
**Bodywork:** roadster, phaeton
**Maximum speed (approx):** 70 mph (113 kph)

**White 15 HP**

**Willys Jeep**

degree V8 engine was heavily inspired by the most advanced European thinking, particularly that of Marc Birkigt, designer of Hispano-Suiza cars and aero-engines. Its engine also boasted a seven-bearing crankshaft and such refinements as a cooling fan which disengaged automatically at speeds of over 40 mph (64 kph), when it was not needed.

But although the Wills Sainte Claire Grey Goose was superbly engineered, its sales were hampered by dull, unadventurous styling; output reached a peak of 1500 units in 1923, and then tailed off.

The 4.3-litre V8 was supplanted by an overhead-camshaft 4.5-litre straight-six in 1925; this unit was capable of similar levels of performance to the V8, and was used on a number of record cross-country runs, culminating in a coast-to-coast dash from New York to San Francisco in 83 hours 12 minutes.

Like the V8, the overhead-cam straight-six was too complex for the average American mechanic, nurtured on a diet of uncomplicated side-valve engines, to service, and was in turn succeeded by a pushrod unit in 1926. The Wills Sainte Claire company managed to stagger on for only a few months more before expiring. Total production was in the region of 16,000 cars.

# WILLYS (WILLYS-OVERLAND)

**Indianapolis/Toledo, USA**
**1908–1956**

In order to save an order for 500 Overland cars, John North Willys of the American Motor Car Sales Company took over the Overland company of Indianapolis, victim of a banking crisis and threatened with being put into receivership. Overland, which had been producing gas buggies since 1903, was then reformed as the Willys-Overland Company in 1908.

Initially, production was concentrated on a $1200 four-cylinder runabout with epicyclic gearing, 465 cars were sold in nine months, and the cash generated thereby enabled two new models, the Overland Six and the 45 hp Willys Six, to be put into production. During 1909, Willys-Overland sold 4000 cars, generating turnover of $5 million and profits of $1 million, and business was so good that by 1910, Willys-Overland had outgrown its 300 ft-long tin shed works, and moved into the old Pope-Toledo factory in Toledo, Ohio.

Sales in 1913 were 35,000, establishing Willys-Overland as leaders in the $625–1500 sector; the following year saw sales more than doubled, to 80,000, thanks mainly to the keenly-priced 3949 cc Overland Model 79 four-cylinder.

The company adopted electric lighting and starting in 1914, claiming: 'In the electrically started and electrically-lighted Overland Coupé, the Women of America have for the first time their ideal motor car . . . .'

In the same year the company introduced a new model called the Willys-Knight; this 4529 cc sleeve-

valve four was developed from the 1912–14 Edwards-Knight, built by a company which had merged with Willys-Overland in 1914. The new marque survived until 1932–33.

In 1920, there was a joint venture with a British company, Crossley of Gorton, Manchester. Known as Willys-Overland-Crossley, the joint company assembled Overland Fours (distinguished by their U-shaped transverse suspension) for the UK market; the 1924 model featured a Morris-Oxford engine.

The US company was hit by a major financial crisis in 1921–23, and only saved by the personal

### 1940 WILLYS JEEP

**Engine:** in-line four-cylinder, side-valve
**Bore × stroke:** 79.4 mm × 111.1 mm
**Capacity:** 2199 cc
**Maximum power:** 60 bhp
**Transmission:** Three-speed manual with high and low ratio and two or four-wheel drive
**Chassis:** ladder frame
**Suspension:** non-independent with live axles and semi-elliptic leaf springs front and rear
**Brakes:** drums all round with transmission brake
**Bodywork:** open four-seater
**Maximum speed (approx):** 70 mph (113 kph)

intervention of John Willys, who, by completely reorganising the production and sales of his company, managed to pay off debts of $17.3 million and generate profits of $13 million.

By April 1925, Willys-Overland was building 250 Overland Sixes and 600 Overland Fours every working day, plus 5200 Willys-Knights each month.

In 1926 the company brought out a new low-priced model, the Whippet, intended to compete with Ford and Chevrolet. Although, at $495, it eventually became the cheapest car on the US market, the Whippet never achieved the anticipated market success.

In 1929 John Willys unloaded his share in the company for £21 million and was appointed US Ambassador to Poland, and soon after the Willys-Overland company collapsed in the slump, and was placed in receivership. John Willys hurried back to try and save the situation again, but this time the company was in too bad a situation even for his entrepreneurial skills. Willys died in 1933, with the company only partially on the road to recovery.

In 1933, the ugly aerodynamically-styled Willys 77 appeared; it was the only model built until 1936, when the receivership was lifted. With more acceptable styling, and rechristened the Willys-American, the 77 survived until 1942.

By then, however, Willys was producing the Jeep for the Allied war effort, and by the end of hostilities had built 361,349 of these 'Blitz Buggies'.

Willys continued building Jeeps for civilian use when hostilities ceased, introducing an enclosed Jeep station wagon in July 1946. The 1948 range included several commercial variants of the Jeeps, plus the Brook Stevens-designed Jeepster Phaeton, powered by side-valve Willys fours and sixes of 2196 cc and 2425 cc respectively, which was listed for four years.

In 1952, Willys introduced a brand-new range of passenger cars which included the side-valve six Aero-Lark, and the Aero-Wing, Aero-Ace and Aero-Eagle, all powered by a 2638 cc overhead-valve six-cylinder engine.

Production of the Aero Willys range reached 31,363 in 1952, rising to 41,735 in 1953. That year, the cars bore a gold W on their grilles to commemorate the 50th anniversary of the founding of the original Overland company.

During the anniversary year, Willys-Overland was taken over by the ailing Kaiser group, though the 1954 models showed little evidence of the merger, except for offering the option of Kaiser's 3703 cc side-valve six.

Some Aero Willys models were supercharged, boosting power output to 140 bhp, while the 1955 models were mildly face-lifted, and the Aero designation replaced by Custom (sedans) and Bermuda (hardtops). However, only 6564 of the 1955 models had been sold when the decision was taken to end passenger-car production in the United States, though the Aero continued to be manufactured in the Willys-Overland factory in Sao Paolo, Brazil, until 1962.

From 1956, Jeeps were the sole North American product of the company, which changed its name to Kaiser-Jeep in 1963.

# WINTON

### Cleveland, USA
### 1896–1924

Scottish marine engineer Alexander Winton jumped ship to seek his fortune in America, and founded a cycle company in Cleveland, Ohio, building an experimental shaft-driven two-cylinder car in 1896.

Winton went into production with light phaetons in 1897, and made his – and, he claimed, the American motor industry's – first sale on 24 March 1898. Production reached twenty-five cars in the first year. The twelfth Winton sold went to a young electrical engineer named James Ward Packard, who, on complaining about certain deficiencies in the vehicle, was told by Winton that if he knew so much, why didn't he build a better car, replied: 'I will, Mr Winton, I will . . .'

From the start, Alexander Winton displayed an engaging preoccupation with pneumatic actuation of controls, and early models featured both a pneumatic governor and pneumatic throttle control.

Winton was an early convert to the belief that the easiest way to promote his products was to compete in racing and endurance runs, and as early as 1897 had driven from Cleveland to New York. In 1899, he challenged top French racing driver Ferdinand Charron to a race over any distance, 'each driver to wager $10,000, winner take all', but failed to respond when Charron called his bluff.

However, the challenge inspired newspaper magnate James Gordon Bennett to inaugurate the international race series bearing his name, and a 3.8-litre single-cylinder Winton duly took part in the 1900 Gordon Bennett race – which Charron won . . .

In 1901, Winton introduced an improved horizontally-opposed twin-cylinder phaeton, and in 1903 the first successful automobile crossing of America was made by one of these cars. This was a spur-of-the-moment venture carried out by an enthusiastic Winton owner named Dr H. Nelson Jackson who, wintering in San Francisco, bet friends $50 that he could drive a Winton car across America. 'The

Mad Doctor' bought a virtually-new 20 hp Winton for $3000 ($500 over list price) and, with the car laden with camping gear and a 22-year-old co-driver named Crocker, headed east, arriving in New York 63 days later; that $50 wager had cost $8000 to win! When, following a well-publicised crossing of America by Packard a few days later, doubts were cast on the validity of Dr Jackson's claim, Alexander Winton offered $25,000 to anyone who could disprove it; the reward was still unclaimed when Winton ceased car manufacture 21 years later.

For the 1903 Gordon Bennett race in Ireland, Winton built two Bullet racers whose ultra-low profile was only spoiled by the upright seating position; the Baby Bullet had a 40 hp 8514 cc horizontal four and two-speed transmission, while Alexander Winton himself drove the 80 hp Bullet, which was powered by a 17,028 cc horizontal straight-eight and had only one speed. Though neither car finished the race, both survive today in the Smithsonian Museum in Washington.

At the end of 1904, Winton discontinued the flat-twin. The only new horizontally-opposed model was a flat-four, the Winton Quad, but it survived only a season before vertical fours of 16/20 hp, 24/30 hp and 50/100 hp were standardised. A link with tradition was the retention of the pneumatic speed control.

One of the advantages claimed for the new Accessible Winton range was that 'you may take out this whole transmission gear of the 1905 Winton *from above*, without

removing the seat, or getting under the car – convenient, isn't it?'

In 1906, Winton concentrated production of the 30 hp 5801 cc Model K, though this was joined by a 45 hp four in 1907. The Six-Teen-Six introduced for 1908 had a displacement of 7817 cc, while in 1909 a 9505 cc six was listed – it carried Winton's love of air-actuated devices a stage further by incorporating pneumatic starting, and by 1911 this model also had a built-in tyre pump.

The Winton marque had now become a somewhat outdated range; only conservatively-engineered pair-cast sixes were built, and their last vestige of individuality vanished in 1915, when they were equipped with electric lighting and starting.

Winton finally ceased car production in 1924 in order to concentrate on the manufacture of marine diesel engines; the company eventually became the diesel division of General Motors.

### 1903 WINTON 20 HP

**Engine:** flat-twin, side-valve
**Bore × stroke:** 133.4 mm × 152.4 mm
**Capacity:** 4256 cc
**Maximum power:** 20 bhp
**Transmission:** two-speed manual (chain drive)
**Chassis:** riveted sheet steel
**Suspension:** non-independent with semi-elliptic leaf springs front and rear
**Brakes:** drums on rear only
**Bodywork:** tourer
**Maximum speed (approx):** 35 mph (56 kph)

**Winton 20 HP**

## WOLSELEY

**Birmingham/Cowley, England**
**1899–1976**

In 1985, Herbert Austin, former engineer of the Australian Wolseley Sheep Shearing Company (founded seven years earlier by the brother of Field-Marshal Sir Garnet Wolseley) and now manager of their newly-formed British operation, began work in Birmingham on a tricar powered by a 1257 cc flat-twin engine and inspired by the French Léon Bollée. In May 1896, the Wolseley directors voted £2000 towards motorcar manufacture, and later that year the Wolseley Autocar Number 1 appeared.

This open-frame three-wheeler was Austin's first truly original design, and though a catalogue was issued, it never went into production but was extensively modified during the ensuing two or three years; four-wheeled prototypes followed in 1899.

One of these, a 3.5 hp single-cylinder car with belt drive, successfully completed the 1000 Miles' Trial of 1900. In March that year, the mighty Vickers, Sons & Maxim organisation took over the machine-tool and motor manufacturing side of the Wolseley company, retaining Austin as manager.

The first cars produced by the reorganised Wolseley company were a 5 hp single and 10 hp twin, of 1303 and 2606 cc respectively. Like all Wolseleys until 1905, these cars had horizontal engines, but John Davenport Siddeley, an importer of the French Peugeot cars who was appointed a Wolseley director that year, insisted on the production of vertical-engined Siddeley cars alongside the archaic horizontal-engined models.

Austin was a staunch proponent of the horizontal engine, and the resultant clash of personalities compelled Austin's resignation in December 1905; ironically, when Austin started building cars under his own name in 1906, they were vertical-engined . . . .

After he left the Wolseley company, its products were known variously as Siddeleys or Wolseley-Siddeleys. This Wolseley-Siddeley liaison proved a costly one, but nevertheless lasted until 1910, building a complex range of two-, four- and six-cylinder cars from a 12 hp vertical twin to a gigantic 15.7-litre four.

The marque was also built in Italy under the name Wolsit, but when Siddeley left in 1911 to build the Siddeley-Deasy, the Wolseley name was revived. By 1913, the 16/20 hp four was the best-selling model, while a subsidiary company was building a wooden-chassis light car, the Stellite, and an experimental gyrocar was built for a Russian inventor, Schilovsky.

During the Great War, Wolseley built the overhead-camshaft Hispano-Suiza V8 aero engine under licence, and this camshaft layout featured on their post-war 1.3-litre 10 hp (which replaced the Stellite), 12 hp and 15 hp models; in 1925 the 10 was developed into the 11/22 hp model.

Although the overhead-camshaft 15 hp was succeeded by a cheaper side-valve 16/35, which also appeared in 1925, a new overhead-camshaft six, the 16/45, appeared in 1927.

Meanwhile, the company had gone bankrupt and been swallowed up by Morris in the face of opposition from Austin; before long, the Wolseley-inspired overhead-camshaft layout began appearing in the contemporary MG and Morris models.

The first new Wolseleys to appear after the merger were the 1928 2.7-litre straight-eight and four-cylinder 12/32 HP. These were followed in 1929 by the 2677 cc 21/60 hp six – a Wolseley precursor of the 1930 Morris Isis – and an ephemeral 4011 cc 32/80 hp straight-eight, offered in chassis form only at £1275 (two-and-a-half times as much as the 21/60 saloon).

A significant innovation in 1930 was the 1.3-litre overhead-camshaft Hornet, while in 1931 Wolseley introduced the 2.0-litre Viper plus new six and eight-cylinder derivatives of the 21/60. The Hornet's swept volume

was later increased to 1.4 litres, while in 1935 there was also a Hornet Special with the power unit from the new Wolseley 14, which had a swept volume of 1604 cc. Disappointingly its twin carburettors and dural conrods only added 2 bhp to the standard model's output of 48 bhp.

A small touch of genius came with the introduction in 1933 of the illuminated oval radiator badge, hallmark of the Wolseley.

Wolseley abandoned the overhead-camshaft engine layout in 1936; it was replaced by Morris-derived pushrod-engined cars which included the Super Six and

the 1.8-litre 14/56.

Launched in 1937, the Wolseley 18 was the first of the marque to be adopted in large numbers by the Metropolitan Police in London. In 1938–39, journalist Humfrey Symons drove a Wolseley 18/85 on the 10,300 mile journey from London to Cape Town in a record 31 days 22 hours, despite losing 12 days when the car fell over 30 ft from a bridge into 'the black, crocodile-infested River Gada' in the Belgian Congo.

The post-war story of Wolseley was increasingly one of badge-engineering; the Wolseley 8 of 1946 was an overhead-valve development of the old side-valve Morris 8 Series E, while from 1949 Wolseley production was transferred to the Morris plant at Cowley. That year's brand new unit-construction Wolseleys, the overhead-camshaft four-cylinder 4/50 and six-cylinder 6/80 were basically upmarket derivatives of the post-war Morris Oxford and Six; the 4/50 engine was a four-cylinder version of the six-cylinder power unit used by Wolseley and Morris.

The 4/44 of 1953 was powered by a detuned MG TD engine, while

the 6/90 of 1955 had a 2.6-litre Austin power unit in a Riley Pathfinder bodyshell. Rationalisation within the British Motor Corporation (formed from a merger between Austin and the Nuffield Group) was further reflected in the Wolseley 1500 of 1958, which was in effect an expanded version of Morris Minor, also produced in Riley guise in Britain, and with Morris and Austin badges in Australia.

Inevitably, there was a Wolseley version of the Mini, which appeared in 1962, bearing the pre-war Hornet name. There were also luxury Wolseley versions of the front wheel drive 1100/1300 and 1800 BMC models bearing the famous illuminated ratiator badge, followed by the transverse-six front-wheel drive 2200.

In 1975 this was replaced by a front-wheel-drive de luxe derivative of the Austin/Morris 18/22. The Wolseley marque vanished six months later when the 18/22 range was renamed Princess.

## Wolseley 5HP

The first production cars to emerge from the Wolseley factory were a 5 hp single and a 10 hp twin; the cars both had horizontal engines and were of similar appearance, though the 10 hp was slightly larger.

Coil ignition with a simple wipe

### 1901 WOLSELEY 5 HP

**Engine:** single-cylinder, transverse and horizontal
**Bore × stroke:** 114.3 mm × 127 mm
**Capacity:** 1303 cc
**Maximum power:** 5 bhp
**Transmission:** three-speed manual
**Chassis:** pressed steel channel
**Suspension:** non-independent with semi-elliptic leaf springs
**Brakes:** rear wheel contracting bands
**Bodywork:** two-seater
**Maximum speed (approx):** 25 mph (40 kph)

**Wolseley 5 HP**

**Wolseley Gyrocar**

contact distributor was standard, as was a float carburettor, both evidence of up-to-date design practice. Indeed, the press commented that the cars displayed 'the highest class of workmanship', though the description of the transmission was somewhat cryptic: 'The motorshaft gears by means of a Renold's silent chain with the slidingshaft in the gear box, and the balance-geared countershaft engages by means of roller chains with the sprockets on the driving wheels.'

Despite that, the hill-climbing ability of the cars was highly praised.

## Wolseley Gyrocar

In 1912 a Russian aristocrat, Peter Paul Schilovsky, commissioned Wolseley to build him a two-wheeled gyroscopically-steadied motorcar which could go where there were no proper roads. Schilovsky already held a number of patents for gyroscopic monorails, and the gyroscope installation in his monocar showed evidence of careful thought. When the car, powered by a modified 16/20 hp Wolseley engine, leaned to either side, the movement of cylindrical pendulums operated a rack-and-pinion gear that caused the gyroscope to precess (the natural tendency for the upper axis to describe a circle when disturbed) rapidly, forcing the vehicle to rise towards the vertical.

After some initial problems, and a problem of torque reaction from the 780 lb flywheel which rendered it impossible for the Gyrocar to negotiate sharp left-hand bends, the system was found to work well, and was even demonstrated in London. Unfortunately the outbreak of war in 1914, followed by the Russian Revolution, meant that the Gyrocar remained forgotten in a corner of the Wolseley works; in 1930 the decision was made to dispose of it, and a hole was dug in the factory railwayt yard into which the Gyrocar was dumped.

---

### 1913 WOLSELEY GYROCAR

**Engine:** in-line four-cylinder, side valve, bi-block
**Bore × stroke:** 90 mm × 121 mm
**Capacity:** 3079 cc
**Maximum power:** 20 bhp
**Transmission:** four-speed manual with gyroscopic stabiliser
**Chassis:** pressed steel channel
**Suspension:** non-independent with reversed quarter-elliptic leaf springs front and cantilever rear
**Brakes:** drums on rear
**Bodywork:** six-seater
**Maximum speed (approx):** not known

---

Oddly, although the hole had been covered by newly-laid railway track, the decision was taken in 1938 to resurrect the Gyrocar. It was dug out and put in the company's museum.

But in 1948, having survived wartime scrap drives and air raids, the Gyrocar was ordered to be scrapped by some mindless Wolseley executive, though in the intervening years rumours that it still survives have never ceased....

## Wolseley Hornet Special

The original Wolseley Hornet appeared in 1930 as a six-cylinder derivative of the Morris Minor; its 1271 cc power unit was then the smallest six in production, and to accommodate it the diminutive (and whippy) Morris chassis was stretched by 12.5 in (31.7 cm).

Hydraulic brakes were an advanced touch, while the overhead-cam power unit was to form the basis of all MG's overhead-cam six-cylinder models.

Sports versions of the Hornet began to appear, but nothing serious happened until a revised Hornet chassis was launched in 1931 in which extra space was created for more spacious bodywork by the simple expedient of moving the engine well forward in the chassis, and shortening the power unit by replacing the vertical kingshaft (which was also the dynamo shaft) with a chain drive.

In April 1932 Wolseley introduced a 'speed chassis for the enthusiast'; it was intended that specialist bodybuiilders should create 'the most modern types of sporting

---

### 1933 WOLSELEY HORNET SPECIAL

**Engine:** in-line six-cylinder, overhead-cam
**Bore × stroke:** 57 mm × 83 mm
**Capacity:** 1271 cc
**Maximum power:** 35 bhp
**Transmission:** four-speed manual
**Chassis:** pressed steel channel
**Suspension:** non-independent with semi-elliptic leaf springs
**Brakes:** drums all round
**Bodywork:** two or four-seater sports
**Maximum speed (approx):** 75 mph (137 kph)

---

**Wolseley Hornet Special**

**Wolseley 4-44**

coachwork' on this low, crab-tracked chassis, the engine of which boasted twin carburettors against the single unit of the standard power unit.

But the Wolseley Hornet Special never achieved the success of the rival MG.

In many ways the Wolseley Hornet was a typical mid-1930s sports model, with a low-geared back axle for good acceleration at the expense of a high-revving engine, and the special bodywork often carried the outward and visible signs that were popularly believed to make a sports car – heavily louvred bonnet, flared scuttle cowlings, remote-control gear lever and stoneguards for headlamps and radiator.

In the final analysis, the equivalent MGs were far more desirable cars, and the Hornet line was discontinued after 1936.

# Wolseley 4/44

The Wolseley 4/44 made its debut at the 1952 Motor Show and, said the press, 'drew attention by the obvious Italian inclucnce in its styling'. The rounded bodywork bore a family resemblance to that of the Z-series MG Magnette, though its makers described it as 'Gracefully modern – distinctively Wolseley'.

The power unit was a detuned version of the MG-TD engine, developing 46 bhp instead of 54.4 bhp; despite that and a weight of 22 cwt (1117 kg) against 17.5 cwt (889 kg), the Wolseley saloon was only 4 mph (6.4 kph) slower than the MG.

In 1955, the 4/44 was joined by the larger 6/90, which shared a common bodyshell with the Riley Pathfinder; for a while, these Wolseley saloons were the archetypal police car.

---

### 1953 WOLSELEY 4/44

**Engine:** in-line four-cylinder, overhead-valve
**Bore × stroke:** 66.5 mm × 90 mm
**Capacity:** 1250 cc
**Maximum power:** 46 bhp
**Transmission:** four-speed manual
**Chassis:** integral
**Suspension:** independent front with coil springs and wishbones. Live rear axle with semi-elliptic leaf springs
**Brakes:** drums all round
**Bodywork:** saloon
**Maximum speed (approx):** 73 mph (118 kph)

---

# Z (ZBROJOVKA)

**Brno-Zidenice, Czechoslovakia
1927–1936**

Though the Ackiova Spolecnost Ceskoslovenska Zbrojovka arms factory was part of the Skoda Group, its cars – happily known simply as Z – had no connection with the automotive products of Skoda. Indeed, all Z cars were two-strokes, though their first model, the Disk, a 660 cc twin-cylinder designed by Novotny, never went into quantity production.

The sporting Z18, with a liberally-drilled U-channel frame, had doorless two-seater bodywork

and a differentialless rear axle; twin quarter-elliptic front springs took the torque reaction of the front-wheel brakes. A Z18 won the under-1000 cc class in the 1927 Ecce Homo and Brno-Sobiesce hill climbs.

In 1928, the first racing Z appeared, the supercharged opposed-piston six-cylinder Z2, which developed 60 bhp from 1100 cc; it was followed in 1932 by the Z13, which had a complex Duplex two-stroke 1.5-litre power unit consisting of four parallel pairs of cylinders with opposed pistons and common combustion chambers. One cylinder in each pair contained the inlet port, fed by either a Cozette or Roots supercharger, while the other cylinder incorporated the exhaust porting. The front semi-elliptic springs passed through the axle beam, while the brake drums were integral with the cast aluminium wheels. Top speed was in the region of 100 mph (161 kph).

---

### 1926 Z18

**Engine:** two-cylinder, two-stroke
**Bore × stroke:** 80 mm × 100 mm
**Capacity:** 987 cc
**Maximum power:** 33 bhp
**Transmission:** four-speed manual
**Chassis:** U-section steel channel, trapezoidal frame
**Suspension:** non-independent with double quarter elliptic leaf springs front and quarter elliptics rear
**Brakes:** drums all round
**Bodywork:** sports two-seater
**Maximum speed (approx):** 75 mph (120 kph)

---

**Z18**

## MODEL
Volkswagen Beetle 1300 (1970)
**UK price:** £585

## ENGINE
**Location:** Rear, longitudinal
**Type:** Air-cooled horizontally-opposed, four cylinder with aluminium cylinder blocks, cast-iron liners and alloy cylinder heads. Four main bearings
**Cubic Capacity:** 1285 cc
**Bore × stroke:** 77 mm × 69 mm
**Compression ratio:** 7.3:1
**Valve gear:** 2 valves per cylinder operated by pushrods from one central camshaft
**Fuel supply:** 1 Solex downdraught single-choke carburettor
**Ignition:** Mechanical by coil and distributor
**Maximum power:** 44 bhp DIN at 4100 rpm
**Maximum torque:** 69 lb ft (SAE) at 2600 rpm

## TRANSMISSION
**Layout:** Gearbox in front of engine driving rear wheels
**Clutch:** Single dry plate
**Gearbox:** Four-speed manual
    1st  3.800:1  3rd  1.260:1
    2nd 2.060:1  4th  0.890:
**Final drive:** Spiral bevel
**Ratio:** 4.375:1

## SUSPENSION
**Front:** Independent twin swinging longitudinal trailing arms with transverse laminated torsion bars, anti-roll bar and telescopic dampers.
**Rear:** Independent swinging semi-axles with longitudinal trailing arms, transverse torsion bars and telescopic dampers

## STEERING
**Type:** Worm and roller. 2.6 turns lock to lock

## BRAKES
**Type:** Drums all round

## WHEELS AND TYRES
**Type:** Steel perforated wheels with 5,60 × 15 in tyres

## BODY/CHASSIS
**Type:** Backbone platform and integral bodyshell. 2-door, 4-seat saloon

## DIMENSIONS AND WEIGHT
**Length:** 160 in (4070 mm)
**Width:** 61 in (1550 mm)
**Wheelbase:** 94.50 in (2400 mm)
**Track – front:** 51.57 in (1310 mm)
     **– rear:** 53.15 in (1350 mm)
**Weight:** 1676 lb (760 kg)

## PERFORMANCE
**Maximum speed:** 75 mph (120 kph)
**Acceleration 0-50 mph:** 14 seconds
**Fuel consumption (approx):** 33 mpg

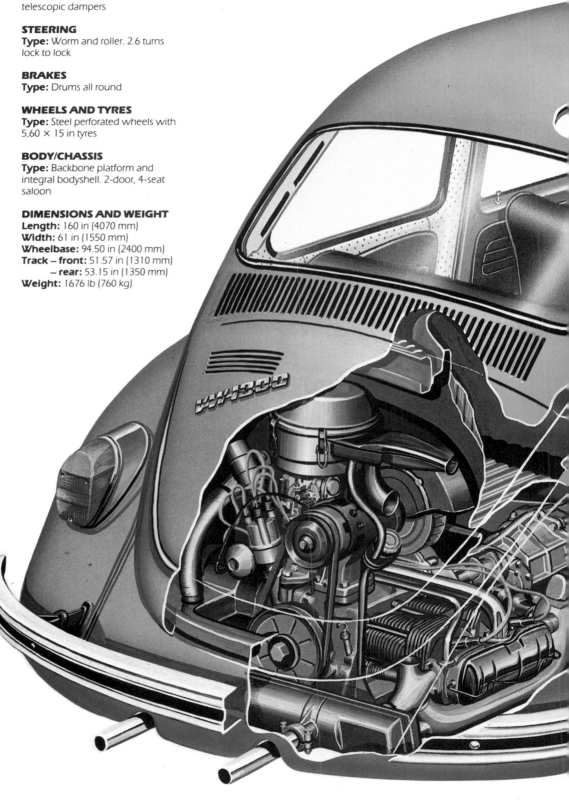

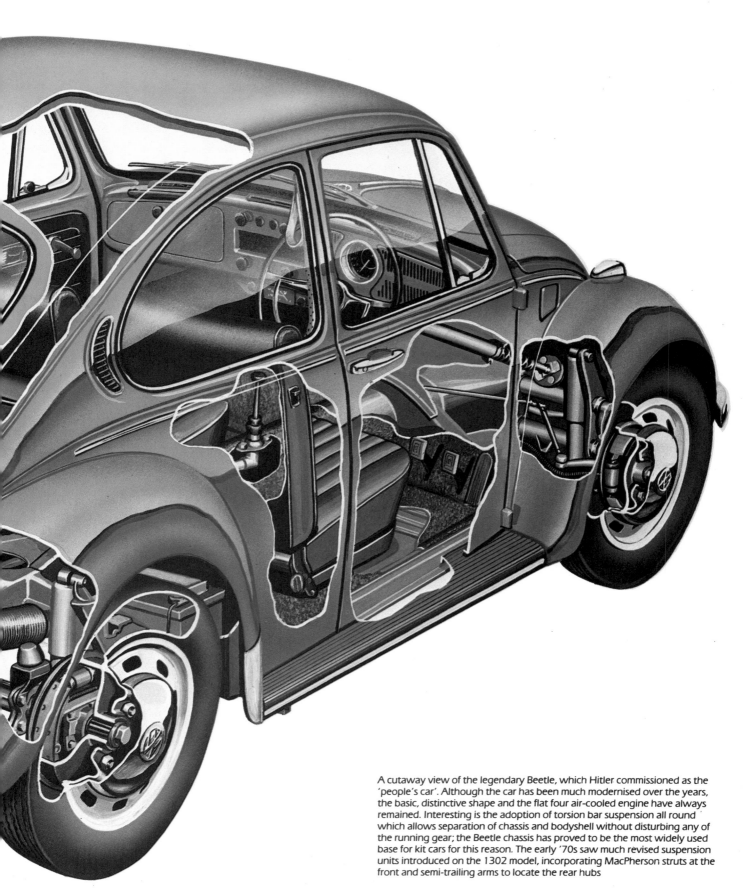

A cutaway view of the legendary Beetle, which Hitler commissioned as the 'people's car'. Although the car has been much modernised over the years, the basic, distinctive shape and the flat four air-cooled engine have always remained. Interesting is the adoption of torsion bar suspension all round which allows separation of chassis and bodyshell without disturbing any of the running gear; the Beetle chassis has proved to be the most widely used base for kit cars for this reason. The early '70s saw much revised suspension units introduced on the 1302 model, incorporating MacPherson struts at the front and semi-trailing arms to locate the rear hubs

# A-Z OF THE CAR

## LE ZEBRE
**Suresnes, France**
**1910–1931**

At a time when French designers were beginning to offer diminutive multi-cylinder cars, the little Zèbre ran counter to the trend by employing a single-cylinder 636 cc four-stroke 5 hp engine. It also had only two speeds in its transmission, although it was shaft-driven.

In 1913, Zèbre at last produced a tiny four-cylinder, initially of 943 cc, but later of just 785 cc, plus a 10 hp of 1743 cc. By now, three-sped gearboxes were common to all Zebres.

The post-war Zèbre had a side-valve 8 hp engine of 998 cc, and was designed by Jules Salomon who was to create the famous 5 hp Citroën after he left Le Zèbre.

Against the competition of the big mass-producers like Renault and Citroën, the 8 hp Le Zèbre failed to maintain headway, and was replaced by the company's last production model, a 1974 cc 10 hp with a Ricardo head and four-speed gearbox. Just before Le Zèbre closed down, they exhibited a prototype at the 1931 Paris Salon, powered by a single-cylinder opposed-piston CLM diesel engine.

### 1913 LE ZEBRE 8 HP
**Engine:** in-line four-cylinder, side-valve
**Bore × stroke:** 50 mm × 100 mm
**Capacity:** 785 cc
**Maximum power:** 12 bhp
**Transmission:** three-speed manual
**Chassis:** pressed steel channel
**Suspension:** non-independent with semi-elliptic leaf springs
**Brakes:** drums on rear only
**Bodywork:** two-seater
**Maximum speed (approx):** 35 mph (56 kph)

## ZIL
**Russia**
**1956 —**

The ZIL (Zavod Imieni Likhatchev) succeeded the ZIS (Zavod Imieni Stalina) of 1936–56, which had been originally inspired by the Buick straight-eight. Since 1945 the car was built using Packard body dies, handed over to the Russians in a fit of over-enthusastic wartime cameraderie. This was the ZIL model 110, which was fitted with a 137 bhp side-valve straight-eight and three-speed synchromesh gearbox. It was virtually identical to the highly successful pre-war Packard Senior 180, and was capable of 90 mph (145 kph). Electric windows and 'occasional'

Le Zèbre

seats were standard in these luxurious cars.

The ZIL, which rivalled the Chaika as prestige transport for high-ranking Soviet officials, retained the Packard inspiration of its forebear until 1963, when it acquired more modern American-inspired styling and reappeared as the 111G. This car was fitted with a 6-litre V8 engine of 230 bhp and had a reputed top speed of 106 mph (170 kph). Its appearance was again very similar to that of GM cars of the period.

In 1967 the 114 seven-seat limousine was introduced, fitted with a 7-litre V8; the still-current and similarly-engined ZIL 117 limousine was launched in 1971.

The Moscow works have been much expanded since 1970, with the addition of hundreds of automated and fully mechanised assembly lines. The paternalistic nature of the Soviet philosophy is evinced by the presence of nearby factory run schools, colleges — one to university standard — and flats.

---

### 1980 ZIL 117

**Engine:** V8, overhead-valve
**Bore × stroke:** 108 mm × 95 mm
**Capacity:** 6962 cc
**Maximum power:** 300 bhp
**Transmission:** three-speed automatic
**Chassis:** X-braced box type ladder frame
**Suspension:** independent front with wishbones and coil springs. Live rear axle with semi-elliptic leaf springs
**Brakes:** discs all round
**Bodywork:** limousine
**Maximum speed (approx):** 124 mph (200 kph)

---

## ZÜNDAPP

**Munich, Germany**
**1957–1958**

---

This leading manufacturer of mopeds and motorcycles took over the production of the unconventional Dornier Delta mini-car, and relaunched it as the Janus (named for the two-headed Roman god of doors), an odd-looking four-seater in which the two rear-seat passengers sat with their backs to those in front, looking through the rear window.

The power unit, a 248 cc single-cylinder Zündapp two-stroke engine, was mounted horizontally between the seats.

The unconventional 'draw-wedge' gear-change had all forward speeds in constant mesh, with the ratios selected by moving a rod inside the hollow layshaft, forcing steel balls out of recesses in the layshaft to key the gearwheel to the shaft.

ZIL 114

**Zündapp**

Roadholding and suspension of
the Janus were claimed to be
'remarkably good', and
performance 'quite lively'; total
production of the Janus was 6900.

# ZÜST

**Milan/Brescia, Italy
1905–1914**

Shortly before the turn of the
century, the Swiss-born engineer
Roberto Züst, who had founded a
precision metal-working machinery
factory at Intra, on Lake Maggiore,
died and left his business to his
sons. Having made some
experiments with road
transportation, they decided to set
up a branch factory in Milan, where
production of automobile
components began in 1903. Two
years later, the entire operation
moved from Intra to Milan, and
manufacture of complete cars and
commercials beghan.

The Milan factory built big pair-
cast four-cylinders of 7432 cc and
11,308 cc, but in 1906 a branch
factory was established at Brescia
to build more economical cars; they
were known as Brixia-Züsts from
the Latin name for Brescia. The
Brescia factory began production
with a 3770 cc 14/18 HP, then in
1908 introduced a four-cylinder

18/24 hp of 3770 cc and a three-
cylinder 10 HP of 1386 cc; in 1910,
the latter model was uprated to
1501 cc, and a fleet of 150 was put
into service as London taxicabs.
Production of the 10 HP, the 14/18
(now of 2297 cc) and the 18/24
(uprated to 4942 cc) ceased in
1911. As Brixia-Züst had been
showing a defecit, the company
was absorbed into the parent Züst
organisation – which had gained
wider fame with the entry of a
28/45 HP in the 1908 New York-
Paris round-the-world race. Max
Pemberton said of this event in
1908: "The Züst car, as all the
world remembers, took a very
creditable part in that far from
creditable burlesque known as the
"New York to Paris" race. This

fiasco permitted many charlatans to
advertise themselves; but it
managed to interest more than one
firm of repute and, among other
achievements, to demonstrate the
durability of the Züst and the pluck
of its driver…The Züst took the
road whenever possible, and
where there was no road it
ploughed its way across the
Siberian desert as the mighty Itala
had done before it."

The car had been driven by
Sirtori, accompanied by his
mechanic Haaga and a journalist
called Scarfoglio. During the drive
across America's Mid-West they
were attacked by wolves, but all
survived to reach Paris. The car,
which had withstood the rigours of
thousands of miles of rough roads,

water and precipices, was
accidentally destroyed in Bromley
Railway Station in England, when a
porter, peering at the famous car
under its tarpaulin, set fire to it with
his lamp.

Production in these years was
centred on Brescia and a three-car
range introduced, consisting of a
2853 cc 15/25 HP, a 35/50 HP
Speciale GS of 6321 cc and a 50/
60 HP (later known as the S235) of
7432 cc.

New in 1913 was the 25/35 hp
S305, with a pear-shaped Fiat-like
radiator and a 4712 cc bi-block
engine, while in 1915–16, Züst
built the 2952 cc 15/25 hp S365.

On 1 October 1917, Züst was
absorbed by the Officine
Meccaniche of Milan.

**Züst 'New York to Paris' Tourer**

## MODEL
Porsche 356C (1965)

## ENGINE
**Location:** Rear, longitudinal
**Type:** Air-cooled flat-four with plain bearings.. Cast-iron block and alloy cylinder heads
**Cubic capacity:** 1582 cc
**Bore × stroke:** 82.5 mm × 74 mm
**Compression ratio:** 8.5:1
**Valve gear:** Two valves per cylinder operated by pushrods and single central camshaft
**Fuel supply:** Two Zenith 32 ND1X carburettors
**Ignition:** Mechanical by coil and distributor
**Maximum power:** 75 bhp at 5200 rpm
**Maximum torque:** 90.4 lb ft at 4200 rpm

## TRANSMISSION
**Layout:** Gearbox ahead of engine
**Clutch:** Single dry plate
**Gearbox:** Four-speed manual
  1st 1.765:1      3rd 1.130:1
  2nd 1.309:1     4th 0.815:1
**Final drive:** Spiral bevel
**Ratio:** 4.428:1

## SUSPENSION
**Front:** Independent with trailing arms, transverse torsion bars, anti-roll bar and telescopic dampers
**Rear:** Independent with swinging half axles, swinging longitudinal trailing arms, transverse torsion bars, telescopic dampers and optional transverse leaf spring fixed to differential

## STEERING
**Type:** Worm and roller

## BRAKES
**Type:** Ate discs front and rear

## WHEELS AND TYRES
**Type:** 5.60 × 15 steel sport wheels with 165/15 crossply tyres

## BODY/CHASSIS
**Type:** Integral with steel two-door coupé body welded to steel floor pan

## DIMENSIONS AND WEIGHT
**Length:** 157.9 in (4011 mm)
**Width:** 65.8 in (1671 mm)
**Wheelbase:** 82.7 in (2101 mm)
**Track – front:** 51.4 in (1305 mm)
        – rear: 50.1 in (1273 mm)
**Weight:** 2040 lb (925 kg)

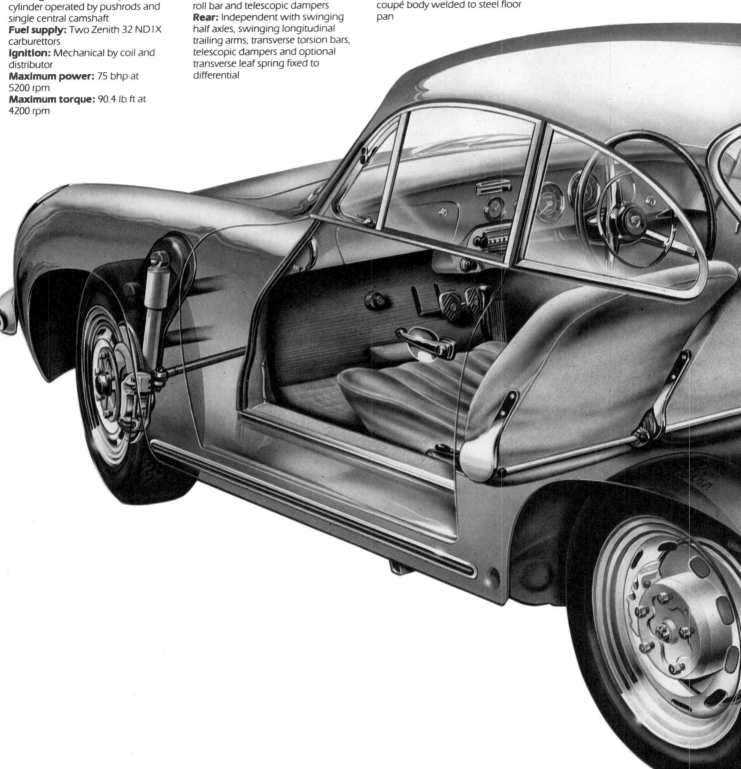